$f(x)=3x-10$

$3x+1=10$

$x^2-x=0$

$x+y=2x-1$

$3x+4=5x+2$

$(a+b)+c=a+(b+c)$

$f(x)=3x-10$

$x2-x=0$

College Algebra

Second Edition

Print ISBN 978-1-934920-86-2

For permission to use material from this text or for general questions about permissions, submit a request on line to http://www.wordsofwisdombooks.com/contact.asp

Publisher: Words of Wisdom, LLC
Book Title: College Algebra
Author: Editorial Board
Rights: Words of Wisdom, LLC
Publication Date: 2014
Edition: 2

Acknowledgments

We would like to thank the Editorial Board for their time
and dedication to the creation of this book.

Socrates Boussios
Stuart Carney
Dr. Gregory Dlabach
Kelly Jirous
Tanya Mifsud
Gail Roach
Cindy Roberts
David Runde
Tom West

TABLE OF CONTENTS

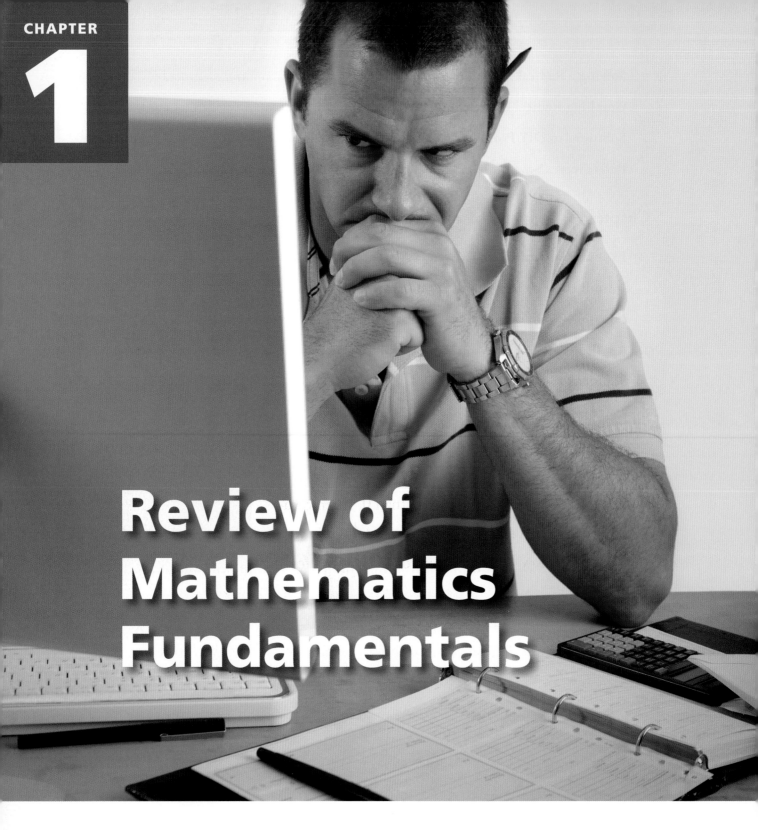

Review of Mathematics Fundamentals

Mr. Kamden is an employee at a large company. He has a family, a house, and a pet. At his company, he is paid on the 1st and 15th of each month. His check is deposited directly into his bank account, and he receives a pay stub showing his gross pay and his net pay. How is his net pay determined?

His pay stub shows a series of deductions, for federal income tax, for Social Security, for insurance for his family, for investment in a retirement plan, and so on. How are these deductions, or subtractions, shown on his stub?

Deductions, subtractions, or withdrawals are generally shown in one of two ways. One way is by showing the amount of the deduction in parentheses, such as ($100.00). Another way is to use the subtraction sign, −, in front of the number, such as −$100.00.

The subtraction sign, −, indicates a negative number. A *negative number* is a number that is less than 0. A temperature reading of −10°F means that the temperature is very cold, 10 degrees below 0. A golf score of −3 is good for a golfer, as it means that his or her score is 3 strokes under par.

Mr. Kamden's net pay is then deposited into his checking account. From this deposit, or addition, to his account balance, he can write checks for the mortgage payment, the utility companies, and whatever other expenses he may have. The checks he writes are deductions, or subtractions, from his account balance. How does his bank statement show these transactions?

The addition sign, +, indicates a *positive number*. A deposit into your account means that your balance is increased, or added to. Often, the + sign is not written in front of a positive number. A temperature of 65°F is the same as +65°F. An account balance of $200.00 is the same as a balance of +$200.00. A negative number will always be indicated with a symbol.

QUESTIONS TO CONSIDER

1. Find a bank account statement. How does it show deposits and withdrawals? Are parentheses used to indicate a withdrawal or is the negative sign, −, used? Is a deposit or a positive balance shown with a + symbol or without it?

2. Suppose a golfer's score is currently 3 under par (−3). What is the golfer's score if on the next hole she scores a birdie (one under par)? What if the golfer scores a bogey (1 over par)? How can signed numbers be used to find the golfer's new score?

3. A temperature reading during the day was 2 degrees above zero. At night, the temperature fell 9 degrees. How can signed numbers help find the new temperature?

4. What other situations might use signed numbers?

KEY TERMS

- absolute value (p. 5)
- integers (p. 4)
- irrational numbers (p. 4)
- negative number (p. 4)
- number line (p. 4)
- positive number (p. 4)
- rational numbers (p. 4)
- real numbers (p. 4)

SIGNED NUMBERS

1.1 POSITIVE NUMBER Any number greater than 0.

1.2 NEGATIVE NUMBER Any number less than 0.

Any number of everyday situations use negative as well as positive numbers. The phrase *signed numbers* represents both. A **positive number** is any number greater than 0. A **negative number** is any number less than 0.

Another way to interpret the negative symbol is to think of it as indicating "the opposite." The opposite of positive is negative, so the opposite of +7, or just 7, is −7, or negative 7. Also, the opposite of −5, written as −(−5), is +5, or 5. Notice that the negative of a number need not itself be negative, so beware!

Integers

1.3 INTEGERS The set of numbers consisting of whole numbers and their opposites.

The set of whole numbers includes the numbers 0, 1, 2, 3, 4, 5, 6, and so on. The opposites of these numbers are 0, −1, −2, −3, −4, and so on. The set of **integers** is the set consisting of whole numbers and their opposites.

Notice that 0 is its own opposite—it is not correct to write −0 or +0. Zero is neither positive nor negative.

Rational Numbers

1.4 RATIONAL NUMBERS The set of numbers that includes all fractions and all decimals that can be written in fractional form.

While an integer is a particular kind of fraction or decimal (for example, $7 = \frac{7}{1} = 7.0$), not all fractions or decimals are integers. The set of **rational numbers** includes all fractions and all decimals that can be written in fractional form.

Numbers such as $4, \frac{2}{5}, -14.75$, and $-1\frac{1}{3}$ are all rational numbers. Fractions and decimals are closely related. Recall that any fraction can be written as a decimal. These decimal equivalents will always terminate or repeat. The fraction $\frac{2}{5} = \frac{4}{10}$ is equivalent to the decimal 0.4, which is a terminating decimal. The mixed number $-1\frac{1}{3}$ is equivalent to −1.333333. . ., or $-1.\overline{3}$, where the ellipsis (. . .) or overbar indicates digits that continue to repeat.

Real Numbers

1.5 IRRATIONAL NUMBERS The set of numbers that includes all nonrepeating, nonending decimals.

When a decimal never ends and never repeats, it cannot be expressed as a fraction, and so is not a rational number. The set of **irrational numbers** includes all nonrepeating, nonending decimals.

Some examples of irrational numbers are the number π (pi), which is used in the calculation of circumference and area of circles and begins 3.14159. . ., and a number such as $\sqrt{2}$, which begins 1.4142135. . . . Observe that the ellipsis here indicates a continuing string of nonrepeating digits, since there are no repetitions shown.

1.6 REAL NUMBERS The set of all rational and irrational numbers.

Note that a number must be either rational or irrational, but cannot be both. There is no overlap between the two classifications. The set of **real numbers** consists of all rational and irrational numbers.

Number Line

1.7 NUMBER LINE A graphical representation of real numbers in order, with every point representing a real number and every real number corresponding to a point on the line.

A **number line** represents real numbers in order, with every point representing a real number and every real number corresponding to a point on the line. On a horizontal number line, it is usual to indicate positive numbers in increasing order moving to the right from a point labeled 0 and negative numbers in decreasing order moving to the left from 0. On a vertical number line, the positive direction from 0 is usually up, and the negative direction is down.

When operating a car, the gears for "drive" and "reverse" are opposites—drive moves the car forward, while reverse moves the car backward.

Suppose the car starts at 0 feet along the number line. The driver shifts the car into drive and moves forward 600 feet (Figure 1.1a). From the original position, the car is now at +600, or 600, feet along the number line.

Suppose a second car starts from the same point at 0 feet along the number line. The driver shifts the car into reverse and moves backward 300 feet (Figure 1.1b). From the original position, the car is now at −300 feet along the number line.

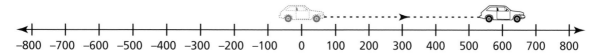

FIGURE 1.1a In Drive Gear, a Car Moves Forward 600 Feet to +600 on the Number Line.

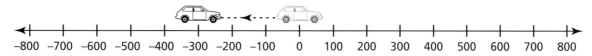

FIGURE 1.1b In Reverse Gear, a Second Car Moves Backward 300 Feet, to –300 on the Number Line.

Absolute Value

But how far is each car in Figure 1.1 from the starting point? The first car is at +600, or 600, so it is 600 feet from the starting point. The second car is at −300, so it is 300 feet from the starting point. To say that the car is −300 feet from the starting point does not make sense. When the context is distance, a negative number does not make sense because distance is always positive.

Consider the integers 12 and −9. On a number line, 12 is located 12 units away from 0 to the right. Similarly, −9 is located 9 units away from 0 but to the left. Note that 12 units away and 9 units away are measures of distance. The distance of a number from 0 is the **absolute value** of the number.

1.8 ABSOLUTE VALUE A number's distance from 0.

Absolute value bars are used to indicate the absolute value of a number. Referring to the car going forward and the car in reverse, the first car is $|600| = 600$ feet from the starting point. The second car is $|-300| = 300$ feet from the starting point.

ADDITION AND SUBTRACTION OF INTEGERS

Adding Integers

Just as whole numbers can be added and subtracted, integers can be added and subtracted.

To remember the rules for adding and subtracting integers, it helps to visualize a number line as in Figure 1.2. When adding integers, measure a positive number that distance to the right and a negative number that distance to the left.

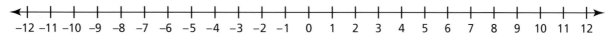

FIGURE 1.2 Number Line

To add integers, always start at 0 on the number line.

Adding Two Positive Integers

Adding two positive integers, such as $3 + 5$, equals another positive integer. Graphing this example on the number line in Figure 1.3, the 3 means to move 3 units to the right from 0, and the 5 means to move 5 more units to the right from 3 to end up at 8.

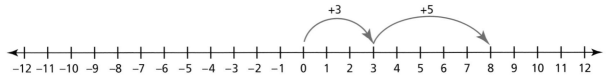

FIGURE 1.3 Adding 3 and 5

Adding Two Negative Integers

To add two negative integers, such as $-4 + (-7)$, on the number line in Figure 1.4, move 4 units left from 0, then 7 more units to the left. The result is -11.

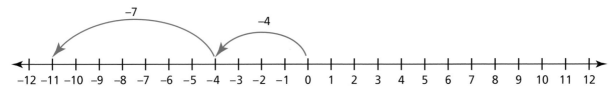

FIGURE 1.4 Adding –4 and –7

Adding negative integers will always involve movements to the left, so the result always will be a negative number. The absolute value of that number is the sum of the absolute values of the integers ($4 + 7 = 11$).

Adding Positive and Negative Integers

When adding one positive integer and one negative integer, there will be one movement to the right and one to the left. If the movement to the right is the greater distance, the result will be positive (Figure 1.5). If the movement to the left is the greater distance, the result will be negative (Figure 1.6). When adding a positive and a negative integer, the sum will have the same sign as the term with the largest absolute value.

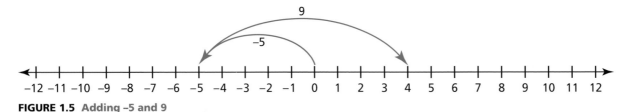

FIGURE 1.5 Adding –5 and 9

The difference in absolute values in Figure 1.5 is $|9| - |-5| = 9 - 5 = 4$. Positive 9 is the greater distance, so the result is positive.

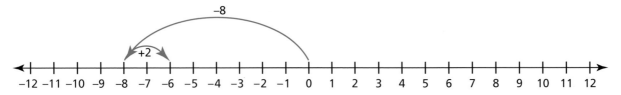

FIGURE 1.6 Adding –8 and 2

The difference in absolute values in Figure 1.6 is $8 - 2 = 6$. Negative 8 is the greater distance, so the result is negative.

In either case, the absolute value of the result is the difference between the absolute values of the two integers: $9 - 5 = 4$ and $8 - 2 = 6$.

Subtracting Integers

Now consider the subtraction $9 - 5 = (+9) - (+5)$. The result is 4, as usual, but notice that it is also equivalent to the work above, and that by the Commutative Property of Addition $-5 + 9 = 9 + (-5)$. Instead of subtracting $+5$, add -5.

Subtracting a Positive Integer

To find $4 - 11$, rewrite the expression as $4 + (-11)$, which is -7. To find $-3 - 9$, rewrite the expression as $-3 + (-9)$, which is -12.

Subtracting a Negative Integer

When subtracting a negative integer, follow the same rule—add the positive number that is the opposite of the negative number. This is sometimes described as *two negatives (the two − symbols) make a positive.*

To find $5 - (-2)$, rewrite the expression as $5 + (2)$, which is 7. To find $-8 - (-10)$, rewrite the expression as $-8 + (10)$, which is 2.

ADDING AND SUBTRACTING INTEGERS

The rules for adding and subtracting integers are as follows:

1. The sum of two positive integers is their positive sum.

2. The sum of two negative integers is the negative of the sum of their absolute values.

3. The sum of a positive and a negative integer is the difference of their absolute values, with the sign of the number with the greater absolute value.

4. To subtract any number, add its negative.

Example 1.1
Find $12 + 42$.

Solution:

Since both integers are positive, this will be two movements to the right on a number line. The sum is 54 (Figure 1.7).

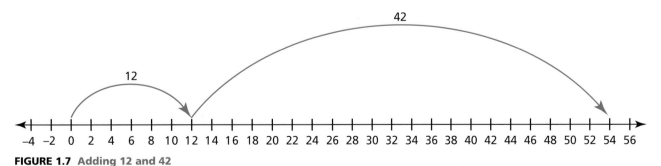

FIGURE 1.7 Adding 12 and 42

Example 1.2
A golfer's score in the tournament is currently 4 under par, or -4. On the next hole, the golfer scores a birdie (1 under par), or -1. What is the golfer's current score?

Solution:

Find $-4 + (-1)$.

Since both integers are negative, this will be two movements to the left on a number line, so the result will be negative. Add the absolute values of the two numbers: $4 + 1 = 5$. So $-4 + (-1) = -5$.

The golfer's current score is -5, or 5 under par (Figure 1.8).

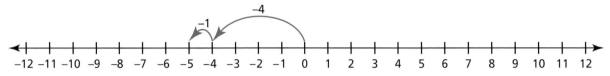

FIGURE 1.8 Adding –4 and –1

Example 1.3
Find $-25 + 14$.

Solution:

Since 25 units to the left is a greater distance than 14 units to the right, the sum will be negative. Find the difference of the absolute values of the two numbers: $25 - 14 = 11$. So $-25 + 14 = -11$ (Figure 1.9).

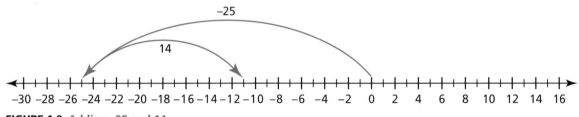

FIGURE 1.9 Adding –25 and 14

Example 1.4
Find $35 - 64 + (-54) - (-2)$.

Solution:

Rewrite, adding -64 instead of subtracting 64, and adding 2 instead of subtracting -2 (two negatives make a positive): $35 - 64 + (-54) - (-2) = 35 + (-64) + (-54) + 2$.

Using the Commutative Property of Addition, first add 35 and 2, getting 37, and then add -64 and -54 getting -118: $35 - 64 + (-54) - (-2) = 37 + (-118)$. Since 118 units to the left is a greater distance than 37 units to the right, the sum will be negative, and the difference of the absolute values is 81.

$35 - 64 + (-54) - (-2) = -81$

General rule for adding signed numbers: Write the expression as a sum of positive and negative numbers, add the positive numbers and add the negative numbers, and finally compute the sum.

Example 1.5
The temperature outside was 13° above 0. With the wind blowing, the temperature felt colder by 29°. What temperature did it feel like outside with the wind blowing?

Solution:

Find $13 - 29$.

Rewrite the expression as an addition by adding the opposite of 29:
$13 - 29 = 13 + (-29) = -16$.
The temperature felt like 16° below 0.

Example 1.6

Find $-51 - 16 + 54 + (-45)$.

Solution:

Rewrite the expression as an addition by adding the opposite of 16: $-51 - 16 + 54 + (-45) = -51 + (-16) + 54 + (-45)$. The only positive term is 54. The sum of the three negative terms is -112. The sum of 54 and -112 is -58.
So $-51 - 16 + 54 + (-45) = -58$.

Example 1.7

Find $20 - (-12) + (-8) - 31$.

Solution:

Rewrite the expression as an addition by adding the opposites of -12 and 31: $20 - (-12) + (-8) - 31 = 20 + 12 + (-8) + (-31)$. The sum of the positive terms is $20 + 12 = 32$. The sum of the negative terms is $(-8) + (-31) = -39$. The sum of 32 and -39 is -7.
So $20 - (-12) + (-8) - 31 = -7$.

Example 1.8

Find $-10 - (-35) - (-72) + (-93)$.

Solution:

Rewrite the expression as an addition, sum the positive and negative terms, and add:
$-10 - (-35) - (-72) + (-93) = -10 + (35) + 72 + (-93) = 107 + (-103) = 4$.

DIY PROBLEMS

1.1 Find $3 + 11$.

1.2 Find $-12 + 12$.

1.3 Find $-8 - (-8)$.

1.4 A golfer's score in the tournament is currently 7 under par, or -7. On the next hole, the golfer scores a birdie (1 under par), or -1. What is the golfer's current score?

1.5 Find $14 + (-50)$.

1.6 Find $-9 - 23 + (-34)$.

1.7 The temperature outside was $12°$ above 0. Overnight, the temperature fell $16°$. What was the temperature the next morning?

1.8 Find $-2 - 33 + 9 - 15$.

1.9 Find $5 - (-7) + (-4) - 8$.

1.10 Find $-10 - (-10) - (-54) + (-54)$.

MULTIPLICATION AND DIVISION OF INTEGERS

Multiplying Integers

Like whole numbers, integers can be multiplied and divided.

Multiplying Positive Integers

To multiply two positive integers, such as 3 and 5, the result is, as always, $3 \cdot 5 = 15$. Recall that multiplication is a short way to write repeated additions: $3 \cdot 5$ means three addends of 5—$5 + 5 + 5$ (or five addends of 3—$3 + 3 + 3 + 3 + 3$). On a number line, either of these would all be movements to the right, so when two positive integers are multiplied, the result is a positive number.

Multiplying Positive and Negative Integers

Now consider $4 \cdot (-6)$. This expression is a short way to write $(-6) + (-6) + (-6) + (-6)$. To add these, all the movements will be to the left, so the result has to be a negative number. Since $4 \cdot 6 = 24$, $4 \cdot (-6) = -24$. Remember that $4 \cdot (-6) = (-6) \cdot 4$ by the Commutative Law of Multiplication. Multiplying a positive number by a negative number results in a negative number.

Multiplying Two Negative Integers

What about multiplying two negative integers, such as $-4 \cdot (-6)$? Recall that one way to interpret a $-$ symbol is as "the opposite of." So if $4 \cdot (-6) = -24$, then $-4 \cdot (-6)$ is the opposite of -24, or 24. The product of two negative integers is always a positive number.

Another way to understand this is to compare it to a word phrase, where the word *not* is an interpretation of the $-$ symbol. Suppose a statement is true. Then a negative symbol would make the statement "not true." A second negative symbol would make the statement "not not true," which is equivalent to the statement being true again.

To summarize, in multiplying two numbers, one negative symbol makes the result negative, while two negative symbols make the result positive.

Dividing Integers

Dividing Two Positive Integers

The sign rules for dividing integers are the same as for multiplication, since dividing by a number is the same as multiplying by its reciprocal. If both integers in the division are positive, the quotient will be positive: $15 \div 5 = 3$.

Dividing Positive and Negative Integers

If one of the integers is negative, the quotient will be negative: $-28 \div 7 = -4$ and $72 \div (-9) = -8$.

Dividing Two Negative Integers

If both of the integers are negative, the quotient will be positive: $-54 \div (-6) = 9$.

Example 1.9
Paul earned $15 per hour at his job. How much did he earn for working nine hours?

MULTIPLYING AND DIVIDING INTEGERS

The rules for multiplying and dividing integers are as follows:

1. The product of two positive numbers is their positive product.

2. The product of two negative numbers is the positive product of their absolute values.

3. The product of a positive and a negative number is the negative of the product of their absolute values.

4. The quotient of two numbers is the product of the dividend and the reciprocal of the divisor.

Solution:

Find $9 \cdot 15$.

Since both integers are positive, the product will be positive: $9 \cdot 15 = 135$.
Paul earned \$135 for working nine hours.

Example 1.10
Find $4 \cdot (-12) \cdot (-3) \cdot (-4)$.

Solution:

Since $4 \cdot (-12) = -48$, $-48 \cdot (-3) = 144$, and $144 \cdot (-4) = -586$, $4 \cdot (-12) \cdot (-3) \cdot (-4) = -586$.

Notice that because the product of two negative numbers is positive, the product of three negative numbers must then be negative.

MULTIPLYING SIGNED NUMBERS

If the number of negative factors is even, the product is positive. If the number of negative factors is odd, the product is negative.

Example 1.11
Find $-5 \cdot 8 \cdot (-6) \cdot (-3) \cdot (-1)$.

Solution:

Since four factors are negative, the product will be positive:
$-5 \cdot 8 \cdot (-6) \cdot (-3) \cdot (-1) = 720$.

Example 1.12
Find $-9 \cdot (-21) \cdot (-2) \cdot 4$.

Solution:

Since three factors are negative, the product will be negative:
$-9 \cdot (-21) \cdot (-2) \cdot 4 = -1512$.

Example 1.13
Find $25 \div 4$.

Solution:

Since both integers are positive, the quotient will be positive: $25 \div 4 = 6.25$.

Example 1.14

Jen owes Yolanda $200. She agrees to pay her back in equal amounts over eight weeks. What integer describes the change in Jen's account balance each week? What will Jen do each week?

Solution:

Find $-200 \div 8$.

    Since one of the integers is negative, the quotient will be negative:

    $-200 \div 8 = -25$.

    Jen will pay back $25 each week.

Example 1.15

Find $63 \div (-9)$.

Solution:

Since one of the integers is negative, the quotient will be negative: $63 \div (-9) = -7$.

Example 1.16

Find $-72 \div (-10)$.

Solution:

Since both integers are negative, the quotient will be positive: $-72 \div (-10) = 7.2$.

Example 1.17

Find $(-2)^3$

Solution:

Since an exponent of 3 indicates three factors of the base (-2), expand: $(-2)(-2)(-2)$. For every two negative factors, the product is even. Since there are three negative factors, the answer is negative.

$(-2)^3 = -8$

DIY PROBLEMS

1.11 Katisha earns $18 per hour at her job. One day she worked a total of ten hours. How much did she earn that day?

1.12 Find $3 \cdot (-4) \cdot (-10) \cdot (-8)$.

1.13 Find $-7 \cdot 3 \cdot (-2) \cdot (-5) \cdot (-1)$.

1.14 Find $-2 \cdot (-31) \cdot (-6) \cdot 2$.

1.15 Find $48 \div 6$.

1.16 Jorge owes Michael $600. He agrees to pay him back in equal amounts over 15 weeks. What integer describes the change in Jorge's account balance each week? What will Jorge do each week?

1.17 Find $27 \div (-6)$.

1.18 Find $-15 \div (-2)$.

1.19 Find $(-1)^5$.

1.20 Find $(-6)^2$.

1.21 Find -4^3.

USING ORDER OF OPERATIONS

When there is more than one operation, the order in which the operations are performed is important. Let's consider the problem $3 + 5 \cdot 2$. If addition is performed first, then $8 \cdot 2 = 16$. However, if multiplication is performed first, then $3 + 10 = 13$. Two different answers would be possible. Which answer is correct?

The following Order of Operations should be applied:

1. Do all operations inside parentheses first.
2. Apply exponential operations.
3. Perform all multiplication and division operations from left to right.
4. Perform all addition and subtraction operations from left to right.

If we apply the correct order of operations to our problem of $3 + 5 \cdot 2$, then we must multiply first, and the correct answer is 13.

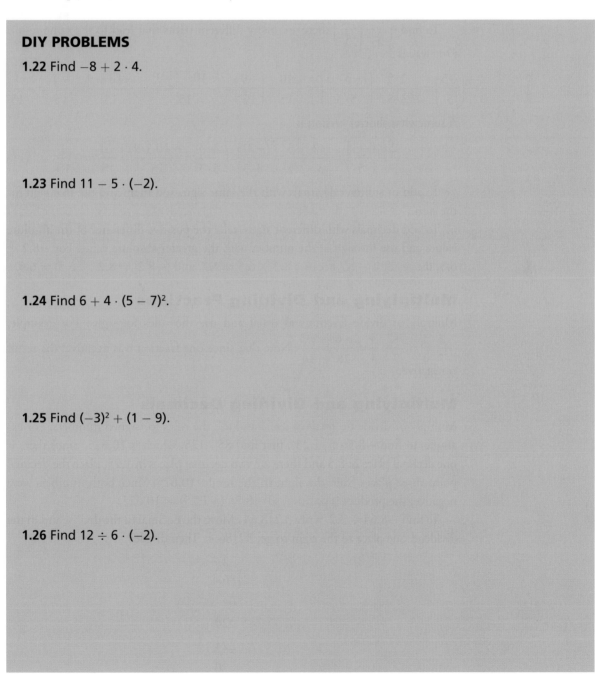

DIY PROBLEMS

1.22 Find $-8 + 2 \cdot 4$.

1.23 Find $11 - 5 \cdot (-2)$.

1.24 Find $6 + 4 \cdot (5 - 7)^2$.

1.25 Find $(-3)^2 + (1 - 9)$.

1.26 Find $12 \div 6 \cdot (-2)$.

OPERATIONS WITH RATIONAL NUMBERS

The rules of signs when adding, subtracting, multiplying, and dividing integers also hold when performing these operations on fractions and their decimal equivalents (and on all real numbers, as well). Notice that $-\frac{3}{4} = \frac{3}{-4} = \frac{-3}{4}$ since a quotient of a positive and a negative integer is negative.

Adding and Subtracting Rational Numbers

When adding or subtracting fractions that are negative, find a common denominator and add or subtract the numerators.

To compute $\frac{3}{4} - \left(-\frac{5}{6}\right)$ rewrite the fractions as 12ths, and then add the opposite of $-\frac{10}{12}$ to $\frac{9}{12}$, so $\frac{3}{4} - \left(-\frac{5}{6}\right) = \frac{9}{12} - \left(-\frac{10}{12}\right) = \frac{9}{12} + \frac{10}{12} = \frac{19}{12} = 1\frac{7}{12}$.

To find $-\frac{2}{3} - \left(\frac{-3}{5}\right)$ there are many different paths that lead to the same result. One way is

$$-\frac{2}{3} - \left(\frac{-3}{5}\right) = -\frac{2 \cdot 5}{3 \cdot 5} - \left(\frac{(-3) \cdot 3}{5 \cdot 3}\right) = -\frac{10}{15} - \left(\frac{-9}{15}\right) = \frac{-10 - (-9)}{15} = \frac{-10 + 9}{15} = \frac{-1}{15} = -\frac{1}{15}$$

A somewhat shorter version is

$$-\frac{2}{3} - \left(\frac{-3}{5}\right) = \frac{-2}{3} + \frac{3}{5} = \frac{(-2)5}{3 \cdot 5} + \frac{3 \cdot 3}{5 \cdot 3} = \frac{-10 + 9}{15} = \frac{-1}{15} = -\frac{1}{15}$$

To add or subtract decimals with the same sign, add them and use that sign for the sum.

To add decimals with different signs, take the positive difference of the absolute values and use the sign of the number with the greater absolute value. For $-8.2 + 6.5$, the result is -1.7 because $8.2 - 6.5 = 1.7$, and $|-8.2| = 8.2 > |6.5| = 6.5$.

Multiplying and Dividing Fractions

Multiply or divide fractions as usual and use the rules for signs. For example, $-\frac{2}{7} \cdot \frac{3}{4} = \frac{-2}{7} \cdot \frac{3}{4} = \frac{-6}{28} = \frac{-3}{14}$. Note that since one fraction was negative, the result is negative.

Multiplying and Dividing Decimals

Multiply or divide decimals as usual and use the rules for signed numbers. For example, to find $-8.5 \cdot (-1.25)$, first find $85 \cdot 125$, which is 10,625. Since there is one decimal place in 8.5 and there are two decimal places in 1.25, place the decimal point three places from the right in the result: 10.625. Since both numbers were negative, the product is positive, so $-8.5 \cdot (-1.25) = 10.625$.

To find $-8.64 \div 3.2$, write $3.2\overline{)8.64}$. Move the decimal in the divisor and in the dividend one place to the right to get $32\overline{)86.4}$. Then divide:

$$
\begin{array}{r}
2.7 \\
32\overline{)86.4} \\
\underline{64} \\
224 \\
\underline{224} \\
0
\end{array}
$$

Since one of the numbers is negative, $-8.64 \div 3.2 = -2.7$.

Example 1.18

Find $3\frac{2}{3} - \left(-7\frac{4}{9}\right)$.

Solution:

Step 1: The least common denominator for 3 and 9 is 9.

Step 2: Write equivalent fractions and add the opposite of $-7\frac{4}{9}$:

$$3\frac{2}{3} + 7\frac{4}{9} = 3\frac{6}{9} + 7\frac{4}{9}.$$

Step 3: Add the whole numbers and add the fractions: $3\frac{6}{9} + 7\frac{4}{9} = 10\frac{10}{9}$.

Step 4: Since $\frac{10}{9} = 1\frac{1}{9}$, the sum is $11\frac{1}{9}$.

Example 1.19

A carpenter had a board that was $8\frac{1}{3}$ feet long. He cut a board from this piece that was $3\frac{3}{4}$ feet long. What is the length of the board that remains?

Solution:

Find $8\frac{1}{3} - 3\frac{3}{4}$.

Step 1: The least common denominator for 3 and 4 is 12.

Step 2: Write equivalent fractions: $8\frac{1}{3} - 3\frac{3}{4} = 8\frac{4}{12} - 3\frac{9}{12}$.

Step 3: Subtract the fractions first, but you cannot take away $\frac{9}{12}$ from only $\frac{4}{12}$.

Rename $8\frac{4}{12}$ as $7\frac{16}{12}$ (the renamed 1 becomes $\frac{12}{12}$, which combines with the $\frac{4}{12}$ to make $\frac{16}{12}$).

Step 4: Now subtract: $8\frac{1}{3} - 3\frac{3}{4} = 8\frac{4}{12} - 3\frac{9}{12} = 7\frac{16}{12} - 3\frac{9}{12} = 4\frac{7}{12}$.

The board is now $4\frac{7}{12}$ feet long.

Example 1.20

Find $-34.8 + (-9.57)$.

Solution:

Rewrite the problem vertically so that the decimal points align:

$$\begin{array}{r} 34.8 \\ +\ \ 9.57 \\ \hline \end{array}$$

The sum is 44.37. Since both decimals were negative, the result is -44.37.

Example 1.21

At the diving competition, a diver scored 152.6 points after two dives. The diver scored 63.45 points on the first dive. What was the diver's score on the second dive?

Solution:

Find $152.6 - 63.45$.

Rewrite the problem vertically so that the decimal points align:

$$152.6$$
$$- \ \ 63.45$$

The difference is 89.15. The diver scored 89.15 on the second dive.

Example 1.22

Find $1\dfrac{3}{5} \cdot \left(-3\dfrac{2}{3}\right)$.

Solution:

Step 1: Write each mixed number as a fraction: $\dfrac{8}{5} \cdot \left(\dfrac{-11}{3}\right)$. Since one number is negative, the result will be negative.

Step 2: Multiply the numerators and the denominators, then simplify:

$$\frac{8}{5} \cdot \left(\frac{-11}{3}\right) = \frac{-88}{15} = -5\frac{13}{15}$$

Example 1.23

Find $-12\dfrac{2}{3} \div \left(-1\dfrac{5}{6}\right)$.

Solution:

Step 1: Write each mixed number as a fraction: $\dfrac{-38}{3} \div \left(\dfrac{-11}{6}\right)$.

Step 2: Rewrite the division as a multiplication by the reciprocal of the divisor:

$$\frac{-38}{3} \div \left(\frac{-11}{6}\right) = \frac{-38}{3} \cdot \left(\frac{-6}{11}\right).$$

Step 3: Since both numbers are negative, the result will be positive. Multiply the numerators and the denominators, then simplify:

$$\frac{-38}{3} \cdot \left(\frac{-6}{11}\right) = \frac{228}{33} = \frac{76}{11} = 6\frac{10}{11}$$

Example 1.24

Find $3.46 \cdot (-0.75)$.

Solution:

Since one number is negative, the result will be negative.

Step 1: Multiply as if there were no decimal points: $346 \cdot 75 = 25{,}950$.

Step 2: There are two decimal places in each number, for a total of four decimal places. Place the decimal four places from the right in the result: $3.46 \cdot (-0.75) = -2.5950$, or -2.595.

Example 1.25

Find $-75.4 \div 1.25$.

Solution:

Step 1: Write in long−division form: $1.25\overline{)75.4}$.

Step 2: Since the divisor has two decimal places, move the decimal two places to the right so that the divisor is a whole number. Move the decimal two places to the right in the dividend as well: $125\overline{)7540}$.

Step 3: Write a decimal point in the quotient directly above the decimal in the dividend and divide:

$$
\begin{array}{r}
60.32 \\
125\overline{)7540.00} \\
\underline{750} \\
400 \\
\underline{375} \\
250 \\
\underline{250} \\
0
\end{array}
$$

So $-75.4 \div 1.25 = -60.32$ since one of the numbers is negative.

DIY PROBLEMS

1.27 Find $6\frac{1}{2} + 4\frac{2}{3}$.

1.28 A frog jumped twice, covering a total of $10\frac{1}{4}$ feet. The frog's first jump was $5\frac{5}{6}$ feet. How long was its second jump?

1.29 Find $-15.78 + -254.9$.

1.30 A gymnast earned a total score of 35.2 points. On the last event, the gymnast earned 8.55 points. What was the gymnast's score prior to the last event?

1.31 Find $-3\frac{3}{5} \cdot \frac{5}{8}$.

1.32 Find $-2\dfrac{2}{5} \div \left(-\dfrac{3}{4}\right)$.

1.33 Find $8.45 \cdot (-0.6)$.

1.34 Find $-9.36 \div 0.9$.

SOLUTIONS TO DIY PROBLEMS

1.1 Find $3 + 11$.

Solution:

Both movements are to the right on a number line, so the result is positive: $3 + 11 = 14$ (Figure 1.10).

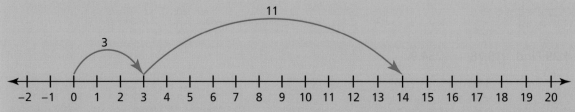

FIGURE 1.10 Adding 3 and 11

1.2 Find $-12 + 12$.

Solution:

The first movement is 12 units to the left on a number line, and the second movement is 12 units to the right on the number line. The result is $-12 + 12 + 0$

1.3 Find $-8 - (-8)$.

Solution:

Rewrite the expression $-8 - (-8)$ as $-8 + 8$. The first movement is 8 units to the left on a number line, and the second movement is 8 units to the right on the number line. The result is $-8 - (-8) = 0$

1.4 A golfer's score in the tournament is currently 7 under par, or −7. On the next hole, the golfer scores a birdie (1 under par), or −1. What is the golfer's current score?

Solution:

Find −7 + (−1).

  Since both integers are negative, this will be two movements to the left on a number line, so the result will be negative.

  Add the absolute values of the numbers: 7 + 1 = 8.

  So −7 + (−1) = −8. The golfer's current score is −8, or 8 under par (Figure 1.11).

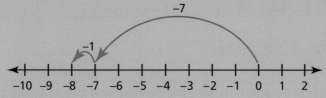

FIGURE 1.11 Adding −7 and −1

1.5 Find 14 + (−50).

Solution:

Since 50 units to the left is a greater distance than 14 units to the right, the sum will be negative. Subtract the absolute values of the two numbers: 50 − 14 = 36 (Figure 1.12).

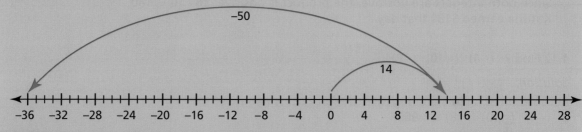

FIGURE 1.12 Adding 14 and −50

So 14 + (−50) = −36.

1.6 Find −9 − 23 + (−34).

Solution:

Rewrite the expression as an addition by adding the opposite of 23: Find −9 + (− 23) + (−34). All the terms are negative, and their sum is −66.

1.7 The temperature outside was 12° above 0. Overnight, the temperature fell 16°. What was the temperature the next morning?

Solution:

Find 12 − 16.

  Rewrite the expression as an addition: 12 + (−16) = −4. The temperature the next morning was 4° below 0.

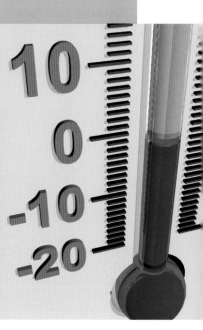

1.8 Find $-2 - 33 + 9 - 15$.

Solution:

Rewrite the expression as an addition and add the negative terms:
$-2 - 33 + 9 - 15 = -2 + (-33) + 9 + (-15) = 9 + (-50) = -41$.

1.9 Find $5 - (-7) + (-4) - 8$.

Solution:

Rewrite the expression as an addition, sum the positive and the negative terms, and add:
$5 - (-7) + (-4) - 8 = 5 + 7 + (-4) + (-8) = 12 + (-12) = 0$.

1.10 Find $-10 - (-10) - (-54) + (-54)$.

Solutions:

Rewrite the expression as an addition, sum the positive and the negative terms, and add:
$-10 - (-10) - (-54) + (-54) = -10 + 10 + 54 + (-54) = 64 + (-64) = 0$. [or, $0 + 0 = 0$]

1.11 Katisha earns $18 per hour at her job. One day, she worked a total of ten hours. How much did she earn that day?

Solution:

Find $18 \cdot 10$.

Since both integers are positive, the product is positive: $18 \cdot 10 = 180$.
Katisha earned $180 that day.

1.12 Find $3 \cdot (-4) \cdot (-10) \cdot (-8)$.

Solution:

Because three factors are negative, the product is negative:
$3 \cdot (-4) \cdot (-10) \cdot (-8) = -960$.

1.13 Find $-7 \cdot 3 \cdot (-2) \cdot (-5) \cdot (-1)$.

Solution:

Because four factors are negative, the product is positive:
$-7 \cdot 3 \cdot (-2) \cdot (-5) \cdot (-1) = 210$.

1.14 Find $-2 \cdot (-31) \cdot (-6) \cdot 2$.

Solution:

Because three factors are negative, the product is negative:
$-2 \cdot (-31) \cdot (-6) \cdot 2 = -744$.

1.15 Find $48 \div 6$.

Solution:

Since both integers are positive, the quotient is positive: $48 \div 6 = 8$.

1.16 Jorge owes Michael $600. He agrees to pay him back in equal amounts over 15 weeks. What integer describes the change in Jorge's account balance each week? What will Jorge do each week?

Solution:

Find $-600 \div 15$.

Since one integer is negative, the quotient is negative:
$-600 \div 15 = -40$.

Jorge will pay back $40 each week.

1.17 Find $27 \div (-6)$.

Solution:

Since one integer is negative, the quotient is negative:
$27 \div (-6) = -4.5$.

1.18 Find $-15 \div (-2)$.

Solution:

Since both integers are negative, the quotient is positive:
$-15 \div (-2) = 7.5$.

1.19 Find $(-1)^5$.

Solution:

Since there are an odd number of negative factors, the answer is negative:
$(-1)(-1)(-1)(-1)(-1) = -1$

1.20 Find $(-6)^2$.

Sine there are an even number of negative factors, the answer is positive: $(-6)(-6) = 36$

1.21 Find $- (4)^3$.

Only 4 is raised to the third power. $- 4^3 = (-1) \cdot 4 \cdot 4 \cdot 4 = -64$

1.22 Find $-8 + 2 \cdot 4$.

Solution:

Multiplication is performed before addition. $-8 + 2 \cdot 4 = -8 + 8 = 0$

1.23 Find $11 - 5 \cdot (-2)$.

Solution:

Multiplication is performed before subtraction.
$11 - 5 \cdot (-2) = 11 - (-10) = 11 + 10 = 21$

1.24 Find $6 + 4 \cdot (5 - 7)^2$.

Solution:

The operation in parenthesis is performed first. Since $5 - 7 = 5 + (-7) = -2$, substitute -2 in the parenthesis. $6 + 4 \cdot (-2)^2$. Exponents is the next operation. Since $(-2)^2 = (-2) \cdot (-2) = 4$, then the problem becomes $6 + 4 \cdot 4$. Multiplication is performed before addition to give $6 + 16 = 22$.

1.25 Find $(-3)^2 + (1 - 9)$.

Solution:

$(-3)^2 + (1 - 9) = (-3)^2 + (-8) = 9 + (-8) = 1$

1.26 Find $12 \div 6 \cdot (-2)$.

Solution:

Since multiplication and division are performed left to right, division is first.

$12 \div 6 \cdot (-2) = 2 \cdot (-2) = -4$

1.27 Find $6\frac{1}{2} - \left(-4\frac{2}{3}\right)$.

Solution:

$$6\frac{1}{2} + 4\frac{2}{3} = 6\frac{3}{6} + 4\frac{4}{6} = 10\frac{7}{6} = 11\frac{1}{6}$$

1.28 A frog jumped twice, covering a total of $10\frac{1}{4}$ feet. The frog's first jump was $5\frac{5}{6}$ feet. How long was its second jump?

Solution:

Find $10\frac{1}{4} - 5\frac{5}{6}$.

$$10\frac{1}{4} - 5\frac{5}{6} = 10\frac{3}{12} - 5\frac{10}{12} = 9\frac{15}{12} - 5\frac{10}{12} = 4\frac{5}{12}$$

The frog jumped $4\frac{5}{12}$ feet on its second jump.

1.29 Find $-15.78 + (-254.9)$.

Solution:

$$
\begin{array}{r}
15.78 \\
+\ 254.9 \\
\hline
270.68
\end{array}
$$

Since both numbers are negative, $-15.78 + (-254.9) = -270.68$.

1.30 A gymnast earned a total score of 35.2 points. On the last event, the gymnast earned 8.55 points. What was the gymnast's score prior to the last event?

Solution:

Find $35.2 - 8.55$.

$$
\begin{array}{r}
35.20 \\
-\ 8.55 \\
\hline
26.65
\end{array}
$$

The gymnast had earned 26.65 points prior to the last event.

1.31 Find $-3\frac{3}{5} \cdot \frac{5}{8}$.

Solution:

$$-\frac{18}{5} \cdot \frac{5}{8} = -\frac{90}{4} = -\frac{9}{4} = -2\frac{1}{4}$$

1.32 Find $-2\dfrac{2}{5} \div \left(-\dfrac{3}{4}\right)$.

Solution:

$$-\frac{12}{5} \div \left(-\frac{3}{4}\right) = -\frac{12}{5} \cdot \left(-\frac{4}{3}\right) = \frac{48}{15} = \frac{16}{5} = 3\frac{1}{5}$$

1.33 Find $8.45 \cdot (-0.6)$.

Solution:

Since one number is negative, the product will be negative. The product will have three decimal places: $845 \cdot 6 = 5070$, so $8.45 \cdot (-0.6) = -5.070$, or -5.07.

1.34 Find $-9.36 \div 0.9$.

Solution:

Since one number is negative, the quotient will be negative. Write as a long division: $0.9\overline{)9.36}$. Move the decimal so that the divisor is a whole number, then divide:

$$
\begin{array}{r}
10.4 \\
9{\overline{)93.6}} \\
\underline{9} \\
036 \\
\underline{36} \\
0
\end{array}
$$

So $-9.36 \div 0.9 = -10.4$.

END OF CHAPTER REVIEW QUESTIONS

Addition and Subtraction of Integers

1.1 Add $(-92) + 92 + (-10)$.

1.2 Add $-2 + (-7) + 4 + (-6)$.

1.3 Add $-126 + (-247) + (-358) + 338.$

1.4 Subtract $-28 - (-28).$

1.5 Subtract $-8 - 30 - (-11) - 7.$

1.6 Subtract $42 - 30 - 65 - (-11).$

1.7 The record high in a certain city in the month of June is 109°F, and the record low in the month of January is −21°F. What is the difference between the two temperatures?

Multiplication and Division of Integers

1.8 Multiply $4(-5)(-2)(-6).$

1.9 Multiply 3(−5)(−4)(9).

1.10 Find (−7)^2.

1.11 Find (−5)^3.

1.12 Find (−1)^9.

1.13 Find −8^2.

1.14 Divide −156 ÷ (−13).

1.15 Find the quotient of 144 and −24.

1.16 The combined scores of the top 11 golfers in a tournament equaled −44. What was the average score among the 11 players?

Operations with Rational Numbers

1.17 Solve $\dfrac{1}{8} + \dfrac{3}{16} - \left(-\dfrac{1}{2}\right)$.

1.18 Multiply $\left(\dfrac{1}{2}\right)\left(-\dfrac{3}{8}\right)\left(\dfrac{2}{5}\right)$.

1.19 Multiply $25.355 \cdot (-0.5)$.

1.20 Divide $-26.22 \div (-6.9)$.

1.21 Eleanor had a balance in her bank account of $1369.23. She paid her bills with checks written for $679.65, $567.35, and $240.34. What is her current account balance?

Using Order of Operations

1.22 Solve $-5 \cdot (3 - 9)$.

1.23 Solve $-12 - 3 + 7$.

1.24 Solve $8 \div 2 \cdot (-3)$.

1.25 Solve $10 + 2 \cdot (15 + (-5))$.

1.26 Solve $(-2)^3 - 20$.

1.27 Solve $-23 - (6 + (-9))$.

1.28 Solve $12 - 2 \cdot (9 - 8)$.

1.29 Solve $-1.5 \cdot (7 - 8)^2$.

1.30 Solve $-4^2 - 5 \cdot (-2)^2$.

1.31 Solve $\dfrac{(6-8)}{(12-9)}$.

1.32 Solve $\dfrac{(15-9)}{(9-1)}$.

1.33 Solve $\dfrac{\left[(2^2)+(-1)\right]}{(6-3)}$.

1.34 Solve $\dfrac{1}{5} \cdot (16 - 21)$.

1.35 Solve $\dfrac{2}{3} \cdot (7 - 10)$.

Introduction to Algebra

Julia wanted to open her own bakery. She did some research to study the costs of starting up a new business. Julia discovered that there are two types of expenses: one–time start–up costs and monthly costs.

The one–time start–up costs include buying the baking machinery, such as ovens, a take–a–number dispenser, counters and display cases, government licenses, and baking tools, such as mixing bowls, spoons, whisks, and so on. She even thought about having a few tables with chairs so customers could sit and enjoy their purchase. This thought led Julia to consider adding the costs for a coffee machine and a juice dispenser.

Then there are the monthly costs, such as rent for her store space, and utilities, such as phone and Internet services, electricity, and natural gas. Other monthly costs are employees; baking ingredients, such as eggs and flour; and boxes and bags for customers to take their purchases.

After a thorough study, Julia estimated her start–up costs to be about $45,000. She further estimated her monthly costs to be about $6,000.

Once she was open for business, Julia predicted that Monday through Thursday would be her slower days, so she estimated income for those days to be $200 each day. She thought that Friday, Saturday, and Sunday would be her busiest days, and estimated that she would earn $500 on each of these three days. This gave her an estimate of $2,300 in income each week, or $9,200 a month.

Julia pondered whether it made sense for her to pursue this dream. She felt that she needed to start showing a profit within six months. She asked her friend Merrill for some advice. He suggested that she use her estimates to figure out the point at which she would break even, or her *breakeven point.*

He explained that, after that length of time, her income would be larger than her expenses, so her business would show a profit.

This chapter will show how to use algebra to write expressions, and how to set up and solve equations like these that will help Julia calculate her breakeven point. For Julia, the critical equations are:

- $E = 45,000 + 6000m$, where m represents number of months in business, and E represents expenses after m months in business
- $I = 9200m$, where m represents number of months in business, and I represents income after m months in business
- The value of m, for which $E = I$ is the number of months it will take Julia to reach the breakeven point

QUESTIONS TO CONSIDER

1. How can an entrepreneur like Julia calculate the breakeven point for a new business? Under what circumstances might the breakeven point change? What effect would this have on Julia's business?

2. Until she launches her business and has actual data to consider, Julia is relying on estimates of her costs and income. What if her estimates are far off the actual numbers? How might Julia use equations to consider best–case and worst–case estimates and their effect on her breakeven point?

KEY TERMS

ALGEBRAIC EXPRESSIONS

Algebraic expressions do not have to contain a variable, but the focus here will be on those that do.

Variable Expressions

Consider the two expressions $3 + 4$ and $x + 4$. The value of $3 + 4$ is 7. The value of $x + 4$ cannot be determined until a value for x is chosen. We call the letter x here a **variable.**

Any letter or symbol can be used as a variable. An expression containing a variable, such as $x + 4$, is called a **variable expression.**

Another name for an addend (something added in an expression) is **term.** In the expression $9t - 4$, the terms are $9t$ and -4. We call the 9 in $9t$ the numerical coefficient, or simply the **coefficient,** of t. A coefficient of a quantity is a multiplier of the quantity. It is also true that t is the coefficient of 9. Note that the second term is -4, not 4; that is, the expression can be stated $9t + (-4)$.

Evaluating Variable Expressions

Evaluating an expression means finding its value. Evaluating a variable expression means finding its value for a certain value of x. For the variable expression $5n$, if $n = 6$, then $5n$ becomes $5 \cdot 6$, which is 30. If $n = -10$, $5(-10) = -50$.

There are two steps in evaluating a variable expression:

1. Substitute the given value for every instance of the variable.
2. Use the Order of Operations to calculate the result.

To evaluate a variable expression such as $x + 4$ when x has the value -9:

1. Replace the x with -9: $x + 4$ becomes $(-9) + 4$
2. Add. The result is -5.

To evaluate the expression $3g - 5$ when the value of $g = 7$:

1. Replace g with 7: $3g - 5$ becomes $3(7) - 5$.
2. First multiply 3 by 7, then add -5: $21 + (-5) = 16$. The result is 16.

Notice that 3 is the coefficient only of g, so 3 multiplies only the 7, not the 5.

Simplifying Variable Expressions

To **simplify** an expression, rewrite it as an **equivalent expression** using algebraic laws and relationships.

Figure 2.1 summarizes several of the key mathematical laws and shows how they apply to a sample algebraic expression.

	ADDITION	MULTIPLICATION
Commutative Law (allows changes in order)	$x + 4$ is the same as $4 + x$ $x + y$ is the same as $y + x$	$4x$ is the same as $x(4)$ xy is the same as yx
Associative Law (allows changes in grouping)	$(a + 5) + 6$ is the same as $a + (5 + 6)$ $a + (b + c)$ is the same as $(a + b) + c$	$(5m)n$ is the same as $5(mn)$ $m(np)$ is the same as $(mn)p$
Identity Law (Adding/Multiplying a number to/by its identity element yields the original number.)	$x + 0$ is equal to x The identity element for addition is 0.	$1 \cdot x$ is equal to x The identity element for multiplication is 1.
Inverse Law (Adding/Multiplying a number to/by its inverse yields the identity element.)	x and $-x$ are additive inverses, or opposites: $-4 + -(-4) = -4 + 4 = 0$, and $x + (-x) = 0$. The sum of a number and its opposite is the additive identity element, 0.	x and $\dfrac{1}{x}$ are multiplicative inverses, or reciprocals: $14 \cdot \dfrac{1}{14} = 1$, $-\dfrac{1}{2} \cdot (-2) = \dfrac{1}{-2} \cdot \dfrac{-2}{1} = 1$, $\dfrac{7}{9} \cdot \dfrac{1}{\frac{7}{9}} = \dfrac{7}{9} \cdot \dfrac{9}{7} = 1$ and $x \cdot \dfrac{1}{x} = 1$. The product of a number and its reciprocal is the multiplicative identity element, 1.

FIGURE 2.1 Laws for Simplifying Algebraic Expressions

The Distributive Law and Factoring

The *Distributive Law* controls multiplication of a sum by another expression. Consider multiplying $(6 + 9)$ by 3, or $(2x + 7)$ by 5:

$3(6 + 9)$	$5(2x + 7)$	Write the multiplication.
$3(6) + 3(9)$ *Distribute* 3 to multiply each term of $(6 + 9)$.	$5(2x) + 5(7)$ *Distribute* 5 to multiply each term of $(2x + 7)$.	Apply the Distributive Law.
	$(5 \cdot 2)x + 5(7)$	Apply the Associative Law of Multiplication.
$18 + 27 = 45$	$10x + 35$	Multiply.

The expression $3(6 + 9)$ is equivalent to the expression $18 + 27$ and equals 45. Both 6 and 9 have been multiplied by 3. (Note that this expression can also be solved by first adding the numbers in parentheses; that is, $3 (6 + 9) = 3 (15) = 45$.)

The expression $5(2x + 7)$ is equivalent to the expression $10x + 35$. Each term in $(2x + 7)$ has been multiplied by the factor 5.

Factoring

Factoring is the reverse of the Distributive Law. To factor an expression, first identify a **common factor** of the terms in the expression. Then write the expression in an equivalent form to show the common factor as a factor of the entire expression.

2.6 COMMON FACTOR A factor in an expression that is common to all terms of the expression.

2.7 FACTORING AN EXPRESSION To find a common factor and rewrite the expression in an equivalent form that shows the common factor.

2.8 GREATEST COMMON FACTOR The product of all the common factors of the terms in the expression.

For example, one can rewrite $10x + 35$ as $5(2x) + 5(7) = 5(2x + 7)$. The common factor of the original two terms $10x$ and 35 is 5.

Any common factor can be used to simplify an expression. However, often it is desirable to find the **greatest common factor.**

For example, if the original expression is $20x + 70$, 5 is a common factor, so one can write $20x + 70 = 5(4x + 14)$. However, there is an additional common factor of 2, since $4x + 14 = 2(2x + 7)$. Therefore, one can write $20x + 70 = 5 \cdot 2(2x + 7) = 10(2x + 7)$. While 2 and 5 are each factors of the terms $20x$ and 70, 10 is the greatest common factor, the product of all the common factors of the two terms.

Combining Like Terms

In algebraic expressions, variables may be the common factors. In the expression $5x^3y + yz$, the variable y is common to both terms.

Consider the expression $5x + 3x$. These terms can be combined as follows:

$5x + 3x$	Write the variable expression.
$5x = 5 \cdot x$ $3x = 3 \cdot x$	Factor each term and identify the common factor(s) in each; x is common factor in each term.
$x(5) + x(3)$	Write each term using the greatest common factor, x.
$x(5 + 3)$	Factor.
$x(8)$	Add inside parentheses.
$8x$	Apply the Commutative Law of Multiplication.

2.9 LIKE TERMS Terms that have the same variables raised to the same powers.

The terms in the expression $5x + 3x$ can be combined to make $8x$. The terms $5x$ and $3x$ are **like terms** since they both have the same variable, x, raised to the same power.

Other examples of like terms are $3pq$ and $7pq$, $4x^5$ and $-8x^5$, and so on.

Example 2.1 Identify the law illustrated by each of the following:
  a. $20x + 50$ is the same as $50 + 20x$
  b. $5n \cdot 1$ is the same as $5n$
  c. $7y + (-7y)$ is the same as 0

Solution:
  a. Since the order in which the terms are added is changed, this is the Commutative Law of Addition.
  b. Since the original quantity is obtained, this is the Identity Law of Multiplication.
  c. Since the additive identity element is obtained, this is the Inverse Law of Addition.

Example 2.2 Simplify the variable expression $5n + 8 - 2n$. Then evaluate the expression $n = -5$.

Solution:

$5n - 2n + 8$	Rewrite the variable expression using the Commutative Law.
$n(5) - n(2) + 8$	Write each like term using the greatest common factor, n.
$n(5 - 2) + 8$	Factor n from the first two terms.
$n(3) + 8$	Add inside parentheses.
$3n + 8$	Apply the Commutative Law.
$3(-5) + 8$ becomes $-15 + 8$, which is -7	Replace n with -5.

DIY PROBLEMS

2.1 Identify the law illustrated by each example.

   a. $4 \cdot 25x$ is the same as $(4 \cdot 25)x$

   b. $4(3x - 7)$ is equivalent to $12x - 28$

   c. $12m + 0$ is the same as $12m$

2.2 Simplify the expression $10a - 7 + 9a$. Then evaluate the expression for $a = 2$.

2.3 Simplify the expression $6m + 9m + 5$. Then evaluate the expression for $m = (-1)$.

2.4 Simplify the expression $-7y + 12 + 2y - 1$. Then evaluate the expression for $y = 3$.

INTRODUCTION TO EQUATIONS

Equations

An **equation** is two expressions set equal to each other. The equals symbol ($=$) is used between the expressions. If one or both of the expressions are variable expressions, the goal is to find a value of the variable that gives both expressions the same value.

To solve an algebraic equation means to find a value of the variable that makes the equation true. An equal sign makes it possible to determine the values that make the equation true. Consider the equation $3x + 5 = 11$. To find the required value of x, isolate the x on one side of the equation. How can the equation be manipulated so that x appears on one side by itself?

Addition Property of Equations

The variable x appears in only one term of the equation, the term $3x$. Also on that side, however, is $+ 5$. How can we make the $+ 5$ "disappear"? Recall the Inverse and Identity laws. The Inverse Law says that $5 + (-5) = 0$, and the Identity Law says that $3x + 0 = 3x$. So if we add -5 to the left side (which is the same as saying "subtract 5 from the left side"), the left side would become $3x$.

$$3x + 5 + (-5) = 3x + 5 - 5 = 3x$$

Can one simply add -5 to the left side? For the equation to remain true (sometimes referred to as *balanced*), -5 must also be added to the right side. The right side becomes $11 + (-5)$, which is 6.

$$11 + (-5) = 11 - 5 = 6$$

Adding the same quantity to (or subtracting it from) the expressions on both sides of an equation keeps the expressions equal (keeps the equation *balanced*—see Figure 2.2). Therefore, $3x = 6$ because

$$3x + 5 = 11$$
$$3x + 5 + (-5) = 11 + (-5)$$
$$3x = 6$$

This is the Addition Property of Equations.

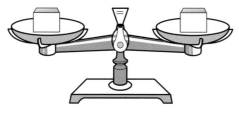

The scale is in balance since the two masses are the same. What would happen if a second mass were added to one side?

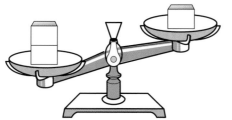

The scale would become unbalanced. In order to maintain balance, whatever happens to one side of the scale also has to happen to the other side. This is true for equations as well.

FIGURE 2.2 Balancing Equations

Multiplication Property of Equations

Now we have the equation $3x = 6$. How can we isolate x? To get x alone, the coefficient 3 must become the coefficient 1. Recall the Inverse and Identity laws. The Inverse Law says that $3 \cdot \frac{1}{3} = 1$, and the Identity Law says that $1 \cdot x = x$. So multiply the left side by $\frac{1}{3}$ (which is the same as saying "divide the left side by 3" because

$$3 \div 3 = \frac{3}{3} = \frac{3}{1} \cdot \frac{1}{3} = 3 \cdot \frac{1}{3} = 1),$$ making the left side x.

$$\frac{1}{3} \cdot 3x = x$$

To keep the equation balanced, the right side also must be multiplied by $\frac{1}{3}$, so it becomes $6 \cdot \frac{1}{3} = 2$.

Therefore, $x = 2$, because

$$3x = 6$$
$$\frac{1}{3} \cdot 3x = 6 \cdot \frac{1}{3}$$
$$x = 2$$

Now, check this answer by substituting 2 into the original equation:

$$3x + 5 = 11$$
$$3(2) + 5 = 11$$
$$6 + 5 = 11$$

$11 = 11$, so the answer $x = 2$ is correct.

Multiplying (or dividing) the expressions on both sides of an equation by the same quantity keeps the expressions equivalent (keeps the equation *balanced).* This is the **Multiplication Property of Equations.**

In applying the Multiplication Property of Equations, it is often useful to remember that dividing by a constant is the same as multiplying by its inverse. So, for example, instead of dividing by 1/10 (or in decimal form, 0.10), one can multiply by 10. Recognizing this sometimes makes the mathematics easier to solve at a glance.

Relatedly, an expression like $\dfrac{x}{4}$ (x divided by 4) is equivalent to $\dfrac{1}{4}x$ (x times the inverse of 4) because $\dfrac{1}{4}x = \dfrac{1}{4} \cdot \dfrac{x}{1} = \dfrac{x}{4}$.

Figure 2.3 summarizes the Addition and Multiplication properties for algebraic equations.

Equations Containing Parentheses

An equation may contain expressions with parentheses, such as $3(2n - 5) + 4n = 6 + 2(3n + 4)$. In this situation, use the Distributive Law to remove the parentheses. Then combine like terms.

	ALGEBRAIC REPRESENTATION	WHAT IT MEANS
Addition Property of Equations	If $a = b$, then $a + c = b + c$ and $a - c = b - c$	The same quantity may be added to or subtracted from both sides of an equation.
Multiplication Property of Equations	If $a = b$, then $a \cdot c = b \cdot c$ and $\dfrac{a}{c} = \dfrac{b}{c}$	The same quantity may be used to multiply or divide both sides of an equation.

FIGURE 2.3 Addition and Multiplication Properties in Algebraic Equations

$3(2n) - 3(5) + 4n = 6 + 2(3n) + 2(4)$	Apply the Distributive Law.
$6n - 15 + 4n = 6 + 6n + 8$	Multiply, using the Associative Law when necessary.
$10n - 15 = 6n + 14$	Combine like terms in each expression, using the Commutative, Associative, and Distributive laws mentally.

The next section discusses how to solve equations of this type.

Example 2.3 Describe how to solve each of the following equations.
  a. $x - 9 = 15$
  b. $\dfrac{n}{4} = 7$

Solution:

  a. Add 9 to both sides of the equation.

  b. Multiply both sides of the equation by 4.

Example 2.4 Simplify the equation $8 - 3(2n + 3) = 7(n - 4) + 2n$.

Solution:

Apply the Distributive Law: $8 - 3(2n) - 3(3) = 7(n) - 7(4) + 2n$
Multiply: $8 - 6n - 9 = 7n - 28 + 2n$
Combine like terms: $-6n - 1 = 9n - 28$

2.6 Describe how to solve each equation.

   a. $7x = 21$
   b. $14 = n + 5$
   c. $\dfrac{c}{2} = 5$
   d. $w - 12 = 3$

2.7 Simplify the equations.

   a. $9 + 3(4c - 2) - 2c = 15 - 2(5c - 1).$
   b. $5(d + 1) = 4(d - 2)$
   c. $(x - 2) = -2(x + 8)$
   d. $2(x + 9) - 4x = 12 - 3(2x + 2)$

GENERAL EQUATIONS

Figure 2.4 summarizes a general method for solving algebraic equations.

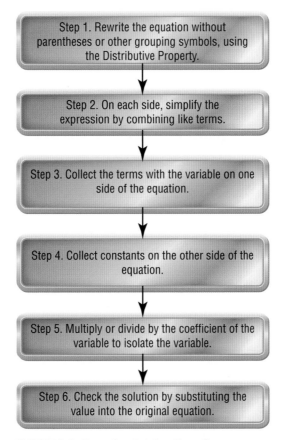

Step 1. Rewrite the equation without parentheses or other grouping symbols, using the Distributive Property.

Step 2. On each side, simplify the expression by combining like terms.

Step 3. Collect the terms with the variable on one side of the equation.

Step 4. Collect constants on the other side of the equation.

Step 5. Multiply or divide by the coefficient of the variable to isolate the variable.

Step 6. Check the solution by substituting the value into the original equation.

FIGURE 2.4 Steps for Solving Equations

Solving Equations in the Form of *ax* + *b* = *c*

Use the outline shown in Figure 2.4 to solve the equation $5n - 7 = 11$. Steps 1, 2, and 3 are already satisfied for this equation: there are no parentheses, there are no like terms to be combined, and the variable is on just one side of the equation. So, begin with Step 4.

Step 4	Add 7 to both sides.	$5n - 7 + 7 = 11 + 7$	Addition Property of Equations
	Simplify by combining the constants.	$5n = 18$	Inverse and Identity laws
Step 5	Divide both sides by 5.	$\dfrac{5n}{5} = \dfrac{18}{5}$	Multiplication Property of Equations
	Simplify by performing the division.	$n = 3.6$	Inverse and Identity laws
Step 6	Check the solution.	$5(3.6) - 7 = 11$	Evaluate for $n = 3.6$.
		$18 - 7 = 11$	
		$11 = 11$	

The solution is $n = 3.6$.

Solving Equations in the Form of *ax* + *b* = *cx* + *d*

Solve the equation $17x - 4 = 13x + 12$. Using the outline, steps 1 and 2 do not apply to this equation. So begin with Step 3.

Step 3	Add $-13x$ to both sides.	$17x - 4 - 13x = 13x + 12 - 13x$	Addition Property of Equations
	Simplify by combining like terms.	$4x - 4 = 12$	Inverse and Identity laws
Step 4	Add 4 to both sides.	$4x - 4 + 4 = 12 + 4$	Addition Property of Equations
	Simplify by combining the constants.	$4x = 16$	Inverse and Identity laws
Step 5	Divide both sides by 4.	$\dfrac{4x}{4} = \dfrac{16}{4}$	Multiplication Property of Equations
	Simplify by performing the division.	$x = 4$	Inverse and Identity laws
Step 6	Check the solution.	$17(4) - 4 = 13(4) + 12$	Evaluate for $x = 4$.
		$68 - 4 = 52 + 12$	
		$64 = 64$	

The solution is $x = 4$.

Solving Equations Containing Parentheses

Use the various properties for rewriting and simplifying equations to rewrite equations containing parentheses.

Example 2.5 Solve the equation $3p + 4 = 7(p + 1) - 2p$.
Use the outline steps.

Step 1	Rewrite without parentheses	$3p + 4 = 7p + 7 - 2p$	Distributive Property
Step 2	Simplify by combining like terms.	$3p + 4 = 5p + 7$	Commutative Property of Addition
Step 3	Subtract $5p$ from both sides.	$3p - 5p + 4 = 5p + 7 - 5p$	Addition Property of Equations
	Simplify by combining like terms.	$-2p + 4 = 7$	Commutative Property of Addition
Step 4	Add -4 to both sides.	$-2p + 4 - 4 = 7 - 4$	Addition Property of Equations
	Simplify by combining the constants.	$-2p = 3$	Inverse and Identity laws
Step 5	Divide both sides by -2.	$\dfrac{-2p}{-2} = \dfrac{3}{-2}$	Multiplication Property of Equations
	Simplify.	$p = -1.5$	Inverse and Identity laws
Step 6	Check the solution.	$3(-1.5) + 4 = 7(-1.5 + 1)$ $- 2(-1.5) -4.5 + 4 = 7\,(-0.5)$ $+ 3 -0.5 = -3.5 + 3 - 0.5$ $= -0.5$	Evaluate for $p = -1.5$

Example 2.6 Solve the equation $3(5x - 4) + 8 = 6x - 2(x - 9)$.

Solution:

Using the outline, begin with Step 1.

Step 1	Distribute.	$3(5x) - 3(4) + 8 =$ $6x - 2(x) - 2(-9)$	Distributive Property
	Multiply.	$15x - 12 + 8 = 6x - 2x + 18$	Associative Law
Step 2	Simplify the expressions on both sides.	$15x - 4 = 4x + 18$	Combine like terms.
Step 3	Subtract $4x$ from both sides.	$15x - 4 - 4x = 4x + 18 - 4x$	Addition Property of Equations
	Simplify.	$11x - 4 = 18$	Associative, Commutative, Inverse, Identity, and Distributive laws
Step 4	Add 4 to both sides.	$11x - 4 + 4 = 18 + 4$	Addition Property of Equations
	Simplify.	$11x = 22$	Inverse and Identity laws
Step 5	Divide both sides by 11.	$\dfrac{11x}{11} = \dfrac{22}{11}$	Multiplication Property of Equations

	Simplify.	$x = 2$	Inverse and Identity laws
Step 6	Check the solution.	$3[5(2) - 4] + 8 = 6(2)$ $- 2[(2) - 9]$ $3(6) + 8 = 12 - 2(-7)$ $18 + 8 = 12 + 14$ $26 = 26$	Evaluate for $x = 2$.

The solution is $x = 2$.

Solving the equation $3(n + 5) = 21$ following these steps gives $3n + 15 = 21$, then $3n = 6$, and $n = 2$.

Notice, though, that the left side of the equation is simply a product of two factors, 3 and $(n + 5)$. An alternate method for solving this equation is as follows:

$3(n + 5) = 21$

$$\dfrac{3(n+5)}{3} = \dfrac{21}{3} \qquad \text{Divide both sides by 3 to isolate the factor } (n + 5).$$

$n + 5 = 7$ Simplify.

$n + 5 - 5 = 7 - 5$ Subtract 5 from both sides.

$n = 2$ Simplify.

Will this method always work? It will only work if the product that involves the variable is isolated.

Solve $6(2x + 1) - 5 = 19$.

$6(2x + 1) - 5 + 5 = 19 + 5$ Add 5 to both sides to isolate the product $6(2x + 1)$.

$6(2x + 1) = 24$ Simplify.

$$\dfrac{6(2x+1)}{6} = \dfrac{24}{6} \qquad \text{Divide both sides by 6 to isolate the factor } (2x + 1).$$

$2x + 1 = 4$ Simplify.

$2x + 1 - 1 = 4 - 1$ Subtract 1 from both sides.

$2x = 3$ Simplify.

$$\dfrac{2x}{2} = \dfrac{3}{2} \qquad \text{Divide both sides by 2.}$$

$x = \dfrac{3}{2}$ or 1.5   Simplify.

$6[2(1.5) + 1] - 5 = 19$ Check the solution.

$6(3 + 1) - 5 = 19$

$6(4) - 5 = 19$

$24 - 5 = 19$

$19 = 19$

Example 2.7

Solve the equation $8 - 3(x + 5) = 11$ in two ways.

Method 1

$8 - 3(x + 5) - 8 = 11 - 8$ Subtract 8 from both sides.

$-3(x + 5) = 3$ Simplify.

$$\frac{-3(x+5)}{-3} = \frac{3}{-3}$$ Divide both sides by -3 to isolate the factor $(x+5)$.

$x + 5 = -1$ Simplify.

$x + 5 - 5 = -1 - 5$ Subtract 5 from both sides.

$x = -6$ Simplify.

$8 - 3(-6 + 5) = 11$ Check the solution.

$8 - 3(-1) = 11$

$8 + 3 = 11$

$11 = 11$

Method 2

$8 - 3(x) + (-3)(5) = 11$ Use the distributive property.

$8 - 3x - 15 = 11 - 7 - 3x = 11$ Simplify.

$-7 - 3x + 7 = 11 + 7$ Add 7 to both sides.

$-3x = 18$ Simplify.

$$\frac{-3x}{-3} = \frac{18}{-3}$$ Divide both sides by -3.

$x = -6$ Simplify.

$8 - 3(-6 + 5) = 11$ Check the solution.

$8 - 3(-1) = 11$

$8 + 3 = 11$

$11 = 11$

Example 2.8

Choose a method to solve $2(3n + 4) - 5 = 12$.

$2(3n + 4) - 5 + 5 = 12 + 5$ Add 5 to both sides.

$2(3n + 4) = 17$ Simplify.

$2(3n) + 2(4) = 17$ Since division by 2 would yield a fraction, use the distributive property.

$6n + 8 = 17$ Simplify.

$6n + 8 - 8 = 17 - 8$ Subtract 8 from both sides.

$6n = 9$ Simplify.

$$\frac{6n}{6} = \frac{9}{6}$$ Divide both sides by 6.

$n = \dfrac{9}{6} = \dfrac{3}{2}$ or $1\dfrac{1}{2}$ or 1.5 Simplify.

$2[3(1.5) + 4] - 5 = 12$ Check the solution.

$2(4.5 + 4) - 5 = 12$

$2(8.5) - 5 = 12$

$17 - 5 = 12$

$12 = 12$

DIY PROBLEMS

2.8 Solve the equation $0.75\,x + 6 = x - 2$.

Step 1: Rewrite the equation without parentheses or other grouping symbols.

Step 2: On each side, simplify the expression by combining like terms.

Step 3: Collect the terms with the variable on one side of the equation.

Step 4: Collect constants on the other side of the equation.

Step 5: Multiply or divide to isolate the variable.

Step 6: Check the solution.

2.9 Solve the equation $12(n - 4) - 5n = 10 - 3n$.

Step 1: Rewrite the equation without parentheses or other grouping symbols.

Step 2: On each side, simplify the expression by combining like terms.

Step 3: Collect the terms with the variable on one side of the equation.

Step 4: Collect constants on the other side of the equation.

Step 5: Multiply or divide to isolate the variable.

Step 6: Check the solution.

2.10 Solve the equation $5m + 7 = -23$.

2.11 Solve the equation $-3(x - 1) = 27$.

2.12 Solve the equation $5(2n - 5) + 4 = 14$ in two ways.

2.13 Solve the equation $12 - 2(x + 4) = 15$.

2.14 Solve the equation $-2(2x + 1) = -3x + 4$.

2.15 Solve the equation $2(x - 3) - 4x = 15 - (x + 6)$.

Translating Sentences into Equations and Solving

Most problems are presented in words, not in equations. To use algebra to solve word problems, follow these five steps:

1. Identify what needs to be found and create a variable for it.
2. Write an equation that represents the problem situation.
3. Solve the equation, using the steps summarized in Figure 2.4.
4. Check the solution.
5. Put the solution back into the context of the problem and answer the question that was asked.

Step 2 is crucial to the success of solving the problem. It is vital to be able to translate problems presented in words into an equation that can be solved. Look for the key words in Figure 2.5 to help choose the operation symbol needed to translate the words to an equation. (Note that in algebraic expressions the variable x can be easily confused with the multiplication symbol, $\times$. For this reason, algebraic expressions often use an alternative symbol to indicate multiplication, such as $*$ or $\cdot$.)

ADDITION (+)	SUBTRACTION (−)	MULTIPLICATION (*, ·, OR ×)	DIVISION (÷, /,) , OR FRACTION BAR)	EQUALS =
Sum	Difference	Product	Quotient	Is
More than	Less than	Times	Divided by	Is the same as
Increased by	Decreased by	Twice		The result is
Together	Minus	of		

FIGURE 2.5 Key Words and Their Associated Mathematical Operations

Example 2.9 The sum of two numbers is 18. The greater number is 2 less than three times the lesser number. What are the numbers?

Solution:

Step 1: Create the variable.	Let n represent the lesser number. Then $3n - 2$ represents the greater number.	"2 less than" means to subtract 2 from "three times the lesser number," n.
Step 2: Write an equation.	$n + 3n - 2 = 18$	"The sum" means to add the two numbers; "is" represents "=."
Step 3: Solve the equation.	$4n - 2 = 18$ $4n - 2 + 2 = 18 + 2$ $4n = 20$ $\dfrac{4n}{4} = \dfrac{20}{4}$ $n = 5$	Use the steps from Figure 2.4.
Step 4: Check the solution.	$5 + 3(5) - 2 = 18$ $5 + 15 - 2 = 18$ Yes, $n = 5$	Substitute 5 for n in the original equation.
Step 5: Answer the question.	The two numbers are 5 and 13.	The lesser number is 5 and the greater number is $3(5) - 2 = 15 - 2 = 13$.

Example 2.10 One number is 6 more than another number. Three times the lesser number added to twice the greater number is 2. What is the greater number?

Solution:

Step 1: Create the variable.	Let n represent the lesser number. Then $n + 6$ represents the greater number.	"6 more than" means to add 6 to the lesser number, n.
Step 2: Write an equation.	$3(n) + 2(n + 6) = 2$	"Three times the lesser number" means to multiply the lesser number by 3; "twice the greater number" means to multiply the greater number by 2; "is" represents "=."
Step 3: Solve the equation.	$3n + 2n + 12 = 2$ $5n + 12 = 2$ $5n + 12 - 12 = 2 - 12$ $5n = -10$ $\dfrac{5n}{5} = \dfrac{-10}{5}$ $n = -2$	Use the steps from Figure 2.4.
Step 4: Check the solution.	$3(-2) + 2(-2 + 6) = 2$ $-6 + 8 = 2$ Yes, $n = -2$	Substitute -2 for n in the original equation.
Step 5: Answer the question.	The greater number is 4.	-2 is the lesser number, so $-2 + 6 = 4$ is the greater number.

Example 2.11 Juanita paid a total of $40.75 for five shirts. Each shirt cost the same amount. How much did she pay for each shirt?

Solution:

Step 1: Create the variable.	Let n represent the cost of one shirt.
Step 2: Write an equation.	$5n = 40.75$
Step 3: Solve the equation.	$\dfrac{5n}{5} = \dfrac{40.75}{5}$
	$n = 8.15$
Step 4: Check the solution.	Is $5(8.15) = 40.75$?
	$5(8.15) = 40.75$
	Yes, 8.15 is the solution.
Step 5: Answer the question.	Juanita paid $8.15 for each shirt.

Example 2.12 Henry paid a total of $68.37 for six pairs of pants. He paid $4.77 in sales tax. If each pair of pants cost the same amount, how much was one pair of pants?

Solution:

Step 1: Create the variable.	Let n represent the cost of one pair of pants.
Step 2: Write an equation.	$6n + 4.77 = 68.37$
Step 3: Solve the equation.	$6n + 4.77 = 68.37$
	$6n + 4.77 - 4.77 = 68.37 - 4.77$
	$6n = 63.6$
	$\dfrac{6n}{6} = \dfrac{63.6}{6}$
	$n = 10.6$
Step 4: Check the solution.	Is $6(10.6) + 4.77 = 68.37$?
	$6(10.6) + 4.77 = 63.6 + 4.77 = 68.37$
	Yes, 10.6 is the solution.
Step 5: Answer the question.	Each pair of pants cost $10.60.

Example 2.13 Penny made a batch of cookies for a bake sale. Pauline made four times the number of cookies that Penny made. Together, they made 150 cookies. How many cookies did Penny make?

Solution:

Let x represent the number of cookies Penny made. Then $4x$ represents the number of cookies Pauline made.

$$x + 4x = 150$$
$$5x = 150$$
$$\frac{5x}{5} = \frac{150}{5}$$
$$x = 30$$

Penny made 30 cookies for the bake sale.

Example 2.14 Jacqueline made a deposit into her checking account that was exactly three times her current balance. Then she wrote a check for $75. After this, her balance was $105.40. What was Jacqueline's beginning balance?

Solution:

Let x represent her original balance.

$$x + 3x - 75 = 105.40$$
$$4x - 75 = 105.40$$
$$4x - 75 + 75 = 105.40 + 75$$
$$4x = 180.40$$
$$\frac{4x}{4} = \frac{180.40}{4}$$
$$x = 45.10$$

She had $45.10 in her checking account originally.

Example 2.15 Pete decided to start a business mowing lawns. He invested $420 in a lawn mower and estimated that he would need $1 of gas per lawn. He decided to charge customers $15 to mow their lawn. How many lawns would Pete have to mow in order to break even?

Solution:

Let n represent the number of lawns.

$$420 + n = 15n$$
$$420 + n - n = 15n - n$$
$$420 = 14n$$
$$\frac{420}{14} = \frac{14n}{14}$$
$$30 = n$$

Pete would have to mow 30 lawns in order to break even.

Example 2.16 One cell phone provider charges a monthly fee of $10 and $0.15 per minute of use. Another provider charges a monthly fee of only $2, but charges $0.25 per minute of use. For what number of minutes of use would the charge be the same for one month?

Solution:

Let n represent the number of minutes of use.

$$10 + 0.15n = 2 + 0.25n$$
$$10 + 0.15n - 0.15n = 2 + 0.25n - 0.15n$$
$$10 = 2 + 0.1n$$
$$10 - 2 = 2 + 0.1n - 2$$
$$8 = 0.1n$$
$$10(8) = 10(0.1n)$$
$$80 = n$$

The charge would be the same for 80 minutes of use.

DIY PROBLEMS

2.16 The sum of two numbers is 25. One number is 8 less than twice the other number. What are the two numbers?

Step 1: Create the variable.

Step 2: Write an equation.

Step 3: Solve the equation.

Step 4: Check the solution.

Step 5: Answer the question.

2.17 One number is 1 less than four times another number. Twice the greater number minus three times the lesser number is 48. What is the greater number?

Step 1: Create the variable.

Step 2: Write an equation.

Step 3: Solve the equation.

Step 4: Check the solution.

Step 5: Answer the question.

2.18 Marge bought 12 cans of soup at the store. Each can cost the same amount. If the total was $8.76, how much was each can of soup?

Step 1: Create the variable.

Step 2: Write an equation.

Step 3: Solve the equation.

Step 4: Check the solution.

Step 5: Answer the question.

2.19 Kendra bought four pairs of socks. She paid a total of $11.88, which included $0.88 sales tax. If each pair of socks cost the same amount, what was the pretax cost of one pair of socks?

Step 1: Create the variable.

Step 2: Write an equation.

Step 3: Solve the equation.

Step 4: Check the solution.

Step 5: Answer the question.

2.20 Keith and Randy set up a lemonade stand. On Saturday, they sold six times the number of cups of lemonade as they sold on Friday. In all, they sold 154 cups of lemonade. How many cups did they sell on Saturday?

Step 1: Create the variable.

Step 2: Write an equation.

Step 3: Solve the equation.

Step 4: Check the solution.

Step 5: Answer the question.

2.21 A breakfast restaurant keeps a certain number of dozens of eggs on hand. The owner placed an order for three times this number of dozens of eggs. One weekend, the restaurant used 75 dozen eggs. This left them with 45 dozen eggs. How many dozens of eggs did the restaurant have originally?

Step 1: Create the variable.

Step 2: Write an equation.

Step 3: Solve the equation.

Step 4: Check the solution.

Step 5: Answer the question.

2.22 Kiki and Delores decided to open a juice stand. They invested $40 for some wood to build the stand. They estimated that each cup of juice sold would cost them $0.25. The girls decided to sell each cup of juice for $0.75. How many cups would they have to sell in order to break even?

Step 1: Create the variable.

Step 2: Write an equation.

Step 3: Solve the equation.

Step 4: Check the solution.

Step 5: Answer the question.

2.23 One health club charges a monthly fee of $75 and an extra $5 for every visit. Another health club charges $119 per month and $1 for every visit. For how many visits will the monthly charge be the same?

Step 1: Create the variable.

Step 2: Write an equation.

Step 3: Solve the equation.

Step 4: Check the solution.

Step 5: Answer the question.

SOLUTIONS TO DIY PROBLEMS

2.1 Identify the law illustrated by each example.

    a. $4 \cdot 25x$ is the same as $(4 \cdot 25)x$
    b. $4(3x - 7)$ is equivalent to $12x - 28$
    c. $12m + 0$ is the same as $12m$

Solution:

    a. Since the grouping is changed, this is the Associative Law.
    b. The Distributive Law; $4(3x - 7)$ is equivalent to $4(3x) - 4(7)$, which is $12x - 28$.
    c. Since the original quantity is obtained, this is the Identity Law.

2.2 Simplify the expression $10a - 7 + 9a$. Then evaluate the expression for $a = 2$.

Solution:

$10a + 9a - 7$	Rewrite the variable expression using the Commutative Law.
$a(10) + a(9) - 7$	Write each like term using the greatest common factor, a.
$a(10 + 9) - 7$	Factor a from the first two terms.
$a(19) - 7$	Add inside parentheses.
$19a - 7$	Apply the Commutative Law.
$19(2) - 7$ becomes $38 - 7$, which is 31	Replace a with 2.

2.3 Simplify the expression $6m + 9m + 5$. Then evaluate the expression for $m = (-1)$.

Solution:

$m(6) + m(9) + 5$	Write each like term using the greatest common factor, m.
$m(6 + 9) + 5$	Factor m from the first two terms.
$m(15) + 5$	Add inside parentheses.
$15m + 5$	Apply the Commutative Law.
$15(-1) + 5$ becomes $-15 + 5$, which is -10	Replace m with -1.

2.4 Simplify the expression $-7y + 12 + 2y - 1$. Then evaluate the expression for $y = 3$.

Solution:

$-7y + 2y + 12 - 1$	Rewrite the variable expression using the Commutative Law.
$y(-7) + y(2) + 11$	Write each like term using the greatest common factor, y, and add the constants.
$y(-7 + 2) + 11$	Factor y from the first two terms.
$y(-5) + 11$	Add inside parentheses.
$-5y + 11$	Apply the Commutative Law.
$-5(3) + 11$ becomes $-15 + 11$, which is -4	Replace y with 3.

2.5 Simplify the expression $-4p + 11 - (-5p) - 2$. Then evaluate the expression for $p = 6$.

Solution:

$-4p + 11 + 5p + (-2)$	Rewrite the variable expression using addition.
$-4p + 5p + 11 + (-2)$	Rewrite the variable expression using the Commutative Law.
$p(-4) + p(5) + 9$	Write each like term using the greatest common factor, p, and add the constants.
$p(-4 + 5) + 9$	Factor p from the first two terms.
$p(-1) + 9$	Add inside parentheses.
$-p + 9$	Apply the Commutative Law.
$-(6) + 9$ becomes $-6 + 9$, which is 3	Replace p with 6.

2.6 Describe how to solve each equation.

   a. $7x = 21$

   b. $14 = n + 5$

   c. $\dfrac{c}{2} = 5$

   d. $w - 12 = 3$

Solution:

a. $7x = 21$	Multiply both sides by $\dfrac{1}{7}$, or divide both sides by 7.
b. $14 = n + 5$	Subtract 5 from both sides, or add -5 to both sides.
c. $\dfrac{c}{2} = 5$	Multiply both sides by 2.
d. $w - 12 = 3$	Add 12 to both sides.

2.7 Simplify the equations.

   a. $9 + 3(4c - 2) - 2c = 15 - 2(5c - 1)$.

Solution a:

$$9 + 3(4c - 2) - 2c = 15 - 2(5c - 1)$$
$$9 + 3(4c) - 3(2) - 2c = 15 - 2(5c) - 2(-1)$$
$$9 + 12c - 6 - 2c = 15 - 10c + 2$$
$$10c + 3 = -10c + 17$$

   b. $5(d + 1) = 4(d - 2)$

Solution b:

$$5(d + 1) = 4(d - 2)$$
$$5d + 5 = 4d - 8$$

c. $3(x - 2) = -2(x + 8)$

Solution c:
$$3(x - 2) = -2(x + 8)$$
$$3x - 6 = -2x - 16$$

d. $2(x + 9) - 4x = 12 - 3(2x + 2)$

Solution d:
$$2(x + 9) - 4x = 12 - 3(2x + 2)$$
$$2(x) + 2(9) - 4x = 12 - 3(2x) - 3(2)$$
$$2x + 18 - 4x = 12 - 6x - 6$$
$$2x - 4x + 18 = -6x + 12 - 6$$
$$-2x + 18 = -6x + 6$$

2.8 Solve the equation $0.75x + 6 = x - 2$.

Solution:
This equation does not have parentheses but does have variables on both sides. Begin by collecting variables.

Subtract 0.75x from both sides.	$0.75x + 6 - 0.75x = x - 2 - 0.75x$
Simplify.	$6 = 0.25x - 2$
Add 2 to both sides.	$6 + 2 = 0.25x - 2 + 2$
Simplify.	$8 = 0.25x$
Multiply both sides by 4.	$4(8) = 4(0.25x)$
Simplify.	$32 = x$
Check the solution.	$0.75(32) + 6 = 32 - 2$
	$24 + 6 = 32 - 2$
	$30 = 30$

The solution is $x = 32$.

2.9 Solve the equation $12(n - 4) - 5n = 10 - 3n$.

Solution:
This equation has parentheses, so begin by distributing.

Apply the Distributive Law.	$12(n) - 12(4) - 5n = 10 - 3n$
Multiply.	$12n - 48 - 5n = 10 - 3n$
Simplify the expressions on both sides.	$7n - 48 = 10 - 3n$
Add 3n to both sides.	$7n - 48 + 3n = 10 - 3n + 3n$

Simplify.	$10n - 48 = 10$
Add 48 to both sides.	$10n - 48 + 48 = 10 + 48$
Simplify.	$10n = 58$
Divide both sides by 10.	$\dfrac{10n}{10} = \dfrac{58}{10}$
Simplify.	$n = 5.8$
Check the solution.	

$$12(5.8 - 4) - 5(5.8) = 10 - 3(5.8)$$
$$12(1.8) - 5(5.8) = 10 - 3(5.8)$$
$$21.6 - 29 = 10 - 17.4$$
$$-7.4 = -7.4$$

The solution is $n = 5.8$.

2.10 Solve the equation $5m + 7 = -23$

Solution:

$$5m + 7 - 7 = -23 - 7$$
$$5m = -30$$
$$\dfrac{5m}{5} = -\dfrac{30}{5}$$
$$m = -6$$

2.11 Solve the equation $-3(x - 1) = 27$

Solution:

Method 1

$$\dfrac{-3(x - 1)}{-3} = \dfrac{27}{-3}$$
$$x - 1 = -9$$
$$x - 1 + 1 = -9 + 1$$
$$x = -8$$

Method 2

$$-3x + 3 = 27$$
$$-3x + 3 - 3 = 27 - 3$$
$$-3x = 24$$
$$\dfrac{-3x}{-3} = \dfrac{24}{-3}$$
$$x = -8$$

2.12 Solve the equation $5(2n - 5) + 4 = 14$ in two ways.

Solution:

Method 1

$$5(2n - 5) + 4 - 4 = 14 - 4$$
$$5(2n - 5) = 10$$
$$\frac{5(2n - 5)}{5} = \frac{10}{5}$$
$$2n - 5 = 2$$
$$2n - 5 + 5 = 2 + 5$$
$$2n = 7$$
$$\frac{2n}{2} = \frac{7}{2}$$
$$n = \frac{7}{2} \text{ or } 3.5$$

Method 2

$$5(2n - 5) + 4 = 14$$
$$10n - 25 + 4 = 14$$
$$10n - 21 = 14$$
$$10n - 21 + 21 = 14 + 21$$
$$10n = 35$$
$$\frac{10n}{10} = \frac{35}{10}$$
$$n = \frac{7}{2} \text{ or } 3.5$$

2.13 Solve the equation $12 - 2(x + 4) = 15$.

Solution:

$$12 - 2(x + 4) - 12 = 15 - 12$$
$$-2(x + 4) = 3$$
$$-2x - 8 = 3$$
$$-2x - 8 + 8 = 3 + 8$$
$$-2x = 11$$
$$-\frac{2x}{2} = \frac{11}{-2}$$
$$x = -\frac{11}{2} \text{ or } -5.5$$

2.14 Solve the equation $-2(2x + 1) = -3x + 4$

Solution:

$$-4x - 2 = -3x + 4$$
$$-4x - 2 + 4x = -3x + 4 + 4x$$
$$-2 = x + 4$$
$$-2 - 4 = x + 4 - 4$$
$$-6 = x$$
$$x = -6$$

2.15 Solve the equation $2(x-3) - 4x = 15 - (x+6)$

Solution:

$$2x - 6 - 4x = 15 - x - 6$$
$$-2x - 6 = -x + 9$$
$$-2x - 6 + 2x = -x + 9 + 2x$$
$$-6 = x + 9$$
$$-6 - 9 = x + 9 - 9$$
$$-15 = x$$
$$x = -15$$

2.16 The sum of two numbers is 25. One number is 8 less than twice the other number. What are the two numbers?

Solution:

Let n represent the number.

Let $2n - 8$ represent the other number.

$$n + 2n - 8 = 25$$
$$3n - 8 = 25$$
$$3n - 8 + 8 = 25 + 8$$
$$3n = 33$$
$$\frac{3n}{3} = \frac{33}{3}$$
$$n = 11$$

The two numbers are 11 and 14.

2.17 One number is 1 less than four times another number. Twice the greater number minus three times the lesser number is 48. What is the greater number?

Solution:

Let n represent the lesser number.

Let $4n - 1$ represent the greater number.

$$2(4n - 1) - 3n = 48$$
$$8n - 2 - 3n = 48$$
$$5n - 2 = 48$$
$$5n - 2 + 2 = 48 + 2$$
$$5n = 50$$
$$\frac{5n}{5} = \frac{50}{5}$$
$$n = 10$$

The greater number is 39.

2.18 Marge bought 12 cans of soup at the store. Each can cost the same amount. If the total was $8.76, how much was each can of soup?

Solution:

Let x represent the cost of one can of soup.

$$12x = 8.76$$
$$\frac{12x}{12} = \frac{8.76}{12}$$
$$x = 0.73$$

Each can of soup cost $0.73.

2.19 Kendra bought four pairs of socks. She paid a total of $11.88, which included $0.88 sales tax. If each pair of socks cost the same amount, what was the pretax cost of one pair of socks?

Solution:

Let x represent the cost of one pair of socks.

$$4x + 0.88 = 11.88$$
$$4x + 0.88 - 0.88 = 11.88 - 0.88$$
$$4x = 11$$
$$\frac{4x}{4} = \frac{11}{4}$$
$$x = 2.75$$

One pair of socks cost $2.75.

2.20 Keith and Randy set up a lemonade stand. On Saturday, they sold six times the number of cups of lemonade as they sold on Friday. In all, they sold 154 cups of lemonade. How many cups did they sell on Saturday?

Solution:

Let c represent the number of cups of lemonade sold on Friday.

Let $6c$ represent the number of cups of lemonade sold on Saturday.

$$c + 6c = 154$$
$$7c = 154$$
$$\frac{7c}{7} = \frac{154}{7}$$
$$c = 22$$

They sold 132 cups of lemonade on Saturday.

2.21 A breakfast restaurant keeps a certain number of dozens of eggs on hand. The owner placed an order for three times this number of dozens of eggs. One weekend, the restaurant used 75 dozen eggs. This left them with 45 dozen eggs. How many dozens of eggs did the restaurant have originally?

Solution:

Let *d* represent the original number of dozens of eggs on hand.

$$d + 3d - 75 = 45$$
$$4d - 75 = 45$$
$$4d - 75 + 75 = 45 + 75$$
$$4d = 120$$
$$\frac{4d}{4} = \frac{120}{4}$$
$$d = 30$$

The restaurant had 30 dozen eggs originally.

2.22 Kiki and Delores decided to open a juice stand. They invested $40 for some wood to build the stand. They estimated that each cup of juice sold would cost them $0.25. The girls decided to sell each cup of juice for $0.75. How many cups would they have to sell in order to break even?

Solution:

Let *n* represent the number of cups of juice.

$$40 + 0.25x = 0.75x$$
$$40 + 0.25x - 0.25x = 0.75x - 0.25x$$
$$40 = 0.5x$$
$$2(40) = 2(0.5x)$$
$$80 = x$$

They would have to sell 80 cups of juice to break even.

2.23. One health club charges a monthly fee of $75 and an extra $5 for every visit. Another health club charges $119 per month and $1 for every visit. For how many visits will the monthly charge be the same?

Solution:

Let *x* represent the number of visits to the health club.

$$75 + 5x = 119 + x$$
$$75 + 5x - x = 119 + x - x$$
$$75 + 4x = 119$$
$$75 + 4x - 75 = 119 - 75$$
$$4x = 44$$
$$\frac{4x}{4} = \frac{44}{4}$$
$$x = 11$$

The cost at each club would be the same for 11 visits.

2.1 Use the Distributive Law to rewrite the following expression: $8(z + 3)$

2.2 Use the Distributive Law to rewrite the following expression: $-9(c - 2)$

2.3 Write the following expression without parentheses: $-(4u - 7v + w)$

2.4 Combine the like terms in the following expression: $20s + 14t - 10s + t$

2.5 Combine the like terms in the following expression: $3x^2 + 5xy - 6yx - 2x^2$

2.6 Simplify the following expression using the Distributive Law and combining like terms: $6x - 7[4(x + 3) - (x - 8)] - 2$

2.7 Solve: $3(1 - x) + 10 = 14 - 2(x + 3)$

2.8 Solve: $\dfrac{2}{3}(x - 2) + \dfrac{3}{4} = \dfrac{5}{4}(2x + 3)$

2.9 Solve using the Addition Property of Equations: $x - 8 = 14$

2.10 Solve using the Addition Property of Equations: $z + \dfrac{5}{8} = \dfrac{15}{16}$

2.11 Solve using the Multiplication Property of Equations: $16c = -48$

2.12 Solve using the Multiplication Property of Equations: $-\dfrac{2}{3}y = 24$

Solve for the variable.

2.13 Solve: $5p - 4 = 16$

2.14 Solve: $-6x + 7 = -41$

2.15 Solve: $-\dfrac{1}{4}y - 1 = 15$

2.16 Solve: $2(x - 3) = 9$

2.17 Solve: $3(2y + 1) = 27$

2.18 Solve: $-2(z + 4) = -12$

2.19 Solve: $-5(-3x + 1) = -45$

2.20 Solve: $\left(-\dfrac{1}{2}\right)(4x + 6) = 10$

2.21 Solve: $-2(x + 1) + x = 12$

2.22 Solve: $4x + 11 = 6x - 3$

2.23 Solve: $-\dfrac{1}{2}z + \dfrac{2}{5} = \dfrac{7}{5}$

2.24 Solve: $-3x + 4 = 2x - 14$

2.25 Solve: $9x - 1 = -x + 49$

2.26 Solve: $11x + 3 = 3x + 35$

2.27 Solve: $4p - 9 = -2p + 21$

2.28 Solve: $5m + 1 = -10m - 19$

2.29 Solve: $-3(x - 4) = 9x$

2.30 Solve: $7(x - 3) = 5(x + 3)$

2.31 Solve: $-2(2x - 3) = 3(x + 1) + 10$

2.32 Solve: $2m - 3(m + 1) = 4(m + 3)$

2.33 Solve: $-4(b + 1) + 2b = 3(2b - 1)$

Solve

2.34 Five times a number is equal to 3 less than twice the number. Find the number.

2.35 Frog Pond Golf Course charges non–members $60.00 for each round of golf. The membership fee is $100.00, and members pay $40.00 for each round of golf. For how many rounds will the total of charges be the same for members and non–members?

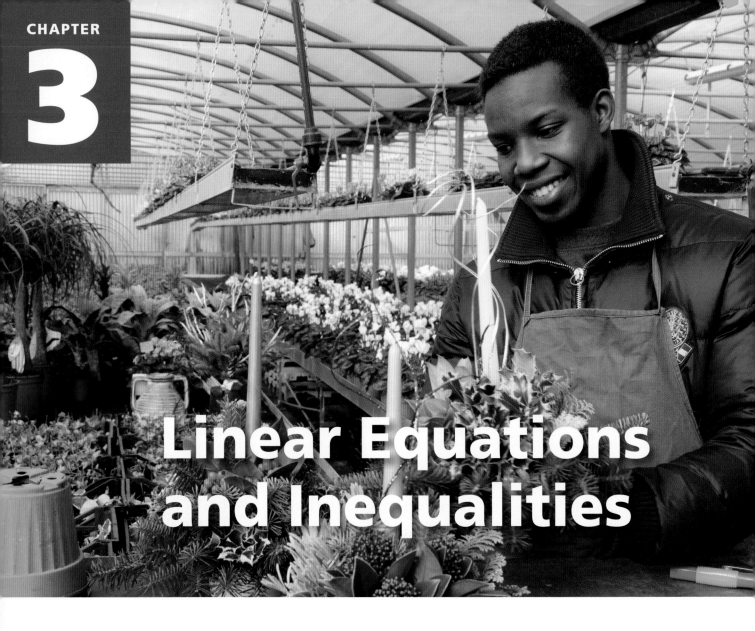

Linear Equations and Inequalities

Anthony is a manager for a garden and landscaping business. The business grows many of the plants that it sells in its own greenhouse facilities. Anthony's job is to know what types of plants to grow and when, have the resources available to grow them, and produce them in the most cost-efficient manner.

In the spring, for example, the business sells several different varieties of lilies, tulips, and geraniums, all grown in the greenhouse. It also grows and sells vegetable plants throughout the spring and summer. In other seasons, different plants such as mums and poinsettias are either grown from seed or raised from young plants in the greenhouse.

What are some of the factors Anthony has to take into account? He has to consider how many square feet are available in the greenhouse to grow different plants, how many hours of labor it takes to maintain the greenhouse and tend the plants, and at what cost.

Anthony might also consult with the sales manager and a business manager. The sales manager would know the selling price of each plant and which plants sell better than others. The business manager would analyze the costs that Anthony reports and the selling prices and demand as reported by the sales manager. The business manager could then decide which plants are the most profitable for the business to produce, and this would affect Anthony's decisions about how to allocate the resources to produce them.

So how can algebra help the garden shop run its business? The business manager must make sure that profits are greater than expenses. Notice that the business manager doesn't just want to know when profits equal expenses but also when profits are *greater than* expenses. In algebra, there are equations and there are inequalities. An equation would show that profits equal expenses. An inequality would show that profits are greater or less than expenses.

1. How does algebra help Anthony with his job? He can write equations or inequalities to represent his conditions and constraints. For example, if each greenhouse worker earns $12 per hour and Anthony has at most $100 per hour to use for labor, how many workers, represented by the variable w, can he hire? The inequality "$12w$ is less than or equal to 100" represents this constraint.

2. What other constraints or conditions might Anthony have to take into consideration? Would these be best represented with an equation or an inequality?

3. In what other areas or businesses might equations and inequalities represent certain conditions? How might equations and inequalities be used in everyday experiences?

KEY TERMS

➤ compound inequality (p. 82)
➤ compound interest (p. 73)
➤ formula (p. 73)
➤ inequality (p. 81)
➤ linear equation (p. 70)
➤ markdown (p. 74)
➤ markup (p. 74)
➤ principal (p. 73)
➤ rate (p. 73)
➤ simple interest (p. 73)
➤ time (p. 73)

LINEAR EQUATIONS

In the equations presented so far, there has been one variable in each equation. This has led to finding one solution. Substituting values for all but one variable in an equation reduces it to an equation in one variable.

Consider an equation that has two variables, such as $y = 3x + 2$. Notice that y is isolated, but its value can only be determined if a value for x is known. So choose a value for x, such as 1. Then y would have the value $3(1) + 2$, which is $3 + 2 = 5$. Choose another value for x, say 6, and then y would be $3(6) + 2 = 18 + 2 = 20$. Is there a limit to the number of possibilities? No, any real number could be used for the independent variable x, resulting in a corresponding value for the dependent variable y. Consider the table in Figure 3.1 that shows values for selected values of x.

x	1	6	10	0	-4	-1	$\frac{1}{3}$
y	5	20	32	2	-10	-1	3

FIGURE 3.1 Table of Values for $y = 3x + 2$

Consider each pair of values as an ordered pair, (x, y). The pairs are $(1, 5)$, $(6, 20)$, $(10, 32)$, $(0, 2)$, $(-4, -10)$, $(-1, -1)$, and $\left(\frac{1}{3}, 3\right)$. Plot these pairs as points on a coordinate plane as shown in Figure 3.2.

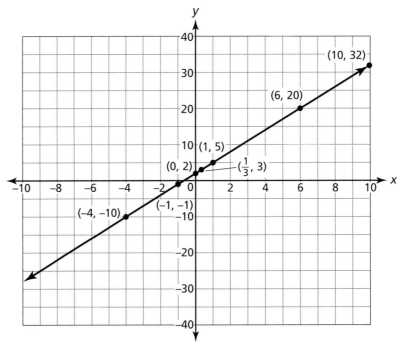

FIGURE 3.2 Graph of Linear Equation $y = 3x + 2$

Notice that all of the points seem to lie along a straight line! In fact, all of the solution pairs generated by the equation $y = 3x + 2$ lie along the same line. This type of equation, one that can be written in the form $y = mx + b$, where x and y are not both 0 and the exponents of x and/or y are 1, is called a **linear equation.** Another chapter will explore graphs in more detail as a tool for analyzing linear equations. This chapter will focus on solving linear equations in formulas.

3.1 LINEAR EQUATION An equation that can be written in the form $y = mx + b$.

To claim that an equation is linear, the dependent variable y must be isolated on one side of the equals (=) sign. After that, both the independent variable x and the dependent variable y must each have an implied exponent of 1. If this situation occurs, then this equation can be referred to as a linear equation.

Either x or y—but not both—may have 0 for an exponent. If $y = x^0 + b$, the graph of $y = 1 + b$ is a horizontal line. If $y^0 = x + b$, then the graph of $x = -b$ is a vertical line.

Example 3.1 Tell whether the equation $y = x^2 - 3$ is linear. Make a table of values for the equation. Graph the points.

Solution:

The equation is not linear since x has exponent 2.
If $x = 2$, then $y = (2)^2 - 3 = 4 - 3 = 1$. If $x = 4$, then $y = (4)^2 - 3 = 16 - 3 = 13$.
Continue. (See Figure 3.3.)

x	2	4	6	0	−1	−3	−4
y	1	13	33	−3	−2	6	13

FIGURE 3.3 Table of Values for $y = x^2 - 3$

The graph is shown in Figure 3.4.

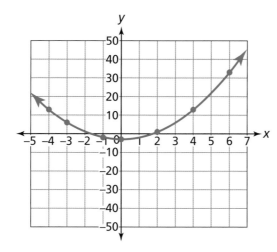

FIGURE 3.4

Example 3.2 Explain why each of the following equations is linear or not linear.
  a. $y = x^3 - 2$
  b. $y = -3x + 5$
  c. $x + y = 7$
  d. $y - x^{-2} = 5$

Solution:
  a. Not linear since x has exponent 3
  b. Linear since both variables have exponent 1
  c. Linear since both variables have exponent 1
  d. Not linear since x has exponent -2

DIY PROBLEMS

3.1 Tell whether the equation $x + y = 3$ is linear. Make a table of values for the equation. Graph the points.

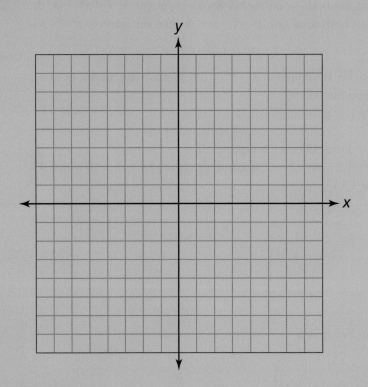

3.2 Explain why each equation is linear or not linear.

   a. $y = 2x^{-4} - 1$

   b. $y - 3x = 15$

   c. $y^2 - x = 9$

   d. $x - y = 1$

APPLICATION: SOLVING PROBLEMS USING FORMULAS

A **formula** is an equation that describes the relationships between several variables. When values for all but one variable are known, the formula becomes an equation in one variable and so has a solution.

For example, to find the perimeter P of a rectangle with corresponding dimensional values l (length) and w (width), use the geometrical formula $P = 2l + 2w$. Given values for l and w allows solving for the rectangle's corresponding value of P. To find the area of the rectangle, use the formula $A = lw$. To find its length or its width, use either formula depending on the known variables.

3.2 FORMULA An equation that describes the relationships between several variables.

Solving Problems Using Financial Formulas

Simple Interest

Investing money to earn more money is common in most financial systems. The amount of money used as the initial investment is the **principal**, P. Multiplying the principal by a percent called the **rate** per time period, r, for a given number of the same **time** periods, t, yields the interest, I.

If the interest earned by the principal over the period of time is not reinvested to earn more interest, the interest earned by the principal is **simple interest.**

The formula $I = Prt$ represents the amount of simple interest I earned when the principal P is invested at a rate r per time period, for a number of periods of time t.

Consider the case of Terrence, who has $2,000 to invest. He invests in a CD that pays 2.5% interest per year. How much simple interest will Terrence earn on his investment in 1 year? In 10 years?

Here, $P = 2000$ and $r = 2.5\% = 0.025$. If he invests for 1 year, $t = 1$ and $I = (2000)(0.025)(1) = 50$, so he would earn $50 in interest in one year.

If he invests for 10 years, $t = 10$ and $I = (2000)(0.025)(10) = 500$, so he would earn $500 in simple interest in 10 years.

Notice that the simple interest for 10 years is 10 times the simple interest for one year.

3.3 PRINCIPAL An initial amount of investment money.

3.4 RATE In an interest formula, the percent used to compute the interest earned by the principal for a given period of time.

3.5 TIME In an interest formula, the number of periods for which the principal will earn interest.

3.6 SIMPLE INTEREST Interest earned on only the principal.

Compound Interest

When interest earned each period is reinvested to earn interest during the next investment period, the amount of money, A, at the end of n investment periods is principal, P, plus **compound interest, C.**

Usually interest rates are stated per year and n is the number of periods per year.

The formulas $A = P\left(1 + \dfrac{r}{n}\right)^{nt}$ and $C = A - P$ represent the relationships between these variables. The ratio $\dfrac{r}{n}$ is the rate per compounding period, and nt is the total number of those periods.

If Terrence invested his $2,000 in a CD at 2.5% that compounded interest every year for 10 years ($t = 10$ and $n = 1$), the amount of money at the end of 10 years would be

$$A = 2000\left(1 + \frac{.025}{1}\right)^{1.10} = 2000(1.025)^{10} = 2560.2$$

3.7 COMPOUND INTEREST Interest earned on accumulated interest.

and the compound interest would be $2560.20 − $2000 = $560.20, which is $60.20 (about 12%) more than he earned in simple interest under the same circumstances.

If Terrence invested $2,000 in a CD at 2.5% that compounded interest monthly for 10 years ($t = 10$ and $n = 12$), he would have a bit more:

$$A = 2000\left(1 + \frac{.025}{12}\right)^{12.10} = 2567.4$$

of which compound interest is $567.40, about 13% more than he earned in simple interest.

Markup/Markdown

3.8 MARKUP An increase in the price of an item.

3.9 MARKDOWN A decrease in the price of an item.

A **markup** is an increase in price that frequently reflects a merchant's need to include expenses and profit in the price of goods sold. Generally it is a percent of the base cost of the item. A **markdown** is a decrease in price that usually reflects a discount or sale. It is usually the discount, or a percent of the current price.

The formula to calculate the percent markup or markdown is

$$m = \frac{\left|\text{Last price} - \text{Original price}\right|}{\text{Original price}}$$

Where c is the original cost, or base price of an item, the markup is mc. Where p is the current price, the markdown is mp.

A store's selling price p for an item is the sum of the cost, or base price, c and the markup mc. The formula for a price after a percent markup is $p = c + mc = c(1 + m)$. For example, the price of an item with a 50% markup whose cost is $4 is $p = 4(1 + 50\%) = 4(1 + 0.5) = 4(1.5) = 6$. The price is $6; the markup is $2.

A store's sale price s for an item is the difference of the current price p and the markdown mp. The formula is $s = p - mp = p(1 - m)$.

Be aware that a markdown mp that equals a markup mc does not reflect the same percent change, or m value. For an item that is $5 and on sale for $4, the *markdown* is 1 but the original amount is 5, so $m = \frac{1}{5}$, or 20%. On the other hand, for an item that is $4 and marked up to $5, the *markup* is 1 and the original amount is 4, so $m = \frac{1}{4}$, or 25%. Even though the change in price is the same, the percent of markup does not equal the percent of markdown because p and c ($4 and $5—the *original amounts*) are different.

Example 3.3

The Andersons invest $10,000 in a CD that pays 3.25% annual interest. They decide to leave the money in the account for 12 years.

a. How much simple interest will they earn?

Solution:
Use the formula $I = Prt$, where P is $10,000, r is 0.0325, and $t = 12$.
$I = 10,000(0.0325)(12) = 3900$
The Andersons will earn $3,900 in simple interest over the 12 years.

b. If interest on the CD were compounded semiannually (twice a year), how much compound interest would they earn?

Solution:

Their compound interest will be the difference between the total value of the investment in 12 years and $10,000. The amount is

$$A = 10,000\left(1 + \frac{.0325}{2}\right)^{2.12} = 10,000(1.01625)^{24} = 14,724$$

The Andersons would earn $4,724 in compound interest after 12 years.

Example 3.4

A store buys a TV from the manufacturer for $400. After applying an 85% markup to the item, the store then tries to sell it to consumers. What is the price of the TV in the store?

Use the formula $p = c(1 + m)$, where c is 400 and m is 85% = 0.85.
$p = 400(1 + 0.85) = 400(1.85) = 740$
The store would sell the TV for $740.

DIY PROBLEMS

3.3 Henry invests $32,000 in an account that pays 2.25% interest per year for 18 months.

    a. How much simple interest will he earn?

    b. If interest is compounded monthly, how much compound interest will he earn?

3.4 Barbara wants to buy a sweater that regularly costs $40. Today, the sweater is on sale for 30% off. What is the sale price of the sweater? What is the markdown?

TRANSLATING SENTENCES INTO EQUATIONS

Solving Integer Problems

Recall that the integers are the numbers: . . . , -3, -2, -1, 0, 1, 2, 3, . . . Suppose that n is an integer. Then the next integer is $n + 1$, then $n + 2$, $n + 3$, and so on. Now suppose that n is an even integer such as 6. Then the next even integer is 8. In relation to n, this is $n + 2$. The next even integer would be 10, which is $n + 4$.

Now suppose that n is an odd integer such as 7. Then the next odd integer is 9. In relation to n, this is also $n + 2$. The next odd integer would be 11, which is $n + 4$. Consecutive even or odd integers can be represented by n, $n + 2$, $n + 4$, $n + 6$, and so on.

Translating a Sentence into an Equation and Solving

To be able to solve word problems, an important skill is to be able to translate the problem situation given in words into an equation.

Figure 3.5 shows a table of some common terms that indicate addition, subtraction, multiplication, division, and equals.

Addition	Subtraction	Multiplication	Division	Equals
Sum	Difference	Product	Quotient	Is
More than	Less than	Times	Divided by	Is the same as
Increased by	Decreased by	Twice		The result is
Together	Minus	Of		

FIGURE 3.5 **Key Words and Their Associated Mathematical Operations**

Example 3.5

The sum of three consecutive odd integers is 39. What are the integers?

Solution:

Let n represent the first odd integer, $n + 2$ the second odd integer, and $n + 4$ the third odd integer.

Represent the three consecutive odd integers.

$n + n + 2 + n + 4 = 39$	Write an equation. The word "is" represents $=$. The "sum of three consecutive integers" precedes the $=$ and means to add the three numbers on the left side of the $=$ symbol. "39" follows the "is" and so is on the right side of $=$.
$3n + 6 = 39$	Simplify.
$3n + 6 - 6 = 39 - 6$	Subtract 6 from both sides.
$3n = 33$	Simplify.
$\dfrac{3n}{3} = \dfrac{33}{3}$	Divide both sides by 3.
$n = 11$	Simplify.
So the integers are 11, 13, and 15.	Check the solution: $11 + 13 + 15 = 39$

Example 3.6

Find four consecutive integers such that four times the least is equal to twice the next least integer minus six times the greatest integer. What are the four integers?

Solution:

Let n represent the first integer, and $n + 1$, $n + 2$, and $n + 3$ the other integers.	Represent the four consecutive integers.
$4n = 2(n + 1) - 6(n + 3)$	Write an equation. The words "is equal to" represents $=$. "Four times the least" precedes the $=$ and means to multiply 4 and the least integer, *n,* on the left side of the $=$ symbol. "Twice the next least integer minus six times the greatest integer" follows the "is equal to" and so is on the right side of $=$. Note the use of parentheses so that the entire representation of the integer is multiplied, not just the first part.
$4n = 2n + 2 - 6n - 18$	Use the distributive property.
$4n = -4n - 16$	Simplify.
$4n + 4n = -4n - 16 + 4n$	Add $4n$ to both sides.
$8n = -16$	Simplify.
$\dfrac{8n}{8} = \dfrac{-16}{8}$	Divide both sides by 8.
$n = -2$	Simplify.
So the integers are -2, -1, 0, and 1.	Check the solution: $4(-2) = 2(-1) - 6(1)$ $$-8 = -2 - 6$$ $$-8 = -8$$

MIXTURE AND UNIFORM MOTION PROBLEMS

Here are some other situations for which linear functions are useful.

Solving Value Mixture Problems

Consider this problem: Cashews cost $8.25 per pound. Almonds cost $4.75 per pound. How many pounds of each are needed to create 4 pounds of a mixture that sells for $6.00 per pound?

Let x represent the number of pounds of cashews. Then $4 - x$ represents the number of pounds of almonds. The value of each part of the mixture is (cost per pound)(number of pounds). So the value of the cashews ($8.25x$) plus the value of the almonds ($4.75(4 - x)$) equals the total value of the mixture ($6 \cdot 4$). Use this reasoning to write an equation.

$$8.25 + 4.75(4 - x) = 6(4)$$
$$825x + 475(4 - x) = 2400$$
$$825x + 1900 - 475x = 2400$$
$$350x + 1900 = 2400$$
$$350x + 1900 - 1900 = 2400 - 1900$$
$$350x = 500$$
$$7x = 10$$
$$x = \frac{10}{7} = 1\frac{3}{7}$$

So the mixture should have $1\frac{3}{7}$ pounds of cashews and $4 - 1\frac{3}{7} = 2\frac{4}{7}$ pounds of almonds.

Solving Percent Mixture Problems

The Johnsons had $10,000 to invest. They invested part in a long-term CD that paid 2.5% annual interest and part in a short-term CD that paid 2% interest per year. After one year, they had earned $236.75 in interest. How much did they invest in each account?

Since the time period is one year, the t in $I = Prt$ is 1 so the interest earned in either account is the principal times the interest rate (written as a decimal). Let x = amount invested at 2.5%. Then $10,000 - x$ is the amount invested at 2%. The amount of interest earned from both accounts totals 236.75. Use this reasoning to write an equation.

$$0.025x + 0.02(10,000 - x) = 236.75$$
$$25x + 20(10,000 - x) = 236,750$$
$$25x + 200,000 - 20x = 236,750$$
$$5x + 200,000 - 200,000 = 236,750 - 200,000$$
$$5x = 36,750$$
$$x = 7350; 10,000 - 7350 = 2650$$

So the Johnsons invested $7,350 in the long-term CD and $2,650 in the short-term CD.

Solving Uniform Motion Problems

Suppose you drive 50 mph for four hours. You would travel a distance of 200 miles. The formula that represents this relationship is $d = rt$, where d represents the distance traveled, r is the rate (often miles per hour), and t is the amount of time (usually expressed in hours).

Aimee starts out in her car driving at 50 mph. Two hours later, Angie starts out along the same route as Aimee driving at 60 mph. How long will it take Angie to catch up with Aimee?

Charts such as Figures 3.6a, 3.6b, and 3.6c can help to organize the information you know. It is given that Aimee drives 50 mph and Angie drives 60 mph.

	RATE, r	TIME, t	DISTANCE, d
Aimee	50		
Angie	60		

FIGURE 3.6a Aimee and Angie's Rates

How can we represent Angie starting out two hours later, or after, Aimee? Since the question is how long it takes Angie to catch up to Aimee, let x represent the amount of time Angie travels. Then $x + 2$ is the amount of time Aimee travels, since she has been driving for two hours longer.

	RATE, r	TIME, t	DISTANCE, d
Aimee	50	$x + 2$	
Angie	60	x	

FIGURE 3.6b Aimee and Angie's Rates and Expressions for Their Travel Times

Once rate and time are known, the distance column can be filled in since $d = rt$.

	RATE, *r*	TIME, *t*	DISTANCE, *d*
Aimee	50	$x+2$	$50(x+2)$
Angie	60	x	$60x$

FIGURE 3.6c Aimee and Angie's Rates, Time Expressions, and Distance Expressions

What equation can be written? Think: what happens when Angie catches up to Aimee? The distance traveled by each is the same, so set the distances equal to each other.

$$50(x+2)=60x$$
$$50x+100=60x$$
$$50x+100-50x=60x-50x$$
$$100=10x$$
$$\frac{100}{10}=\frac{10x}{10}$$
$$10=x$$

So Angie will catch up to Aimee in 10 hours.

Example 3.7

The Tomlinsons invested $20,000 in two mutual funds. One was higher risk but had an average return on investment of 8% per year. The other was lower risk and had an average return of 4.5% per year. After one year, the Tomlinsons had earned $1,328.75 on their investments. How much did they invest in the higher-risk mutual fund?

Solution:

Let x represent the amount invested at 8% and $20,000 - x$ the amount invested at 4.5%.

$$0.08x+0.045(20,000-x)=1328.75$$
$$0.08x+900-0.045x=1328.75$$
$$0.035x+900=1328.75$$
$$0.035x+900-900=1328.75-900$$
$$0.035x=428.75$$
$$\frac{0.035x}{0.035}=\frac{428.75}{0.035}$$
$$x=12,250$$

So the Tomlinsons invested $12,250 in the higher-risk mutual fund.

Example 3.8

Kate and Allie live 595 miles apart. They agree to meet somewhere between them. They leave at the same time, with Kate averaging 40 mph and Allie averaging 45 mph. When they meet, how far will Kate have driven?

Solution: Make a table (Figure 3.7).

	RATE, *r*	TIME, *t*	DISTANCE, *d*
Kate	40	x	$40x$
Allie	45	x	$45x$

FIGURE 3.7

Notice that the time traveled is the same for both women since they left at the same time. Even though the question asks how far Kate drives, the variable represents the amount of time traveled. The equation here has to represent that the distance Kate drives plus the distance Allie drives totals 595 miles.

$$40x + 45x = 595$$
$$85x = 595$$
$$\frac{85x}{85} = \frac{595}{85}$$
$$x = 7$$

They each drove for seven hours. So Kate drove 280 miles.

DIY PROBLEMS

3.8 Robyn keeps her money in two accounts. Her money market account pays 3.15% annual interest and her savings/checking account pays 1.25% annual interest. Last year she had a total of $25,000 invested in these two accounts. She earned a total of $624.10 in interest. How much did she invest in the money market account?

3.9 Two trains are in cities that are 800 miles apart. They are each traveling on tracks straight toward the other city. Train A starts at 1:00 pm traveling at 125 mph. Train B starts out one hour later traveling at 100 mph. What time will it be when the two trains pass each other?

FIRST DEGREE INEQUALITIES

An **inequality** is a sentence using one of the four symbols: $<$ (is less than), $>$ (is greater than), $\leq$ (is less than or equal to), or $\geq$ (is greater than or equal to).

Inequalities describe infinite sets of real numbers. Compare the sentences $x = 3$, $x > 3$, and $x \geq 3$. The sentence $x = 3$ names one specific value for x; $x > 3$ names an infinite number of values for x, all greater than 3 but not including 3; $x \geq 3$ names an infinite number of values for x and does include the value 3.

3.10 INEQUALITY A sentence using one of the four symbols: $<$ (is less than), $>$ (is greater than), $\leq$ (is less than or equal to), or $\geq$ (is greater than or equal to).

Solving an Inequality in One Variable

Solving an inequality is very much the same as solving an equation. The goal is still to isolate the variable on one side of the inequality. The same steps are used: adding or subtracting the same quantity from both sides and multiplying or dividing both sides by the same quantity. The only difference is that when multiplying or dividing by a negative number, the inequality symbol is reversed.

Consider the inequality $8 > 4$. No matter what you add or subtract on each side, the inequality symbol will be preserved: $8 + 7 > 4 + 7$ or $8 - 5 > 4 - 5$ and so on. Multiplying or dividing both sides by a positive number also preserves the inequality symbol: $8 \cdot 5 > 4 \cdot 5$ or $8 \div 2 > 4 \div 2$. When multiplying or dividing both sides by a negative number, the inequality symbol has to be reversed: $8 \cdot -3 < 4 \cdot -3$ since $-24 < -12$, or $8 \div -2 < 4 \div -2$ since $-4 < -2$.

Solving a Compound Inequality

3.11 COMPOUND INEQUALITY Two inequalities joined by either "and" or "or."

A **compound inequality** is two inequalities joined by either "and" or "or." The conjunction "and" means that any solution has to satisfy both inequalities, not just one. The conjunction "or" means that any solution has to satisfy one inequality or the other, but not necessarily both.

Consider the compound inequality $x > 2$ and $x < 9$. Any real number between 2 and 9 is a solution. The compound inequality $x > 2$ or $x < 9$ would include all real numbers as solutions, since a number such as 10 or -3 would satisfy one inequality, while the numbers between 2 and 9 satisfy both inequalities.

For the compound inequality $x < -2$ or $x > 5$, values such as -3, -10, 7, and 12 would all be solutions since they satisfy one of the two inequalities. There are an infinite number of solutions, all the numbers less than -2 and all the numbers greater than 5. However, the compound inequality $x < -2$ and $x > 5$ would have no solutions since there are no values that satisfy both inequalities.

Example 3.9

Landscape manager Anthony in our opening story has \$100 per hour to allocate to for labor in the greenhouse. Two employees each earn \$18 per hour. What is the greatest number of additional employees earning \$9 per hour Anthony can use?

Solution:

Let x represent the number of employees that earn \$9 per hour. Note the use of $\leq$; Anthony can use up to and including \$100 but not more.

$$2(18) + 9x \leq 100$$
$$36 + 9x \leq 100$$
$$36 + 9x - 36 \leq 100 - 36$$
$$9x \leq 64$$
$$\frac{9x}{9} \leq \frac{64}{9}$$
$$x \leq 7\frac{1}{9}$$

The greatest number of employees earning \$9 per hour that Anthony can hire is seven.

Example 3.10

Solve the compound inequality. List four possible solutions.
$$6x - 4(2x - 5) < 10 \text{ or } 5x + 9 < 2x - 21$$

Solution:

Solve each inequality separately.

$6x - 4(2x - 5) < 10$	or	$5x + 9 < 2x - 21$
$6x - 8x + 20 < 10$	or	$5x + 9 - 2x < 2x - 21 - 2x$
$-2x + 20 < 10$	or	$3x + 9 < -21$
$-2x + 20 - 20 < 10 - 20$	or	$3x + 9 - 9 < -21 - 9$
$-2x < -10$	or	$3x < -30$
$\dfrac{-2x}{-2} > \dfrac{-10}{-2}$	or	$\dfrac{3x}{3} < \dfrac{-30}{3}$
$x > 5$	or	$x < -10$

Four possible solutions are -15, -12, 7, and 10.

DIY PROBLEMS

Solve:

3.10 $2x - 3 < 19$

3.11 $-5x + 1 \geq -24$

3.12 $-3(x - 2) > -2(x + 1)$

3.13 $6(3x + 9) - 8x \leq -6$

3.14 A clothing manufacturer produces one type of sweater that earns $4 profit for each one sold. The business manager requires that a profit of at least $100 be earned every hour. The product manager estimates that the expenses for running the machine are $45 per hour. What is the least number of sweaters that must be produced each hour to earn a profit of at least $100?

Solve the compound inequalities:

3.15 $12x - 7 > 5$ or $6x \leq -6$

3.16 $4(x - 1) \geq 8$ and $-3x + 4 > -2$

3.17 List four possible solutions.
$2x - 3(2x - 5) \leq 7$ and $3x - 1 \geq 5x - 7$

ABSOLUTE VALUE EQUATIONS AND INEQUALITIES

Recall that $|x|$, read *the absolute value of x*, means the distance that x is from 0, and since it is a distance it must always be 0 or positive.

Solving an Absolute Value Equation

To solve an equation such as $|x| = 5$, you must rewrite the equation without absolute value bars. There are two cases to consider: if x is positive, then $|x| = x$; if x is negative, then $|x| = -x$. Rewrite an absolute value equation as two equations without absolute value bars.

To solve $|x| = 5$, rewrite the equation as $x = 5$ or $-x = 5$.

The first equation is already simplified, and dividing both sides of the second equation by -1 yields $x = -5$. There are two solutions to the absolute value equation, 5 or -5. Note the use of the conjunction "or."

Solving an Absolute Value Inequality

To solve an inequality such as $|x| \geq 8$, follow the same reasoning—rewrite the inequality without absolute value bars. There will be two separate inequalities.

To solve $|x| \geq 8$, rewrite the inequality as $x \geq 8$ or $-x \geq 8$.

The first inequality is already simplified, and dividing both sides of the second inequality by -1 yields $x \leq -8$.

The solutions then are all values of x that are 8 and greater or all values of x that are -8 or less. Notice the use of the conjunction "or." The $\geq$ symbol in an absolute value inequality requires "or." If the conjunction were "and," there would be no solutions since no values would satisfy both inequalities.

To solve an inequality such as $|x| < 3$, rewrite the inequality without the absolute value bars: $x < 3$ and $-x < 3$.

The first inequality is already simplified, and dividing both sides of the second inequality by -1 yields $x > -3$.

The only values that satisfy both inequalities are the values of x between -3 and 3, not including -3 and 3. Notice the use of the $<$ symbol and the conjunction "and." If the conjunction were "or," the solutions would be all real numbers.

Example 3.11

What numbers on a number line are 7 units away from 4?

Solution:

Since the distance from 4 is 7 units, write an absolute value equation.

$$|x-4| = 7$$

$$\begin{array}{lll} x-4=7 & \text{or} & -(x-4)=7 \\ x-4+4=7+4 & \text{or} & (x-4)=-7 \text{ (dividing both sides by } -1) \\ x=11 & \text{or} & x-4+4=-7+4 \\ x=11 & \text{or} & x=-3 \end{array}$$

Both 11 and -3 are 7 units away from 4.

Example 3.12

Solve the inequality $14 - 2|2x-5| > 8$.

Solution:

First, isolate the absolute value.

$$14 - 2|2x-5| - 14 > 8 - 14$$
$$-2|2x-5| > -6$$
$$\frac{-2|2x-5|}{-2} < \frac{-6}{-2}$$

Note that the inequality symbol is reversed since both sides are divided by -2.

$$\begin{array}{lll} |2x-5| < 3 & & \\ 2x-5 < 3 \text{ and } -(2x-5) < 3 & & \text{(Use "and" since the inequality has } <.) \\ 2x-5+5 < 3+5 & \text{and} & 2x-5 > -3 \text{ (Divide both sides by } -1.) \\ 2x < 8 & \text{and} & 2x-5+5 > -3+5 \\ \dfrac{2x}{2} < \dfrac{8}{2} & \text{and} & 2x > 2 \\ x < 4 & \text{and} & \dfrac{2x}{2} > \dfrac{2}{2} \\ x < 4 & \text{and} & x > 1 \end{array}$$

DIY PROBLEMS

3.18 What numbers on a number line are 10.5 units away from 6?

Solve the Inequalities:

3.19 $|x+3| \geq 7$

3.20 $|x - 4| - 3 < 9$

3.21 $-|2x - 1| \leq -13$

3.22 $3\,|3x + 4| > 12.$

SOLUTIONS TO DIY PROBLEMS

3.1 Tell whether the equation $x + y = 3$ is linear. Make a table of values for the equation. Graph the points.

Solution:
Possible points:

x	0	1	3	5	−1	−3	−4
y	3	2	0	−2	4	6	7

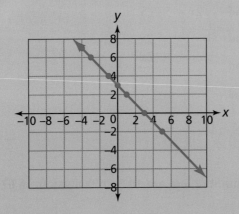

The equation is linear.

3.2 Explain why each equation is linear or not linear.

    a. $y = 2x^{-4} - 1$
    b. $y - 3x = 15$
    c. $y^2 - x = 9$
    d. $x - y = 1$

Solution:

    a. Not linear since x has an exponent -4
    b. Linear since both variables have exponent 1
    c. Not linear since y has an exponent 2
    d. Linear since both variables have an exponent 1

3.3 Henry invests $32,000 in an account that pays 2.25% interest per year for 18 months.
   a. How much simple interest will he earn?

Solution:

18 months is 1.5 years, so
$I = 32,000(0.0225)(1.5)$
$I = 1080$
  Henry will earn $1,080 in simple interest in 18 months.
  b. If interest is compounded monthly, how much compound interest will he earn?

Solution:

The amount of money at the end of 18 months is

$$A = 32,000\left(1 + \frac{.0225}{18}\right)^{12 \cdot 1.5} = 33,097.39$$

Henry will earn $1097.39 in compound interest in 18 months.

3.4 Barbara wants to buy a sweater that regularly costs $40. Today, the sweater is on sale for 30% off. What is the sale price of the sweater? What is the markdown?

Solution:

Sale price $= 40(1 - 0.30)$
Sale price $= 40(0.70)$
Sale price $= 28$
The sweater is on sale for $28. The markdown is $40 − $28 = $12.

3.5 The sum of three consecutive integers is -18. What are the integers?

Solution:

Let n, $n + 1$, and $n + 2$ represent the integers.
$$n + n + 1 + n + 2 = -18$$
$$3n + 3 = -18$$
$$3n + 3 - 3 = -18 - 3$$
$$3n = -21$$
$$\frac{3n}{3} = \frac{-21}{3}$$
$$n = -7$$
The integers are -7, -6, and -5.

3.6 Find three consecutive odd integers such that twice the largest is three less than three times the smallest.

Solution:

Let x, $x + 2$, and $x + 4$ represent the three odd integers.
Twice the largest is represented by $2(x + 4)$.
Three less than three times the smallest is represented by $3x - 3$.

This gives $2(x + 4) = 3x - 3$
$$2x + 8 = 3x - 3$$
$$2x + 8 - 2x = 3x - 3 - 2x$$
$$8 = x - 3$$
$$8 + 3 = x - 3 + 3$$
$$11 = x$$
The three integers are 11, 13, and 15.

3.7 Find four consecutive even integers such that twice the greatest decreased by the least is equal to three times the second integer minus the third.

Solution:

Let x, $x + 2$, $x + 4$, and $x + 6$ represent the four even integers.

$$2(x + 6) - x = 3(x + 2) - (x + 4)$$
$$2x + 12 - x = 3x + 6 - x - 4$$
$$x + 12 = 2x + 2$$
$$x + 12 - x = 2x + 2 - x$$
$$12 = x + 2$$
$$12 - 2 = x + 2 - 2$$
$$10 = x$$

The integers are 10, 12, 14, and 16.

3.8 Robyn keeps her money in two accounts. Her money market account pays 3.15% annual interest and her savings/checking account pays 1.25% annual interest. Last year she had a total of $25,000 invested in these two accounts. She earned a total of $624.10 in interest. How much did she invest in the money market account?

Solution:

Let x represent the amount invested in the money market account and $25,000 - x$ represent the amount invested in the savings/checking account.

$$0.0315x + 0.0125(25,000 - x) = 624.10$$
$$0.0315x + 312.5 - 0.0125x = 624.10$$
$$0.019x + 312.5 = 624.10$$
$$0.019x + 312.5 - 312.5 = 624.10 - 312.5$$
$$0.019x = 311.6$$
$$\frac{0.019x}{0.019} = \frac{311.6}{0.019}$$
$$x = 16,400$$

Robyn invested $16,400 in the money market account.

3.9 Two trains are in cities that are 800 miles apart. They are each traveling on tracks straight toward the other city. Train A starts at 1:00 pm traveling at 125 mph. Train B starts out one hour later traveling at 100 mph. What time will it be when the two trains pass each other?

Solution:

	RATE, *r*	TIME, *t*	DISTANCE, *d*
Train A	125	x	$125x$
Train B	100	$x - 1$	$100(x - 1)$

$$125x + 100(x - 1) = 800$$
$$125x + 100x - 100 = 800$$
$$225x - 100 = 800$$
$$225x - 100 + 100 = 800 + 100$$
$$225x = 900$$
$$\frac{225x}{225} = \frac{900}{225}$$
$$x = 4$$

Since Train A traveled for four hours, the time was 5:00 pm when the trains passed each other.

3.10 $2x - 3 < 19$.

Solution:
$$2x - 3 + 3 < 19 + 3$$
$$2x < 22$$
$$\frac{2x}{2} < \frac{22}{2}$$
$$x < 11$$

3.11 $-5x + 1 \geq -24$.

Solution:
$$-5x + 1 - 1 \geq -24 - 1$$
$$-5x \geq -25$$
$$\frac{-5x}{-5} \geq \frac{-25}{-5}$$
$$x \leq 5$$

3.12 $-3(x - 2) > -2(x + 1)$.

Solution:
$$-3x + 6 > -2x - 2$$
$$-3x + 6 + 3x > -2x - 2 + 3x$$
$$6 > x - 2$$
$$6 + 2 > x - 2 + 2$$
$$8 > x$$
$$x < 8$$

3.13 $6(3x + 9) - 8x \leq -6$.

Solution:
$$18x + 54 - 8x \leq -6$$
$$10x + 54 \leq -6$$
$$10x + 54 - 54 \leq -6 - 54$$
$$10x \leq -60$$
$$\frac{10x}{10} \leq \frac{-60}{10}$$
$$x \leq -6$$

3.14 A clothing manufacturer produces one type of sweater that earns $4 profit for each one sold. The business manager requires that a profit of at least $100 be earned every hour. The product manager estimates that the expenses for running the machine are $45 per hour. What is the least number of sweaters that has to be produced each hour to earn a profit of at least $100?

Solution:

Let x represent the number of sweaters to be produced.
$$4x - 45 \geq 100$$
$$4x - 45 + 45 \geq 100 + 45$$
$$4x \geq 145$$
$$\frac{4x}{4} \geq \frac{145}{4}$$
$$x \geq 36.25$$
The least number of sweaters is 37.

3.15 $12x - 7 > 5$ or $6x \leq -6$.

Solution:

$12x - 7 + 7 > 5 + 7$ or $\dfrac{6x}{6} \leq \dfrac{-6}{6}$

$\quad\quad 12x > 12$ x $x \leq -1$

$\quad\quad \dfrac{12x}{12} > \dfrac{12}{12}$

$\quad\quad\quad x > 1$ or $x \leq -1$

x > 1 or x ≤ -1

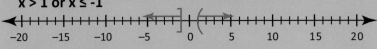

3.16 $4(x - 1) \geq 8$ and $-3x + 4 > -2$.

Solution:

$\quad\quad 4x - 4 \geq 8$ and $-3x + 4 - 4 > -2 - 4$

$4x - 4 + 4 \geq 8 + 4$ $-3x > -6$

$\quad\quad\quad 4x \geq 12$ $\dfrac{-3x}{-3} > \dfrac{-6}{-3}$

$\quad\quad\quad \dfrac{4x}{4} \geq \dfrac{12}{4}$ $x < 2$

$\quad\quad\quad\quad x \geq 3$ and $x < 2$

Since there are no numbers that will satisfy both conditions, there is no solution.

3.17 Solve the compound inequality. List four possible solutions.
$2x - 3(2x - 5) \leq 7$ and $3x - 1 \geq 5x - 7$

Solution:

$\quad 2x - 6x + 15 \leq 7$ and $3x - 1 - 3x \geq 5x - 7 - 3x$

$\quad\quad -4x + 15 \leq 7$ and $-1 \geq 2x - 7$

$-4x + 15 - 15 \leq 7 - 15$ and $-1 + 7 \geq 2x - 7 + 7$

$\quad\quad\quad\quad -4x \leq -8$ and $6 \geq 2x$

$\quad\quad\quad\quad \dfrac{-4x}{-4} \geq \dfrac{-8}{-4}$ and $\dfrac{6}{2} \geq \dfrac{2x}{2}$

$\quad\quad\quad\quad\quad x \geq 2$ and $3 \geq x$

$\quad\quad\quad\quad\quad x \geq 2$ and $x \leq 3$

Four possible solutions are 2, 2.3, 2.6, and 3.

3.18 What numbers on a number line are 10.5 units away from 6?

Solution:

$\quad\quad |x - 6| = 10.5$

$\quad\quad\quad x - 6 = 10.5$ or $-(x - 6) = 10.5$

$\quad x - 6 + 6 = 10.5 + 6$ or $-x + 6 = 10.5$

$\quad\quad\quad\quad x = 16.5$ or $-x + 6 - 6 = 10.5 - 6$

                    or $-x = 4.5$

                    or $\dfrac{-x}{-1} = \dfrac{4.5}{-1}$

$\quad\quad\quad\quad x = 16.5$ or $x = -4.5$

3.19 $|x + 3| \geq 7$.

Solution:

$x + 3 \geq 7$	or	$-(x + 3) \geq 7$
$x + 3 - 3 \geq 7 - 3$	or	$-x - 3 + 3 \geq 7 + 3$
$x \geq 4$	or	$-x \geq 10$
$x \geq 4$	or	$x \leq -10$

3.20 $|x - 4| - 3 < 9$.

Solution:

$|x - 4| - 3 + 3 < 9 + 3$

$\quad |x - 4| < 12$

$x - 4 < 12$	and	$-(x - 4) < 12$
		$-x + 4 < 12$
$x - 4 + 4 < 12 + 4$	and	$-x + 4 - 4 < 12 - 4$
$x < 16$	and	$-x < 8$
$x < 16$	and	$x > 8$

3.21 $-|2x - 1| \leq -13$.

Solution:

$-|2x - 1| \leq -13$

$(-1)(-|2x - 1|) \leq (-13)(-1)$

$\quad |2x - 1| \geq 13$

$2x - 1 \geq 13$	or	$-(2x - 1) \geq 13$
		$-2x + 1 \geq 13$
$2x - 1 + 1 \geq 13 + 1$	or	$-2x + 1 - 1 \geq 13 - 1$
$2x \geq 14$	or	$-2x \geq 12$
$x \geq 7$	or	$x \leq -6$

3.22 Solve the inequality $3|3x + 4| > 12$.

Solution:

$\dfrac{3|3x + 4|}{3} > \dfrac{12}{3}$

$|3x + 4| > 4$

$3x + 4 > 4$	or	$-(3x + 4) > 4$
$3x + 4 - 4 > 4 - 4$	or	$(3x + 4) < -4$
$3x > 0$	or	$3x + 4 - 4 < -4 - 4$
$\dfrac{3x}{3} > \dfrac{0}{3}$	or	$3x < -8$
$x > 0$	or	$\dfrac{3x}{3} < -\dfrac{8}{3}$
$x > 0$	or	$x < -\dfrac{8}{3}$

Introduction to Linear Equations

3.1 Solve $2x - 3 = 15$.

3.2 Solve $0.3x + 20 = 1.2x - 25$.

Application: Solving Problems Using Formulas

3.3 Set up an equation and solve. The length of a rectangle is twice its width. If the perimeter is 36 meters, what are its dimensions?

3.4 Set up an equation and solve. The width of a rectangle is 3 more than twice its length. The perimeter is 60 feet. Find the width and length of the rectangle.

3.5 Set up an equation and solve. Three consecutive odd integers have a sum of 51; find the integers.

3.6 Set up an equation and solve. Find three consecutive even integers such that twice the largest is equal to two more than three times the smallest.

Translating Sentences into Equations

3.7 Translate the following English phrase into an algebraic expression: three more than twice some number.

3.8 Translate the following English phrase into an algebraic expression: four less than five times some number.

3.9 Translate and solve. Nine more than three times a number is −3. Find the number.

3.10 Translate and solve. Four less than twice the sum of a number and 2 is 10. Find the number.

3.11 Translate and solve. Twice a number is fifteen less than three times the number. Find the number.

3.12 If a person invested a third of her money at 6% and two thirds at 9% and received $450 in interest, find the total money invested.

3.13 A coffee shop has two types of coffee. Coffee A sells for $4 per pound and Coffee B sells for $13 per pound. Mix 90 pounds of Coffee B with Coffee A to get a mixture that will sell for $10 per pound. How many pounds of Coffee A should be used?

Mixture and Uniform Motion Problems

3.14 Set up an equation and solve. How much 20% acid must be mixed with 5% acid to make 30 mL of 12% acid?

3.15 Set up an equation and solve. A plane leaves Chicago flying due east at 200 mph while a train that left two hours earlier is going due west at 70 mph. How much time will it take for them to be 545 miles apart?

3.16 On a 425 mile trip, John drove for 4 hours and Barry drove for 3 hours. John's rate of speed was 10 mph faster than Barry's rate. Find the rates in miles per hour. How many miles did each drive?

3.17 Set up an equation and solve. There are 125 cast members for the play Oliver! 30 members came down with the flu. What percent of cast members had the flu?

3.18 A team lost 8 of the 40 games they played. What percent of games did they win?

3.19 How much needs to be invested into a simple interest account paying 4% for 3 years that would result in $540 in interest?

3.20 Brand A of herbal tea costs $2.00 per ounce, and Brand B costs $4.00 per ounce. A merchant would like to create a mixture of the teas to yield 100 ounces that would sell for $2.70 per ounce. How much of each brand would be needed?

First Degree Inequalities

3.21 Solve and graph the solutions. $3x + 1 < 10$.

3.22 Solve and graph the solutions. $10x + 9 > -15x + 34$.

3.23 Solve and graph the solutions. $3(6 - x) \leq -12$.

3.24 Solve and graph the solutions. $9x - 7 > 5(x + 5)$.

3.25 Solve and graph the solutions. $-2(2x - 9) + 3 < 6x + 5$.

3.26 Solve and graph the solutions. $2 - 3(x - 4) \leq 11$.

3.27 Solve and graph the solutions. $5(4 - x) - 2x \geq 3 - (x - 1)$.

3.28 Solve and graph the solutions. $12x - 7(x - 3) + 3 > 4 - (2x + 1)$.

Absolute Value Equations and Inequalities

3.29 Solve and graph the solutions. $|x + 5| = 8$.

3.30 Solve and graph the solutions. $|2x - 3| = 5$.

3.31 Solve and graph the solutions. $|x + 3| < 2$.

3.32 Solve and graph the solutions. $|x - 3| + 7 = 15$.

3.33 Solve and graph the solutions. $|3x - 4| \geq 7$.

3.34 Solve and graph the solutions. $-|x - 6| > -13$.
Solution:

3.35 Solve and graph the solutions. $|x - 1| + 9 \geq 20$.

Graphing Linear Equations and Inequalities

Travis pays his credit card balance in full every month, so the only expense he has related to the card is the annual fee, which is $30. The card awards Travis 4 percent cash back on all of his purchases, so if Travis charges enough to his card during the year, he will actually make money.

Suppose that Travis charges $1,000 to his credit card during the year. Since 4%· $1000 = $40, he earns $40 cash back. In this case, after taking into account the fee and the cash back, Travis would be ahead $10. Next, suppose that Travis charges $2,000 to his credit card during the year, earning $80 cash back. This time Travis would be ahead $50. Likewise, if Travis charges $3,000 to his card during the year, he would be ahead $90.

How can Travis accurately predict how far "ahead" or "behind" he will be at the end of the year based on how much he charges to his card? One way is to represent the amount of money Travis charges to his credit card during the year by a visual aid such as a graph. The visual aid also would account for the amount of money he is ahead or behind for the year, including the fee and the cash back.

QUESTIONS TO CONSIDER

1. Suppose Travis decides to use his card only for emergencies and ends up charging $0 to his card during the year. How far ahead or behind is he?

2. If Travis charges $750 to his card during the year, how far ahead or behind is he?

3. At what point will he be neither ahead nor behind (the breakeven point)?

KEY TERMS

INTRODUCTION TO THE CARTESIAN PLANE

A graph is usually drawn on a **Cartesian plane,** which is a two-dimensional coordinate system. A horizontal number line forms the **x-axis** of the plane, and a vertical number line forms the **y-axis.** The axes intersect at their 0 points; this coordinate is called the **origin.** Every point in the plane can be defined by its x and y **coordinates.** The **x-coordinate** of a point is the point's distance in the x direction from the y-axis. Similarly, the **y-coordinate** of a point is the point's distance in the y direction from the x-axis.

It is customary to use ordered pairs (x, y) to represent the coordinates of a point in the plane. The x-coordinate is the first coordinate, and the y-coordinate is the second coordinate.

For the case of Travis's credit card records, the numbers along the x-axis could represent the amount of money Travis charges to his credit card during the year, and the numbers along the y-axis could represent the amount of money he is ahead or behind for the year.

Referring back to the chapter opening, when Travis charges $1,000 during the year, he is $10 ahead at the end of the year. The point representing this scenario would have an x-coordinate of 1000 and a y-coordinate of 10 and would be written (1000, 10). The point is 1000 units in the x direction from the y-axis, and 10 units in the y direction from the x-axis. To graph this point, begin at the origin and move to 1000 on the x-axis, and then move up 10 units, parallel to the y-axis (Figure 4.1).

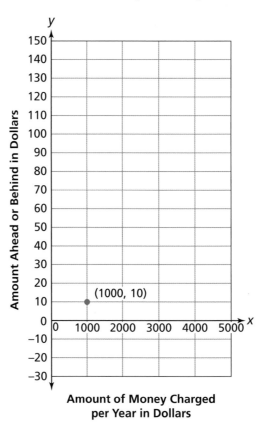

FIGURE 4.1 Graph If Travis Charges $1,000 per Year

Other ways of describing plotting the point (1000, 10) are "right 1000, up 10," or "over 1000, up 10."

If Travis spent $2,000 during the year, he was ahead by $50. The point to graph that represents this information is (2000, 50)—right 2000, up 50 (Figure 4.2).

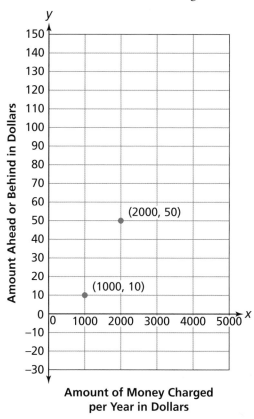

FIGURE 4.2 Graph If Travis Charges $2,000 per Year

If Travis charges $3,000 per year, the point to graph is (3000, 90) (Figure 4.3).

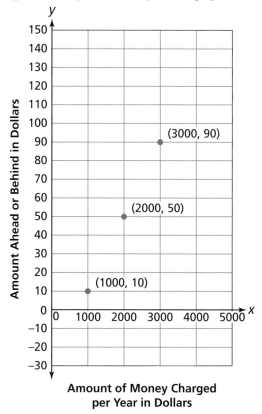

FIGURE 4.3 Graph If Travis Charges $3,000 per Year

When the points (1000, 10), (2000, 50), and (3000, 90) are plotted on a Cartesian plane, it becomes apparent that every time the x-coordinate increases by 1000, the y-coordinate increases by 40.

With this in mind, how much would Travis be ahead if he charges $4,000 to his card during the year? Since the x-coordinate would now be 4000, which is 1000 greater than the x-coordinate of the point (3000, 90), the y-coordinate would now be 130, that is, 40 greater than the y-coordinate of (3000, 90) (Figure 4.4).

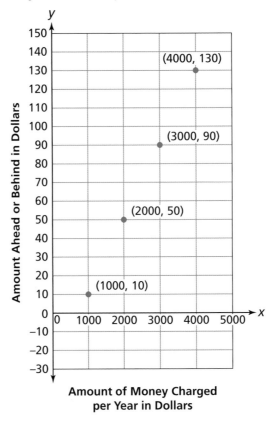

FIGURE 4.4 Graph If Travis Charges $4,000 per Year

Identifying the coordinates of points on a graph, as well as plotting points when given their coordinates, are valuable skills.

Example 4.1
What are the coordinates of points *A*, *B*, *C*, and *D* plotted on the Cartesian plane in Figure 4.5?

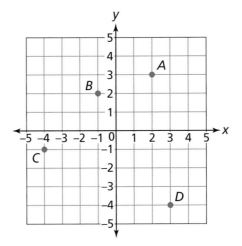

FIGURE 4.5

Solution:

    a. Point *A* is 2 units to the right of the *y*-axis and 3 units above the *x*-axis, so its coordinates are (2, 3).

    b. Point *B* is 1 unit to the left of the *y*-axis and 2 units above the *x*-axis, so its coordinates are (−1, 2).

    c. Point *C* is 4 units to the left of the *y*-axis and 1 unit below the *x*-axis, so its coordinates are (−4, −1).

    d. Point *D* is 3 units to the right of the *y*-axis and 4 units below the *x*-axis, so its coordinates are (3, −4).

Example 4.2

The *x*-axis and the *y*-axis of a Cartesian plane intersect at the origin and form four **quadrants.** Determine in what quadrant of the Cartesian plane in Figure 4.6 the points *A* (−3, 3), *B* (2, 4), *C* (−1, −3), and *D* (4, −1) are located.

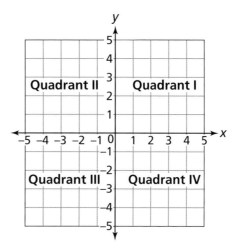

FIGURE 4.6

Solution:

    a. Since point *A* (−3, 3) will be 3 units to the left of the *y*-axis and 3 units above the *x*-axis, it will be in quadrant II.

    b. Since point *B* (2, 4) will be 2 units to the right of the *y*-axis and 4 units above the *x*-axis, it will be in quadrant I.

    c. Since point *C* (−1, −3) will be 1 unit to the left of the *y*-axis and 3 units below the *x*-axis, it will be in quadrant III.

    d. Since point *D* (4, −1) will be 4 units to the right of the *y*-axis and 1 unit below the *x*-axis, it will be in quadrant IV.

Example 4.3

Plot the points *A* (−2, −3), *B* (−4, 1), *C* (1, 3), and *D* (4, −2) on a Cartesian plane.

Solution:

For each of the points, perform the following steps.

    a. Move left or right along the *x*-axis to the point's *x*-coordinate.

    b. Move up or down parallel to the *y*-axis to the point's *y*-coordinate.

    c. Plot the point.

Figure 4.7 shows the results when these steps are performed for each of the points.

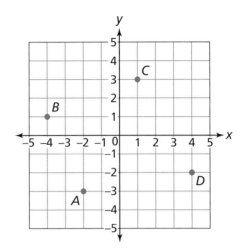

FIGURE 4.7

DIY PROBLEMS

4.1 What are the coordinates of points *A*, *B*, *C*, and *D* plotted on the Cartesian plane in Figure 4.8?

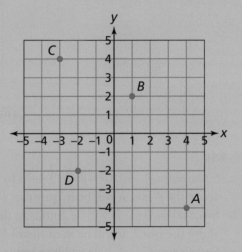

FIGURE 4.8

A (____, ____)   C (____, ____)
B (____, ____)   D (____, ____)

4.2 Determine in what quadrant the points *A* (1, −4), *B* (−3, 1), *C* (2, 2), and *D* (−4, −3) will be when plotted.
Point *A*: Quadrant ____   Point *C*: Quadrant ____
Point *B*: Quadrant ____   Point *D*: Quadrant ____

4.3 Plot the points *A* (4, 1), *B* (−1, 3), *C* (−2, −4), and *D* (3, −2) on the following Cartesian plane.

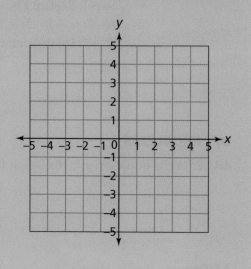

INTRODUCTION TO FUNCTIONS

Function Notation

A **function** *f* is a collection of ordered pairs $(x, f(x))$ for which every first coordinate is paired with a unique second coordinate. The **function notation** *f(x)* is read "*f* of *x*" or "*f* is a function of (the variable) *x*."

The first coordinate, *x*, is the input to the function, and the second coordinate, $f(x)$, is the output of the function. It is correct to use either *y* or $f(x)$ as the second coordinate; $y = f(x)$.

4.7 FUNCTION f A collection of ordered pairs $(x, f(x))$ for which every first coordinate is paired with a unique second coordinate.

4.8 FUNCTION NOTATION *f(x)* Read "*f* of *x*" or "*f* is a function of (the variable) *x*"; *x* is the input, *f(x)* is the output.

Evaluating Functions

To evaluate a function for a given input value, substitute the value for the variable. An example of a function is $f(x) = x + 2$.

Suppose that $x = 3$. Substituting 3 for *x*, $f(3) = 3 + 2$, so $f(3) = 5$. Likewise, $f(-3) = -3 + 2$, so $f(-3) = -1$. The ordered pairs (3, 5) and (−3, −1) belong to the function *f*.

Example 4.4
Write the equation $y = 4x - 1$ in function notation.

Solution:

Step 1: First choose a letter to identify the function. The most common letter is *f*, but any letter will do. In this case, choose *g*.
Step 2: Replace *y* with the function notation, using *g*. The equation is $g(x) = 4x - 1$.

Example 4.5

Evaluate the function $f(x) = -3x + 5$ when $x = -2$.

Solution:

Step 1: Replace x by -2.
$f(-2) = -3(-2) + 5$
Step 2: Do the arithmetic.
$f(-2) = -3(-2) + 5 = 6 + 5 = 11$

DIY PROBLEMS

4.4 Write the equation $y = 10x + 3$ in function notation.

4.5 Evaluate the function $g(x) = 7x - 9$ for $x = 4$.

4.6 Evaluate the function $h(x) = \left(\dfrac{1}{2}\right)x - 3$ for $x = 10$.

LINEAR FUNCTIONS

Linear Functions f(x) = y

4.9 LINEAR FUNCTION A function $f(x)$ for which 1 is the greatest power of x in the equation.

A function $f(x)$ is a **linear function** if 1 is the greatest power of x in the equation.

For example, $f(x) = 8x - 15$ is a linear function, because x is raised to the power 1 (recall that $x^1 = x$). Also, $g(x) = 8$ is a linear function because x is raised to the 0 power (recall that $x^0 = 1$, so $g(x)$ is equivalent to $g(x) = 8x^0$). The graph of any linear function is a line.

Example 4.6 Graph the linear function $f(x) = -x + 6$.

Solution:

Step 1: Evaluate the function for at least two values of x, because two points determine a line. Any values of x can be chosen; use $x = 2$ and $x = 3$.

$f(2) = -(2) + 6 = -2 + 6 = 4$
$f(3) = -(3) + 6 = -3 + 6 = 3$

Step 2: This means that the coordinates of two points on the graph of the function are (2, 4) and (3, 3). Plot these points on a Cartesian plane and draw a line through them (Figure 4.9).

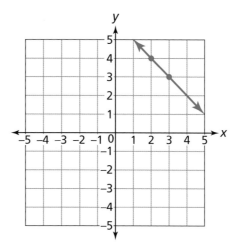

FIGURE 4.9

Example 4.7 Graph the linear function $g(x) = 5x - 2$.

Solution:

a. Again, evaluate the function for two values of x; use $x = 0$ and $x = 1$.
$g(0) = 5(0) - 2 = 0 - 2 = -2$
$g(1) = 5(1) - 2 = 5 - 2 = 3$

b. Since $g(x) = y$, when $x = 0$, $y = -2$, and when $x = 1$, $y = 3$. This means that the coordinates of two points on the graph of the function are $(0, -2)$ and $(1, 3)$. Plot these points on a Cartesian plane and draw a line through them (Figure 4.10).

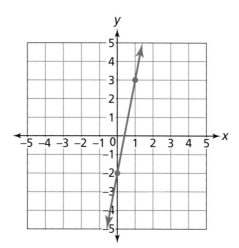

FIGURE 4.10

DIY PROBLEMS

4.7 Graph the linear function $f(x) = 3x - 4$.

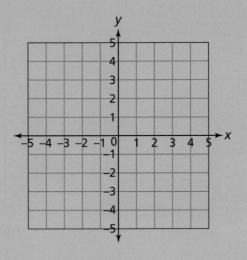

4.8 Graph the linear function $g(x) = -2x + 1$.

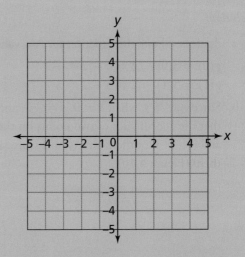

4.9 Graph the linear function $h(x) = \left(-\dfrac{1}{2}\right)x + 2$.

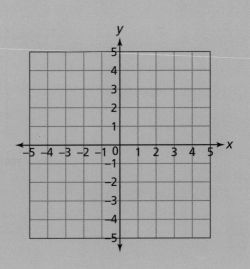

Linear Equations

Another form of linear equation involves only first powers of x and/or y. A linear equation in the form $Ax + By = C$, where A, B, and C are constants, can also be graphed by finding the coordinates of two points, plotting the points on a Cartesian plane, and drawing a line through them.

Graphing a Linear Equation: Ax + By = C

There are two parallel techniques for graphing $Ax + By = C$. Consider the equation $3x + 2y = 5$.

1. Choose x, and solve for y.

   Step 1: Let $x = 1$ and substitute 1 for x in the equation. Then, $3(1) + 2y = 5$. Solving for y, $3 - 3 + 2y = 5 - 3$, so $2y = 2$. Dividing by 2, $y = 1$. The point $(1, 1)$ is on the graph.

   Let $x = -1$ and substitute 1 for x in the equation. Then, $3(-1) + 2y = 5$. Solving for y, $2y = 5 + 3 = 8$, so $y = 4$. The point $(-1, 4)$ is on the graph.

   Step 2: Graph the two points and draw a line through them (Figure 4.11).

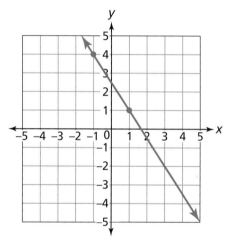

FIGURE 4.11

2. Choose y, and solve for x.

   Alternately, choose values for y and solve for x. Check that if $y = 1$, $x = 1$, and if $y = 4$, $x = -1$, repeating the coordinates found above for two points on the graph.

   In addition, let $y = 0$. Then $3x = 5$, and x is approximately 1.7. If $x = 0$, $y = 2.5$. Observe that the points $(1.7, 0)$ and $(0, 2.5)$ appear to fall on the line graphed in Figure 4.11 where the graph intersects the axes.

Example 4.8 Graph the linear equation $8x + 2y = 4$.

Solution:

Step 1: Choose a value for x, substitute 0 for x, and solve for y.

$8(0) + 2y = 4$
$0 + 2y = 4$
$2y = 4$
$y = 2$

Because $y = 2$ when $x = 0$, the coordinates of the first point are $(0, 2)$, a point on the y-axis.

Step 2: To find the coordinates of the second point, use $y = 0$.

$$8x + 2(0) = 4$$
$$8x = 4$$
$$x = 0.5$$

Since $x = 0.5$ when $y = 0$, the coordinates of the second point are $(0.5, 0)$, a point on the x-axis.

Step 3: Plot these points on a Cartesian plane and draw a line through them (Figure 4.12).

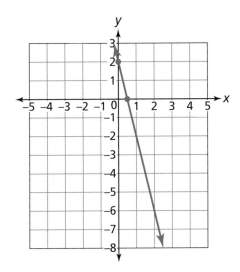

FIGURE 4.12

Notice that dividing the common factor of 2 out of all the terms in the equation simplifies the problem. The equation becomes $4x + y = 2$, so that giving x a value makes finding y very easy. When $x = 0$, $y = 2$, and when $x = \frac{1}{2}$, $y = 0$.

Example 4.9
Graph the linear equation $x - 3y = 5$.

Solution:

Step 1: To find the coordinates of the first point, plug in $y = 0$.

$$x - 3(0) = 5$$
$$x = 5$$

Since $x = 5$ when $y = 0$, the coordinates of the first point are $(5, 0)$, a point on the x-axis.

Step 2: To find the coordinates of the second point, plug in $y = -2$.

$$x - 3(-2) = 5$$
$$x + 6 = 5$$
$$x + 6 - 6 = 5 - 6$$
$$x = -1$$

Since $x = -1$ when $y = -2$, the coordinates of the second point are $(-1, -2)$.

Step 3: Plot these points on a Cartesian plane and draw a line through them (Figure 4.13).

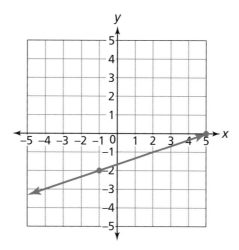

FIGURE 4.13

DIY PROBLEMS

4.10 Graph the linear equation $4x - y = 1$.

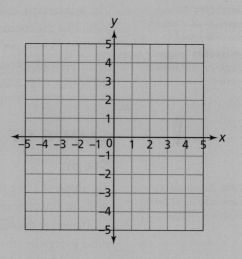

4.11 Graph the linear equation $2x + 4y = 6$.

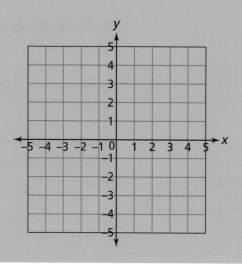

4.12 Graph the linear equation $x - 2y = 4$.

Finding the *x*- and *y*-Intercepts of a Line

The **x-intercept** and **y-intercept** of a linear equation or a linear function are the points (or the coordinate values) where the line intersects the x-axis and y-axis.

Since points on the x-axis have coordinates $(x, 0)$, substitute $y = 0$ in the equation and solve for x to find the x-intercept. Similarly, substitute $x = 0$ in the equation and solve for y to find the y-intercept $(0, y)$.

SLOPE OF A LINE

Slope

The **slope** of a line is a measure of the line's steepness and whether the line goes up or down from left to right.

The larger the absolute value of the measure, the steeper the line. If the slope of a line is negative, the line descends from left to right, and if the slope is positive, the line ascends from left to right.

Calculating the Slope of a Line

"Rise over run" is a phrase that describes the slope of a line. Given two points on the line, the ratio of the difference in the y-coordinates (the vertical distance between the points, or the *rise*) to the difference in the x-coordinates (the horizontal distance between the points, or the *run*) is the slope.

Finding the Slope Given Two Points

To calculate the slope of a line, use the coordinates of any two points on the line. It is customary to use **subscripts** to identify general coordinates of the points.

Instead of using many different letters, subscripts often identify a series of variables of the same type. Read n_3 as "*n*-sub-3."

In this case, the *x* and *y* variables have subscripts 1 and 2 (for first and second points). Given two points (x_1, y_1) and (x_2, y_2) that lie on the line, the line's slope is the difference of the *y*-coordinates over the difference of the *x*-coordinates, or $\dfrac{y_2 - y_1}{x_2 - x_1}$.

For example, given two points with coordinates $(4, 7)$ and $(-6, 9)$, the slope of the line that contains them is $\dfrac{9-7}{-6-4} = \dfrac{2}{-10} = -\dfrac{1}{5}$. Tracing the line from left to right, the line goes down 1 unit (the *rise*—here a *fall*) for every 5 units to the right (the *run*). Notice that it is important that the order of the coordinates be the same in the numerator and the denominator. Above, the coordinates of the first point are subtracted form the coordinates of the second point.

Example 4.10
The coordinates of two points on a line are $(-3, 7)$ and $(1, 0)$. Find the slope of the line and describe what it represents.

Solution:
The slope is $\dfrac{0-7}{1-(-3)} = -\dfrac{7}{4}$, which represents a *fall* of 7 units for each *run* of 4 units.

Example 4.11
A line's slope is $\dfrac{1}{2}$, and a point on the line is $(-3, 1)$. Graph the line.

Solution:

Step 1: Plot the point $(-3, 1)$ on a Cartesian plane (Figure 4.14).

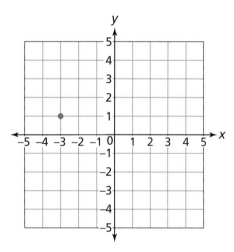

FIGURE 4.14

Step 2: Next, recall that the slope $\dfrac{1}{2}$ represents a *rise* of 1 vertical unit for every horizontal *run* of 2 units. So, from the point $(-3, 1)$, move 1 unit up and 2 units to the right to arrive at the point $(-1, 2)$. Plot this point and draw a line through the points (Figure 4.15).

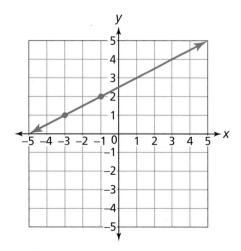

FIGURE 4.15

Example 4.12

A line's slope is −4, and a point on the line is (−2, 2). Graph the line.

Solution:

Step 1: Plot the point (−2, 2) on a Cartesian plane (Figure 4.16).

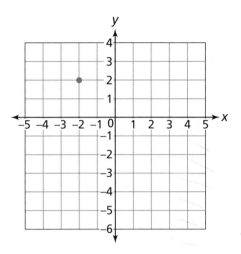

FIGURE 4.16

Step 2: Next, recall that the slope $-4 = -\dfrac{4}{1}$ represents a *rise* of −4 vertical units (that is, a *fall* in this case) for every horizontal *run* of 1 unit. So, from the point (−2, 2), move 4 units down and 1 unit to the right to arrive at the point (−1, −2). Plot this point and draw a line through the points (Figure 4.17).

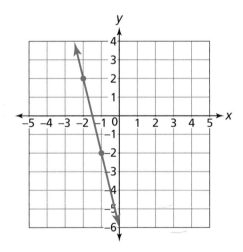

FIGURE 4.17

DIY PROBLEMS

4.13 The coordinates of two points on a line are (−3, 0) and (1, 6). Find the slope of the line and describe what it represents.

4.14 The coordinates of two points on a line are (−4, 0) and (3, −1). Find the slope of the line and describe what it represents.

4.15 The coordinates of two points on a line are (−2, 1) and (3, 1). Find the slope of the line and describe what it represents.

4.16 A line's slope is $\frac{1}{3}$, and a point on the line is (−4, −1). Graph the line.

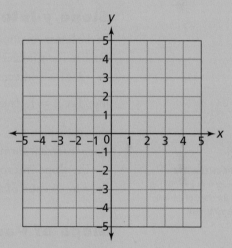

4.17 A line's slope is −2, and a point on the line is (1, 3). Graph the line.

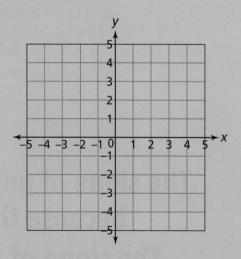

4.18 A line's slope is $-\dfrac{1}{2}$, and a point on the line is $(-1, 3)$. Graph the line.

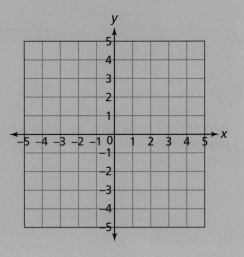

Slope y-Intercept Form

In the linear equation $y = f(x) = 9x - 2$, the constants 9 and -2 have direct connections to the y-intercept and slope of the graph of the equation. When $x = 0$, $y = -2$, so -2 is the y-intercept of the graph. To find the slope, identify a second point on the line. Let $x = 1$. Then $y = 7$. The slope of the line is $\dfrac{y_2 - y_1}{x_2 - x_1} = \dfrac{-2 - 7}{0 - 1} = \dfrac{-9}{-1} = 9$, the coefficient of x. This equation is an instance of an equation of a line written in slope-intercept form.

The **slope-intercept form** of a line is $y = mx + b$, where m is the slope and b is the y-intercept. For the example above, the slope 9 is m, and the y-intercept -2 is b.

4.14 SLOPE-INTERCEPT FORM The formula $y = mx + b$, where m is the slope of the line and b is the y-intercept.

Slope of Parallel and Perpendicular Lines

Parallel lines are lines in the same plane that never intersect. It makes sense, then, that the slopes of parallel lines are equal, since intuitively the rise over run ratios will be equal. In fact, an alternate definition of parallel lines is "lines that have the same slope." For example, the lines $y = 8x - 5$ and $y = 8x + 1$ are parallel; they both have slope 8.

It is true, but more difficult to explain, that perpendicular lines have slopes that are *negative reciprocals* of each other. The lines $y = 5x - 7$ and $y = -\dfrac{1}{5}x + 3$ are perpendicular. An alternate definition of perpendicular lines is "lines whose slopes have product -1."

The slope of any horizontal line is 0, because the *rise* equals 0.
The slope of any vertical line is undefined because the *run* equals 0.

Slope of Horizontal and Vertical Lines

A horizontal line is parallel to the *x*-axis. For all values of *x*, *y* is a constant. The equation of a horizontal line is $y = b$. The *y*-intercept of the line is *b*, and the slope *m* is 0. All points on the line are of the form (x, b). There is no change in *y* values (the *rise*) for any difference of *x* values (the *run*). The slope ratio is $\dfrac{b - b}{x_2 - x_1} = \dfrac{0}{x_2 - x_1} = 0$.

On the other hand, a vertical line is parallel to the *y*-axis. For all values of *y*, *x* is a constant. The equation of a vertical line is $x = c$, for *c* a constant. All points on the line are of the form (c, y). There is no *y*-intercept, and no change in *x* values for any difference of *y* values. The slope ratio is $\dfrac{y_2 - y_1}{c - c} = \dfrac{y_2 - y_1}{0}$. Since division by zero is undefined, a vertical line has slope that is undefined.

Example 4.13

Write the equation of the line with *y*-intercept 10 that is parallel to the line shown in Figure 4.18. Also write the equation for the line with *y*-intercept 10 that is perpendicular to the line shown.

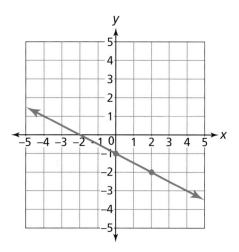

FIGURE 4.18

Solution:

Step 1: Determine the slope of the line shown. It appears that $(0, -1)$ and $(2, -2)$ are on the line. Since the graph moves down 1 unit for every 2 units it moves to the right, the slope is $-\dfrac{1}{2}$.

Step 2: Since the line with intercept 10 parallel to the one shown has the same slope, its equation is $y = -\dfrac{1}{2}x + 10$.

Step 3: Since the line with intercept 10 perpendicular to the one shown has a slope that is the negative reciprocal of $-\dfrac{1}{2}$, its equation is $y = 2x + 10$.

Example 4.14

What are the slopes of lines parallel and perpendicular to the line shown in Figure 4.19?

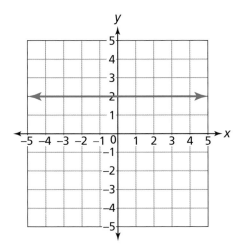

FIGURE 4.19

Solution:

Step 1: The line shown is horizontal, so its slope is 0.

Step 2: Since a line parallel to the one shown would also be horizontal, its slope would also be 0.

Step 3: Since a line perpendicular to the one shown would be vertical, its slope would be undefined.

Example 4.15

Graph the equation $y = 4x - 3$.

Solution:

Step 1: Plot the point $(0, -3)$, which is the line's y-intercept in Figure 4.20, on a Cartesian plane.

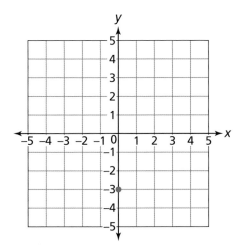

FIGURE 4.20

Step 2: Using the slope 4, from the point $(0, -3)$ move 4 units up and 1 unit to the right to arrive at the point $(1, 1)$. Plot this point and draw a line through the points (Figure 4.21).

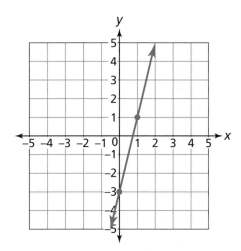

FIGURE 4.21

Example 4.16

Graph the function $f(x) = -x + 1$.

Solution:

Step 1: Plot the point $(0, 1)$, which is the line's y-intercept, on a Cartesian plane (Figure 4.22).

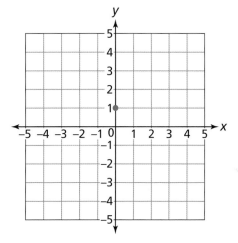

FIGURE 4.22

Step 2: Using the slope -1, from the point $(0, 1)$ move 1 unit down and 1 unit to the right to arrive at the point $(1, 0)$. Plot this point and draw a line through the points (Figure 4.23).

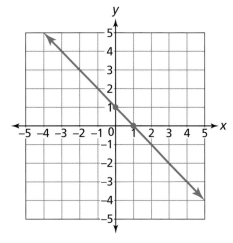

FIGURE 4.23

DIY PROBLEMS

4.19 Identify the slope and *y*-intercept for the linear equation $y = \left(-\dfrac{2}{3}\right)x + 4$.

Slope = _____
y-intercept = _____

4.20 Identify the slope and *y*-intercept for the linear equation $y = 5x - 2$.

Slope = _____
y-intercept = _____

4.21 Identify the slope and *y*-intercept for the linear equation $2y = 3x + 4$.

Slope = _____
y-intercept = _____

4.22 Write the equation of the line that is parallel to the line $y = -x + 3$ and contains the point (2, 1).

4.23 Write the equations of the lines with *y*-intercepts of -9 that are parallel and perpendicular to the line shown in Figure 4.24.

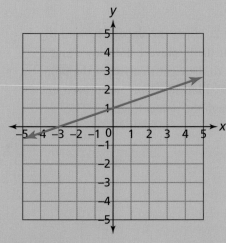

FIGURE 4.24

Parallel line: _____
Perpendicular line: _____

4.24 What are the slopes of lines parallel and perpendicular to the one shown in Figure 4.25?

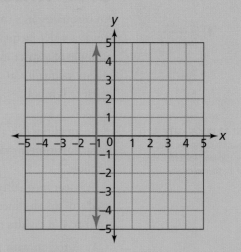

FIGURE 4.25

4.25 Graph the equation $y = x - 4$.

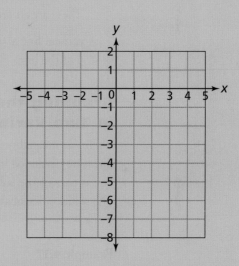

4.26 Graph the function $f(x) = -6x + 4$.

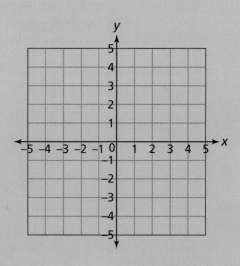

GRAPHING LINEAR INEQUALITIES

An inequality in a single variable uses the *less than* or *greater than* symbols, $<$ or $>$, if it is a strict inequality (that is, the given value is not included as a solution). An example of a strict inequality in one variable is $t > 4$.

An inequality in a single variable uses the *less than or equal to* or *greater than or equal to* symbols, $\leq$ or $\geq$, if the given value is included as a solution. An example is $t \geq 4$.

4.15 LINEAR INEQUALITY A linear equation in two variables with the = symbol replaced by one of the four inequality symbols.

Inequalities can also exist in two variables and be linear. A **linear inequality** is a linear equation in two variables with the = symbol replaced by one of the inequality symbols.

A linear inequality can be visualized on a Cartesian plane, building on techniques used to graph linear equations. In slope-intercept form, the linear equation $y = mx + b$ divides the plane into two regions:

1. A region with y values *greater than* those on the related line for a given x value. These are all points *above* the line and included in the inequality $y > mx + b$.
2. A region with y values *less than* those on the related line for a given x value. These are all *below* the line and included in the inequality $y < mx + b$.

A vertical line $x = c$ divides the plane into regions to the right ($x > c$) and left ($x < c$) of the line.

Graphing the Solution Set of a Linear Inequality in Two Variables

If a linear inequality is a strict inequality, graph the related line as a dashed line (the line is not included in the solution set). Otherwise, graph the line as a solid line (the line is part of the solution set). Then, in either case, shade the appropriate region. The solution set of the linear inequality $y > 4x + 9$ is the region above the dashed line $y = 4x + 9$.

Example 4.17
Graph the linear inequality $y < 3x - 2$.

Solution:

Step 1: Mark the point $(0, -2)$, which is the line's y-intercept, on a Cartesian plane (Figure 4.26).

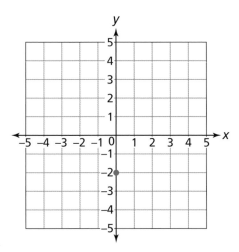

FIGURE 4.26

Step 2: Using the slope 3, from the point (0, −2) move 3 units up and 1 unit to the right to arrive at the point (1, 1). Mark this point and draw a dashed line through the points. Do not leave bullets at these points, as they are not part of the solution set (Figure 4.27).

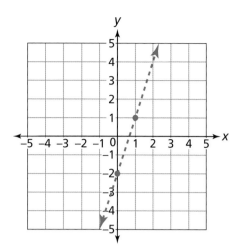

FIGURE 4.27

Step 3: Since the symbol in the expressions is <, shade the region below the dashed line (Figure 4.28).

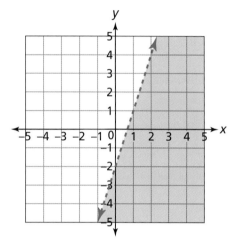

FIGURE 4.28

All the points below the line, when plugged into the inequality, should make a true statement. Pick points $(1, -2)$ and $(3, 3,)$ in the region as a partial check of the solution: For $(1, -2)$, $-2 < (3)1 - 2 = 1$ is true. For $(3, 3,)$, $3 < 3(3) - 2 = 7$ is true. Or, pick $(0, 0)$ as a point outside of the region and observe that $0 < 3(0) - 2 = -2$ is not true.

Example 4.18

Graph the linear inequality $y \geq -\dfrac{3}{4}x + 2$.

Solution:

Step 1: Plot the point $(0, 2)$, which is the line's y-intercept, on a Cartesian plane (Figure 4.29).

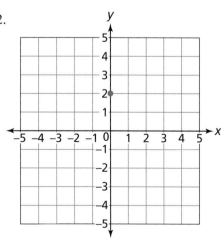

FIGURE 4.29

Step 2: Using the slope $-\dfrac{3}{4}$, from the point $(0, 2)$ move 3 units down and 4 units to the right to arrive at the point $(4, -1)$. Plot this point and draw a solid line through the points (Figure 4.30).

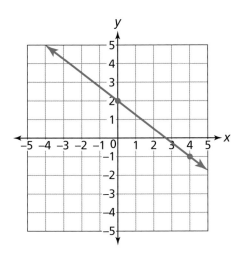

FIGURE 4.30

Step 3: Since the symbol in the inequality is $\geq$, shade the region above the solid line (Figure 4.31).

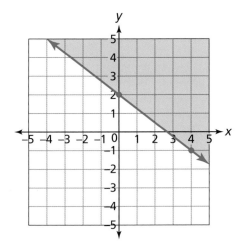

FIGURE 4.31

DIY PROBLEMS

4.27 Graph the linear inequality.

$y > -\dfrac{1}{3}x + 3.$

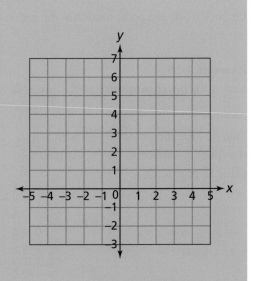

4.28 Graph the linear inequality.

$y \leq 4x - 1$.

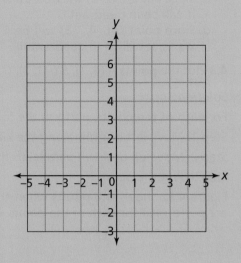

SOLUTIONS TO DIY PROBLEMS

4.1 What are the coordinates of points A, B, C, and D plotted on the Cartesian plane below?

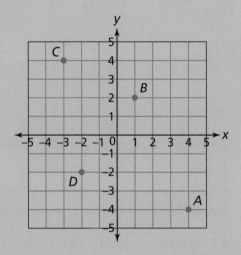

Solution:
   a. Point A is 4 units to the right of the y-axis and 4 units below the x-axis, so its coordinates are (4, −4).
   b. Point B is 1 unit to the right of the y-axis and 2 units above the x-axis, so its coordinates are (1, 2).
   c. Point C is 3 units to the left of the y-axis and 4 units above the x-axis, so its coordinates are (−3, 4).
   d. Point D is 2 units to the left of the y-axis and 2 units below the x-axis, so its coordinates are (−2, −2).

4.2 Determine in what quadrant the points A (1, −4), B (−3, 1), C (2, 2), and D (−4, −3) will be when plotted.

   a. Since point A (1, −4) will be 1 unit to the right of the y-axis and 4 units below the x-axis, it will be in quadrant IV.
   b. Since point B (−3, 1) will be 3 units to the left of the y-axis and 1 unit above the x-axis, it will be in quadrant II.

c. Since point C (2, 2) will be 2 units to the right of the y-axis and 2 units above the x-axis, it will be in quadrant I.

d. Since point D (−4, −3) will be 4 units to the left of the y-axis and 3 units below the x-axis, it will be in quadrant III.

4.3 Plot the points A (4, 1), B (−1, 3), C (−2, −4), and D (3, −2) on the Cartesian plane below.

Solution:

For each of the points, perform the following steps:

Step 1: Move left or right along the x-axis to the point's x-coordinate.

Step 2: Move up or down parallel to the y-axis to the point's y-coordinate.

Step 3: Plot the point.

Figure 4.32 shows the results when these steps are performed for each of the points.

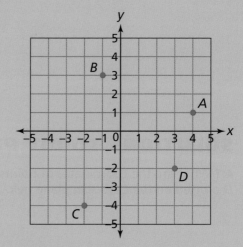

FIGURE 4.32

4.4 Write the equation $y = 10x + 3$ in function notation.

Solution:

Step 1: Choose a letter to identify the function; in this case, choose f.

Step 2: Replace y by f(x). The equation in function notation is $f(x) = 10x + 3$.

4.5 Evaluate the function $g(x) = 7x − 9$ for $x = 4$.

Solution:

Step 1: Substitute 4 for x in the function.
$g(4) = 7(4) − 9$

Step 2: Do the arithmetic.
$g(4) = 7(4) − 9 = 28 − 9 = 19$

4.6 Evaluate the function $h(x) = \left(\dfrac{1}{2}\right)x − 3$ for $x = 10$.

Solution:

Step 1: Substitute 10 for x in the function.

Evaluate the function $h(10) = \left(\dfrac{1}{2}\right)(10) − 3$

Step 2: Do the arithmetic.
$h(10) = 5 − 3 = 2$

4.7 Graph the linear function $f(x) = 3x - 4$.

Solution:

Step 1: Evaluate the function for two values of x; use $x = 1$ and $x = 2$.

$f(1) = 3(1) - 4 = 3 - 4 = -1$

$f(2) = 3(2) - 4 = 6 - 4 = 2$

Step 2: This means that the coordinates of two points on the graph of the function are $(1, -1)$ and $(2, 2)$. Plot these points on a Cartesian plane and draw a line through them (Figure 4.33).

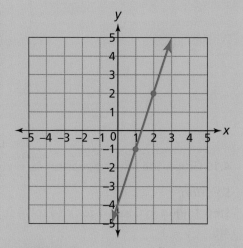

FIGURE 4.33

4.8 Graph the linear function $g(x) = -2x + 1$.

Solution:

Step 1: Evaluate the function for two values of x; use $x = -1$ and $x = 0$.

$g(-1) = -2(-1) + 1 = 2 + 1 = 3$

$g(0) = -2(0) + 1 = 0 + 1 = 1$

Step 2: This means that the coordinates of two points on the graph of the function are $(-1, 3)$ and $(0, 1)$. Plot these points on a Cartesian plane and draw a line through them (Figure 4.34).

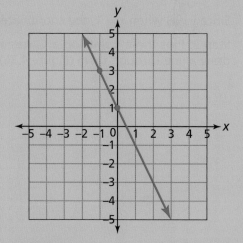

FIGURE 4.34

4.9 Graph the linear function $h(x) = \left(-\dfrac{1}{2}\right)x + 2$.

Solution:

Step 1: Evaluate the function for two values of x; use $x = -2$ and $x = 0$.

$h(-2) = \left(-\dfrac{1}{2}\right)(-2) + 2 = 1 + 2 = 3$

$h(0) = \left(-\dfrac{1}{2}\right)(0) + 2 = 0 + 2 = 2$

Step 2: This means that the coordinates of two points on the graph of the function are (−2, 3) and (0, 2). Plot these points on a Cartesian plane and draw a line through them (Figure 4.35).

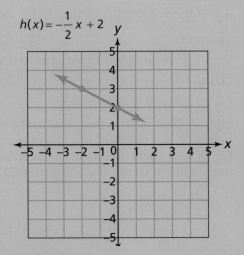

$h(x) = -\dfrac{1}{2}x + 2$

FIGURE 4.35

4.10 Graph the linear equation $4x - y = 1$.

Solution:

Step 1: Plug in 0 and 1 for x to solve for y.

$$4(0) - y = 1$$
$$0 - y = 1$$
$$-y = 1$$
$$y = -1$$

Since $y = -1$ when $x = 0$, the coordinates of one point are (0, −1).

$$4(1) - y = 1$$
$$4 - y = 1$$
$$-y = -3$$
$$y = 3$$

Since $y = 3$ when $x = 1$, the coordinates of another point are (1, 3).

Step 2: Plot these points on a Cartesian plane and draw a line through them (Figure 4.36).

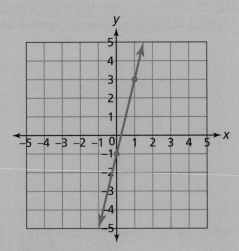

FIGURE 4.36

4.11 Graph the linear equation $2x + 4y = 6$.

Solution:

Step 1: Substitute 0 and 1 for y and solve for x.

$$2x + 4(0) = 6$$
$$2x + 0 = 6$$
$$2x = 6$$
$$x = 3$$

Since $x = 3$ when $y = 0$, the coordinates of one point are (3, 0).

$$2x + 4(1) = 6$$
$$2x + 4 = 6$$
$$2x + 4 - 4 = 6 - 4$$
$$2x = 2$$
$$x = 1$$

Since $x = 1$ when $y = 1$, the coordinates of another point are (1, 1).

Step 2: Plot these points on a Cartesian plane and draw a line through them (Figure 4.37).

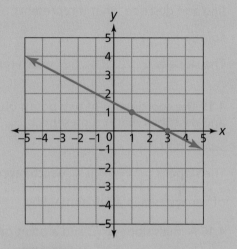

FIGURE 4.37

This exercise can be simplified by dividing out the factor of 2 from each term of the equation. The result is $x + 2y = 3$. This makes it very easy to find x when y has a value. For example, if $y = 0$, $x = 3$, and if $y = 4$, $x = -5$.

4.12 Graph the linear equation $x - 2y = 4$.

Solution:

Step 1: Substitute 0 and 1 for y and solve for x.

$$x - 2(0) = 4$$
$$x - 0 = 4$$
$$x = 4$$

Since $x = 4$ when $y = 0$, the coordinates of one point are (4, 0).

$$x - 2(1) = 4$$
$$x - 2 = 4$$
$$x - 2 + 2 = 4 + 2$$
$$x = 6$$

Since $x = 6$ when $y = 1$, the coordinates of another point are (6, 1).

Step 2: Plot these points on a Cartesian plane and draw a line through them (Figure 4.38).

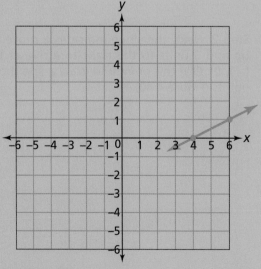

FIGURE 4.38

4.13 The coordinates of two points on a line are (−3, 0) and (1, −6). Find the slope of the line and describe what it represents.

Solution:

The slope is, $\dfrac{-6-0}{1-(-3)} = -\dfrac{6}{4} = -\dfrac{3}{2}$ which represents a *fall* of 3 units for each *run* of 2 units.

4.14 The coordinates of two points on a line are (−4, 0) and (3, −1). Find the slope of the line and describe what it represents.

Solution:

The slope is $\dfrac{(-1-0)}{(3-(-4))} = -\dfrac{1}{7}$ which represents a fall of 1 unit for each run of 7 units.

4.15 The coordinates of two points on a line are (−2, 1) and (3, 1). Find the slope of the line and describe what it represents.

Solution:

The slope is $\dfrac{(1-1)}{(3-(-2))} = \dfrac{0}{5}$ which represents a fall of 0 units for each run of 5 units. A slope of zero results in a horizontal line.

4.16 A line's slope is $\dfrac{1}{3}$, and a point on the line is (−4, −1). Graph the line.

Solution:

Step 1: First plot the point (−4, −1) on a Cartesian plane (Figure 4.39).

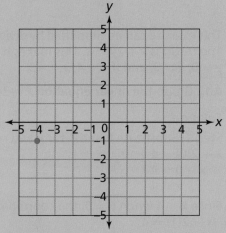

FIGURE 4.39

Step 2: Next, the slope indicates a move of 1 unit up and 3 units to the right to arrive at the point (−1, 0). Plot this point and draw a line through the points (Figure 4.40).

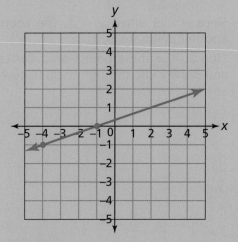

FIGURE 4.40

4.17 A line's slope is −2, and a point on the line is (1, 3). Graph the line.

Solution:

Step 1: Plot the point (1, 3) on a Cartesian plane (Figure 4.41).

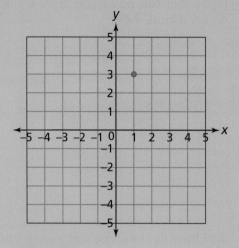

FIGURE 4.41

Step 2: Next, the slope indicates a move of 2 units down and 1 unit to the right to arrive at the point (2, 1). Plot this point and draw a line through the points (Figure 4.42).

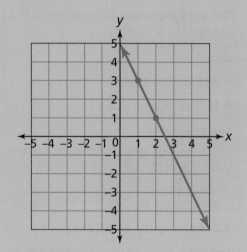

FIGURE 4.42

4.18 A line's slope is $-\frac{1}{2}$, and a point on the line is (−1, 3). Graph the line.

Solution:

Step 1: Plot the point (−1, 3) on a Cartesian plane (Figure 4.43).

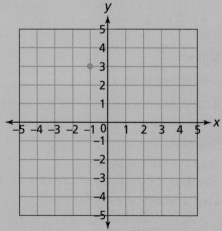

FIGURE 4.43

Step 2: Next, the slope indicates a move of 1 unit down and 2 units to the right to arrive at the point (1, 2). Plot this point and draw a line through the points (Figure 4.44).

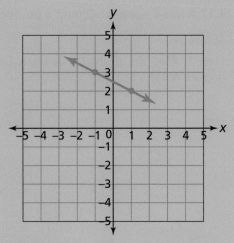

FIGURE 4.44

4.19 Identify the slope and y-intercept for the linear equation $y = \left(-\dfrac{2}{3}\right)x + 4$.

Solution:

Since the equation is solved for y, the coefficient of x is $-\dfrac{2}{3}$ which gives the slope, and the y Intercept is (0, 4)

Slope $= -\dfrac{2}{3}$

y-intercept $=$ (0, 4)

4.20 Identify the slope and y-intercept for the linear equation $y = 5x - 2$.

Solution:

Since the equation is solved for y, the coefficient of x is 5 which gives the slope, and the y Intercept is (0, −2)

Slope $= 5$

y-intercept $=$ (0, −2)

4.21 Identify the slope and y-intercept for the linear equation $2y = 3x + 4$.

Solution:

Solve for y:

$$\frac{2y}{2} = \frac{3x}{2} + \frac{4}{2}$$

$$y = \frac{3}{2}x + 2$$

Slope $= \dfrac{3}{2}$

y-intercept $=$ (0, 2)

4.22 Write the equation of the line that is parallel to the line $y = -x + 3$ and contains the point (2, 1).

Solution:

Step 1: Find the slope
The slope of the line $y = -x + 3$ is −1. Since the lines are parallel, the slope will be equal to −1.

Step 2: Substitute −1 for the slope, $x = 2$, $y = 1$, and solve for b.

$$1 = -1(2) + b$$
$$1 = -2 + b$$
$$1 + 2 = -2 + b + 2$$
$$3 = b$$

Step 3: Write the equation using the slope and y-intercept.
$y = -x + 3$

4.23 Write the equations of the lines with y-intercepts of -9 that are parallel and perpendicular to the line shown in Figure 4.24.

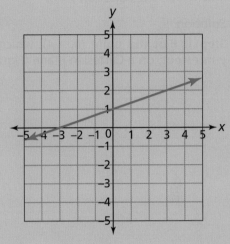

Solution:

Step 1: Determine the slope of the line shown. It appears that (0, 1) and (3, 2) are on the line. Since the line moves up 1 unit for every 3 units it moves to the right, the slope is $\frac{1}{3}$.

Step 2: Since the line with intercept -9 parallel to the one shown has the same slope, its equation is $y = \frac{1}{3}x - 9$.

Step 3: Since the line with intercept -9 perpendicular to the one shown has a slope that is the negative reciprocal of $\frac{1}{3}$, its equation is $y = -3x - 9$.

4.24 What are the slopes of lines parallel and perpendicular to the one shown in Figure 4.25?

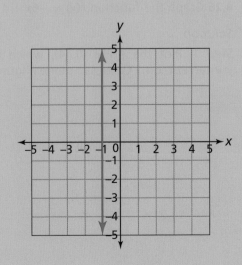

Solution:

Step 1: The line shown is vertical, so its slope is undefined.

Step 2: Since a line parallel to the one shown would also be vertical, its slope would also be undefined.

Step 3: Since a line perpendicular to the one shown would be horizontal, its slope would be 0.

4.25 Graph the equation $y = x - 4$.

Solution:

Step 1: Plot the point $(0, -4)$, which is the line's y-intercept, on a Cartesian plane (Figure 4.45).

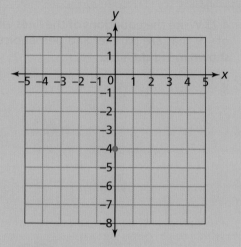

FIGURE 4.45

Step 2: Using the slope 1, from the point $(0, -4)$ move 1 unit up and 1 unit to the right to arrive at the point $(1, -3)$. Plot this point and draw a line through the points (Figure 4.46).

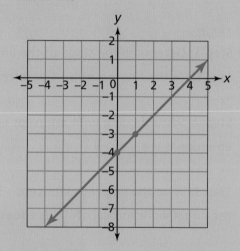

FIGURE 4.46

4.26 Graph the function $f(x) = -6x + 4$.

Solution:

Step 1: Plot the point $(0, 4)$, which is the line's y-intercept, on a Cartesian plane (Figure 4.47).

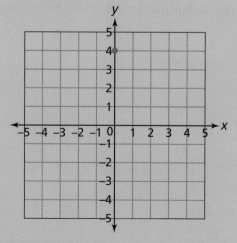

FIGURE 4.47

Step 2: Using the slope −6, from the point (0, 4) move 6 units down and 1 unit to the right to arrive at the point (1, −2). Plot this point and draw a line through the points (Figure 4.48).

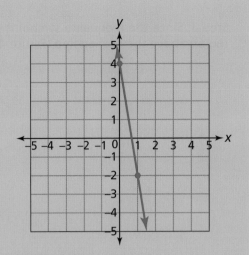

FIGURE 4.48

4.27 Graph the linear inequality $y > -\frac{1}{3}x + 3$.

Solution:

Step 1: Mark the point (0, 3), which is the line's *y*-intercept, on a Cartesian plane (Figure 4.49).

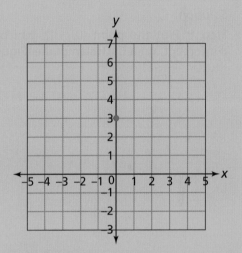

FIGURE 4.49

Step 2: Using the slope $-\frac{1}{3}$, from the point (0, 3) move 1 unit down and 3 units to the right to arrive at the point (3, 2). Mark this point and draw a dashed line through the points (Figure 4.50). Graph shows bullets.

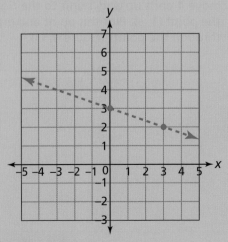

FIGURE 4.50

Step 3: Since the inequality symbol is >, shade the region above the dashed line (Figure 4.51).

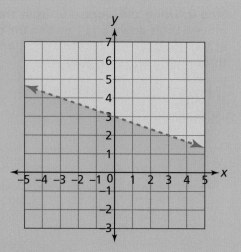

FIGURE 4.51

4.28 Graph the linear inequality $y \leq 4x - 1$.

Solution:

Step 1: Plot the point $(0, -1)$, which is the line's y-intercept, on a Cartesian plane (Figure 4.52).

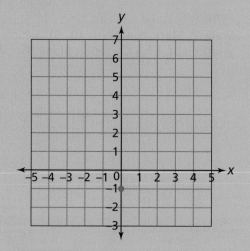

FIGURE 4.52

Step 2: Using the slope 4, from the point $(0, -1)$ move 4 units up and 1 unit to the right to arrive at the point $(1, 3)$. Plot this point and draw a solid line through the points (Figure 4.53).

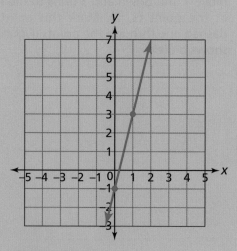

FIGURE 4.53

Step 3: Since the inequality symbol is $\leq$, shade the region below the solid line (Figure 4.54).
As a partial check, notice that $(0, 0)$ is not in the solution set: $0 \leq 0 - 1 = -1$ is not true.

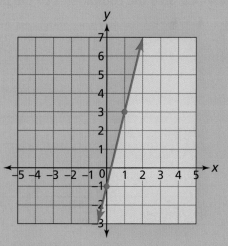

FIGURE 4.54

END OF CHAPTER REVIEW QUESTIONS

Introduction to the Cartesian Plane

For questions 4.1–4.3, graph the ordered pairs on coordinate axes and indicate in which quadrant they are located.

4.1 (4, 7).

4.2 (0, −8).

4.3 (−2, 5).

4.4–4.6 Give the coordinates of the points in the plane shown in Figure 4.55.

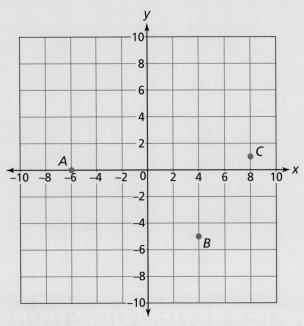

FIGURE 4.55

Introduction to Functions

For questions 4.7 and 4.8, evaluate the functions for the given values of the variables.

4.7 $f(x) = 11 - 2x$, for $x = 5$ and $x = -3$.

4.8 $g(x) = x^2 - 4x - 15$, for $x = 0$ and $x = 2$.

4.9 Determine whether each of the following is a function and explain why or why not.

a.

x	y
2	4
3	8
2	−3

b.

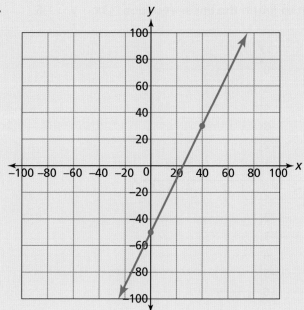

Linear Functions

4.10 Find three points that satisfy the equation, plot them, and graph the line: $y = -2x + 5$.

4.11 Use the *x*-intercept and *y*-intercept to graph the linear equation $2x - y = 4$.

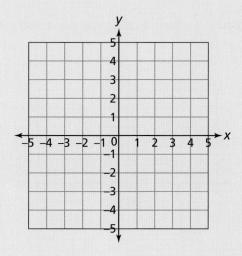

4.12 Use the *x*-intercept and *y*-intercept to graph the linear equation $-3x + y = -6$.

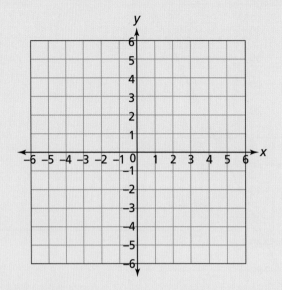

4.13 Use the *x*-intercept and *y*-intercept to graph the linear equation $5x - 2y = -10$.

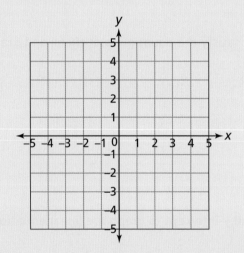

4.14 Graph the linear equation $y = -3x + 1$ using the slope and *y*-intercept.

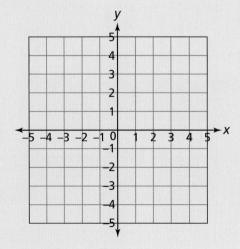

4.15 Graph the linear equation $y = \left(\dfrac{2}{3}\right)x - 4$ using the slope and y-intercept.

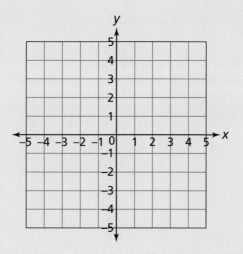

4.16 Graph the linear equation $2y = -x + 6$ using the slope and y-intercept.

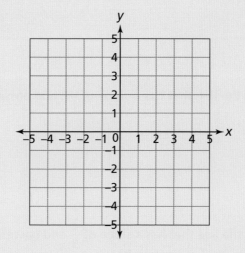

4.17 Graph the linear equation $4x - 3y = 9$ using the slope and y-intercept.

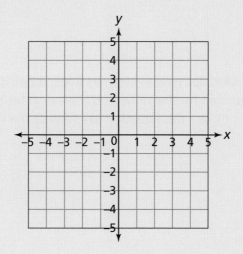

4.18 Graph the linear equation $y = -3$ using the slope and y-intercept.

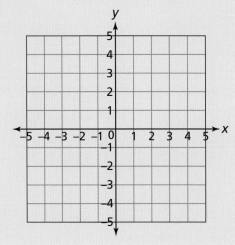

4.19 Write the equation of the line that has a slope of $\frac{1}{2}$ and y-intercept of $(0, -3)$.

4.20 Write the equation of the line that has a slope of -2 and passes through the point $(2, 1)$.

4.21 Write the equation of the line that has a slope of $\frac{2}{3}$ and passes through the point $(-3, 1)$.

4.22 The corporate jet cost \$400,000 new in 2005. By 2009, it had depreciated to a value of \$260,000. Write a linear equation for the value of the plane in terms of the number of years after its purchase ($V = mt + b$). Use this equation to estimate the value of the plane in 2012.

Slope of a Straight Line

4.23 Determine the slopes of the lines joining the following pairs of points:

   a. (2, 5) and (−3, 10)

   b. (2, 5) and (2, 10)

4.24 Write the equation of the line that passes through the points (0, 2) and (−1, −1).

4.25 Write the equation of the line that passes through the points (1, 1) and (−2, 10).

4.26 Write the equation of the line that passes through the points (3, 2) and (2, 3).

4.27 Write the equation of the line that passes through the points (2, −4) and (−2, −2).

4.28 Find the slope of a line that is parallel to the line $2x - y = 3$.

4.29 Write the equation of the line that passes through the point $(-2, 1)$ and is parallel to the line $y = 3x - 2$.

4.30. Give the slopes of the lines that are perpendicular to the following lines:

   a. $3x + 5y = 15$

   b. $x = 7$

4.31 Write the equation of the line that passes through the point $(1, 3)$ and is perpendicular to the line $y = \dfrac{1}{2}x - 1$.

Graphing Inequalities

4.32 Graph the inequality $y \leq \dfrac{1}{2}x + 3$.

4.33 Graph the inequality 2*x* + *y* > 1.

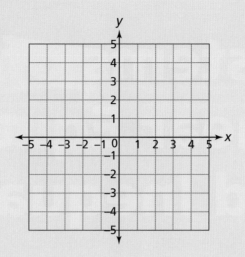

4.34 Graph the inequality 3*x* − *y* > 2.

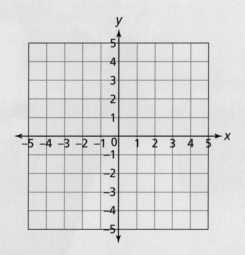

4.35 An insurance company has policies that cost $40 and $60 per month. Graph the inequality that shows the region where the number of polices sold will generate a monthly revenue in excess of $5,000.

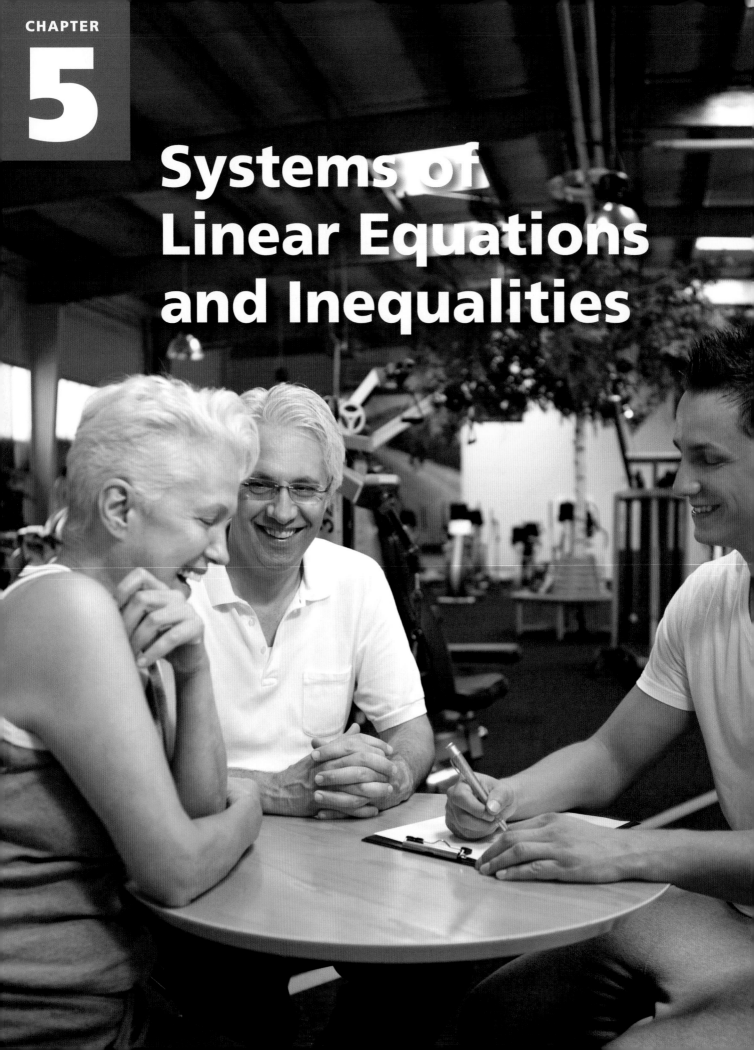

Systems of Linear Equations and Inequalities

The members of a fitness center have mentioned to the staff that they would like to be able to buy sports drinks after their workouts. For this reason, the fitness center has decided to spend $2,000 to purchase a vending machine. The fitness center can buy sports drinks for $0.75 each to sell from the vending machine, and the members are willing to pay $1.25 for each drink.

The center's operating costs have risen to $10,800 a month. To cope with the higher costs, the center decides to raise the current monthly fee of $65 by $10 for new members. Current members will continue to pay $65.

Will the fitness club's new income streams balance or exceed its new expenses? Using systems of linear equations helps in finding the answer to questions such as this.

1. How can the fitness center determine the number of sports drinks the members will need to buy in order for it to recover the cost of the vending machine?

2. If the center wants to end up with 150 members, how many old, and how many new, members must it have to meet expenses?

KEY TERMS

SOLVING SYSTEMS OF LINEAR EQUATIONS

Many physical settings can be expressed in terms of linear equations, and if they concern the same or similar information, some may be used together to solve various problems.

A **system of linear equations** is a group of linear equations that use the same variables. Assume that the graphs of equations in a system are all in the same plane. The **solution of a system** is the collection of points that satisfy all the equations of the system.

5.1 SYSTEM OF LINEAR EQUATIONS A group of linear equations (in the same plane) that use the same variables.

5.2 SOLUTION OF A SYSTEM The collection of points or their coordinates that satisfy all the equations of the system.

Solving a System of Linear Equations by Graphing

It is possible to use graphing to solve a system of linear equations. There are three possible situations for the graphs of lines in a system: the graphs are parallel lines, they are the same line, or the lines intersect at a unique point.

If the lines are parallel, their graphs have no points in common and there is no solution to the system. (Recall that parallel lines have the same slope.)

Lines with the same slope and same y-intercept are not only parallel but also the same line. The graphs are the same line and the system has an infinite number of solutions—the coordinates of all the points on the line.

If the graphs of the lines share one common point, the solution of the system is the coordinates of the point where the graphs of the equations intersect. It is correct to refer to the solution as either the point or as the coordinates of the point.

While finding both intercepts is a possible technique to produce a graph of a line, it is usually a good idea to convert the equations of a system to slope-intercept form. Comparing the slopes and intercepts of the lines in the system allows identification of parallel and coincident lines directly—no need to graph to find the solution.

When to Use This Method

Graphing shows the solution of any system of equations. Since graphing by hand can be inexact, it is necessary to check the coordinates of an apparent solution in the equations of the system to verify that it is a true solution. Even solving a system by graphing with a calculator will give a solution that is accurate only to a certain number of decimal places.

Example 5.1

Solve the system of linear equations $\begin{cases} -2x + y = -5 \\ x + y = 1 \end{cases}$ by graphing.

Solution:

Step 1: Convert $-2x + y = -5$ to slope-intercept form.

$$-2x + y = -5$$
$$-2x + y + 2x = -5 + 2x$$
$$y = -5 + 2x$$
$$y = 2x - 5$$

Step 2: Convert $x + y = 1$ to slope-intercept form.

$$x + y = 1$$
$$x + y - x = 1 - x$$
$$y = 1 - x$$
$$y = -x + 1$$

Step 3: Graph $y = 2x - 5$ through $(0, -5)$, with slope 2 (Figure 5.1).

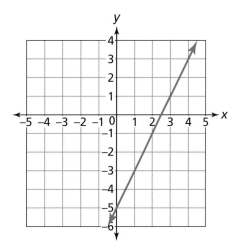

FIGURE 5.1

Step 4: Graph $y = -x + 1$ through $(0, 1)$ with slope -1, on the same Cartesian plane (Figure 5.2).

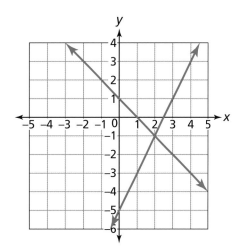

FIGURE 5.2

Step 5: The lines appear to intersect at the point $(2, -1)$, and a check $(-1 = 4 - 5$ and $-1 = -2 + 1)$ shows that this point satisfies both equations, so this is the solution.

Example 5.2

Solve the system $\begin{cases} x + 2y = 6 \\ 2x + 4y = -4 \end{cases}$ by graphing.

Solution:

Step 1: Convert $x + 2y = 6$ to slope-intercept form.

$$x + 2y = 6$$
$$x + 2y - x = 6 - x$$
$$2y = 6 - x$$
$$\frac{2y}{2} = \frac{6-x}{2}$$
$$y = 3 - \frac{x}{2}$$
$$y = -\frac{x}{2} + 3$$

Step 2: Convert $2x + 4y = -4$ to slope-intercept form.

$$2x + 4y = -4$$
$$2x + 4y - 2x = -4 - 2x$$
$$4y = -4 - 2x$$
$$\frac{4y}{4} = \frac{-4-2x}{4}$$
$$y = -1 - \frac{x}{2}$$
$$y = -\frac{x}{2} - 1$$

Step 3: Graph $y = -\dfrac{x}{2} + 3$ through $(0, 3)$ with slope $-\dfrac{1}{2}$ (Figure 5.3).

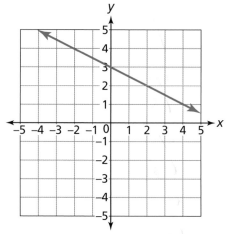

FIGURE 5.3

Step 4: Graph $y = -\dfrac{x}{2} - 1$ through $(0, -1)$ with slope $-\dfrac{1}{2}$ on the same Cartesian plane (Figure 5.4).

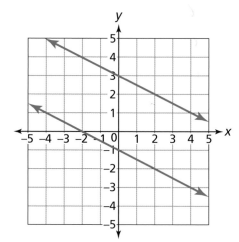

FIGURE 5.4

Step 5: Notice that both equations have the same slope and different intercepts, so the lines are parallel. The graphs do not intersect, so the system has no solution.

If the directions had asked only for a solution of the system, without asking for graphs, it would be sufficient to show that the lines have equal slopes and different intercepts and conclude that the system has no solution.

DIY PROBLEMS

5.1 Determine if the coordinates (1, 1) is a solution to the system.

$2x - 3y = -1$
$5x + y = 6$

5.2 Solve the system $\begin{cases} 2x + y = -4 \\ -x + y = 2 \end{cases}$ by graphing.

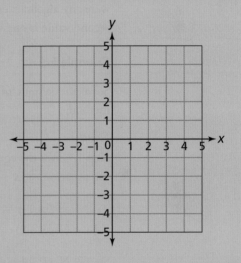

5.3 Solve the system $\begin{cases} 3x + y = -1 \\ 9x + 3y = -3 \end{cases}$ by graphing.

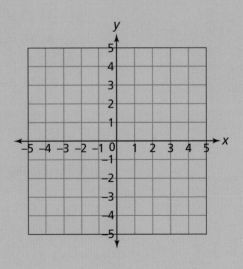

Solving a System of Linear Equations by the Substitution Method

5.3 SUBSTITUTION METHOD (for solving a system) A procedure that requires solving for a variable in one equation and substituting that value in the other equation.

An algebraic method for solving a system of linear equations is the substitution method. The **substitution method** for solving a system of equations is a procedure that requires solving for a variable in one equation, and substituting that value in the other equation. Solve the resulting equation for the other variable and substitute back in either of the original equations to find a value for the first variable.

If the result of the first substitution is an equation that is never true, the system has no solution, and if the result is an equation that is always true, the system has an infinite number of solutions. Otherwise, the point whose coordinates are the values found for the variables is the solution of the system.

When to Use This Method

Use this method when one of the equations is already solved for one of the variables. Use similar operations with the goal of finding values for all the variables if the system has more than two equations. Note that there is no need to check the solution since the algebraic methods are accurate. (However, a check is a help in case there were any algebraic errors. Checking the values in the equation not used to find the second value is one technique.)

Example 5.3

Solve the system of linear equations $\begin{cases} -5x + y = -8 \\ y = -4x + 1 \end{cases}$ by using the substitution method.

Solution:

Step 1: Since the equation $y = -4x + 1$ is already solved for y, plug $-4x + 1$ into the equation $-5x + y = -8$ for y.

$$-5x + y = -8$$
$$-5x + (-4x + 1) = -8$$

Step 2: Next, solve the equation $-5x + (-4x + 1) = -8$ for x.

$$-5x + (-4x + 1) = -8$$
$$-5x - 4x + 1 = -8$$
$$-9x + 1 = -8$$
$$-9x + 1 - 1 = -8 - 1$$
$$-9x = -9$$
$$\frac{-9x}{-9} = \frac{-9}{-9}$$
$$x = 1$$

Step 3: Finally, plug the value of x back into the equation $y = -4x + 1$ and solve for y.

$$y = -4x + 1$$
$$y = -4(1) + 1$$
$$y = -4 + 1$$
$$y = -3$$

This means that the solution to the system is $(1, -3)$.

Example 5.4

Solve the system $\begin{cases} x = 5 - \dfrac{1}{2}y \\ 2x + y = 10 \end{cases}$ by using the substitution method.

Solution:

Step 1: Since the equation $x = 5 - \dfrac{1}{2}y$ is already solved for x, plug $5 - \dfrac{1}{2}y$ into the equation $2x + y = 10$ for x.

$$2x + y = 10$$
$$2\left(5 - \frac{1}{2}y\right) + y = 10$$

Step 2: Solve the equation $2\left(5 - \dfrac{1}{2}y\right) + y = 10$ for y.

$$2\left(5 - \frac{1}{2}y\right) + y = 10$$
$$10 - y + y = 10$$
$$10 = 10$$

Step 3: Since $10 = 10$ is always true, the system has an infinite number of solutions. The two equations actually describe the same line, written in two different ways. So their intersection is the entire line.

DIY PROBLEMS

5.4 Solve the system $\begin{cases} y = x - 4 \\ 2x + y = 5 \end{cases}$ by using the substitution method.

5.5 Solve the system of linear equations $\begin{cases} y = 9x + 2 \\ 6x + y = -13 \end{cases}$ by using the substitution method.

5.6 Solve the system $\begin{cases} 2x - 16y = -10 \\ x = 8y + 2 \end{cases}$ by using the substitution method.

5.7 Solve the system $\begin{cases} y = 3x - 4 \\ -6x + 2y = -8 \end{cases}$ by using the substitution method.

5.8 Solve the system $\begin{cases} x - 2y = 9 \\ y = \dfrac{1}{2}x + 2 \end{cases}$ by using the substitution method.

Solving by the Elimination Method

Another algebraic method for solving a system of linear equations is the elimination method. The **elimination method** for solving a system of equations is a procedure that requires adding a multiple of one equation to the other in order to eliminate one variable. Solve the resulting equation for the other variable and substitute back in either of the original equations to find a value for the first variable.

Again, if the result is an equation that is never true, the system has no solution, and if the result is an equation that is always true, the system has an infinite number of solutions.

When to Use the Elimination Method

Use this method when it is easy to eliminate one of the variables by adding a multiple of one of the equations to the other equation. The idea is to make the coefficient of one of the variables in one equation the opposite of that variable's coefficient in the other equation, so that they cancel each other out.

Essentially the process finds the LCM of the two coefficients. For example, for the system $\begin{cases} 6x - 7y = 40 \\ 4x - 3y = 15 \end{cases}$, multiplying the first equation by 4 and the second by -6 makes the coefficients of x 24 and -24, but also makes the rest of the numbers in the equations very large. Multiplying the first equation by 2 and the second equation by -3, because the LCM of 6 and 4 is 12, makes the system $\begin{cases} 12x - 14y = 80 \\ -12x + 9y = -45 \end{cases}$, and adding the equations gives $-5y = 35$, so $y = -7$.

Note again that there is no need to check the solution since the algebraic methods are accurate. But also again, a check might be a help in case there were any algebraic errors. Checking the values in the equation not used to find the second value is one technique.

Example 5.5

Solve the system of linear equations $\begin{cases} 7x - 2y = 4 \\ 4x + y = 13 \end{cases}$ a by using the elimination method.

Solution:

Step 1: Note that the coefficient of the y term in the first equation is -2 and in the second equation it is 1. If we multiply the second equations by 2, we can make the coefficient of y 2, the opposite of the coefficient of y in the first equation.

$$4x + y = 13$$
$$2(4x + y) = 2(13)$$
$$8x + 2y = 26$$

Step 2: Add the equations $7x - 2y = 4$ and $8x + 2y = 26$.

$$\begin{aligned} 7x - 2y &= 4 \\ + 8x + 2y &= 26 \\ \hline 15x \quad\;\; &= 30 \end{aligned}$$

Step 3: Solve the equation $15x = 30$ for x.

$$15x = 30$$
$$\frac{15x}{15} = \frac{30}{15}$$
$$x = 2$$

Step 4: Finally, plug the value of x into either of the original equations and solve for y.

$$4x + y = 13$$
$$4(2) + y = 13$$
$$8 + y = 13$$
$$8 + y - 8 = 13 - 8$$
$$y = 5$$

This means that the solution to the system is (2, 5). This checks in $7x - 2y = 4$: $7 \cdot 2 - 2 \cdot 5 = 14 - 10 = 4$.

Example 5.6

Solve the system of linear equations $\begin{cases} 2x - y = 9 \\ 6x - 3y = 18 \end{cases}$ by using the elimination method.

Solution:

Step 1: Multiply both sides of the equation $2x - y = 9$ by –3 so that the y terms in both equations have the same coefficient.

$$2x - y = 9$$
$$-3(2x - y) = -3(9)$$
$$-6x + 3y = -27$$

Step 2: Add the equations $-6x+3y=-27$ and $6x-3y=18$.

$$-6x+3y=-27$$
$$+ \quad \underline{6x-3y=18}$$
$$0 \qquad = -9$$

Step 3: Since $0 = -9$ is never true, the system has no solution. On a Cartesian plane, the graphs for each equation are parallel. Dividing the second equation by 3 to begin with gives $2x - y = 6$, an immediate way of showing that the two graphs differ only in their y-intercepts, that is, they are parallel.

DIY PROBLEMS

5.9 Solve the system of linear equations $\begin{cases} -15x - 12y = -48 \\ 5x + 4y = 16 \end{cases}$ by using the elimination method.

5.10 Solve the system $\begin{cases} 10x - 3y = 9 \\ 5x + 2y = 29 \end{cases}$ by using the elimination method.

5.11 Solve the system $\begin{cases} 2x + 3y = 1 \\ x - 2y = 11 \end{cases}$ by using the elimination method.

5.12 Solve the system $\begin{cases} -3x + y = -1 \\ x - 2y = 2 \end{cases}$ by using the elimination method.

A variant technique for solving a system of equations without using a calculator, when neither substitution nor elimination seems reasonable, is to solve each equation for the same variable and solve the equation that results from equating those values.

For instance, in Example 5.5 the resulting equation, setting the y vales equal to each other, is

$$\frac{7}{2}x - 2 = -4x + 13$$

$$\frac{7}{2}x + \frac{8}{2}x = 2 + 13$$

$$\frac{2}{15} \cdot \frac{15}{2}x = \frac{2}{15} \cdot 15$$

$$x = 2$$

and substituting shows that when $x = 2$, $y = 5$.

Matrices

It is also possible to represent and solve a system of linear equations by using matrices. A **matrix** is a rectangular array of numbers, often representing a system of equations.

5.5 MATRIX A rectangular array of numbers, often representing a system of equations.

Matrices (plural of matrix) are set in brackets and identified by the number of rows and columns they have. For example, $A = \begin{bmatrix} 2 & -1 & 4 \\ 4 & 5 & 1 \end{bmatrix}$ is a 2×3 matrix that can be interpreted as representing the system $\begin{cases} 2x - y = 4 \\ 4x + 5y = 1 \end{cases}$. The constants in the equations are the numbers in the matrix. Each equation is represented in one row, and each variable or constant term is in one column. Note that the equations must be written in $Ax + By = C$ form.

The elimination method for solving a system justifies methods of writing equivalent matrices. For example, any row can be multiplied or divided by the same number. Multiplying the first row of A by 5: $\begin{bmatrix} 2 & -1 & 4 \\ 4 & 5 & 1 \end{bmatrix} \rightarrow \begin{bmatrix} 10 & -5 & 20 \\ 4 & 5 & 1 \end{bmatrix}$.

This provides the y terms with opposite coefficients. As in adding equations in the elimination method, add the rows in the matrix, replacing one row with the sum: $\begin{bmatrix} 10 & -5 & 20 \\ 4 & 5 & 1 \end{bmatrix} \rightarrow \begin{bmatrix} 14 & 0 & 21 \\ 4 & 5 & 1 \end{bmatrix}$. Since the first row now has a common factor of 7, again rewrite the matrix, dividing out the 7 and then dividing the row by 2: $\begin{bmatrix} 14 & 0 & 21 \\ 4 & 5 & 1 \end{bmatrix} \rightarrow \begin{bmatrix} 2 & 0 & 3 \\ 4 & 5 & 1 \end{bmatrix} \rightarrow \begin{bmatrix} 1 & 0 & \frac{3}{2} \\ 4 & 5 & 1 \end{bmatrix}$. Now the first row represents the equation $x = \frac{3}{2}$. Then substitute $\frac{3}{2}$ for x in the equation represented by the second row of the matrix, $4x + 5y = 1$, to find the value of y:

$$4 \cdot \frac{3}{2} + 5y = 1$$

$$6 + 5y = 1$$

$$5y = -5$$

$$y = -1$$

It is possible to manipulate the matrix $\begin{bmatrix} 1 & 0 & \frac{3}{2} \\ 4 & 5 & 1 \end{bmatrix}$ (from which we read the value

of x) further so that an equivalent form is $\begin{bmatrix} 1 & 0 & \frac{3}{2} \\ 4 & 5 & 1 \end{bmatrix} \rightarrow \begin{bmatrix} 1 & 0 & \frac{3}{2} \\ 0 & 1 & -1 \end{bmatrix}$. This form

provides the values of x and y at a glance since their coefficients are each 1.

The final section of this chapter includes a more detailed explanation of this method.

SOLVING SYSTEMS OF LINEAR INEQUALITIES

Graphing the Solution Set of Linear Inequalities

5.6 SYSTEM OF LINEAR INEQUALITIES A group of linear inequalities that use the same variables.

A **system of linear inequalities** is a group of linear inequalities that use the same variables. To solve a system of linear inequalities, graph each of the inequalities in the system on the same Cartesian plane and determine the region of the graph that satisfies all the inequalities. This region is the solution to the system.

Example 5.7

Solve the system of linear inequalities $\begin{cases} -x + 3y > -3 \\ 2x + y < 1 \end{cases}$.

Solution:

Step 1: Convert $-x + 3y > -3$ to slope-intercept form.

$$-x + 3y > -3$$
$$-x + 3y + x > -3 + x$$
$$3y > -3 + x$$
$$\frac{3y}{3} > \frac{-3 + x}{3}$$
$$y > -1 + \frac{1}{3}x$$
$$y > \frac{1}{3}x - 1$$

Step 2: Graph $y > \frac{1}{3}x - 1$ (Figure 5.5).

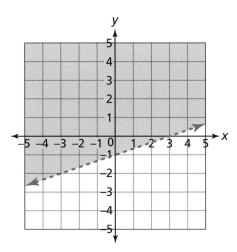

FIGURE 5.5

Step 3: Convert $2x + y < 1$ to slope-intercept form.

$$2x + y < 1$$
$$2x + y - 2x < 1 - 2x$$
$$y < 1 - 2x$$
$$y < -2x + 1$$

Step 4: Graph $y < -2x + 1$ on the same Cartesian plane (Figure 5.6).

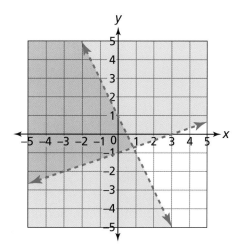

FIGURE 5.6

Step 5: The solution is the region of the graph that satisfies both inequalities (Figure 5.7).

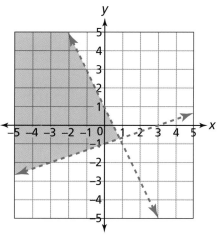

FIGURE 5.7

Example 5.8

Solve the system of linear inequalities $\begin{cases} y \leq x + 3 \\ y \leq -2x \\ y \geq 0 \end{cases}$.

Solution:

Step 1: Graph $y \leq x + 3$ (Figure 5.8).

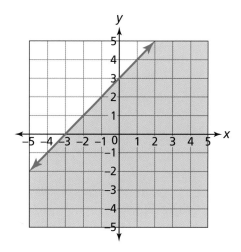

FIGURE 5.8

Step 2: Graph $y \leq -2x$ on the same Cartesian plane (Figure 5.9).

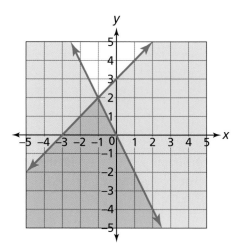

FIGURE 5.9

Step 3: Now determine the region of the graph that satisfies both $y \leq x + 3$ and $y \leq -2x$ (Figure 5.10).

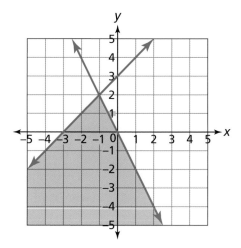

FIGURE 5.10

Step 4: Since the region of the graph that satisfies the inequality $y \geq 0$ is everything at or above the *x*-axis, the solution includes only this portion of the previous graph (Figure 5.11).

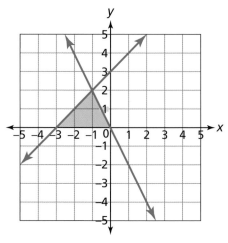

FIGURE 5.11

DIY PROBLEMS

5.13 Solve the system of linear inequalities $\begin{cases} x + y > -2 \\ -2x + y > 3 \end{cases}$.

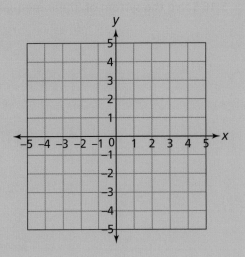

5.14 Solve the system of linear inequalities $\begin{cases} y \geq \dfrac{1}{2}x - 3 \\ y \geq -\dfrac{1}{2}x - 1 \\ y \leq 0 \end{cases}$.

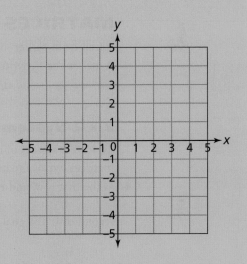

5.15 Solve the system of linear inequalities $\begin{cases} y \leq 2x \\ y < -x + 1 \end{cases}$.

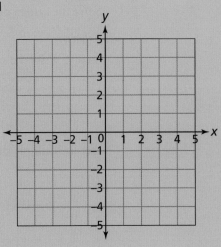

5.16 Solve the system of linear inequalities $\begin{cases} 2y > x - 8 \\ 2x + y \le 3 \end{cases}$.

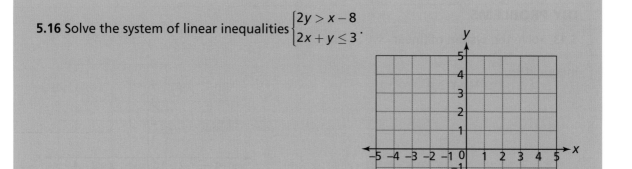

MATRICES

Recall from earlier in the chapter that matrices can represent systems of equations. A matrix can be written as an equivalent matrix by multiplying or dividing a row by any nonzero value and by adding (or subtracting) rows.

2 × 2 Systems of Equations

To solve a system of two linear equations, each in the form $Ax + By = C$, by using matrices, write a matrix, with the coefficients and the constant of the first equation as the first row, and the coefficients and the constant of the second equation as the second row. The goal is to then transform the matrix into the form $\begin{bmatrix} 1 & 0 & a \\ 0 & 1 & b \end{bmatrix}$. This is equivalent to the system $\begin{cases} x = a \\ y = b \end{cases}$, so (a, b) is the solution to the system.

Example 5.9

Solve the system of equations $\begin{cases} x - 5y = -8 \\ 6x + y = -17 \end{cases}$ using matrices.

Solution:

Step 1: Write the system as a matrix.

$$\begin{bmatrix} 1 & -5 & -8 \\ 6 & 1 & -17 \end{bmatrix}$$

Step 2: Multiply the top row by –6 and add it to the bottom row.

$$\begin{bmatrix} 1 & -5 & -8 \\ 6+(1)(-6) & 1+(-5)(-6) & -17+(-8)(-6) \end{bmatrix} \rightarrow \begin{bmatrix} 1 & -5 & -8 \\ 0 & 31 & 31 \end{bmatrix}$$

Step 3: Multiply the bottom row by $\dfrac{1}{31}$.

$$\begin{bmatrix} 1 & -5 & -8 \\ 0 \cdot \dfrac{1}{31} & 31 \cdot \dfrac{1}{31} & 31 \cdot \dfrac{1}{31} \end{bmatrix} \rightarrow \begin{bmatrix} 1 & -5 & -8 \\ 0 & 1 & 1 \end{bmatrix}$$

Step 4: Finally, multiply the bottom row by 5 and add it to the top row.

$$\begin{bmatrix} 1+(0)(5) & -5+(1)(5) & -8+(1)(5) \\ 0 & 1 & 1 \end{bmatrix} \rightarrow \begin{bmatrix} 1 & 0 & -3 \\ 0 & 1 & 1 \end{bmatrix}$$

This means that the solution to the system is (–3, 1).

Example 5.10

Solve the system of equations $\begin{cases} 2x - y = 1 \\ x + 3y = 11 \end{cases}$ using matrices.

Solution:

Step 1: Write the system as a matrix.

$$\begin{bmatrix} 2 & -1 & 1 \\ 1 & 3 & 11 \end{bmatrix}$$

Step 2: Multiply the top row by $-\dfrac{1}{2}$ and add it to the bottom row.

$$\begin{bmatrix} 2 & -1 & 1 \\ 1+(2)\left(-\dfrac{1}{2}\right) & 3+(-1)\left(-\dfrac{1}{2}\right) & 11+(1)\left(-\dfrac{1}{2}\right) \end{bmatrix} \rightarrow \begin{bmatrix} 2 & -1 & 1 \\ 0 & \dfrac{7}{2} & \dfrac{21}{2} \end{bmatrix}$$

Step 3: Multiply the bottom row by $\dfrac{2}{7}$.

$$\begin{bmatrix} 2 & -1 & 1 \\ 0 \cdot \dfrac{2}{7} & \dfrac{7}{2} \cdot \dfrac{2}{7} & \dfrac{21}{2} \cdot \dfrac{2}{7} \end{bmatrix} \rightarrow \begin{bmatrix} 2 & -1 & 1 \\ 0 & 1 & 3 \end{bmatrix}$$

Step 4: Add the bottom row to the top row.

$$\begin{bmatrix} 2+0 & -1+1 & 1+3 \\ 0 & 1 & 3 \end{bmatrix} \rightarrow \begin{bmatrix} 2 & 0 & 4 \\ 0 & 1 & 3 \end{bmatrix}$$

Step 5: Multiply the top row by $\dfrac{1}{2}$.

$$\begin{bmatrix} 2 \cdot \dfrac{1}{2} & 0 \cdot \dfrac{1}{2} & 4 \cdot \dfrac{1}{2} \\ 0 & 1 & 3 \end{bmatrix} \rightarrow \begin{bmatrix} 1 & 0 & 2 \\ 0 & 1 & 3 \end{bmatrix}$$

This means that the solution to the system is (2, 3).

5.17 Solve the system of equations $\begin{cases} 8x - y = 3 \\ 2x + 3y = 17 \end{cases}$ using matrices.

5.18 Use matrices to solve the system of equations $\begin{cases} 5x - 2y = -21 \\ x + 7y = 18 \end{cases}$.

5.19 Use matrices to solve the system of equations $\begin{cases} -x + y = 4 \\ 3x - 2y = -5 \end{cases}$.

Gaussian Elimination

5.7 GAUSSIAN ELIMINATION A procedure for finding the solution to a system of equations by forming a matrix with zeros below the diagonal going down from top-left to right.

Gaussian elimination is similar to the previous work with matrices. It is a procedure for finding the solution to a system of equations by forming a matrix with zeros below the diagonal going down from top, left to right. The bottom row of the matrix then supplies the solution for the last variable. Use substitution to solve for other variables in the system.

Example 5.11

Solve the system of equations $\begin{cases} x + 9y = 14 \\ 3x - 8y = 7 \end{cases}$ using Gaussian elimination.

Solution:

Step 1: Write the system as a matrix.

$$\begin{bmatrix} 1 & 9 & 14 \\ 3 & -8 & 7 \end{bmatrix}$$

Step 2: Multiply the top row by –3 and add it to the bottom row to get 0 in the second row, first column.

$$\begin{bmatrix} 1 & 9 & 14 \\ 3 + (1)(-3) & -8 + (9)(-3) & 7 + (14)(-3) \end{bmatrix} \rightarrow \begin{bmatrix} 1 & 9 & 14 \\ 0 & -35 & -35 \end{bmatrix}$$

Step 3: This means that $-35y = -35$. Solve this equation for y.

$$-35y = -35$$

$$\frac{-35y}{-35} = \frac{-35}{-35}$$

$$y = 1$$

Step 4: Now plug the value of y into the equation $x + 9y = 14$ and solve for x.

$$x + 9y = 14$$
$$x + 9(1) = 14$$
$$x + 9 = 14$$
$$x + 9 - 9 = 14 - 9$$
$$x = 5$$

So, the solution to the system is (5, 1).

Example 5.12

Solve the system of equations $\begin{cases} 7x - 2y = -24 \\ 5x + y = -22 \end{cases}$ using Gaussian elimination.

Solution:

Step 1: Write the system as a matrix.

$$\begin{bmatrix} 7 & -2 & -24 \\ 5 & 1 & -22 \end{bmatrix}$$

Step 2: Multiply the top row by $-\dfrac{5}{7}$ and add it to the bottom row to make the second row x coefficient 0.

$$\begin{bmatrix} 7 & -2 & -24 \\ 5 + (7)\left(-\dfrac{5}{7}\right) & 1 + (-2)\left(-\dfrac{5}{7}\right) & -22 + (-24)\left(-\dfrac{5}{7}\right) \end{bmatrix} \rightarrow \begin{bmatrix} 7 & -2 & -24 \\ 0 & \dfrac{17}{7} & -\dfrac{34}{7} \end{bmatrix}$$

Step 3: This means that $\dfrac{17}{7}y = -\dfrac{34}{7}$. Solve this equation for y.

$$\frac{17}{7}y = -\frac{34}{7}$$
$$\frac{17}{7}y \cdot \frac{7}{17} = -\frac{34}{7} \cdot \frac{7}{17}$$
$$y = -2$$

Step 4: Now plug the value of y into the equation $7x - 2y = -24$ and solve for x.

$$7x - 2y = -24$$
$$7x - 2(-2) = -24$$
$$7x + 4 = -24$$
$$7x + 4 - 4 = -24 - 4$$
$$7x = -28$$
$$\frac{7x}{7} = \frac{-28}{7}$$
$$x = -4$$

This means that the solution to the system is (−4, −2).

5.20 Solve the system of equations $\begin{cases} 2x - 9y = 5 \\ -10x + y = 19 \end{cases}$ using Gaussian elimination.

5.21 Use Gaussian elimination to solve the system of equations $\begin{cases} -4x - y = 4 \\ 7x + 2y = -5 \end{cases}$.

5.22 Use Gaussian elimination to solve the system of equations $\begin{cases} x - 2y = 10 \\ 3x + y = 9 \end{cases}$.

3 × 3 Systems of Equations

The use of Gaussian elimination can also produce a solution to a 3×3 system of equations where each equation is in the form $Ax + By + Cz = D$.

Example 5.13

Solve the system of equations $\begin{cases} 2x - y + 3z = -1 \\ x - 2y - 5z = 14 \\ -3x + 2y + z = -10 \end{cases}$ using Gaussian elimination.

Solution:

Remember that the goal is to write an equivalent matrix with 0s below the diagonal beginning at 2 at the upper left.

Step 1: Write the system as a matrix.

$$\begin{bmatrix} 2 & -1 & 3 & -1 \\ 1 & -2 & -5 & 14 \\ -3 & 2 & 1 & -10 \end{bmatrix}$$

Step 2: Multiply the top row by $-\dfrac{1}{2}$ and add it to the middle row. This creates 0 in the second row, below the 2 at the upper left.

$$\begin{bmatrix} 2 & -1 & 3 & -1 \\ 1+(2)\left(-\dfrac{1}{2}\right) & -2+(-1)\left(-\dfrac{1}{2}\right) & -5+(3)\left(-\dfrac{1}{2}\right) & 14+(-1)\left(-\dfrac{1}{2}\right) \\ -3 & 2 & 1 & -10 \end{bmatrix} \rightarrow \begin{bmatrix} 2 & -1 & 3 & -1 \\ 0 & -\dfrac{3}{2} & -\dfrac{13}{2} & \dfrac{29}{2} \\ -3 & 2 & 1 & -10 \end{bmatrix}$$

Step 3: Now multiply the top row by $\frac{3}{2}$ and add it to the bottom row. This completes creating 0s below 2 in the first column.

$$\begin{bmatrix} 2 & -1 & 3 & -1 \\ 0 & -\dfrac{3}{2} & -\dfrac{13}{2} & \dfrac{29}{2} \\ -3+(2)\left(\dfrac{3}{2}\right) & 2+(-1)\left(\dfrac{3}{2}\right) & 1+(3)\left(\dfrac{3}{2}\right) & -10+(-1)\left(\dfrac{3}{2}\right) \end{bmatrix} \rightarrow \begin{bmatrix} 2 & -1 & 3 & -1 \\ 0 & -\dfrac{3}{2} & -\dfrac{13}{2} & \dfrac{29}{2} \\ 0 & \dfrac{1}{2} & \dfrac{11}{2} & -\dfrac{23}{2} \end{bmatrix}$$

Step 4: Next, multiply the middle row by $\frac{1}{3}$ and add it to the bottom row. This creates 0 below $\frac{3}{2}$, the next element in the diagonal.

$$\begin{bmatrix} 2 & -1 & 3 & -1 \\ 0 & -\dfrac{3}{2} & -\dfrac{13}{2} & \dfrac{29}{2} \\ 0+(0)\left(\dfrac{1}{3}\right) & \dfrac{1}{2}+\left(-\dfrac{3}{2}\right)\left(\dfrac{1}{3}\right) & \dfrac{11}{2}+\left(-\dfrac{13}{2}\right)\left(\dfrac{1}{3}\right) & -\dfrac{23}{2}+\left(\dfrac{29}{2}\right)\left(\dfrac{1}{3}\right) \end{bmatrix} \rightarrow \begin{bmatrix} 2 & -1 & 3 & -1 \\ 0 & -\dfrac{3}{2} & -\dfrac{13}{2} & \dfrac{29}{2} \\ 0 & 0 & \dfrac{10}{3} & -\dfrac{20}{3} \end{bmatrix}$$

Step 5: This means that $\frac{10}{3}z = -\frac{20}{3}$. Solve this equation for z.

$$\frac{10}{3}z = -\frac{20}{3}$$
$$\frac{10}{3}z \cdot \frac{3}{10} = -\frac{20}{3} \cdot \frac{3}{10}$$
$$z = -2$$

Step 6: It also means that $-\frac{3}{2}y - \frac{13}{2}z = \frac{29}{2}$. Plug the value of z into this equation and solve for y.

$$-\frac{3}{2}y - \frac{13}{2}z = \frac{29}{2}$$
$$-\frac{3}{2}y - \frac{13}{2}(-2) = \frac{29}{2}$$
$$-\frac{3}{2}y + 13 = \frac{29}{2}$$
$$-\frac{3}{2}y + 13 - 13 = \frac{29}{2} - 13$$
$$-\frac{3}{2}y = \frac{3}{2}$$
$$-\frac{3}{2}y \cdot \left(-\frac{2}{3}\right) = \frac{3}{2} \cdot \left(-\frac{2}{3}\right)$$
$$y = -1$$

Step 7: Now plug the values of y and z into the equation $2x - y + 3z = -1$ and solve for x.

$$2x - y + 3z = -1$$
$$2x - (-1) + 3(-2) = -1$$
$$2x + 1 - 6 = -1$$
$$2x - 5 = -1$$
$$2x - 5 + 5 = -1 + 5$$
$$2x = 4$$
$$\frac{2x}{2} = \frac{4}{2}$$
$$x = 2$$

This means that the solution to the system is $x = 2$, $y = -1$, and $z = -2$.

Example 5.14

Solve the system of equations $\begin{cases} 4x + 2y - z = 23 \\ -x - 5y + 4z = -14 \\ 3x + y + 10z = 6 \end{cases}$ using Gaussian elimination.

Solution:

Step 1: Write the system as a matrix.

$$\begin{bmatrix} 4 & 2 & -1 & 23 \\ -1 & -5 & 4 & -14 \\ 3 & 1 & 10 & 6 \end{bmatrix}$$

Step 2: Multiply the top row by $\dfrac{1}{4}$ and add it to the middle row.

$$\begin{bmatrix} 4 & 2 & -1 & 23 \\ -1+(4)\left(\frac{1}{4}\right) & -5+(2)\left(\frac{1}{4}\right) & 4+(-1)\left(\frac{1}{4}\right) & -14+(23)\left(\frac{1}{4}\right) \\ 3 & 1 & 10 & 6 \end{bmatrix} \rightarrow \begin{bmatrix} 4 & 2 & -1 & 23 \\ 0 & -\frac{9}{2} & \frac{15}{4} & -\frac{33}{4} \\ 3 & 1 & 10 & 6 \end{bmatrix}$$

Step 3: Multiply the top row by $-\dfrac{3}{4}$ and add it to the bottom row.

$$\begin{bmatrix} 4 & 2 & -1 & 23 \\ 0 & -\frac{9}{2} & \frac{15}{4} & -\frac{33}{4} \\ 3+(4)\left(-\frac{3}{4}\right) & 1+(2)\left(-\frac{3}{4}\right) & 10+(-1)\left(-\frac{3}{4}\right) & 6+(23)\left(-\frac{3}{4}\right) \end{bmatrix} \rightarrow \begin{bmatrix} 4 & 2 & -1 & 23 \\ 0 & -\frac{9}{2} & \frac{15}{4} & -\frac{33}{4} \\ 0 & -\frac{1}{2} & \frac{43}{4} & -\frac{45}{4} \end{bmatrix}$$

Step 4: Multiply the middle row by $-\dfrac{1}{9}$ and add it to the bottom row.

$$\begin{bmatrix} 4 & 2 & -1 & 23 \\ 0 & -\frac{9}{2} & \frac{15}{4} & -\frac{33}{4} \\ 0+(0)\left(-\frac{1}{9}\right) & -\frac{1}{2}+\left(-\frac{9}{2}\right)\left(-\frac{1}{9}\right) & \frac{43}{4}+\left(\frac{15}{4}\right)\left(-\frac{1}{9}\right) & -\frac{45}{4}+\left(-\frac{33}{4}\right)\left(-\frac{1}{9}\right) \end{bmatrix} \rightarrow \begin{bmatrix} 4 & 2 & -1 & 23 \\ 0 & -\frac{9}{2} & \frac{15}{4} & -\frac{33}{4} \\ 0 & 0 & \frac{31}{3} & -\frac{31}{3} \end{bmatrix}$$

Step 5: This means that $\dfrac{31}{3}z = -\dfrac{31}{3}$. Solve this equation for z.

$$\dfrac{31}{3}z = -\dfrac{31}{3}$$

$$\dfrac{31}{3}z \cdot \dfrac{3}{31} = -\dfrac{31}{3} \cdot \dfrac{3}{31}$$

$$z = -1$$

Step 6: It also means that $-\dfrac{9}{2}y + \dfrac{15}{4}z = -\dfrac{33}{4}$. Plug the value of z into this equation and solve for y.

$$-\dfrac{9}{2}y + \dfrac{15}{4}z = -\dfrac{33}{4}$$

$$-\dfrac{9}{2}y + \dfrac{15}{4}(-1) = -\dfrac{33}{4}$$

$$-\dfrac{9}{2}y - \dfrac{15}{4} = -\dfrac{33}{4}$$

$$-\dfrac{9}{2}y - \dfrac{15}{4} + \dfrac{15}{4} = -\dfrac{33}{4} + \dfrac{15}{4}$$

$$-\dfrac{9}{2}y = -\dfrac{9}{2}$$

$$-\dfrac{9}{2}y \cdot \left(-\dfrac{2}{9}\right) = -\dfrac{9}{2} \cdot \left(-\dfrac{2}{9}\right)$$

$$y = 1$$

Step 7: Now plug the values of y and z into the equation $4x + 2y - z = 23$ and solve for x.

$$4x + 2y - z = 23$$

$$4x + 2(1) - (-1) = 23$$

$$4x + 2 + 1 = 23$$

$$4x + 3 = 23$$

$$4x + 3 - 3 = 23 - 3$$

$$4x = 20$$

$$\dfrac{4x}{4} = \dfrac{20}{4}$$

$$x = 5$$

This means that the solution to the system is $x = 5$, $y = 1$, and $z = -1$.

DIY PROBLEMS

5.23 Solve the system of equations $\begin{cases} x + 8y - 2z = -25 \\ 5x - y + 4z = -3 \\ 3x + 2y - z = -2 \end{cases}$ using Gaussian elimination.

5.24 Solve the system of equations $\begin{cases} 4x - 2y + 5z = 16 \\ -x + 10y - 3z = 9 \\ 2x - 9y + 7z = -9 \end{cases}$ using Gaussian elimination.

Determinants

5.8 DETERMINANT A number representing a square matrix.

5.9 SQUARE MATRIX An $n \times n$ matrix.

A numerical method for solving a system of equations involves determinants of matrices. A **determinant** is a number representing a **square matrix,** that is, an $n \times n$ matrix. A square matrix has the same number of rows as columns.

The determinant of the 2×2 matrix $\begin{bmatrix} a & b \\ c & d \end{bmatrix}$ is $\begin{vmatrix} a & b \\ c & d \end{vmatrix} = ad - cb$. Vertical lines instead of brackets enclose the array, and the value of the determinant is the product of the numbers in the diagonal going down from left to right minus the product of the numbers in the diagonal going up from left to right.

The determinant of the 3×3 matrix $\begin{bmatrix} a & b & c \\ d & e & f \\ g & h & i \end{bmatrix}$ is $\begin{vmatrix} a & b & c \\ d & e & f \\ g & h & i \end{vmatrix}$. To calculate its value, repeat the first two columns, copying them to the right of the determinant,

to produce $\begin{vmatrix} a & b & c \\ d & e & f \\ g & h & i \end{vmatrix}\begin{matrix} a & b \\ d & e \\ g & h \end{matrix}$. The determinant is equal to the product of the numbers in the 3-number diagonals going down from left to right minus the product of the numbers in the 3-number diagonals going up from left to right, or $aei + bfg + cdh - gec - hfa - idb$.

Example 5.15

Calculate the value of the determinant of the matrix $\begin{bmatrix} 2 & -9 \\ 5 & 1 \end{bmatrix}$.

Solution:

Step 1: Write the determinant of the matrix.

$\begin{vmatrix} 2 & -9 \\ 5 & 1 \end{vmatrix}$

Step 2: Calculate the value of the determinant.

$(2)(1) - (5)(-9) = 2 - (-45) = 2 + 45 = 47$

Example 5.16

Calculate the value of the determinant of the matrix $\begin{vmatrix} 1 & 8 & 2 \\ -2 & -3 & 4 \\ 5 & -1 & 6 \end{vmatrix}$.

Solution:

Step 1: Write the determinant of the matrix with the first two columns appended on the right.

$$\begin{vmatrix} 1 & 8 & 2 \\ -2 & -3 & 4 \\ 5 & -1 & 6 \end{vmatrix} \begin{matrix} 1 & 8 \\ -2 & -3 \\ 5 & -1 \end{matrix}$$

Step 2: Calculate the value of the determinant.

$$(1)(-3)(6) + (8)(4)(5) + (2)(-2)(-1) - (5)(-3)(2) - (-1)(4)(1) - (6)(-2)(8) =$$
$$-18 + 160 + 4 - (-30) - (-4) - (-96) = -18 + 160 + 4 + 30 + 4 + 96 = 276$$

DIY PROBLEMS

5.25 Calculate the value of the determinant of the matrix $\begin{bmatrix} -4 & 8 \\ 7 & -9 \end{bmatrix}$.

5.26 Calculate the value of the determinant of the matrix $\begin{bmatrix} 3 & 2 & 6 \\ -1 & 5 & -4 \\ -3 & -2 & 1 \end{bmatrix}$.

Cramer's Rule

Cramer's Rule is a way of calculating the solution of a system of equations by using determinants. Each equation in the system must be arranged with the variables in the same order on the left of the equal sign, and the constant term to the right of the equal sign. Using Cramer's Rule involves calculating, for each variable, the quotient of two determinants. The denominator is always C, consisting of the coefficients of the variables in the system.

5.10 CRAMER'S RULE
A method of using determinants to solve a system of equations.

For example, for the system $\begin{cases} 5x - 2y = -21 \\ x + 7y = 18 \end{cases}$, $C = \begin{vmatrix} 5 & -2 \\ 1 & 7 \end{vmatrix} = 35 - (-2) = 37$.

For each variable, the numerator is the determinant formed by substituting the constant terms for its coefficients in C. Here,

$$x = \frac{\begin{vmatrix} -21 & -2 \\ 18 & 7 \end{vmatrix}}{37} = \frac{-147 + 36}{37} = -3 \text{ and } y = \frac{\begin{vmatrix} 5 & -21 \\ 1 & 18 \end{vmatrix}}{37} = \frac{90 + 21}{37} = 3,$$

so the solution of the system is $(-3, 3)$.

Example 5.17

Solve the system of equations $\begin{cases} -6x + y = 26 \\ 3x - 2y = -7 \end{cases}$ by using Cramer's Rule.

Solution:

Step 1: Write the coefficient matrix for the system.

$$\begin{bmatrix} -6 & 1 \\ 3 & -2 \end{bmatrix}$$

Step 2: Calculate the value of its determinant.

$$\begin{vmatrix} -6 & 1 \\ 3 & -2 \end{vmatrix}$$

$$(-6)(-2) - (3)(1) = 12 - 3 = 9$$

Step 3: Replace the first column of the coefficient matrix with the equations' constants.

$$\begin{vmatrix} 26 & 1 \\ -7 & -2 \end{vmatrix}$$

Step 4: Calculate the value of the determinant of this matrix.

$$\begin{vmatrix} 26 & 1 \\ -7 & -2 \end{vmatrix}$$

$$(26)(-2) - (-7)(1) = -52 - (-7) = -52 + 7 = -45$$

Step 5: Divide the value from the previous step by the value of the determinant of the coefficient matrix to get the value of x.

$$x = \frac{-45}{9} = -5$$

Step 6: Now replace the second column of the coefficient matrix with the equations' constants.

$$\begin{vmatrix} -6 & 26 \\ 3 & -7 \end{vmatrix}$$

Step 7: Calculate the value of the determinant of this matrix.

$$\begin{vmatrix} -6 & 26 \\ 3 & -7 \end{vmatrix}$$

$$(-6)(-7) - (3)(26) = 42 - 78 = -36$$

Step 8: Divide the value from the previous step by the value of the determinant of the coefficient matrix to get the value of y.

$$y = \frac{-36}{9} = -4$$

This means that the solution to the system is (–5, –4).

Example 5.18

Solve the system of equations $\begin{cases} -x + 9y - 2z = 12 \\ 4x - y + 5z = -4 \\ 2x + 7y + z = 10 \end{cases}$ by using Cramer's Rule.

Solution:

Step 1: Write the coefficient matrix for the system.

$$\begin{bmatrix} -1 & 9 & -2 \\ 4 & -1 & 5 \\ 2 & 7 & 1 \end{bmatrix}$$

Step 2: Calculate the value of its determinant.

$$\left.\begin{vmatrix} -1 & 9 & -2 \\ 4 & -1 & 5 \\ 2 & 7 & 1 \end{vmatrix}\right| \begin{matrix} -1 & 9 \\ 4 & -1 \\ 2 & 7 \end{matrix}$$

$(-1)(-1)(1) + (9)(5)(2) + (-2)(4)(7) - (2)(-1)(-2) - (7)(5)(-1) - (1)(4)(9) =$

$1 + 90 + (-56) - 4 - (-35) - 36 = 1 + 90 - 56 - 4 + 35 - 36 = 30$

Step 3: Replace the first column of the coefficient matrix with the equations' constants.

$$\begin{bmatrix} 12 & 9 & -2 \\ -4 & -1 & 5 \\ 10 & 7 & 1 \end{bmatrix}$$

Step 4: Calculate the value of the determinant of this matrix.

$$\left.\begin{vmatrix} 12 & 9 & -2 \\ -4 & -1 & 5 \\ 10 & 7 & 1 \end{vmatrix}\right| \begin{matrix} 12 & 9 \\ -4 & -1 \\ 10 & 7 \end{matrix}$$

$(12)(-1)(1) + (9)(5)(10) + (-2)(-4)(7) - (10)(-1)(-2) - (7)(5)(12) - (1)(-4)(9) =$

$-12 + 450 + 56 - 20 - 420 + 36 = 90$

Step 5: Divide the value from the previous step by the value of the determinant of the coefficient matrix to get the value of x.

$$x = \frac{90}{30} = 3$$

Step 6: Replace the second column of the coefficient matrix with the equations' constants.

$$\begin{bmatrix} -1 & 12 & -2 \\ 4 & -4 & 5 \\ 2 & 10 & 1 \end{bmatrix}$$

Step 7: Calculate the value of the determinant of this matrix.

$$\begin{vmatrix} -1 & 12 & -2 \\ 4 & -4 & 5 \\ 2 & 10 & 1 \end{vmatrix} \begin{matrix} -1 & 12 \\ 4 & -4 \\ 2 & 10 \end{matrix}$$

$(-1)(-4)(1)+(12)(5)(2)+(-2)(4)(10)-(2)(-4)(-2)-(10)(5)(-1)-(1)(4)(12)=$
$4+120+(-80)-16-(-50)-48=4+120-80-16+50-48=30$

Step 8: Divide the value from the previous step by the value of the determinant of the coefficient matrix to get the value of y.

$$y=\frac{30}{30}=1$$

Step 9: Now replace the third column of the coefficient matrix with the equations' constants.

$$\begin{bmatrix} -1 & 9 & 12 \\ 4 & -1 & -4 \\ 2 & 7 & 10 \end{bmatrix}$$

Step 10: Calculate the value of the determinant of this matrix.

$$\begin{vmatrix} -1 & 9 & 12 \\ 4 & -1 & -4 \\ 2 & 7 & 10 \end{vmatrix} \begin{matrix} -1 & 9 \\ 4 & -1 \\ 2 & 7 \end{matrix}$$

$(-1)(-1)(10)+(9)(-4)(2)+(12)(4)(7)-(2)(-1)(12)-(7)(-4)(-1)-(10)(4)(9)=$
$10+(-72)+336-(-24)-28-360=10-72+336+24-28-360=-90$

Step 11: Divide the value from the previous step by the value of the determinant of the coefficient matrix to get the value of z.

$$z=\frac{-90}{30}=-3$$

This means that the solution to the system is $x=3$, $y=1$, and $z=-3$.

DIY PROBLEMS

5.27 Solve the system of equations $\begin{cases} -2x-7y=-25 \\ x+8y=35 \end{cases}$ by using Cramer's Rule.

5.28 Solve the system of equations $\begin{cases} -9x-y+2z=13 \\ 3x+4y-z=-12 \\ 7x+2y+3z=-8 \end{cases}$ by using Cramer's Rule.

SOLUTIONS TO DIY PROBLEMS

5.1 Determine if the coordinates (1, 1) is a solution to the system.

$2x - 3y = -1$
$5x + y = 6$

Solution:

Substitute $x = 1$ and $y = 1$ in both equations:

$$2(1) - 3(1) = -1 \qquad 5(1) + (1) = 6$$
$$2 - 3 = -1 \qquad\qquad 5 + 1 = 6$$
$$-1 = -1 \qquad\qquad\quad 6 = 6$$

The point (1,1) is a solution to both equations, and therefore is a solution to the system.

5.2 Solve the system $\begin{cases} 2x + y = -4 \\ -x + y = 2 \end{cases}$ by graphing.

Solution:

Step 1: Convert $2x + y = -4$ to slope-intercept form.

$$2x + y = -4$$
$$2x + y - 2x = -4 - 2x$$
$$y = -4 - 2x$$
$$y = -2x - 4$$

Step 2: Convert $-x + y = 2$ to slope-intercept form.

$$-x + y = 2$$
$$-x + y + x = 2 + x$$
$$y = 2 + x$$
$$y = x + 2$$

Step 3: Graph $y = -2x - 4$ through $(0, -4)$ with slope -2 (Figure 5.12).

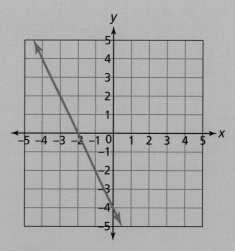

FIGURE 5.12

Step 4: Graph $y = x + 2$ with y-intercept (0, 2) and slope 1 on the same Cartesian plane (Figure 5.13).

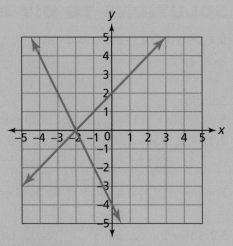

FIGURE 5.13

Step 5: Since the lines appear to intersect at the point (–2, 0), and checking shows that these coordinates satisfy both equations, this is the solution to the system.

5.3 Solve the system $\begin{cases} 3x + y = -1 \\ 9x + 3y = -3 \end{cases}$ by graphing.

Solution:

Step 1: Convert $3x + y = -1$ to slope-intercept form.

$$3x + y = -1$$
$$3x + y - 3x = -1 - 3x$$
$$y = -1 - 3x$$
$$y = -3x - 1$$

Step 2: Convert $9x + 3y = -3$ to slope-intercept form.

$$9x + 3y = -3$$
$$9x + 3y - 9x = -3 - 9x$$
$$3y = -3 - 9x$$
$$\frac{3y}{3} = \frac{-3 - 9x}{3}$$
$$y = -1 - 3x$$
$$y = -3x - 1$$

Step 3: Graph $y = -3x - 1$ with intercept (0, −1) and slope −3. (Figure 5.14)

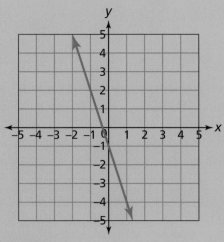

FIGURE 5.14

Step 4: Notice that the form of the second equation is now the same as that of the first equation; the slope and intercept of the second equation are the same as those of the first equation.
Since the graphs are the same line, the system has an infinite number of solutions.

5.4 Solve the system $\begin{cases} y = x - 4 \\ 2x + y = 5 \end{cases}$ by using the substitution method.

Solution:

Step 1: Since the equation $y = x - 4$ is already solved for y, substitute $x - 4$ into the equation $2x + y = 5$ for y. Then solve for x.

$$2x + (x - 4) = 5$$
$$3x - 4 = 5$$
$$3x - 4 + 4 = 5 + 4$$
$$3x = 9$$
$$\frac{3x}{3} = \frac{9}{3}$$
$$x = 3$$

Step 2: Substitute the value of 3 for x in the equation $y = x - 4$ and solve for y.
$$y = 3 - 4$$
$$y = -1$$
This means that the solution to the system is $(3, -1)$

5.5 Solve the system of linear equations $\begin{cases} y = 9x + 2 \\ 6x + y = -13 \end{cases}$ by using the substitution method.

Solution:

Step 1: Since the equation $y = 9x + 2$ is already solved for y, plug $9x + 2$ into the equation $6x + y = -13$ for y. Then solve for x.

$$6x + y = -13$$
$$6x + (9x + 2) = -13$$
$$6x + 9x + 2 = -13$$
$$15x + 2 = -13$$
$$15x + 2 - 2 = -13 - 2$$
$$15x = -15$$
$$\frac{15x}{15} = \frac{-15}{15}$$
$$x = -1$$

Step 2: Plug –1 into the equation $y = 9x + 2$ for x and solve for y.
$$y = 9x + 2$$
$$y = 9(-1) + 2$$
$$y = -9 + 2$$
$$y = -7$$

This means that the solution to the system is $(-1, -7)$.

5.6 Solve the system $\begin{cases} 2x - 16y = -10 \\ x = 8y + 2 \end{cases}$ by using the substitution method.

Solution:

Since the equation $x = 8y + 2$ is already solved for x, plug $8y + 2$ into the equation $2x - 16y = -10$ for x. Then attempt to solve for y.

$$2x - 16y = -10$$
$$2(8y + 2) - 16y = -10$$
$$16y + 4 - 16y = -10$$
$$4 = -10$$

Since $4 = -10$ is never true, the system has no solution.

5.7 Solve the system $\begin{cases} y = 3x - 4 \\ -6x + 2y = -8 \end{cases}$ by using the substitution method.

Solution:

Step 1: Since the equation $y = 3x - 4$ is already solved for y, substitute $3x - 4$ for y in the equation $-6x + 2y = -8$ and solve for x.

$$-6x + 2(3x - 4) = -8$$
$$-6x + 6x - 8 = -8$$
$$-8 = -8$$

There are infinite solutions for x, therefore, the two equations are the same line.

5.8 Solve the system $\begin{cases} x - 2y = 9 \\ y = \dfrac{1}{2}x + 2 \end{cases}$ by using the substitution method.

Solution:

Step 1: Since the equation $y = \dfrac{1}{2}x + 2$ is already solved for y, substitute $\dfrac{1}{2}x + 2$ for y in the equation $x - 2y = 9$ and solve for x.

$$x - 2\left(\dfrac{1}{2}x + 2\right) = 9$$
$$x - x - 4 = 9$$
$$-4 = 9$$

Since there are no solutions to the system, the lines are parallel and do not intersect.

5.9 Solve the system of linear equations $\begin{cases} -15x - 12y = -48 \\ 5x + 4y = 16 \end{cases}$ by using the elimination method.

Solution:

Step 1: Multiply both sides of the equation $5x + 4y = 16$ by 3.

$$5x + 4y = 16$$
$$3(5x + 4y) = 3(16)$$
$$15x + 12y = 48$$

Step 2: Add the equations $-15x - 12y = -48$ and $15x + 12y = 48$ together.

$$\begin{array}{r} -15x - 12y = -48 \\ +\ \underline{15x + 12y = 48} \\ 0 \quad\ = 0 \end{array}$$

Step 3: Since $0 = 0$ is always true, the system has an infinite number of solutions, the line $5x + 4y = 16$ itself. Dividing the first equation by the common factor 3 to begin with makes this apparent.

5.10 Solve the system $\begin{cases} 10x - 3y = 9 \\ 5x + 2y = 29 \end{cases}$ by using the elimination method.

Solution:

Step 1: Multiply both sides of the equation $5x + 2y = 29$ by -2.

$$5x + 2y = 29$$
$$-2(5x + 2y) = -2(29)$$
$$-10x - 4y = -58$$

Step 2: Add the equations $10x - 3y = 9$ and $-10x - 4y = -58$.

$$\begin{array}{r} 10x - 3y = 9 \\ + \underline{-10x - 4y = -58} \\ -7y = -49 \end{array}$$

Step 3: Solve the equation $-7y = -49$ for y.

$$-7y = -49$$
$$\frac{-7y}{-7} = \frac{-49}{-7}$$
$$y = 7$$

Step 4: Finally, plug the value of y into either of the original equations and solve for x.

$$10x - 3y = 9$$
$$10x - 3(7) = 9$$
$$10x - 21 = 9$$
$$10x - 21 + 21 = 9 + 21$$
$$10x = 30$$
$$\frac{10x}{10} = \frac{30}{10}$$
$$x = 3$$

This means that the solution to the system is (3, 7).

5.11 Solve the system $\begin{cases} 2x + 3y = 1 \\ x - 2y = 11 \end{cases}$ by using the elimination method.

Solution:

Step 1: to eliminate x, multiply both sides of the equation $x - 2y = 11$ by -2:

$$(-2)(x - 2y) = 11(-2)$$
$$-2x + 4y = -22$$

Step 2: add the equations $2x + 3y = 1$ and $-2x + 4y = -22$:

$$\begin{array}{r} 2x + 3y = 1 \\ + \underline{-2x + 4y = -22} \\ 7y = -21 \end{array}$$
$$\frac{7y}{7} = -\frac{21}{7}$$
$$y = -3$$

Step 3: Substitute $y = -3$ in one of the original equations and solve for x:

$$2x + 3y = 1$$
$$2x + 3(-3) = 1$$
$$2x - 9 = 1$$
$$2x - 9 + 9 = 1 + 9$$
$$2x = 10$$
$$\frac{2x}{2} = \frac{10}{2}$$
$$x = 5$$

The solution to the system is $(5, -3)$

5.12 Solve the system $\begin{cases} -3x + y = -1 \\ x - 2y = 2 \end{cases}$ by using the elimination method.

Solution:

Step 1: to eliminate y: multiply the equation $-3x + y = -1$ by 2:

$$(2)(-3x + y) = (-1)(2)$$
$$-6x + 2y = -2$$

Step 2: add the equations $-6x + 2y = -2$ and $x - 2y = 2$:

$$\begin{array}{r} -6x + 2y = -2 \\ + \quad x - 2y = -2 \\ \hline -5x = 0 \\ x = 0 \end{array}$$

Step 3: Substitute $x = 0$ in one of the original equations:

$$x - 2y = 2$$
$$0 - 2y = 2$$
$$-2y = 2$$
$$\frac{-2y}{(-2)} = \frac{2}{(-2)}$$
$$y = -1$$

The solution to the system is $(0, -1)$

5.13 Solve the system of linear inequalities $\begin{cases} x + y > -2 \\ -2x + y > 3 \end{cases}$.

Solution:

Step 1: Convert $x + y > -2$ to slope-intercept form and graph it (Figure 5.15).

$$x + y > -2$$
$$x + y - x > -2 - x$$
$$y > -2 - x$$
$$y > -x - 2$$

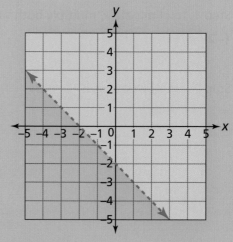

FIGURE 5.15

Step 2: Convert $-2x + y > 3$ to slope-intercept form and graph it on the same Cartesian plane (Figure 5.16).

$$-2x + y > 3$$
$$-2x + y + 2x > 3 + 2x$$
$$y > 3 + 2x$$
$$y > 2x + 3$$

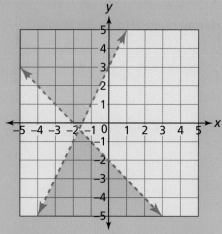

FIGURE 5.16

Step 3: The solution is the region of the graph that satisfies both inequalities (Figure 5.17).

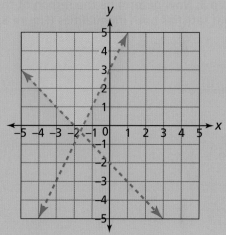

FIGURE 5.17

5.14 Solve the system of linear inequalities $\begin{cases} y \geq \dfrac{1}{2}x - 3 \\ y \geq -\dfrac{1}{2}x - 1 \\ y \leq 0 \end{cases}$.

Solution:

Step 1: Graph $y \geq \dfrac{1}{2}x - 3$ (Figure 5.18).

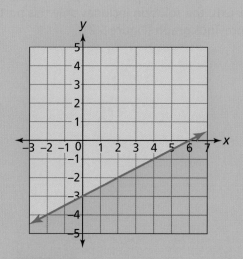

FIGURE 5.18

Step 2: Graph $y \geq -\dfrac{1}{2}x - 1$ on the same

Cartesian plane (Figure 5.19).

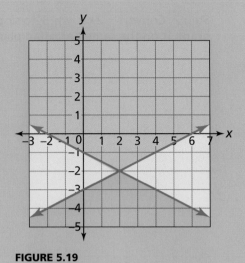

FIGURE 5.19

Step 3: Now determine the region of the graph that satisfies both inequalities (Figure 5.20).

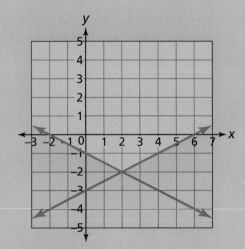

FIGURE 5.20

Step 4: Since the region of the graph that satisfies the inequality $y \leq 0$ is everything at or below the x-axis, the solution includes only this portion of the previous graph (Figure 5.21).

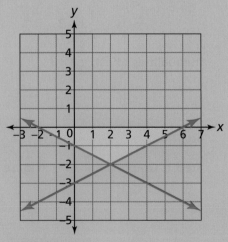

FIGURE 5.21

5.15 Solve the system of linear inequalities $\begin{cases} y \leq 2x \\ y < -x + 1 \end{cases}$

Solution:

Graph $y \leq 2x$ (Figure 5.22).

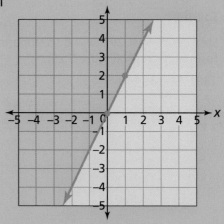

FIGURE 5.22

Graph $y < -x + 1$ (Figure 5.23).

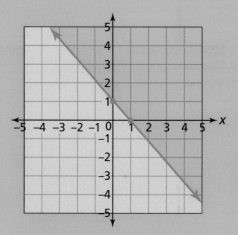

FIGURE 5.23

Determine the region of the graph that satisfies both inequalities (Figure 5.24).

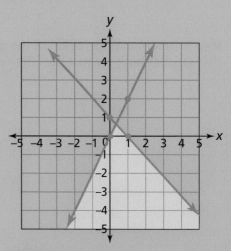

FIGURE 5.24

5.16 Solve the system of linear inequalities $\begin{cases} 2y > x - 8 \\ 2x + y \leq 3 \end{cases}$

Solution:

Step 1: Convert $2y > x - 8$ to slope-intercept form and graph (Figure 5.25).

$$\frac{2y}{2} > \frac{(x-8)}{2}$$

$$y > \frac{1}{2}x - 4$$

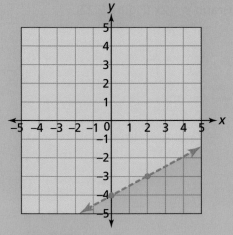

FIGURE 5.25

Step 2: Convert $2x + y \leq 3$ to slope-intercept form and graph (Figure 5.26).

$$2x + y - 2x \leq 3 - 2x$$

$$y \leq -2x + 3$$

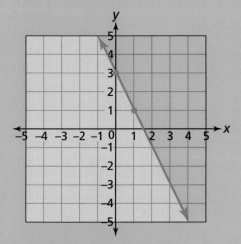

FIGURE 5.26

Step 3: Determine the region of the graph that satisfies both inequalities (Figure 5.27).

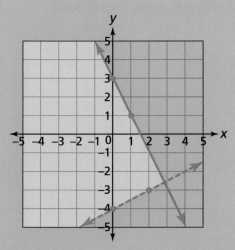

FIGURE 5.27

5.17 Solve the system of equations $\begin{cases} 8x - y = 3 \\ 2x + 3y = 17 \end{cases}$ using matrices.

Solution:

Step 1: Write the system as a matrix.

$$\begin{bmatrix} 8 & -1 & 3 \\ 2 & 3 & 17 \end{bmatrix}$$

Step 2: Multiply the bottom row by $\frac{1}{3}$ and add it to the top row.

$$\begin{bmatrix} 8+(2)\left(\frac{1}{3}\right) & -1+(3)\left(\frac{1}{3}\right) & 3+(17)\left(\frac{1}{3}\right) \\ 2 & 3 & 17 \end{bmatrix} \rightarrow \begin{bmatrix} \frac{26}{3} & 0 & \frac{26}{3} \\ 2 & 3 & 17 \end{bmatrix}$$

Step 3: Multiply the top row by $\frac{3}{26}$.

$$\begin{bmatrix} \frac{26}{3} \cdot \frac{3}{26} & 0 \cdot \frac{3}{26} & \frac{26}{3} \cdot \frac{3}{26} \\ 2 & 3 & 17 \end{bmatrix} \rightarrow \begin{bmatrix} 1 & 0 & 1 \\ 2 & 3 & 17 \end{bmatrix}$$

Step 4: Multiply the top row by -2 and add it to the bottom row.

$$\begin{bmatrix} 1 & 0 & 1 \\ 2+(1)(-2) & 3+(0)(-2) & 17+(1)(-2) \end{bmatrix} \rightarrow \begin{bmatrix} 1 & 0 & 1 \\ 0 & 3 & 15 \end{bmatrix}$$

Step 5: Finally, multiply the bottom row by $\frac{1}{3}$.

$$\begin{bmatrix} 1 & 0 & 1 \\ 0 \cdot \frac{1}{3} & 3 \cdot \frac{1}{3} & 15 \cdot \frac{1}{3} \end{bmatrix} \rightarrow \begin{bmatrix} 1 & 0 & 1 \\ 0 & 1 & 5 \end{bmatrix}$$

This means that the solution to the system is (1, 5).

5.18 Use matrices to solve the system of equations $\begin{cases} 5x - 2y = -21 \\ x + 7y = 18 \end{cases}$.

Solution:

Step 1: Write the system as a matrix.

$$\begin{bmatrix} 5 & -2 & -21 \\ 1 & 7 & 18 \end{bmatrix}$$

Step 2: Multiply the top row by $-\frac{1}{5}$ and add it to the bottom row.

$$\begin{bmatrix} 5 & -2 & -21 \\ 1+(5)\left(-\frac{1}{5}\right) & 7+(-2)\left(-\frac{1}{5}\right) & 18+(-21)\left(-\frac{1}{5}\right) \end{bmatrix} \rightarrow \begin{bmatrix} 5 & -2 & -21 \\ 0 & \frac{37}{5} & \frac{111}{5} \end{bmatrix}$$

Step 3: Multiply the bottom row by $\frac{5}{37}$.

$$\begin{bmatrix} 5 & -2 & -21 \\ 0 \cdot \frac{5}{37} & \frac{37}{5} \cdot \frac{5}{37} & \frac{111}{5} \cdot \frac{5}{37} \end{bmatrix} \rightarrow \begin{bmatrix} 5 & -2 & -21 \\ 0 & 1 & 3 \end{bmatrix}$$

Step 4: Multiply the bottom row by 2 and add it to the top row.

$$\begin{bmatrix} 5+(0)(2) & -2+(1)(2) & -21+(3)(2) \\ 0 & 1 & 3 \end{bmatrix} \rightarrow \begin{bmatrix} 5 & 0 & -15 \\ 0 & 1 & 3 \end{bmatrix}$$

Step 5: Finally, multiply the top row by $\dfrac{1}{5}$.

$$\begin{bmatrix} 5 \cdot \dfrac{1}{5} & 0 \cdot \dfrac{1}{5} & -15 \cdot \dfrac{1}{5} \\ 0 & 1 & 3 \end{bmatrix} \rightarrow \begin{bmatrix} 1 & 0 & -3 \\ 0 & 1 & 3 \end{bmatrix}$$

This means that the solution to the system is $(-3, 3)$.

5.19 Use matrices to solve the system of equations $\begin{cases} -x+y=4 \\ 3x-2y=-5 \end{cases}$

Solution:

Step 1: Write the system as a matrix:

$$\begin{bmatrix} -1 & 1 & 4 \\ 3 & -2 & -5 \end{bmatrix}$$

Step 2: Multiply the top row by 2 and add it to the bottom row:

$$\begin{bmatrix} (2)(-1)+3 & (2)(1)+(-2) & (2)(4)-5 \\ 3 & -2 & -5 \end{bmatrix} \rightarrow \begin{bmatrix} 1 & 0 & 3 \\ 3 & -2 & -5 \end{bmatrix}$$

Step 3: Multiply the top row by -3 and add it to the bottom row:

$$\begin{bmatrix} 1 & 0 & 3 \\ (-3)(1)+3 & (-3)(0)-2 & (-3)(3)-5 \end{bmatrix} \rightarrow \begin{bmatrix} 1 & 0 & 3 \\ 0 & -2 & -14 \end{bmatrix}$$

Step 4: divide the bottom row by -2:

$$\begin{bmatrix} 1 & 0 & 3 \\ \dfrac{0}{(-2)} & -\dfrac{2}{(-2)} & -\dfrac{14}{(-2)} \end{bmatrix} \rightarrow \begin{bmatrix} 1 & 0 & 3 \\ 0 & 1 & 7 \end{bmatrix}$$

This means the solution to the system is $(3, 7)$

5.20 Solve the system of equations $\begin{cases} 2x-9y=5 \\ -10x+y=19 \end{cases}$ using Gaussian elimination.

Solution:

Step 1: Write the system as a matrix.

$$\begin{bmatrix} 2 & -9 & 5 \\ -10 & 1 & 19 \end{bmatrix}$$

Step 2: Multiply the top row by 5 and add it to the bottom row.

$$\begin{bmatrix} 2 & -9 & 5 \\ -10+(2)(5) & 1+(-9)(5) & 19+(5)(5) \end{bmatrix} \rightarrow \begin{bmatrix} 2 & -9 & 5 \\ 0 & -44 & 44 \end{bmatrix}$$

Step 3: This means that $-44y = 44$. Solve this equation for y.

$$-44y = 44$$
$$\frac{-44y}{-44} = \frac{44}{-44}$$
$$y = -1$$

Step 4: Now plug the value of y into the equation $2x - 9y = 5$ and solve for x.

$$2x - 9y = 5$$
$$2x - 9(-1) = 5$$
$$2x + 9 = 5$$
$$2x + 9 - 9 = 5 - 9$$
$$2x = -4$$
$$\frac{2x}{2} = \frac{-4}{2}$$
$$x = -2$$

This means that the solution to the system is (–2, –1).

5.21 Use Gaussian elimination to solve the system of equations $\begin{cases} -4x - y = 4 \\ 7x + 2y = -5 \end{cases}$.

Solution:

Step 1: Write the system as a matrix.

$$\begin{bmatrix} -4 & -1 & 4 \\ 7 & 2 & -5 \end{bmatrix}$$

Step 2: Multiply the top row by $\frac{7}{4}$ and add it to the bottom row.

$$\begin{bmatrix} -4 & -1 & 4 \\ 7 + (-4)\left(\frac{7}{4}\right) & 2 + (-1)\left(\frac{7}{4}\right) & -5 + (4)\left(\frac{7}{4}\right) \end{bmatrix} \rightarrow \begin{bmatrix} -4 & -1 & 4 \\ 0 & \frac{1}{4} & 2 \end{bmatrix}$$

Step 3: This means that $\frac{1}{4}y = 2$. Solve this equation for y.

$$\frac{1}{4}y = 2$$
$$\frac{1}{4}y \cdot 4 = 2 \cdot 4$$
$$y = 8$$

Step 4: Now plug the value of y into the equation $-4x - y = 4$ and solve for x.

$$-4x - y = 4$$
$$-4x - (8) = 4$$
$$-4x - 8 = 4$$
$$-4x - 8 + 8 = 4 + 8$$
$$-4x = 12$$
$$\frac{-4x}{-4} = \frac{12}{-4}$$
$$x = -3$$

This means that the solution to the system is (–3, 8).

5.22 Use Gaussian elimination to solve the system of equations $\begin{cases} x - 2y = 10 \\ 3x + y = 9 \end{cases}$

Solution:

Step 1: Write the system as a matrix:

$$\begin{bmatrix} 1 & -2 & 10 \\ 3 & 1 & 9 \end{bmatrix}$$

Step 2: Multiply the top row by -3 and add it to the bottom row:

$$\begin{bmatrix} 1 & -2 & 10 \\ (-3)(1)+3 & (-3)(-2)+1 & (-3)(10)+9 \end{bmatrix} \rightarrow \begin{bmatrix} 1 & -2 & 10 \\ 0 & 7 & -21 \end{bmatrix}$$

This means that $7y = -21$, Solve the equation for y:

$$\frac{7y}{7} = -\frac{21}{7}$$
$$y = -3$$

Step 3: Substitute the value $y = -3$ into the equation $x - 2y = 10$

$$x - 2(-3) = 10$$
$$x + 6 = 10$$
$$x + 6 - 6 = 10 - 6$$
$$x = 4$$

This means the solution to the system is $(4, -3)$

5.23 Solve the system of equations $\begin{cases} x + 8y - 2z = -25 \\ 5x - y + 4z = -3 \\ 3x + 2y - z = -2 \end{cases}$ using Gaussian elimination.

Solution:

Step 1: Write the system as a matrix.

$$\begin{bmatrix} 1 & 8 & -2 & -25 \\ 5 & -1 & 4 & -3 \\ 3 & 2 & -1 & -2 \end{bmatrix}$$

Step 2: Multiply the top row by -5 and add it to the middle row.

$$\begin{bmatrix} 1 & 8 & -2 & -25 \\ 5+(1)(-5) & -1+(8)(-5) & 4+(-2)(-5) & -3+(-25)(-5) \\ 3 & 2 & -1 & -2 \end{bmatrix} \rightarrow \begin{bmatrix} 1 & 8 & -2 & -25 \\ 0 & -41 & 14 & 122 \\ 3 & 2 & -1 & -2 \end{bmatrix}$$

Step 3: Multiply the top row by -3 and add it to the bottom row.

$$\begin{bmatrix} 1 & 8 & -2 & -25 \\ 0 & -41 & 14 & 122 \\ 3+(1)(-3) & 2+(8)(-3) & -1+(-2)(-3) & -2+(-25)(-3) \end{bmatrix} \rightarrow \begin{bmatrix} 1 & 8 & -2 & -25 \\ 0 & -41 & 14 & 122 \\ 0 & -22 & 5 & 73 \end{bmatrix}$$

Step 4: Multiply the middle row by $-\dfrac{22}{41}$ and add it to the bottom row.

$$\begin{bmatrix} 1 & 8 & -2 & -25 \\ 0 & -41 & 14 & 122 \\ 0+(0)\left(-\dfrac{22}{41}\right) & -22+(-41)\left(-\dfrac{22}{41}\right) & 5+(14)\left(-\dfrac{22}{41}\right) & 73+(122)\left(-\dfrac{22}{41}\right) \end{bmatrix} \rightarrow \begin{bmatrix} 1 & 8 & -2 & -25 \\ 0 & -41 & 14 & 122 \\ 0 & 0 & -\dfrac{103}{41} & \dfrac{309}{41} \end{bmatrix}$$

Step 5: This means that $-\dfrac{103}{41}z = \dfrac{309}{41}$. Solve this equation for z.

$$-\frac{103}{41}z = \frac{309}{41}$$
$$-\frac{103}{41}z \cdot \left(-\frac{41}{103}\right) = \frac{309}{41} \cdot \left(-\frac{41}{103}\right)$$
$$z = -3$$

Step 6: It also means that $-41y + 14z = 122$. Plug the value of z into this equation and solve for y.

$$-41y + 14z = 122$$
$$-41y + 14(-3) = 122$$
$$-41y + (-42) = 122$$
$$-41y - 42 = 122$$
$$-41y - 42 + 42 = 122 + 42$$
$$-41y = 164$$
$$\frac{-41y}{-41} = \frac{164}{-41}$$
$$y = -4$$

Step 7: Now plug the values of y and z into the equation $x + 8y - 2z = -25$ and solve for x.

$$x + 8y - 2z = -25$$
$$x + 8(-4) - 2(-3) = -25$$
$$x + (-32) - (-6) = -25$$
$$x - 32 + 6 = -25$$
$$x - 26 = -25$$
$$x - 26 + 26 = -25 + 26$$
$$x = 1$$

This means that the solution to the system is $x = 1$, $y = -4$, and $z = -3$.

5.24 Solve the system of equations $\begin{cases} 4x - 2y + 5z = 16 \\ -x + 10y - 3z = 9 \\ 2x - 9y + 7z = -9 \end{cases}$ using Gaussian elimination.

Solution:

Step 1: Write the system as a matrix.

$$\begin{bmatrix} 4 & -2 & 5 & 16 \\ -1 & 10 & -3 & 9 \\ 2 & -9 & 7 & -9 \end{bmatrix}$$

Step 2: Multiply the top row by $\frac{1}{4}$ and add it to the middle row.

$$\begin{bmatrix} 4 & -2 & 5 & 16 \\ -1+(4)\left(\frac{1}{4}\right) & 10+(-2)\left(\frac{1}{4}\right) & -3+(5)\left(\frac{1}{4}\right) & 9+(16)\left(\frac{1}{4}\right) \\ 2 & -9 & 7 & -9 \end{bmatrix} \rightarrow \begin{bmatrix} 4 & -2 & 5 & 16 \\ 0 & \frac{19}{2} & -\frac{7}{4} & 13 \\ 2 & -9 & 7 & -9 \end{bmatrix}$$

Step 3: Multiply the top row by $-\frac{1}{2}$ and add it to the bottom row.

$$\begin{bmatrix} 4 & -2 & 5 & 16 \\ 0 & \frac{19}{2} & -\frac{7}{4} & 13 \\ 2+(4)\left(-\frac{1}{2}\right) & -9+(-2)\left(-\frac{1}{2}\right) & 7+(5)\left(-\frac{1}{2}\right) & -9+(16)\left(-\frac{1}{2}\right) \end{bmatrix} \rightarrow \begin{bmatrix} 4 & -2 & 5 & 16 \\ 0 & \frac{19}{2} & -\frac{7}{4} & 13 \\ 0 & -8 & \frac{9}{2} & -17 \end{bmatrix}$$

Step 4: Multiply the middle row by $\frac{16}{19}$ and add it to the bottom row.

$$\begin{bmatrix} 4 & -2 & 5 & 16 \\ 0 & \frac{19}{2} & -\frac{7}{4} & 13 \\ 0+(0)\left(\frac{16}{19}\right) & -8+\left(\frac{19}{2}\right)\left(\frac{16}{19}\right) & \frac{9}{2}+\left(-\frac{7}{4}\right)\left(\frac{16}{19}\right) & -17+(13)\left(\frac{16}{19}\right) \end{bmatrix} \rightarrow \begin{bmatrix} 4 & -2 & 5 & 16 \\ 0 & \frac{19}{2} & -\frac{7}{4} & 13 \\ 0 & 0 & \frac{115}{38} & -\frac{115}{19} \end{bmatrix}$$

Step 5: This means that $\frac{115}{38}z = -\frac{115}{19}$. Solve this equation for z.

$$\frac{115}{38}z = -\frac{115}{19}$$
$$\frac{115}{38}z \cdot \frac{38}{115} = -\frac{115}{19} \cdot \frac{38}{115}$$
$$z = -2$$

Step 6: It also means that $\frac{19}{2}y - \frac{7}{4}z = 13$. Plug the value of z into this equation and solve for y.

$$\frac{19}{2}y - \frac{7}{4}z = 13$$
$$\frac{19}{2}y - \frac{7}{4}(-2) = 13$$
$$\frac{19}{2}y + \frac{7}{2} = 13$$
$$\frac{19}{2}y + \frac{7}{2} - \frac{7}{2} = 13 - \frac{7}{2}$$
$$\frac{19}{2}y = \frac{19}{2}$$
$$y = 1$$

Step 7: Now plug the values of y and z into the equation $4x - 2y + 5z = 16$ and solve for x.

$$4x - 2y + 5z = 16$$
$$4x - 2(1) + 5(-2) = 16$$
$$4x - 2 + (-10) = 16$$
$$4x - 2 - 10 = 16$$
$$4x - 12 = 16$$
$$4x - 12 + 12 = 16 + 12$$
$$4x = 28$$
$$\frac{4x}{4} = \frac{28}{4}$$
$$x = 7$$

This means that the solution to the system is $x = 7$, $y = 1$, and $z = -2$.

5.25 Calculate the value of the determinant of the matrix $\begin{bmatrix} -4 & 8 \\ 7 & -9 \end{bmatrix}$.

Solution:

Step 1: Write the determinant of the matrix.

$$\begin{vmatrix} -4 & 8 \\ 7 & -9 \end{vmatrix}$$

Step 2: Calculate the value of the determinant.

$$(-4)(-9) - (7)(8) = 36 - 56 = -20$$

5.26 Calculate the value of the determinant of the matrix $\begin{bmatrix} 3 & 2 & 6 \\ -1 & 5 & -4 \\ -3 & -2 & 1 \end{bmatrix}$.

Solution:

Step 1: Write the determinant of the matrix with the first two columns added on at the right.

$$\begin{vmatrix} 3 & 2 & 6 \\ -1 & 5 & -4 \\ -3 & -2 & 1 \end{vmatrix} \begin{matrix} 3 & 2 \\ -1 & 5 \\ -3 & -2 \end{matrix}$$

Step 2: Calculate the value of the determinant.

$$(3)(5)(1) + (2)(-4)(-3) + (6)(-1)(-2) - (-3)(5)(6) - (-2)(-4)(3) - (1)(-1)(2) =$$
$$15 + 24 + 12 - (-90) - 24 - (-2) = 15 + 24 + 12 + 90 - 24 + 2 = 119$$

5.27 Solve the system of equations $\begin{cases} -2x - 7y = -25 \\ x + 8y = 35 \end{cases}$ by using Cramer's Rule.

Solution:

Step 1: Write the coefficient matrix for the system.

$$\begin{bmatrix} -2 & -7 \\ 1 & 8 \end{bmatrix}$$

Step 2: Calculate the value of its determinant.

$$\begin{vmatrix} -2 & -7 \\ 1 & 8 \end{vmatrix}$$

$$(-2)(8) - (1)(-7) = -16 - (-7) = -16 + 7 = -9$$

Step 3: Replace the first column of the coefficient matrix with the equations' constants.

$$\begin{vmatrix} -25 & -7 \\ 35 & 8 \end{vmatrix}$$

Step 4: Calculate the value of the determinant of this matrix.

$$\begin{vmatrix} -25 & -7 \\ 35 & 8 \end{vmatrix}$$

$$(-25)(8) - (35)(-7) = -200 - (-245) = -200 + 245 = 45$$

Step 5: Divide the value from the previous step by the value of the determinant of the coefficient matrix to get the value of x.

$$x = \frac{45}{-9} = -5$$

Step 6: Replace the second column of the coefficient matrix with the equations' constants.

$$\begin{vmatrix} -2 & -25 \\ 1 & 35 \end{vmatrix}$$

Step 7: Calculate the value of the determinant of this matrix.

$$\begin{vmatrix} -2 & -25 \\ 1 & 35 \end{vmatrix}$$

$$(-2)(35) - (1)(-25) = -70 - (-25) = -70 + 25 = -45$$

Step 8: Divide the value from the previous step by the value of the determinant of the coefficient matrix to get the value of y.

$$y = \frac{-45}{-9} = 5$$

This means that the solution to the system is $(-5, 5)$.

5.28 Solve the system of equations $\begin{cases} -9x - y + 2z = 13 \\ 3x + 4y - z = -12 \\ 7x + 2y + 3z = -8 \end{cases}$ by using Cramer's Rule.

Solution:

Step 1: Write the coefficient matrix for the system.

$$\begin{bmatrix} -9 & -1 & 2 \\ 3 & 4 & -1 \\ 7 & 2 & 3 \end{bmatrix}$$

Step 2: Calculate the value of its determinant.

$$\begin{vmatrix} -9 & -1 & 2 \\ 3 & 4 & -1 \\ 7 & 2 & 3 \end{vmatrix} \begin{matrix} -9 & -1 \\ 3 & 4 \\ 7 & 2 \end{matrix}$$

$(-9)(4)(3) + (-1)(-1)(7) + (2)(3)(2) - (7)(4)(2) - (2)(-1)(-9) - (3)(3)(-1) =$
$-108 + 7 + 12 - 56 - 18 - (-9) = -108 + 7 + 12 - 56 - 18 + 9 = -154$

Step 3: Replace the first column of the coefficient matrix with the equations' constants.

$$\begin{bmatrix} 13 & -1 & 2 \\ -12 & 4 & -1 \\ -8 & 2 & 3 \end{bmatrix}$$

Step 4: Calculate the value of the determinant of this matrix.

$$\begin{vmatrix} 13 & -1 & 2 \\ -12 & 4 & -1 \\ -8 & 2 & 3 \end{vmatrix} \begin{matrix} 13 & -1 \\ -12 & 4 \\ -8 & 2 \end{matrix}$$

$(13)(4)(3) + (-1)(-1)(-8) + (2)(-12)(2) - (-8)(4)(2) - (2)(-1)(13) - (3)(-12)(-1) =$
$156 + (-8) + (-48) - (-64) - (-26) - 36 = 156 - 8 - 48 + 64 + 26 - 36 = 154$

Step 5: Divide the value from the previous step by the value of the determinant of the coefficient matrix to get the value of x.

$$x = \frac{154}{-154} = -1$$

Step 6: Replace the second column of the coefficient matrix with the equations' constants.

$$\begin{bmatrix} -9 & 13 & 2 \\ 3 & -12 & -1 \\ 7 & -8 & 3 \end{bmatrix}$$

Step 7: Calculate the value of the determinant of this matrix.

$$\begin{vmatrix} -9 & 13 & 2 \\ 3 & -12 & -1 \\ 7 & -8 & 3 \end{vmatrix} \begin{matrix} -9 & 13 \\ 3 & -12 \\ 7 & -8 \end{matrix}$$

$(-9)(-12)(3) + (13)(-1)(7) + (2)(3)(-8) - (7)(-12)(2) - (-8)(-1)(-9) - (3)(3)(13) =$
$324 + (-91) + (-48) - (-168) - (-72) - 117 = 324 - 91 - 48 + 168 + 72 - 117 = 308$

Step 8: Divide the value from the previous step by the value of the determinant of the coefficient matrix to get the value of y.

$$y = \frac{308}{-154} = -2$$

Step 9: Replace the third column of the coefficient matrix with the equations' constants.

$$\begin{bmatrix} 0 & -1 & 13 \\ 3 & 4 & -12 \\ 7 & 2 & -8 \end{bmatrix}$$

Step 10: Calculate the value of the determinant of this matrix.

$$\begin{vmatrix} -9 & -1 & 13 \\ 3 & 4 & -12 \\ 7 & 2 & -8 \end{vmatrix} \begin{matrix} -9 & -1 \\ 3 & 4 \\ 7 & 2 \end{matrix}$$

$(-9)(4)(-8) + (-1)(-12)(7) + (13)(3)(2) - (7)(4)(13) - (2)(-12)(-9) - (-8)(3)(-1) =$

$288 + 84 + 78 - 364 - 216 - 24 = -154$

Step 11: Divide the value from the previous step by the value of the determinant of the coefficient matrix to get the value of z.

$$z = \frac{-154}{-154} = 1$$

This means that the solution to the system is $x = -1$, $y = -2$, and $z = 1$.

END OF CHAPTER REVIEW QUESTIONS

5.1 Determine if the point (5, 1) is a solution to the systems of equations.

$x + y = 6$
$x - y = 4$

5.2 Determine if the point (3, −1) is a solution to the system of equations.

$x - 2y = 1$
$2x - y = 5$

5.3 Graph the following systems of equations to determine the solution.

$2x - y = 2$
$-x + y = 1$

5.4 Graph the following systems of equations to determine the solution.

$2x - y = 2$

$6x - 3y = -18$

5.5 Graph the following systems of equations to determine the solution.

$2x - y = 2$

$4x - 2y = 4$

5.6 Use the substitution method to solve the following system of equations.

$y = 2x + 6$

$-3x - y = 4$

5.7 Substitute $x = 2$ in the equation $y = 2x + 6$:

$y = 2(-2) + 6$

$y = -4 + 6$

$y = 2$

5.8 Use the substitution method to solve the following system of equations.

$x = y - 3$

$-4x - y = -8$

5.9 Use the substitution method to solve the following system of equations.

$$4x + 2y = 6$$
$$y = -2x + 3$$

5.10 Use the substitution method to solve the following systems of equations.

$$3x + y = 4$$
$$x - 2y = 4$$

5.11 Use the elimination method to solve the following systems of equations.

$$5x + y = 5$$
$$5x + 3y = 15$$

5.12 Use the elimination method to solve the following system of equations.

$$6x - 2y = 2$$
$$-3x + 3y = 9$$

5.13 Use the elimination method to solve the following system of equations.

$$5x - 2y = -1$$
$$-2x + 3y = -4$$

5.14 Use the elimination method to solve the following system of equations.

$5x - 5y = 40$

$x + 3y = 0$

5.15 Use the elimination method to solve the following system of equations.

$-4x + 2y = 20$

$3x + 5y = -15$

5.16 Use the elimination method to solve the following system of equations.

$3x - y = 12$

$-6x + 2y = 6$

5.17 Solve the systems of equations with method of choice.

$\dfrac{1}{5}x + \dfrac{2}{5}y = 1$

$\dfrac{1}{4}x - \dfrac{1}{3}y = -\dfrac{5}{12}$

5.18 Solve the systems of equations with method of choice.

$0.2x + 0.3y = 1$

$x - 0.5y = 3$

5.19 The demand and supply for a certain product is given by the following systems of equations:

$D(p) = 1500 - 5p$
$S(p) = 300 + p$

Find the price at the equilibrium point for each function and then find the value of the demand at this price.

5.20 Graph the systems of inequalities and shade the feasible solution.

$y > -3$
$x < 2$

5.21 Graph the systems of inequalities and shade the feasible solution.

$y \geq 3x - 2$
$y < -2x + 3$

5.22 Graph the systems of inequalities and shade the feasible solutions.

$x - y \geq 2$
$x + y \leq 6$

5.23 Graph the systems of inequalities and shade the feasible solution.

$2x - y < -1$

$x - y > -2$

5.24 Graph the systems of inequalities and shade the feasible solution.

$y \geq -4$

$x - y < 5$

5.25 Graph the systems of inequalities and shade the feasible solution.

$x \leq -2$

$x - y \geq 2$

5.26 Graph the systems of inequalities and shade the feasible solution.

$2x - 3y < -6$

$x + 2y \leq 1$

5.27 Graph the systems of inequalities and shade the feasible solutions.

$x \geq 1$

$y \geq 2$

$4 \leq 2x + y$

$2x + y \leq 6$

5.28 Solve the systems of equations using matrix row operations.

$2x + y = 2$

$x - y = 7$

5.29 Members of book clubs purchased a total of about 110 million books in 2010. Paperback sales exceeded sales of hardbacks by about 40 million books. How many copies of each type of book were published?

5.30 Solve the following systems of equations:

$3x + y - 2z = 13$

$x - 2y + 3z = -9$

$2x + 2y + z = 3$

5.31 Solve the following systems of equations:

$-2x + 3y + z = -10$

$5x + y - z = 19$

$2x - y + 2z = -2$

5.32 Solve the following systems of equations:

$2x - y + 4z = -3$

$x - 2y - 10z = -6$

$3x + 4z = 7$

5.33 Solve the following systems of equations:

$x + y + z = 2$

$6x - 4y + 5z = 31$

$5x + 2y + 2z = 13$

5.34 Find the determinants of the following system of equations:

$2x - 3y = -9$

$-3x + 4y = 10$

5.35 Find the determinants of the following system of equations:

$5x - 2y = 10$

$3x + 2y = 6$

5.36 Use the Gaussian method to solve the system of equations:

$2x + y = 2$

$-x + y = 5$

Polynomials

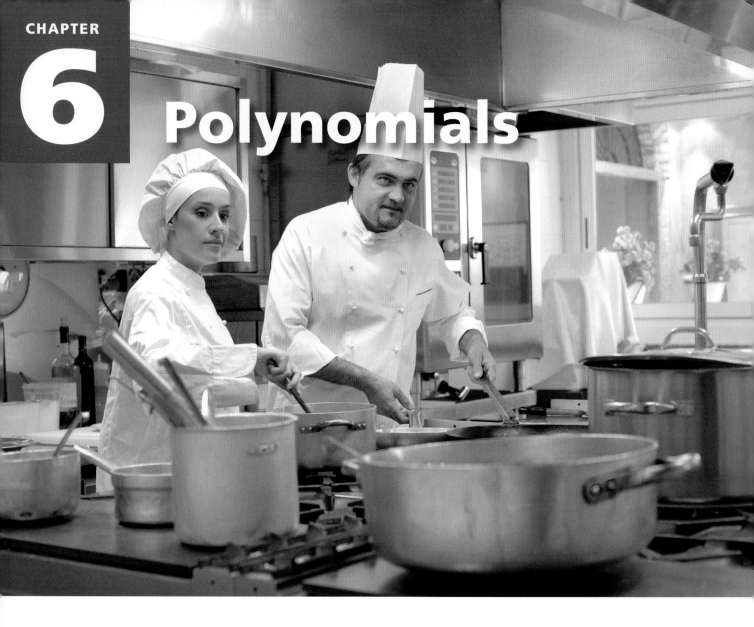

Jared is a professional chef who owns and operates his own catering business, which specializes in making soups. He has found that it is most convenient and efficient to measure the amount of soup he makes and sells in terms of its volume.

Jared packages his soup in three different box-shaped containers, or cartons. Rather than trying to remember the various volumes of the cartons, he realizes that he can use the formula for the volume of a box to compute each volume he needs. For a box with height h, and a rectangular base with length l, and width w, the volume formula is $V = lwh$.

The smallest carton has a square base with sides of s inches and a height of d inches. So the volume of the smallest carton is ds^2 cubic inches. The medium-sized carton has a square base with sides of $2s$ inches and a height of d inches. Consequently, its volume is $d(2s)^2 = 4ds^2$ cubic inches. Finally, the largest carton has a height of d inches and a rectangular base with length l, and width $2s$ inches. The volume of the largest carton, then, is $V = 2dls$ cubic inches.

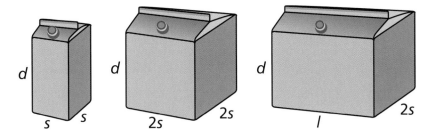

Jared's kitchen also contains eight large cylindrical stockpots, one for each of the eight soups he makes. The stockpots are of identical size, and Jared needs to know how their volume relates to the volume of the soup cartons. That is, he needs to know how many small, medium, or large cartons can be filled from a single stockpot, so he can ensure sufficient portions for each catered event. Each stockpot has a volume of $\pi r^2 h$, where h is its height and r is the radius of the (circular) base.

Although he makes a large variety of soups, Jared only sells soup meals in two different sizes, regular and hearty. The regular meal consists of two small cartons of soup and one medium carton, and the hearty meal consists of one large carton, one medium carton, and one small carton.

QUESTIONS TO CONSIDER

1. Jared knows the volume of each carton that he uses. How would he create an expression that tells him how much soup each *meal* contains?

2. Jared decides that the hearty meal and the regular meal are too close in size. How can he determine how much greater the volume of the hearty meal is than the regular meal?

3. As his business expands, Jared decides to hire another chef and to increase the number of soups he sells. To achieve this, he decides to buy some smaller stockpots with radius and depth each half of those of his existing pots. What is the difference in volume between the old and new stockpots?

The general answer to all these questions is that Jared can write polynomial expressions to relate the volumes of cartons, meals, and stockpots in his catering business. This chapter introduces polynomials, their elements, and how to evaluate, add, subtract, multiply, and divide them.

KEY TERMS

EXPONENTS

Laws of Exponents

Exponents are a convenient and powerful notation used throughout mathematics. An **exponent** is a superscript number written to the right of the **base**, the number on which it acts. The exponent indicates the power to which the base is raised.

In the expression x^n, n is the exponent for the base x. Read the expression as "x (raised) to the *nth* power" or "x to the *nth.*" In the simplest case, n is a positive integer. In this case, x^n means n x's multiplied together. The cases when $n = 2$ or $n = 3$ have special names. Read $x^2 = x \cdot x$ as x squared and $x^3 = x \cdot x \cdot x$ as x cubed.

Reading x^2 as "x squared" is a result of the most common geometric occurrence of x^2, finding the area of a square whose sides are of length x.

Similarly, reading x^3 as "x cubed" is a result of the most common geometric occurrence of x^3, finding the volume of a cube whose edges are of length x.

When the base for an exponent is positive, the value of the expression is always positive. You can check that $4^1 = 4 > 0$, $4^2 = 16 > 0$, $4^3 = 64 > 0$, and so on.

When the base for an exponent is negative, the value of the expression is negative for odd exponents and positive for even exponents. You can check that $(-2)^1 = -2 < 0$ because 1 is odd, $(-2)^2 = (-2)(-2) = 4 > 0$ because 2 is even, $(-2)^3 = (-2)(-2)(-2) = -8 < 0$ because 3 is odd, and so on.

The rule is sometimes stated: Odd exponents preserve the sign of the base; even exponents yield a positive result.

Exponents obey three basic laws, which are all consequences of the Associative and Commutative Laws of Multiplication and Division. (Note: 0^0 has no meaning.)

1. $(x^a)^b = x^{ab}$ A power of a power is the same as the product of the powers.
2. $(abc\ldots)^n = a^n b^n c^n \ldots$ An exponent can be distributed across multiplication.
3. $\left(\dfrac{x}{y}\right)^n = \dfrac{x^n}{y^n}$ An exponent can be distributed across division.

There are four additional laws governing exponents, each of which requires some explanation.

4. $x^0 = 1$, $x \neq 0$ The zero power of a nonzero number is always 1.
5. $x^{-n} = \dfrac{1}{x^n} = \left(\dfrac{1}{x}\right)^n$, $x \neq 0$ Exponents can be negative numbers. If $x = 0$ and n is positive, $x^n = 0$.
6. $\sqrt[q]{x} = x^{\frac{1}{q}}$, where both are defined ($q \neq 0$, and $x \geq 0$ if q is even)
7. $x^{\frac{p}{q}} = \left(x^{\frac{1}{q}}\right)^p = \left(x^p\right)^{\frac{1}{q}}$, where $x \geq 0$ if $p \neq 1$

Explanations

4. *Nonzero numbers.* To see why $x^0 = 1$, $x \neq 0$, consider this pattern when x is 2:

$$\frac{2^3}{2} = 2^2$$

$$\frac{2^2}{2} = 2^1$$

$$\frac{2^1}{2} = 2^0$$

However, $\dfrac{2^1}{2} = \dfrac{2}{2} = 1$, so $2^0 = 1$. This pattern holds for any nonzero value of x.

5. *Negative exponents.* Exponents can be negative numbers. Continuing the pattern from the last paragraph, $\frac{2^0}{2} = 2^{-1}$, but $\frac{2^0}{2} = \frac{1}{2}$, so we let $2^{-1} = \frac{1}{2}$. The rule is: A nonzero x raised to the $-n$ power equals 1 divided by x^n. This is written as

$$x^{-n} = \frac{1}{x^n} = \left(\frac{1}{x}\right)^n$$

Note that for all values of x, n itself may be either positive or negative.

6 and 7. Rational exponents. Exponents can also be rational numbers $\frac{p}{q}$, where p and q are integers and q is not zero. Rational exponents $\frac{p}{q}$ in which q is an even number have three special properties:

i. Because q is even, the base x must be positive. There is no real number that, when raised to an even power, will result in a negative number. See the rule stated above. For example, let $p = 1$. If $q = 2$, there is no value of x for which

$$x^2 = -64 = \left[(-64)^{\frac{1}{2}}\right]^2.$$ But if q is 3, $x^3 = -64 = \left[(-64)^{\frac{1}{3}}\right]^3$ and $x = -4$.

Note $x \geq 0$ if $p \neq 1$.

ii. Therefore, where both expressions are defined, $\sqrt[q]{x} = x^{\frac{1}{q}}$.
To see this, raise both sides of the equation to the qth power:

$$\left(\sqrt[q]{x}\right)^q = \left(x^{\frac{1}{q}}\right)^q$$

$$x = x^1$$

$$x = x$$

Either form is called the qth root of x. It is the number that, when it is raised to the qth power, equals x. If $p = 1$ and $q = 2$, $x^{\frac{1}{2}}$ is the square root of x, written $\sqrt[2]{x} = \sqrt{x}$. If $q = 3$, $x^{\frac{1}{3}}$ is the cube root of x, or $\sqrt[3]{x}$.

iii. The solution of any equation of the form $x^2 = k$, k a constant yields two roots. To see that this is true, take the simple example $x^2 = 4$. Here, x represents the number that equals 4 when multiplied by itself. Two numbers satisfy this requirement: 2 and -2. The form $\sqrt[2]{4} = \sqrt{4}$ is always 2, the positive square root of 4 (the principal square root of 4). However, when solving an equation such as $x^2 = 4$, you must consider both possibilities.

For every q and x for which the expressions are defined, we can use the Power of a Power Property to write

$$x^{\frac{p}{q}} = \left(x^{\frac{1}{q}}\right)^p = (x^p)^{\frac{1}{q}}$$

(Notice that it is always true that for nonzero x, $x^{\frac{p}{q}} = \frac{1}{x^{-\frac{p}{q}}}$.)

SCIENTIFIC NOTATION

Scientific notation is shorthand used by scientists and engineers to represent (usually very large and very small) numbers using a finite number of significant figures. There are two forms used to write a number in scientific notation: $x \times 10^n$ and $x\mathrm{E}n$ (seen most often on calculators), where the coefficient x is a rational number with absolute value from 1 to 10 (including 1, but not 10), and the exponent n is any integer. Figure 6.1 gives the decimal representations of several numbers in both forms of scientific notation.

6.3 SCIENTIFIC NOTATION A shorthand way of writing decimal numbers.

DECIMAL	SCIENTIFIC NOTATION I	SCIENTIFIC NOTATION II
18600000	1.86×10^7	1.86E7
.000000003882	3.882×10^{-9}	3.882E−9
−98500	-9.85×10^4	−9.85E4

FIGURE 6.1 Comparison of Decimals and Scientific Notations

Multiplying Monomials

A **monomial** is any one term expression that is the product of a constant and various variables, each raised to some power. The form is $ax_1^{r_1} x_2^{r_2} x_3^{r_3} \ldots x_n^{r_n}$. Read $ax_1^{r_1}$ as "a times x-sub-one to the r-sub-one", and so on. The simplest form is ax^r which is read "a times x to the r" or "$a x$ to the r." Since, for m and n positive integers, x^m represents m multiples of x, and x^n represents n multiples of x, their product must be $m + n$ multiples of x. So, in general, to multiply monomials in the same variable add their exponents:

$$x^a x^b = x^{a+b}$$

This is also true for the multiplication of more general monomials containing more than one base. For example, $(3x^3 y)(5x^2) = 15x^5 y$ and $(x^a y^c)(x^b y^d) = (x^a x^b)(y^c y^d) = x^{a+b} y^{c+d}$.

Dividing Monomials

You can divide monomials with the same base(s) by subtracting the exponents, using the rules for negative exponents and multiplying monomials:

$$\frac{x^a}{x^b} = x^a x^{-b} = x^{a-b}$$

Example 6.1

Multiply the monomials $\dfrac{4x^3}{y^3}$ and $3xy^4$.

Solution:

Step 1: Multiply the monomials and group the like variable bases together using the Commutative and Associative Properties of Multiplication.

$$\left(\frac{4x^3}{y^3}\right)(3xy^4) = (4 \cdot 3)(x^3 \cdot x)\left(\frac{y^4}{y^3}\right)$$

Step 2: Simplify by adding and subtracting the exponents using the appropriate rules.

$$(4 \cdot 3)(x^3 \cdot x)\left(\frac{y^4}{y^3}\right) = 12x^{3+1} y^{4-3} = 12x^4 y$$

Example 6.2

Divide $\dfrac{z^3}{\sqrt[3]{y}}$ by $\dfrac{z^{\frac{1}{2}} y^{-\frac{1}{3}}}{x^2}$.

Solution:

Step 1: Remember that dividing by a fraction is the same as multiplying by the inverse of that fraction. Thus,

$$\frac{z^3}{\sqrt[3]{y}} \div \frac{z^{\frac{1}{2}}y^{-\frac{1}{3}}}{x^2} = \left(\frac{z^3}{\sqrt[3]{y}}\right)\left(\frac{x^2}{z^{\frac{1}{2}}y^{-\frac{1}{3}}}\right)$$

Step 2: Group like variables and remember that $\sqrt[3]{y} = y^{\frac{1}{3}}$.

$$\left(\frac{z^3}{\sqrt[3]{y}}\right)\left(\frac{x^2}{z^{\frac{1}{2}}y^{-\frac{1}{3}}}\right) = \left(\frac{z^3}{z^{\frac{1}{2}}}\right)\left(\frac{1}{y^{\frac{1}{3}}y^{-\frac{1}{3}}}\right)x^2$$

Step 3: Simplify by applying the rules for multiplying and dividing monomials, and adding and subtracting exponents.

$$z^{3-\frac{1}{2}}\left(\frac{1}{y^{\frac{1}{3}-\frac{1}{3}}}\right)x^2 = \frac{x^2 z^{\frac{5}{2}}}{y^0} = x^2 z^{\frac{5}{2}} \text{, since } y^0 = 1$$

DIY PROBLEMS

6.1 Simplify: $(xy^3)(x^3y)$.

6.2 Simplify: $(9xy^4)(-3x^2y^2)$.

6.3 Multiply the monomials $\sqrt[3]{3w}x^2$ by $\dfrac{w}{x^{-3}}$.

6.4 Simplify: $\dfrac{9x^5}{12x^8}$.

6.5 Simplify: $\dfrac{y^{-2}}{y^6}$.

6.6 Divide the monomials $\dfrac{x^2}{y^{-6}}$ by $\dfrac{x^{\frac{2}{3}}}{y^4}$.

INTRODUCTION TO POLYNOMIALS

6.5 POLYNOMIALS Sums of monomials.

Polynomials are sums of monomials. Other names for these monomials are *terms* or *addends*. In standard form, a polynomial in one variable is written $a_n x^n + a_{n-1} x^{n-1} + a_{n-2} x^{n-2} + \ldots + a_1 x + a_0$, where n is a positive integer and a_0 through a_n are real number coefficients whose subscripts match the exponent of the variable in their term. (Subscripts are a convenient way of naming a set of related variables. Instead of a, b, c, and so on, we use a_0, a_1, a_2, and so on.) The **order**, or **degree**, of this polynomial is n.

6.6 ORDER OR DEGREE OF A SINGLE-VARIABLE POLYNOMIAL The value of the greatest exponent of the polynomial. For polynomials with several variables, the order is the greatest sum of exponents among the monomial terms.

If a polynomial has more than one variable, its order is the greatest of the set of sums of the exponents in each term. For example, the degree of $3x^2y + xy - 0.4xy^3$ is 4 because the first term has degree $2 + 1 = 3$, the second term has degree $1 + 1 = 2$, and the third term has degree $1 + 3 = 4$.

Polynomials never contain terms with negative exponents and always have a finite number of terms. Just as a monomial is a single term, a binomial is the sum of two terms, and a trinomial is the sum of three terms.

Evaluating Polynomials

To evaluate a polynomial, substitute given values for each variable.

Example 6.3a
Evaluate the polynomial $x^2 - 5x + 6$ for $x = -1$.

Solution:

To evaluate the polynomial at $x = -1$, substitute -1 for each x:

$$x^2 - 5x + 6 = (-1)^2 - 5(-1) + 6 = 1 + 5 + 6 = 12$$

Example 6.3b
Evaluate the polynomial $x^2 - 5x + 6$ for $x - 4$.

Solution:

Similarly, to evaluate the polynomial at $x = 4$, substitute 4 for each x:

$$x^2 - 5x + 6 = 4^2 - 5 \cdot 4 + 6 = 16 - 20 + 6 = 2$$

Example 6.4a
Evaluate the polynomial $x^2 - 2xy + \sqrt{2}x + y^2$ for $x = y$.

Solution:

As in Examples 6.3a and 6.3b, we simply substitute y for x everywhere x appears.

$$x^2 - 2xy + \sqrt{2}x + y^2 = y^2 - 2y \cdot y + \sqrt{2}y + y^2 = 2y^2 - 2y^2 + \sqrt{2}y = \sqrt{2}y$$

Example 6.4b
Evaluate the polynomial $x^2 - 2xy + \sqrt{2}x + y^2$ for $x = \sqrt{2}$.

Solution:

Similarly, to evaluate the polynomial at $x = \sqrt{2}$, substitute $\sqrt{2}$ for each x:

$$x^2 - 2xy + \sqrt{2}x + y^2 = \left(\sqrt{2}\right)^2 - 2\sqrt{2}y + \sqrt{2}\sqrt{2} + y^2 = 4 - 2\sqrt{2}y + 4 + y^2$$
$$= y^2 - 2\sqrt{2}y + 8$$

DIY PROBLEMS

6.7 Evaluate the polynomial $x^3 - 3x^2y + 3xy^2 - y^3$ for $y = 3$.

6.8a Evaluate the polynomial $x^2 + 2\sqrt{3}x - 9$ for $x = \sqrt{3}$.

6.8b Evaluate the polynomial $x^2 + 2\sqrt{3}x - 9$ for $x = -2\sqrt{3}$.

Addition and Subtraction of Polynomials

The sum or difference of two or more polynomials can be found by adding the coefficients of **like terms.**

The monomials $3x^3yz^2$ and $-3\sqrt{14}z^2yx^3$ are like terms because they differ only in their coefficients; xy and $-7xz$ are not like terms because they have different variables;. $42x^2$ and $13x^5$ are not like terms because the variable has different powers. Figure 6.2 summarizes these examples of like and unlike terms.

6.7 LIKE TERMS Terms having the same variables raised to the same powers.

TERM 1	TERM 2	LIKE TERMS OR UNLIKE TERMS?	REASON
$3x^3yz^2$	$-3\sqrt{14}z^2yx^3$	Like terms	The terms share the same variables raised to the same powers.
xy	$-7xz$	Unlike terms	The terms do not share y or z.
$42x^2$	$13x^5$	Unlike terms	The terms share only x^2 (two factors of x), not x^5 (an additional three factors of x).
$42x^2$	$13x^2$	Like terms	The terms share the same variable raised to the same power.

FIGURE 6.2 Examples of Like and Unlike Terms

When adding and subtracting polynomials, it is often useful to write a 1 when the coefficient of a term equals 1, and a 0 for the coefficients of terms that are not present. For example, the polynomial

$$x^3 - 2x + 1$$

can be rewritten as

$$1x^3 + 0x^2 - 2x + 1$$

to supply a coefficient for the third power of x and a term for the second power of x.

Example 6.5

In order to ensure that his prices are reasonable, Jared wishes to know the volume of soup in his regular and hearty meals. What are the expressions for the volume of each of his meals?

Solution:

Remember from the opening scenario that Jared packages soup in three different cartons. The small carton has volume ds^2, the medium $4ds^2$, and the large $2dls$ (see Figure 6.3). His regular meal has one medium carton and two small cartons, and his hearty meal has one carton of each size.

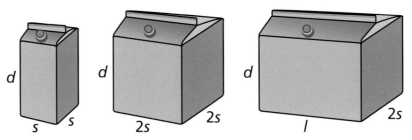

FIGURE 6.3 JARED'S SMALL, MEDIUM, AND LARGE SOUP CARTONS

To find the volume of each meal, sum the volumes of each carton used. For the regular meal $V_r = 4ds^2 + ds^2 + ds^2$, where V_r identifies the volume of a regular meal.

Notice that all the terms are like terms, meaning that summing the terms amounts to summing their coefficients.

$$V_r = 4ds^2 + 1ds^2 + 1ds^2 = 6ds^2$$

For the hearty meal:

$$V_h = 2dls + 4ds^2 + ds^2$$

where V_h identifies the volume of a hearty meal

In this case, only the last two terms are like terms.

$$V_h = 2dls + 4ds^2 + 1ds^2 = 2dls + 5ds^2$$

Example 6.6

Jared thinks the size of his regular meal might be too close to the size of his hearty meal. To check this, he wants to derive a polynomial for the difference between the volumes of his two meals. What is this expression?

Solution:

To find this expression, subtract the volume of the regular meal from the volume of the hearty meal.

$$V_h - V_r = 2dls + 5ds^2 - 6ds^2 = 2dls - 1ds^2$$

Dropping the coefficient 1 leaves

$$V_h - V_r = 2dls - ds^2$$

So Jared knows that the difference in volume between his hearty meal and his regular meal is $2dls - ds^2$.

DIY PROBLEMS

6.9 Subtract $2x^2 - 3x$ from $4x^2 + 5x$.

6.10 Subtract $x^3 - 9x^2 + 2$ from $\sqrt{2}x^3 - x + 2$.

6.11 Subtract $-3x + 14$ from $x^2 - 1$.

MULTIPLICATION OF POLYNOMIALS

Multiplying a Polynomial by a Monomial

Because multiplication is distributive, the first step in multiplying a polynomial by a monomial is to distribute the monomial to each term of the polynomial. Then simplify the terms. The final polynomial should have as many terms as the original polynomial (as long as the monomial is nonzero).

Example 6.7
Multiply $3x^2 + 2x + 1$ by $4x$.

Solution:

Step 1: Distribute the monomial to each term of the polynomial:

$$4x(3x^2 + 2x + 1) = (4x)(3x^2) + (4x)(2x) + (4x)(1)$$

Step 2: Simplify each term to get $12x^3 + 8x^2 + 4x$.

Example 6.8
Multiply $5z^2 - 2xz + y^3$ by $-2x^2yz$.

Solution:

Step 1: Distribute the monomial to each term of the polynomial:

$$(-2x^2yz)(5z^2 - 2xz + y^3) = (-2x^2yz)(5z^2) + (-2x^2yz)(-2xz) + (-2x^2yz)(y^3)$$

Step 2: Simplify each term to get $-10x^2yz^3 + 4x^3yz^2 - 2x^2y^4z$.

6.12 Multiply $3x + 2$ by 4.

6.13 Multiply $9x^2 + 3x - 7$ by $2x$.

6.14 Multiply $x^3 - 2x - 1$ by $\dfrac{x^4}{2}$.

Multiplying Two Polynomials

To multiply two polynomials, break the work into several problems, each only requiring the multiplication of a monomial by a polynomial. Then sum the results of these simpler problems to give the answer.

6.8 FOIL A shortcut way of finding the product of two binomials.

There is a pattern called **FOIL** that many use to find the product $(ax + b)(cx + d)$ of two binomials.

In the acronym FOIL:

- F stands for the product of the first terms of each binomial: $axcx = acx^2$.
- O stands for the product of the outside terms: axd.
- I stands for the product of the inside terms: bcx.
- L stands for the product of the last terms: bd.

The sum of the O and I products is $(ad + bc)x$.

The sum of all four products is $acx^2 + (ad + bc)x + bd = (ax + b)(cx + d)$.

Example 6.9
Multiply $x + 2$ by $x - 3$.

First Solution:

Step 1: Distribute the first polynomial to each term of the second polynomial:

$$(x + 2)(x - 3) = (x + 2)(x) + (x + 2)(-3)$$

Step 2: Apply the rule for multiplying a monomial and a polynomial twice:

$$(x + 2)(x) = x^2 + 2x \text{ and } (x + 2)(-3) = -3x - 6$$

Step 3: Add the two expressions to get the answer:

$$
\begin{aligned}
1x^2 + 2x + 0 & \\
+ (0x^2 - 3x - 6) & \\
\hline
1x^2 - 1x - 6 &
\end{aligned}
$$

Thus, the final answer is $x^2 - x - 6$.

Second Solution:

Use the FOIL method. The F product is x^2. The O product is $-3x$. The I product is $2x$. The L product is -6. Adding them, $x^2 - 3x + 2x - 6 = x^2 - x - 6$.

Example 6.10

Multiply $-2x^2 + x - 3$ by $-x^2 - 1$.

Solution:

Step 1: Distribute the second polynomial to each term of the first polynomial:

$$(-x^2 - 1)(-2x^2 + x - 3) = (-x^2)(-2x^2 + x - 3) + (-1)(-2x^2 + x - 3)$$

Step 2: Apply the rule for multiplying a monomial by a polynomial twice:

$$(-x^2)(-2x^2 + x - 3) = 2x^4 - x^3 + 3x^2$$

and

$$(-1)(-2x^2 + x - 3) = 2x^2 - x + 3$$

Step 3: Add the two results:

$$\begin{array}{r} 2x^4 - 1x^3 + 3x^2 + 0x + 0 \\ + (0x^4 + 0x^3 + 2x^2 - 1x + 3) \\ \hline 2x^4 - 1x^3 + 5x^2 - 1x + 3 \end{array}$$

The answer is $2x^4 - x^3 + 5x^2 - x + 3$.

DIY PROBLEMS

6.15 Multiply $2x + 3$ and $3x - 2$.

6.16 Multiply $x + 3y$ and $x + 2$.

6.17 Multiply $x - 3z$ and $2x + 2z$.

6.18 Multiply $x^2 - 2x + 2$ and $x^2 + 7x + 1$.

Multiplying Polynomials with Special Products

The multiplication of certain types of polynomials results in especially simple or recognizable products. The products are referred to as special products, and often have terms that are recognizable as perfect squares or cubes.

Example 6.11

Multiply $3x + 2$ and $3x - 2$ (the product of the sum and difference of two terms).

First Solution:

Step 1: Distribute, following the same procedure as above:

$$(3x + 2)(3x - 2) = (3x)(3x - 2) + (2)(3x - 2)$$

Step 2: Distribute the monomials:

$$(3x)(3x - 2) = 9x^2 - 6x$$

and

$$(2)(3x - 2) = 6x - 4$$

Step 3: Sum the two expressions:

$$\begin{array}{r} 9x^2 - 6x + 0 \\ + (0x^2 + 6x - 4) \\ \hline 9x^2 + 0x - 4 \end{array}$$

Second Solution:

FOIL gives $9x^2 - 6x + 6x - 4 = 9x^2 - 4$.

The answer is $9x^2 - 4$. The product of the sum and difference of two terms is the difference of their squares.

Example 6.12a

Multiply $ax + by$ by $ax + by$ [that is: $(ax + by)^2$].

Solution:

Step 1: Distribute, following the same procedure as above:

$$(ax + by)(ax + by) = (ax)(ax + by) + (by)(ax + by)$$

Step 2: Distribute the monomials:

$$(ax)(ax + by) = a^2 x^2 + abxy$$

and

$$(by)(ax + by) = abx + b^2 y^2$$

Step 3: Add the two expressions:

$$\begin{array}{r} a^2x^2 + abxy + 0 \\ + (0x^2 + abxy + b^2 y^2) \\ \hline a^2x^2 + 2abxy + b^2 y^2 \end{array}$$

FOIL gives the same result.

This is a fairly common special form. The square of a binomial sum is the trinomial that is the sum of the squares of the two terms plus twice their product.

Example 6.12b

Multiply $ax - by$ by $ax - by$ [that is: $(ax - by)^2$].

Solution:

Step 1: Translate into an algebraic expression:

$$(ax - by)(ax - by)$$

Step 2: Distribute, following the same procedure as above:

$$(ax - by)(ax - by) = (ax)(ax - by) - (by)(ax - by)$$

Step 3: Distribute the monomials:

$$(ax)(ax - by) = a^2 x^2 - abxy$$

and

$$(by)(ax - by) = abx - b^2 y^2$$

Step 4: Subtract the two expressions:

$$\begin{array}{r} a^2 x^2 - abxy + 0 \\ - (0x^2 + abxy - b^2 y^2) \\ \hline a^2 x^2 - 2abxy + b^2 y^2 \end{array}$$

FOIL gives the same result.

This is a fairly common special form. The square of a binomial difference is the trinomial that is the sum of the squares of the two terms minus twice their product.

$$(a - b)^2 = a^2 - 2ab + b^2$$

DIY PROBLEMS

6.19 Multiply $2 + x$ by $2 + x$.

6.20a Multiply $ax + by$ by $ax - by$, where a and b are real numbers.

6.20b Multiply $x + 3y$ by $x + 3y$.

6.21 Multiply $a^2 + 2a + 4$ by $a - 2$.

DIVISION OF POLYNOMIALS

Dividing a Polynomial by a Monomial

Dividing a polynomial by a monomial is very similar to multiplying a polynomial by a monomial. Distribute the monomial division to the terms of the polynomial and reduce the problem to several cases of dividing one monomial by another.

Example 6.13

Divide $3x^2 - 2x$ by $4x$.

Solution:

Step 1: Write out the operation, then distribute the division into each term in the polynomial:

$$(3x^2 - 2x) \div 4x = \frac{3x^2 - 2x}{4x}$$

$$= \frac{3x^2}{4x} - \frac{2x}{4x}$$

Step 2: Using the familiar rules for exponents, this reduces to $\dfrac{3x}{4} - \dfrac{1}{2}$.

Example 6.14

Jared knows that the volume of 50 of his hearty meals is equal to the volume of one of his large stockpots. Algebraically,

$$\pi r^2 h = 50(2lds + 5ds^2) = 100lds + 250ds^2$$

Given this fact, find an expression for how many medium cartons of soup he can fill with one stockpot.

Solution:

Step 1: To find the number of medium cartons in a whole stockpot, divide the volume of the stockpot by the volume of the medium carton.

$$\# \text{ of cartons} = \pi r^2 h \div 4ds^2$$

Step 2: Substitute the given expression for volume into the equation.

$$\# \text{ of cartons} = (100lds + 250ds^2) \div 4ds^2$$

Step 3: Distribute the division into each term in the polynomial.

$$(100lds + 250ds^2) \div 4ds^2 = \frac{100lds}{4ds^2} + \frac{250ds^2}{4ds^2}$$

Step 4: Simplify the expression where possible.

$\dfrac{100lds}{4ds^2} + \dfrac{250ds^2}{4ds^2} = 25\dfrac{l}{s} + 62.5$, number of medium cartons one stockpot will fill

Dividing Polynomials

Dividing one polynomial by another presents a more complicated problem. As a general case, take the problem of

$$\frac{a_nx^n + a_{n-1}x^{n-1} + a_{n-2}x^{n-2} + \ldots + a_1x + a_0}{b_mx^m + b_{m-1}x^{m-1} + b_{m-2}x^{m-2} + \ldots + b_1x + b_0}$$

The first step is to check that the order of the dividend (numerator) is greater than or equal to the order of the divisor (denominator), that is, that $n \geq m$. If it is not, then no division can be performed. If it is, then one can apply the method of polynomial long division.

First, write the polynomials in standard long division form.

$$b_mx^m + b_{m-1}x^{m-1} + b_{m-2}x^{m-2} + \ldots + b_1x + b_0 \overline{\big)a_nx^n + a_{n-1}x^{n-1} + a_{n-2}x^{n-2} + \ldots + a_1x + a_0}$$

Then, divide the first term in the dividend by the first term in the divisor. Place the result in the quotient's spot above the term with the same order in the dividend, as in numerical long division. Then, just as with numerical long division, multiply the divisor by the new term in the quotient and subtract that product from the dividend. Bring down the next term from the dividend. Repeat the process until the order of the divisor is greater than the order of the difference. This final difference is the remainder.

Two examples will illustrate this process.

Example 6.15
Divide $x - 5$ by $x - 6$.

Solution:

Step 1: First, check the order of the polynomials—both are of the first degree. Then write in long division form:

$$1x - 6 \overline{\big)1x - 5}$$

Step 2: Divide the first term in the dividend by the first term in the divisor, then place that result in the quotient's spot:

$$1x-6\overline{)\,1x-5}^{\;1}$$

Step 3: Multiply the newest term in the quotient by the divisor, then subtract that from the dividend:

$$
\begin{array}{r}
1 \\
1x-6\overline{)\,1x-5} \\
-1x-6 \\
\hline
0x+1
\end{array}
$$

Step 4: $0x + 1$ has a lower order than $x - 6$, and there are no more terms in the dividend to bring down, which means the problem is finished. The quotient and remainder are both 1, so write the quotient plus the remainder over the divisor:

$$\frac{x-5}{x-6} = 1 + \frac{1}{x-6}$$

Example 6.16
Divide $x^2 - 5x + 6$ by $x - 2$.

Solution:

Step 1: The dividend is a second order polynomial, and the divisor is first order, so division can be performed. Write the two polynomials in long division form:

$$1x-2\overline{)\,1x^2-5x+6}$$

Step 2: Divide the first term of the dividend by the first term of the divisor. Write this result in the quotient's spot above the term of the same order in the dividend:

$$1x-2\overline{)\,1x^2-5x+6}^{\;1x}$$

Step 3: Multiply the new term in the quotient by the divisor, align the terms of this product under the like terms of the dividend, and subtract:

$$
\begin{array}{r}
1x \\
1x-2\overline{)\,1x^2-5x+6} \\
-1x^2-2x+0 \\
\hline
\end{array}
$$

Which results in:

$$
\begin{array}{r}
1x \\
1x-2\overline{)\,1x^2-5x+6} \\
-1x^2-2x+0 \\
\hline
0x^2-3x+6
\end{array}
$$

Step 4: Repeat the process and divide the first term in the difference by the first term in the divisor:

$$\frac{-3x}{1x} = -3$$

Then write -3 in the appropriate spot in the quotient, multiply the divisor by it, and subtract that from the previous difference:

$$
\begin{array}{r}
1x - 3 \\
1x - 2 \overline{)\,1x^2 - 5x + 6} \\
-\quad\ \ 1x^2 - 2x + 0 \\
\hline
0x^2 - 3x + 6 \\
-\quad\quad\ -3x + 6 \\
\hline
0x + 0
\end{array}
$$

The difference this time is zero, and there are no more terms in the dividend to bring down, so the remainder is zero, and the process is finished. The result is

$$
\frac{x^2 - 5x + 6}{x - 2} = x - 3
$$

DIY PROBLEMS

6.25 Divide $3x^2 + 4x + 6$ by $x - 7$.

6.26 Divide $x^3 + 27$ by $x + 3$.

Dividing Polynomials Using Synthetic Division

Synthetic division is a shorthand method that allows the quick division of a polynomial by a first order expression of the form $x - d$. This method drops the variables in the polynomials and uses only their coefficients to calculate the quotient. The result of a synthetic division problem is a set of coefficients that determines the quotient and the remainder of the problem. A few examples will help to explain the process.

6.9 SYNTHETIC DIVISION A shortcut method for dividing a polynomial by a first order expression of the form $x - d$.

Example 6.17
Divide polynomial $x^2 - 2x - 6$ by $x - 3$.

Solution:

Step 1: Set up the problem using the notation of synthetic division. Write d from $x - d$ in a box to the left of the coefficients of the polynomial. Here, $x - d = x - 3$, so $d = 3$. Be sure the polynomial is in standard form:

$$
\underline{3|}\quad 1\quad -2\quad -6
$$

Step 2: Bring down the first coefficient in the dividend:

$$\begin{array}{r|rrr} 3 & 1 & -2 & -6 \\ & \downarrow & & \\ \hline & 1 & & \end{array}$$

Step 3: Multiply this number by the boxed number and write it on the line under the next coefficient to the right:

$$\begin{array}{r|rrr} 3 & 1 & -2 & -6 \\ & & 3 & \\ \hline & 1 & & \end{array}$$

Step 4: Add the second column and write the sum below the line:

$$\begin{array}{r|rrr} 3 & 1 & -2 & -6 \\ & & 3 & \\ \hline & 1 & & \end{array}$$

Step 5: Multiply the sum by the boxed number and place the product in the next column to the right above the line:

$$\begin{array}{r|rrr} 3 & 1 & -2 & -6 \\ & & 3 & 3 \\ \hline & 1 & 1 & \end{array}$$

Step 6: Add up the new column and write the sum below the line:

$$\begin{array}{r|rrr} 3 & 1 & -2 & -6 \\ & & 3 & 3 \\ \hline & 1 & 1 & -3 \end{array}$$

Step 7: Read off the coefficients and write the answer as a polynomial. The easiest way to do this is to read the numbers under the line from right to left. The first number is the remainder, the second number from the right is the constant term, the third number from the right is the first order term, and so on.

Thus, the answer is:

$$\frac{x^2 - 2x - 6}{x - 3} = x + 1 - \frac{3}{x - 3}$$

Notice that the degree of the quotient polynomial is always the difference between the degrees of the dividend and the divisor.

Example 6.18
Divide $2x^4 + 3x + 2$ by $x + 2$.

Solution:

Step 1: First note that the second and third order terms of the dividend have coefficients of zero. Remember to include them when writing the problem! Also, take note of the fact that the notation of synthetic division relies on a divisor of the form $x - d$. To satisfy this requirement, rewrite $x + 2$ as $x - (-2)$. Now write the problem in the notation of synthetic division:

$$\begin{array}{r|rrrrr} -2 & 2 & 0 & 0 & 3 & 2 \end{array}$$

Step 2: Bring down the lead coefficient:

$$\begin{array}{r|rrrrr} -2 & 2 & 0 & 0 & 3 & 2 \\ \hline & 2 & & & & \end{array}$$

Step 3: Multiply the new number by the boxed number and place the product above the line in the column to the right. Add the column and write the sum below the line:

$$\begin{array}{r|rrrrr} -2 & 2 & 0 & 0 & 3 & 2 \\ & & -4 & & & \\ \hline & 2 & -4 & & & \end{array}$$

Step 4: Repeat step 3:

$$\begin{array}{r|rrrrr} -2 & 2 & 0 & 0 & 3 & 2 \\ & & -4 & 8 & & \\ \hline & 2 & -4 & 8 & & \end{array}$$

Step 5: Repeat step 3:

$$\begin{array}{r|rrrrr} -2 & 2 & 0 & 0 & 3 & 2 \\ & & -4 & 8 & -16 & \\ \hline & 2 & -4 & 8 & -13 & \end{array}$$

Step 6: Repeat step 3:

$$\begin{array}{r|rrrrr} -2 & 2 & 0 & 0 & 3 & 2 \\ & & -4 & 8 & -16 & 26 \\ \hline & 2 & -4 & 8 & -13 & 28 \end{array}$$

Step 7: Read off the coefficients from right to left, remembering that the rightmost number represents the remainder. Thus, the answer is:

$$\frac{2x^4 + 3x + 2}{x + 2} = 2x^3 - 4x^2 + 8x - 13 + \frac{28}{x + 2}$$

DIY PROBLEMS

6.27 Divide $-3x^4 + x^3 - 5x^2 + 16x$ by $x - 2$.

6.28 Divide $x^4 - b^4$ by $x - b$.

SOLUTIONS TO DIY PROBLEMS

6.1 Simplify: $(xy^3)(x^3y)$

Solution:
Use the Commutative and Associative Properties of Multiplication to rearrange and group factors.

$$(xy^3)(x^3y) = (x^1 x^3)(y^3 y) = (x^{1+3})(y^{3+1}) = x^4y^4$$

6.2 Simplify: $(9xy^4)(-3x^2y^2)$

Solution:

$$(9xy^4)(-3x^2y^2) = (9)(-3)(x^1 x^2)(y^4 y^2) = -27(x^{1+2})(y^{4+2}) = -27x^3y^6$$

6.3 Multiply $\sqrt[3]{3w}\, x^2$ by $\dfrac{w}{x^{-3}}$.

Solution:
Rewrite the radical expression using exponents:

$$\sqrt[3]{3w}\, x^2 = 3^{\frac{1}{3}} w^{\frac{1}{3}} x^2$$

Multiply:

$$\left(\frac{w}{x^{-3}}\right)\left(3^{\frac{1}{3}} w^{\frac{1}{3}} x^2\right) = 3^{\frac{1}{3}}\left(w \cdot w^{\frac{1}{3}}\right)\left(\frac{x^2}{x^{-3}}\right)$$

Add and subtract the exponents as necessary:

$$3^{\frac{1}{3}}\left(w^{1+\frac{1}{3}}\right)\left(x^{2-(-3)}\right) = 3^{\frac{1}{3}} w^{\frac{4}{3}} x^5$$

6.4 Simplify: $\dfrac{9x^5}{12x^8}$

Solution:
Write $\dfrac{9}{12}$ in simplest form. Subtract the exponents on like bases.

$$\frac{9x^5}{12x^8} = \frac{3x^{5-8}}{4} = \frac{3x^{-3}}{4} = \frac{3}{4x^3}$$

6.5 Simplify: $\dfrac{y^{-2}}{y^6}$

Solution:

$$\frac{y^{-2}}{y^6} = \frac{y^{-2-6}}{1} = y^{-8} = \frac{1}{y^8}$$

6.6 Divide $\dfrac{x^2}{y^{-6}}$ by $\dfrac{x^{\frac{2}{3}}}{y^4}$.

Solution:
Because dividing by a fraction is the same as multiplying by its inverse, write:

$$\frac{x^2}{y^{-6}} \div \frac{x^{\frac{2}{3}}}{y^4} = \left(\frac{x^2}{y^{-6}}\right)\left(\frac{y^4}{x^{\frac{2}{3}}}\right)$$

Group like variables and simplify:

$$\left(\frac{y^4}{y^{-6}}\right)\left(\frac{x^2}{x^{\frac{2}{3}}}\right) = y^{4-(-6)}x^{2-\frac{2}{3}} = y^{10}x^{\frac{4}{3}}$$

6.7 Evaluate the polynomial $x^3 - 3x^2y + 3xy^2 - y^3$ for $y = 3$.

Solution:
Substitute 3 for every y in the equation:

$$x^3 - 3x^2y + 3xy^2 - y^3 = x^3 - 3x^2 \cdot 3 + 3x \cdot 3^2 - 3^3 = x^3 - 9x^2 + 27x - 27$$

6.8a Evaluate the polynomial $x^2 + 2\sqrt{3}x - 9$ for $x = \sqrt{3}$.

Solution:
Substitute $\sqrt{3}$ for every x in the equation:

$$x^2 + 2\sqrt{3}x - 9 = \left(\sqrt{3}\right)^2 + 2\sqrt{3}\sqrt{3} - 9 = 3 + 2 \cdot 3 - 9 = 0$$

6.8b Evaluate the polynomial $x^2 + 2\sqrt{3}x - 9$ for $x = -2\sqrt{3}$.

Solution:
Substitute $-2\sqrt{3}$ in for every x:

$$x^2 + 2\sqrt{3}x - 9 = \left(-2\sqrt{3}\right)^2 + \left(2\sqrt{3}\right)\left(-2\sqrt{3}\right) - 9 = 12 - 12 - 9 = -9$$

6.9 Subtract $2x^2 - 3x$ from $4x^2 + 5x$.

Solution:

$$4x^2 + 5x - (2x^2 - 3x) = 4x^2 + 5x + (-2x^2 + 3x)$$

Combine like terms.

$$2x^2 + 8x$$

6.10 Subtract $x^3 - 9x^2 + 2$ from $\sqrt{2}x^3 - x + 2$.

Solution:
Rewrite each of the polynomials so that each has the same number of terms:

$x^3 - 9x^2 + 2 = 1x^3 - 9x^2 + 0x + 2$ and $\sqrt{2}x^3 - x + 2 = \sqrt{2}x^3 + 0x^2 - 1x + 2$

Subtract:

$$
\begin{array}{r}
\sqrt{2}x^3 + 0x^2 - 1x + 2 \\
- \ (1x^3 - 9x^2 + 0x + 2) \\
\hline
\left(\sqrt{2} - 1\right)x^3 + 9x^2 - 1x + 0
\end{array}
$$

The difference is:

$$\left(\sqrt{2} - 1\right)x^3 + 9x^2 - x$$

6.11 Subtract $-3x + 14$ from $x^2 - 1$.

Solution:
Rewrite each of the polynomials so that each has like terms, and subtract:

$$\begin{array}{r} 1x^2 + 0x - 1 \\ -\ (0x^2 - 3x + 14) \\ \hline 1x^2 + 3x - 15 \end{array}$$

Therefore, the difference is: $x^2 + 3x - 15$.

6.12 Multiply $3x + 2$ by 4.

Solution:
Distribute the 4 to each term of the polynomial.

$$(4)(3x) + (4)(2) = 12x + 8$$

6.13 Multiply $9x^2 + 3x - 7$ by $2x$.

Solution:
Distribute the monomial to each term of the polynomial:

$$(9x^2 + 3x - 7)(2x) = (9x^2)(2x) + (3x)(2x) + (-7)(2x)$$

Simplify the terms:

$$(9x^2)(2x) + (3x)(2x) + (-7)(2x) = 18x^3 + 6x^2 - 14x$$

6.14 Multiply $x^3 - 2x - 1$ by $\dfrac{x^4}{2}$.

Solution:
Distribute the monomial to each term of the polynomial:

$$(x^3 - 2x - 1)\left(\frac{x^4}{2}\right) = (x^3)\left(\frac{x^4}{2}\right) + (-2x)\left(\frac{x^4}{2}\right) + (-1)\left(\frac{x^4}{2}\right)$$

Simplify the terms:

$$(x^3)\left(\frac{x^4}{2}\right) + (-2x)\left(\frac{x^4}{2}\right) + (-1)\left(\frac{x^4}{2}\right) = \frac{x^7}{2} - x^5 - \frac{x^4}{2}$$

6.15 Multiply $2x + 3$ and $3x - 2$

Solution:
Using the FOIL method. The F product is $6x^2$. The O product is $-4x$. The I product is $9x$. The L product is -6. Adding them, $6x^2 - 4x + 9x - 6 = 6x^2 + 5x - 6$.

6.16 Multiply $x + 3y$ and $x + 2$

Solution:
Using the FOIL method. The F product Is x^2. The O product is $2x$. The I product Is $3xy$. The L product is $6y$.
Adding them,

$$x^2 + 2x + 3xy + 6y$$

6.17 Multiply $x - 3z$ by $2x + 2z$.

First Solution:
Distribute the second polynomial to each term of the first polynomial:

$$(x - 3z)(2x + 2z) = (x)(2x + 2z) + (-3z)(2x + 2z)$$

Distribute the monomials, and then add like terms:

$$(2x^2 + 2xz) + (-6xz - 6z^2) = 2x^2 - 4xz - 6z^2$$

Second Solution:
FOIL gives $2x^2 - 6xz + 2xz - 6z^2 = 2x^2 - 4xz - 6z^2$.

6.18 Multiply $x^2 - 2x + 2$ and $x^2 + 7x + 1$.

Solution:
Distribute the second polynomial to each term of the first polynomial:

$$(x^2 - 2x + 2)(x^2 + 7x + 1) = (x^2)(x^2 + 7x + 1) + (-2x)(x^2 + 7x + 1) + (2)(x^2 + 7x + 1)$$

Distribute the monomials:

$$(x^2)(x^2 + 7x + 1) = 1x^4 + 7x^3 + 1x^2 + 0x + 0$$

$$(-2x)(x^2 + 7x + 1) = 0x^4 - 2x^3 - 14x^2 - 2x + 0$$

$$(2)(x^2 + 7x + 1) = 0x^4 + 0x^3 + 2x^2 + 14x + 2$$

Add the three results together to get the final polynomial:

$$
\begin{array}{r}
1x^4 + 7x^3 + 1x^2 + 0x + 0 \\
0x^4 - 2x^3 - 14x^2 - 2x + 0 \\
+ \quad 0x^4 + 0x^3 + 2x^2 + 14x + 2 \\
\hline
1x^4 + 5x^3 - 11x^2 + 12x + 2
\end{array}
$$

Thus the product is: $x^4 + 5x^3 - 11x^2 + 12x + 2$.

6.19 Multiply $2 + x$ by $2 + x$

Solution:

$$(2 + x)(2 + x) = 4 + 2x + 2x + x^2 = 4 + 4x + x^2 = x^2 + 4x + 4$$

6.20a Multiply $ax + by$ by $ax - by$, where a and b are real numbers.

Solution:
Distribute one polynomial to the terms of the other:

$$(ax + by)(ax - by) = (ax)(ax - by) + (by)(ax - by)$$

Distribute the monomials. The first expression is:

$$(ax)(ax - by) = a^2x^2 - abxy$$

And the second expression is:

$$(by)(ax - by) = abxy - b^2y^2$$

Add the two expressions:

$$a^2x^2 - abxy + abxy - b^2y^2 = a^2x^2 - b^2y^2$$

6.20b Multiply $x + 3y$ by $x + 3y$.

Solution:
The result can be found directly by using the conclusion at the end of Example 6.12a: the square of a binomial sum is the trinomial that is the sum of the squares of the two terms plus twice their product. Otherwise proceed as above.

Step 1: To find $(x + 3y)^2$, distribute the second polynomial to each term of the first polynomial:

$$(x + 3y)(x + 3y) = (x)(x + 3y) + (3y)(x + 3y)$$

Step 2: Distribute the monomials:

$$(x)(x + 3y) = x^2 + 3xy \text{ and } (3y)(x + 3y) = 3xy + 3^2 y^2$$

Step 3: Add the two expressions:
$$\begin{array}{r} x^2 + 3xy + 0 \\ + \ (0x^2 + 3xy + 3^2 y^2) \\ \hline x^2 + 2 \cdot 3xy + 3^2 y^2 = x^2 + 6xy + 9y^2 \end{array}$$

This is the sum of the squares of the two terms plus twice their product. FOIL gives the same result.

6.21 Multiply $a^2 + 2a + 4$ by $a - 2$.

Solution:
Distribute one polynomial to the terms of the other:

$$(a - 2)(a^2 + 2a + 4) = (a)(a^2 + 2a + 4) + (-2)(a^2 + 2a + 4)$$

Distribute the monomials. The first expression yields:

$$(a)(a^2 + 2a + 4) = a^3 + 2a^2 + 4a$$

And the second expression yields:

$$(-2)(a^2 + 2a + 4) = -2a^2 - 4a - 8$$

Summing the two expressions yields:

$$a^3 + 2a^2 + 4a - 2a^2 - 4a - 8 = a^3 - 8$$

6.22 Divide $4x^2 - 2x$ by $2x$

Solution:
Step 1: Write out the operation, then distribute the division into each term in the polynomial:

$$(4x^2 - 2x) \div 2x = \frac{4x^2 - 2x}{2x} = \frac{4x^2}{2x} - \frac{2x}{2x}$$

Step 2 : Using the familiar rules for exponents, this reduces to $2x - 1$.

6.23 Divide $6x^4 + 10x^3$ by $2x$.

Solution:
Distribute the division:

$$6x^4 + 10x^3 \div 2x = \frac{6x^4}{2x} + \frac{10x^3}{2x}$$

Simplify:

$$\frac{6x^4}{2x} + \frac{10x^3}{2x} = 3x^3 + 5x^2$$

6.24 Divide $3x^6 y^2 + 5x^3 y^3 - 2xy^4$ by $-7xy^2$.

Solution:
Distribute the division:

$$(3x^6y^2 + 5x^3 y^3 - 2xy^4) \div (-7xy^2) = \frac{3x^6y^2}{-7xy^2} + \frac{5x^3y^3}{-7xy^2} - \frac{2xy^4}{-7xy^2}$$

Simplify:

$$-\frac{3}{7}x^{6-1}y^{2-2} - \frac{5}{7}x^{3-1}y^{3-2} + \frac{2}{7}x^{1-1}y^{4-2}$$

$$= -\frac{3}{7}x^5 y^0 - \frac{5}{7}x^2 y^1 + \frac{2}{7}x^0 y$$

$$= -\frac{3}{7}x^5 - \frac{5}{7}x^2 y + \frac{2}{7}y^2$$

6.25 Divide $3x^2 + 4x + 6$ by $x - 7$.

Solution:
Step 1: Write the problem in the notation of long division:

$$x - 7 \overline{)3x^2 + 4x + 6}$$

Step 2: Divide the highest term of the dividend by the highest term of the divisor and place that in the quotient:

$$\begin{array}{r} 3x \\ x - 7 \overline{)3x^2 + 4x + 6} \end{array}$$

Step 3: Multiply the new quotient term by the divisor and subtract from the dividend. Then bring down the next term from the dividend:

$$\begin{array}{r} 3x \\ x - 7 \overline{)3x^2 + 4x + 6} \\ - \underline{3x^2 - 21x + 0} \\ 0x^2 + 25x + 6 \end{array}$$

Step 4: Repeat Step 3:

$$\begin{array}{r} 3x + 25 \\ x - 7 \overline{)3x^2 + 4x + 6} \\ - \underline{3x^2 - 21x + 0} \\ 0x^2 + 25x + 6 \\ - \underline{25x - 175} \\ 181 \end{array}$$

Thus the answer is: $3x + 25 + \dfrac{181}{x - 7}$.

6.26 Divide $x^3 + 27$ by $x + 3$.

Solution:

Step 1: Fill in the missing powers of x with coefficient zero and write in long division form:

$$x+3\overline{)1x^3 + 0x^2 + 0x + 27}$$

Step 2: Divide the highest term of the dividend by the highest term of the divisor and place the result in the quotient:

$$\begin{array}{r} 1x^2 \\ x+3\overline{)1x^3 + 0x^2 + 0x + 27} \end{array}$$

Step 3: Multiply the new quotient term by the divisor and subtract from the dividend. Then bring down the next term from the dividend:

$$\begin{array}{r} 1x^2 \\ x+3\overline{)1x^3 + 0x^2 + 0x + 27} \\ -\underline{1x^3 + 3x^2 } \\ 0x^3 - 3x^2 + 0x \end{array}$$

Step 4: Repeat Step 3:

$$\begin{array}{r} 1x^2 - 3x \\ x+3\overline{)1x^3 + 0x^2 + 0x + 27} \\ -\underline{1x^3 + 3x^2 } \\ 0x^3 - 3x^2 + 0x \\ -\underline{-3x^2 - 9x } \\ 0x^2 + 9x + 27 \end{array}$$

Step 5: Repeat Step 3:

$$\begin{array}{r} 1x^2 - 3x + 9 \\ x+3\overline{)1x^3 + 0x^2 + 0x + 27} \\ -\underline{1x^3 + 3x^2 } \\ 0x^3 - 3x^2 + 0x \\ -\underline{-3x^2 - 9x } \\ 0x^2 + 9x + 27 \\ -\underline{9x + 27} \\ 0x + 0 \end{array}$$

Thus the quotient is: $x^2 - 3x + 9$.

6.27 Divide $-3x^4 + x^3 - 5x^2 + 16x$ by $x - 2$.

Solution:

Step 1: Write the coefficients in the notation of synthetic division:

$\underline{2|}$ -3 1 -5 16 0

Step 2: Bring the first coefficient down under the line:

$$\underline{2|} \quad -3 \quad 1 \quad -5 \quad 16 \quad 0$$

$$\quad\quad -3$$

Step 3: Multiply the number below the line by the number in the box and place above the line in the column to the right. Add the column and put the sum below the line:

$$\underline{2|} \quad -3 \quad 1 \quad -5 \quad 16 \quad 0$$

$$\quad\quad\quad\quad -6$$
$$\overline{\quad -3 \quad -5}$$

Step 4: Repeat Step 3:

$$\underline{2|} \quad -3 \quad 1 \quad -5 \quad 16 \quad 0$$

$$\quad\quad\quad\quad -6 \quad -10$$
$$\overline{\quad -3 \quad -5 \quad -15}$$

Step 5: Repeat Step 3:

$$\underline{2|} \quad -3 \quad 1 \quad -5 \quad 16 \quad 0$$

$$\quad\quad\quad\quad -6 \quad -10 \quad -30$$
$$\overline{\quad -3 \quad -5 \quad -15 \quad -14}$$

Step 6: Repeat Step 3:

$$\underline{2|} \quad -3 \quad 1 \quad -5 \quad 16 \quad 0$$

$$\quad\quad\quad\quad -6 \quad -10 \quad -30 \quad -28$$
$$\overline{\quad -3 \quad -5 \quad -15 \quad -14 \quad -28}$$

The answer is: $-3x^3 - 5x^2 - 15x - 14 - \dfrac{28}{x-2}$

6.28 Divide $x^4 - b^4$ by $x - b$.

Solution:
Step 1: Write out the problem. Notice that you need to supply terms for the first, second, and third powers of x:

$$\underline{b|} \quad 1 \quad 0 \quad 0 \quad 0 \quad -b^4$$

Step 2: Bring down the first coefficient:

$$\underline{b|} \quad 1 \quad 0 \quad 0 \quad 0 \quad -b^4$$

$$\quad 1$$

Step 3: Multiply the number below the line by the number in the box and place above the line in the column to the right. Add the column and put the sum below the line:

$$\underline{b|} \quad 1 \quad 0 \quad 0 \quad 0 \quad b^4$$

$$\quad\quad\quad b$$
$$\overline{\quad 1 \quad b}$$

Step 4: Repeat Step 3:

$$\begin{array}{c|ccccc} \underline{b|} & 1 & 0 & 0 & 0 & b^4 \\ & & b & b^2 & & \\ \hline & 1 & b & b^2 & & \end{array}$$

Step 5: Repeat Step 3:

$$\begin{array}{c|ccccc} \underline{b|} & 1 & 0 & 0 & 0 & b^4 \\ & & b & b^2 & b^3 & \\ \hline & 1 & b & b^2 & b^3 & \end{array}$$

Step 6: Repeat Step 3:

$$\begin{array}{c|ccccc} \underline{b|} & 1 & 0 & 0 & 0 & b^4 \\ & & b & b^2 & b^3 & -b^4 \\ \hline & 1 & b & b^2 & b^3 & 0 \end{array}$$

Therefore, the answer is: $x^3 + bx^2 + b^2x + b^3$.

END OF CHAPTER REVIEW QUESTIONS

6.1 Simplify 5^{-3}.

6.2 Simplify $\dfrac{2}{x^{-4}}$.

6.3 Simplify $\dfrac{1}{2x^0}$.

6.4 Simplify $(3m^2n^4)(-2mn^6)$.

6.5 Simplify $(4x^6y^4)(-3x^{-1}y^2)$.

6.6 Simplify $(x^2y^{-4})^2$.

6.7 Simplify $\left(\dfrac{2}{3}\right)^3$.

6.8 Simplify $\dfrac{x^3y}{xy^4}$.

6.9 Simplify $\dfrac{2x^{-3}}{6x^{-2}}$.

6.10 Write .000057 in scientific notation.

6.11 Write 2.72 × 10^{-3} in decimal notation.

6.12 Evaluate the polynomial: 2x^3 − 5x + 11 for x = −2.

6.13 Evaluate the polynomial: 15 + 2x − x^2 for x = 5.

6.14 Perform the indicated operation and simplify: (2x^2 − 5x + 7) + (3x^2 − 11x − 17).

6.15 Perform the indicated operation and simplify: (3x^3 − x + 8) − (x^3 − 2x^2 − 5x − 11).

6.16 Perform the indicated operation and simplify: $2x(x - 3)$.

6.17 Perform the indicated operation and simplify: $4x(x^2 - 3x + 5)$.

6.18 Perform the indicated operation and simplify: $-4ab(5a - 3b)$.

6.19 Perform the indicated operation and simplify: $4a^3 + 2a(a^2 - 5a - 3)$.

6.20 Perform the indicated operation and simplify: $(2x - 5)(x + 3)$.

6.21 Simplify $(x - 2y)(x + 5y)$.

6.22 Perform the indicated operation and simplify: $(x^2 + 2)(x^2 - x - 3)$.

6.23 Perform the indicated operation and simplify: $(3x - 5)(3x + 5)$.

6.24 Perform the indicated operation and simplify: $(x^2 - 3)(x^2 - 3)$.

6.25 Perform the indicated operation and simplify: $y^2 - (x - y)^2$.

6.26 Divide: $\dfrac{5m^4 n^2}{25mn^2}$.

6.27 Divide: $\dfrac{4m^3 n^5 - 20m^2 n^2}{4m^2 n^2}$.

6.28 Divide: $\dfrac{3pq^3 + 18p^2q^2 - pq}{3pq}$.

6.29 Divide: $(x^2 + 3x - 40) \div (x - 5)$.

6.30 Divide: $(x^2 + 5x - 7) \div (x + 3)$.

6.31 The following polynomial describes the height of an object t seconds after being thrown straight up with an initial velocity of 96 feet per second: $H(t) = -16t^2 + 96t$. Find the height of the object after 5 seconds.

6.32 The demand for a particular item is given by $x = 100 - p$, where p is the price of the product. Revenue can be found by taking the number of items sold times the price of each item. Find the revenue. Then find the revenue if the particular item sold for $28.

REFERENCES

Burzynski, D., & Ellis, W. (2009). Factoring polynomials: Factoring two special products. Retrieved from http://cnx.org/content/m21903/latest/

Cajori, F., & Odell, L. R. (1917). *Elementary algebra*. New York, NY: Macmillan.

Rietz, H. L., & Crathorne, A. R. (1909). *College algebra*. New York, NY: Henry Holt and Company.

Factoring Polynomials

Fatima is the veterinarian at an animal clinic. Her clinic specializes in the treatment and rehabilitation of wild animals. Although her clinic regularly treats rabbits, raccoons, foxes, turtles, songbirds, and hawks, she recently received an unusual animal. A severe windstorm knocked a screech owl's nest out of a tree, and the owl with it. A family surveying the damage to their property the next morning found the owl dragging its wing in their yard, and brought it to Fatima's animal clinic.

After setting the screech owl's wing and immobilizing it with a splint, Fatima set the owl up in its temporary home, a nest box inside a small cage in her clinic. Over the course of the next several weeks, the owl's wing began to heal nicely. Before it could be released, however, the owl needed to spend two weeks regaining the strength in its newly healed wing and relearning how to fly. Never having cared for owls before, Fatima set about planning and constructing a new, outdoor flight cage for the bird.

Once Fatima and her assistants erected a simple, pavilionlike structure with a roof and no walls, she began thinking about what the sides should be made of. Flight cages are sometimes constructed with sides made out of a thick, mesh cloth stretched between the cage's supports. Since the recuperating bird was weak and lacked control, the cloth sides in the cage would allow it to have the occasional accident as it relearned how to fly without injuring itself again.

Fatima wanted each side of the flight cage to be a square with total area of 225 square feet, but she also knew that she must reinforce the sides of each square by folding them over, much like the hems in clothing. If she didn't do this, the cloth might tear under its own weight. She decided to fold over the top and bottom edges by one foot, and both of the other sides by half a foot. With these specifications in mind, Fatima is ready to place an order for the flight cage's cloth.

QUESTIONS TO CONSIDER

1. Given that each square has a hem of one foot on its top and bottom edges, and a hem of half a foot on each of its sides, what are the dimensions of the initial piece of cloth?

2. What is the area of each of the initial pieces of cloth?

3. Since Fatima wants the flight cage to have four identical sides, how much cloth should she order?

KEY TERMS

COMMON FACTORS

Factoring a Monomial from a Polynomial

If a polynomial is a product of polynomials, it is often useful to factor it. The simplest kind of factor to look for is a monomial, which will be a factor of each term of the polynomial.

Greatest Common Factor

Before diving into factoring polynomials, it is important to understand greatest common factors. Recall that the **greatest common factor** (GCF) of an expression is the product of all the common factors of the terms in the expression. If the GCF of all the terms of a polynomial is nontrivial, that is, not 1, then it can be factored out of the polynomial. Two examples will illustrate this process.

Example 7.1

Factor the monomial from $3x^4 + x^2$.

Solution:

Step 1: First find the greatest common factor of the terms in the polynomial. Remember that positive exponents indicate repeated multiplication, so

$3x^4 = 3 \cdot x \cdot x \cdot x \cdot x$

and

$x^2 = x \cdot x$.

Step 2: Each of the above monomials has at least two factors of x, so the GCF is x^2. Now factor the GCF out of the polynomial.

$3x^4 + x^2 = x^2(3x^2 + 1)$

Example 7.2

Factor the monomial from the polynomial $4x^3 - 12x^2 - 6x$.

Solution:

Step 1: Find the GCF of the terms in the polynomial. Examining each term, observe that

$4x^3 = 2 \cdot 2 \cdot x \cdot x \cdot x,$
$-12x^2 = -2 \cdot 2 \cdot 3 \cdot x \cdot x,$
and
$-6x = -2 \cdot 3 \cdot x.$

Step 2: The GCF of these three monomials is $2x$, so factor that out of the polynomial.

$4x^3 - 12x^2 - 6x = 2x(2x^2 - 6x - 3)$

DIY PROBLEMS

7.1 Factor the monomial from $4x^3 + 4x$.

7.2 Factor the monomial from $2x^2y - 10xy - 5xy^2$.

7.3 Factor the monomial from $12x^4 - 108x^2$.

Factoring by Grouping

It is sometimes possible to factor a polynomial of order 3 or greater using the method of factoring by grouping. This method separates a polynomial into the sum of two or more polynomials, and then finds a GCF of each. After the GCF has been factored out of each of the new polynomials, the remaining polynomials should be identical. Then, factoring the identical polynomial multiplies the sum of the GCFs.

Example 7.3

Factor $x^3 - 2x^2 + x - 2$.

Solution:

Step 1: Group the polynomial into a sum of polynomials.

$$x^3 - 2x^2 + x - 2 = (x^3 - 2x^2) + (x - 2)$$

Step 2: Find a GCF of each new polynomial. In the first, the factors of the terms are

$$x^3 = x \cdot x \cdot x$$

and

$$2x^2 = 2 \cdot x \cdot x.$$

The GCF of these two terms is x^2. In the second polynomial, the factors of the terms are x and 2, so the GCF is 1.

Step 3: Factor each GCF out of its respective polynomial.

$$(x^3 - 2x^2) + (x - 2) = x^2(x - 2) + 1(x - 2)$$

Step 4: Use the distributive property of multiplication to factor the common polynomial out of each term.

$$x^2(x - 2) + 1(x - 2) = (x^2 + 1)(x - 2)$$

Example 7.4

Factor $6x^4 + 18x^3 - 12x^2 - 36x$.

Solution:

Step 1: Group the polynomial into a sum of polynomials.

$$6x^4 + 18x^3 - 12x^2 - 36x = (6x^4 + 18x^3) + (-12x^2 - 36x)$$

Step 2: Find the GCF of each new polynomial. In the first, the factors of the terms are

$$6x^4 = 2 \cdot 3 \cdot x \cdot x \cdot x \cdot x$$

and

$$18x^3 = 2 \cdot 3 \cdot 3 \cdot x \cdot x \cdot x.$$

The greatest common factor is $6x^3$.

In the second polynomial, the factors of the terms are

$$-12x^2 = -2 \cdot 2 \cdot 3 \cdot x \cdot x$$

and

$$-36x = -2 \cdot 2 \cdot 3 \cdot 3 \cdot x.$$

The greatest common factor is $-12x$.

Step 3: Factor each GCF out of its respective polynomial.

$$(6x^4 + 18x^3) + (-12x^2 - 36x) = 6x^3(x+3) - 12x^2(x+3)$$

Step 4: Use the Distributive Law of Multiplication to factor out the common polynomial factor.

$$6x^3(x+3) - 12x^2(x+3) = (6x^3 - 12x^2)(x+3)$$

Step 5: For the sake of completeness, factor the $6x^2$ out of the first factor to get

$$6x^2(x-2)(x+3).$$

DIY PROBLEMS

7.4 Factor $4x(x - 2) - 7(x - 2)$.

7.5 Factor $-12x^5 + 3x^3 + 4x^2 - 1$ by grouping.

7.6 Factor $3x^4 + x^3 - 9x^2 - 3x$ by grouping.

FACTORING SECOND-DEGREE TRINOMIALS WITH LEADING COEFFICIENT OF 1

Factoring a Trinomial in the Form $x^2 + bx + c$

The goal in factoring a second-degree trinomial is to write it as the product of two binomials. Since the x^2 term in the trinomial has coefficient 1, so do the x terms in each binomial. To complete the binomials, one must find two numbers whose sum is b and whose product is c. More mathematically, the binomials must have constant terms d and f such that $d + f = b$ and $df = c$.

So, rewrite $x^2 + bx + c$ as $(x + d)(x + f) = x + (d + f)x + df$ and find d and f. Notice that b, c, d, and f may each be either positive or negative.

First set up the binomial product framework: $(x)(x)$, omitting the $+$ and/or $-$ signs and d and f.

Consider that if c is positive both operators must be the same, since a positive product requires factors of the same sign. Therefore, d and f will have the same sign, and their sum is b.

If c is negative, a little more thought is required to decide which of the possible factors of c yields the correct value for b.

This method of factoring is most useful for trinomials with relatively small, rational coefficients. It can also be extended easily to trinomials of the form $-x^2 + bx + c$, since these can immediately be written as $-(x^2 - bx - c)$.

Example 7.5

Factor $x^2 + 3x + 2$.

Solution:

Step 1: Choose two numbers whose product is 2. The only choice is the pair 2 and 1 (say $d = 1$, and $f = 2$). Write the binomial product in the following form:
$(x \quad 1)(x \quad 2)$.

Step 2: Fill in the correct choice of $+$ and/or $-$ to achieve $d + f = b = 3$. Since $c = 2 > 0$, both signs must be the same, and since $b = 3 > 0$, the signs must be positive, so
$(x + 1)(x + 2)$
since $1 \cdot 2 = 2$ and $1 + 2 = 3$.

Example 7.6

Factor $x^2 + x - 20$.

Solution:

Step 1: Choose two numbers whose product is 20. Take 2 and 10 and write the binomials:
$(x \quad 2)(x \quad 10)$.

Step 2: Fill in the binomials with the correct combination of $+$ and $-$ to achieve $b = 1$. In this case, $c = -20$, so one must be a plus sign and the other a minus sign. Unfortunately, neither $(x - 2)(x + 10)$ nor $(x + 2)(x - 10)$ gives the correct result. The former results in $b = 8$ and the latter in $b = -8$. Clearly, 2 and 10 were poor choices.

Step 3: Choose two new numbers with a product of 20. Notice that since c is negative, the numbers will have opposite signs, and since $b = 1$, 4 and 5 are a better choice. Write the binomials with no operators: $(x \quad 4)(x \quad 5)$.

Step 4: Fill in the blanks with $+$ and $-$ signs that yield $c = -20$ and $b = 1$. The correct binomials are $(x - 4)(x + 5)$.

DIY PROBLEMS

7.7 Factor $x^2 + 5x + 6$.

7.8 Factor $x^2 + 17x + 60$.

7.9 Factor $x^2 - 4x + 4$.

7.10 Factor $x^2 - 2x - 48$.

Factoring Completely

Occasionally a trinomial of degree greater than 2 can be reduced to a second-degree polynomial through the removal of a common factor. In this case, the first step in factoring is to remove the common factor from the terms, and then to factor the resulting trinomial.

Example 7.7
Completely factor the polynomial $3x^3 + 24x^2 + 45x$.

Solution:

Step 1: Find the GCF of the three terms and factor it out of the trinomial. The GCF in this case is $3x$, and factoring it out results in $3x(x^2 + 8x + 15)$.

Step 2: Choose two numbers that have a product of 15 and a sum of 8. Write $3x(x\ 3)(x\ 5)$.

Step 3: Choose the appropriate operations in each binomial that result in $b = 8$ and $c = 15$. Both operations must be addition, so the answer is $3x(x + 3)(x + 5)$.

Example 7.8
Factor $-6x^6 + 18x^5 + 168x^4$ completely.

Solution:

Step 1: Find the GCF of the three terms and factor it out of the polynomial. The GCF here is $-6x^4$, and factoring it out results in

$-6x^4(x^2 - 3x - 28)$.

Step 2: Since c is negative, choose two numbers that have a product of 28 and differ by 3; 4 and 7 are the appropriate numbers in this case. Write the factors without operators:

$-6x^4(x\ 4)(x\ 7)$.

Step 3: Choose the appropriate operations in each binomial that result in $b = -3$ and $c = -28$. This results in $-6x^4(x + 4)(x - 7)$.

DIY PROBLEMS

7.11 Factor $2x^2 + 6x + 4$ completely.

7.12 Factor $3x^4 + 6x^3 - 72x^2$ completely.

7.13 Factor $-7x^7 - 84x^6 - 245x^5$ completely.

FACTORING SECOND-DEGREE TRINOMIALS WITH LEADING COEFFICIENT GREATER THAN 1

Factoring a Trinomial in the Form $ax^2 + bx + c$

The form $ax^2 + bx + c$ indicates a second-degree trinomial that may not have a leading coefficient of 1. Factoring these polynomials is similar to factoring those with leading coefficient 1, except that the constants a and c are both products.

Trial Method

Many second-degree trinomials are simple enough that they can be solved using the **trial method.** The following examples will illustrate the process.

7.2 TRIAL METHOD A method of factoring polynomials through practice and educated guesses.

Example 7.9
Factor $2x^2 - 3x + 1$.

Solution:

Step 1: Find the GCF of the trinomial. It is 1, so proceed to the next step.

Step 2: Find the factors of a and c. In this case, a has factors 1 and 2, and the only factor c has is 1.

Step 3: Starting with the framework $(x)(x)$, place the chosen factors of a in front of the variables. Write $(1x\ )(2x\ )$.

Step 4: Repeat the above process with the factors of c. They are both 1, so there is only one possibility: $(1x\ 1)(2x\ 1)$.

Step 5: Fill in the blanks with addition or subtraction symbols in such a way that the coefficients of the x terms produced by multiplying the binomials together will add up to b. Since c is positive and b is negative, the only choice is $(1x - 1)(2x - 1) = (x - 1)(2x - 1)$.

Use FOIL to check that this product yields the original expression:
$x(2x) - 1x - 1(2x) + (-1)(-1) = 2x^2 - 3x + 1$.

Example 7.10

Factor $8x^3 - 22x^2 - 30x$.

Solution:

Step 1: Find the GCF of the trinomial. In this case the GCF is $2x$, so write $2x(4x^2 - 11x - 15)$.

Step 2: Find the factors of a and c. There are two pairs of factors for $a = 4$: 4 and 1, and 2 and 2. There are also two pairs of factors for $c = 15$: 1 and 15, and 3 and 5.

Step 3: Starting with the framework $2x(x\ )(x\ )$ choose a pair of factors for a and place them in front of the x terms in the framework. Use 4 and 1 to write $2x(4x\ )(1x\ )$.

Step 4: Where should the factors of 15 be placed? Taking an educated guess, try using 3 and 5 as the factors of 15 and place them like this: $2x(4x\ 5)(1x\ 3)$.

Step 5: Now put plus and minus signs in the appropriate places. The two components of b are $4 \cdot 3 = 12$ and $5 \cdot 1 = 5$. Placing the minus sign in front of the 3 and the plus sign in front of the 5 results in 12 being negative, 5 being positive, and their sum being -7. So the answer is $2x(4x + 5)(1x - 3)$.

DIY PROBLEMS

7.14 Factor $-3x^3y + 7x^2y + 6xy$.

7.15 Factor $12x^3 + 24x^2 + 9x$.

A-C Method

7.3 A-C METHOD A method of factoring a second-degree trinomial that uses the product of the constants a and c. The two factors of $a \times c$ that have a sum or difference of b are used to rewrite the trinomial, which is then factored by grouping.

The **A-C method** of factoring is a somewhat more methodical way to factor trinomials.

The A-C method is useful because it immediately makes clear whether the trinomial can be factored at all, and provides all the possible factors if it is factorable.

The A-C method poses this question: Are there two factors of ac that have a sum or difference that is the absolute value of b? If ac is positive, then $|b|$ should be the sum of two of its factors, and if ac is negative, then $|b|$ should be the difference of two of its factors. Using the correct factors for ac, rewrite the bx term in the trinomial as a sum or difference. Finally, factor the polynomial by grouping to get the answer.

Example 7.11

Factor $6x^2 - x - 12$ using the A-C method.

Solution:

Step 1: The GCF is 1, so proceed to the next step.

Step 2: $ac = -72$. Since the product is negative, the goal is to find a pair of factors that have a difference of $|b| = 1$. Organize this search using a table. For the remainder of this step, ignore signs.

In this table, the two factors of 72 go in the left column and their difference goes in the right column.

72, 1	71
36, 2	34
24, 3	21
18, 4	14
12, 6	6
9, 8	1

The numbers 8 and 9 are the necessary factors, since their difference is one.

Step 3: Rewrite the original trinomial with the bx term expressed as a difference: $6x^2 - x - 12 = 6x^2 + 8x - 9x - 12$. The order of the first-degree terms does not matter.

Step 4: Find the GCF of the first two terms and the GCF of the last two terms and factor them out. The GCF of $6x^2$ and $8x$ is $2x$, and the GCF of $-9x$ and -12 is -3, so write
$6x^2 + 8x - 9x - 12 = 2x(3x + 4) - 3(3x + 4)$.

Step 5: Using the distributive property of multiplication, factor out $(3x + 4)$ from both terms to get $2x(3x + 4) - 3(3x + 4) = (2x - 3)(3x + 4)$.

Example 7.12
Factor $12x^3 + 34x^2 + 14x$ using the A-C method.

Solution:

Step 1: The GCF of this trinomial is $2x$, so write $2x(6x^2 + 17x + 7)$.

Step 2: $ac = 42$. Since the product is positive, find two factors that sum to 17. Do this using a table that has pairs of factors in the left column and sums in the right column.

42, 1	43
21, 2	23
14, 3	17
7, 6	13

14 and 3 are the correct factors.

Step 3: Rewrite the trinomial with the bx term expressed as a sum.
$2x(6x^2 + 17x + 7) = 2x(6x^2 + 14x + 3x + 7)$

Step 4: Find the GCF of the first two terms and the last two terms. Factor each GCF out of its respective pair.

The GCF of $6x^2$ and $14x$ is $2x$, and the GCF of $3x$ and 7 is 1, so write $2x(6x^2 + 14x + 3x + 7) = 2x[2x(3x + 7) + 1(3x + 7)]$.

Step 5: Factor $3x + 7$ out of each term to get the final result.
$2x[2x(3x + 7) + 1(3x + 7)] = 2x(2x + 1)(3x + 7)$

Box Method

7.4 BOX METHOD A method of factoring a second-degree trinomial that parallels the A-C method but arranges the four resulting terms in a 2 × 2 array. The GCF of each row and column of the array is a term of the binomial factors.

The **box method** of factoring also provides a straightforward way to calculate the coefficients of binomial factors. The box method is very similar to the A-C method, but more visual. The technique will be outlined in the following examples.

Example 7.13

Factor $21x^2 - x - 2$ using the box method.

Solution:

Step 1: Factor out any common factors in the trinomial. This example has none, so proceed to the next step.

Step 2: In a 2 × 2 table, write the second-degree term in the upper left cell and the constant term in the lower right cell.

$21x^2$	
	-2

Step 3: $ac = -42$, so find the two factors of 42 that have a difference of -1, just as in the A-C method. These two factors are 7 and 6.

Step 4: Write the one of the first-degree terms in the upper right corner and the other in the lower left corner. It does not matter which term goes in which corner, just be careful that the signs are correct.

$21x^2$	$-7x$
$6x$	-2

Step 5: Find the GCF of each row and write it on the left of its row. The GCF of the first row is $7x$, and the GCF of the second row is 2.

$7x$	$21x^2$	$-7x$
2	$6x$	-2

Step 6: Find the GCF of each column and write it above the column. The GCF of the first column is $3x$, and the GCF of the second column is -1.

$3x$	-1
$21x^2$	$-7x$
$6x$	-2

Step 7: Read off the new row and the new column. These are the two factors of the original trinomial.

$$21x^2 - x - 2 = (7x + 2)(3x - 1)$$

Example 7.14

Factor $2x^2 + 7x + 3$ using the box method.

Solution:

Step 1: Check the trinomial to make sure its GCF is 1. In this case it is, so move on to the next step.

Step 2: In a 2×2 table, write the second-degree term in the upper left cell and the constant term in the lower right cell.

$2x^2$	
	3

Step 3: $a \times c = 6$, so find the two factors of 6 that have a sum of 7. These two factors are 1 and 6.

Step 4: Write the factors in the remaining corners of the table.

$2x^2$	$6x$
$1x$	3

Step 5: Find the GCF of each row and write it to the left of that row.

$2x$	$2x^2$	$6x$
1	$1x$	3

Step 6: Find the GCF of each column and write it above its column.

	x	3
$2x$	$2x^2$	$6x$
1	$1x$	3

Step 7: Read off the new row and new column. These are the factors of the trinomial.

$$2x^2 + 7x + 3 = (x + 3)(2x + 1)$$

DIY PROBLEMS

7.20 Factor $2x^2 + 11x + 5$ using the box method.

7.21 Factor $6x^2 + 7x + 2$ using the box method.

FACTORING SPECIAL PRODUCTS

After some practice, certain patterns begin to emerge connecting trinomials and their binomial factors. This section will explore some of the most common patterns.

Factoring the Difference of Two Perfect Squares

The form $a^2x^2 - b^2$ is a very common and appears in many different types of problems. With the application of the A-C method of factoring, one can see that $a^2x^2 - b^2 = (ax + b)(ax - b)$. The following examples show this.

Example 7.15

Factor $x^2 - 4$ using the A-C method.

Solution:

Step 1: In this problem, $a = 1$, $b = 0$, and $c = -4$. Since $ac = -4$, the A-C method requires two factors of 4 that have a difference of 0. These must be 2 and 2. Remember to make one factor positive and one negative, since c is negative.

$x^2 - 4 = x^2 + 2x - 2x - 4$

Step 2: Find the GCF of the first two terms and the GCF of the second two terms. Factor both out.

$x^2 + 2x - 2x - 4 = x(x + 2) - 2(x + 2)$

Step 3: Factor the common binomial out of both terms.

$x(x + 2) - 2(x + 2) = (x - 2)(x + 2)$

Example 7.16

Factor $9x^2 - 16$ using the A-C method.

Solution:

Step 1: In this problem, $a = 9$, $b = 0$, and $c = -16$. Since $ac = -144$, the A-C method requires two factors of 144 that have a difference of 0. These factors are 12 and 12. Write $9x^2 - 16 = 9x^2 - 12x + 12x - 16$.

Step 2: Find the GCF of the first two terms and the GCF of the second two terms. Factor both out.

$9x^2 - 12x + 12x - 16 = 3x(3x - 4) + 4(3x - 4)$

Step 3: Factor the common binomial out of both terms.

$3x(3x - 4) + 4(3x - 4) = (3x + 4)(3x - 4)$

Factoring a Perfect Square Trinomial

What happens when a binomial is squared? Try it with the binomial $px + q$:

$$\left(px + q\right)^2 = \left(px + q\right)\left(px + q\right) = p^2x^2 + 2pqx + q^2$$

This very recognizable form can also be factored easily using the A-C method.

Example 7.17

Factor $x^2 + 2x + 1$.

Solution:

Step 1: The coefficients for the basic trinomial are $a = 1$, $b = 2$, and $c = 2$. Following the A-C method, $ac = 1$, meaning that the two factors must be 1 and 1. Indeed, their sum is 2.

$x^2 + 2x + 1 = x^2 + x + x + 1$

Step 2: Find the GCF of the first two terms and the GCF of the last two terms. Factor both out.

$x^2 + x + x + 1 = x(x + 1) + 1(x + 1)$

Step 3: Factor the common binomial out of both terms.

$x(x + 1) + 1(x + 1) = (x + 1)(x + 1) = (x + 1)^2$

This follows the form indicated above with $p = 1$ and $q = 1$.

Example 7.18

Factor $4x^2 - 12x + 9$.

Solution:

Step 1: The coefficients are $a = 4$, $b = -12$, and $c = 9$. Following the A-C method, $ac = 36$, meaning that the two factors must be -6 and -6, since their sum must equal -12.

$4x^2 - 12x + 9 = 4x^2 - 6x - 6x + 9$

Step 2: Find the GCF of the first two terms and the GCF of the last two terms. Factor both out.

$4x^2 - 6x - 6x + 9 = 2x(2x - 3) - 3(2x - 3)$

Step 3: Factor out the common binomial from each term.

$2x(2x - 3) - 3(2x - 3) = (2x - 3)(2x - 3) = (2x - 3)^2$

Again, this follows the pattern outlined above with $p = 2$ and $q = -3$.

DIY PROBLEMS

7.25 Factor $x^2 + 12x + 36$.

7.26 Factor $9x^2 - 42x + 49$.

Factoring the Sum or Difference of Two Perfect Cubes

Sums and differences of perfect cubes follow recognizable patterns as well: $a^3 - b^3 = (a - b)(a^2 + ab + b^2)$ and $a^3 + b^3 = (a + b)(a^2 - ab + b^2)$.

Notice that the second-degree trinomials on the right-hand side of each equation do not factor.

Example 7.19
Factor $x^3 - 27$.

Solution:

Notice that $3^3 = 27$. The polynomial can be written as the difference of two cubes.

$x^3 - 27 = x^3 - 3^3$

Following the formula, $x^3 - 3^3 = (x - 3)(x^2 + 3x + 9)$. This can be verified by multiplying the factors using the distributive property.

Example 7.20
Factor $8x^3 + 64$.

Solution:

Notice that $8 = 2^3$ and $64 = 4^3$, so the polynomial can be written as the sum of two cubes.

$8x^3 + 64 = (2x)^3 + 4^3$

Following the formula, see that $(2x)^3 + 4^3 = (2x + 4)(4x^2 - 8x + 16)$. This can be verified by multiplying the factors using the distributive property.

DIY PROBLEMS

7.27 Factor $x^3 y^3 - 27$.

7.28 Factor $216x^3 - 1$.

7.29 Factor $8x^3 - 343$.

SOLVING QUADRATIC EQUATIONS BY FACTORING

Second-degree trinomials occur in many fields outside of mathematics. They are often referred to as *quadratic expressions* and are very useful. The next three sections will explore several real-world applications of **quadratic functions** and put to use some of the skills acquired in this chapter.

Solving a **quadratic equation** requires finding the values of the variables that make the equation true. Equivalently, these values make the function equal 0.

Since this same number makes the related quadratic function have the value 0, sometimes the number is called a *zero* of the function.

Solving a factorable quadratic equation is based on the **Zero Product Property.** When a quadratic equation is reduced to a product that equals zero, then one or both factors must equal 0. Solving the two linear equations gives the **roots** of the polynomial. For example, consider $m^2 - m + 12 = (m - 3)(m + 4) = 0$. Then $m - 3 = 0$ so m $= 3$, or $m + 4 = 0$ so $m = -4$. The roots of the quadratic equation $m^2 - m + 12 = 0$ are 3 and -4.

A slightly different use of the word *root* occurs when considering the **square root** of a quantity.

This concept is useful in finding the roots of any equation of the form $x^2 = k^2$. Looking at $x^2 = k^2$ as $x^2 - k^2 = 0$, then $(x - k)(x + k) = 0$, and the roots of the equation are k and $-k$. This justifies finding the roots of an equation such as $x^2 = 9$ by taking the square root of both sides of the equation. Write:

$$\sqrt{x^2} = \sqrt{9}$$

$$x = \pm 3$$

For $(x + 2)^2 = 36$, then $x + 2 = \pm 6$; the roots of the equation are $x = 4$ or -8.

Gravity Problems: Ballistics

Near the Earth's surface, a quadratic function known as the **ballistics equation** describes the motions of objects in free fall, meaning objects that are only under the

7.5 QUADRATIC FUNCTION A polynomial function of degree 2.

7.6 QUADRATIC EQUATION A quadratic function set equal to 0.

7.7 ZERO PRODUCT PROPERTY If $xy = 0$, then either x or y (or both) are equal to 0.

7.8 ROOT (of an equation) Value of the variable which makes the equation true.

7.9 SQUARE ROOT Written $\sqrt[2]{x}$ or $\sqrt{x}$, the number r such that $r^2 = (\sqrt{x})^2 = x$.

7.10 BALLISTICS EQUATION The equation of motion $x(t) = \frac{1}{2}at^2 + v_0 t + x_0$, where t is time in seconds and $x(t)$ is the height of the object at time t.

influence of gravity. Since the acceleration due to gravity is constant near the Earth's surface, the equation of motion can be written in the form $x(t) = \frac{1}{2}at^2 + v_0 t + x_0$, where t is time in seconds and $x(t)$ is the height of the object at time t.

In this equation, x_0 represents the initial position of an object (initial height), v_0 represents the initial velocity (positive direction is up) in meters per second, and a represents acceleration due to gravity. For the remainder of this section, take $a = -10\frac{m}{s^2}$. (This is very close to the actual value.)

It is often desirable to factor this equation, since it is much easier to determine what values of t result in the position becoming 0 when it is in its factored form.

Example 7.21
A penny is dropped with no initial velocity from a 20-meter-high balcony into a fountain. How long does it take for the penny to reach the fountain?

Solution:

Step 1: The problem statement indicates that $v_0 = 0$ and $x_0 = 20$. Write the equation of motion as $x(t) = \frac{1}{2}(-10)t^2 + 20 = -5t^2 + 20$.

Step 2: Factor out the GCF, -5.
$x(t) = -5t^2 + 20 = -5(t^2 - 4)$

Step 3: Notice the familiar form inside the parentheses, which becomes
$x(t) = -5(t^2 - 4) = -5(t + 2)(t - 2)$.

Step 4: Since the problem asks for the time when x is 0, set the equation equal to 0:
$-5(t + 2)(t - 2) = 0$.

This implies that $x(t) = 0$ when $t = \pm 2$ seconds. Negative time is physically impossible, so keep only the positive result. It takes 2 seconds for the penny to reach the fountain.

Example 7.22
A man standing on a 24-meter cliff by the ocean throws a stone straight up with initial velocity of 19 meters per second. How long will it take the stone to reach the water below?

Solution:

Step 1: The problem statement indicates that $v_0 = 19$ and $x_0 = 24$. Write the equation of motion as

$$x(t) = \frac{1}{2}(-10)t^2 + 19t + 24 = -5t^2 + 19t + 24.$$

Step 2: Note that $ac = -120$. The A-C method requires two factors of 60 that have a difference of 19. Setting up a difference table of the factors yields the following:

120, 1	119
60, 2	58
40, 3	37
30, 4	26
24, 5	19
20, 6	14
15, 8	7
12, 10	2

So the factors are 24 and 5.

Step 3: Rewrite the quadratic equation with the two new terms.

$x(t) = -5t^2 + 19t + 24 = -5t^2 - 5t + 24t + 24$

Step 4: Find the GCF of the first two terms and the GCF of the second two terms. Factor out each.

$x(t) = -5t^2 - 5t + 24t + 24 = -5t(t + 1) + 24(t + 1)$

Step 5: Factor out the common binomial.

$x(t) = -5t(t + 1) + 24(t + 1) = (-5t + 24)(t + 1)$

Step 6: Set the equation equal to 0 and solve for t.

$(-5t + 24)(t + 1) = 0$

This implies that $x(t) = 0$ when $t = -1$ or $t = 4.8$. Again, negative time is not real, so the answer is $t = 4.8$ seconds.

DIY PROBLEMS

7.30 A volleyball player hits a ball straight up with an initial velocity of $v_0 = 30\frac{m}{s}$. How long will it take for the ball to return to the ground? Assume that its initial height is 0.

7.31 A hunter fires a rifle straight up. The bullet's initial velocity is $1000\frac{m}{s}$. If he fired the bullet from ground level, how high is it after 5 seconds? After 10?

Light Intensity Problems

The **light intensity equation** is often used to determine the distance from a light source of known power. In standard units, distance is in meters, power is in watts, and intensity is in watts per square meter.

7.11 LIGHT INTENSITY EQUATION The equation $I = \frac{k}{4\pi r^2}$ that describes light intensity, where I is the intensity, k is the power of the light source, and r is the distance to the light source.

Example 7.23

A certain type of streetlight is rated at 200 watts of power output. If an observer measures the intensity of the light to be $\frac{1}{2\pi}\frac{\text{watts}}{\text{meter}^2}$ how far is she from the streetlight?

Solution:

Step 1: In this problem $k = 200$ watts and. $I = \frac{1}{2\pi}\frac{\text{watts}}{\text{meter}^2}$. Substitute these values 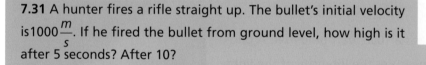 into the given equation. Drop the units until the solution is found.

$$I = \frac{k}{4\pi r^2} \rightarrow \frac{1}{2\pi} = \frac{200}{4\pi r^2}$$

Step 2: Multiply both sides of the equation by $2\pi r^2$.

$$(2\pi r^2)\frac{1}{2\pi} = (2\pi r^2)\frac{200}{4\pi r^2} \rightarrow r^2 = 100$$

Step 3: Since both sides of the equation are perfect squares, take the square root of both sides.

Observe that this equation is true only when $r = \pm 10$.

Step 4: Negative distances are impossible, so the streetlight must be 10 meters away.

Example 7.24

An astronomer measures the intensity of the light coming from a star to be $4.4 \cdot 10^{-10} \frac{\text{watts}}{\text{meter}^2}$. If the power output of the star is roughly half that of the sun, say $2 \cdot 10^{26}$ w, what is the approximate distance of the star?

Step 1: Rearrange the intensity equation, solving for r^2.

$$r^2 = \frac{k}{4\pi I}$$

Step 2: Substitute the known values and solve for r. Drop the units until the solution is achieved.

$$r^2 = \frac{2 \cdot 10^{26}}{4\pi(4.4 \cdot 10^{-10})} = 3.4172 \cdot 10^{34}$$

Taking the square root of both sides of the equation, $r \approx 1.8 \cdot 10^{17}$ m.

DIY PROBLEMS

7.32 A certain lighthouse has a 1000-watt bulb in it. A photodiode on a ship at sea measures the intensity of the light from the lighthouse to be $\frac{1}{4000\pi} \frac{\text{watts}}{\text{meter}^2}$. How far is the ship from the lighthouse?

7.33 Find the distance from the observer of a 60-watt light bulb with intensity $4.77 \cdot 10^{-10}$.

SOLUTIONS TO DIY PROBLEMS

7.1 Factor the monomial from $4x^3 + 4x$.

Solution:
Step 1: Find the factors of each monomial in the polynomial, and then determine the GCF.

$4x^3 = 4 \cdot x \cdot x \cdot x$

and

$4x = 4 \cdot x$

Step 2: The GCF of the above monomials is $4x$, so factor that out of the polynomial.

$4x^3 + 4x = 4x(x^2 + 1)$

7.2 Factor the monomial from $2x^2y - 10xy - 5xy^2$.

Solution:
Step 1: Find the factors of each monomial in the polynomial, and then determine the GCF.

$2x^2y = 2 \cdot x \cdot x \cdot y$

$-10xy = -2 \cdot 5 \cdot x \cdot y$

and

$-5xy^2 = -5 \cdot x \cdot y \cdot y$

By inspection, the GCF is xy.

Step 2: Factor out the GCF.

$2x^2y - 10xy - 5xy^2 = 2x(xy) - 10(xy) - 5y(xy) = xy(2x - 10 - 5y)$

7.3 Factor the monomial from $12x^4 - 108x^2$.

Solution:
Step 1: Find the factors of each monomial, and then determine the GCF.

$12x^4 = 2 \cdot 2 \cdot 3 \cdot x \cdot x \cdot x \cdot x$

and

$-108x^2 = -2 \cdot 2 \cdot 3 \cdot 3 \cdot 3 \cdot x \cdot x$

The GCF is $12x^2$.

Step 2: Factor out the GCF.

$12x^4 - 108x^2 = 12x^2 \cdot x^2 - 12x^2 \cdot 9 = 12x^2(x^2 - 9)$

7.4 Factor $4x(x - 2) - 7(x - 2)$.

Solution:
x − 2 is the common binomial factor

$4x(x - 2) - 7(x - 2) = (x - 2)(4x - 7)$

7.5 Factor $-12x^5 + 3x^3 + 4x^2 - 1$ by grouping.

Solution:
Step 1: Group the terms into two polynomials.

$-12x^5 + 3x^3 + 4x^2 - 1 = (-12x^5 + 3x^3) + (4x^2 - 1)$

Step 2: Find a GCF of each new polynomial.

$-12x^5 = -2 \cdot 2 \cdot 3 \cdot x \cdot x \cdot x \cdot x \cdot x$

and

$3x^3 = 3 \cdot x \cdot x \cdot x$

So the GCF is $-3x^3$.

Likewise, $4x^2 = 2 \cdot 2 \cdot x \cdot x$ and $-1 = -1$, so the GCF is 1.

Step 3: Factor the GCF out of each new polynomial.

$(-12x^5 + 3x^3) + (4x^2 - 1) = -3x^3(4x^2 - 1) + 1(4x^2 - 1)$

Step 4: Factor the common binomial out of each term.

$-3x^3(4x^2 - 1) + 1(4x^2 - 1) = (-3x^3 + 1)(4x^2 - 1)$

7.6 Factor $3x^4 + x^3 - 9x^2 - 3x$ by grouping.

Solution:
Step 1: Group the terms into two polynomials.

$3x^4 + x^3 - 9x^2 - 3x = (3x^4 + x^3) + (-9x^2 - 3x)$

Step 2: Find the GCF of each new polynomial.

$3x^4 = 3 \cdot x \cdot x \cdot x \cdot x$

and

$x^3 = x \cdot x \cdot x$

So the GCF of the first is x^3.

Likewise, $-9x^2 = -3 \cdot 3 \cdot x \cdot x \cdot x$ and $-3x = -3 \cdot x$, so the GCF of the second is $-3x$.

Step 3: Factor the GCFs out of each new polynomial.

$(3x^4 + x^3) + (-9x^2 - 3x) = x^3(3x + 1) - 3x(3x + 1)$

Step 4: Factor the common binomial out of both terms.

$x^3(3x + 1) - 3x(3x + 1) = (x^3 - 3x)(3x + 1)$

Step 5: For the sake of completeness, factor the x out of the first binomial.

$(x^3 - 3x)(3x + 1) = x(x^2 - 3)(3x + 1)$

7.7 Factor $x^2 + 5x + 6$.

Solution:
Step 1: The choices for d and f so that $df = 6$ are 1 and 6, 2 and 3.

Step 2: The only choice that satisfies $d + f = 5$ is $d = 2$ and $f = 3$. Fill in the blanks with $+$ signs so that the x term is $5x$. This requires addition in both cases, since 6 and 5 are both positive, so the correct factoring is $(x + 2)(x + 3)$.

7.8 Factor $x^2 + 17x + 60$.

Solution:
Step 1: The choices for d and f so that $df = 60$ are 1 and 60, 2 and 30, 3 and 20, 4 and 15, 5 and 12, and 6 and 10. Write $(x \; 5)(x \; 12)$.

Step 2: The only choice that satisfies $d + f = 17$ is $d = 5$ and $f = 12$. Fill in the blanks with $+$ and/or $-$ signs so that the x term becomes $17x$. This requires addition in both cases, since 60 and 17 are both positive, so the correct factoring is $(x + 5)(x + 12)$.

7.9 Factor $x^2 - 4x + 4$.

Solution:

Step 1: The choices of d and f so that $df = 4$ are 1 and 4, 2 and 2, −2 and −2, −1 and −4.

Step 2: The only choice that satisfies $d + f = -4$ is $d = -2$ and $f = -2$. So the correct factoring is $(x - 2)(x - 2)$

7.10 Factor $x^2 - 2x - 48$.

Solution:

Step 1: Choose two numbers with product 48. Since both b and c are negative, one must be negative, and their difference must be 2. The pairs of factors of 48 are 1 and 48, 2 and 24, 3 and 16, 4 and 12, and 6 and 8. Write the framework for the problem using one + and one − symbol.

$(x + \ )(x - \ )$

Step 2: Fill in the blanks with a pair of factors of 48 so that the x term is $-2x$;
$(x + 6)(x - 8)$ is the solution.

7.11 Factor $2x^2 + 6x + 4$ completely.

Solution:

Step 1: Find the GCF of the trinomial and factor it out. The GCF is 2, so write $2(x^2 + 3x + 2)$.

Step 2: The two factors of 2 whose sum is 3 are 2 and 1.

$2(x^2 + 3x + 2) = 2(x + 1)(x + 2)$

7.12 Factor $3x^4 + 6x^3 - 72x^2$ completely.

Solution:

Step 1: Find the GCF of the trinomial and factor it out. The GCF is $3x^2$, so write
$3x^2(x^2 + 2x - 24)$.

Step 2: Since c is negative, choose two factors of 24 that differ by 2; 4 and 6 are good choices:
$3x^2(x\ 4)(x\ 6)$.

Step 3: Choose operators that result in the x term being $2x$: $3x^2(x - 4)(x + 6)$.

7.13 Factor $-7x^7 - 84x^6 - 245x^5$ completely.

Solution:

Step 1: Find the GCF of the trinomial and factor it out. The GCF is $-7x^5$, so write $-7x^5(x^2 + 12x + 35)$.

Step 2: Choose two factors of 35 whose sum is 12; 5 and 7 work: $-7x^5(x\ 5)(x\ 7)$.

Step 3: Choose plus and/or minus operators so that the x term is $12x$. Both must be pluses:
$-7x^5(x + 5)(x + 7)$.

7.14 Factor $-3x^3y + 7x^2y + 6xy$.

Solution:

Step 1: Find the GCF of the trinomial and factor it out. The GCF is xy, so write

$xy(-3x^2 + 7x + 6)$.

Step 2: Find the factors of a. They are −1 and 3. Write them in the problem framework:
$xy(-1x\ )(3x\ )$.

Step 3: Find the factors of c. They could be 6 and 1, or 2 and 3. Try 2 and 3 first. Make an educated guess as to where they should go: $xy(-1x\ 3)(3x\ 2)$.

Step 4: Since both b and c are positive, fill in the blanks with plus signs so that the x term equals $7x$: $xy(-1x + 3)(3x + 2)$.

7.15 Factor $12x^3 + 24x^2 + 9x$.

Solution:
Step 1: The GCF of this trinomial is $3x$, so factor it out.

$3x(4x^2 + 8x + 3)$

Step 2: The factors of c are 1 and 3. Write them in the problem framework:

$3x(x\ 1)(x\ 3)$.

Step 3: The factors of a are 2 and 2, or 1 and 4. The better choice is 2 and 2, so write them in the problem framework as well: $3x(2x\ 1)(2x\ 3)$.

Step 4: Now choose the appropriate operators so that the x term has a coefficient of 8. Since b and c are positive, both operations must be addition.

$3x(2x + 1)(2x + 3)$

7.16 Factor $3x^2 + 7x + 2$ using the A-C method.

Find two positive factors of 6 ($a \cdot c = 3 \cdot 2 = 6$) whose sum is 7.

Positive factors of 6	Sum
1,6	7
2,3	5

Use the factors of 6 whose sum is 7 to write $7x$ as $1x + 6x$.

$3x^2 + 7x + 2 = 3x^2 + 1x + 6x + 2$

Factor by grouping

$= x(3x + 1) + 2(3x + 1) = (3x + 1)(x + 2)$

7.17 Factor $-10x^2 + 17x - 3$ using the A-C method.

Solution:
Step 1: The GCF of this trinomial is 1, so proceed to the next step.

Step 2: The product of a and c is 30, so list all its factors and their sums.

30, 1	31
15, 2	17
10, 3	13
6, 5	11

Step 3: Factors 15 and 2 sum to 17, so rewrite the trinomial using those numbers as follows:

$-10x^2 + 17x - 3 = -10x^2 + 15x + 2x - 3$

Step 4: Find the GCF of the first two terms and the GCF of the second two terms. Factor each out.

$-10x^2 + 15x + 2x - 3 = -5x(2x + 3) + 1(2x + 3)$

Step 5: Factor the common binomial out of both terms to get the final answer.

$-5x(2x + 3) + 1(2x + 3) = (-5x + 1)(2x + 3)$

7.18 Factor $9x^2 + 3x + 2$ using the A-C method.

Solution:
Nonfactorable over the integers.

7.19 Factor $9x^2 + 13x - 10$ using the A-C method.

Solution:
Step 1: The GCF of this trinomial is 1, so proceed to the next step.

Step 2: The product of a and c is -90. Create a table with factors of 90 in the left column and their difference in the right column.

90, 1	89
45, 2	43
30, 3	27
18, 5	13
15, 6	9
10, 9	1

Step 3: Factors 18 and 5 are correct, so write the $13x$ term as the difference of $18x$ and $5x$.

$$9x^2 + 13x - 10 = 9x^2 + 18x - 5x - 10$$

Step 4: Find and factor out the GCF of the first two terms and the last two terms.

$$9x^2 + 18x - 5x - 10 = 9x(x + 2) - 5(x + 2)$$

Step 5: Factor the binomial out of both terms.

$$9x(x + 2) - 5(x + 2) = (9x - 5)(x + 2)$$

7.20 Factor $2x^2 + 11x + 5$ using the box method.

Solution:
Step 1: The GCF of this trinomial is 1, so proceed to the next step.

Step 2: In a two-by-two table, write the second-degree term in the upper left cell and the constant term in the lower right cell.

$2x^2$	
	5

Step 3: $ac = 10$, so find two factors of 10 that sum to 11. These factors are 10 and 1. Write them in the remaining corners of the box.

$2x^2$	$10x$
$1x$	5

Step 4: Find the GCF of each row and write it to the left of its row.

$2x$	$2x^2$	$10x$
1	$1x$	5

Step 5: Find the GCF of each column and write it above its column.

	$1x$	5
$2x^2$	$2x^2$	$10x$
1	$1x$	5

Step 6: Read off the new column and the new row. These are the binomial factors of the trinomial.

$$2x^2 + 11x + 5 = (2x + 1)(x + 5)$$

7.21 Factor $6x^2 - 7x + 2$ using the box method.

Solution:
Step 1: The GCF of this trinomial is 1, so proceed to the next step.

Step 2: In a 2 × 2 table, write the second-degree term in the upper left cell and the constant term in the lower right cell.

$6x^2$	
	2

Step 3: $ac = 12$, so find two products of 12 that have a sum of -7. These are -3 and -4. Write them in the remaining corners.

$6x^2$	$-3x$
$-4x$	2

Step 4: Find the GCF of each row and write it to the left of the row.

$3x$	$6x$	$-3x$
-2	$-4x$	2

Step 5: find the GCF of each column and write it above the column.

	$2x$	-1
$3x$	$6x^2$	$-3x$
-2	$-4x$	2

Step 6: Read off the new column and new row. These are the binomial factors of the trinomial.
$6x^2 - 7x + 2 = (2x - 1)(3x - 2)$

7.22 Factor $x^2 - 64$.

Solution:
Step 1: Rewrite the polynomial to make the squares more obvious.
$x^2 - 64 = x^2 - (8)^2$

Step 2: Using the formulas for the difference of two squares, factor the polynomial.
$x^2 - (8)^2 = (x - 8)(x + 8)$

7.23 Factor $16x^2 - 49$.

Solution:
Step 1: Rewrite the polynomial to make the squares more obvious.
$16x^2 - 49 = (4x)^2 - 7^2$

Step 2: Using the formulas for the difference of two squares, factor the polynomial.
$(4x)^2 - 7^2 = (4x - 7)(4x + 7)$

7.24 Factor $25x^2 - 4y^2$.

Solution:
Step 1: Rewrite the polynomial to make the squares obvious.
$25x^2 - 4y^2 = (5x)^2 - (2y)^2$

Step 2: Using the formula for the difference of two squares, factor the polynomial.
$(5x)^2 - (2y)^2 = (5x - 2y)(5x + 2y)$

7.25 Factor $x^2 + 12x + 36$.

Solution:
Step 1: Rewrite the polynomial to make the squares more obvious.

$x^2 + 12x + 36 = (1x)^2 + 2 \cdot 1 \cdot 6 \cdot x + 6^2$

Step 2: Using the formula for a perfect square trinomial, write the trinomial as the product of two binomials.

$(1x)^2 + 2 \cdot 1 \cdot 6 \cdot x + 6^2 = (x + 6)(x + 6) = (x + 6)^2$

7.26 Factor $9x^2 - 42x + 49$.

Solution:
Step 1: Rewrite the polynomial to make the squares more obvious.

$9x^2 - 42x + 49 = (3x)^2 - 2 \cdot 3 \cdot 7 \cdot x + (-7)^2$

Step 2: Using the formula for a perfect square trinomial, write the polynomial as the product of two binomials.

$(3x)^2 - 2 \cdot 3 \cdot 7 \cdot x + (-7)^2 = (3x - 7)(3x - 7) = (3x - 7)^2$

7.27 Factor $x^3y^3 - 27$.

Solution:
Step 1: Rewrite the polynomial so that the cubes are more obvious.

$x^3y^3 - 27 = x^3y^3 - (3)^3$

Step 2: Using the formula for the difference of two cubes, write the polynomial as the product of two polynomials.

$x^3y^3 - (3)^3 = (xy - 3)(x^2y^2 + 3xy + 9)$

7.28 Factor $216x^3 - 1$.

Solution:
Step 1: Rewrite the polynomial so that the cubes are more obvious.

$216x^3 - 1 = (6x)^3 - 1^3$

Step 2: Using the formula for the difference of two cubes, write the polynomial as the product of two polynomials.

$(6x)^3 - 1^3 = (6x - 1)(36x^2 + 6x + 1)$

7.29 Factor $8x^3 - 343$.

Solution:
Step 1: Rewrite the polynomial to make the cubes more obvious.

$8x^3 - 343 = (2x)^3 + (-7)^3$

Step 2: Using the formula for the difference of two cubes, rewrite the polynomial as the product of two polynomials.

$(2x)^3 + (-7)^3 = (2x - 7)(4x^2 + 14x + 49)$

7.30 A volleyball player hits a ball straight up with an initial velocity of $v_0 = 30\frac{m}{s}$. How long will it take for the ball to return to the ground? Assume that its initial height is 0.

Solution:
Step 1: Write out the ballistics equation with $v_0 = 30\frac{m}{s}$ and $x_0 = 0$.

$$x(t) = -5t^2 + 30t$$

Step 2: Factor out the GCF of the right-hand side.

$$x(t) = -5t^2 + 30t = -5t(t - 6)$$

Step 3: In order to find the times when the ball is at ground level, set $x(t) = 0$, leaving: $5t(t - 6) = 0$.

This equation is true when $t = 0$ and $t = 6$. The time $t = 0$ represents the instant the ball was hit, so the answer is $t = 6$ seconds.

7.31 A hunter fires a rifle straight up. The bullet's initial velocity is $1000 \frac{m}{s}$. If he fired the bullet from ground level, how high is it after 5 seconds? After 10?

Solution:
Step 1: Observe that $v_0 = 1000 \frac{m}{s}$ and $x_0 = 0$. Write out the ballistics equation with these values.

$$x(t) = -5t^2 + 1000t$$

Step 2: Find the height of the bullet after 5 seconds.

$$x(5) = -5(5)^2 + 1000(5) = -125 + 5000 = 4875$$

After 5 seconds the bullet is 4,875 meters high.

Step 3: Find the height of the bullet after 10 seconds.

$$x(10) = -5(10)^2 + 1000(10) = -500 + 10,000 = 9500$$

After 10 seconds the bullet is 9,500 meters high.

7.32 A certain lighthouse has a 1000-watt bulb in it. A photodiode on a ship at sea measures the intensity of the light from the lighthouse to be $\frac{1}{4000\pi} \frac{\text{watts}}{\text{meter}^2}$. How far is the ship from the lighthouse?

Solution:

Step 1: Note that the problem states that $k = 1000$ watts and $I = \frac{1}{4000\pi} \frac{\text{watts}}{\text{meter}^2}$. Substitute these values into the light intensity equation and ignore the units until the final step.

$$\frac{1}{4000\pi} = \frac{1000}{4\pi r^2}$$

Step 2: To begin solving for r, multiply both sides by $4000\,\pi r^2$.

$$(4000\pi r^2)\frac{1}{4000\pi} = (4000\pi r^2)\frac{1000}{4\pi r^2} \rightarrow r^2 = 1000000$$

Step 3: Take the square root of both sides of the equation. This equation is only true when $r = \pm 1000$.

Step 4: The negative value is impossible, so the ship must be 1,000 meters (which is 1 kilometer) from the lighthouse.

7.33 Find the distance from the observer of a 60-watt light bulb with intensity $4.77 \cdot 10^{-10} \dfrac{\text{watts}}{\text{meter}^2}$.

Solution:

Step 1: Rearrange the intensity equation, solving for r^2.

$$r^2 = \frac{k}{4\pi I}.$$

Step 2: Substitute the known values and solve for r. Drop the units until the solution is achieved.

$$r^2 = \frac{60}{4\pi(4.77 \cdot 10^{-10})} = 1.0010 \cdot 10^{10}$$

Taking the square root of both sides of the equation, $r \approx 100050$ m

END OF CHAPTER REVIEW QUESTIONS

7.1 Factor completely: $8x - 24$.

7.2 Factor a monomial from a polynomial: $16 - 8x^2$.

7.3 Factor a monomial from a polynomial: $2x^4 - 4x$.

7.4 Factor the monomial from a polynomial: $9x^2 + 81$.

7.5 Factor completely: $\dfrac{x}{2} + \dfrac{3x^2}{4}$.

7.6 Factor completely: $10x^2 - 25x^3$.

7.7 Factor completely: $x(y + 2) + 4(y + 2)$.

7.8 Factor completely: $3x^2(c - d) + 5(c - d)$.

7.9 Factor completely: $x(x - 1) + y(1 - x)$.

7.10 Factor completely: $2x^4 - 4x^3 - x^2 + 2x$.

7.11 Factor completely: $x^2 + 7x + 12$.

7.12 Factor completely: $x^2 + 8x + 16$.

7.13 Factor completely: $t^2 - 8t + 15$.

7.14 Factor completely: $b^2 + 12b + 27$.

7.15 Factor completely: $y^2 - y - 2$.

7.16 Factor completely: $x^2 + 27x + 72$.

7.17 Factor completely: $2x^2 + 10x + 8$.

7.18 Factor completely: $xy^2 + 5xy + 6x$.

7.19 Factor completely: $5x^2 + 7x + 2$.

7.20 Factor completely: $2x^2 - 5x + 3$.

7.21 Factor completely: $6x^2 + 5x - 1$.

7.22 Factor completely: $7x^2 + 50x + 7$.

7.23 Factor completely: $6y^2 - 7y - 3$.

7.24 Factor completely: $-2x^2 - 7x - 5$.

7.25 Factor the following expression: The equivalent resistance R of two electric circuits is given by $2R^2 - 3R + 1$.

7.26 Factor completely: $4x^2 - 25$.

7.27 Factor completely: $125x^3 + 64y^3$.

7.28 Factor completely: $8x^3 - 27$.

7.29 Solve: $(x + 3)(x + 2) = 0$.

7.30 Solve: $x^2 - 81 = 0$.

7.31 Solve the following by factoring: $x^2 + 6x + 8 = 0$.

7.32 Solve the following by factoring: $2x^2 + x - 36 = 0$.

7.33 Solve the following by factoring: $12x^2 + 5x - 3 = 0$.

7.34 The square of a positive number is four more than three times the positive number. Find the number.

7.35 Find the dimensions of a rectangle with width = 2x + 1 and length = x + 3 and an area of 7 square feet.

REFERENCES

Arny, T., & Schneider, S. (2010). Explorations: *An introduction to astronomy* (6th ed.). New York, NY: McGraw-Hill.

Cajori, F., & Odell, L. R. (1917). *Elementary algebra.* New York, NY: Macmillan.

Rietz, H. L., & Crathorne, A. R. (1909). *College algebra.* New York, NY: Henry Holt and Company.

Stapel, E. (n.d). Factoring quadratics: The hard case (examples). Retrieved from Purplemath website: http:// www.purplemath.com/modules/factquad3.htm

Quadratic Functions

asimir owns and operates a large farm where he grows vegetables. He supplies local markets with fresh vegetables, including peppers, onions, and potatoes. He sometimes offers discounts to those who place large orders. His onions, for example, are priced according to the equation $R(x) = -0.00006x^2 + 0.5x$, where x is the number of pounds of onions sold and $R(x)$ represents the revenue generated by that sale. This quadratic function indicates that base cost of a pound of onions is 50 cents, but that large orders are discounted.

Years of meticulous record keeping allow Casimir to make precise estimates of his costs. According to his best estimate, the sale of x pounds of onions costs him $C(x) = 0.02x + 40$. This function indicates that each pound of onions costs 20 cents to grow, and the delivery of each order costs about $40. Being rather mathematically inclined, he realizes that he can determine how much profit he makes from one pound of onions by subtracting his costs from his equation for revenue. He does so, and comes up with the profit function $P(x) = -0.00006x^2 + 0.3x - 40$.

Casimir knows that he grows 6,000 pounds of onions in a year, and plugs that number into his function as one large bulk sale. To his shock and dismay, he finds that this sale will actually cost him $400!

1. How would Casimir calculate the breakeven point in his profit function?

2. Casimir decides that he wants to encourage people to buy vegetables in amounts that maximize his profits. How will he determine what order size maximizes his profits?

3. Suppose Casimir wanted to know how many pounds of peppers he would have to sell in order to generate $1,000 of revenue. How would he calculate this amount?

KEY TERMS

INTRODUCTION TO QUADRATIC EQUATIONS

Quadratic Functions and Quadratic Equations

A *quadratic function* is a polynomial function of degree 2. Quadratic functions $f(x) = ax^2 + bx + c$ turn up in many real-world applications and are common in science.

A *quadratic equation* is a quadratic function set equal to 0. A quadratic equation is one of the few types of polynomial equations that can be explicitly solved. Solving a quadratic equation refers to finding the *roots* of the equation, that is, the values that make the equation true.

Solving quadratic equations offers a good starting point to develop the skill necessary to graph and manipulate more general polynomial functions. There are several different forms in which to write quadratic functions, and each is useful in a different context. The graph of a quadratic function is called a **parabola.**

A parabola is roughly U-shaped. For now we consider only parabolas that open up or down (Figure 8.1). For these it is easy to use a form of the equation of the function to identify the coordinates of the maximum or minimum point on the parabola. The **vertex** of a parabola that opens upward is its minimum point; the vertex of a parabola that opens downward is its maximum point.

8.1 PARABOLA The name of the graph of a quadratic function.

8.2 VERTEX The maximum point of a parabola that opens downward or the minimum point of a parabola that opens upward.

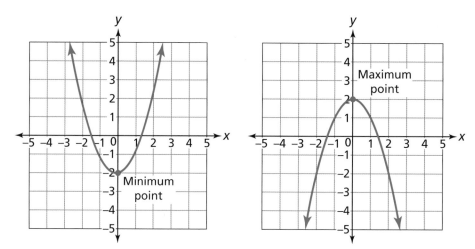

FIGURE 8.1 Parabolas Opening Up or Down

Translations

The most basic way to manipulate a quadratic function is with a translation. A **translation** of a graph is a vertical or horizontal shift of the graph, reflecting a change in the basic equation.

Vertical translations refer to movement up or down parallel to the *y*-axis, and horizontal translations refer to movement left or right parallel to the *x*-axis.

8.3 TRANSLATION A vertical or horizontal shift of a graph, reflecting a change in its basic equation.

GRAPHING THE QUADRATIC FUNCTION

Standard Form

The **standard form** of a quadratic function is $y = f(x) = ax^2 + bx + c$. The coefficients b and c can both be zero, but the a is always nonzero. There must be an x^2 term

8.4 STANDARD FORM (of a quadratic function) $f(x) = ax^2 + bx + c$

or else the equation is not quadratic. The basic form of the function is $y = x^2$, where $a = 1$, and b and c are 0.

Example 8.1

Write the quadratic function with coefficients $a = 2$, $b = -5$, and $c = 1$ in general form.

Solution:

Using the form above, $f(x) = 2x^2 - 5x + 1$.

Example 8.2

What are the coefficients of the quadratic function $y = x^2 + 7x - 3$?

Solution:

By analogy to the general form, $a = 1$, $b = 7$, and $c = -3$.

DIY PROBLEMS

8.1 Write the quadratic function with coefficients $a = -\dfrac{3}{2}$, $b = -\dfrac{1}{3}$, and $c = 5$.

8.2 What are the coefficients of the quadratic function $y = 9x^2 + 2x - 15$?

Vertex Form

The **vertex form** of a quadratic function is $f(x) = a(x - h)^2 + k$. The name of the form refers to the fact that the point (h, k) is the vertex of the parabola. Identifying the vertex gives the most convenient starting point when graphing a parabola. In addition, each of the constants a, h, and k controls a potential change in the basic graph.

A change in the basic graph $y = x^2$ of a quadratic function related to one of the constants a, h, or k is termed a **transformation.** The *translations* caused by h and/or k are particular kinds of transformations.

8.5 VERTEX FORM (of a quadratic function) The formula $y = a(x - h)^2 + k$, where the point (h, k) is the vertex.

8.6 TRANSFORMATION (of a parabola) A change in the basic graph $y = x^2$ of a quadratic function related to one of the constants a, h, or k.

Example 8.3

Find the vertex of the quadratic function $y = (x + 1)^2 - 2$. Draw the graph of the parabola.

Solution:

Step 1: For clarity, rewrite the equation with the same signs as the definition given above.

$$y = (x + 1)^2 - 2 \rightarrow y = \left(x - (-1)\right)^2 + (-2)$$

Step 2: By analogy to the definition, see that $h = -1$ and $k = -2$. Thus the vertex is at the point $(h, k) = (-1, -2)$.

Step 3: Make a table of (x, y) coordinates that lie along the graph. Choose at least two points on either side of the vertex to indicate the shape of the parabola.

x	y
−3	2
−2	−1
−1	−2
0	−1
1	2

Step 4: Plot these points and draw a curve through them (Figure 8.2).

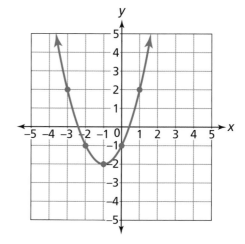

FIGURE 8.2

Example 8.4

Find the vertex of the equation $y = 2(x - 1)^2 + 4$. Draw a graph of the parabola.

Solution:

Step 1: In vertex form, read off h and k. $(h, k) = (1, 4)$

Step 2: Make a table of x and y coordinates.

x	y
−1	12
0	6
1	4
2	6
3	12

Step 3: Plot the points on a coordinate plane and connect them to form the graph of the parabola (Figure 8.3).

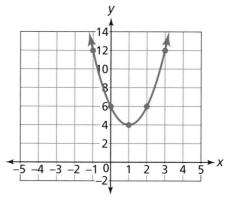

FIGURE 8.3

DIY PROBLEMS

8.3 Find the vertex of $y = (x + 3)^2 - 5$. Draw the graph of the parabola.

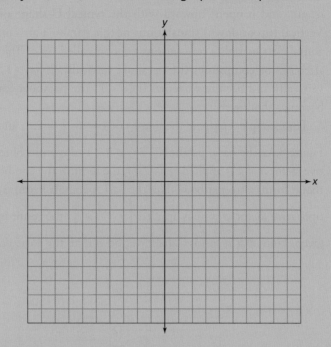

8.4 Find the vertex of the equation $y = 3(x + 2)^2 + 3$.

8.5 Find the vertex of $y = 3x^2 + 2$. Draw the graph of the parabola.

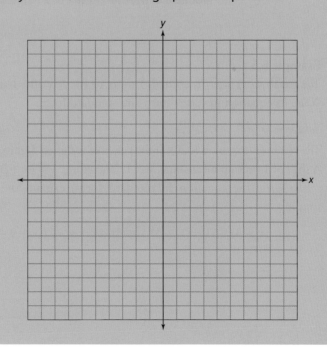

Transformations

The constants h, k, and a all control transformations of the basic parabola $y = x^2$. In vertex form, $y = x^2 = 1(x - 0)^2 + 0$. Its vertex is at $(h, k) = (0, 0)$, the origin, and it opens upward with the typical U-shape of a quadratic function. Vertical (up or down) translations of this parabola are controlled by k, and horizontal (left or right) translations are controlled by h. The multiplicative factor a stretches or compresses the parabola vertically. If $|a| > 1$, the parabola stretches vertically and becomes steeper. If $|a| < 1$, the parabola compresses vertically and becomes shallower.

For example, compare the graphs of $y = x^2$, $y = 2x^2$, and $y = \frac{1}{2}x^2$, as shown in Figure 8.4. The basic parabola, $y = x^2 w$, is shown in blue. When the multiplicative factor $a = 2$ is applied ($y = 2x^2$), the result is the parabola shown in pink. Note that it forms a steeper bowl than the basic parabola because $|a| > 1$. When the multiplicative factor $a = \frac{1}{2}$ is applied $\left(y = \frac{1}{2}x^2\right)$, the result is the parabola shown in green. Note that it forms a shallower bowl than the basic parabola because $|a| < 1$.

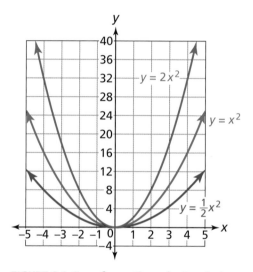

FIGURE 8.4 Transformation of a Parabola

Example 8.5

The parabola $y = x^2$ is shifted 3 units to the left and 1 unit up from the origin. Write its equation in vertex form and standard form.

Solution:

The vertex of $y = x^2$ is (0, 0). If the parabola is shifted 3 units to the left, then $h = -3$. A shift of 1 unit up means that $k = 1$. Therefore, $y = (x + 3)^2 + 1$.

To write the equation in standard form, expand the squared binomial and simplify.

$$y = (x + 3)^2 + 1 = (x + 3)(x + 3) + 1 = x^2 + 6x + 9 + 1 = x^2 + 6x + 10$$

Example 8.6

The parabola $y = x^2$ shifts 2 units down and 6 units to the right from the origin. It is stretched to be twice as steep as the original parabola. Write its equation in vertex form and standard form.

Solution:

A shift of 2 units down means that $k = -2$, and a shift of 6 units to the right means that $h = 6$. If the parabola is twice as steep, this indicates that $a = 2$.

In vertex form, the equation is $y = 2(x - 6)^2 - 2$.

Expanding and simplifying this yields $y = 2(x^2 - 12x + 36) - 2 = 2x^2 - 24x + 72 - 2$. So, $y = 2x^2 - 24x + 70$ in standard form.

DIY PROBLEMS

8.6 The parabola $y = x^2$ is shifted 2 units to the right and 2 units up from the origin. Write its equation in vertex form.

8.7 The parabola $y = x^2$ shifts 4 units left and 1 unit down. It is also compressed by a factor of $\frac{1}{2}$. Write its equation in vertex form and standard form.

8.8 The parabola $y = x^2$ is shifted 1.5 units up and 0.75 units to the right. It is otherwise untransformed. Write its equation in vertex form and standard form.

Axis of Symmetry

A parabola is symmetric about a line that runs vertically through its vertex. The **axis of symmetry** of a parabola is the vertical line through the vertex.

If the quadratic function is in vertex form, the axis of symmetry is $x = h$. If the quadratic function is in standard form, the axis of symmetry is $x = -\frac{b}{2a}$. Knowing the axis of symmetry of a parabola is useful because it halves the number of points necessary to accurately draw the graph.

8.7 AXIS OF SYMMETRY A vertical line through the vertex of the parabola, given by $x = h$ in vertex form and $x = -\frac{b}{2a}$ in standard form.

Example 8.7

Find the axis of symmetry of $y = (x-2)^2 - 5$.

Solution:

Since $h = 2$ in this equation, the axis of symmetry is the line $x = 2$ (Figure 8.5).

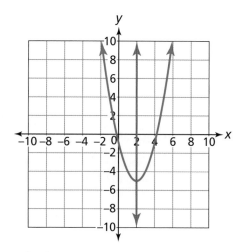

FIGURE 8.5

Example 8.8

Find the axis of symmetry of $y = 4x^2 + 16x + 25$.

Solution:

For quadratic functions in standard form, the axis of symmetry is $x = -\dfrac{b}{2a}$. In this case, $-\dfrac{b}{2a} = -\dfrac{16}{2 \cdot 4} = -2$. Thus, the axis of symmetry is the line $x = -2$ (Figure 8.6).

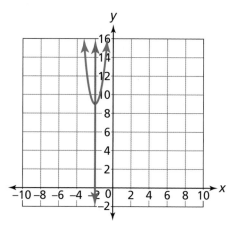

FIGURE 8.6

DIY PROBLEMS

8.9 Find the axis of symmetry of the parabola given by $y = 6(x + 2)^2 - 1$.

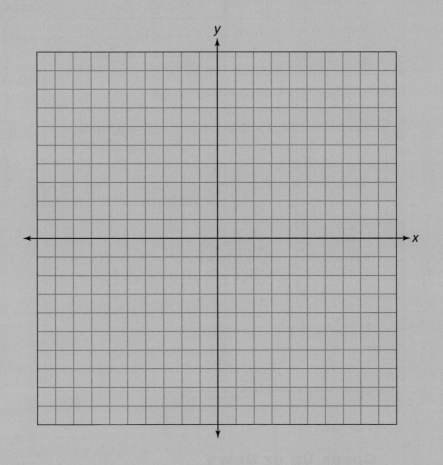

8.10 Find the axis of symmetry of the parabola given by $y = (x - 3)^2 - 4$.

8.11 Find the axis of symmetry of the parabola given by $y = -2x^2 + x - 3$.

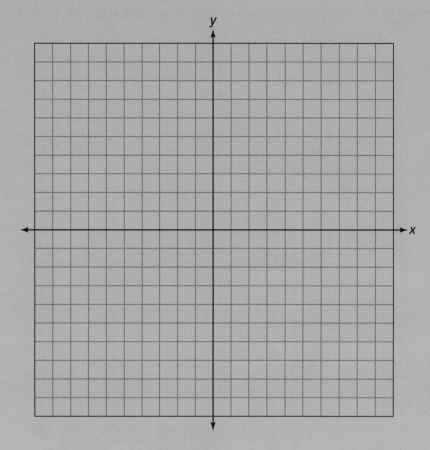

Opens Up or Down

In both forms of the quadratic function, the sign of a controls whether the parabola opens up or down. If $a > 0$, the parabola opens upward, and is $a < 0$, it opens downward.

Example 8.9

Does the parabola given by $y = -2(x-6)^2 + 5$ open up or down?

Solution:

In this equation $a = -2$, so the parabola opens down and is twice as steep as $y = x^2$ (Figure 8.7).

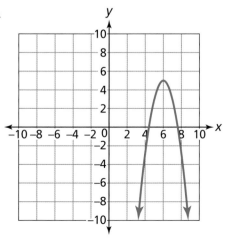

FIGURE 8.7

Example 8.10

Does the parabola given by $y = x^2 - 3x + 5$ open up or down?

Solution:

In this case $a = 1$, so the parabola opens up (Figure 8.8).

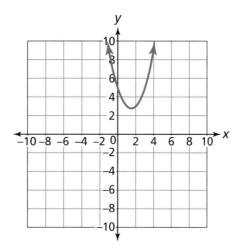

FIGURE 8.8

DIY PROBLEMS

8.12 Which way does the parabola given by $y = 3(x - 5)^2 + 1$ open?

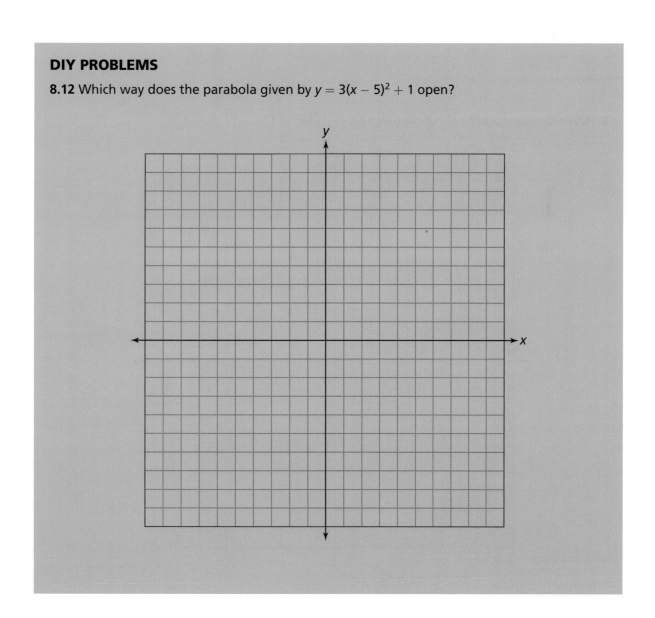

8.13 Does the parabola given by $y = (x + 3)^2 + 2$ open up or down?

8.14 Which way does the parabola given by $y = -6x^2 + 19x - 17$ open?

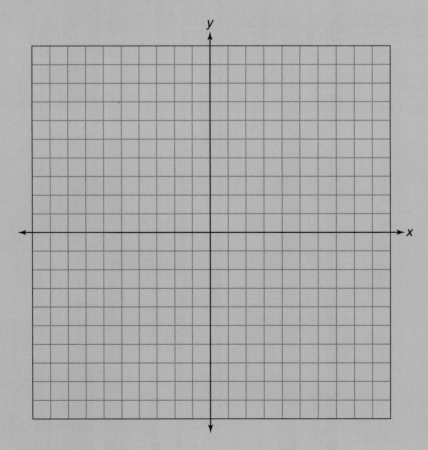

Discriminant

The **discriminant** of a quadratic function in standard form is the quantity $b^2 - 4ac$. The discriminant indicates the number of roots of the equation. A *root* is a value where the parabola intersects the x-axis and the quadratic equation has value 0. If $b^2 - 4ac < 0$, then the equation has no real roots and the graph of the parabola lies completely above or below the x-axis. If $b^2 - 4ac = 0$, the equation has one root and the vertex is on the x-axis. And finally, if $b^2 - 4ac > 0$, the equation has two roots and the graph of the parabola crosses the x-axis in two places. From now on we will refer to the roots of a quadratic function as well as the roots of the related equations.

8.8 DISCRIMINANT The quantity $b^2 - 4ac$, which determines the number of roots of a quadratic equation in standard form.

Example 8.11

How many roots does $y = 2x^2 + 3x - 5$ have?

Solution:

Calculate the value of the discriminant.

$b^2 - 4ac = 3^2 - 4 \cdot 2 \cdot (-5) = 49$

This is greater than 0, so the quadratic equation has two roots (Figure 8.9).

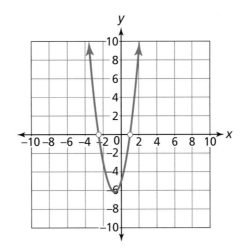

FIGURE 8.9

Example 8.12

How many roots does the equation $y = -2(x - 3)^2$ have?

Solution:

Step 1: Expand the equation into standard form.

$y = -2(x - 3)^2$
$y = -2(x - 3)(x - 3)$
$y = -2(x^2 - 6x + 9)$
$y = -2x^2 + 12x - 18$

Step 2: Calculate the discriminant.

$b^2 - 4ac = 12^2 - 4 \cdot (-2) \cdot (-18) = 0$

The discriminant is 0, so the equation has one root.
Notice that if $y = -2(x - 3)^2$ is set equal to 0, then $-2(x - 3)^2 = 0$. Using the Zero Product Property, the only solution will be $x = 3$. This reflects the fact that if $k = 0$ in the vertex form of a quadratic function, the vertex is unmoved from the x-axis, so there is a single solution.

SOLVING BY COMPLETING THE SQUARE

Completing the square of a quadratic function transforms the equation from standard form into vertex form. This method is useful for solving quadratic equations and putting the function in an easy-to-graph form. In general, the method of completing the square proceeds as follows.

Step 1 Set the standard form of the quadratic equal to zero.

$ax^2 + bx + c = 0$

Step 2 Factor out the leading coefficient a from the *first two terms* of the equation.

$$ax^2 + bx + c = 0 \rightarrow a\left(x^2 + \frac{b}{a}x\right) + c = 0$$

Making the expression inside the parentheses into a perfect square trinomial requires some care to ensure that the resulting equation is equivalent to the original. Remember that a perfect square trinomial with $a = 1$ has the form $x^2 + 2qx + q^2 = (x + q)^2$. So if $2q = \dfrac{b}{a}$, then $q = \dfrac{b}{2a}$ and $q^2 = \dfrac{b^2}{4a^2}$.

Step 3 So add $\dfrac{b^2}{4a^2}$ inside the parentheses.

In order for the equations to remain equivalent, whatever term has been added by adding $\dfrac{b^2}{4a^2}$ inside the parentheses must be subtracted as well. The term that is added is the product of a and $\dfrac{b^2}{4a^2}$.

Step 4 So subtract $a \cdot \dfrac{b^2}{4a^2} = \dfrac{b^2}{4a}$.

$$a\left(x^2 + \frac{b}{a}x\right) + c = 0 \rightarrow a\left(x^2 + \frac{b}{a}x + \frac{b^2}{4a^2}\right) + c - \frac{b^2}{4a} = 0$$

Notice that there is a check for this work: if the constant a is distributed inside the parentheses, the two new terms sum to 0 and the original equation is recovered.

Step 5 Factor the perfect square trinomial inside the parentheses using the formula shown above: $x^2 + 2qx + q^2 = (x+q)^2$.

$$a\left(x^2 + \frac{b}{a}x + \frac{b^2}{4a^2}\right) + c - \frac{b^2}{4a} = 0 \rightarrow a\left(x + \frac{b}{2a}\right)^2 + c - \frac{b^2}{4a} = 0$$

Compare this equation to vertex form and notice that $h = -\dfrac{b}{2a}$ and $k = c - \dfrac{b^2}{4a}$.

Example 8.13

Use the method of completing the square to solve the equation $x^2 + 2x - 3 = 0$.

Solution:

Step 1: Put the first two terms in the quadratic equation in parentheses.

$(x^2 + 2x) - 3 = 0$

Step 2: Note that $a = 1$. Find the term that is needed to create a perfect square trinomial. Here $\dfrac{b^2}{4a^2} = \dfrac{2^2}{4 \cdot 1^2} = 1$, so write

$(x^2 + 2x + 1) - 3 - 1 = 0 \rightarrow (x^2 + 2x + 1) - 4 = 0$

Step 3: Factor the trinomial into the square of a binomial.

$(x^2 + 2x + 1) - 4 = 0 \rightarrow (x+1)^2 - 4 = 0$

Step 4: To solve for x, first add 4 to both sides of the equation.

$(x+1)^2 - 4 + 4 = 4 \rightarrow (x+1)^2 = 4$

Step 5: Take the square root of both sides.

$\sqrt{(x+1)^2} = \sqrt{4} \rightarrow x + 1 = \pm 2$

Step 6: Subtract 1 from both sides and find the solutions.

$x + 1 - 1 = -1 \pm 2 \rightarrow x = 1, x = -3$

Step 7: Check these possible solutions in the original equation $x^2 + 2x - 3 = 0$. Both are roots of the quadratic equation since $1 + 2 - 3 = 0$ and $9 - 6 - 3 = 0$. Figure 8.10 shows the graph of the related quadratic function.

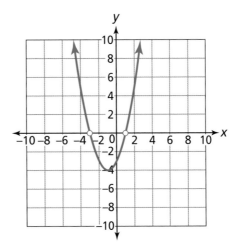

FIGURE 8.10

Example 8.14

Use the method of completing the square to solve $\frac{1}{2}x^2 - \frac{3}{2}x - 5 = 0$.

Solution:

Step 1: Put the first two terms in parentheses.

$$\frac{1}{2}x^2 - \frac{3}{2}x - 5 = 0 \rightarrow \left(\frac{1}{2}x^2 - \frac{3}{2}x\right) - 5 = 0$$

Step 2: Factor $\frac{1}{2}$ out of the term in parentheses.

$$\left(\frac{1}{2}x^2 - \frac{3}{2}x\right) - 5 = 0 \rightarrow \frac{1}{2}(x^2 - 3x) - 5 = 0$$

Step 3: In this example, $\frac{b^2}{4a^2} = \frac{(-3)^2}{4 \cdot 1^2} = \frac{9}{4}$ and the term added is $\frac{1}{2} \cdot \frac{9}{4} = \frac{9}{8}$, so write

$$\frac{1}{2}\left(x^2 - 3x + \frac{9}{4}\right) - \frac{9}{8} - 5 = 0 \rightarrow \frac{1}{2}\left(x^2 - 3x + \frac{9}{4}\right) - \frac{49}{8} = 0$$

Step 4: Factor the trinomial in parentheses and add $\frac{49}{8}$ to both sides of the equation.

$$\frac{1}{2}\left(x^2 - 3x + \frac{9}{4}\right) - \frac{49}{8} = 0 \rightarrow \frac{1}{2}\left(x - \frac{3}{2}\right)^2 = \frac{49}{8}$$

Step 5: Multiply both sides of the equation by two and take the square root of each side.

$$\sqrt{\left(x - \frac{3}{2}\right)^2} = \sqrt{\frac{49}{4}} \rightarrow x - \frac{3}{2} = \pm\frac{7}{2}$$

Step 6: Add three halves to both sides and find the solutions.

$$x - \frac{3}{2} + \frac{3}{2} = \frac{3}{2} \pm \frac{7}{2} \rightarrow x = 5, x = -2$$

Step 7: Check. Both values are roots of the equation.

DIY PROBLEMS

8.18 Complete the square for $x^2 + 16x$ and then factor the resulting perfect square trinomial.

8.19 Find the solutions of $6x^2 + 12x = 0$ by completing the squares.

8.20 Find the solutions of $-2x^2 + 12x - 10 = 0$.

SOLVING BY USING THE QUADRATIC FORMULA

After completing the square, it is possible to apply a little more algebra to generate a formula for the zeros of a quadratic equation.

Beginning with the final step in the previous section, move the constants to the right-hand side of the equation.

$$a\left(x+\frac{b}{2a}\right)^2 + c - \frac{b^2}{4a} = 0 \rightarrow a\left(x+\frac{b}{2a}\right)^2 = \frac{b^2}{4a} - c$$

Dividing both sides by a yields

$$\left(x+\frac{b}{2a}\right)^2 = \frac{b^2}{4a^2} - \frac{c}{a}$$

Combine the fractions on the right-hand side of the equation into one fraction by multiplying the second term by $\frac{4a}{4a}$.

$$\left(x+\frac{b}{2a}\right)^2 = \frac{b^2}{4a^2} - \frac{c}{a}\frac{4a}{4a} \rightarrow \left(x+\frac{b}{2a}\right)^2 = \frac{b^2-4ac}{4a^2}$$

Take the square root of both sides.

$$\sqrt{\left(x+\frac{b}{2a}\right)^2} = \sqrt{\frac{b^2-4ac}{4a^2}} \rightarrow x+\frac{b}{2a} = \frac{\pm\sqrt{b^2-4ac}}{2a}$$

Subtracting $\frac{b}{2a}$ from both sides yields the **quadratic formula:**

$$x = -\frac{b}{2a} \pm \frac{\sqrt{b^2-4ac}}{2a} = \frac{-b\pm\sqrt{b^2-4ac}}{2a}$$

> **8.10 QUADRATIC FORMULA**
> For a quadratic equation
> $ax^2 + bx + c = 0$, the quadratic
> formula is $x = -\frac{b}{2a} \pm \frac{\sqrt{b^2-4ac}}{2a}$
> $= \frac{-b\pm\sqrt{b^2-4ac}}{2a}$.

Notice that the radicand is the discriminant. This formula can be used to directly calculate the roots of any quadratic equation, provided $b^2 - 4ac \geq 0$. The discriminant *discriminates* between quadratic equations with solutions and those without. If it is less than 0, then there are no real solutions to the equation, since taking the square root of a negative number does not yield a real number. If it equals 0, then the whole second term is 0, and there is only one solution.

Example 8.15

Find the roots of $2x^2 + 10x - 28 = 0$ using the quadratic formula.

Solution:

Step 1: Identify the constants: $a = 2, b = 10, c = -28$.

Step 2: Plug the constants into the quadratic formula and solve.

$$x = -\frac{10}{4} \pm \frac{\sqrt{100 - 4 \cdot 2 \cdot (-28)}}{4} = -\frac{5}{2} \pm \frac{\sqrt{324}}{4} = -\frac{5}{2} \pm \frac{9}{2} \rightarrow x = -7, x = 2$$

Example 8.16

Find the roots of $-3x^2 + 12x - 10 = 0$ using the quadratic formula.

Solution:

Step 1: Identify the constants: $a = -3, b = 12, c = -10$.

Step 2: Plug the constants into the quadratic formula and solve.

$$x = -\frac{12}{2 \cdot (-3)} \pm \frac{\sqrt{144 - 4 \cdot (-3) \cdot (-10)}}{2 \cdot (-3)} = 2 \pm \frac{\sqrt{24}}{6} = 2 \pm \frac{\sqrt{6}}{3} \rightarrow x \approx 2.94, x \approx 1.057$$

DIY PROBLEMS

8.21 Identify the value of *a*, *b*, and *c* in each quadratic equation.

    a.) $3x^2 + 4x + 2 = 0$

    b.) $x^2 + 7x = 0$

8.22 Find the roots of $4x^2 - 12x + 9 = 0$ using the quadratic formula.

8.23 Find the roots of $-2x^2 - 12x + 10 = 0$ using the quadratic formula.

SOLVING BY USING THE SQUARE ROOT METHOD

8.11 SQUARE ROOT METHOD A method of solving quadratic equations by taking the square root of both sides of the equation, such that the square of a variable or linear binomial is one side of the equation and the other side contains no variable.

Most quadratic equations cannot be solved by factoring because their roots are not whole numbers. In addition to the quadratic formula, another method to use for these types of problems is the **square root method.**

The square root method for solving a quadratic equation takes the square root of both sides of the equation, where the square of a variable or linear binomial is one side and the other side contains no variable.

It is then relatively straightforward to solve the equation. In a previous chapter, the square root method was used for equations that had no first-degree term. This is reviewed in Example 8.17. Example 8.18 expands the method to a quadratic equation written in vertex form, which suggests that by using completing the square, this method will solve any quadratic equation.

Example 8.17

Find the roots of the function $y = 2x^2 - 16$ using the square root method.

Solution:

Step 1: Set the quadratic expression equal to zero.

$$y = 2x^2 - 16 \rightarrow 2x^2 - 16 = 0$$

Step 2: Add 16 to both sides, and then divide both sides by 2 to get:

$$2x^2 = 16 \rightarrow x^2 = 8$$

Step 3: Take the square root of both sides in order to get the x alone. Remember that taking square roots of both sides of an equation yields a positive and negative result.

$$x^2 = 8 \rightarrow \sqrt{x^2} = \sqrt{8} \rightarrow x = \pm\sqrt{8} \approx \pm 2.828$$

Example 8.18

Find the roots of the function $f(x) = 3(x + 2)^2 - 9$ using the square root method.

Solution:

Step 1: Set the function equal to zero.

$$f(x) = 3(x + 2)^2 - 9 \rightarrow 3(x + 2)^2 - 9 = 0$$

Step 2: Add 9 to both sides and divide both sides by 3 to get:

$$(x + 2)^2 = 3$$

Step 3: Take the square root of both sides.

$$(x + 2)^2 = 3 \rightarrow \sqrt{(x + 2)^2} = \sqrt{3} \rightarrow x + 2 = \pm\sqrt{3}$$

Step 4: Subtract 2 from both sides and evaluate the roots.

$$x = \sqrt{3} - 2 \rightarrow x \approx -.268, x \approx -3.732$$

DIY PROBLEMS

8.24 Solve $x^2 = 25$.

8.25 Find the roots of the function $f(x) = 9x^2 - 16$.

8.26 Find the roots of the function $y = (x - 3)^2 - 2$.

8.27 Find the roots of the function $y = 6(x + 1)^2 - 17$.

APPLICATIONS OF THE QUADRATIC EQUATION

Maximum/Minimum Revenue/Cost Problems

Economists often use revenue functions and cost functions. The cost function, often denoted $C(x)$, indicates the amount of money required to produce x items. The revenue function, $R(x)$, gives the amount of money made from the sale of x items. Economists define the profit function as the difference of the revenue function and the cost function: $P(x) = R(x) - C(x)$.

In many cases the cost function is a second-order equation. Economists use these functions to find the minimum number of items that must be sold to cover production costs. This value is called the break-even point, and it occurs when the profit is zero: $P(x) = R(x) - C(x) = 0$.

Marginal quantities are also useful economics concepts to which the methods of this chapter apply. Refer to the marginal revenue as $R'(x)$, the marginal cost as $C'(x)$, and the marginal profit as $P'(x)$. The **marginal cost,** for example, is the amount of money required to produce one additional unit. Mathematically,

$$C'(x) = \frac{C(x+1) - C(x)}{1}.$$

The numerator represents the change in cost, and the denominator represents the change in the number of items produced. Marginal profit, $P'(x)$, and marginal revenue, $R'(x)$, have parallel definitions.

Marginal quantities are useful because they allow economists to calculate the number of items that must be sold to maximize the profit function.

Consider the marginal profit $P'(x) = \dfrac{P(x+1) - P(x)}{1}$. The maximum profit is the point where adding one more unit won't increase the profit anymore. This means that the marginal profit must be zero at that point. Since $P'(x) = R'(x) - C'(x)$, if the marginal profit is 0, then $R'(x) - C'(x) = 0$, and the methods outlined in this chapter are again useful.

8.12 MARGINAL QUANTITIES Functions derived from the cost, revenue, and profit functions that indicate the change in each of these quantities from the production of one more unit.

8.13 MARGINAL COST The difference between successive costs as production increases by one unit, expressed by the equation $C'(x) = \frac{C(x+1) - C(x)}{1}$.

Example 8.19

Suppose that a certain manufacturing process has a cost function, $C(x) = -.1x^2 + 2x + 100$. This corresponds to fixed costs of $100 and variable costs that depend on the number of units produced. Assume that the revenue function is $R(x) = 4x$, meaning that each item sells for $4. Find the profit function and calculate the break-even point.

Solution:

Step 1: Calculate the profit function. The profit function is the difference of the revenue function and the cost function, so

$$P(x) = R(x) - C(x) = 4x + .1x^2 - 2x - 100 = .1x^2 + 2x - 100 \cdot$$

Step 2: The break-even point occurs when the profit equals 0, so set the profit function equal to 0 and solve.

$$P(x) = .1x^2 + 2x - 100 = 0$$

Since this problem uses standard quadratic function notation but cannot be easily factored, it is best tackled with the quadratic equation. Substitute the coefficient values into the quadratic equation.

$$x = -\frac{2}{2 \cdot (.1)} \pm \frac{\sqrt{4 - 4 \cdot (.1) \cdot (-100)}}{2 \cdot (.1)} = -10 \pm 5\sqrt{44} = -10 \pm 10\sqrt{11}$$

This yields $x \approx 23.17, x \approx -43.17$.

The negative value is not a plausible solution for this problem, so at least 24 items must be sold in order to make a profit.

Example 8.20

Now imagine that a certain product has a cost function $C(x) = .02x^2 + x + 300$, meaning that there are $300 of fixed costs and that the variable cost tends to increase as the number of items is increased. If this product sells for $7 per item, so $R(x) = 7x$, find the number of units that maximizes the profit and what that profit is.

Solution:

Step 1: This is a marginal profit problem, so first find the profit function.

$$P(x) = R(x) - C(x) = 7x - .02x^2 - x - 300 = -.02x^2 + 6x - 300$$

Step 2: Find the marginal profit function.

$$P'(x) = \frac{P(x+1) - P(x)}{1} = -.02(x+1)^2 + 6(x+1) - 300 - (-.02x^2 + 6x - 300)$$

$$= -.02(x^2 + 2x + 1) + 6x + 6 - 300 + .02x^2 - 6x + 300 = -.04x + 5.98$$

Step 3: Set this equal to 0 and solve to find the number of items sold that results in the maximum profit.

$$P'(x) = -.04x + 5.98 = 0 \rightarrow x = 149.5$$

This indicates that both 149 and 150 items will produce the nearly maximum profit.

Step 4: Choose 150 as the number of items and substitute that into the profit function to find the actual profit.

$$P(150) = .02(150)^2 + 6(150) - 300 = 1050$$

Thus the maximum profit is $1,050.

DIY Problems

8.28 The manufacture of a certain product has a cost function of $C(x) = -.3x^2 + 2x + 500$. This corresponds to fixed costs of \$500 and variable costs that tend to decrease with increased production. Assume that the revenue function is $R(x) = 12x$, meaning that each item sells for \$12. Find the profit function and calculate the break-even point.

8.29 A certain industrial product has a cost function of $C(x) = .001x^2 + 200x + 12000$, meaning that there are \$12,000 dollars of fixed costs and that the variable cost tends to increase as the number of items is increased due to the costs of replacing precision machinery used in the manufacturing process. If this product sells for \$4,000 per item, find the number of units that maximizes the profit and what that profit is.

SOLUTIONS TO DIY PROBLEMS

8.1 Write the quadratic function with coefficients $a = -\dfrac{3}{2}$, $b = -\dfrac{1}{3}$, and $c = 5$.

Solution:
Insert the constants into the general form of the quadratic equation.

$$y = -\frac{3}{2}x^2 - \frac{1}{3}x + 5$$

8.2 What are the coefficients of the quadratic function $y = 9x^2 + 2x - 15$?

Solution:
Compare this equation to the general form and read off the constants: $a = 9$, $b = 2$, and $c = -15$.

8.3 Find the vertex of $y = (x + 3)^2 - 5$. Draw the graph of the parabola.

Solution:
Step 1: For clarity, write the equation with the same signs as the definition of vertex form.

$$y = (x + 3)^2 - 5 \rightarrow y = (x - (-3))^2 + (-5)$$

Step 2: Read off h and k from the rearranged equation: $h = -3$, $k = -5$.
Step 3: Make a table of x and y values.

x	y
−5	−1
−4	−4
−3	−5
−2	−4
−1	−1

Step 4: Graph the function using the values above (Figure 8.11).

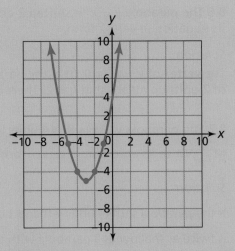

FIGURE 8.11

8.4 Find the vertex of the equation $y = 3(x + 2)^2 + 3$.

Solution:

Step 1: For clarity, rewrite the equation with the same signs as the definition given above.

$y = 3(x + 2)^2 + 3 \rightarrow y = 3(x - (-2))^2 + 3$

Step 2: By analogy to the definition, see that $h = -2$ and $k = 3$. Thus the vertex is at the point $(h, k) = (-2, 3)$.

8.5 Find the vertex of $y = 3x^2 + 2$. Draw the graph of the parabola.

Solution:

Step 1: $y = 3x^2 + 2$ can be written as $3(x - 0)^2 + 2$. This means $h = 0$ and $k = 2$.

Step 2: Make a table of x and y values.

x	y
−2	14
−1	5
0	2
1	5
2	14

Step 3: Graph the function using these values (Figure 8.12).

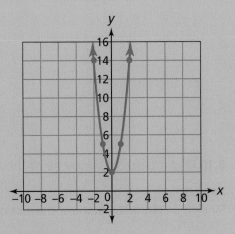

FIGURE 8.12

8.6 The parabola $y = x^2$ is shifted 2 units to the right and 2 units up from the origin. Write its equation in vertex form.

Solution:
The vertex of $y = x^2$ is (0, 0), If the parabola is shifted 2 units to the right, then $h = 2$. A shift of 2 units up means that $k = 2$. Therefore, $y = (x - 2)^2 + 2$.

8.7 The parabola $y = x^2$ shifts 4 units left and 1 unit down. It is also compressed by a factor of $\frac{1}{2}$. Write its equation in vertex form and standard form.

Solution:
If the parabola shifts 4 units left and 1 unit down, then $h = -4$ and $k = -1$. Since the parabola is twice as shallow as a parabola with coefficient 1, $a = \frac{1}{2}$.

In vertex form, the equation is $y = \frac{1}{2}(x + 4)^2 - 1$. Expanding into general form yields $y = \frac{1}{2}x^2 + 4x + 7$.

8.8 The parabola $y = x^2$ is shifted 1.5 units up and 0.75 units to the right. It is otherwise untransformed. Write its equation in vertex form and standard form.

Solution:
The vertex is $(h, k) = (.75, 1.5)$, so the quadratic equation in vertex form is $y = (x - .75)^2 + 1.5$. Expanding into standard form yields $y = x^2 - 1.5x + 2.0625$.

8.9 Find the axis of symmetry of the parabola given by $y = 6(x + 2)^2 - 1$.

Solution:
The axis of symmetry is a vertical line running through the vertex $(-2, -1)$. So the axis of symmetry is $x = -2$ (Figure 8.13).

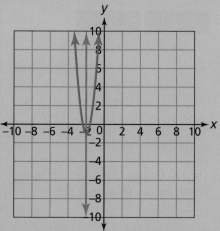

FIGURE 8.13

8.10 Find the axis of symmetry of the parabola given by $y = (x - 3)^2 - 4$.

Solution:
Since $h = 3$ in this equation, the axis of symmetry is the line $x = 3$.

8.11 Find the axis of symmetry of the parabola given by $y = -2x^2 + x - 3$.

Solution:

The axis of symmetry is given by $x = -\dfrac{b}{2a}$. In this problem $-\dfrac{b}{2a} = \dfrac{1}{4}$, so the axis of symmetry is $x = \dfrac{1}{4}$ (Figure 8.14).

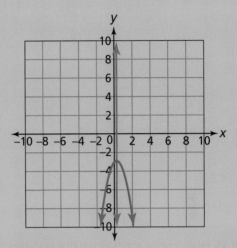

FIGURE 8.14

8.12 Which way does the parabola given by $y = 3(x - 5)^2 + 1$ open?

Solution:

The 3 is greater than 0, so the parabola opens upward (Figure 8.15).

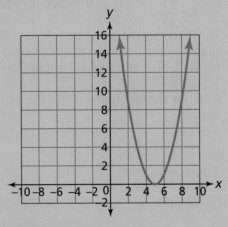

FIGURE 8.15

8.13 Does the parabola given by $y = (x + 3)^2 + 2$ open up or down?

Solution:
In this case $a = 1$, so the parabola opens up.

8.14 Which way does the parabola given by $y = -6x^2 + 19x - 17$ open?

Solution:

The -6 is less than 0, so the parabola opens downward (Figure 8.16).

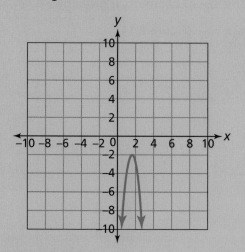

FIGURE 8.16

8.15 How many roots does the equation $y = 2(x - 3)^2 + 5$ have?

Solution:

Step 1: Expand the equation into standard form.

$$y = 2(x - 3)^2 + 5 = 2(x^2 - 6x + 9) + 5 = 2x^2 - 12x + 23$$

Step 2: Find the discriminant.

$$b^2 - 4ac = (-12)^2 - 4 \cdot 2 \cdot 23 = 144 - 184 = -40$$

The discriminant is less than 0, so this quadratic equation has no roots. This means that the graph of the parabola does not cross the x-axis, which is not a surprise. Notice that the vertex is (3, 5), and $a = 2 > 0$ implies the parabola opens up, so the vertex is a minimum.

8.16 Use the discriminant to determine the number of x-intercepts of the graph of the equation.

$$y = 2x^2 + 2x - 1$$

Solution:

$$b^2 - 4ac = 2^2 - 4(2)(-1) = 12$$

This is greater than 0, so the quadratic equation has two roots.

8.17 At how many points does the equation $f(x) = 9x^2 + 42x + 49$ cross the x-axis?

Solution:

Find the discriminant.

$$b^2 - 4ac = 42^2 - 4 \cdot 9 \cdot 49 = 1764 - 1764 = 0$$

This equation only has one root, so its graph only touches the x-axis at one point. This means that its vertex is on the x-axis.

8.18 Complete the square for $x^2 + 16x$ and then factor the resulting perfect square trinomial.

Solution:
The coefficient of the x-term is 16. Half of 16 is 8 and $8^2 = 64$. Add 64

$$x^2 + 16x + 64 = (x + 8)^2$$

8.19 Find the solutions of $6x^2 + 12x = 0$ by completing the square.

Solution:
Step 1: Put the first two terms in parentheses.

$$y = (6x^2 + 12x)$$

Step 2: Factor 6 out of the first two terms.

$$y = (6x^2 + 12x) \rightarrow y = 6(x^2 + 2x)$$

Step 3: In this problem $\dfrac{b^2}{4a^2} = 1$. Add this quantity inside the parentheses and subtract $\dfrac{b^2}{4a} = 6$ outside.

$$y = 6(x^2 + 2x) \rightarrow y = 6(x^2 + 2x + 1) - 6$$

Step 4: Now factor the terms inside the parentheses according to the rule for a perfect square trinomial.

$$y = 6(x^2 + 2x + 1) - 6 = 6(x + 1)^2 - 6$$

Step 5: Set y equal to 0 and begin to solve.

$$6(x + 1)^2 - 6 = 0 \rightarrow 6(x + 1)^2 = 6 \rightarrow (x + 1)^2 = 1$$

Step 6: Take the square root of both sides and solve for x.

$$\sqrt{(x + 1)^2} = \sqrt{1} \rightarrow x + 1 = \pm 1 \rightarrow x = -1 \pm 1 \rightarrow x = 0, x = -2$$

Step 7: Check. Both values are roots of the equation.

8.20 Find the solutions of $-2x^2 + 12x - 10 = 0$ using the method of completing the square.

Solution:
Step 1: Write the first two terms inside parentheses.

$$y = (-2x^2 + 12x) - 10$$

Step 2: Factor the a term out of the parentheses.

$$y = -2(x^2 - 6x) - 10$$

Step 3: Since $\dfrac{b^2}{4a^2} = 9$ and $\dfrac{b^2}{4a} = -18$, add 9 inside the parentheses and add 18 outside the parentheses.

$$y = -2(x^2 - 6x) - 10 \rightarrow y = -2(x^2 - 6x + 9) - 10 + 8 \rightarrow y = -2(x^2 - 6x + 9) + 8$$

Step 4: Factor the perfect square trinomial.

$$y = -2(x^2 - 6x + 9) + 8 \rightarrow y = -2(x-3)^2 + 8$$

Step 5: Set y equal to 0 and begin to solve.

$$-2(x-3)^2 + 8 = 0 \rightarrow -2(x-3)^2 = -8 \rightarrow (x-3)^2 = 4$$

Step 6: Take the square root of both sides and solve for x.

$$\sqrt{(x-3)^2} = \sqrt{4} \rightarrow x - 3 = \pm 2 \rightarrow x = 3 \pm 2 \rightarrow x = 5, x = 1$$

Step 7: Check. Both values are roots of the equation.

8.21 Identify the value of a, b, and c in each quadratic equation.

   a.) $3x^2 + 4x + 2 = 0$

   b.) $x^2 + 7x = 0$

Solution:
   a.) $a = 3$, $b = 4$, $c = 2$

   b.) $a = 1$, $b = 7$, $c = 0$

8.22 Find the roots of $4x^2 - 12x + 9 = 0$ using the quadratic formula.

Solution:
Step 1: Read off the coefficients: $a = 4$, $b = -12$, and $c = 9$.
Step 2: Plug the coefficients into the quadratic formula.

$$x = -\frac{-12}{2 \cdot 4} \pm \frac{\sqrt{(-12)^2 - 4 \cdot 4 \cdot 9}}{2 \cdot 4} = \frac{3}{2} \pm \frac{\sqrt{144 - 144}}{8} = \frac{3}{2}$$

This equation has one root, so the vertex of the related parabola must be on the x-axis at the point $\left(\frac{3}{2}, 0\right)$.

8.23 Find the roots of $-2x^2 - 12x + 10 = 0$ using the quadratic formula.

Solution:
Step 1: Read off the coefficients: $a = -2$, $b = -12$, and $c = 10$.
Step 2: Plug the coefficients into the quadratic formula.

$$x = -\frac{-12}{2 \cdot (-2)} \pm \frac{\sqrt{(-12)^2 - 4 \cdot (-2) \cdot 10}}{2 \cdot (-2)} = -3 \pm \frac{\sqrt{144 + 80}}{-4} = -3 + \sqrt{14}$$

Therefore, $x \approx -6.74$, $x \approx .742$.

8.24 Solve $x^2 = 25$.

Solution:

$$x^2 = 25$$
$$\sqrt{x^2} = \sqrt{25}$$
$$|x| = 5$$

The solutions of $|x| = 5$ and -5. Therefore, the solutions of $x^2 = 25$ are -5 and 5.

8.25 Find the roots of the function $f(x) = 9x^2 - 16$.

Solution:

$$9x^2 - 16 = 0$$
$$9x^2 = 16$$
$$x^2 = \frac{16}{9}$$
$$\sqrt{x^2} = \sqrt{\frac{16}{9}}$$
$$x = \pm\frac{4}{3}$$

8.26 Find the roots of the equation $y = (x - 3)^2 - 2$.

Solution:
Step 1: Set the equation equal to 0: $(x - 3)^2 - 2 = 0$.
Step 2: Add 2 to both sides of the equation to get $(x - 3)^2 = 2$.
Step 3: Take the square root of both sides to get rid of the square. Remember that the square root of a number yields a positive and a negative root!

$$\sqrt{(x-3)^2} = \sqrt{2} \rightarrow x - 3 = \pm\sqrt{2}$$

Step 4: Add 3 to both sides of the equation and solve.

$$x = 3 \pm \sqrt{2} \rightarrow x \approx 4.414, x \approx 1.586$$

8.27 Find the roots of the equation $y = 6(x + 1)^2 - 17$.

Solution:
Step 1: Set the equation equal to 0: $6(x + 1)^2 - 17 = 0$.
Step 2: Add 17 to both sides and divide both sides by 6.

$$6(x + 1)^2 - 17 = 0 \rightarrow (x + 1)^2 = \frac{17}{6}$$

Step 3: Take the square root of both sides to get rid of the square. Remember to include both positive and negative roots.

$$\sqrt{(x+1)^2} = \sqrt{\frac{17}{6}} \rightarrow x + 1 = \pm\sqrt{\frac{17}{6}}$$

Step 4: Subtract 1 from both sides and evaluate x.

$$x = \sqrt{\frac{17}{6}} - 1 \rightarrow x \approx .683, -2.683$$

8.28 The manufacture of a certain product has a cost function of $C(x) = -.03x^2 + 2x + 500$. This corresponds to fixed costs of $500 and variable costs that tend to decrease with increased production. Assume that the revenue function is $R(x) = 12x$, meaning that each item sells for $12. Find the profit function and calculate the break-even point.

Solution:

Step 1: Calculate the profit function, which is the difference of the revenue function and the cost function.

$$P(x) = R(x) - C(x) = 12x + .03x^2 - 2x - 500 = .03x^2 + 10x - 500$$

Step 2: The break-even point occurs when the profit equals 0, so set the profit function equal to 0 and solve.

$$P(x) = .03x^2 + 10x - 500 = 0$$

This problem is best tackled with the quadratic equation, so substitute the values into the equation.

$$x = -\frac{10}{2\cdot(.03)} \pm \frac{\sqrt{100 - 4\cdot(.03)\cdot(-500)}}{2\cdot(.03)} = -\frac{-1000}{6} \pm 200\sqrt{\frac{10}{3}} \approx -166.67 \pm 210.82$$

Therefore, $x \approx -44.15$, $x \approx -377.45$. At least 45 items must be sold to make a profit.

8.29 A certain industrial product has a cost function of $C(x) = .001x^2 + 200x + 12,000$, meaning that there are $12,000 of fixed costs and that the variable cost tends to increase as the number of items is increased due to the costs of replacing precision machinery used in the manufacturing process. If this product sells for $4,000 per item, find the number of units that maximizes the profit and what that profit is.

Solution:

Step 1: This is a marginal profit problem, so first find the profit function:
$R(x) = 4000x$.

$$P(x) = R(x) - C(x) = 4000x - .001x^2 - 200x - 12000 = -.001x^2 + 3800x - 12000$$

Step 2: Find the marginal profit function.

$$P'(x) = \frac{P(x+1) - P(x)}{1} = (-.001)(x+1)^2 + 3800(x+1) - 12000 -$$
$$(-.001x^2 + 3800x - 12000) = -.001x^2 + (-.001)2x + (-.001) +$$
$$3800x + 3800 - 12000 + .001x^2 - 3800x + 12000 = -.002x - 3799.999$$

Step 3: Set this equal to 0 and solve to find the number of items sold that results in the maximum profit.

$$P'(x) = -.002x + 3799.999 = 0 \rightarrow x = 1,899,999.999$$

This indicates that both 1,899,999 and 1,900,000 items will produce the nearly maximum profit.
Step 4: Choose 1,900,000 as the number of items and substitute that into the profit function to find the actual profit.

$$P(1,900,000) = -.001(1,900,000)^2 + 3800(1,900,000) - 12,000 = 3.61\cdot10^9.$$

Thus the maximum profit is $3,610,000,000.

8.1 Write the quadratic function with coefficients $a = 8$, $b = 3$, and $c = 4$ in general form.

8.2 What are the coefficients of the quadratic function $y = 2x^2 + 3x + 10$.

8.3 The parabola $y = x^2$ is shifted 2 units to the left and 5 unit up from the origin. Write its equation in vertex form.

8.4 The parabola $y = x^2$ shifts 1 unit down and 3 units to the right from the origin. It is stretched to be three times as steep as the original parabola. Write its equation in vertex form.

8.5 If $f(x) = x^2$ is shown in Figure 8.17, graph $f(x) + 5$.

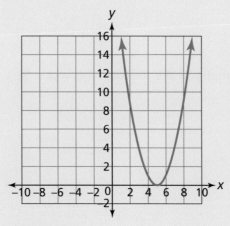

FIGURE 8.17

8.6 If the graph of $f(x) = 2x^2$ is shown in Figure 8.18, graph $f(x - 1)$.

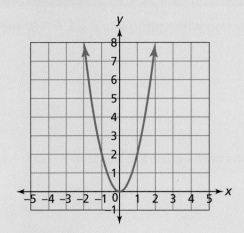

FIGURE 8.18

8.7 Figure 8.19 shows the graph of $f(x) = x^2 + 2$. Graph $-f(x)$.

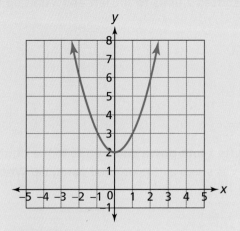

FIGURE 8.19

8.8 What is the axis of symmetry of the quadratic function $f(x) = -\frac{1}{2}x^2$?

8.9 What is the axis of symmetry of the function $f(x) = (x - 3)^2 - 4$.

8.10 What is the axis of symmetry of the function $f(x) = x^2 + 4x + 4$?

8.11 What is the axis of symmetry of the function $f(x) = 2x^2 + 3x + 1$.

8.12 Does the parabola given by $x^2 - 3x + 2$ open up or down?

8.13 Does the quadratic function $f(x) = -3x^2 + 2x + 5$ open up or open down?

8.14 Will the graph of the function $f(x) = \frac{3}{4}(x - 7)^2$ open upward or downward?

8.15 Find the vertex of the quadratic function $y = (x + 2)^2 - 4$.

8.16 Find the vertex of the equation $y = 3(x - 2)^2 + 3$.

8.17 How many x-intercepts can the graph of $f(x) = ax^2 + bx + c$ have?

8.18 How many y-intercepts does the graph of $f(x) = ax^2 + bx + c$ have?

8.19 Use the discriminant to determine the number of solutions of $3x^2 + 2x - 2 = 0$.

8.20 Use the discriminant to determine the number of solutions of $x^2 - 6x + 9 = 0$.

8.21 Use the discriminant to determine the number of solutions of $5x^2 + 1 = 0$.

8.22 Determine the coordinates of the vertex for the quadratic function $f(x) = \dfrac{3}{4}(x-7)^2$.

8.23 Determine the coordinates of the vertex for the quadratic function $f(x) = x^2 + 4x + 6$.

8.24 What number completes the square in the expression $x^2 + 18x$?

8.25 Find the number that will make the following a perfect square: $y^2 - \dfrac{1}{5}y + ?$

8.26 Complete the square for $x^2 + 10x$ then factor to the resulting perfect square trinomial.

8.27 Solve the following quadratic equation by completing the square: $x^2 - 8x = -12$.

8.28 Solve by completing the square: $x^2 - 14x - 4 = 0$.

8.29 Solve by completing the square: $2x^2 - 13x - 5 = 0$.

8.30 Identify the value of a, b, and c in the quadratic equation $x^2 - 7 = 0$.

8.31 Use the quadratic formula to solve $9x^2 - 7x - 3 = 0$.

8.32 Use the quadratic formula to solve $0.6x^2 = 1.2x + 0.06$.

8.33 Use the square root property to solve $x^2 = -4$.

8.34 Use the square root property to solve $x^2 - 16 = 0$.

8.35 Use the square root property to solve $3x^2 = 9$.

8.36 Use the square root property to solve $(x - 4)^2 = 25$.

REFERENCES

Cajori, F., & Odell, L. R. (1917). *Elementary algebra*. New York, NY: Macmillan.

Rietz, H. L., & Crathorne, A. R. (1909). *College algebra*. New York, NY: Henry Holt and Company.

Graphing Higher-Order Polynomials

QUESTIONS TO CONSIDER

1. How long should Andreas tell his patient to wait before taking the second drug if she takes it without eating?

2. How long should Andreas tell his patient to wait before taking the second drug if she takes it with food?

3. In both cases, when will drug A reach its maximum concentration in the patient's bloodstream?

4. In both cases, how long will it take for drug A to be completely gone from the patient's body?

KEY TERMS

➤ continuous (p. 314)
➤ even function (p. 318)
➤ local maximum (p. 329)
➤ local minimum (p. 329)
➤ multiplicity (p. 325)
➤ odd function (p. 318)
➤ polynomial function (p. 314)
➤ power function (p. 315)
➤ turning points (p. 329)
➤ zero (p. 321)

A ndreas works in a hospital pharmacy. The patients that he serves often come to his pharmacy with several prescriptions for very different medicines to be filled at the same time. Consequently, one of his most important tasks is to ensure that the medicines he dispenses do not have harmful interactions with each other. To this end, he dutifully checks up on all the medicines a patient is currently taking and cross-references all of them. Many medicines are absorbed by the body in very predictable ways, and he often has an equation that models the concentration of a certain drug in the bloodstream after the patient takes it.

Andreas has a patient who needs to take both drug A and drug B. Unfortunately, she cannot take drug B until drug A wears off, that is, when its concentration in her bloodstream is less than 0.025%. Andreas knows that his patient is a 135 lb female, so the concentration of drug A in her bloodstream is given by $f(x) = -.001x^4 + .05x$, where $f(x)$ is the concentration and x is the number of hours since the patient took the drug. This equation only holds if the patient takes the medicine without food. If the patient takes the medicine right before a meal, for example, its concentration in the patient is given by $f(x) = -.0001x^4 + .02x$.

DEFINITION OF POLYNOMIAL FUNCTIONS

9.1 POLYNOMIAL FUNCTION A function of the form $f(x) = a_n x^n + a_{n-1} x^{n-1} + a_{n-2} x^{n-2} + \ldots + a_1 x + a_0,$ where n is a nonnegative integer and a_n through a_0 are constant coefficients. The constant coefficients of a polynomial function can be any real numbers.

9.2 CONTINUOUS Polynomial functions for which the graph has no breaks, jumps, or holes.

A polynomial function *in one variable*—from now on a **polynomial function**—is a sum of terms that are constant multiples of nonnegative integer powers of a variable. If a function is **continuous**, its graph can be traced without lifting a pencil from the graph. Evaluating a function for a given value of the variable means substituting the value for the variable and computing the result.

Example 9.1
Which of these functions are polynomial functions?

a. $f(x) = x^4 - 10x^2 + 9$

b. $g(x) = x^{-2}y - p$

c. $h(x) = 4 - 0.56x + x^2$

d. $k(x) = 3x^{\frac{1}{2}} - x^{\frac{1}{2}}$

Solution:

Functions f and h follow the form of definition 9.1 and so are polynomial functions. In function g, x has a negative exponent, and in function k the exponents for x are not integers.

Example 9.2
Find the value of the function $f(x) = x^3 - x^2 - 9x + 9$ at $x = -3$.

Solution:

Substitute -3 into the function.

$$f(-3) = (-3)^3 - (-3)^2 - 9 \cdot (-3) + 9 = -27 - 9 + 27 + 9 = 0$$

DIY PROBLEMS

9.1 Which of these functions are polynomial functions?

a. $f(x) = \sqrt{7}x^2 + x^3 + x - 34$

b. $f(x) = 2x^5 - 7x^2 + 13$

c. $h(x) = 3 - x$

d. $k(x) = -5x^5 - 4x^4 - 3x^3 - 2x^2$

9.2 Extra problem:

Find the leading coefficient, the constant term, and the degree of the polynomial function $F(x) = 6x^3 - 4x^2 + 2x - 4$

9.3 Find the value of $f(x) = -x^4 - x^3 + 4x^2 + 3x - 7$ at $x = 2$.

9.4 Given $s(t) = t^3 - 3t + 4$, evaluate $s(a)$.

9.5 Evaluate $P(z) = 3z - 6$ when $z = 2 + h$.

POWER FUNCTIONS

A **power function** is a polynomial function with only one term. A power function has the form $f(x) = ax^n$.

Example 9.3

Graph the function $f(x) = \dfrac{1}{2}x$.

Solution:

Step 1: Make a table of several values of x and $f(x)$.

x	f(x)
−3	−1.5
−2	−1
−1	−0.5
0	0
1	0.5
2	1
3	1.5

Step 2: Plot these points on a coordinate plane (Figure 9.1).

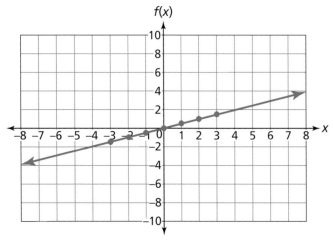

FIGURE 9.1

The function is a linear function, so the graph is a line.

Example 9.4

Graph the function $f(x) = \dfrac{1}{4}x^4$.

x	f(x)
−3	20.25
−2	4
−1	0.25
0	0
1	0.25
2	4
3	20.25

Step 2: Graph these points. Notice that the y-axis in Figure 9.2 only shows points with y-coordinates up to 10, so the points $(-3, 20.25)$ and $(3, 20.25)$ are not shown.

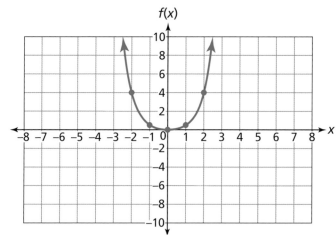

FIGURE 9.2

DIY PROBLEMS

9.6 Graph the power function $\dfrac{2}{3}x$.

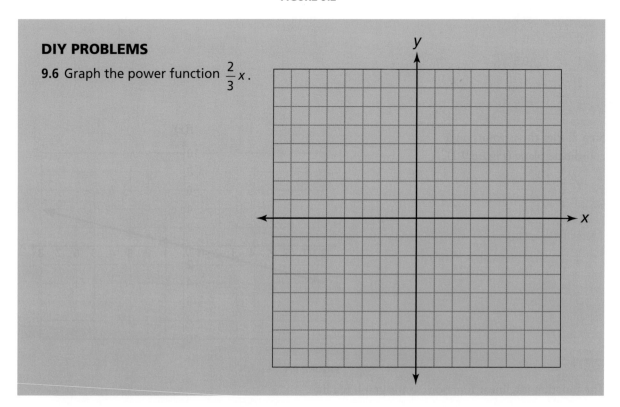

9.7 Graph the power function $f(x) = 2x^2$.

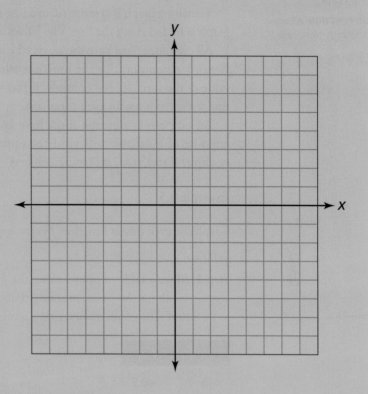

9.8 Graph the power function $f(x) = \dfrac{1}{4}x^3$.

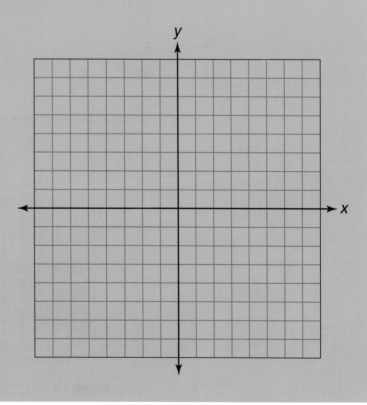

Properties of Power Functions

Functions are divided into two categories, **even functions** and **odd functions.** These two types of functions have different properties.

Visually, a graph is symmetric to a line if the halves of the graph match when the graph is folded along the line. The halves are mirror images of each other.

All even functions have the *y*-axis (the line $x = 0$) as their axis of symmetry since $f(-x) = f(x)$ means that the function value is the same for a positive or a negative value of the variable. For example, if $f(x) = x^4$, $f(2) = f(-2) = 16$. A power function is even if it has an even exponent.

An odd power function must have an odd exponent, so that substituting the opposite of a variable will yield the opposite of the original function value. For example, if $g(x) = x^5$, $g(2) = 32$, while $g(-2) = -32 = -g(2)$

Example 9.5

Graph the even power function $f(x) = -\dfrac{1}{2}x^4$.

Solution:

Step 1: Make a table of points along the graph. Remember that even functions are symmetric about the *y*-axis, meaning that only points on one side of the *y*-axis need to be found. The graph on one side is a mirror image of the graph on the other side.

x	f(x)
−3	−40.5
−2	−8
−1	−0.5
0	0
1	−0.5
2	−8
3	−40.5

Step 2: Plot the points and connect them to form the graph (Figure 9.3).

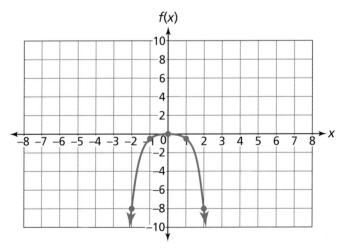

FIGURE 9.3

Example 9.6

Graph the odd power function $f(x) = \dfrac{1}{2}x^3$.

Solution:

Step 1: Make a table of points along the graph. Remember to use the property of odd power functions to reduce the number of points that must be calculated.

x	f(x)
−3	−13.5
−2	−4
−1	−0.5
0	0
1	0.5
2	4
3	13.5

Step 2: Plot the points and connect them to form the graph.

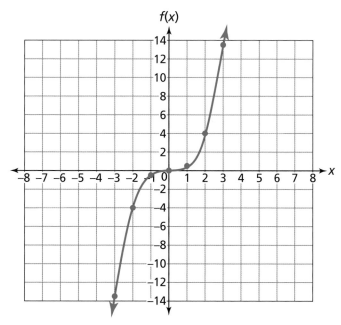

FIGURE 9.4

9.9 Determine if the function $f(x) = x^6$ is even, odd or neither.

9.10 Determine if the function $f(x) = x^5$ is even, odd or neither.

9.11 Graph the even power function $f(x) = x^2$.

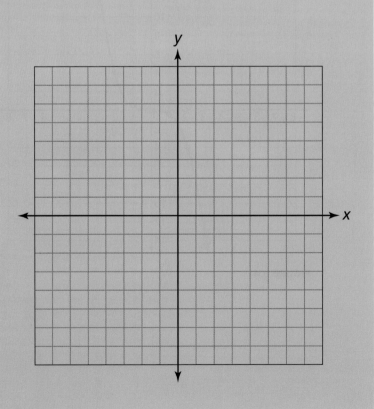

9.12 Graph the odd power function $f(x) = 2x$.

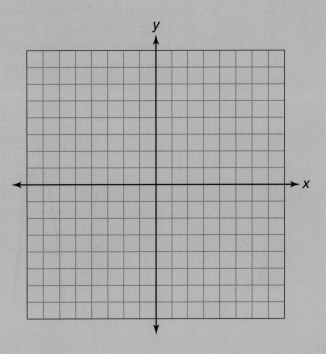

9.13 Graph the even power function $f(x) = -0.5x^2$.

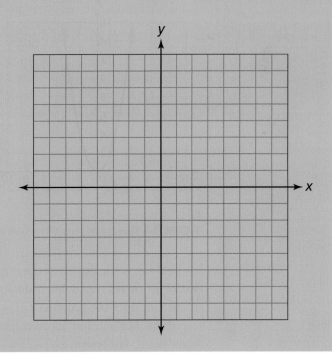

ZEROS OF POLYNOMIALS

Graphing the Zeros of a Polynomial

A **zero** of a function is a value of the variable that makes the value of the function 0.

Graphically, since at any point where the graph of the function crosses the x-axis the value of the function is 0, the zeros of a function are the points $(x_1, 0)$, $(x_2, 0)$, $(x_3, 0)$, and so on, that satisfy the function.

9.6 ZERO (of a function) The value of the variable that makes the value of the function equal 0.

The degree of a polynomial function determines how many zeros it can have. Recall that a linear function $y = f(x) = mx + b$ is a polynomial function of degree 1, and that every (nonhorizontal) line crosses the x-axis exactly once. So a linear function has 1 zero. If n is 2, then the polynomial may have no zeros, or one or two zeros. (Recall the possible graphs of a quadratic function: the parabola may have its vertex above or below the x-axis as either a max or a min point of the function [0 or 2 zeros], or vertex on the x-axis [1 zero]; see Figure 9.5.) Any polynomial of degree n can have *at most n* zeros.

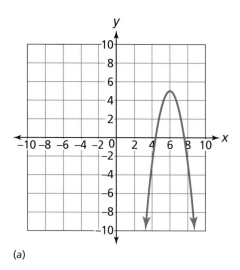

(a)

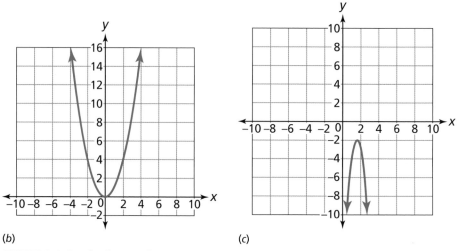

(b)   (c)

FIGURE 9.5 Quadratic Functions Can Have Two, One, or No Zeros

Looking at the degree of the exponent to determine evenness or oddness only works for power functions. It does not work for other types of polynomial functions. Consider the function $f(x) = x^2 - x$. Its highest-degree term has an even exponent, but it is not an even function since it does not obey $f(-x) = f(x)$ at every point. For instance, $f(-2) = (-2)^2 - (-2) = 6$ while $f(2) = 2^2 - 2 = 2$.

The quadratic formula, or factoring, will determine the zeros of second-degree equations. For example, if $f(x) = x^2 - x$, factoring gives $f(x) = x(x - 1)$, so $x = 0$ and $x = 1$ are the zeros of the function.

Formulas exist to factor degree 3 and degree 4 polynomials. However, they are very complicated to do by hand. For polynomials with degree 5 or higher, there is no explicit formula. In general, graphing the function in question to get a sense of its behavior can yield a decent guess as to the value of its zeros.

Example 9.7 Graph the equation $f(x) = x^3 - 3x + 1$ and estimate the location of its zeros.

Solution:

Step 1: Tabulate the values of x and $f(x)$.

x	f(x)
−3	−17
−2	−1
−1	3
0	1
1	−1
2	3
3	19

Step 2: Notice the values of x between which the value $f(x)$ changes sign. An instance of $f(x) = 0$ will occur somewhere between the points $(-2, -1)$ and $(-1, 3)$, somewhere between $(0, 1)$ and $(1, -1)$, and somewhere between $(1, -1)$ and $(2, 3)$ (Figure 9.6).

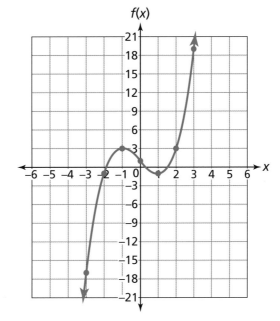

FIGURE 9.6

Step 3: Estimate the zeros based on the graph. They appear to be $x = -1.9$, $x = 0.4$, and $x = 1.6$. In higher math, estimates such as these can be very useful in finding more precise values of the zeros of higher-order polynomials. Some of the most powerful methods for finding the zeros of polynomials are iterative methods that require a good first guess as the initial input.

Example 9.8 Graph the function $f(x) = x^4 - 5x - 3$ and estimate its zeros.

Solution:

Step 1: Tabulate values of x and $f(x)$.

x	f(x)
−2	23
−1	3
0	−3
1	−7
2	3
3	63

Step 2: Plot the points and create the graph of the function (Figure 9.7).

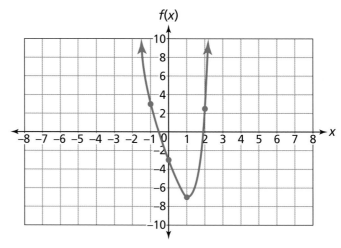

FIGURE 9.7

Step 3: Estimate the zeros of the graph. It appears that the zeros are at roughly -0.6 and 1.9.

DIY PROBLEMS

9.14 Determine if the function $f(x) = x^3 + x^2 + 1$ is even, odd or neither.

9.15 Graph the function $f(x) = x^2 + 6x - 3$ and estimate its zeros.

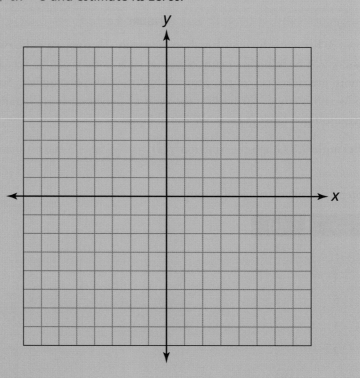

9.16 Graph the function $f(x) = x^3 - 2x^2 + 4x - 3$ and estimate its zeros.

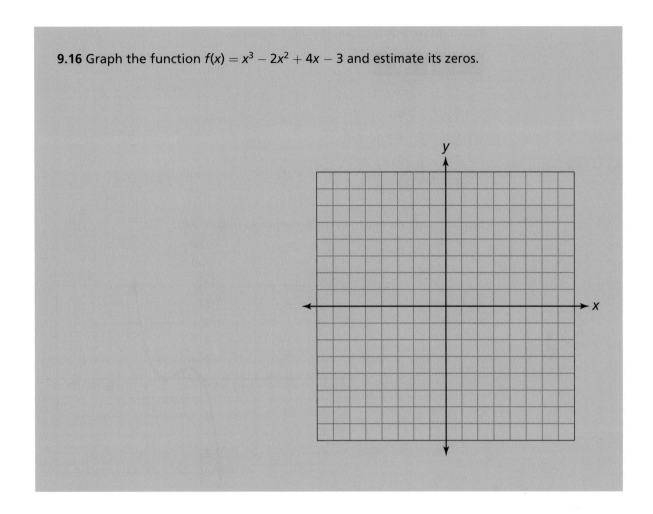

Multiplicity of Zeros

The **multiplicity** of a factor is the power to which that factor is raised in a factored polynomial function. Since the factors of a polynomial determine its zeros, the zeros are said to have the same multiplicity as the associated factors. The *multiplicity* of a zero refers to the number of times the factor corresponding to the zero occurs in the factored form of a polynomial.

9.7 MULTIPLICITY (of a factor) The power to which that factor is raised in a factored polynomial function.

Example 9.9

Find the multiplicity of the factors of $f(x) = x^3 - 4x^2 + 4x$ and graph the function.

Solution:

Step 1: Factor the polynomial by first removing the common factor of x.

$$f(x) = x^3 - 4x^2 + 4x = x(x^2 - 4x + 4)$$

Step 2: The trinomial product is a perfect square trinomial. Rewrite it as

$$f(x) = x(x^2 - 4x + 4) = x(x - 2)^2$$

The factor of x only occurs once, so it has a multiplicity of 1. The factor $(x - 2)$, however, is squared, so it has a multiplicity of two. Since the factors determine the roots/zeros of the function, it is also said that the zero at $x = 0$ has multiplicity 1, and the zero at $x = 2$ has multiplicity 2.

Step 3: Make a table of points along the graph.

x	f(x)
−1	−9
0	0
1	1
2	0
3	3

Step 4: Graph the equation using the points (Figure 9.8).

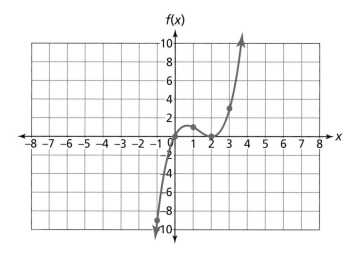

FIGURE 9.8

Notice that the graph just touches the x-axis at the zero with multiplicity 2 and crosses the x-axis at the zero with multiplicity 1.

Example 9.10 Find the multiplicity of the factors of $f(x) = x^2 + 6x + 9$ and graph the function.

Solution:

Step 1: This is a perfect square trinomial. Factor it.

$$f(x) = x^2 + 6x + 9 = (x + 3)^2$$

Step 2: The factor $(x + 3)$ is squared and therefore has multiplicity 2. This means that the associated zero at $x = -3$ also has multiplicity 2.

Step 3: Make a table of points.

x	f(x)
−6	9
−5	4
−4	1
−3	0
−2	1
−1	4
0	9

Step 4: Plot the graph (Figure 9.9).

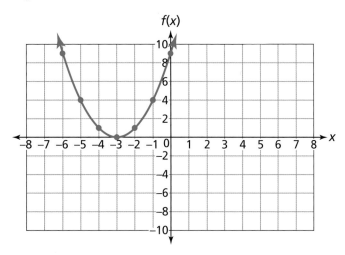

FIGURE 9.9

Notice again that the graph just touches the axis at the zero with multiplicity 2.

Most polynomials are difficult if not impossible to factor, and little can be said about the multiplicity of their factors. However, one can always tell whether the multiplicity of a zero is even or odd based on the graph's behavior around the zero. If the graph just touches the x-axis and then returns back in the direction from which it came, the zero has even multiplicity. However, if the graph crosses the x-axis, then the corresponding zero has odd multiplicity.

DIY PROBLEMS

9.17 Find the roots and multiplicity of the function $f(x) = (x − 3)^4 (x − 5)$.

9.18 Graph the function $f(x) = x^4 - 5x^2 + 4$ and find the multiplicity of its zeros.

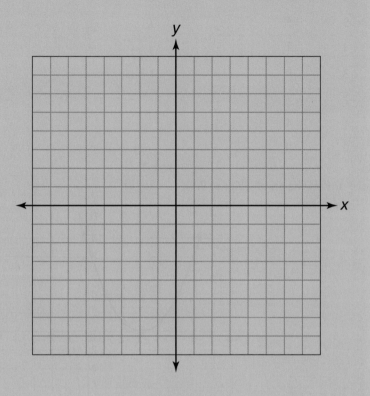

9.19 Graph the function $f(x) = x^3 + 3x^2 - 4$ and find the multiplicity of its zeros.

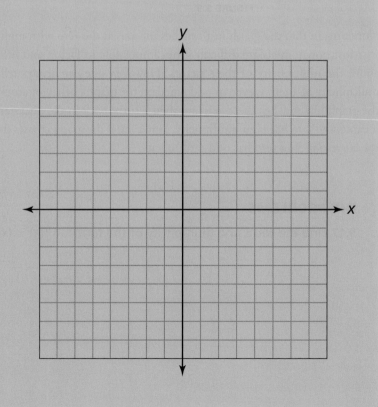

TURNING POINTS AND EQUATIONS

Turning Points and Behavior

The **turning points** of a graph are the local maximums/minimums of the graph. A **local maximum** point has the greatest function value in its immediate neighborhood; a **local minimum** point has the least function value in its immediate neighborhood.

Imagine tracing a finger along the graph of a function. The turning points are the points at which the finger reverses its vertical direction—motion along the graph "turns around" at these points. These points are also the local maximums and minimums of a graph, meaning that they are the "lowest" or "highest" points in a small region that surrounds them.

9.8 LOCAL MAXIMUM The point having the greatest function value in its immediate neighborhood on a graph.

9.9 LOCAL MINIMUM The point having the least function value in its immediate neighborhood on a graph.

9.10 TURNING POINTS The local maximums/minimums of the graph.

Example 9.11

Find the turning point on the graph of $f(x) = x^2 - 9$.

Solution:

Step 1: Make a table of values.

x	f(x)
−4	7
−3	0
−2	−5
−1	−8
0	−9
1	−8
2	−5
3	0
4	7

Step 2: Plot the points and form the graph (Figure 9.10).

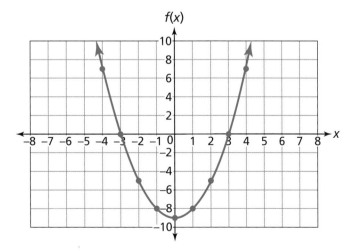

FIGURE 9.10

Step 3: Find the turning point. The minimum of this graph occurs at $x = 0$. Not only is this a local minimum, it is also *the* minimum value of the function. This is possible for polynomials that have a highest-degree term that is even.

Example 9.12

Find the turning points of $f(x) = x^3 + 1.5x^2 - 6x - 3$.

Solution:

Step 1: Make a table of points along the graph.

x	f(x)
−4	−19
−3	1.5
−2	7
−1	3.5
0	−3
1	−6.5
2	−1
3	19.5

Step 2: Plot the points and use them to form the graph (Figure 9.11).

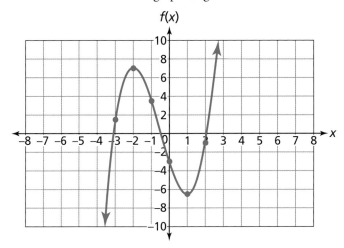

FIGURE 9.11

Step 3: Find the turning points. It may be helpful to use a ruler to draw a vertical line through turning point down to the *x*-axis to verify where it is. The turning points of this function are located at $x = -2$ and $x = 1$.

DIY PROBLEMS

9.20 Find the turning point of $f(x) = x^2 + 1$.

9.21 Find the turning points of $f(x) = \dfrac{1}{2}x^4 - x^2 - 4$.

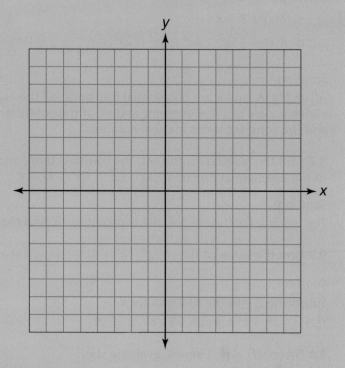

9.22 Find the turning points of $f(x) = x^3 - 3x - 4$.

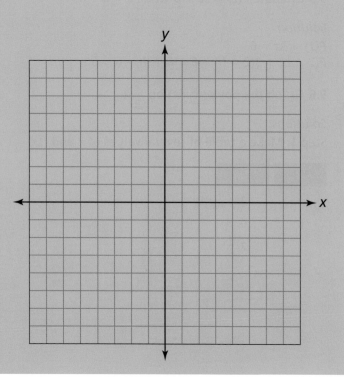

SOLUTIONS TO DIY PROBLEMS

9.1 Which of these functions are polynomial functions?

    a. $f(x) = \sqrt{7}x^2 + x^3 + x - 34$

    b. $g(x) = 2x^5 - 7x^2 + 13$

    c. $h(x) = 3 - x$

    d. $k(x) = -5x^5 - 4x^4 - 3x^3 - 2x^2$

Solution:

All of *f, g, h,* and *k* are polynomial functions; all the exponents for the variable *x* are positive integers; and all of the coefficients of *x* and the constant terms are real numbers.

9.2 Find the leading coefficient, the constant term, and the degree of the polynomial function $F(x) = 6x^3 - 4x^2 + 2x - 4$.

Solution:

The leading coefficient is 6, the constant is −4, and the degree is 3.

9.3 Find the value of $f(x) = -x^4 - x^3 + 4x^2 + 3x - 7$ at $x = 2$.

Solution:

Substitute 2 into the function for *x*.

$f(2) = -2^4 - 2^3 + 4 \cdot 2^2 + 3 \cdot 2 - 7 = -9$

9.4 Given $s(t) = t^3 - 3t + 4$, evaluate $s(a)$.

Solution:

$s(a) = a^3 - 3(a) + 4$

9.5 Evaluate $P(z) = 3z - 6$ when $z = 2 + h$.

Solution:

$P(z) = 3z - 6$
$P(2 + h) = 3(2 + h) - 6 = 6 + 3h - 6 = 3h$

9.6 Graph the power function $\frac{2}{3}x$.

Solutions:

Step 1: Make a table of several values of *x* and *f(x)*

x	f(x)
−3	−2
0	0
3	2

Step 2: Plot these points on a coordinate plane.

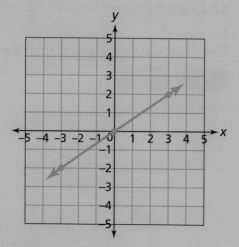

FIGURE 9.12

9.7 Graph the power function $f(x) = 2x^2$.

Solution:
Step 1: Tabulate some values of this function.

x	f(x)
−3	18
−2	8
−1	2
0	0
1	2
2	8
3	18

Step 2: Graph the function using the calculated points (Figure 9.13).

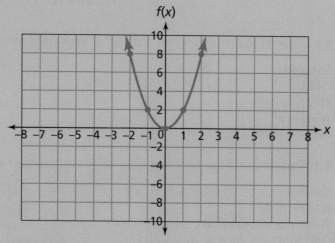

FIGURE 9.13

The function is a quadratic function, so the graph is a parabola.

9.8 Graph the power function $f(x) = \frac{1}{4}x^3$.

Solution:
Step 1: Tabulate some points from the function.

x	f(x)
−3	−6.75
−2	−2
−1	−0.25
0	0
1	0.25
2	2
3	6.75

Step 2: Graph the function using these points (Figure 9.14).

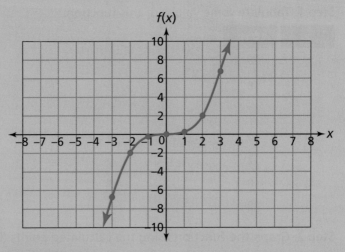

FIGURE 9.14

9.9 Determine if the function $f(x) = x^6$ is even, odd or neither.

Solution:
$f(x) = x^6$
$f(-x) = (-x)^6$
$f(-x) = x^6$
Even function since $f(-x) = f(x)$

9.10 Determine if the function $f(x) = x^5$ is even, odd or neither.

Solution:
$f(-x) = (-x)^5$
$f(-x) = (-x)\,(-x)\,(-x)\,(-x)\,(-x) = -x^5$
Odd function since $f(-x) = -f(x)$

9.11 Graph the even power function $f(x) = x^2$.

Solution:
Step 1: Make a table of several values of x and $f(x)$.

x	f(x)
−2	4
−1	1
0	0
1	1
2	4

Step 2: Plot these points on a coordinate plane.

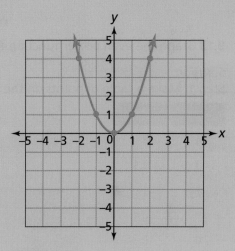

FIGURE 9.15

9.12 Graph the odd power function $f(x) = 2x$.

Solution:
Step 1: Tabulate several points from the function.

x	f(x)
−4	−8
−3	−6
−2	−4
−1	−2
0	0
1	2
2	4
3	6
4	8

Step 2: Plot these points and form the graph of the function (Figure 9.16).

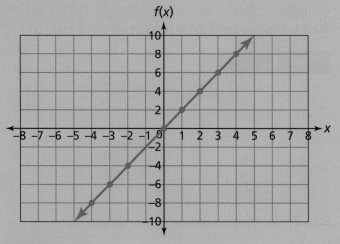

FIGURE 9.16

9.13 Graph the even power function $f(x) = -0.5x^2$.

Solution:
Step 1: Make a table of points on the graph of this function.

x	f(x)
−4	−8
−3	−4.5
−2	−2
−1	−0.5
0	0
1	−0.5
2	−2
3	−4.5
4	−8

Step 2: Graph the function using these points (Figure 9.17).

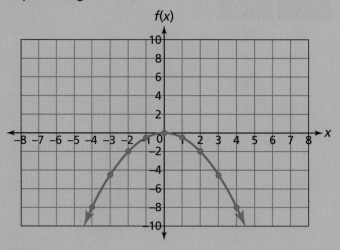

FIGURE 9.17

9.14 Determine if the function $f(x) = x^3 + x^2 + 1$ is even, odd or neither.

Solution:

$$f(x) = x^3 + x^2 + 1$$
$$f(-x) = (-x)^3 + (-x)^2 + 1 = -x^3 + x^2 + 1$$

Note that $-x^3$ is the opposite of x^3 and x^2 is the same as the original function. Therefore, the function is neither.

9.15 Graph the function $f(x) = x^2 + 6x - 3$ and estimate its zeros.

Solution:

Step 1: Make a table of points.

x	f(x)
−7	4
−6	−3
−5	−8
−4	−11
−3	−12
−2	−11
−1	−8
0	−3
1	4

Step 2: Plot the points on a graph (Figure 9.18).

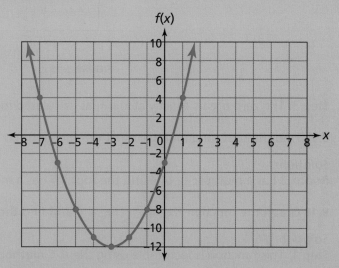

FIGURE 9.18

Step 3: Estimate the zeros of the function. They appear to be at about −6.5 and 0.5.

9.16 Graph the function $f(x) = x^3 - 2x^2 + 4x - 3$ and estimate its zeros.

Solution:
Step 1: Make a table of points.

x	f(x)
−2	−27
−1	−10
0	−3
1	0
2	5
3	18

Step 2: Plot the points and form the graph (Figure 9.19).

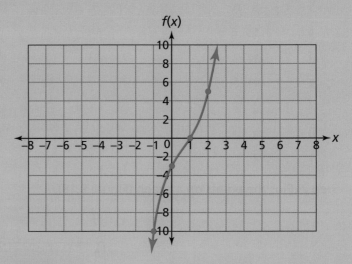

FIGURE 9.19

Step 3: The zero occurs exactly at $x = 1$, as calculated in the table.

9.17 Find the roots and multiplicity of the function $f(x) = (x - 3)^4 (x - 5)$.

Solution:
Root +3 has a multiplicity of 4 and the root +5 has a multiplicity of 1.

9.18 Graph the function $f(x) = x^4 - 5x^2 + 4$ and find the multiplicity of its zeros.

Solution:
Step 1: This function is factorable using the A-C method. It becomes

$$f(x) = x^4 - 5x^2 + 4 = (x^2 - 1)(x^2 - 4)$$

Step 2: Each of these binomials is the difference of two squares and can be factored as such.

$$f(x) = (x^2 - 1)(x^2 - 4) = (x - 1)(x + 1)(x - 2)(x + 2)$$

All of these factors have multiplicity 1.

Step 3: Tabulate some points for the graph.

x	f(x)
−3	40
−2	0
−1.5	−2.1875
−1	0
0	4
1	0
1.5	−2.1875
2	0
3	40

Step 4: Graph the function using these points (Figure 9.20).

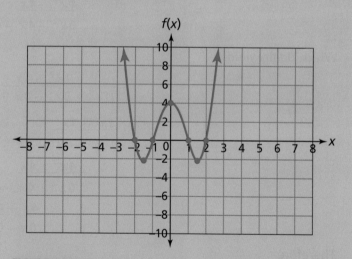

FIGURE 9.20

Notice that this graph crosses the x-axis at all of its zeros. All of these zeros have (odd) multiplicity 1.

9.19 Graph the function $f(x) = x^3 + 3x^2 - 4$ and find the multiplicity of its zeros.

Solution:
Step 1: A quick test reveals that $x = 1$ is a zero of this function. Use polynomial long division to factor out $(x - 1)$.

$$x-1\overline{)1x^3 + 3x^2 + 0x - 4} \rightarrow x-1\overline{)\begin{array}{l}1x^2\\ 1x^3 + 3x^2 + 0x - 4\end{array}}$$

This yields:

$$\begin{array}{r}1x^2\phantom{{}+0x-4}\\ x-1\overline{)1x^3 + 3x^2 + 0x - 4}\\ -\underline{1x^3 - 1x^2}\\ 0x^3 + 4x^2\end{array}$$

Which in turn yields:

$$\begin{array}{r}1x^2 + 4x\phantom{{}-4}\\ x-1\overline{)1x^3 + 3x^2 + 0x - 4}\\ -\underline{1x^3 - 1x^2}\\ 0x^3 + 4x^2 + 0x\\ -\underline{4x^2 - 4x}\\ 0x^2 + 4x - 4\end{array}$$

Which finally yields:

$$\begin{array}{r}1x^2 + 4x + 4\\ x-1\overline{)1x^3 + 3x^2 + 0x - 4}\\ -\underline{1x^3 - 1x^2}\\ 0x^3 + 4x^2 + 0x\\ -\underline{4x^2 - 4x}\\ 0x^2 + 4x - 4\\ -\underline{-4x + 4}\\ 0x + 0\end{array}$$

Therefore

$$f(x) = x^3 + 3x^2 - 4 = (x - 1)(x^2 + 4x + 4)$$

Step 2: The term on the right is a perfect square trinomial.

$$f(x) = (x - 1)(x^2 + 4x + 4) = (x - 1)(x + 2)^2$$

The first factor has multiplicity 1, and the second has multiplicity 2.

Step 3: Make a table of points.

x	f(x)
−3	−4
−2	0
−1	−2
0	−4
1	0
2	16

Step 4: Graph the function (Figure 9.21).

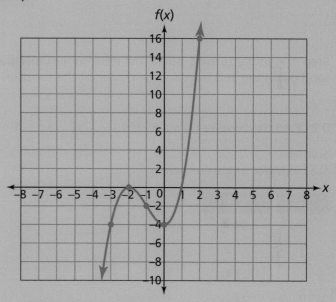

FIGURE 9.21

Step 5: The zero at −2 has multiplicity 2. Notice that the graph just touches the axis at this point. The zero at $x = 1$ has multiplicity 1.

9.20 Find the turning point of $f(x) = x^2 + 1$.

Solution:
Step 1: Make a table of values.

x	f(x)
−2	5
−1	2
0	1
1	2
2	5

Step 2: Plot the points and form the graph

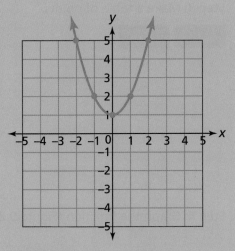

FIGURE 9.22

Step 3: Find the turning point. The minimum of this graph occurs at $x = 0$. This is the local minimum and the minimum value of the function.

9.21 Find the turning points of $f(x) = \frac{1}{2}x^4 - x^2 - 4$.

Solution:
Step 1: Make a table of points.

x	f(x)
−3	27.5
−2	0
−1	−4.5
0	−4
1	−4.5
2	0
3	27.5

Step 2: Draw the graph using these points (Figure 9.23).

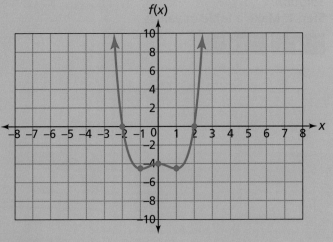

FIGURE 9.23

Step 3: Identify the turning points. Comparing the graph and the table, the turning points occur at −1, 0, and 1.

9.22 Find the turning points of $f(x) = x^3 - 3x - 4$.

Solution:
Step 1: Make a table of points.

x	f(x)
−2	−6
−1	−2
0	−4
1	−6
2	−2
3	14

Step 2: Draw the graph of the function using these points (Figure 9.24).

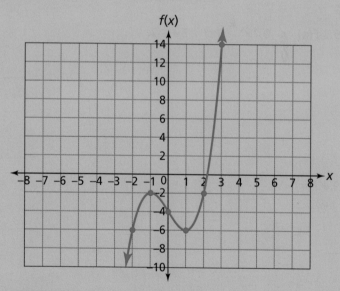

FIGURE 9.24

Step 3: Comparing the graph and the table, note that the turning points occur at −1 and 1.

For the following polynomials:
   a. Classify the polynomial functions as constant, linear, quadratic, cubic, or quartic.
   b. Find the leading term.
   c. Find the leading coefficient.
   d. Give the degree of the polynomial.

9.1 $f(x) = -x^2 - 3x + 5$.

9.2 $f(x) = 5 - x$.

9.3 $f(x) = -0.7x^4 - 3x^2 + 5x - 7$.

9.4 $f(x) = -\dfrac{2}{3}$.

9.5 $f(x) = x^3 + 5x^2 - x + 9$.

9.6 Given $f(x) = 5x - 3$, evaluate $f(3)$.

9.7 Given $F(x) = x^2 + 3x - 4$, evaluate $F(-3) =$

9.8 Given $H(x) = \dfrac{3x}{x+2}$, evaluate $H(-3)$.

9.9 Determine which of the following are polynomials. For those that are polynomials, give the degree, and for those that are not polynomials, explain why not.

   a. $f(x) = 2 - 3x^2$

   b. $f(x) = 5$

   c. $f(x) = \dfrac{x-2}{x^2+5}$

9.10 Graph the following power functions and determine if they are even or odd functions.

   a. $f(x) = x^2$

   b. $f(x) = x^4$

   c. $f(x) = x^3$

9.11 Determine algebraically whether the function $f(x) = -2x^2$ is even, odd or neither.

9.12 Determine algebraically whether the function $f(x) = 2x^3 - 2x$ is even, odd or neither.

9.13 Determine algebraically whether the function $f(x) = -3x^2 + 2$ is even, odd or neither.

9.14 Graph $f(x) = \dfrac{3}{4}x + 1$.

9.15 Graph $f(x) = -\dfrac{1}{2}x + 3$.

9.16 Graph the polynomial $f(x) = \dfrac{1}{2}(x - 1)^4$ using transformations. Show each stage of the function being transformed and explain the transformation.

9.17 Graph the polynomial $f(x) = 1 - x^3$ using transformations. Show each stage of the function being transformed and explain the transformation.

9.18 Find a polynomial of degree 3 whose zeros are −2, 3, and 4. Then graph the polynomial to verify your result.

9.19 Find a polynomial of degree 4 whose zeros are −4, −1, 2, 3. Then graph the polynomial to verify your result.

9.20 Find the zeros and state the multiplicity of the polynomial $f(x) = -2(x - 4)^3 (x + 5)$.

9.21 Find the zeros and state the multiplicity of the polynomial $f(x) = x^2 (x + 2) (x+2) (x + 2)$.

9.22 Find a polynomial of degree 3 whose zeros are −2, multiplicity 2; 4, multiplicity 1. Then graph the polynomial to verify your result.

9.23 Find and identify the number of turning points for the function $f(x) = x^2 (x - 2)$. Verify with the graph of the function.

9.24 For the polynomial $f(x) = x^3 - x^2 - 12x$, find the intercepts and determine the maximum number of turning points.

9.25 For the function $f(x) = 3(x - 7)(x + 3)^2$:
    a. List each real zero and its multiplicity.

    b. Find the x-intercept.

    c. Determine the maximum number of turning points.

9.26 Find the turning point of $f(x) = x^2 - 2x$ and graph its function.

REFERENCES

Cajori, F., & Odell, L. R. (1917). *Elementary algebra*. New York, NY: Macmillan.

Rietz, H. L., & Crathorne, A. R. (1909). College algebra. New York, NY: Henry Holt and Company.

Rational Expressions and Equations

A local clothing store has offered Sarah a contract to sell her handmade charm bracelets in their stores. The contract stipulates that Sarah must sell every piece she makes for exactly $25. Her fixed costs, including rent on a design studio, utilities, and wages for her part-time assistant, total $1,000 a month. Each charm bracelet costs her $5 in materials to make. The average cost, C, of a bracelet is given by the equation $C = \dfrac{1000 + 5x}{x} = \dfrac{1000}{x} + 5$, where x is the number of bracelets made and $5x$ is the cost of making them all.

QUESTIONS TO CONSIDER

1. How would Sarah's production have to change if the selling price of the bracelet were $15?

2. How many bracelets would Sarah have to make per month to break even?

3. As the average selling price of her bracelets goes down, what happens to the number of bracelets that Sarah would have to make to break even?

KEY TERMS

- ➤ asymptote (p. 364)
- ➤ average cost (p. 363)
- ➤ direct variation (p. 361)
- ➤ extraneous solution (p. 358)
- ➤ inverse variation (p. 361)
- ➤ joint variation (p. 361)
- ➤ proportion (p. 360)
- ➤ ratio (p. 360)
- ➤ rational expression (p. 352)

INTRODUCTION TO RATIONAL EXPRESSIONS AND EQUATIONS

Definition of Rational Expressions

The situation in the chapter opener is an application that uses rational expressions. A **rational expression** is a function of the form $f(x) = \dfrac{a(x)}{b(x)}$, where $a(x)$ and $b(x)$ are polynomials and $b(x)$ can never equal 0.

The following are examples of rational expressions:

$$\frac{x^2 + 1}{x^2 - 1} \quad \text{and} \quad \frac{1}{x}$$

The presence of a fraction may indicate a rational expression. However, even though the following expressions contain fractions, they are *not* examples of rational expressions because either the numerator or the denominator is not a polynomial:

$$\frac{\sqrt{x^2 + 1}}{2x} \quad \text{and} \quad \frac{1}{1 + \dfrac{1}{x}}$$

Since any nonzero integer is a polynomial of degree zero, rational numbers are technically rational expressions.

10.1 RATIONAL EXPRESSION A function of the form $f(x) = \dfrac{a(x)}{b(x)}$, where $a(x)$ and $b(x)$ are polynomials and $b(x)$ can never equal 0.

Simplest Form

Rational expressions, like numerical fractions, are in simplest form when the numerator, $a(x)$, and the denominator, $b(x)$, share only the common factor 1. In order to express the answers in simplest form, rational expressions require frequent use of the factoring techniques.

MULTIPLICATION AND DIVISION OF RATIONAL EXPRESSIONS

Simplifying a Rational Expression

Rational expressions are in final form when they are simplified. To do this, factor all polynomials in the numerator and denominator completely and divide out common factors. When simplifying numerical fractions such as $\dfrac{14}{21}$, first factor the numerator as $(7)(2)$ and factor the denominator as $(7)(3)$. The common factor of 7 is divided out because $\dfrac{7}{7}$ is equal to 1. Use the same process to simplify a rational expression:

$$\frac{r^3 + 2r}{r^4} \Rightarrow \frac{r(r^2 + 2)}{(r)(r)(r)(r)} \Rightarrow \frac{\cancel{r}(r^2 + 2)}{\cancel{r}(r)(r)(r)} \Rightarrow \frac{r^2 + 2}{r^3}$$

A common mistake is to "simplify" further to $\dfrac{r + 2}{r^2}$. That thinking is erroneous because the perceived common factor r is not a factor of the *entire* quantity in the numerator. For this reason, it may help to put parentheses around the quantities, such as $\dfrac{(r^2 + 2)}{(r^3)}$, to avoid making this mistake of dividing out common factors from individual terms.

On the other hand, if the expression were $\dfrac{r^2 + 2r}{r^3}$, r would be a common factor of the numerator and denominator because $r^2 + 2r = r(r+2)$, so $\dfrac{r^2 + 2r}{r^3} = \dfrac{r(r+2)}{r^3} = \dfrac{r+2}{r^2}$.

Multiplying a Rational Expression

Simplifying rational expressions follows the same logic and process as with numerical fractions, and the same is true for multiplying and dividing them. Recall that the multiplication property is $\dfrac{a}{b} \cdot \dfrac{c}{d} = \dfrac{ac}{bd}$. Multiplying numerical fractions such as $\dfrac{7}{21} \cdot \dfrac{24}{9}$ directly results in $\dfrac{168}{189}$. Proceed to simplify by factoring to $\dfrac{(7)(3)(2)(2)(2)}{(7)(3)(3)(3)}$ and then dividing out the common factors of 7 and 3, writing the final answer as $\dfrac{8}{9}$. A better alternative to this process would be to simplify first and then multiply, as in $\dfrac{7}{3(7)} \cdot \dfrac{3(8)}{3(3)} = \dfrac{1}{3} \cdot \dfrac{8}{3} = \dfrac{8}{9}$. This process will make working with rational expressions more manageable.

Dividing a Rational Expression

The same alternative approach is also better for dividing rational expressions. Recall that dividing by a fraction is equivalent to multiplying by its reciprocal. The division property is

$$\frac{a}{b} \div \frac{c}{d} = \frac{a}{b} \cdot \frac{d}{c} = \frac{ad}{bc}$$

Example 10.1 Simplify $\dfrac{3ab^2}{4 - a^2} \cdot \dfrac{a - 2}{6a^2 b^2}$.

Solution:

Step 1: Factor all expressions. $\dfrac{(3)(a)(b)(b)}{(2-a)(2+a)} \cdot \dfrac{(a-2)}{(2)(3)(a)(a)(b)(b)}$

Step 2: Divide out factors common to the numerators and the denominators. Note that $(a - 2)$ is rewritten as $(2 - a)(-1)$. $\dfrac{(\cancel{3})(\cancel{a})(\cancel{b})(\cancel{b})}{(\cancel{2-a})(2+a)} \cdot \dfrac{(\cancel{2-a})(-1)}{(2)(\cancel{3})(\cancel{a})(a)(\cancel{b})(\cancel{b})}$

Step 3: Write the final product. $\dfrac{-1}{2a(2+a)}$

Step 4: Check that answer is in simplest form by looking for any missed common factors.

Example 10.2 Simplify $\dfrac{2x^2 + 5x - 25}{3x^2 + 5x + 2} \cdot \dfrac{3x^2 + 2x}{x + 5} \div \dfrac{x^2}{(x+1)^2}$.

Solution:

Step 1: Factor all expressions. $\dfrac{(2x-5)(x+5)}{(3x+2)(x+1)} \cdot \dfrac{x(3x+2)}{(x+5)} \div \dfrac{(x)(x)}{(x+1)(x+1)}$

Step 2: Instead of dividing by the third expression, multiply by its reciprocal.

$\dfrac{(2x-5)(x+5)}{(3x+2)(x+1)} \cdot \dfrac{x(3x+2)}{(x+5)} \cdot \dfrac{(x+1)(x+1)}{(x)(x)}$

Step 3: Divide out any factors common to the numerators and the denominators.

$\dfrac{(2x-5)\cancel{(x+5)}}{\cancel{(3x+2)}\cancel{(x+1)}} \cdot \dfrac{\cancel{x}\cancel{(3x+2)}}{\cancel{(x+5)}} \cdot \dfrac{\cancel{(x+1)}(x+1)}{(\cancel{x})(x)}$

Step 4: Write the final product. $\dfrac{(2x-5)(x+1)}{x}$

Step 5: Check that answer is in simplest form by looking for any missed common factors.

DIY PROBLEMS

10.1 Simplify $\dfrac{2x^2y^3}{4x^4y}$.

10.2 Simplify $\dfrac{x^2+4x+16}{x+4}$.

10.3 Simplify $\dfrac{10x^2}{9y^3} \cdot \dfrac{3y^2}{5x^3}$.

10.4 Find the quotient when $\dfrac{7x^2}{3b}$ is divided by $\dfrac{2}{3x}$.

10.5 Simplify $\dfrac{\dfrac{2m^2+2m-12}{12m}}{\dfrac{m^2-9}{3m^2}}$.

10.6 Simplify $\dfrac{a+3b}{2a-2b} \div \dfrac{a^2+3ab}{b^2-a^2} \cdot ab$.

ADDITION AND SUBTRACTION OF RATIONAL EXPRESSIONS

Rewriting Rational Expressions in Terms of the Common Denominator

Adding and subtracting rational expressions also follow the same process as adding and subtracting numerical fractions. If the expressions have common denominators, the work is simple:

$$\text{Addition } \frac{a}{b} + \frac{c}{b} = \frac{a+c}{b} \quad \text{Subtraction } \frac{a}{b} - \frac{c}{b} = \frac{a-c}{b}$$

If the expressions do not have common denominators, then write the expressions in factored form (and simplify where possible). Remember that a least common denominator (LCD) must contain all the factors of each denominator. For each denominator of one of the expressions, identify the factors it is missing that are factors of any other denominator. Then rewrite the expression, multiplying by the product of those factors divided by that same product. These new expressions are equivalent to the originals but should now all have the same denominators. This LCD is the product of the factors the denominators originally shared and all the "missing" factors.

Adding and Subtracting Rational Expressions

Once the expressions have common denominators, combine the numerators using the indicated operations. An important step to remember when subtracting a polynomial is to distribute the subtraction to every term in the subtracted numerator. Therefore, the correct use of parentheses is crucial.

Example 10.3

　　a. What is the common denominator of the following rational expressions?

$$\frac{1}{5a^2} \text{ and } \frac{a}{15ab}$$

　　b. What is the common denominator of the following rational expressions?

$$\frac{2x-3}{x^2-3x-4} \text{ and } \frac{6}{x^2-2x-8}$$

Solution:

　　a. Step 1: Factor each denominator.
　　　$5a^2 = (5)(a)(a)$, and
　　　$15ab = (3)(5)(a)(b)$

Step 2: Recognize what factors the first denominator is missing that are in the second denominator: 3 and b. The second fraction's denominator is missing a second factor of a.

Step 3: Rewrite the expressions: multiply $\dfrac{1}{5a^2}$ by 1 in the form $\dfrac{3b}{3b}$, and multiply $\dfrac{a}{15ab}$ by 1 in the form $\dfrac{a}{a}$. So the LCD is $(3)(5)(a)(a)(b) = 15a^2b$; the original denominators shared 5 and a as factors, and the "missing" factors were 3, b, and a.

b. Step 1: Factor each denominator. $(x-4)(x+1)$ and $(x-4)(x+2)$

Step 2: Recognize what factors the first denominator is missing that are in the second denominator: $(x+2)$. The second fraction's denominator is missing $(x+1)$.

Step 3: Rewrite the expressions, multiplying the first by $\dfrac{x+2}{x+2}$, and the second by $\dfrac{x+1}{x+1}$. So the LCD is $(x-4)(x+1)(x+2)$; the original denominators shared $x-4$ as a factor, and the "missing" factors were $x+1$ and $x+2$.

Example 10.4 Add or subtract as indicated.

Numerical fractions

a. $\dfrac{1}{14}+\dfrac{5}{14}$

c. $\dfrac{29}{35}-\dfrac{2}{5}$

e. $\dfrac{12}{13}+\dfrac{2}{3}$

Rational expressions

b. $\dfrac{x+2}{14}+\dfrac{6x+5}{14}$

d. $\dfrac{4x+2}{x^2+4x+3}-\dfrac{5}{x+3}$

f. $\dfrac{10}{x+7}+\dfrac{10}{x-7}$

Solution:

Numerical fractions

a. Step 1: Rewrite each fraction with the LCD.
Not needed

Step 2: Add. $\dfrac{1+5}{14}=\dfrac{6}{14}$

Step 3: Simplify and check for simplest form.
$$\dfrac{(\cancel{2})(3)}{(\cancel{2})(7)}=\dfrac{3}{7}$$

c. Step 1: Factor the denominators. $\dfrac{29}{(7)(5)}-\dfrac{2}{5}$

Step 2: Rewrite each fraction with the LCD 7(5).
$$\dfrac{29}{(7)(5)}-\dfrac{2(7)}{5(7)}=\dfrac{29}{35}-\dfrac{14}{35}$$

Step 3: Subtract. $\dfrac{29}{35}-\dfrac{14}{35}=\dfrac{15}{35}$

Step 4: Simplify and check for simplest form.
$$\dfrac{15}{35}=\dfrac{(3)(\cancel{5})}{(7)(\cancel{5})}=\dfrac{3}{7}$$

Rational expressions

b. Step 1: Rewrite each expression with the LCD.
Not needed

Step 2: Add. $\dfrac{x+2+6x+5}{14}=\dfrac{7x+7}{14}$

Step 3: Simplify and check for simplest form.
$$\dfrac{\cancel{7}(x+1)}{(\cancel{7})(2)}=\dfrac{x+1}{2}$$

d. Step 1: Factor the denominators.
$$\dfrac{4x+2}{(x+1)(x+3)}-\dfrac{5}{x+3}$$

Step 2: Rewrite each fraction with the LCD $(x+1)(x+3)$.
$$\dfrac{4x+2}{(x+1)(x+3)}-\dfrac{5(x+1)}{(x+3)(x+1)}$$

Step 3: Subtract.
$$\dfrac{4x+2}{(x+1)(x+3)}-\dfrac{5(x+1)}{(x+3)(x+1)}=\dfrac{4x+2-5(x+1)}{(x+1)(x+3)}$$
$$=\dfrac{-x-3}{(x+1)(x+3)}$$

Step 4: Simplify and check for simplest form.
$$\dfrac{-1(\cancel{x+3})}{(x+1)(\cancel{x+3})}=\dfrac{-1}{x+1}$$

e. Step 1: Factor the denominators. In this case, the LCD is the product of the two denominators since there are no factors common to the given denominators.

Step 2: Rewrite each fraction with the LCD.

$$\frac{12(3)}{13(3)} + \frac{2(13)}{3(13)} = \frac{36}{39} + \frac{26}{39}$$

Step 3: Add. $\frac{62}{39}$

Step 4: Simplify and check for simplest form.

$$\frac{(2)(31)}{(3)(13)} = \frac{62}{39}$$

f. Step 1: Factor the denominators. In this case, the LCD is the product of the two denominators since there are no factors common to the given denominators.

Step 2: Rewrite each fraction with the LCD.

$$\frac{10(x-7)}{(x+7)(x-7)} + \frac{10(x+7)}{(x-7)(x+7)}$$
$$= \frac{10x-70}{(x+7)(x-7)} + \frac{10x+70}{(x+7)(x-7)}$$

Step 3: Add. $\dfrac{20x}{(x+7)(x-7)}$

Step 4: Simplify and check for simplest form.

$$\frac{(2)(2)(5)(x)}{(x+7)(x-7)} = \frac{20x}{(x+7)(x-7)}$$

DIY PROBLEMS

10.7 Find the Lowest Common Multiple (LCM) of $9x^2y^2$ and $12\,xy^3$.

10.8 Add the rational expressions $\dfrac{2x+1}{12} + \dfrac{3x+2}{12}$.

10.9 Perform the indicated operation and simplify $\dfrac{3}{4} + \dfrac{-5}{6}$.

10.10 Simplify $\dfrac{4t}{t^2-4} + \dfrac{t}{t+2}$.

10.11 Simplify $\dfrac{5x}{3x^2-x-2} - \dfrac{x-2}{x^2+4x-5}$.

SOLVING EQUATIONS CONTAINING FRACTIONS

Solving an Equation Containing Fractions

The process of finding the LCD is crucial to not only adding and subtracting rational expressions but also to solving equations containing rational expressions. These equations appear in applications such as the one in the opening scenario.

The process for solving equations with fractions first requires the following steps:

Step 1: Find the least common denominator.

Step 2: Multiply the entire equation by that LCD.

Step 3: Finally, solve the remaining equation (which will then have no rational expressions).

Step 4: Check the solution. For all fractions, the denominator cannot equal 0; therefore, it is necessary to check the solutions in the original equation to ensure they do not produce a 0 denominator.

One important concept to keep in mind when solving rational equations is to answer the question, Are there are any restrictions on the variable? If a solution yields a denominator of 0 at any step in the equation solving process, that solution is extraneous. A solution of an equation is **extraneous** if it does not make sense mathematically or in the context of a physical situation.

Later we will discuss how extraneous solutions affect graphs of rational expressions.

10.2 EXTRANEOUS SOLUTION A solution of an equation that does not make sense mathematically or in the context of a physical situation.

Example 10.5 Solve the following:

a. $\dfrac{x}{5} + 8x = 12$

b. $\dfrac{6}{x^2 - 5x} + \dfrac{3}{x} = \dfrac{x-3}{x-5}$

c. $\dfrac{1}{a+2} + 8 = \dfrac{4}{3a}$

Solution:

Notice that in every case, multiplying by the LCD clears the equations of all fractions, as promised.

a. Step 1: Factor the denominators to find the LCD; here they are factored (supply the 1s): $\dfrac{x}{5} + \dfrac{8x}{1} = \dfrac{12}{1}$

So the LCD is 5.

Step 2: Multiply each quantity in the equation by the LCD.

$$5\left(\dfrac{x}{5} + \dfrac{8x}{1} = \dfrac{12}{1}\right) \Rightarrow \dfrac{\cancel{5}x}{\cancel{5}} + \dfrac{40x}{1} = \dfrac{60}{1} \Rightarrow x + 40x = 60$$

Step 3: Solve: $41x = 60$ and $x = \dfrac{60}{41} \approx 1.46$

Step 4: Since the denominators are constants, there is no chance of an extraneous solution; $x \approx 1.46$ is the solution.

b. Step 1: Factor the denominators to find the LCD:

$$\dfrac{6}{x(x-5)} + \dfrac{3}{x} = \dfrac{x-3}{x-5}$$

So the LCD is $x(x - 5)$. Note that the terms x and $x - 5$ must be nonzero.

Step 2: Multiply each quantity in the equation by the LCD.

$$[x(x-5)]\left(\frac{6}{x(x-5)}+\frac{3}{x}=\frac{x-3}{x-5}\right)\Rightarrow\frac{6x(x\cancel{-5})}{x(x\cancel{-5})}+\frac{3x(x-5)}{\cancel{x}}=\frac{x(x\cancel{-5})(x-3)}{x\cancel{-5}}\Rightarrow 6+3(x-5)=x(x-3)$$

Step 3: Solve:

$$6+3x-15=x^2-3x$$

$$3x-9=x^2-3x$$

$$x^2-6x+9=0$$

$$(x-3)^2=0$$

$$x=3$$

Step 4: The original equation restricts x to any real number except 0 or 5 (because these values would produce a denominator of 0). The solution is $x = 3$.

   c. Step 1: Factor the denominators to find the LCD:

$$\frac{1}{a+2}+8=\frac{4}{(3)(a)}$$

So the LCD is $(3)(a)(a + 2)$. Note that the terms $a + 2$ and a must be nonzero.

Step 2: Multiply each quantity in the equation by the LCD.

$$[3a(a+2)]\left(\frac{1}{a+2}+8=\frac{4}{(3)(a)}\right)\Rightarrow\frac{3a(a\cancel{+2})(1)}{a\cancel{+2}}+8(3a)(a+2)=\frac{4(3\cancel{a})(a+2)}{3\cancel{a}}\Rightarrow 3a+8(3a)(a+2)=4(a+2)$$

Step 3: Solve:

$$3a+24a^2+48a=4a+8$$

$$24a^2+51a-4a-8=0$$

$$24a^2+47a-8=0$$

This quadratic expression does not factor (has no rational zeros). Using the quadratic formula:

$$a=\frac{-47\pm\sqrt{47^2-4(24)(-8)}}{2(24)}\approx 0.16,-2.12$$

Step 4: The original equation restricts a to any real number except 0 or -2, which would produce denominators of 0. So 0.16 and -2.12 are valid solutions.

Example 10.6

Solve $\dfrac{2}{x-3}+\dfrac{1}{x}=\dfrac{x-1}{x-3}$.

Solution:

Step 1: Factor the denominators to find the LCD. In this equation, none of the denominators can be factored further, so the LCD is $x(x - 3)$. Note that the terms $x - 3$ and x must be nonzero.

Step 2: Multiply each quantity in the equation by the LCD.

$$[x(x-3)]\left(\frac{2}{x-3}+\frac{1}{x}=\frac{x-1}{x-3}\right)$$

$$\frac{2x(x\cancel{-3})}{x\cancel{-3}}+\frac{x(x-3)}{\cancel{x}}=\frac{x(x\cancel{-3})(x-1)}{x\cancel{-3}}$$

$$2x+x-3=x(x-1)$$

Step 3: Solve:

$$2x + x - 3 = x(x-1)$$
$$3x - 3 = x^2 - x$$
$$0 = x^2 - 4x + 3$$
$$0 = (x-3)(x-1)$$
$$x = 3, 1$$

Step 4: Check the solutions in the original problem to determine extraneous solutions.

$$\frac{2}{1-3} + \frac{1}{1} = \frac{1-1}{1-3}$$
$$-1 + 1 - = 0$$

$$\frac{2}{3-3} + \frac{1}{3} = \frac{3-1}{3-3}$$

So $x = 1$ is a valid solution, and $x = 3$ is extraneous because it yields a denominator of 0.

DIY PROBLEMS

10.12 Solve $b + \dfrac{4}{b} = -5$.

10.13 Solve $\dfrac{1}{t+1} = \dfrac{2}{t^2-1} - \dfrac{1}{t-1}$.

RATIO AND PROPORTION

Solving a Proportion

10.3 RATIO A fraction comparing two quantities measured in the same units.

10.4 PROPORTION An equation setting two ratios equal to each other.

A common application of rational equations involves ratios and proportions. A **ratio** is a fraction that compares two quantities measured in the same units. A **proportion** is an equation setting two ratios equal to each other.

When solving a proportion $\dfrac{a}{b} = \dfrac{c}{d}$, it is easiest to cross-multiply. Multiplying the entire equation by the LCD bd illustrates this: $\dfrac{a}{b} = \dfrac{c}{d} \Rightarrow ad = bc$.

Example 10.7

A patient's heart beats 24 times in 20 seconds. Using a proportion, what is the patient's heart rate per 1 minute?

Solution:

Step 1: Write an equation, keeping the placement of the quantities and *units* consistent (1 minute = 60 seconds). Let x be the number of the patient's heartbeats in 60 seconds:

$$\frac{24}{20} = \frac{x}{60}$$

Step 2: Solve by cross-multiplying.

$$(24)(60) = 20x$$
$$1440 = 20x$$
$$72 = x$$

So $x = 72$ beats per minute.

Step 3: Check the answer for validity and logic; 72 is a solution.

Variation Problems

In **direct variation,** quantities y and x *vary directly*, or are *directly proportional*, when $y = kx$ or $\frac{y}{x} = k$, where $k \uparrow 0$. The constant of variation, k, is often called the proportionality constant.

The equation distance = (rate)(time), or $d = rt$, is a familiar use of direct variation. In the distance formula, d is directly proportional to t with proportionally constant r. Similarly, d is directly proportional to r with proportionality constant t.

Two other kinds of variation exist: inverse and joint. In **inverse variation,** quantities y and x *vary inversely* when $y = \frac{k}{x}$ or $xy = k$, where $k \neq 0$. In the distance formula, r and t vary inversely with $k = d$.

In **joint variation,** quantity y *varies jointly* with x and z when $y = kxz$, where $k \neq 0$. In the example $d = rt, d$ varies jointly with r and t, with $k = 1$.

> **10.5 DIRECT VARIATION** Quantities y and x vary directly, or are directly proportional, when $y = kx$ or $\frac{y}{x} = k$, where $k \neq 0$.

> **10.6 INVERSE VARIATION** Quantities y and x vary inversely when $y = \frac{k}{x}$ or $xy = k$, where $k \neq 0$.

> **10.7 JOINT VARIATION** Quantity y varies jointly with x and z when $y = kxz$, where $k \neq 0$.

Example 10.8

   a. Quantities x and y vary directly. If $x = 20$ and $y = 8$:
      i. Find k.
      ii. Write an equation relating x and y.
      iii. Complete the chart.

x	1	2	3	4
y				

   b. Quantities x and y vary inversely. If $x = 20$ and $y = 8$:
      i. Find k.
      ii. Write an equation relating x and y.
      iii. Complete the chart.

x	1	2	3	4
y				

Solution:

a. Step 1: Using the general direct variation equation, substitute for x and y and solve for k.

$$8 = k(20)$$
$$8 \div 20 = k$$
$$2 \div 5 = k$$
$$k = 0.4$$

Step 2: Substitute k into the general equation, leaving y and x as variables. $y = \frac{2}{5}x$

Step 3: Multiply each x value by 0.4.

x	1	2	3	4
y	0.4	0.8	1.2	1.6

b. Step 1: Using the general inverse variation equation, substitute for x and y and solve for k.

$$8 = k \div 20$$
$$160 = k$$

Step 2: Substitute k into the general equation, leaving y and x as variables. $y = \frac{160}{x}$

Step 3: Divide 160 by each x value.

x	1	2	3	4
y	160	80	$53\frac{1}{3}$	40

DIY PROBLEMS

10.14 Solve the proportion $\dfrac{6}{x} = \dfrac{2}{3}$.

10.15 Solve the proportion $\dfrac{x+3}{4} = \dfrac{x}{8}$.

10.16 The monthly loan for a boat is $35 for each $1000 borrowed. At this rate, find the monthly payment for a $10,000 loan.

10.17 The commission a real estate agent makes varies directly with the price of the house. The agent made $5,100 on a sale of $85,000.

    a. Find k.

    b. For a $1,000,000 house, what is the commission?

10.18 The number of words that fit on a typed crime report varies inversely with the font size. At size 12, 200 words fit.

    a. Find k.

    b. The police chief wants to maximize one page while still keeping it readable. If a report of 686 words is put on one page, what is the corresponding font size and is it readable?

GRAPHING

Figure 10.1 is a graph of the average cost function from the opening scenario. The **average cost** per bracelet is modeled by the equation $C = \dfrac{1000 + 5x}{x}$, where x is the number of bracelets made.

10.8 AVERAGE COST The quotient of the total of fixed and variable costs and the number of items made.

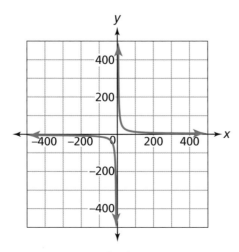

FIGURE 10.1 Graph of an Average Cost Function

Using the graph in Figure 10.1, consider the following questions. (Notice that the graph only makes sense for the cost scenario when $x > 0$; there is no such thing as making -3 bracelets.)

■ Will the average cost of the bracelets ever equal 0? Can an average be calculated for 0 bracelets? If $C = 0$, the equation becomes $-5x = 1000$, or $x = -200$; but x cannot be negative. And x cannot equal 0, since then a denominator would equal 0.

■ What happens to the average cost as the number of bracelets increases or decreases?

■ As x increases, the average cost decreases, getting closer and closer to 0. As x decreases through positive numbers toward 0, the average cost gets larger and larger.

Asymptotes

The answers to the last question are characteristic of rational functions and their asymptotes. An **asymptote** is a line to which the graph of a function becomes arbitrarily close for appropriate values of the variable.

A horizontal asymptote $(y = k)$ involves the end behavior of a function, as the variable values become very large and/or very small. For the cost function, the x-axis $(y = 0)$ is a horizontal asymptote as x gets greater and greater. (If we were considering negative values of x in some other context, the x-axis is also the horizontal asymptote as x decreases without bound.)

A vertical asymptote $(x = k)$ occurs when k is a value that makes the denominator, but not the numerator, of a rational function equal 0. The y-axis $(x = 0)$ is a vertical asymptote for the cost function as x takes on values closer and closer to 0.

10.9 ASYMPTOTE A line to which the graph of a function becomes arbitrarily close for appropriate values of the variable.

Graphing a Rational Expression

To graph a simplified function:

1. Plot the x-intercept and y-intercept, the points where the graph crosses the axes; find them by setting y and then x equal to zero.
2. A hole is a break in the curve where the function has no value. A hole exists at the value where both the denominator and the numerator equal 0.
3. Vertical asymptotes occur at the value where the denominator equals 0.
4. Horizontal or slant asymptotes occur depending on the *degree* of the numerator (n) and the degree of the denominator (m):
   ■ If $n < m$, then $y = 0$ is an asymptote.
   ■ If $n = m$, then $y =$ the ratio of the leading coefficients (the coefficients of the terms of degree m).
   ■ If $n > m$, there is no horizontal asymptote. A special case of a slant asymptote occurs when $n = m + 1$. Long division of the expression, excluding the remainder, produces the linear equation of the slant asymptote.

Notice that the cost function has no intercepts [though if x could be negative, $(-200, 0)$ is the x-intercept] and no holes, but has one vertical and one horizontal asymptote. Since $n = m = 1$, $y = 1$ is the horizontal asymptote.

The above information may be enough to form an accurate graph. If not, it will be necessary to plot points.

Example 10.9

a. Graph $y = \dfrac{8}{x^2 - x - 6}$.

b. Graph $y = \dfrac{2x^2 - x - 3}{x^2 - 1}$.

Solution:

a. Step 1: Find x and y intercepts. The x-intercept is

$$0 = \frac{8}{x^2 - x - 6}$$

There is no x-intercept since there is no value of x that makes the equation true. The graph will not cross the x-axis.

The y-intercept is

$$y = \frac{8}{0^2 - 0 - 6}$$
$$y = -\frac{4}{3}$$

The point $\left(0, -\dfrac{4}{3}\right)$ is on the graph.

Step 2: Find holes.

$$y = \frac{8}{(x - 3)(x + 2)}$$

There is no value that makes both the numerator and denominator equal 0.

Step 3: Find vertical asymptote(s). Set the denominator equal to 0 and solve for x.

$$y = \frac{8}{(x - 3)(x + 2)}$$
$$(x - 3)(x + 2) = 0$$
$$x = 3, x = -2$$

Step 4: Find horizontal or slant asymptote(s). Because $n < m$, $y = 0$ is the asymptote.

Step 5: Plot points.

x	y
−4	0.57
−1	−2
1	−1.33
4	1.33

Step 6: Graph (Figure 10.2).

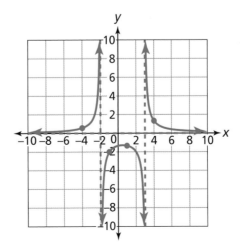

FIGURE 10.2

b. Step 1: Find x and y intercepts after simplifying.

$$y = \frac{2x^2 - x - 3}{x^2 - 1} \Rightarrow \frac{(2x-3)(x+1)}{(x-1)(x+1)} \Rightarrow \frac{2x-3}{x-1}$$

The x-intercept is

$$0 = \frac{2x-3}{x-1}$$

$$0 = 2x - 3$$

$$3 = 2x$$

$$\frac{3}{2} = x$$

So $(1.5, 0)$ is on the graph.

The y-intercept is

$$y = \frac{2(0) - 3}{(0) - 1}$$

$$y = \frac{-3}{-1}$$

$$y = 3$$

So $(0, 3)$ is on the graph.

Step 2: Find holes. Remember to consider all the steps produced in the simplification process.

$$y = \frac{2x^2 - x - 3}{x^2 - 1} \Rightarrow \frac{(2x-3)(x+1)}{(x-1)(x+1)} \Rightarrow \frac{2x-3}{x-1}$$

Because $x + 1$ is a common factor of the numerator and denominator, $x = -1$ makes both the numerator and the denominator equal 0. At $x = -1$, there is a hole.

Step 3: Find vertical asymptote(s) by setting the denominator equal to 0.

$$y = \frac{2x-3}{x-1}$$

$$0 = x - 1$$

$$1 = x$$

Step 4: Find horizontal or slant asymptote(s). Because $n = m$, there is an asymptote at $y = 2$.

Step 5: Plot points.

x	y
−4	2.2
0.5	4
4	1.67

Step 6: Graph (Figure 10.3).

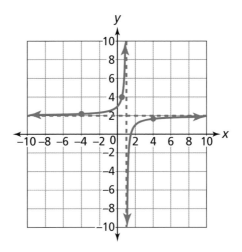

FIGURE 10.3

Example 10.10

Graph $y = \dfrac{x^2 + 11x + 18}{x + 1}$.

Solution:

Step 1: Find x and y intercepts.

The x-intercepts are

$$0 = \frac{x^2 + 11x + 18}{x + 1}$$

$$0 = x^2 + 11x + 18$$

$$0 = (x + 9)(x + 2)$$

$$x = -9, \ -2$$

So $(-9, 0)$ and $(-2, 0)$ are on the graph.

The y-intercept is

$$y = \frac{0^2 + 11(0) + 18}{0 + 1}$$

$$y = \frac{18}{1}$$

$$y = 18$$

So $(0, 18)$ is on the graph.

Step 2: Find holes.

$$y = \frac{(x + 9)(x + 2)}{x + 1}$$

There are no common factors and so no holes.

Step 3: Find vertical asymptote(s).

$$y = \frac{(x + 9)(x + 2)}{x + 1}$$

$$0 = x + 1$$

$$-1 = x$$

Step 4: Find the horizontal or slant asymptote(s). Because $n = m + 1$, there is a slant asymptote. Dividing,

$$\frac{x^2 + 11x + 18}{x + 1} = x + 10 + \frac{8}{x + 1}$$

So the equation of the asymptote is $y = x + 10$.

Step 5: Plot points.

x	y
−4	3.33
−2.5	2.17
4	15.6

Step 6: Graph (Figure 10.4).

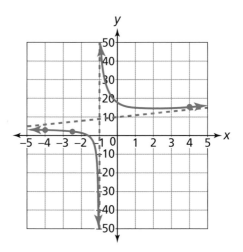

FIGURE 10.4

DIY PROBLEMS

10.19 Graph $p(x) = \dfrac{1}{2x^2 + 10x + 8}$.

10.20 Graph $q(x) = \dfrac{x^2 + 6x + 8}{x^2 - 6x + 8}$.

APPLICATION PROBLEMS

Application Types

Besides variation, proportion, and the average cost, there are other applications of rational functions. Some involve specific formulas while others require an equation constructed from given information. Applications using specific formulas include the following:

■ *Photography.* When an object is in focus, its distance from the lens of a camera, p, and the distance from the lens to the image, q, is given by the formula:

$\frac{1}{p}+\frac{1}{q}=\frac{1}{f}$, where f is the focal length, the distance from the lens to the focal point in the camera. The focal point is where light rays meet after passing through the lens. Figure 10.5 illustrates this.

■ *Finance.* The principal or starting amount P that will grow to value A after n years of simple interest at a yearly interest rate r is given by the formula: $P=\dfrac{A}{1+nr}$.

■ *Package engineering.* When a cylindrical can has volume, V, and base radius, r, its height is given by the formula: $h=\dfrac{V}{\pi r^2}$.

■ *Motion.* The time, t, needed to travel distance, d, at rate, r, is modeled by the equation: $t=\dfrac{d}{r}$.

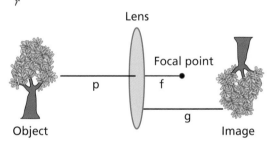

FIGURE 10.5 Schematic Details of the Lens Equation

Example 10.11

a. A wedding photographer sets the focal length at 5 cm and knows that the distance to the wedding cake is triple the distance to its image. Using the lens equation above, how far away is the wedding cake from the camera's lens?

b. Using the simple interest formula above, what is the interest rate on the Taylor family's college fund if they invested $10,000 18 years ago and now the account totals $27,640?

c. A grocery store has asked a manufacturing company to produce a 350 cm³ can with a 6 cm diameter base that fits on its shelves measuring 10 cm in height. Can such a container be created?

d. A moving truck drove 1,000 miles to Chicago from Denver at a rate 10 miles slower than on the return trip. If the trip took 24 hours total, using the time formula above, how fast was the truck going in each direction?

Solution:

a. Step 1: Substitute for all known variables, defining x as the distance to the image.

$$\frac{1}{3x}+\frac{1}{x}=\frac{1}{5}$$

Step 2: Solve the equation.

$$[(3)(x)(5)]\frac{1}{3x} + \frac{1}{x} = \frac{1}{5}$$

$$\frac{(\cancel{3})(\cancel{x})(5)}{\cancel{3x}} + \frac{(3)(\cancel{x})(5)}{\cancel{x}} = \frac{(3)(x)(\cancel{5})}{\cancel{5}}$$

$$5 + 15 = 3x$$

$$20 = 3x$$

$$6\frac{2}{3} = x$$

Since x is the distance to the image and the distance to the object is triple the distance to x, the answer is 20 cm.

Step 3: Check the solution in the original equation. It is correct.

b. Step 1: Substitute for all known variables.

$$10{,}000 = \frac{27{,}640}{1 + (18)r}$$

Step 2: Solve the equation using cross-multiplying.

$$\frac{10{,}000}{1} = \frac{27{,}640}{1 + (18)r}$$

$$10{,}000(1 + 18r) = 27{,}640$$

$$10{,}000 + 180{,}000r = 27{,}640$$

$$180{,}000r = 17{,}640$$

$$r = .098$$

The interest rate is 9.8%.

Step 3: Check the solution in the original equation. It is correct.

c. Step 1: Substitute for all known variables, finding the radius by dividing the diameter by 2.

$$h = \frac{350}{\pi(3)^2}$$

Step 2: Solve for h by simplifying the fraction.

$$h = \frac{350}{\pi(3)^2}$$

$$h = \frac{350}{9\pi}$$

$$h \approx 12.38$$

The height of the produced can will be 12.38 cm, more than 2 cm taller than the shelves. Therefore, it is not possible to create a can with the given measurements.

d. Step 1: Substitute for all known variables, adding the fractions representing the time for the truck's trips in each direction.

$$24 = \frac{1000}{r-10} + \frac{1000}{r}$$

Step 2: Solve the equation.

$$[r(r-10)]\left(24 = \frac{1000}{r-10} + \frac{1000}{r}\right)$$

$$24r(r-10) = \frac{1000r(r-10)}{r-10} + \frac{1000r(r-10)}{r}$$

$$24r^2 - 240r = 1000r + 1000r - 10000$$

$$24r^2 - 240r = 2000r - 10000$$

$$24r^2 - 2240r + 10000 = 0$$

$$2(12r^2 - 1120r + 5000) = 0$$

$$12r^2 - 1120r + 5000 = 0$$

$$r = \frac{1120 \pm \sqrt{(-1120)^2 - 4(12)(5000)}}{2(12)}$$

$$r \approx 88.63, \ 4.7$$

Step 3: Check the solutions in the original equation to show that r cannot equal 4.7 because it would yield a negative time for the outbound trip. Therefore, the rate of the truck was 78.63 mph going there and 88.63 mph returning.

The other set of applications of rational functions concerns situations where no direct formulas are given. Rather, use specific information to model the scenario with an equation that can be manipulated and solved.

Example 10.12

a. *Work problem:* The lead pharmacist needs to organize the stockroom before the winter's flu season. Employee A can organize the entire stockroom in 8 hours, while Employee B can complete it in 6 hours. How long will it take them, working together, to organize the stockroom?

b. *Average cost:* A former boxer is opening a new boxing gym where there is a one-time enrollment fee of $50 plus a monthly cost of $15. After how many months of membership would the average cost be under $20?

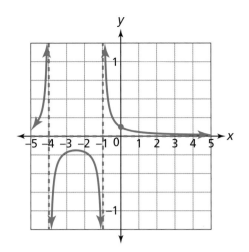

FIGURE 10.6

c. *Percentages:* Currently at the city's only culinary school, 34 out of 50 incoming students are female. If the admissions officers and the president would like to see 50% incoming male students, how many more first-year male students need to enroll?

Solution:

a. Step 1: Write a rational equation from the information. Each hour, Employee A does one-eighth of the work, and Employee B does one-sixth of the work. Let x be the hours it takes them when working together. Then the amount of work they do together in one hour will equal the sum of the amounts each does in one hour. The equation is

$$\frac{1}{8} + \frac{1}{6} = \frac{1}{x}$$

Step 2: Solve the equation.

$$[(8)(6)(x)]\left(\frac{1}{8} + \frac{1}{6} = \frac{1}{x}\right)$$

$$\frac{(\cancel{8})(6)(x)}{\cancel{8}} + \frac{(8)(\cancel{6})(x)}{\cancel{6}} = \frac{(8)(6)(\cancel{x})}{\cancel{x}}$$

$$6x + 8x = 48$$

$$14x = 48$$

$$x \approx 3.4$$

Together, it will take them about 3.4 hours.

Step 3: Check the solution. It is correct.

b. Step 1: Write a rational equation from the information where m is the number of months of membership.

$$20 = \frac{50 + 15m}{m}$$

Step 2: Solve the equation by cross-multiplying.

$$\frac{20}{1} = \frac{50 + 15m}{m}$$

$$20m = 50 + 15m$$

$$5m = 50$$

$$m = 10$$

After 10 months of membership, average cost will be $20. For more than 10 months of membership, average cost will be less than $20.

Step 3: Check the solution. It is correct.

    c. Step 1: Write a rational equation from the information, where x is the number of incoming male students.

$$\frac{50}{100} = \frac{16+x}{50+x}$$

Step 2: Solve the equation by cross-multiplying.

$$\frac{50}{100} = \frac{16+x}{50+x}$$

$$50(50+x) = 100(16+x)$$

$$2500 + 50x = 1600 + 100x$$

$$900 = 50x$$

$$18 = x$$

The culinary school needs 18 male students to enroll.

Step 3: Check the solution. It is correct.

    Checking the solution is not only helpful to see if the solution is extraneous, but also to see if the answer realistically makes sense for the problem. If it does not, this is a telltale sign of an error in problem solving.

DIY PROBLEMS

10.21 How long would it take an account earning simple interest at an interest rate of 5.25% to triple in value?

10.22 It takes a bike courier one hour to make a delivery 8 miles away and return to the home office. If the courier is riding into a 6 mph wind on the way to the delivery and with the 6 mph wind on the way back to the office, what is the courier's rate in each direction? Assume that the courier rides at the same rate throughout the trip.

SOLUTIONS TO DIY PROBLEMS

10.1 Simplify $\frac{2x^2y^3}{4x^4y}$.

Solution:
Use the rules of exponents.

$$\frac{2x^2y^3}{4x^4y} = \frac{y^2}{2x^2}$$

10.2 Simplify $\dfrac{x^2 + 4x + 16}{x + 4}$.

Solution:

$$\frac{x^2 + 8x + 16}{x + 4} = \frac{(x+4)(x+4)}{(x+4)} = x + 4$$

10.3 Simplify $\dfrac{10x^2}{9y^3} \cdot \dfrac{3y^2}{5x^3}$.

Solution:

Step 1: Factor all expressions $\dfrac{(5)(2)(x)(x)}{(3)(3)(y)(y)(y)} \cdot \dfrac{(3)(y)(y)}{(5)(x)(x)(x)}$.

Step 2: Divide out factors common to the numerator and denominators and write out the final product.

The final product is $\dfrac{2}{3xy}$

10.4 Find the quotient when $\dfrac{7x^2}{3b}$ is divided by $\dfrac{2}{3x}$.

Solution:

$$\frac{7x^2}{3b} \div \frac{2}{3x} = \frac{7x^2}{3b} \cdot \frac{3x}{2}$$

$$= \frac{21x^3}{6b}$$

$$= \frac{7x^3}{2b}$$

10.5 Simplify $\dfrac{\dfrac{2m^2 + 2m - 12}{12m}}{\dfrac{m^2 - 9}{3m^2}}$.

Solution:

$$\frac{2m^2 + 2m - 12}{12m} \cdot \frac{3m^2}{m^2 - 9}$$

$$= \frac{2(m-2)(m+3)}{(2)(2)(3)(m)} \cdot \frac{(3)(m)(m)}{(m+3)(m-3)}$$

$$= \frac{m(m-2)}{2(m-3)}$$

10.6 Simplify $\dfrac{a + 3b}{2a - 2b} \div \dfrac{a^2 + 3ab}{b^2 - a^2} \cdot ab$.

Solution:

$$\frac{a+3b}{2a-2b} \cdot \frac{b^2 - a^2}{a^2 + 3ab} \cdot \frac{ab}{1}$$

$$\frac{(a+3b)}{2(a-b)} \cdot \frac{(b+a)(a-b)(-1)}{a(a+3b)} \cdot \frac{(a)(b)}{1}$$

$$\frac{-b(b+a)}{2}$$

10.7 Find the Lowest Common Multiple (LCM) of $9x^2y^2$ and $12\,xy^3$.

Solution:
Step 1: Factor each monomial and identify the common factors
$9x^2y^2 = 3 \cdot 3 \cdot x \cdot x \cdot y \cdot y$
$12xy^3 = 2 \cdot 2 \cdot 3 \cdot x \cdot y \cdot y \cdot y$
The common factors 3, x, y, y

Step 2: Create the LCM by first writing the common factors and then writing the remaining factors of each monomial.
$3 \cdot 2 \cdot 2 \cdot 3 \cdot x \cdot y \cdot y \cdot x \cdot y = 36x^2y^3$

10.8 Add the rational expressions $\dfrac{2x+1}{12} + \dfrac{3x+2}{12}$.

Solution:
$$\frac{2x+1}{12} + \frac{3x+2}{12} = \frac{5x+3}{12}$$

10.9 Perform the indicated operation and simplify $\dfrac{3}{4} + \dfrac{-5}{6}$.

Solution:
$$\frac{3}{4} + \frac{-5}{6} = \frac{9}{12} + \frac{-10}{12} = -\frac{1}{12}$$

10.10 Simplify $\dfrac{4t}{t^2-4} + \dfrac{t}{t+2}$.

Solution:
$$\frac{4t}{(t+2)(t-2)} + \frac{t(t-2)}{(t+2)(t-2)}$$
$$= \frac{4t+t^2-2t}{(t+2)\,(t-2)}$$
$$= \frac{t^2+2t}{(t+2)(t-2)}$$
$$= \frac{t(t+2)}{(t+2)(t-2)}$$
$$= \frac{t}{t-2}$$

10.11 Simplify $\dfrac{5x}{3x^2-x-2} - \dfrac{x-2}{x^2+4x-5}$.

Solution:
$$\frac{5x(x+5)}{(3x+2)(x-1)(x+5)} - \frac{(x-2)(3x+2)}{(x+5)(x-1)(3x+2)}$$
$$\frac{5x^2+25x-(3x^2-4x-4)}{(3x+2)(x-1)(x+5)}$$
$$\frac{2x^2+29x+4}{(3x+2)(x-1)(x+5)}$$

10.12 Solve $b + \dfrac{4}{b} = -5$.

Solution:

$$b\left(b + \frac{4}{b} = -5\right)$$
$$b^2 + 4 = -5b$$
$$b^2 + 5b + 4 = 0$$
$$(b + 1)(b + 4) = 0$$
$$b = -1, -4$$

10.13 Solve $\dfrac{1}{t + 1} = \dfrac{2}{t^2 - 1} - \dfrac{1}{t - 1}$.

Solution:

$$[(t + 1)(t - 1)]\left(\frac{1}{t + 1} = \frac{2}{t^2 - 1} - \frac{1}{t - 1}\right)$$
$$t - 1 = 2 - (t + 1)$$
$$t - 1 = 2 - t - 1$$
$$2t = 2$$
$$t = 1$$

However, when plugged back into the original equation, $t = 1$ is extraneous because it causes two denominators to equal 0. So there is no solution to this equation.

10.14 Solve the proportion $\dfrac{6}{x} = \dfrac{2}{3}$.

Solution:
Solve by cross-mulitiplying

$$(6)(3) = 2x$$
$$18 = 2x$$
$$x = 9$$

The solution is 9

10.15 Solve the proportion $\dfrac{x + 3}{4} = \dfrac{x}{8}$.

Solution:
Solve by cross-multiplying

$$8(x + 3) = 4x$$
$$8x + 24 = 4x$$
$$4x = -24$$
$$x = -6$$

The solution is -6

10.16 The monthly loan for a boat is \$35 for each \$1000 borrowed. At this rate, find the monthly payment for a \$10,000 loan.

Solution:
P represents the monthly boat payments.

$$\frac{\$35}{\$1,000} = \frac{P}{\$10,000}$$
$$(\$35)(\$10,000) = (P)(\$1,000)$$
$$P = \$350$$

10.17 The commission a real estate agent makes varies directly with the price of the house. The agent made $5,100 on a sale of $85,000.

Solution:
  a. Find k.

$$5100 = k(85,000)$$
$$0.06 = k$$

  b. For a $1,000,000 house, what is the commission?

$$y = (0.06)(1,000,000)$$
$$y = \$60,000$$

10.18 The number of words that fit on a typed crime report varies inversely with the font size. At size 12, 200 words fit.

Solution:
  a. Find k.

$$12 = \frac{k}{200}$$
$$2400 = k$$

  b. The police chief wants to maximize one page while still keeping it readable. If a report of 686 words is put on one page, what is the corresponding font size and is it readable?

$$y = \frac{2400}{x}$$
$$y = \frac{2400}{686}$$
$$y = 3.5$$

Therefore, at font size 3.5, the crime report will not be readable by anyone except a mouse.

10.19 Graph $p(x) = \dfrac{1}{2x^2 + 10x + 8}$.

Solution:
There is no x-intercept when $y = p(x) = 0$. The y-intercept is at (0, 1/8).

There are no holes in the graph because even though the denominator factors into $2(x + 4)(x + 1)$, there are no common factors with the numerator other than 1.

There are vertical asymptotes at $x = -4$ and $x = -1$. There is a horizontal asymptote at $y = 0$ since $n < m$. (See Figure 10.7.)

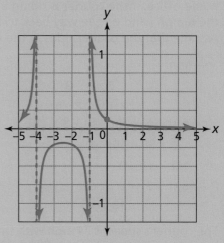

FIGURE 10.7

10.20 Graph $q(x) = \dfrac{x^2 + 6x + 8}{x^2 - 6x + 8}$.

Solution:

The *x*-intercepts are at $(-2, 0)$ and $(-4, 0)$. The *y*-intercept is at $(0, 1)$.

There are no holes in the graph because even though both the numerator and denominator factor, there are no common factors.

There are vertical asymptotes at $x = 4$ and $x = 2$. The horizontal asymptote is at $y = 1$. (See Figure 10.8.)

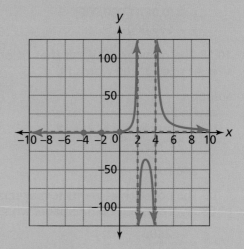

FIGURE 10.8

10.21 How long would it take an account earning simple interest at an interest rate of 5.25% to triple in value?

Solution:

$$1 = \frac{3}{1 + n(0.0525)}$$

$$1 + n(0.0525) = 3$$

$$0.0525n = 2$$

$$n = 38.1$$

It would take 38.1 years to triple the investment.

10.22 It takes a bike courier one hour to make a delivery 8 miles away and return to the home office. If the courier is riding into a 6 mph wind on the way to the delivery and with the 6 mph wind on the way back to the office, what is the courier's rate in each direction? Assume that the courier rides at the same rate throughout the trip.

Solution:

$$1 = \frac{8}{r+6} + \frac{8}{r-6}$$

$$(r+6)(r-6) = 8(r-6) + 8(r+6)$$

$$r^2 - 36 = 16r$$

$$r^2 - 16r - 36 = 0$$

$$(r-18)(r+2) = 0$$

$$r = 18, r = -2$$

The courier's speed is 24 mph with the wind and 12 mph without the wind. The solution for $r = -2$ is an extraneous one because the courier's rate cannot be negative in this scenario.

10.1 Write $\dfrac{3}{8a^2}$ with a denominator of $16a^4$.

10.2 Simplify the following: $\dfrac{12x^2}{15x^4}$.

10.3 Simplify the following: $\dfrac{3x-2}{2-3x}$.

10.4 Simplify the following: $\dfrac{(x+2)^2}{(x+2)^3}$.

10.5 Simplify the following: $\dfrac{6x-8}{9x^2-16}$.

10.6 Simplify the following: $\dfrac{2a^2-ab-b^2}{a^2-b^2}$.

10.7 Simplify the following: $1 + \dfrac{x}{1 + \dfrac{1}{1 + x}}$.

10.8 Find the LCM of $2x^3y^2$ and $3x^2y^4$.

10.9 Find the LCM of $x^2 + 3x$ and $x^2 + 8x + 15$.

10.10 Perform the Indicated operation and simplify $\dfrac{3}{5} + \dfrac{1}{10}$.

10.11 Simplify the following: $\dfrac{5}{3x} + \dfrac{2}{3x}$.

10.12 Simplify the following: $\dfrac{x}{x+2} - \dfrac{3x+1}{x+2}$.

10.13 Add: $\dfrac{3}{2x+4} + \dfrac{2}{x+2}$.

10.14 Subtract: $\dfrac{4x}{x+1} - \dfrac{3}{x-1}$.

10.15 Multiply: $\dfrac{3}{x} \cdot \dfrac{5}{y}$.

10.16 Multiply: $\dfrac{4x}{3y} \cdot \dfrac{5}{8x^2}$.

10.17 Multiply: $\dfrac{2x^2 - 4x}{x^2 - 5x + 6} \cdot \dfrac{x^2 - 9}{2x^2}$.

10.18 Divide: $\dfrac{4}{y} \div \dfrac{x}{2}$.

10.19 Divide: $\dfrac{x^2}{y^2-1} \div \dfrac{x^2}{y+1}$.

10.20 Divide: $\dfrac{8x^3 + 27y^3}{64x^3 - y^3} \div \dfrac{4x^2 - 9y^2}{16x^2 + 4xy + y^2}$.

10.21 Solve: $\dfrac{x}{4} + 5 = \dfrac{2x}{3}$.

10.22 Solve the following: $\dfrac{1}{x} = \dfrac{1}{3x} + \dfrac{1}{2}$.

10.23 Solve the following: $\dfrac{4}{9} = \dfrac{x}{27}$.

10.24 Solve the following: $\dfrac{4}{x} = \dfrac{8}{x+1}$.

10.25 Solve the following: $\dfrac{3}{2} = \dfrac{6}{x+5}$.

10.26 Solve the following: $\dfrac{4}{x-1} = \dfrac{14}{2x+1}$.

10.27 The total amount of time t that is required for two workers to complete a job working together, if one worker can complete it alone in c hours and the other in d hours, can be expressed with the following equation: $\dfrac{1}{t} = \dfrac{1}{c} + \dfrac{1}{d}$. Solve the equation for t. Then use the solved equation to answer the following problem. If Mark can mow his lawn in 2 hours and his brother can mow it in 3 hours, how long will it take them to mow the lawn working together?

10.28 A blueprint uses a scale of 3/4 inch = 2 feet. Find the scaled-down dimensions of a room that is 10 feet by 12 feet.

10.29 A boat travels 30 miles downstream in the same time it takes to go 20 miles upstream. If the river current flows at 5 miles per hour, what is the boat's speed in still water?

10.30 Graph the following rational equations:

a. $y = \dfrac{1}{x}$

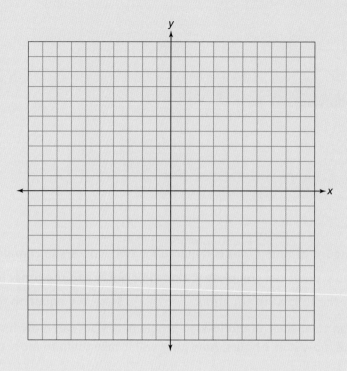

b. $y = \dfrac{1}{x^2}$

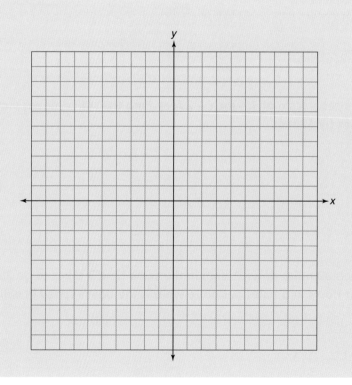

10.31 Graph the rational equation: $y = \dfrac{x+1}{x-1}$.

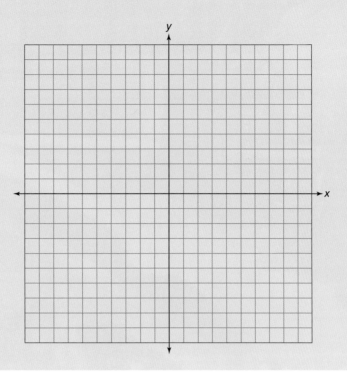

REFERENCES

Definitions. (n.d.). In *Encarta online dictionary.* Retrieved from http://encarta.msn.comDodge, W. (1998). Worksheets of algebra 1. New Trier High School, Winnetka, IL.

Harris, T. (n.d.). How cameras work. Retrieved from http://electronics.howstuffworks.com/camera2.htm

Larson, R., Boswell, L., Kanold, T., & Stiff, L. (2007). *Algebra 2*. Evanston, IL: McDougal Littell. Major, N. (2004). Algebra I notes 2nd semester. Cherry Creek High School, Greenwood Village, CO.

Math Forum @ Drexel. (n.d.). Distance, rate, and time. Retrieved from http://mathforum.org/dr.math/faq/faq.distance.html

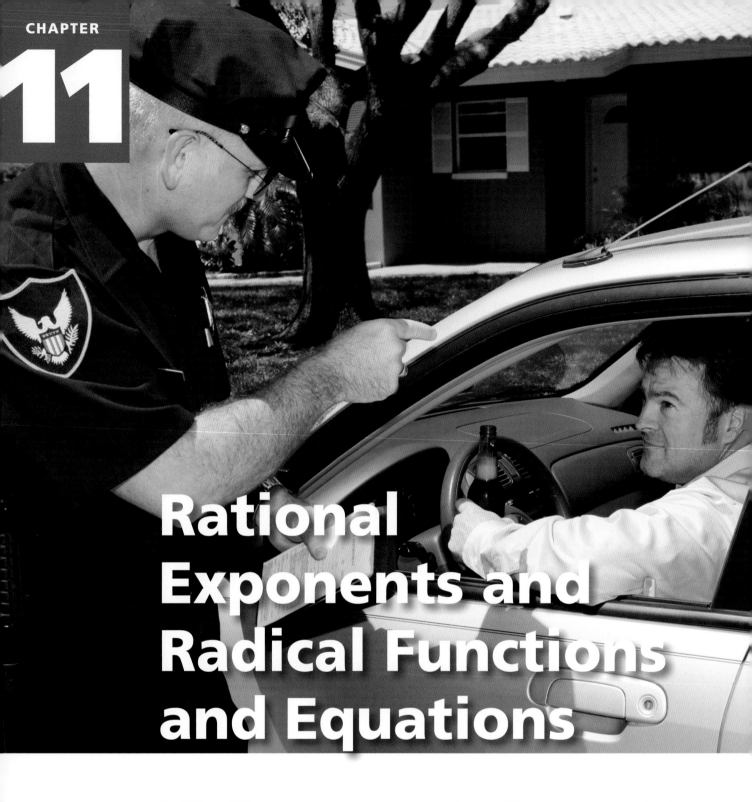

Rational Exponents and Radical Functions and Equations

I. Officer Velazquez is investigating an accident on Vista Avenue in a school zone where the speed limit is 25 mph. A driver with open alcohol in his vehicle struck and seriously injured a child on a bicycle. Officer Velazquez needs to find out the exact speed of the vehicle in order to complete his report and charge the driver. After an unsatisfactory interview with the driver, he measures the length of the delivery van's skid marks and determines it is 72 feet.

Officer Velazquez knows he can use an equation that should provide a very good estimate of the car's speed at the time of the accident. The equation is $s = \sqrt{30\,fd}$, where s is the speed of the car in miles per hour, f is the coefficient of friction, and d is the distance in feet that the car skidded. He already knows that $d = 72$ feet. He consults a transportation reference and determines that the coefficient of friction on the road's surface can be estimated as $f = 0.8$.

II. A pharmaceutical company is redesigning the shape of its daily multivitamin from the current rectangular shape to a new spherical one with the same volume of 1.5 cubic millimeters. The formula for the radius of a sphere of volume V is $r = \left(\dfrac{3V}{4\pi}\right)^{\frac{1}{3}}$, Market research with consumers showed that consumers prefer the pill to be less than 1 millimeter in diameter.

This chapter focuses on the connection between rational exponents and radicals, and on work with radicals, using mathematical operations, equations, and graphing.

QUESTIONS TO CONSIDER

I. Officer Velazquez

1. Use a calculator to find s to the nearest tenth of a mile per hour.

2. Knowing this approximate speed, should Officer Velazquez charge the driver with exceeding the speed limit?

3. Use a calculator and the values shown at left to find the value to the nearest tenth of a mile per hour of the expression $s = (30fd)^{\frac{1}{2}}$. How does it compare to the answer to question 1?

4. If the officer wanted an exact value for the speed of the car without decimals, is there a way to find it?

5. Are there any values that s could not equal?

6. Are there any values that $30fd$ could not equal?

7. What would the graph of the equation above look like?

8. Is there a way to manipulate the formula to solve for d?

II. Pharmaceutical Company

1. Using the formula shown at left what would the radius of the new spherical pill be?

2. Can this company keep the volume constant and still satisfy its customers?

3. Would the new design satisfy the researched customers?

4. Solve the given formula for V.

5. Graph the function in question 4. How does it compare in shape to the graph of the police investigation in the previous scenario?

6. Use a calculator to find the radius using the formula $r = \sqrt[3]{\dfrac{3V}{4\pi}}$. Is it the same value as the answer in question 1?

KEY TERMS

- equivalent exponential and radical expressions (p. 391)
- index (p. 388)
- *n*th root of *x* (p. 388)
- parent function (p. 398)
- Product Property of Radicals (p. 393)
- Quotient Property of Radicals (p. 393)
- radical (p. 388)
- radical expression (p. 388)
- radicand (p. 388)
- simplified radical form (p. 388)

RATIONAL EXPONENTS

Definition of Radical Expressions

Radical four, or $\sqrt{4}$, or *the square root of 4*, or *root 4*, or the principal square root of 4, are all equivalent expressions for the value 2 because $2^2 = 4$. Similarly, $\sqrt{36} = 6$, $\sqrt{121} = 11$, $\sqrt{625} = 25$, and so on. Note $(2)^2 = 4$, but $\sqrt{4} \neq -2$. Both the symbol $\sqrt{}$ and expressions using the symbol, such as $\sqrt[4]{16}$ or $\sqrt{3t}$, are referred to as **radicals.**

In the radical form $\sqrt[n]{x}$, the integer n is the **index** of the radical and indicates which root of x. When $n = 2$, the expression is read "the square root of x." When $n = 3$, it is "the cube root of x." For $n = 4, 5, 6, \ldots$, the expression is read "the 4th, 5th, 6th,… root of x. Use the phrases *radical x* and *root x* only for $\sqrt{x}$. It is customary to omit the index 2, although it is certainly not incorrect to write, for example, $\sqrt[2]{64} = 8$.

In the radical form $\sqrt[n]{x}$, the value x under the radical symbol is called the **radicand.** Recall from Chapter 6 that odd roots of a negative radicand will be negative: $((-32)^{\frac{1}{5}} = \sqrt[5]{-32} = -2)$ and that even roots of a negative radicand are not real; there is no real number whose 4th power is -16 $((-16)^{\frac{1}{4}} = \sqrt[4]{-16} \neq -2)$. From now on assume that an even index implies a nonnegative radicand.

A radical expression is any expression that contains a radical. A radical is in **simplified radical form** when the radicand has no factors with power greater than or equal to the index, there is no radical in the denominator, and the radicand is not a fraction.

To evaluate or simplify a radical, factor the radicand into prime factors and rewrite every group of factors whose power is the index using the property that for $x \geq 0$, $\left(\sqrt[n]{x}\right)^n = \sqrt[n]{x^n} = x$.

For example:

$$\sqrt[3]{54} = \sqrt[3]{2 \cdot 27} = \sqrt[3]{3^3 \cdot 2} = \sqrt[3]{3^3} \cdot \sqrt[3]{2} = 3\sqrt[3]{2}$$

and

$$\sqrt[4]{x^5 yz^4} = \sqrt[4]{xx^4 yz^4} = \sqrt[4]{xy(xz)^4} = \sqrt[4]{xy} \cdot \sqrt[4]{(xz)^4} = xz\sqrt[4]{xy}$$

In the opening scenario, the radical equation for speed, $s = \sqrt{30fd}$, relates to the proposed question: "If the officer wanted an exact value for the speed of the car without decimals, is there a way to find it?" Realistically, for this investigation finding the answer to this question would not be helpful, but in some cases an exact answer is desirable.

For the given equation, $s = \sqrt{30fd} = \sqrt{(30)(0.8)(72)} = \sqrt{1728}$. Since 1728 is not a perfect square, factor the radicand using methods of prime factorization and then simplify:

$$\sqrt{1728} = \sqrt{9 \cdot 192} = \sqrt{9 \cdot 6 \cdot 32} = \sqrt{2^6 3^3} = \sqrt{\left(2^3\right)^2 \cdot 3^2 \cdot 3} = 2^3 \cdot 3\sqrt{3} = 24\sqrt{3}$$

11.1 RADICAL The symbol $\sqrt{}$ used to indicate finding the principal root of a number. Expressions such as $\sqrt[4]{16}$ or $\sqrt{3t}$ are also referred to as radicals.

11.2 nTH ROOT OF x Written $\sqrt[n]{x}$, the quantity r such that $r^n = (\sqrt[n]{x})^n = x$.

11.3 INDEX Of a radical, the integer n greater than 1 in the expression $\sqrt[n]{x}$ that identifies the type of root.

11.4 RADICAND The value under the radical symbol.

11.5 RADICAL EXPRESSION Any expression that contains a radical.

11.6 SIMPLIFIED RADICAL FORM A radical for which the radicand has no factors with power greater than or equal to the index, there is no radical in the denominator, and the radicand is not a fraction.

The exact answer to the question is $\sqrt{1728} = 24\sqrt{3}$ in simplified radical form.

To write an expression as a radical expression, reverse the process. To rewrite $3xh^2$ as an expression using a 5th root of $3h^2$, write $3xh^2 = x\sqrt[5]{3^5\left(h^2\right)^5} = x\sqrt[5]{243h^{10}}$.

Simplifying Expressions with Rational Exponents

To add or subtract exponential expressions (such as r^2 and $3r^2$), they have to be *like terms*. Recall that like terms are quantities with the same variables raised to the same powers.

Exponents can also be rational numbers of the form $\dfrac{p}{q}$, where p and q are integers and q is not zero. For example, $3a^{\frac{2}{3}}b^4 - a^2b^{\frac{4}{5}} - a^{\frac{2}{3}}b^4 + 7a^2b^{\frac{4}{5}} = 2a^{\frac{2}{3}}b^4 + 6a^2b^{\frac{4}{5}}$.

Example 11.1 Simplify the following:

   a. $\sqrt{8} - \sqrt{32}$

Solution:

Step 1: Factor the radicands.
$$\sqrt{8} - \sqrt{32} = \sqrt{2^3} - \sqrt{2^5}$$

Step 2: Use the index as the power for as many factors in the radicands as possible.
$$\sqrt{2^3} - \sqrt{2^5} = \sqrt{2 \cdot 2^2} - \sqrt{2^2 \cdot 2^2 \cdot 2}$$

Step 3: Rewrite those factors using the rule $\sqrt[n]{x^n} = x$, for $x \geq 0$.
$$\sqrt{2 \cdot 2^2} - \sqrt{2^2 \cdot 2^2 \cdot 2} = 2\sqrt{2} - 2 \cdot 2\sqrt{2} = -2\sqrt{2}$$

The ability to combine steps 1 and 2, and steps 3 and 4, comes with experience.

   b. $\sqrt[4]{81x^5yz^{10}}$

Solution:

Step 1: Factor the radicand, using the index as the power for as many factors as possible.
$$\sqrt[4]{81x^5yz^{10}} = \sqrt[4]{3^4 \cdot x \cdot x^4 yz^2 z^4 z^4}$$

Step 2: Write in simplified radical form.
$$\sqrt[4]{3^4 \cdot x \cdot x^4 yz^2 z^4 z^4} = 3xz^2\sqrt[4]{xyz^2}$$

Example 11.2 Simplify $3x^{\frac{1}{2}}y^2 - x^{\frac{1}{2}}y^{\frac{1}{2}} + x^{\frac{1}{2}}y^2$.

Solution:

Notice that only the first and last terms are like terms.
$$3x^{\frac{1}{2}}y^2 - x^{\frac{1}{2}}y^{\frac{1}{2}} + x^{\frac{1}{2}}y^2 = 4x^{\frac{1}{2}}y^2 - x^{\frac{1}{2}}y^{\frac{1}{2}}$$

11.1 Simplify the following:

a. $\sqrt[3]{81} + \sqrt[3]{216}$

b. $\sqrt{12x^6 y^5 z^2}$

11.2 Simplify $2x^{\frac{2}{3}} y^{\frac{1}{3}} - x^{\frac{2}{3}} y^{\frac{1}{3}} + x^{\frac{1}{3}} y^{\frac{2}{3}} + 4x^{\frac{2}{3}} y^{\frac{1}{3}} - x^{\frac{2}{3}} y^{\frac{1}{3}}$.

RELATIONSHIP BETWEEN POWERS AND ROOTS

Writing Exponential Expressions as Radical Expressions

Expressions with a rational exponent have equivalent radical expressions. Recall these two rules of exponents from Chapter 6:

Rule 6. $\sqrt[q]{x} = x^{\frac{1}{q}}$, $q \uparrow 0$, and if q is even, $x \geq 0$

Rule 7. $x^{\frac{p}{q}} = \left(x^{\frac{1}{q}} \right)^p = \left(x^p \right)^{\frac{1}{q}}$, $q \uparrow 0$ and if $x < 0$, q is odd and $p = 1$

Rule 6 equates an expression with a rational exponent to the radical expression whose radicand is the base of the exponent and whose index is the inverse of the exponent. To see that both expressions represent the same value, raise both sides of the equation to the qth power:

$$\left(\sqrt[q]{x} \right)^q = \left(x^{\frac{1}{q}} \right)^q$$

By definition, $\left(\sqrt[q]{x} \right)^q = x$. By the Power of a Power Property, $\left(x^{\frac{1}{q}} \right)^p = x^{\frac{q}{q}} = x^1$.

Since $x = x^1$, both sides of the equation are equal. Both $\sqrt[q]{x}$ and $x^{\frac{1}{q}}$ are called the qth root of x, although $x^{\frac{1}{q}}$ is also read "x to the 1 over q." They represent the number that when it is raised to the qth power equals x.

For a negative exponent,

$$x^{-\frac{1}{q}} = \frac{1}{\sqrt[q]{x}}$$

again if x and q are not 0.

(Remember that negative exponents do not imply negative values. Also recall that if q is 2 (or any even integer), x must be nonnegative.)

Notice that

$$a = a^1 = (a^{\frac{1}{2}})^2 = (\sqrt{a})^2 = a^1 = a$$

$$a = a^1 = (a^{\frac{1}{3}})^3 = (\sqrt[3]{a})^3 = a^1 = a$$

and in general,

$$a = a^1 = \left(a^{\frac{1}{n}}\right)^n = (\sqrt[n]{a})^n = a^1 = a \quad \text{(for } a \geq 0 \text{ if } n \text{ is even)}$$

Rule 7 applies the Power of a Power Property to rational exponents under the appropriate conditions, using the equivalent expressions $\frac{p}{q} = p \cdot \frac{1}{q} = \frac{1}{q} \cdot p$.

Look at $4^{\frac{3}{2}}$ as an example. Using the Power of a Power Property, rewrite $4^{\frac{3}{2}}$ as $(4^{\frac{1}{2}})^3$ or as $(4^3)^{\frac{1}{2}}$.

Using Rule 6, the expression $(4^{\frac{1}{2}})^3$ becomes $(\sqrt{4})^3 = 2^3 = 8$. The expression $(4^3)^{\frac{1}{2}}$ becomes $\sqrt{4^3} = \sqrt{64} = 8$. Note that the exponent can be written either inside the radical sign or above it as long as the radicand is positive.

Writing Radical Expressions as Exponential Expressions

When an expression is in radical form, use the **equivalent exponential and radical expression** equations shown in definition 11.7 to write the expression in exponential form. For instance, $\sqrt[5]{2t}$ in exponential form is $(2t)^{\frac{1}{5}}$.

Example 11.3 Rewrite each exponential expression as a radical expression and evaluate.

a. $4^{\frac{5}{2}}$

Solution:

Step 1: Rewrite as a radical. $4^{\frac{5}{2}} = (\sqrt{4})^5$

Step 2: Evaluate. $(\sqrt{4})^5 = 2^5 = 32$

b. $(xyz)^{-\frac{2}{3}}$

Solution:

Step 1: Rewrite as a radical. $\dfrac{1}{(xyz)^{\frac{2}{3}}} = \dfrac{1}{\sqrt[3]{(xyz)^2}}$

Step 2: Simplify. $\dfrac{1}{\sqrt[3]{(xyz)^2}}$ cannot be simplified because the power of the radicand is less than the index.

11.7 EQUIVALENT EXPONENTIAL AND RADICAL EXPRESSIONS If $a \geq 0$, then

$$(\sqrt[n]{a})^m = a^{\frac{m}{n}} = \sqrt[n]{a^m}.$$

If $a^{-\frac{m}{n}}$ exists and $a \neq 0$, then

$$a^{-\frac{m}{n}} = \frac{1}{(\sqrt[n]{a})^m} = \frac{1}{(\sqrt[n]{a^m})}.$$

c. $-16^{\frac{9}{4}}$

Solution:

Step 1: Rewrite as a radical. $-16^{\frac{9}{4}} = -(\sqrt[4]{16})^9$

Step 2: Evaluate. $-(\sqrt[4]{16})^9 = -\left(\sqrt[4]{2^4}\right)^9 = -(2)^9 = -512$

d. $(-32)^{\frac{7}{5}}$

Solution:

Step 1: Rewrite as a radical. $(-32)^{\frac{7}{5}} = (\sqrt[5]{(-32)})^7$

Step 2: Evaluate. $(\sqrt[5]{(-32)})^7 = \left(\sqrt[5]{(-2)^5}\right)^7 = (-2)^7 = -128$

Example 11.4 Rewrite each radical expression as an exponential expression and simplify.

a. $\sqrt[4]{81^3}$

Solution:

Step 1: Rewrite in exponential form. $\sqrt[4]{81^3} = (81)^{\frac{3}{4}}$

Step 2: Evaluate using the power property of exponents.

$$(81)^{\frac{3}{4}} = (3^4)^{\frac{3}{4}} = 3^3 = 27$$

b. $\sqrt[3]{6z^6}$

Solution:

Step 1: Rewrite in exponential form. $\sqrt[3]{6z^6} = (6z^6)^{\frac{1}{3}}$

Step 2: Evaluate using the power property of exponents.

$$(6z^6)^{\frac{1}{3}} = 6^{\frac{1}{3}} z^2$$

c. $\left(\sqrt[4]{\dfrac{256}{625}}\right)^3$

Solution:

Step 1: Rewrite in exponential form.

$$\left(\sqrt[4]{\frac{256}{625}}\right)^3 = \left(\frac{256}{625}\right)^{\frac{3}{4}}$$

Step 2: Evaluate using the power property of exponents.

$$\left(\frac{256}{625}\right)^{\frac{3}{4}} = \left(\frac{2^8}{5^4}\right)^{\frac{3}{4}} = \frac{2^6}{5^3} = \frac{64}{125}$$

d. $\sqrt{-25^3}$

Solution:

Step 1: There is no real number square root of a negative number.

e. $\sqrt[3]{-27^2}$

Solution:

Step 1: Rewrite in exponential form. $-(27)^{\frac{2}{3}}$

Step 2: Evaluate using the Power Property of Exponents. $-(3^3)^{\frac{2}{3}} = -3^2 = -9$

DIY PROBLEMS

11.3 Rewrite in radical form and evaluate. $-343^{-\frac{2}{3}}$.

11.4 Rewrite in exponential form and simplify. $\sqrt[7]{128k^7z^{14}}$.

SOLVING EQUATIONS WITH RADICALS

Adding or Subtracting Radical Expressions

Radical terms are *like terms* when their indices (plural of index) and their radicands are each the same; for example, $\sqrt{r}$ and $3\sqrt{r}$. When like terms exist, treat the radical as a variable, adding and subtracting the coefficients of the radical; for example,

$$\sqrt{r} + 3\sqrt{r} = 1\sqrt{r} + 3\sqrt{r} = (1+3)\sqrt{r} = 4\sqrt{r}$$

Simplify all radicals in an expression to determine if there are like terms; for example

$$\sqrt{52} - \sqrt{13} = \sqrt{(4)(13)} - \sqrt{13} = 2\sqrt{13} - \sqrt{13} = \sqrt{13}$$

Multiplying Radical Expressions

The **Product Property of Radicals** states that $\sqrt[n]{a^m} \cdot \sqrt[n]{b^m} = \sqrt[n]{(ab)^m}$ whenever the radicals exist. When the bases are the same, the simplified product is $\sqrt[n]{a^m} \cdot \sqrt[n]{a^p} = \sqrt[n]{a^{m+p}}$. The exponential forms of the equations, $a^{\frac{m}{n}} \cdot b^{\frac{m}{n}} = (ab)^{\frac{m}{n}}$ and $a^{\frac{m}{n}} \cdot a^{\frac{p}{n}} = a^{\frac{m+p}{n}}$, may seem more familiar.

11.8 PRODUCT PROPERTY OF RADICALS
$\sqrt[n]{a^m} \cdot \sqrt[n]{b^m} = \sqrt[n]{(ab)^m}$ whenever the radicals exist. When the bases are the same, the simplified product is $\sqrt[n]{a^m} \cdot \sqrt[n]{a^p} = \sqrt[n]{a^{m+p}}$.

Dividing Radical Expressions

The Quotient Property of Exponents, $\left(\dfrac{a}{b}\right)^r = \dfrac{a^r}{b^r}$, $b \uparrow 0$, is true for rational exponents as well as integer exponents.

The **Quotient Property of Radicals** states that $\sqrt[n]{\dfrac{a}{b}} = \dfrac{\sqrt[n]{a}}{\sqrt[n]{b}}$, where $b \uparrow 0$. Comparing the two expressions, $r = \dfrac{1}{n}$.

11.9 QUOTIENT PROPERTY OF RADICALS $\sqrt[n]{\dfrac{a}{b}} = \dfrac{\sqrt[n]{a}}{\sqrt[n]{b}}$, where $b \neq 0$.

However, $\dfrac{\sqrt[n]{a}}{\sqrt[n]{b}}$ is not in simplified radical form because of the radical in the denominator. Rewrite the fraction as an equivalent fraction with denominator b.

Recall that $\sqrt[n]{a^m} \cdot \sqrt[n]{a^p} = \sqrt[n]{a^{m+p}}$ and $\sqrt[n]{a^n} = a$ and consider some examples:

$$\sqrt{x} \cdot \sqrt{x} = \sqrt{x^2} = x$$

$$\sqrt[3]{x} \cdot \sqrt[3]{x^2} = \sqrt[3]{x^3} = x$$

$$\sqrt[4]{x} \cdot \sqrt[4]{x^3} = \sqrt[4]{x^4} = x$$

$$\sqrt[5]{x} \cdot \sqrt[5]{x^4} = \sqrt[5]{x^5} = x$$

When $m + p = n$, then $\sqrt[n]{a^m} \cdot \sqrt[n]{a^p} = \sqrt[n]{a^{m+p}} = \sqrt[n]{a^n} = a$.

Therefore, multiply $\dfrac{\sqrt[n]{a}}{\sqrt[n]{b}}$ by 1 in the form of $\dfrac{\sqrt[n]{b^{n-1}}}{\sqrt[n]{b^{n-1}}}$:

$$\frac{\sqrt[n]{a}}{\sqrt[n]{b}} = \frac{\sqrt[n]{a}}{\sqrt[n]{b}} \cdot \frac{\sqrt[n]{b^{n-1}}}{\sqrt[n]{b^{n-1}}} = \frac{\sqrt[n]{ab^{n-1}}}{\sqrt[n]{bb^{n-1}}} = \frac{\sqrt[n]{ab^{n-1}}}{\sqrt[n]{b^n}} = \frac{\sqrt[n]{ab^{n-1}}}{b}$$

This process is "rationalizing the denominator" and is necessary to achieve a simplified answer.

Example 11.5 Evaluate each expression using the following quantities. Assume all variables are nonnegative.

$$a = \sqrt{98} \quad b = \sqrt{8} \quad c = 3\sqrt{32mnp^5} \quad d = 2\sqrt{50mp^5} \quad e = \sqrt[3]{24} \quad f = \sqrt[3]{81}$$

a. $a + b$

Solution:

Step 1: Substitute the values. $a + b = \sqrt{98} + \sqrt{8}$

Step 2: Rewrite each quantity in simplest form. $\sqrt{98} = \sqrt{49}\sqrt{2} = 7\sqrt{2}$
$$\sqrt{8} = \sqrt{4}\sqrt{2} = 2\sqrt{2}$$

Step 3: Add. $7\sqrt{2} + 2\sqrt{2} = 9\sqrt{2}$

Step 4: Check for simplified radical form.

b. $b \cdot a$

Solution:

Step 1: Substitute the values. $b \cdot a = \sqrt{8} \cdot \sqrt{98}$

Step 2 (optional): Rewrite each quantity in simplest form. $\sqrt{8} = \sqrt{4}\sqrt{2} = 2\sqrt{2}$
$$\sqrt{98} = \sqrt{49}\sqrt{2} = 7\sqrt{2}$$

Step 3: Multiply. $2\sqrt{2} \cdot 7\sqrt{2} = 14\sqrt{4}$

Step 4: Check for simplified radical form. $14\sqrt{4}$ can be simplified to

$$14\sqrt{4} = 14 \cdot 2 = 28.$$

c. $d \cdot c$

Solution:

Step 1: Substitute the values. $d \cdot c = 2\sqrt{50mp^5} \cdot 3\sqrt{32mnp^5}$

Step 2 (optional): Rewrite each quantity in simplest form.

$$2\sqrt{50mp^5} = 2\sqrt{25}\sqrt{2}\sqrt{m}\sqrt{p^2}\sqrt{p^2}\sqrt{p} = 10p^2\sqrt{2mp}$$

$$3\sqrt{32mnp^5} = 3\sqrt{16}\sqrt{2}\sqrt{m}\sqrt{n}\sqrt{p^2}\sqrt{p^2}\sqrt{p} = 12p^2\sqrt{2mnp}$$

Step 3: Multiply. $10p^2\sqrt{2mp} \cdot 12p^2\sqrt{2mnp} = 120p^4\sqrt{4m^2np^2}$

Step 4: Check for simplified radical form. $120p^4\sqrt{4m^2np^2}$ can be simplified to $240mp^5\sqrt{n}$.

　　d. $e - f$

Solution:

Step 1: Substitute the values. $e - f = \sqrt[3]{24} - \sqrt[3]{81}$

Step 2: Rewrite in simplest form. $\sqrt[3]{24} = \sqrt[3]{8}\sqrt[3]{3} = 2\sqrt[3]{3}$

$$\sqrt[3]{81} = \sqrt[3]{27}\sqrt[3]{3} = 3\sqrt[3]{3}$$

Step 3: Subtract. $2\sqrt[3]{3} - 3\sqrt[3]{3} = -1\sqrt[3]{3}$

Step 4: Check for simplified radical form. $-1\sqrt[3]{3} = -\sqrt[3]{3}$

　　e. $e \cdot f$

Solution:

Step 1: Substitute the values. $e \cdot f = \sqrt[3]{24} \cdot \sqrt[3]{81}$

Step 2 (optional): Rewrite in simplest form. $\sqrt[3]{24} = \sqrt[3]{8}\sqrt[3]{3} = 2\sqrt[3]{3}$

$$\sqrt[3]{81} = \sqrt[3]{27}\sqrt[3]{3} = 3\sqrt[3]{3}$$

Step 3: Multiply. $2\sqrt[3]{3} \cdot 3\sqrt[3]{3} = 6\sqrt[3]{9}$

Step 4: Check for simplified radical form.

　　f. $\dfrac{a}{\sqrt{3}}$

Solution:

Step 1: Substitute the values. $\dfrac{a}{\sqrt{3}} = \dfrac{\sqrt{98}}{\sqrt{3}}$

Step 2 (optional): Rewrite in simplest form. $\dfrac{7\sqrt{2}}{\sqrt{3}}$

Step 3: Rationalize the denominator. $\dfrac{7\sqrt{2}}{\sqrt{3}} \cdot \dfrac{\sqrt{3}}{\sqrt{3}} = \dfrac{7\sqrt{6}}{3}$

Step 4: Check for simplified radical form.

　　g. $\dfrac{1}{f}$

Solution:

Step 1: Substitute the values. $\dfrac{1}{f} = \dfrac{1}{\sqrt[3]{81}}$

Step 2 (optional): Rewrite in simplest form. $\dfrac{1}{\sqrt[3]{81}} = \dfrac{1}{3\sqrt[3]{3}}$

Step 3: Rationalize the denominator. $\dfrac{1}{3\sqrt[3]{3}} \cdot \dfrac{\sqrt[3]{9}}{\sqrt[3]{9}} = \dfrac{\sqrt[3]{9}}{3\sqrt[3]{27}} = \dfrac{\sqrt[3]{9}}{3(3)} = \dfrac{\sqrt[3]{9}}{9}$

Step 4: Check for simplified radical form.

SOLVING A RADICAL EQUATION

In the second scenario of the chapter opener, the fourth question was to solve for V in the formula $r = \sqrt[3]{\dfrac{3V}{4\pi}}$. The four steps to solving a radical equation are as follows:

1. Isolate the radical that contains the variable in the radicand.
2. Raise each side of the equation to the power of the index of that radical.
3. Solve.
4. Check the solution in the original equation for *extraneous* solutions. Extraneous solutions are solutions that are not possible mathematically, realistically or contextually.

To answer the question about the opening scenario, we can follow these four steps. The radical is isolated, so the next step calls for cubing both sides of the equation to yield $r^3 = \dfrac{3V}{4\pi}$. Solving for V requires multiplying by 4π and then dividing by 3, which leads to a final formula of $\dfrac{4\pi r^3}{3} = V$. Not all radical equations will be as straightforward but following the four steps above will help.

Example 11.6 Solve the following expressions:

    a. $3\sqrt{x} - 1 = 8$

Solution:

Step 1: Isolate the radical. $3\sqrt{x} - 1 = 8 \Rightarrow 3\sqrt{x} = 9 \Rightarrow \sqrt{x} = 3$

Step 2: Square both sides. $\left(\sqrt{x}\right)^2 = (3)^2$

Step 3: Solve. $x = 9$

Step 4: Check. $3\sqrt{9} - 1 = 8 \Rightarrow 3(3) - 1 = 8 \Rightarrow 9 - 1 = 8 \Rightarrow 8 = 8$. This is a true statement so the solution to this equation is 9.

    b. $x = \sqrt{x+4} - 2$

Solution:

Step 1: Isolate the radical. $x = \sqrt{x+4} - 2 \Rightarrow x + 2 = \sqrt{x+4}$

Step 2: Square both sides. $(x+2)^2 = \left(\sqrt{x+4}\right)^2 \Rightarrow x^2 + 4x + 4 = x + 4$

Step 3: Combine like terms. $x^2 + 3x = 0$

Step 4: Solve by factoring out the greatest common factor. $x(x+3) = 0 \Rightarrow x = -3, 0$

Step 5: Check. $0 = \sqrt{0+4} - 2 \Rightarrow 0 = 2 - 2 \Rightarrow 0 = 0$

$$-3 = \sqrt{-3+4} - 2 \Rightarrow -3 = 1 - 2 \Rightarrow -3 \neq -1$$

Therefore, the equation has one solution, $x = 0$.

    c. $\sqrt{x} = -168 - \sqrt{x}$

Solution:

Step 1: Isolate the radical. $\sqrt{x} = -168 - \sqrt{x} \Rightarrow 2\sqrt{x} = -168 \Rightarrow \sqrt{x} = -84$

Step 2: Square both sides. $(\sqrt{x})^2 = (-84)^2$

Step 3: Solve. $x = 7056$

Step 4: Check. $\sqrt{7056} = -168 - \sqrt{7056} \Rightarrow 84 = -168 - 84 \Rightarrow 84 = -252$. This is not a true statement so this equation has no solution.

d. $\sqrt[3]{x^2 - 36} + 6\sqrt{2} = \sqrt{72}$

Solution:

Step 1: Isolate the radical. $\sqrt[3]{x^2 - 36} + 6\sqrt{2} = \sqrt{72} \Rightarrow \sqrt[3]{x^2 - 36} = 0$

Step 2: Cube both sides. $(\sqrt[3]{x^2 - 36})^3 = (0)^3$

Step 3: Solve. $x^2 - 36 = 0 \Rightarrow x^2 = 36 \Rightarrow x = \pm 6$

Step 4: Check. $\sqrt[3]{6^2 - 36} + 6\sqrt{2} = \sqrt{72}$

$$\sqrt{72} = \sqrt{72}, \text{ and}$$

$$\sqrt[3]{(-6)^2 - 36} + 6\sqrt{2} = \sqrt{72}$$

$$\sqrt{72} = \sqrt{72}$$

So this equation has two solutions, -6 and 6.

e. $\sqrt{3x - 8} + 1 = \sqrt{x + 5}$

Solution:

Step 1: Isolate the radical. $\sqrt{3x - 8} + 1 = \sqrt{x + 5}$

In this case with two radicals, the steps may have to be completed more than once.

Step 2: Square both sides. $(\sqrt{3x - 8} + 1)^2 = (\sqrt{x + 5})^2$

Step 3: Solve.
$$(\sqrt{3x - 8} + 1)(\sqrt{3x - 8} + 1) = x + 5$$
$$3x - 8 + 2\sqrt{3x - 8} + 1 = x + 5$$
$$2\sqrt{3x - 8} = -2x + 12$$
$$\sqrt{3x - 8} = -x + 6$$

Step 4: The radical is already isolated, so perform step 2 and square both sides:
$$(\sqrt{3x - 8})^2 = (-x + 6)^2$$
$$3x - 8 = x^2 - 12x + 36$$
$$0 = x^2 - 15x + 44$$
$$0 = (x - 11)(x - 4)$$
$$11, 4 = x$$

Step 5: Check. $\sqrt{3(11) - 8} + 1 = \sqrt{11 + 5}$ $\qquad$ $\sqrt{3(4) - 8} + 1 = \sqrt{(4) + 5}$

$\qquad\qquad\qquad 6 \neq 4$ $\qquad\qquad\qquad\qquad\qquad 3 = 3$

Therefore, the equation has one solution, $x = 4$.

f. $-4(x + 10)^{\frac{1}{3}} + 3 = 15$

Solution:

Step 1: Isolate the radical. $-4(x + 10)^{\frac{1}{3}} + 3 = 15$ Rewrite as $\sqrt[3]{(x + 10)} = -3$.

Step 2: Cube both sides. $(\sqrt[3]{(x + 10)})^3 = (-3)^3$

Step 3: Solve. $x + 10 = -27$

$\qquad\qquad\quad x = 37$

Step 4: Check. $-4(-37 + 10)^{\frac{1}{3}} + 3 = 15$. The solution is $x = -37$.

$$15 = 15$$

GRAPHING RADICAL FUNCTIONS

11.10 PARENT FUNCTION A function in its most basic standard form.

A **parent function** is a function in its most basic standard form. Some examples are:

$$y = x, \quad y = \frac{1}{x}, \quad y = \sqrt{x}, \quad y = x^2.$$

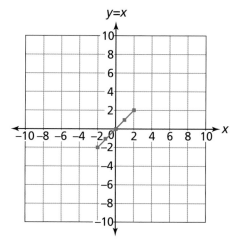

FIGURE 11.1

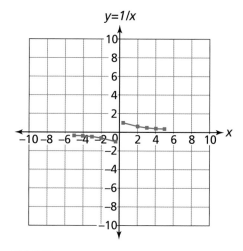

FIGURE 11.2

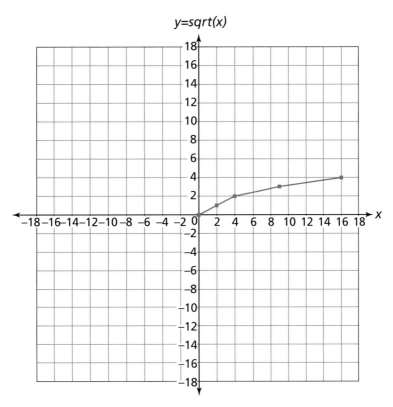

FIGURE 11.3

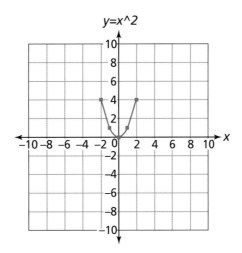

FIGURE 11.4

Figure 11.5 is the graph of $y = 2\sqrt{x+1} - 5$ compared to its parent function graph of $y = \sqrt{x}$. Figure 11.6 is the graph of $y = \sqrt[3]{x-2} + 3$ compared to its parent function graph of $y = \sqrt[3]{x}$. In both figures, the parent function graph is drawn with a heavier line.

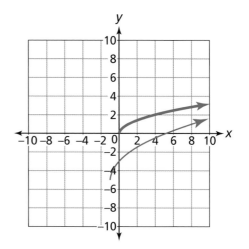

FIGURE 11.5 Graphs of $y = \sqrt{x}$ and $y = 2\sqrt{x+1} - 5$

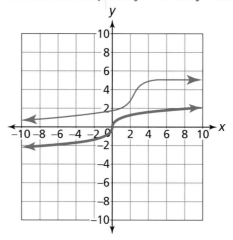

FIGURE 11.6 Graphs of $y = \sqrt[3]{x}$ and $y = \sqrt[3]{x-2} + 3$

How does the graph of each function differ from that of its parent function? In the graph of $y = 2\sqrt{x+1} - 5$ in Figure 11.5, the parent function is $y = \sqrt{x}$. The graph of $y = \sqrt{x}$ is vertically stretched by a factor of 2, shifted horizontally to the left 1 unit, and shifted vertically down 5 units. In the graph of $y = \sqrt[3]{x-2} + 3$ in Figure 11.6, the graph of the parent function, $y = \sqrt[3]{x}$, is shifted horizontally to the right 2 units, and shifted vertically up 3 units. These shifts and stretches are determined by the constants in the equations.

Graphing Radical Functions

The parent function for any radical equation is $y = \sqrt[n]{x}$. The standard form is $y = a\sqrt[n]{x-h} + k$, where in reference to the parent function a represents a vertical stretch $(a > 1)$ or shrink $(0 < a < 1)$, h the horizontal shift, and k the vertical shift. If $a < 0$, then the graph is also flipped, often called *reflected*, over the x-axis.

Example 11.7 Describe how the graph of $y = -(x-4)^{\frac{1}{2}} - 7$ is different from $y = \sqrt{x}$ and graph.

Solution:

Step 1: Rewrite the function in standard form. $y = -1\sqrt{(x-4)} + (-7)$

Step 2: The initial negative sign represents a reflection of the graph over the x-axis.

Step 3: The 4 in the radicand represents a horizontal shift to the right 4 units.

Step 4: The -7 in the equation represents a vertical shift down 7 units.

Step 5: Graph the function (Figure 11.7).

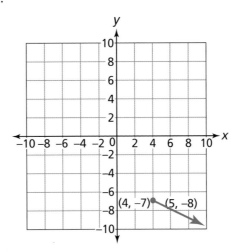

FIGURE 11.7

Example 11.8 What equation will match the graph of Figure 11.8 if the parent function is $y = \sqrt[3]{x}$ (see Figure 11.6)?

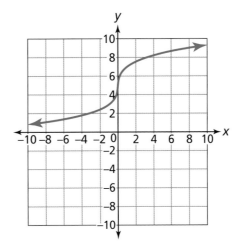

FIGURE 11.8

Solution:

The y-intercept is at $(0, 5)$, not $(0, 0)$, and there appears to be a vertical stretch of 2 units. A difference of 1 in original y-coordinates is 2 in the new y-coordinates: $(0, 0) \rightarrow (0, 5)$ and $(1, 1) \rightarrow (1, 7)$, and $(-1, -1) \rightarrow (-1, 3)$ while $(8, 2) \rightarrow (8, 9)$, so a difference of 2 in original y-coordinates is now 4, a difference of 3 is now 6, and so on. $y = 2\sqrt[3]{x - 0} + 5$

DIY PROBLEMS

11.7 Describe what happens in the graph of $y = -4(x-3)^{\frac{1}{3}} - 1$ as compared to the parent function $y = x^{\frac{1}{3}}$.

11.8 What is the equation that would match the graph of Figure 11.9 if the parent function is $y = \sqrt{x}$?

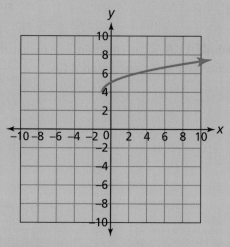

FIGURE 11.9

SOLUTIONS TO DIY PROBLEMS

11.1 Simplify the following:

   a. $\sqrt[3]{81} + \sqrt[3]{216}$

Solution:

Step 1: Factor the radicands.

$$\sqrt[3]{81} + \sqrt[3]{216} = \sqrt[3]{3 \cdot 3^3} + \sqrt[3]{3^3 \cdot 2^3}$$

Notice the index is used as a power when possible.

Step 2: Rewrite every group of factors whose power is the index using the property that $(\sqrt[n]{x})^n = x$ for $x \geq 0$:

$$\sqrt[3]{3 \cdot 3^3} + \sqrt[3]{3^3 \cdot 2^3} = 3\sqrt[3]{3} + 3(2) = 3\sqrt[3]{3} + 6$$

No further simplifying is possible.

b. $\sqrt{12x^6y^5z^2}$.

Solution:

Step 1: Factor the radicand using the index as a power when possible.

$$\sqrt{12x^6y^5z^2} = \sqrt{2^2 \cdot 3\left(x^3\right)^2 \left(y^2\right)^2 yz^2}$$

Step 2: Write in simplified radical form.

$$\sqrt{2^2 \cdot 3\left(x^3\right)^2 \left(y^2\right)^2 yz^2} = 2x^3y^2z\sqrt{3y}$$

No further simplifying is possible.

11.2 Simplify $2x^{\frac{2}{3}}y^{\frac{1}{3}} - x^{\frac{2}{3}}y^{\frac{1}{3}} - x^{\frac{1}{3}}y^{\frac{2}{3}} + 4x^{\frac{2}{3}}y^{\frac{1}{3}} - x^{\frac{1}{3}}y^{\frac{2}{3}}$.

Solution:

$$2x^{\frac{2}{3}}y^{\frac{1}{3}} - x^{\frac{2}{3}}y^{\frac{1}{3}} - x^{\frac{1}{3}}y^{\frac{2}{3}} + 4x^{\frac{2}{3}}y^{\frac{1}{3}} - x^{\frac{1}{3}}y^{\frac{2}{3}} = 5x^{\frac{2}{3}}y^{\frac{1}{3}} - 2x^{\frac{1}{3}}y^{\frac{2}{3}}$$

11.3 Rewrite in radical form and evaluate. $-343^{-\frac{2}{3}}$.

Solution:

$$-343^{-\frac{2}{3}} = \frac{1}{-343^{\frac{2}{3}}} = \frac{1}{-(\sqrt[3]{343})^2} = \frac{1}{-(7)^2} = -\frac{1}{49}$$

11.4 Rewrite in exponential form and simplify. $\sqrt[7]{128k^7z^{14}}$.

Solution:

$$\sqrt[7]{128k^7z^{14}} = (128k^7z^{14})^{\frac{1}{7}} = \left(2^7\right)^{\frac{1}{7}} (k^7)^{\frac{1}{7}} (z^{14})^{\frac{1}{7}} = 2kz^2$$

11.5 Simplify $(2\sqrt{3})^2 + \sqrt{24} - \frac{18}{2\sqrt{6}}$.

Solution:

$$(2\sqrt{3})^2 + \sqrt{24} - \frac{18}{2\sqrt{6}} = 12 + 2\sqrt{6} - \frac{18}{2\sqrt{6}} \cdot \frac{\sqrt{6}}{\sqrt{6}}$$

$$= 12 + 2\sqrt{6} - \frac{18\sqrt{6}}{12}$$

$$= 12 + 2\sqrt{6} - \frac{3\sqrt{6}}{2}$$

$$= 12 + \frac{\sqrt{6}}{2}$$

11.6 Solve $\sqrt{x+2} = 2 - x^{\frac{1}{2}}$.

Solution:

$$\sqrt{x+2} = 2 - \sqrt{x}$$
$$x+2 = (2-\sqrt{x})^2$$
$$x+2 = 4 - 4\sqrt{x} + x$$
$$-2 = -4\sqrt{x}$$
$$\frac{1}{2} = \sqrt{x}$$
$$\frac{1}{4} = x$$

Check:

$$\sqrt{\frac{1}{4}+2} = 2 - \left(\frac{1}{4}\right)^{\frac{1}{2}}$$

$$\sqrt{\frac{9}{4}} = \frac{3}{2}; \ 2 - \frac{1}{2} = \frac{3}{2}$$

11.7 Describe what happens to the graph of $y = -4(x-3)^{\frac{1}{3}} - 1$ as compared to the parent function $y = x^{\frac{1}{3}}$.

Solution:

As compared to the parent function, the graph is reflected over the x-axis, vertically stretched by a factor of 4, shifted to the right 3 units, and shifted down 1 unit.

11.8 What is the equation that would match the graph of Figure 11.9 if the parent function is $y = \sqrt{x}$?

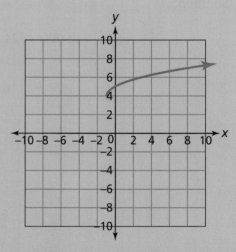

FIGURE 11.9

Solution:

$y = \sqrt{x+1} + 4$

Rational Exponents/Connection between Powers and Roots

11.1 Evaluate: $625^{\frac{1}{4}}$.

11.2 Evaluate: $1024^{\frac{1}{5}}$.

11.3 Evaluate: $25^{\frac{3}{2}}$.

11.4 Evaluate: $27^{\frac{5}{3}}$.

11.5 Evaluate: $32^{\frac{3}{4}}$.

11.6 Evaluate: $243^{\frac{3}{4}}$.

11.7 Evaluate: $\left(\sqrt{10x}\right)^{2}$.

11.8 Evaluate: $\sqrt{500}$.

11.9 Evaluate: $\left(\sqrt{(x+6)}\right)^{2}$.

11.10 Evaluate: $\left(\sqrt[3]{x^{2}+5x-9}\right)^{3}$.

11.11 Evaluate: $\sqrt[3]{64\,x^{5}yz^{7}}$.

11.12 Simplify: $9\sqrt{8z}-4\sqrt{50z}$.

11.13 Simplify: $\sqrt{18} - \sqrt{50}$.

11.14 Simplify: $3\sqrt{32x} + 5\sqrt{50x}$.

11.15 Simplify: $\sqrt[3]{216x^4y^7} - \sqrt[3]{125x^4y^{10}}$.

11.16 Simplify: $\dfrac{\sqrt{8y^{21}}}{\sqrt{2y}}$.

11.17 Simplify: $\left(\dfrac{125}{729}\right)^{\frac{2}{3}}$.

11.18 Simplify: $\dfrac{\sqrt{12x^{18}}}{\sqrt{3x^2}}$.

11.19 Simplify: $\dfrac{\sqrt{20}}{\sqrt{3}}$.

Solving Equations with Radicals

11.20 Solve: $\sqrt{x} = 11$.

11.21 Solve: $\sqrt{x} = 18$.

11.22 Solve: $\sqrt{x} - 3 = 22$.

11.23 Solve: $\sqrt{x} - 6 = 30$.

11.24 Solve: $\sqrt{z + 12} = 3$.

11.25 Solve: $\sqrt{z-10} = 4$.

11.26 Solve: $\sqrt{5y+6} = 6$.

11.27 Solve: $\sqrt{3y+1} = 5$.

11.28 Solve: $\sqrt[3]{3x-7} = 2$.

11.29 Solve: $\sqrt{x} = \sqrt{4x-6}$.

11.30 Solve: $\sqrt{5x-3} = \sqrt{2x}$.

11.31 Solve: $\sqrt{z+10} - z = 8$.

11.32 Solve: $\sqrt{x - 1} + 3 = x$.

11.33 Solve: $2\sqrt{y - 4} - y = -4$.

Radical Functions

11.34 Given the formula for the base of a square pyramid $b = \sqrt{\dfrac{3v}{h}}$, where b is the length of the side of the base, h is the height of the pyramid, and V is the volume of the pyramid. What is the volume of the pyramid if the base is 8 feet and the height is 6 feet?

11.35 Given the following formula: $y = \sqrt{x - h} + k$. Solve for x if $h = 2$, $k = 0$, and $y = 5$.

Graphing Radical Functions

11.36 Describe what happens to the graph of $y = -(x + 6)^{\frac{1}{2}} - 4$ as compared to the parent function $y = x^{\frac{1}{2}}$.

REFERENCES

Definitions. (n.d.). In *Encarta online dictionary*. Retrieved from http://encarta.msn.com

Dodge, W. (1998). Worksheets of algebra 1. New Trier High School, Winnetka, IL.

Larson, R., Boswell, L., Kanold, T., & Stiff, L. (2007). *Algebra 2*. Evanston, IL: McDougal Littell.

Major, N. (2004). Algebra I, 2nd semester [Lecture notes]. Cherry Creek High School, Greenwood Village, CO.

Exponential and Logarithmic Functions

At the beginning of the month three months ago, Oksana opened a savings account at her local bank that pays *inter-est* at an annual rate of 2.4%, compounded monthly, and deposited $5,000. She hasn't made any additional deposits or withdrawals since then. After one month, the bank sent her a statement that said her balance was $5,010. In other words, during the first month Oksana earned $10 in interest from the bank. For this reason, when she received her next bank statement one month later, she expected to have earned $10 in interest again. However, when she looked at her balance, she was surprised to see that it was $5,020.02. In other words, she made $10.02 in interest during the second month instead of the $10 she made during the first month.

Oksana wondered why the amount of interest she earned increased by $0.02, and she was very curious about what her balance would be when she received her third bank statement.

The balance on her third bank statement was $5,030.06. In other words, during the third month, she made $10.04 interest. Oksana wondered why the amount of interest she earned each month kept increasing.

The interest increased each month because it was *compound interest*. With compound interest, the interest Oksana earns each month is added back into her *principal*. This means that during the second month, Oksana was earning interest on $5,010, not the $5,000 she was earning interest on during the first month. Likewise, during the third month, she was earning interest on $5,020.02. Because her principal increased each month, the amount of interest she earned increased as well. What will her balance be when she receives her fourth monthly statement? Since she made $10.04 in interest during the third month, she is sure to make more than that during the fourth month, so her balance will be greater than $5,040.10. Oh, the power of compound interest!

1. How many times does Oksana's savings account pay interest in one year? How about in five years?

2. Is there a formula to use to calculate the balance of Oksana's savings account given her original principal, the annual interest rate, the number of times per year that she receives interest, and the number of years that have passed?

3. Will the amount of interest Oksana earns per month always be $0.02 more than the amount of interest she earned during the previous month?

KEY TERMS

➤ annuity (p. 429)
➤ common logarithm (p. 419)
➤ compound interest (general formula) (p. 425)
➤ continuously compounded interest (p. 427)
➤ e (p. 414)
➤ exponential function (p. 414)
➤ exponential growth (p. 414)
➤ future value (p. 429)
➤ logarithmic function (p. 418)
➤ natural logarithm (p. 419)
➤ present value (p. 429)

EXPONENTIAL FUNCTIONS

Definition of Exponential Function

A function in the form $f(x) = a^x$, where the base a is a positive number, is an **exponential function.** The case $a = 1$ is the function $f(x) = 1$ and does not demonstrate exponential growth or decay, so we will consider only the cases when a is a positive number not equal to 1. Often the base is e, a constant with an approximate value of 2.71828 that occurs frequently in natural settings in biology, botany, physics, and so on.

The exponent x in $f(x) = a^x$ can be any real number because there are no restrictions on the exponent of any positive number, and $a > 0$ by definition. The possible values of the function are all real numbers greater than 0 because all powers of positive numbers are positive.

Evaluating an Exponential Function

Evaluate the function $f(x) = a^x$ in the usual way: for $x = b$, plug in b for x to get $f(b) = a^b$. For example, if $f(x) = 9^x$, then $f(1) = 9$, $f(2) = 81$, and $f(0.5) = 3$.

Graphing an Exponential Function

The graph of the function $f(x) = a^x$, $a \neq 1$, has the x-axis as an *asymptote*, and $f(x) = a^x$ passes through the point $(0, 1)$, since any nonzero number raised to the power 0 equals 1. If $a > 1$, the value of $f(x)$ increases from left to right, and if $0 < a < 1$, the value of $f(x)$ decreases from left to right. It is possible to transform the function $f(x) = a^x$ in a manner similar to the transformations of parabolas to produce functions such as $f(x) = ca^x$, $f(x) = a^{dx}$, $f(x) = a^{x-h}$, $f(x) = a^x + k$, or combinations of these, with c, d, h, and k as constants. All of these functions are exponential functions as well.

Example 12.1
Evaluate the function $f(x) = \left(\dfrac{1}{2}\right)6^x + 15$ for each of the following values of x.

   a. $x = -1$

Solution:

Step 1: Substitute -1 for x to get $f(-1) = \left(\dfrac{1}{2}\right)6^{-1} + 15$.

Step 2: Simplify the right side of the equation.

$$f(-1) = \left(\frac{1}{2}\right)6^{-1} + 15 = \left(\frac{1}{2}\right)\left(\frac{1}{6}\right) + 15 = \frac{1}{12} + 15 = 15\frac{1}{12}$$

This means when $x = -1$ the function $f(x) = \left(\dfrac{1}{2}\right)6^x + 15$ is equal to $15\dfrac{1}{12}$.

   b. $x = 0$

Solution:

Step 1: Substitute 0 for x to get $f(0) = \left(\dfrac{1}{2}\right)6^0 + 15$.

Step 2: Simplify the right side of the equation.

$$f(0) = \left(\frac{1}{2}\right)6^0 + 15 = \left(\frac{1}{2}\right)(1) + 15 = \frac{1}{2} + 15 = 15\frac{1}{2}$$

This means when $x = 0$ the function $f(x) = \left(\dfrac{1}{2}\right)6^x + 15$ is equal to $15\dfrac{1}{2}$.

   c. $x = 3$

Solution:

Step 1: Substitute 3 for x to get $f(3) = \left(\dfrac{1}{2}\right)6^3 + 15$.

Step 2: Simplify the right side of the equation.

$$f(3) = \left(\dfrac{1}{2}\right)6^3 + 15 = \left(\dfrac{1}{2}\right)(216) + 15 = 108 + 15 = 123$$

This means when $x = 3$ the function $f(x) = \left(\dfrac{1}{2}\right)6^x + 15$ is equal to 123.

Example 12.2

Graph both of the following functions.

   a. $f(x) = 2^{2x-1}$

Solution:

Step 1: Make a table of values for the function. Choose values of x for which the function is easy to evaluate (Figure 12.1).

x	f(x)
−2	$2^{2(-2)-1} = 2^{-4-1} = 2^{-5} = \dfrac{1}{32}$
−1	$2^{2(-1)-1} = 2^{-2-1} = 2^{-3} = \dfrac{1}{8}$
0	$2^{2(0)-1} = 2^{0-1} = 2^{-1} = \dfrac{1}{2}$
1	$2^{2(1)-1} = 2^{2-1} = 2^{1} = 2$
2	$2^{2(2)-1} = 2^{4-1} = 2^{3} = 8$

FIGURE 12.1

Step 2: Plot the points from Figure 12.1 on a Cartesian plane (Figure 12.2).

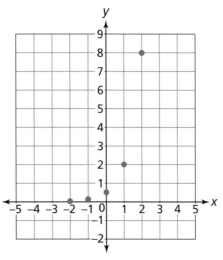

FIGURE 12.2

Step 3: Finally, draw a curve through the points (Figure 12.3).

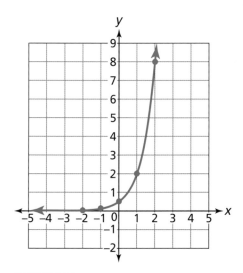

FIGURE 12.3

b. $f(x) = (9)\left(\dfrac{1}{3}\right)^x - 1$

Solution:

Step 1: Make a table of values for the function. Choose values of x for which the function is easy to evaluate (Figure 12.4).

x	$f(x)$
-1	$(9)\left(\dfrac{1}{3}\right)^{-1} - 1 = (9)(3) - 1 = 27 - 1 = 26$
0	$(9)\left(\dfrac{1}{3}\right)^{0} - 1 = (9)(1) - 1 = 9 - 1 = 8$
1	$(9)\left(\dfrac{1}{3}\right)^{1} - 1 = (9)\left(\dfrac{1}{3}\right) - 1 = 3 - 1 = 2$
2	$(9)\left(\dfrac{1}{3}\right)^{2} - 1 = (9)\left(\dfrac{1}{9}\right) - 1 = 1 - 1 = 0$
3	$(9)\left(\dfrac{1}{3}\right)^{3} - 1 = (9)\left(\dfrac{1}{27}\right) - 1 = \dfrac{1}{3} - 1 = -\dfrac{2}{3}$

FIGURE 12.4

Step 2: Plot the points on a Cartesian plane (Figure 12.5).

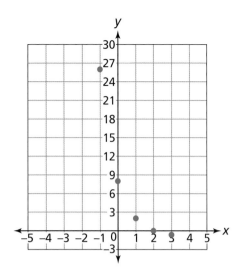

FIGURE 12.5

Step 3: Draw a curve through the points (Figure 12.6).

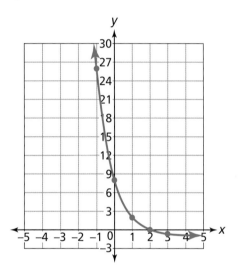

FIGURE 12.6

DIY PROBLEMS

12.1 Evaluate the function $f(x) = 6\left(\dfrac{1}{4}\right)^x - 12$ for each of the following values of x.

a. $x = -2$

b. $x = 0$

c. $x = 2$

12.2a Graph $f(x) = \left(\dfrac{1}{2}\right)^{3x-2}$.

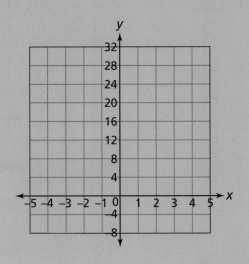

12.2b Graph $f(x) = \left(\dfrac{1}{25}\right)5^x + 1$.

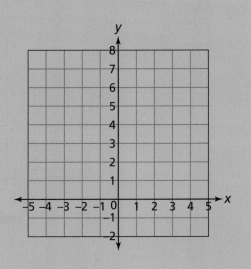

INTRODUCTION TO LOGARITHMS

Definition of Logarithmic Functions

An equivalent equation for the exponential function $y = a^x$ is $\log_a y = x$. Any function of the form $y = f(x) = \log_a x$ is called a **logarithmic function.** It is equivalent to the exponential function $g(y) = a^y = x$.

Read $y = \log_a x$ as "y equals log (logarithm) to the base a of x." Notice that in the equivalent exponential equation $a^y = x$, the base of the exponent is the same a that is the base of the logarithm, and the exponent y is the value of the logarithm of x. A logarithm is an exponent. What exponent? It is the exponent to apply to the base to yield x.

It is customary to omit a multiplication sign when writing $3 \cdot \log(x)$ or $m \cdot \log(x)$ and simply write $3\log(x)$ or $m\log(x)$.

Introduction to Logarithms

Just as with an exponential function, the base a is a positive number. There are special names for logarithms with base 10 or base e.

If a is equal to 10, the logarithm function is written $f(x) = \log x$. The base is not written but is understood to be 10. A base 10 logarithm is a **common logarithm.**

If a is equal to the constant e, the function is written $f(x) = \ln x$, read "el n of x" or "natural log (logarithm) of x."

Recall that the exponential equation equivalent to $y = f(x) = \log_a x$ is $g(y) = a^y = x$. Because $x > 0$ in the exponential equation, it must also be true that $x > 0$ in $y = f(x) = \log_a x$. Likewise, because y is any real number in the exponential equation, the possible values of the logarithm function are all real numbers.

When it is possible to evaluate the function $y = f(x) = \log_a x$ for $x = b$ without using a calculator, write the equivalent equation $a^y = x$. Then, substitute b for x to evaluate $a^y = b$.

12.4 COMMON LOGARITHM A logarithm with base equal to 10.

12.5 NATURAL LOGARITHM A logarithm with base equal to e.

Example 12.3

Evaluate the function $f(x) = \log_6 x$ for $x = 36$.

Solution:

Step 1: Consider the function as $y = \log_6 x$. Then write the form $x = 6^y$.
Step 2: Substitute 36 for x so that the equation becomes $36 = 6^y$, or $6^y = 36$. Since $6^2 = 36$, the solution is $y = 2$.

Example 12.4

Evaluate the function $f(x) = \log x$ for $x = \dfrac{1}{1000}$.

Solution:

Step 1: Rewrite the function as $y = \log x$. Remember, $\log x$ means that the log base is $a = 10$, or $y = \log_{10} x$. So rewrite as $x = 10^y$.

Step 2: Substitute $\dfrac{1}{1000}$ for x so that the equation becomes $\dfrac{1}{1000} = 10^y$, or $10^y = \dfrac{1}{1000}$. Since $10^{-3} = \dfrac{1}{1000}$, the solution is $y = -3$.

DIY PROBLEMS

12.3 Evaluate the function $f(x) = \log_3 x$ for $x = 81$.

12.4 Evaluate the function $f(x) = \ln x$ for $x = \dfrac{1}{e}$.

Graphing Logarithmic Functions

The graph of the function $f(x) = \log_a x$ has the y-axis as an asymptote and passes through the point $(1, 0)$. If $a > 1$, the value of $f(x)$ increases from left to right, and if $0 < a < 1$, the value of $f(x)$ decreases from left to right. Again, it is possible to transform the function $f(x) = \log_a x$ to produce functions such as $f(x) = c \cdot \log_a x$, $f(x) = \log_a(dx)$, $f(x) = \log_a(x - h)$, $f(x) = \log_a x + k$, or combinations of these, with c, d, h, and k as constants. All of these functions are logarithmic functions as well.

Example 12.5 Graph the function $f(x) = \log_2(2x) + 1$.

Solution:

Step 1: Make a table of values for the function. Choose values of x for which the function is easy to evaluate (Figure 12.7).

x	$f(x)$
$\dfrac{1}{8}$	$\log_2\left(2 \cdot \dfrac{1}{8}\right) + 1 = \log_2\left(\dfrac{1}{4}\right) + 1 = -2 + 1 = -1$
$\dfrac{1}{4}$	$\log_2\left(2 \cdot \dfrac{1}{4}\right) + 1 = \log_2\left(\dfrac{1}{2}\right) + 1 = -1 + 1 = 0$
1	$\log_2(2 \cdot 1) + 1 = \log_2 2 + 1 = 1 + 1 = 2$
4	$\log_2(2 \cdot 4) + 1 = \log_2 8 + 1 = 3 + 1 = 4$
8	$\log_2(2 \cdot 8) + 1 = \log_2 16 + 1 = 4 + 1 = 5$

FIGURE 12.7

Step 2: Plot the points on a Cartesian plane (Figure 12.8).

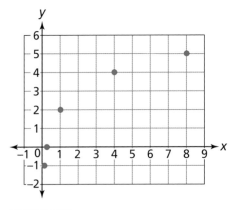

FIGURE 12.8

Step 3: Draw a curve through the points (Figure 12.9).

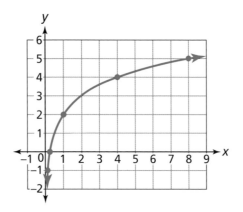

FIGURE 12.9

Example 12.6

Graph the function $f(x) = \frac{1}{2}\log_{\frac{1}{2}}(x-1)$.

Solution:

Step 1: Make a table of values for the function. Choose values of x for which the function is easy to evaluate (Figure 12.10).

x	$f(x)$
$\frac{5}{4}$	$\frac{1}{2}\log_{\frac{1}{2}}\left(\frac{5}{4}-1\right)=\frac{1}{2}\log_{\frac{1}{2}}\left(\frac{1}{4}\right)=\frac{1}{2}\cdot 2=1$
$\frac{3}{2}$	$\frac{1}{2}\log_{\frac{1}{2}}\left(\frac{3}{2}-1\right)=\frac{1}{2}\log_{\frac{1}{2}}\left(\frac{1}{2}\right)=\frac{1}{2}\cdot 1=\frac{1}{2}$
2	$\frac{1}{2}\log_{\frac{1}{2}}(2-1)=\frac{1}{2}\log_{\frac{1}{2}}(1)=\frac{1}{2}\cdot 0=0$
3	$\frac{1}{2}\log_{\frac{1}{2}}(3-1)=\frac{1}{2}\log_{\frac{1}{2}}(2)=\frac{1}{2}\cdot(-1)=-\frac{1}{2}$
5	$\frac{1}{2}\log_{\frac{1}{2}}(5-1)=\frac{1}{2}\log_{\frac{1}{2}}(4)=\frac{1}{2}\cdot(-2)=-1$

FIGURE 12.10

Step 2: Plot the points on a Cartesian plane (Figure 12.11).

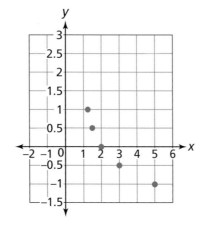

FIGURE 12.11

Step 3: Draw a curve through the points (Figure 12.12).

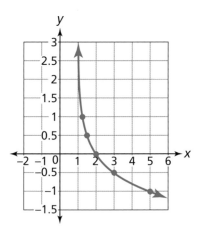

FIGURE 12.12

DIY PROBLEMS

12.5 Graph the function $f(x) = \log_2(4x) - 3$.

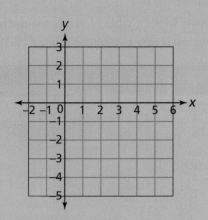

12.6 Graph the function $f(x) = 2\log_{\frac{1}{2}}(x + 5)$.

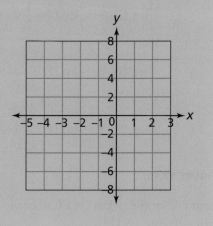

EQUATIONS CONTAINING EXPONENTIAL AND LOGARITHMIC EXPRESSIONS

Solving an Exponential Equation

There are a number of rules for manipulating logarithms. Following are two that will help to solve an equation containing an exponential expression:

1. $\log_b(a^n) = n\log_b(a)$. In words, the log of the *n*th power of a number is the product of the power and the log of the number.

This is true because if $y = \log_b(a^n)$, then the equivalent exponential equation is $a^n = b^y$. Taking the nth root of both sides of the equation gives:

$$a^n = b^y$$

$$a^{n \cdot \frac{1}{n}} = b^{y \cdot \frac{1}{n}}$$

$$a = b^{y \cdot \frac{1}{n}}$$

$$\log_b a = y \cdot \frac{1}{n}$$

$$n \log_b a = y$$

Therefore, $\log_b(a^n) = n\log_b(a)$.

2. $\log_b(b) = 1$. In words, if the base of the log of a number is the number, the value of the logarithm is 1.

Remembering that the value of a logarithm of a number is the exponent to which the base must be raised to yield the number, notice that $b^1 = b$. The formal way to show this is to set $y = \log_b(b)$, write the exponential form as $b^y = b$, and so conclude that $y = 1$. Specifically, $\log(10) = \ln(e) = 1$.

The first step in solving an equation that contains an exponential expression is to isolate the exponential expression on one side of the equation and then take the logarithm of both sides. It is generally advisable to use base 10 or base e, since most calculators have keys for these bases. The key for base 10 is usually LOG, and the key for base e is usually LN. However, the process is true using any base.

Next use the property $\log_b(a^n) = n\log_b(a)$, which makes it possible to write the exponent n as a factor when taking the logarithm of the exponential expression. Finally, solve for the unknown variable.

For example, to solve $4^x = 100$ for x, take logs to the base 10 of both sides of the equation (because 100 is a power of 10). The result is $x\log(4) = \log(10^2) = 2\log 10 = 2$. Therefore, $x = 2 \div \log(4) \approx 3.32$.

Solving a Logarithmic Equation

To solve an equation containing a logarithmic expression, first isolate the logarithmic expression on one side of the equation and then rewrite $y = \log_a$ as $x = a^y$.

Example 12.7

Solve the equation $(5)(4^x) - 32 = 5088$ for x.

Solution:

Step 1: Isolate 4^x on one side of the equation.

$$(5)(4^x) - 32 = 5088$$

$$(5)(4^x) - 32 + 32 = 5088 + 32$$

$$(5)(4^x) = 5120$$

$$\frac{(5)(4^x)}{5} = \frac{5120}{5}$$

$$4^x = 1024$$

Step 2: Take the logarithm of both sides. This example is taking the natural logarithm.

$4^x = 1024$

$\ln(4^x) = \ln(1024)$

Step 3: Use the property $\ln(a^x) = x \cdot \ln a$ to rewrite the equation.

$\ln 4^x = \ln(1024)$

$x \cdot \ln(4) = \ln(1024)$

Step 4: Solve for x. Use a calculator when necessary.

$$x \ln 4 = \ln 1024$$

$$\frac{x \ln 4}{\ln 4} = \frac{\ln 1024}{\ln 4}$$

$$x \approx \frac{6.93}{1.39} \approx 4.99$$

Check for yourself that taking log base 10 of both sides of the equation would have produced the same answer.

Example 12.8

Solve the equation $2\log_7 x + 25 = 19$ for x.

Solution:

Step 1: Isolate $\log_7 x$ on one side of the equation.

$$2 \log_7 x + 25 = 19$$

$$2 \log_7 x + 25 - 25 = 19 - 25$$

$$2 \log_7 x = -6$$

$$\frac{2 \log_7 x}{2} = \frac{-6}{2}$$

$$\log_7 x = -3$$

Step 2: Consider that $y = \log_a x$ can be rewritten as $x = a^y$. So $\log_7 x = -3$ is equivalent to $x = 7^{-3}$.

Step 3: Evaluate x.

$$x = 7^{-3}$$

$$x = \frac{1}{343}$$

DIY PROBLEMS

12.7 Solve the equation $\left(\frac{1}{9}\right)(3^x) + 14 = 95$ for x.

12.8 Solve the equation $20\log_5 x - 6 = 34$ for x.

APPLICATIONS

Compound Interest

Exponential and logarithmic functions have many applications, one of which is compound interest.

The general formula for **compound interest** is $A = P\left(1 + \dfrac{r}{n}\right)^{nt}$, where A is the total amount of money including interest, P is the original principal, r is the annual interest rate, n is the number of times interest is compounded per year, and t is the number of years for which the money is invested.

12.6 COMPOUND INTEREST

$A = P\left(1 + \dfrac{r}{n}\right)^{nt}$

Example 12.9

Tim invested $2,500 for 10 years at an annual interest rate of 2%, compounded quarterly. How much money did he have after 10 years?

Solution:

Step 1: Plug the numbers into the formula.

$$A = P\left(1 + \frac{r}{n}\right)^{nt}$$

$$= \$2500.00\left(1 + \frac{0.02}{4}\right)^{4 \cdot 10}$$

Step 2: Solve for A.

$$A = \$2500.00\left(1 + \frac{0.02}{4}\right)^{4 \cdot 10} = \$2500.00(1.005)^{40} \approx \$2500.00(1.22079) \approx \$3051.98$$

This means that Tim had $3,051.98 after 10 years.

Example 12.10

Lisa invested some money 8 years ago at 3% interest, compounded semiannually, and she now has $5,075.94. How much money did she initially invest?

Solution:

Step 1: Plug the numbers into the formula.

$$A = P\left(1 + \frac{r}{n}\right)^{nt}$$

$$\$5{,}075.84 = P\left(1 + \frac{0.03}{2}\right)^{2.8}$$

Step 2: Solve for P.

$$\$5075.84 = P\left(1 + \frac{0.03}{2}\right)^{2.8}$$

$$\$5075.84 = P(1.015)^{16}$$

$$\$5075.84 \approx P(1.26899)$$

$$\frac{\$5075.84}{1.26899} \approx \frac{P(1.26899)}{1.26899}$$

$$P \approx \$3999.91$$

This means that Lisa initially invested about $4,000.

Example 12.11

John invested $7,000 at an annual interest rate of 1.8%, compounded monthly, and he ended up with $7,522.18. For how many years did he invest the money?

Solution:

Step 1: Plug the numbers into the formula.

$$A = P\left(1 + \frac{r}{n}\right)^{nt}$$

$$\$7522.18 = \$7000.00\left(1 + \frac{0.018}{12}\right)^{12 \cdot t}$$

Step 2: Solve for t.

$$\$7522.18 = \$7000.00\left(1 + \frac{0.018}{12}\right)^{12 \cdot t}$$

$$\frac{\$7522.18}{\$7000.00} = \frac{\$7000.00(1.0015)^{12 \cdot t}}{\$7000.00}$$

$$1.074597 \approx 1.0015^{12 \cdot t}$$

$$\ln(1.074597) = \ln\left(1.0015^{12 \cdot t}\right)$$

$$\ln(1.074597) = (12 \cdot t) \cdot \ln(1.0015)$$

$$\frac{\ln(1.074597)}{\ln(1.0015)} = \frac{(12 \cdot t) \cdot \ln(1.0015)}{\ln(1.0015)}$$

$$\frac{\ln(1.074597)}{\ln(1.0015)} = 12 \cdot t$$

$$48 \approx 12 \cdot t$$

$$\frac{48}{12} = \frac{12 \cdot t}{12}$$

$$t = 4$$

This means that John invested the money for four years.

12.9 Mary invested $6,500 for five years at an annual interest rate of 3.4%, compounded semiannually. How much money did she have after five years?

12.10 Peter invested some money 14 years ago at 1.2% interest, compounded monthly, and he now has $9,341.06. How much money did he initially invest?

12.11 Judith invested $2,000 at an annual interest rate of 2.8%, compounded quarterly, and she ended up with $3,039.47. For how many years did she invest the money?

Continuously Compounded Interest

The formula for **continuously compounded interest** is $A = Pe^{rt}$, where A is the total amount of money including interest, P is the original principal, r is the annual interest rate, and t is number of years.

12.7 CONTINUOUSLY COMPOUNDED INTEREST $A = Pe^{rt}$

Example 12.12
Jake invested $4,500 for three years at an annual interest rate of 2.3%, compounded continuously. How much money did he have after three years?

Solution:

Step 1: Plug the numbers into the formula.

$A = Pe^{rt}$

$\quad = \$4500.00 \cdot e^{0.023 \cdot 3}$

Step 2: Solve for A.

$A = \$4500.00 \cdot e^{0.023 \cdot 3} = \$4500.00 \cdot e^{0.069} \approx \$4500.00 \cdot 1.071436 = \$4821.46$

This means that Jake had about $4,800 after three years.

Example 12.13

Michelle invested some money six years ago at 1.9% interest, compounded continuously, and she now has $13,022.92. How much money did she initially invest?

Solution:

Step 1: Plug the numbers into the formula.

$$A = Pe^{rt}$$

$$\$13{,}022.92 = P \cdot e^{0.019 \cdot 6}$$

Step 2: Solve for P.

$$\$13{,}022.92 = P \cdot e^{0.019 \cdot 6}$$

$$\$13{,}022.92 = P \cdot e^{0.114}$$

$$\$13{,}022.92 \approx P \cdot 1.120752$$

$$\frac{\$13{,}022.92}{1.120752} = \frac{P \cdot 1.120752}{1.120752}$$

$$P \approx \$11{,}619.81$$

This means that Michelle initially invested $11,619.81.

Example 12.14

Jeff invested $1,500 for 18 years in an account that compounded interest continuously, and he ended up with $1,828.44. At what annual interest rate did he invest the money?

Solution:

Step 1: Plug the numbers into the formula.

$$A = Pe^{rt}$$

$$\$1828.44 = \$1500.00 \cdot e^{r \cdot 18}$$

Step 2: Solve for r.

$$\$1828.44 = \$1500.00 \cdot e^{r \cdot 18}$$

$$\frac{\$1828.44}{\$1500.00} = \frac{\$1500.00 \cdot e^{r \cdot 18}}{\$1500.00}$$

$$1.21896 \approx e^{r \cdot 18}$$

$$\ln(1.21896) = \ln\left(e^{r \cdot 18}\right)$$

$$\ln(1.21896) = r \cdot 18$$

$$\frac{\ln(1.21896)}{18} = \frac{r \cdot 18}{18}$$

$$\frac{\ln(1.21896)}{18} = r$$

$$\frac{0.197998}{18} \approx r$$

$$r \approx 0.011$$

This means that Jeff invested the money at an annual interest rate of 1.1%.

DIY PROBLEMS

12.12 Janet invested $10,500 for seven years at an annual interest rate of 3.5%, compounded continuously. How much money did she have after seven years?

12.13 Eric invested some money 20 years ago at 2.6% interest, compounded continuously, and he now has $11,529.46. How much money did he initially invest?

12.14 Karen invested $5,500 for nine years in an account that compounded interest continuously, and she ended up with $7,140.25. At what annual interest rate did she invest the money?

Present/Future Value of Annuity

An **annuity** is an investment that involves someone making and/or receiving monthly payments over a specified period. The **present value** of an annuity is the amount that a person has to invest now in order to receive a certain monthly payment in the future. The **future value** of an annuity is the amount a person will receive in the future if he or she makes a certain monthly payment now.

The formula for present value is $PV = \dfrac{M\left((1+r)^n - 1\right)}{r(1+r)^n}$, and the formula for future value is $FV = \dfrac{M\left((1+r)^n - 1\right)}{r}$. In both formulas, M is the monthly payment, r is the monthly interest rate, and n is the number of months.

12.8 ANNUITY An investment that involves someone making and/or receiving monthly payments over a specified period.

12.9 PRESENT VALUE The amount that a person has to invest now in an annuity in order to receive a certain monthly payment in the future.

12.10 FUTURE VALUE The amount a person will receive in the future if he or she makes a certain monthly payment in an annuity now.

Example 12.15

Jason wants to receive monthly payments of $3,250.00 for 15 years. How much does he have to invest now in an annuity that offers an annual interest rate of 3.6%? Round your answer to the nearest $100.

Solution:

Step 1: Calculate the number of months in 15 years and the monthly interest rate that the annuity offers.

$$15 \text{ years} \cdot 12 \, \frac{\text{months}}{\text{year}} = 180 \text{ months}$$

$$\frac{3.6\%}{12 \text{ months}} = 0.3\% \text{ per month}$$

Step 2: Plug the numbers into the formula.

$$PV = \frac{M\left((1+r)^n - 1\right)}{r(1+r)^n}$$

$$= \frac{\$3{,}250.00\left((1+0.003)^{180} - 1\right)}{0.003(1+0.003)^{180}}$$

Step 3: Solve for PV, or the present value.

$$PV = \frac{\$3250.00\left((1+0.003)^{180} - 1\right)}{0.003(1+0.003)^{180}}$$

$$= \frac{\$3250.00\left((1.003)^{180} - 1\right)}{0.003(1.003)^{180}}$$

$$\approx \frac{\$3250.00(1.71462 - 1)}{0.003(1.71462)}$$

$$= \frac{\$3250.00(0.71462)}{0.003(1.71462)}$$

$$\approx \frac{\$2322.52}{0.00514386}$$

$$\approx \$451{,}513.07$$

This means that Jason has to invest about $451,500.

Example 12.16

Carol plans to make monthly payments of $800 for the next 25 years into an annuity offering an annual interest rate of 4.8%. How much money will she have in 25 years? Round to the nearest $100.

Solution:

Step 1: Calculate the number of months in 25 years and the monthly interest rate that the annuity offers.

$$25 \text{ years} \cdot 12 \, \frac{\text{months}}{\text{year}} = 300 \text{ months}$$

$$\frac{4.8\%}{12 \text{ months}} = 0.4\% \text{ per month}$$

Step 2: Plug the numbers into the formula.

$$FV = \frac{M\left((1+r)^n - 1\right)}{r}$$

$$= \frac{\$800.00\left((1+0.004)^{300} - 1\right)}{0.004}$$

Step 3: Solve for FV, or the future value.

$$FV = \frac{\$800.00\left((1+0.004)^{300}-1\right)}{0.004}$$

$$= \frac{\$800.00\left((1.004)^{300}-1\right)}{0.004}$$

$$\approx \frac{\$800.00\left(3.31218-1\right)}{0.004}$$

$$= \frac{\$800.00\left(2.31218\right)}{0.004}$$

$$\approx \frac{\$1849.74}{0.004}$$

$$\approx \$462,435.00$$

This means that Carol will have about $462,400.

Example 12.17

Garry wants to have $750,000 in 30 years. How much does he have to invest per month in an annuity with an annual interest rate of 2.4%? Round to the nearest dollar.

Solution:

Step 1: Calculate the number of months in 30 years and the monthly interest rate that the annuity offers.

$$30 \text{ years} \cdot 12 \ \frac{\text{months}}{\text{year}} = 360 \text{ months}$$

$$\frac{2.4\%}{12 \text{ months}} = 0.2\% \text{ per month}$$

Step 2: Plug the numbers into the formula.

$$FV = \frac{M\left((1+r)^{n}-1\right)}{r}$$

$$\$750,000.00 = \frac{M\left((1+0.002)^{360}-1\right)}{0.002}$$

Step 3: Solve for M, or the monthly payment.

$$\$750,000.00 = \frac{M\left((1+0.002)^{360}-1\right)}{0.002}$$

$$\$750,000.00 \cdot 0.002 = \frac{M\left((1+0.002)^{360}-1\right)}{0.002} \cdot 0.002$$

$$\$1500.00 = M\left((1+0.002)^{360}-1\right)$$

$$\$1500.00 = M\left((1.002)^{360}-1\right)$$

$$\$1500.00 \approx M\left(2.05296-1\right)$$

$$\$1,500.00 = M(1.05296)$$

$$\frac{\$1,500.00}{1.05296} = \frac{M(1.05296)}{1.05296}$$

$$M \approx \$1,424.56$$

This means that Garry will have to invest about $1,425 per month.

DIY PROBLEMS

12.15 Rachael wants to receive monthly payments of $2,775 for 20 years. How much does she have to invest now in an annuity that offers an annual interest rate of 6%? Round your answer to the nearest $100.

12.16 Kevin plans to make monthly payments of $1,400 for the next 10 years into an annuity offering an annual interest rate of 1.2%. How much money will he have in 10 years? Round your answer to the nearest $100.

12.17 Cathy wants to have $1,000,000 in 40 years. How much does she have to invest per month in an annuity with an annual interest rate of 7.2%? Round your answer to the nearest dollar.

Exponential Growth

One formula for exponential growth is $N = N_0 (1 + r)^t$, while another, for continuous exponential growth, is $N = N_0 e^{kt}$.

In both formulas, N is the final amount, N_0 is the initial amount, and t is the amount of time passed. In the first formula, r is the percent growth per time period, and in the second formula, k is the growth constant.

Example 12.18

The population of a country is increasing at a rate of 15% per year. If the population is currently 5,000,000, what will be the population in eight years?

Solution:

Step 1: Plug the numbers into the formula $N = N_0 (1 + r)^t$.
$N = 5{,}000{,}000(1 + 0.15)^8$

Step 2: Solve for N.
$N = 5{,}000{,}000(1 + 0.15)^8 = 5{,}000{,}000(1.15)^8 \approx 5{,}000{,}000(3.059023) \approx 15{,}295{,}115$
This means that the population will be 15,295,115 people.

Example 12.19

The number of visitors to a website increased at a rate of 40% per day, going from 100 per day to 100,000 per day. How many days did it take to go from 100 to 100,000 visitors per day? Round your answer to the nearest day.

Solution:

Step 1: Plug the numbers into the formula $N = N_0 (1 + r)^t$.

$100{,}000 = 100(1 + 0.4)^t$

Step 2: Solve for t.

$$100{,}000 = 100(1 + 0.4)^t$$
$$100{,}000 = 100(1.4)^t$$
$$\frac{100{,}000}{100} = \frac{100(1.4)^t}{100}$$
$$1{,}000 = 1.4^t$$
$$\ln(1000) = \ln(1.4^t)$$
$$\ln(1000) = t \cdot \ln(1.4)$$
$$\frac{\ln(1{,}000)}{\ln(1.4)} = \frac{t \cdot \ln(1.4)}{\ln(1.4)}$$
$$\frac{\ln(1000)}{\ln(1.4)} = t$$
$$\frac{6.90776}{0.33647} \approx t$$
$$t \approx 20.5$$

This means that it took about 21 days.

Example 12.20

The number of bacteria in a Petri dish increased exponentially from 250 to 9500 in a span of three hours. What is the growth constant for the bacteria? Round your answer to the nearest 100th.

Solution:

Step 1: Plug the numbers into the formula $N = N_0 e^{kt}$.
$9{,}500 = 250 e^{k \cdot 3}$

Step 2: Solve for k.

$$9500 = 250e^{k \cdot 3}$$

$$\frac{9500}{250} = \frac{250e^{k \cdot 3}}{250}$$

$$38 = e^{k \cdot 3}$$

$$\ln(38) = \ln\left(e^{k \cdot 3}\right)$$

$$\ln(38) = (k \cdot 3) \cdot \ln(e)$$

$$\ln(38) = (k \cdot 3) \cdot 1$$

$$\ln(38) = (k \cdot 3)$$

$$\frac{\ln(38)}{3} = \frac{(k \cdot 3)}{3}$$

$$\frac{\ln(38)}{3} = k$$

$$\frac{3.63759}{3} \approx k$$

$$k \approx 1.21$$

This means that the growth constant is about 1.21.

DIY PROBLEMS

12.18 The population of a country is increasing at a rate of 5% per year. If the population is currently 7,000,000, what will be the population in 12 years?

12.19 The number of visitors to a website increased at a rate of 60% per day, going from 30 per day to 30,000 per day. How many days did it take to go from 30 to 30,000 visitors per day? Round your answer to the nearest day.

12.20 The number of bacteria in a Petri dish increased exponentially from 850 to 7650 in a span of four hours. What is the growth constant for the bacteria? Round your answer to the nearest 100th.

BENFORD'S LAW

If you looked at a long list of numbers from a real-world source, what would be the most common first digit of the numbers? It might seem that the digits 1 through 9 would occur with the same frequency, but this is not the case. Benford's law says that the probability of a number having the first digit D is $\log\left(1 + \dfrac{1}{D}\right)$. If you work it out, you will see that 1 is the most frequent first digit, occurring more than 30% of the time! Figure 12.13 shows the probability of each of the digits.

DIGIT	PROBABILITY
1	0.3010
2	0.1761
3	0.1249
4	0.0969
5	0.0792
6	0.0669
7	0.0580
8	0.0512
9	0.0458

FIGURE 12.13 Probability of First Digits in a Numerical List (Benford's Law)

SOLUTIONS TO DIY PROBLEMS

12.1 Evaluate the function $f(x) = 6\left(\dfrac{1}{4}\right)^x - 12$ for each of the following values of x.

a. $x = -2$

Solution:
First, substitute -2 for x to get $f(-2) = 6\left(\dfrac{1}{4}\right)^{-2} - 12$. Next, simplify the right side of the equation.

$$f(-2) = 6\left(\frac{1}{4}\right)^{-2} - 12 = 6(16) - 12 = 96 - 12 = 84$$

b. $x = 0$

Solution:
First, substitute 0 for x to get $f(0) = 6\left(\dfrac{1}{4}\right)^0 - 12$. Next, simplify the right side of the equation.

$$f(0) = 6\left(\frac{1}{4}\right)^0 - 12 = 6(1) - 12 = 6 - 12 = -6$$

c. $x = 2$

Solution:
First, substitute 2 for x to get $f(2) = 6\left(\dfrac{1}{4}\right)^2 - 12$. Next, simplify the right side of the equation.

$$f(2) = 6\left(\frac{1}{4}\right)^2 - 12 = 6\left(\frac{1}{16}\right) - 12 = \frac{6}{16} - 12 = \frac{3}{8} - 12 = -11\frac{5}{8}$$

12.2 Graph both of the following functions.

a. $f(x) = \left(\dfrac{1}{2}\right)^{3x-2}$

Solution:

First, make a table of values for the function. Choose values of x for which the function is easy to evaluate (Figure 12.14).

x	f(x)
−1	$\left(\dfrac{1}{2}\right)^{3(-1)-2} = \left(\dfrac{1}{2}\right)^{-3-2} = \left(\dfrac{1}{2}\right)^{-5} = 32$
0	$\left(\dfrac{1}{2}\right)^{3(0)-2} = \left(\dfrac{1}{2}\right)^{0-2} = \left(\dfrac{1}{2}\right)^{-2} = 4$
1	$\left(\dfrac{1}{2}\right)^{3(1)-2} = \left(\dfrac{1}{2}\right)^{3-2} = \left(\dfrac{1}{2}\right)^{1} = \dfrac{1}{2}$
2	$\left(\dfrac{1}{2}\right)^{3(2)-2} = \left(\dfrac{1}{2}\right)^{6-2} = \left(\dfrac{1}{2}\right)^{4} = \dfrac{1}{16}$
3	$\left(\dfrac{1}{2}\right)^{3(3)-2} = \left(\dfrac{1}{2}\right)^{9-2} = \left(\dfrac{1}{2}\right)^{7} = \dfrac{1}{128}$

FIGURE 12.14

Next, plot the points on a Cartesian plane (Figure 12.15).

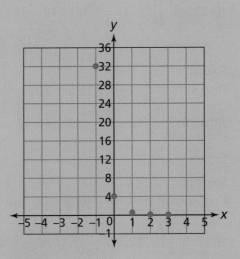

FIGURE 12.15

Finally, draw a curve through the points (Figure 12.16).

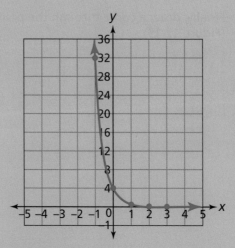

FIGURE 12.16

b. $f(x) = \left(\dfrac{1}{25}\right)5^x + 1$

Solution:

First, make a table of values for the function. Choose values of x for which the function is easy to evaluate (Figure 12.17).

x	$f(x)$
-1	$\left(\dfrac{1}{25}\right)5^{-1} + 1 = \left(\dfrac{1}{25}\right)\left(\dfrac{1}{5}\right) + 1 = \dfrac{1}{125} + 1 = 1\dfrac{1}{125}$
0	$\left(\dfrac{1}{25}\right)5^{0} + 1 = \left(\dfrac{1}{25}\right)(1) + 1 = \dfrac{1}{125} + 1 = 1\dfrac{1}{125}$
1	$\left(\dfrac{1}{25}\right)5^{1} + 1 = \left(\dfrac{1}{25}\right)(5) + 1 = \dfrac{5}{25} + 1 = \dfrac{1}{5} + 1 = 1\dfrac{1}{5}$
2	$\left(\dfrac{1}{25}\right)5^{2} + 1 = \left(\dfrac{1}{25}\right)(25) + 1 = \dfrac{25}{25} + 1 = 1 + 1 = 2$
3	$\left(\dfrac{1}{25}\right)5^{3} + 1 = \left(\dfrac{1}{25}\right)(125) + 1 = \dfrac{125}{25} + 1 = 5 + 1 = 6$

FIGURE 12.17

Next, plot the points on a Cartesian plane (Figure 12.18).

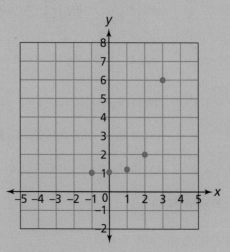

FIGURE 12.18

Finally, draw a curve through the points (Figure 12.19).

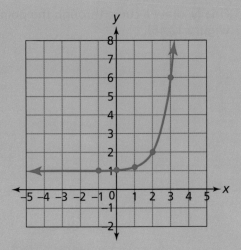

FIGURE 12.19

12.3 Evaluate the function $f(x) = \log_3 x$ for $x = 81$.

Solution:

First, rewrite the function as $y = \log_3 x$, and then write $x = 3^y$. Next, substitute 81 for x so that the equation becomes $81 = 3^y$, or $3^y = 81$. Since $3^4 = 81$, the answer is 4.

12.4 Evaluate the function $f(x) = \ln x$ for $x = \dfrac{1}{e}$.

Solution:

First, rewrite the function as $y = \ln x$, and then write $x = e^y$. Next, substitute $\dfrac{1}{e}$ for x so that the equation becomes $\dfrac{1}{e} = e^y$, or $e^y = \dfrac{1}{e}$. Since $e^{-1} = \dfrac{1}{e}$, the answer is $y = -1$.

12.5 Graph the function $f(x) = \log_2(4x) - 3$.

Solution:

First, make a table of values for the function. Choose values of x for which the function is easy to evaluate (Figure 12.20).

x	$f(x)$
$-\dfrac{1}{8}$	$\log_2\left(4 \cdot \dfrac{1}{8}\right) - 3 = \log_2\left(\dfrac{4}{8}\right) - 3 = \log_2\left(\dfrac{1}{2}\right) - 3 = -1 - 3 = -4$
$\dfrac{1}{4}$	$\log_2\left(4 \cdot \dfrac{1}{4}\right) - 3 = \log_2(1) - 3 = 0 = -3$
1	$\log_2(4 \cdot 1) - 3 = \log_2(4) - 3 = 2 - 3 = -1$
2	$\log_2(4 \cdot 2) - 3 = \log_2(8) - 3 = 3 - 3 = 0$
4	$\log_2(4 \cdot 4) - 3 = \log_2(16) - 3 = 4 - 3 = 1$

FIGURE 12.20

Next, plot the points on a Cartesian plane (Figure 12.21).

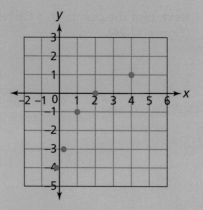

FIGURE 12.21

Finally, draw a curve through the points (Figure 12.22).

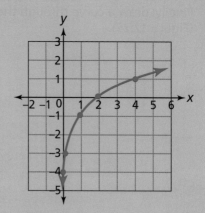

FIGURE 12.22

12.6 Graph the function $f(x) = 2\log_{\frac{1}{2}}(x+5)$.

Solution:

First, make a table of values for the function. Choose values of x for which the function is easy to evaluate (Figure 12.23).

x	$f(x)$
$-\dfrac{19}{4}$	$2\log_{\frac{1}{2}}\left(-\dfrac{19}{4}+5\right) = 2\log_{\frac{1}{2}}\left(-\dfrac{19}{4}+\dfrac{20}{4}\right) = 2\log_{\frac{1}{2}}\left(\dfrac{1}{4}\right) = 2\cdot 2 = 4$
$-\dfrac{9}{2}$	$2\log_{\frac{1}{2}}\left(-\dfrac{9}{2}+5\right) = 2\log_{\frac{1}{2}}\left(-\dfrac{9}{2}+\dfrac{10}{2}\right) = 2\log_{\frac{1}{2}}\left(\dfrac{1}{2}\right) = 2\cdot 1 = 2$
-4	$2\log_{\frac{1}{2}}(-4+5) = 2\log_{\frac{1}{2}}(1) = 2\cdot 0 = 0$
-3	$2\log_{\frac{1}{2}}(-3+5) = 2\log_{\frac{1}{2}}(2) = 2\cdot(-1) = -2$
-1	$2\log_{\frac{1}{2}}(-1+5) = 2\log_{\frac{1}{2}}(4) = 2\cdot(-2) = -4$

FIGURE 12.23

Next, plot the points on a Cartesian plane (Figure 12.24).

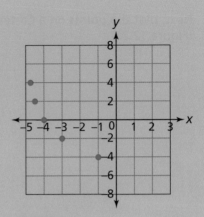

FIGURE 12.24

Finally, draw a curve through the points (Figure 12.25).

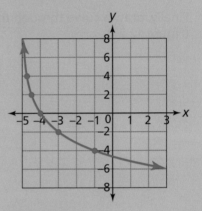

FIGURE 12.25

12.7 Solve the equation $\left(\dfrac{1}{9}\right)(3^x) + 14 = 95$ for x.

Solution:

Step 1: Isolate 3^x on one side of the equation.

$$\left(\frac{1}{9}\right)(3^x) + 14 = 95$$

$$\left(\frac{1}{9}\right)(3^x) + 14 - 14 = 95 - 14$$

$$\left(\frac{1}{9}\right)(3^x) = 81$$

$$\left(\frac{1}{9}\right)(3^x) \cdot 9 = 81 \cdot 9$$

$$3^x = 729$$

Step 2: Take the natural logarithm of both sides.

$$3^x = 729$$

$$\ln\left(3^x\right) = \ln(729)$$

Step 3: Use the property $\ln(a^x) = x \cdot \ln a$ to rewrite the equation.

$$\ln(3^x) = \ln(729)$$

$$x \cdot \ln(3) = \ln(729)$$

Step 4: Solve for x. Use a calculator when necessary.

$$x\ln(3) = \ln(729)$$

$$\frac{x\ln(3)}{\ln(3)} = \frac{\ln(729)}{\ln(3)}$$

$$x = \frac{\ln(729)}{\ln(3)} \approx \frac{6.592}{1.10} \approx 6$$

12.8 Solve the equation $20\log_5 x - 6 = 34$ for x.

Solution:

First, isolate $\log_5 x$ on one side of the equation.

$$20\log_5 x - 6 = 34$$

$$20\log_5 x - 6 + 6 = 34 + 6$$

$$20\log_5 x = 40$$

$$\frac{20\log_5 x}{20} = \frac{40}{20}$$

$$\log_5 x = 2$$

Next, use the fact that another way of writing $y = \log_a x$ is $x = a^y$. This means that another way of writing $\log_5 x = 2$ is $x = 5^2$.

Finally, solve for x.

$$x = 5^2$$

$$x = 25$$

12.9 Mary invested $6,500.00 for five years at an annual interest rate of 3.4%, compounded semiannually. How much money did she have after five years?

Solution:

Step 1: Plug the numbers into the formula.

$$A = P\left(1 + \frac{r}{n}\right)^{nt}$$

$$= \$6500.00\left(1 + \frac{0.034}{2}\right)^{2 \cdot 5}$$

Step 2: Solve for A.

$$A = \$6500.00\left(1 + \frac{0.034}{2}\right)^{2 \cdot 5} = \$6500.00(1.017)^{10} \approx \$6500.00(1.18361) \approx \$7693.47$$

This means that Mary had $7,693.47 after five years.

12.10 Peter invested some money 14 years ago at 1.2% interest, compounded monthly, and he now has $9,341.06. How much money did he initially invest?

Solution:

Step 1: Plug the numbers into the formula.

$$A = P\left(1 + \frac{r}{n}\right)^{nt}$$

$$\$9,341.06 = P\left(1 + \frac{0.012}{12}\right)^{12 \cdot 14}$$

Step 2: Solve for P.

$$\$9341.06 = P\left(1 + \frac{0.012}{12}\right)^{12 \cdot 14}$$

$$\$9341.06 = P(1.001)^{168}$$

$$\$9341.06 \approx P(1.18284)$$

$$\frac{\$9341.06}{1.18284} = \frac{P(1.18284)}{1.18284}$$

$$P \approx \$7897.15$$

This means that Peter initially invested $7,897.15.

12.11 Judith invested $2,000 at an annual interest rate of 2.8%, compounded quarterly, and she ended up with $3,039.47. For how many years did she invest the money?

Solution:

Step 1: Plug the numbers into the formula.

$$A = P\left(1 + \frac{r}{n}\right)^{nt}$$

$$\$3039.47 = \$2000.00\left(1 + \frac{0.028}{4}\right)^{4 \cdot t}$$

Step 2: Solve for t.

$$\$3039.47 = \$2000.00\left(1 + \frac{0.028}{4}\right)^{4 \cdot t}$$

$$\frac{\$3039.47}{\$2000.00} = \frac{\$2000.00(1.007)^{4 \cdot t}}{\$2000.00}$$

$$1.519735 \approx 1.007^{4 \cdot t}$$

$$\ln(1.519735) = \ln(1.007^{4 \cdot t})$$

$$\ln(1.519735) = (4 \cdot t) \cdot \ln(1.007)$$

$$\frac{\ln(1.519735)}{\ln(1.007)} = \frac{(4 \cdot t) \cdot \ln(1.007)}{\ln(1.007)}$$

$$\frac{\ln(1.519735)}{\ln(1.007)} = 4 \cdot t$$

$$60 \approx 4 \cdot t$$

$$\frac{60}{4} \approx \frac{4 \cdot t}{4}$$

$$t \approx 15$$

This means that Judith invested the money for 15 years.

12.12 Janet invested $10,500.00 for seven years at an annual interest rate of 3.5%, compounded continuously. How much money did she have after seven years?

Solution:

Step 1: Plug the numbers into the formula.

$$A = Pe^{rt}$$

$$= \$10,500.00 \cdot e^{0.035 \cdot 7}$$

Step 2: Solve for *A*.

$$A = \$10{,}500.00 \cdot e^{0.035 \cdot 7} = \$10{,}500.00 \cdot e^{0.245} \approx \$10{,}500.00 \cdot 1.277621 \approx \$13{,}415.02$$

This means that Janet had $13,415.02 after seven years.

12.13 Eric invested some money 20 years ago at 2.6% interest, compounded continuously, and he now has $11,529.46. How much money did he initially invest?

Solution:
Step 1: Plug the numbers into the formula.

$$A = Pe^{rt}$$

$$\$11{,}529.46 = P \cdot e^{0.026 \cdot 20}$$

Step 2: Solve for *P*.

$$\$11{,}529.46 = P \cdot e^{0.026 \cdot 20}$$

$$\$11{,}529.46 = P \cdot e^{0.52}$$

$$\$11{,}529.46 \approx P \cdot 1.682028$$

$$\frac{\$11{,}529.46}{1.682028} = \frac{P \cdot 1.682028}{1.682028}$$

$$P \approx \$6{,}854.50$$

This means that Eric initially invested $6,854.50.

12.14 Karen invested $5,500 for nine years in an account that compounded interest continuously, and she ended up with $7,140.25. At what annual interest rate did she invest the money?

Solution:
Step 1: Plug the numbers into the formula.

$$A = Pe^{rt}$$

$$\$7{,}140.25 = \$5{,}500.00 \cdot e^{r \cdot 9}$$

Step 2: Solve for *r*.

$$\$7140.25 = \$5500.00 \cdot e^{r \cdot 9}$$

$$\frac{\$7140.25}{\$5500.00} = \frac{\$5500.00 \cdot e^{r \cdot 9}}{\$5500.00}$$

$$1.29823 = e^{r \cdot 9}$$

$$\ln(1.29823) = \ln\left(e^{r \cdot 9}\right)$$

$$\ln(1.29823) = r \cdot 9$$

$$\frac{\ln(1.29823)}{9} = \frac{r \cdot 9}{9}$$

$$\frac{\ln(1.29823)}{9} = r$$

$$\frac{0.261002}{9} \approx r$$

$$r \approx 0.029$$

This means that Karen invested the money at an annual interest rate of 2.9%.

12.15 Rachael wants to receive monthly payments of $2,775 for 20 years. How much does she have to invest now in an annuity that offers an annual interest rate of 6%? Round your answer to the nearest $100.

Solution:
Step 1: Calculate the number of months in 20 years and the monthly interest rate that the annuity offers.

$$20 \text{ years} \cdot 12 \ \frac{\text{months}}{\text{year}} = 240 \text{ months}$$

$$\frac{6\%}{12 \text{ months}} = 0.5\% \text{ per month}$$

Step 2: Plug the numbers into the formula.

$$PV = \frac{M\left((1+r)^n - 1\right)}{r(1+r)^n}$$

$$= \frac{\$2775.00\left((1+0.005)^{240} - 1\right)}{0.005(1+0.005)^{240}}$$

Step 3: Solve for *PV*, or the present value.

$$PV = \frac{\$2775.00\left((1+0.005)^{240} - 1\right)}{0.005(1+0.005)^{240}}$$

$$= \frac{\$2775.00\left((1.005)^{240} - 1\right)}{0.005(1.005)^{240}}$$

$$\approx \frac{\$2775.00(3.31020 - 1)}{0.005(3.31020)}$$

$$= \frac{\$2775.00(2.31020)}{0.005(3.31020)}$$

$$= \frac{\$6410.81}{0.016551}$$

$$= \$387,336.72$$

This means that Rachael has to invest about $387,300.

12.16 Kevin plans to make monthly payments of $1,400 for the next 10 years into an annuity offering an annual interest rate of 1.2%. How much money will he have in 10 years? Round your answer to the nearest $100.

Solution:
Step 1: Calculate the number of months in 10 years and the monthly interest rate that the annuity offers.

$$10 \text{ years} \cdot 12 \ \frac{\text{months}}{\text{year}} = 120 \text{ months}$$

$$\frac{1.2\%}{12 \text{ months}} = 0.1\% \text{ per month}$$

Step 2: Plug the numbers into the formula.

$$FV = \frac{M\left((1+r)^n - 1\right)}{r}$$

$$= \frac{\$1400.00\left((1+0.001)^{120} - 1\right)}{0.001}$$

Step 3: Solve for *FV*, or the future value.

$$FV = \frac{\$1400.00\left((1+0.001)^{120} - 1\right)}{0.001}$$

$$= \frac{\$1400.00\left((1.001)^{120} - 1\right)}{0.001}$$

$$\approx \frac{\$1400.00\left(1.12743 - 1\right)}{0.001}$$

$$= \frac{\$1400.00\left(0.12743\right)}{0.001}$$

$$\approx \frac{\$178.40}{0.001}$$

$$\approx \$178{,}400.00$$

This means that Kevin will have about $178,400.

12.17 Cathy wants to have $1,000,000 in 40 years. How much does she have to invest per month in an annuity with an annual interest rate of 7.2%? Round your answer to the nearest dollar.

Solution:

Step 1: Calculate the number of months in 40 years and the monthly interest rate that the annuity offers.

$$40 \text{ years} \cdot 12 \; \frac{\text{months}}{\text{year}} = 480 \text{ months}$$

$$\frac{7.2\%}{12 \text{ months}} = 0.6\% \text{ per month}$$

Step 2: Plug the numbers into the formula.

$$FV = \frac{M\left((1+r)^n - 1\right)}{r}$$

$$\$1{,}000{,}000.00 = \frac{M\left((1+0.006)^{480} - 1\right)}{0.006}$$

Step 3: Solve for M, or the monthly payment.

$$\$1,000,000 = \frac{M\left((1+0.006)^{480} - 1\right)}{0.006}$$

$$\$1,000,000 \cdot 0.006 = \frac{M\left((1+0.006)^{480} - 1\right)}{0.006} \cdot 0.006$$

$$\$6000 = M\left((1+0.006)^{480} - 1\right)$$

$$\$6000 \approx M(17.66163 - 1)$$

$$\$6000 = M(16.66163)$$

$$\frac{\$6000}{16.66163} = M\frac{16.66163}{16.66163}$$

$$M \approx \$360.11$$

This means that Cathy will have to invest about $360 per month.

12.18 The population of a country is increasing at a rate of 5% per year. If the population is currently 7,000,000, what will be the population in 12 years?

Solution:
Step 1: Plug the numbers into the formula $N = N_0(1 + r)^t$.

$$N = 7,000,000(1+0.05)^{12}$$

Step 2: Solve for N.

$$N = 7,000,000(1+0.05)^{12} = 7,000,000(1.05)^{12} \approx 7,000,000(1.795856) \approx 12,570,992$$

This means that the population will be 12,570,992 people.

12.19 The number of visitors to a website increased at a rate of 60% per day, going from 30 per day to 30,000 per day. How many days did it take to go from 30 to 30,000 visitors per day? Round your answer to the nearest day.

Solution:
Step 1: Plug the numbers into the formula $N = N_0(1 + r)^t$.

$$30,000 = 30(1+0.6)^t$$

Step 2: Solve for t.

$$30,000 = 30(1+0.6)^t$$

$$30,000 = 30(1.6)^t$$

$$\frac{30,000}{30} = \frac{30(1.6)^t}{30}$$

$$1000 = 1.6^t$$

$$\ln(1,000) = \ln(1.6^t)$$

$$\ln(1,000) = t \cdot \ln(1.6)$$

$$\frac{\ln(1,000)}{\ln(1.6)} = \frac{t \cdot \ln(1.6)}{\ln(1.6)}$$

$$\frac{\ln(1,000)}{\ln(1.6)} = t$$

$$\frac{6.90776}{0.470004} \approx t$$

$$t \approx 14.7$$

This means that it took about 15 days.

12.20 The number of bacteria in a Petri dish increased exponentially from 850 to 7,650 in a span of four hours. What is the growth constant for the bacteria? Round your answer to the nearest 100th.

Solution:
Step 1: Plug the numbers into the formula $N = N_0 e^{kt}$.

$$7,650 = 850 e^{k \cdot 4}$$

Step 2: Next, solve for k.

$$7650 = 850 e^{k \cdot 4}$$

$$\frac{7650}{850} = \frac{850 e^{k \cdot 4}}{850}$$

$$9 = e^{k \cdot 4}$$

$$\ln(9) = \ln\left(e^{k \cdot 4}\right)$$

$$\ln(9) = (k \cdot 4) \cdot \ln(e)$$

$$\ln(9) = (k \cdot 4) \cdot 1$$

$$\ln(9) = (k \cdot 4)$$

$$\frac{\ln(9)}{4} = \frac{(k \cdot 4)}{4}$$

$$\frac{\ln(9)}{4} = k$$

$$\frac{2.19722}{4} \approx k$$

$$k \approx 0.55$$

This means that the growth constant is about 0.55.

12.1 Find the inverse for the equation $y = 5x + 3$.

12.2 Graph the following functions and determine if they are increasing or decreasing.
   a. $f(x) = 2^x$

   b. $f(x) = \left(\dfrac{1}{2}\right)^x$

12.3 Graph the following functions and determine if they are increasing or decreasing:
   a. $f(x) = e^x$

   b. $f(x) = e^{-x}$

12.4 Explain why the two functions are similar in problems 12.2 and 12.3.

12.5 The formula $A = Pe^{rt}$ is used in business for calculating interest on an invested (or owed) amount that is compounded continuously, where P is the amount invested (or owed), r is the interest rate, and t is the time in years the amount has been invested. If an individual invests $1,000 compounded continuously for three years at 6%, what is the amount of the investment at the end of the three years? Round to the nearest cent.

12.6 The formula $A = Pe^{rt}$ is used in business for calculating interest on an invested (or owed) amount that is compounded continuously, where P is the amount invested (or owed), r is the interest rate, and t is the time in years the amount has been invested. If an individual invests $3,300 compounded continuously for four years at 2%, what is the amount of the investment at the end of the four years? Round to the nearest cent.

12.7 The formula $A = Pe^{rt}$ is used in business for calculating interest on an invested (or owed) amount that is compounded continuously, where P is the amount invested (or owed), r is the interest rate, and t is the time in years the amount has been invested. If an individual invests $6,000 at a rate of 3.5% compounded continuously, how long will it take to double their money?

12.8 The formula $A = P\left(1+\dfrac{r}{n}\right)^{nt}$ is used in business for calculating interest on an invested (or owed) amount that is compounded a certain number, n, times per year, where P is the amount invested (or owed), r is the interest rate, and t is the time in years the amount has been invested. If an individual invests $1,000 compounded quarterly for three years at 6%, what is the amount of the investment at the end of three years? Round to the nearest cent.

12.9 The formula $A = P\left(1+\dfrac{r}{n}\right)^{nt}$ is used in business for calculating interest on an invested (or owed) amount that is compounded a certain number, n, times per year, where P is the amount invested (or owed), r is the interest rate, and t is the time in years the amount has been invested. If an individual invests $4,200 compounded semiannually for three years at 4.1%, what is the amount of the investment at the end of three years? Round to the nearest cent.

12.10 If the population for a certain town is given by the equation $P = 1500(2^{0.3t})$, where t is the time in years from 1980, find the population in 1985.

12.11 Simplify the following:
   a. $\log_2(16)$

   b. $\log_5(25)$

c. $\log_{10}(0.001)$

d. $\log_4\left(\dfrac{1}{4}\right)$

12.12 Simplify $\log_3 243$

12.13 Simplify $\log_9 81$

12.14 Simplify $\log_3 \dfrac{1}{27}$

12.15 Solve the following equations for x.
    a. $\log_3(x) = 2$

b. $\log_2(x) = -3$

c. $\log_{32}(x) = \dfrac{1}{5}$

d. $\log_4(x) = \dfrac{1}{2}$

12.16 Solve $\log_{27} x = \dfrac{1}{3}$

12.17 Solve $\log_4 x = 5$

12.18 Solve $\log_4 2x = 3$

12.19 Solve $\log_5 (3x + 7) = 2$

12.20 Solve the following for x:
$\log_3(4x - 7) = 2$

12.21 Solve the following for x:
$\log_x(64) = 2$

12.22 Solve $\log_x 81 = 4$

12.23 Solve the following for x:
$2^x = 5$

12.24 Solve $4^x = 10$

12.25 Solve $e^x = 9$

12.26 Solve $8^{2x+5} = 30$. Round to three decimal places.

12.27 Solve $9e^{x+1} = 108$

12.28 The following formula represents the number N of cells in a culture after a time t has passed, where N_0 is the initial number of cells and k represents the positive growth rate of the cells.

$$N(t) = N_0 e^{kt} \text{ where } k > 0$$

If a colony of bacteria is modeled by the function $N(t) = 130e^{0.045t}$, determine the initial amount of bacteria.

12.29 The following formula represents the number N of cells in a culture after a time t has passed, where N_0 is the initial number of cells and k represents the positive growth rate of the cells.

$N(t) = N_0 e^{kt}$ where $k > 0$

If a colony of bacteria is modeled by the function $N(t) = 130e^{0.045t}$, what is the growth rate of the bacteria?

12.30 The following formula represents the number N of cells in a culture after a time t has passed, where N_0 is the initial number of cells and k represents the positive growth rate of the cells.

$N(t) = N_0 e^{kt}$ where $k > 0$

If a colony of bacteria is modeled by the function $N(t) = 130e^{0.045t}$, how long will it take the population to reach 160 grams?

12.31 The formula $A = Pe^{rt}$ is used in business for calculating interest on an invested (or owed) amount that is compounded continuously, where P is the amount invested (or owed), r is the interest rate, and t is the time in years the amount has been invested.

If an individual invests \$4,000 compounded continuously at 3%, how many years was the money Invested if the return was \$5,399.44.

12.32 The following formula represents exponential growth, where $k > 0$. A is the amount after time t has passed, A_0 is the initial amount and k is the growth constant. $A = A_0 e^{kt}$ where $k > 0$.

There were 10 rabbits living on an island. After 7 months there were 50 rabbits. Determine how many rabbits there will be in 15 months.

12.33 The following formula represents exponential depreciation of worth, where $k < 0$. A is the amount of worth after time t has passed, A_0 is the initial amount and k is depreciation constant. $A = A_0 e^{kt}$ where $k < 0$.

If Christina purchases a car for $45,000 and two years later it has depreciated exponentially to $30,000, find the depreciation constant. Round to three decimal places.

12.34 The following formula represents exponential depreciation of worth, where $k < 0$. A is the amount of worth after time t has passed, A_0 is the initial amount and k is depreciation constant. $A = A_0 e^{kt}$ where $k < 0$.

If James purchases a car for $36,000 and two years later it has depreciated exponentially to $26,000, how much will the car be worth five years from the date of purchase? Round to three decimal places.

12.35 The population of a country is increasing at a rate of 2.5% per year. If the population is currently 5,000,000, how many years will it take for the population to reach 6,500,000?

APPENDIX A

ALGEBRA REFERENCE TOPICS

REAL NUMBERS

Real numbers are those numbers that have a decimal form. The set of real numbers includes all integers, fractions, and irrational numbers. (See Figure A.1.)

Real numbers can be broadly classified as irrational or rational numbers.

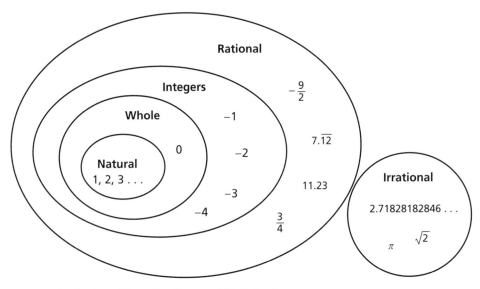

FIGURE A.1 **The Set of Real Numbers and Its Subsets**

Natural numbers are sometimes referred to as *counting numbers*. The set of whole numbers differs from the set of natural numbers only by including zero.

The set of integers includes the set of natural numbers, their opposites, and zero. Zero is its own opposite; it is neither positive nor negative.

The set of rational numbers is the set of all fractions (ratios of integers). Their decimal equivalents are either terminating or repeating decimals. Examples of fractions include $\frac{2}{3}, -\frac{4}{3}$, 0.34, and $-3.121212....$

The set of irrational numbers is the set of all nonrepeating, nonterminating decimals. Examples of irrational numbers include $\sqrt{2} = 1.414...$, $-\sqrt{3} = -1.732...$, and $4.5151151115111151111115111111....$

A number line represents all real numbers in order. Every real number is represented by a point on the line. Every point on the line represents exactly one real number. Some unit of measure marks off intervals on the line, with positive numbers to the right of a point chosen to represent 0 and negative numbers to the left of it. (See Figure A.2.)

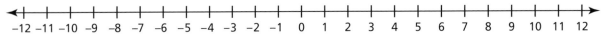

FIGURE A.2 **Number Line**

An interval is a set of all the real numbers that lie between two numbers called the endpoints. The endpoints may or may not be in the interval. For example, the set of real numbers that satisfy the conditions $0 < x < 2$ is the set of all real numbers greater than 0 and less than 2, but not including 0 or 2. The set of real numbers that satisfies the conditions $-5 \leq x < 5$ is the set of all real numbers greater than or equal to -5 and less than 5.

In Figure A.3, a thick line shows values that are included in the interval $0 < x \leq 20$. A filled circle shows inclusion of an endpoint. An open circle shows exclusion of an endpoint. Parentheses and brackets also indicate intervals; a parenthesis shows that the endpoint is not included; a bracket shows that the endpoint is included. The notation $(0, 20]$ is another way of writing $0 < x \leq 20$.

FIGURE A.3 The Interval (0, 20] or 0 < x ≤ 20

For intervals that include all the numbers greater than or less than some number (sometimes called "infinite intervals," use the symbol ∞ or $-\infty$ (∞ is read "infinity"). Infinity is not a number, so a parenthesis or one of the symbols < or > are always used with it in interval notation. Figure A.4 shows two such intervals.

FIGURE A. 4 Infinite Intervals

a. $(3, \infty) = 3 \leq x < \infty$
b. $(-\infty, 2) \cup (3, \infty) = -\infty < x \leq 2$ or $3 < x < \infty$. The symbol $\cup$ is read "union" and indicates that points may belong to one interval or the other.

EXPONENTS

Exponentiation is a mathematical operation that involves two numbers, the exponent and the base. An exponential expression is written a^n. Here the base is a and the exponent is n. If n is an integer, a^n represents a multiplied by itself n times.

$$a^n = \underbrace{a \times \ldots \times a}_{n},$$

The term a^n is read "a raised to the nth power" or "a to the nth." In particular, a^2 is read "a-squared" and a^3 is read "a-cubed."

- The term *odd power* means that the exponent is odd. In a^n, n is odd.
- The term *negative power* means that the exponent is negative. In a^n, n is negative.
- The term *positive power* means that the exponent is positive. In a^n, n is positive.

Important properties:

- Dividing powers of the same base: $\dfrac{a^n}{a^m} = a^{n-m}$

- Multiplying powers of the same base: $a^m \times a^n = a^{n+m}$
- Any number raised to the power 1 is the number itself: $a^1 = a$
- Any nonzero number raised to the power 0 is 1: $a^0 = 1$
- Raising a nonzero number to a negative power is the positive power of the reciprocal of the number: $a^{-1} = \dfrac{1}{a}$
- $\left(\dfrac{a}{b}\right)^m = \dfrac{a^n}{b^n}$

- $a^{-n} = \dfrac{1}{a^n}$
- $(a \times b)^n = a^n b^n$
- $[(a^m)]^n = a^{mn}$

Example A.1
Simplify: $a^3 \times a^5$

Solution:

$a^3 \times a^5 = a^{3+5} = a^8$

Example A.2

Simplify: $[(a^2)]^3$

Solution:

$[(a^2)]^3 = a^{2 \times 3} = a^6$

RADICALS

Radicals *undo* exponentiation. The radical sign, $\sqrt[n]{a}$, is used to indicate "the *n*th root of *a*," the number that equals *a* when raised to the *n*th power. If *n* is omitted, the radical is the square root of *a*; *n* is understood to equal 2.

The expression $\sqrt[n]{x}$ is a **radical expression.** The symbol $\sqrt{}$ is the **radical sign.** The expression under the radical sign is the **radicand,** and *n* is the **index.**

If $x = \sqrt[n]{a}$, then $x^n = a$. For example, $4 = \sqrt[2]{16}$ since $4^2 = 16$.

Adding or Subtracting Radical Expressions

When like terms exist, adding and subtracting change the coefficient of the radical but not the radical itself.

$a\sqrt{x} + b\sqrt{x} = (a+b)\sqrt{x}$

$3\sqrt[n]{x} - 7\sqrt[n]{x} = -4\sqrt[n]{x}$

Perform mathematical operations on a radical as if the radical was a variable.

Multiplying Radical Expressions

The Product Property of Radicals is $\sqrt[n]{a} \cdot \sqrt[n]{b} = \sqrt[n]{ab}$, where all radicals have the same index *n*, $a \geq 0$ and $b \geq 0$.

Dividing Radical Expressions

The Quotient Property states that $\left(\sqrt[n]{\dfrac{a}{b}}\right) = \dfrac{\sqrt[n]{a}}{\sqrt[n]{b}}$ where $b \neq 0$.

The fraction must be rationalized (meaning that there are no fractional radicands and no radical signs used in the denominator). Therefore, the numerator and denominator need to be multiplied by $\sqrt[n]{b}$ $n - 1$ times so that the denominator becomes *b*.

$$\left(\sqrt[n]{\frac{a}{b}}\right) = \frac{\sqrt[n]{a}}{\sqrt[n]{b}} = \frac{\sqrt[n]{a}\left(\sqrt[n]{b}\right)^{n-1}}{b}$$

POLYNOMIALS

Polynomials are sums of monomials. Other names for these monomials are *terms* or *addends*. In standard form, a polynomial in one variable is written

$$a_n x^n + a_{n-1} x^{x-1} + a_{n-2} x^{n-2} + \ldots + a_1 x + a_0$$

where *n* is a positive integer and a_0 through a_n are real number coefficients.

The **order** or **degree** of a single-variable polynomial is the value of the greatest exponent of the polynomial.

If a polynomial has more than one variable, its order is the greatest of the set of sums of the exponents in each term.

For example, the degree of $7x^2 + y - 10xy^4$ is 5 since the first term has degree 2, the second term has degree 1, and the third term has degree $1 + 4 = 5$.

Addition and Subtraction of Polynomials

To add polynomials, add the coefficients of like terms (terms with the same variables raised to the same powers). For example, $4xy - 9xy + 4xp = -5xy + 4xp$.

Multiplication of Polynomials

Multiplying a Polynomial by a Monomial

To multiply a polynomial by a monomial, distribute the monomial to each term of the polynomial. The final polynomial should have as many terms as the original polynomial (as long as the monomial is nonzero).

Example A.3

Multiply: $3x^2 - 7x + 4$ by $2x$

Solution:

Distribute the monomial to multiply each term of the polynomial:
$2x(3x^2) - 2x(7x) + 2x(4) = 6x^3 - 14x^2 + 8x$

Multiplying Two Polynomials

To multiply two polynomials, break the work into several problems. Each requires the multiplication of a monomial by a polynomial. Then add the results of these simpler problems to get the answer.

Example A.4

Multiply: $7x + 5$ and $3x - 1$

Solution:

$(7x + 6)(3x - 1) = 7x(3x - 1) + 6(3x - 1) = 7x(3x) + 7x(-1) + 6(3x) + 6(-1) = 21x^2 - 7x + 18x - 6$
$= 21x^2 + 11x - 6$

Division of Polynomials

Dividing a Polynomial by a Monomial

Dividing a polynomial by a monomial is very similar to multiplying a polynomial by a monomial. Distribute the monomial division to the terms of the polynomial. Then reduce the problem to several cases of dividing one monomial by another.

Dividing Polynomials Using Synthetic Division

Synthetic division is a shorthand method that allows the quick division of a polynomial by a first order term of the form $x - d$. This method drops the variables in the polynomials and uses only their coefficients to calculate the quotient. The result of a synthetic division problem is a set of coefficients that determines the quotient and the remainder of the problem.

Example A.5

Divide: $3x^4 + x + 7$ by $x + 1$

Solution:

$3x^4 + x + 7 \div x + 1$ is written as shown below, and the result gives the coefficients of a polynomial of degree 3, one less than the degree of the dividend. The zeros are placeholders for x^3 and x^2 terms. The value of d in this example is -1. That is, the divisor $x + 1$ is rewritten as $x - (-1)$ to meet the required form $x - d$ for synthetic division.

$$\begin{array}{r|rrrrr} -1 & 3 & 0 & 0 & 1 & 7 \\ & & -3 & 3 & -3 & 2 \\ \hline & 3 & -3 & 3 & -2 & 9 \end{array}$$

First, bring down the leading coefficient of the polynomial to the third row.

$$\begin{array}{r|rrrrr} -1 & 3 & 0 & 0 & 1 & 7 \\ \hline & 3 & & & & \end{array}$$

Next, multiply this unchanged leading coefficient by the value of d, in this case -1. $3 \cdot -1 = -3$. Write this value above the line in the next column.

$$
\begin{array}{r|rrrrr}
-1 & 3 & 0 & 0 & 1 & 7 \\
   &   & -3 &   &   &   \\
\hline
   & 3 &   &   &   &
\end{array}
$$

Add the values in this column. $0 + (-3) = -3$. Write this value at the end of the column.

$$
\begin{array}{r|rrrrr}
-1 & 3 & 0 & 0 & 1 & 7 \\
   &   & -3 &   &   &   \\
\hline
   & 3 & -3 &   &   &
\end{array}
$$

Multiply the -3 from the last step by -1. $(-3) \cdot (-1) = 3$. Write this value above the line in the next column.

$$
\begin{array}{r|rrrrr}
-1 & 3 & 0 & 0 & 1 & 7 \\
   &   & -3 & 3 &   &   \\
\hline
   & 3 & -3 &   &   &
\end{array}
$$

Add the values in the column: $0 + 3 = 3$. Write this value at the end of the column.

$$
\begin{array}{r|rrrrr}
-1 & 3 & 0 & 0 & 1 & 7 \\
   &   & -3 & 3 &   &   \\
\hline
   & 3 & -3 & 3 &   &
\end{array}
$$

Multiply the 3 from the last step by -1. $3 \cdot (-1) = -3$. Write this value above the line in the next column.

$$
\begin{array}{r|rrrrr}
-1 & 3 & 0 & 0 & 1 & 7 \\
   &   & -3 & 3 & -3 &   \\
\hline
   & 3 & -3 & 3 &   &
\end{array}
$$

Add the values in the column. $1 + (-3) = -2$. Write this value at the end of the column.

$$
\begin{array}{r|rrrrr}
-1 & 3 & 0 & 0 & 1 & 7 \\
   &   & -3 & 3 & -3 &   \\
\hline
   & 3 & -3 & 3 & -2 &
\end{array}
$$

Multiply -2 by -1. $(-2) \cdot (-1) = 2$. Write this value above the line in the next column.

$$
\begin{array}{r|rrrrr}
-1 & 3 & 0 & 0 & 1 & 7 \\
   &   & -3 & 3 & -3 & 2 \\
\hline
   & 3 & -3 & 3 & -2 &
\end{array}
$$

Add the values in the column: $7 + 2 = 9$. Write this value at the end of column. It is the remainder.

$$
\begin{array}{r|rrrrr}
-1 & 3 & 0 & 0 & 1 & 7 \\
   &   & -3 & 3 & -3 & 2 \\
\hline
   & 3 & -3 & 3 & -2 & 9
\end{array}
$$

This result means that $(3x^4 + x + 7) \div (x + 1) = 3x^3 - 3x^2 + 3x - 2$ with a remainder of 9.

FACTORING

Factoring involves writing a polynomial as the product of polynomials and/or monomials.

Factoring a Monomial from a Polynomial

The simplest kind of factor of a polynomial is a monomial. The monomial must be a factor of each term of the polynomial.

Factoring by Grouping

The method of grouping rewrites a polynomial as a product of two or more polynomials. The method involves first finding a greatest common factor (GCF) of the polynomial. Once the GCF has been factored out, the remaining polynomial can be rewritten as the sum of two (or more) polynomial terms, each containing the same factor. Treating that factor as a single variable, these like terms can then be combined.

Example A.6

Factor $2x^4 - 4x^3 + 2x^2 - 4x$.

Solution:

$= 2x(x^3 - 2x^2 + x - 2)$
$= 2x[x^2(x - 2) + 1(x - 2)]$
$= 2x(x^2 + 1)(x - 2)$

Factoring Second-Degree Trinomials with Leading Coefficient of 1

Factoring a Trinomial in the Form $x^2 + bx + c$

Rewrite the expression as the product of two binomials. To complete the binomials, find the numbers whose sum is b and product c.

Example A.7

Factor $x^2 + 3x + 2$.

Solution:

$x^2 + 3x + 2 = (x + f)(x + g)$

The conditions that f and g must satisfy are:

$fg = 2$
$f + g = 3$

The solution is $f = 1$ and $g = 2$.
The expression factors as:
$(x + 1)(x + 2)$

There are many ways of arranging factoring work. Any second-degree trinomial can be reduced to a second-degree trinomial with a leading coefficient of 1 by factoring out the leading coefficient from the trinomial. For example, $3x^2 + 6x + 12$ can be rewritten as $3(x^2 + 2x + 4)$.

Factoring Special Products

Factoring the Difference of Two Perfect Squares

$a^2x^2 - b^2 = (ax + b)(ax - b)$

Factoring a Perfect Square Trinomial

$(px + q)^2 = (px + q)(px + q) = p^2x^2 + 2pqx + q^2$

Factoring the Sum or Difference of Two Perfect Cubes

$a^3 - b^3 = (a - b)(a^2 + ab + b^2)$
$a^3 + b^3 = (a + b)(a^2 - ab + b^2)$

FOIL

FOIL is a method used to find the product of two binomials.
$$(ax + b)(cx + d) = acx^2 + (ad + bc)x + bd$$

In the acronym FOIL:

- F stands for the product of the first terms of each binomial: $ax \cdot cx = acx^2$.
- O stands for the product of the outside terms: adx.
- I stands for the product of the inside terms: bcx.
- L stands for the product of the last terms: bd.

The sum of the O and I products is $(ad + bc)x$.
The sum of all four products is $acx^2 + (ad + bc)x + bd = (ax + b)(cx + d)$.

Example A.8
Multiply: $(x + 4)$ by $(x + 3)$

Solution:
$(ax + b)(cx + d) = acx^2 + (ad + bc)x + bd$
For this example, $a = 1$, $b = 4$, $c = 1$, and $d = 3$.
The solution is $(x + 4)(x + 3) = x^2 + 7x + 12$.

FORMS OF FUNCTIONS

Linear

A *linear function* is a first-degree polynomial function of one variable. The graph of a linear function is a straight line.

A linear function written as $y = f(x) = mx + b$ is in slope-intercept form. The graph of $y = mx + b$ intersects the y-axis at the intercept $(0, b)$, b units from the x-axis. The slope of the line is m. (See Figure A.5.)

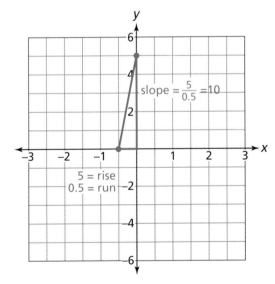

FIGURE A.5 Graph of Linear Function $y = 10x + 5$

Quadratic

A quadratic function has the form $f(x) = ax^2 + bx + c$, where a, b, and c are real numbers and a is not equal to zero.

- $f(x) = ax^2 + bx + c$ is called the **general form.**
- $f(x) = a(x - h)^2 + k$ is called the **vertex form** (or **standard form**), where h and k are the x- and y-coordinates of the vertex, respectively.

The graph of a quadratic function is a curve called a **parabola.** All parabolas are symmetric with respect to a line called the **axis of symmetry.** A parabola intersects its axis of symmetry at a point called the **vertex** of the parabola.

For $f(x) = ax^2 + bx + c$:

- If $a > 0$ (is a positive number), the parabola opens upward.
- If $a < 0$ (is a negative number), the parabola opens downward.

The axis of symmetry is the line $x = -\dfrac{b}{2a}$.

Figure A.6 shows upward- and downward-opening parabolas.

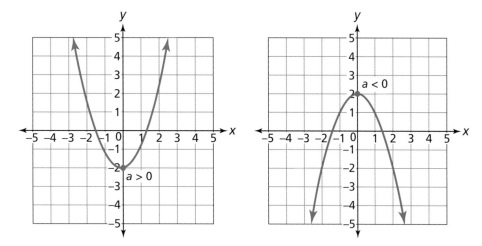

FIGURE A.6 Parabola Graphs

Cubic

Cubic functions have the form $ax^3 + bx^2 + cx + d$. The formula to find the roots of a cubic function is very long and involved.

The graph of a cubic function is shown in Figure A.7. Notice that it intersects the *x*-axis at three points, giving three roots. But also notice that if it is shifted up or down, it may have only one or two distinct roots.

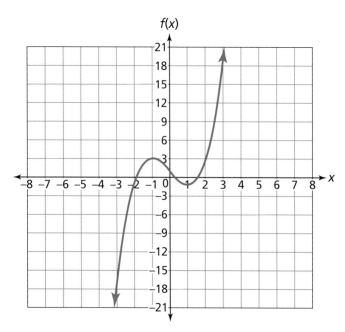

FIGURE A.7 Cubic Graph

Exponential

Exponential Functions

An **exponential function** is a function in the form $f(x) = a^x$. The **base,** a, is a positive number not equal to 1. Often the value of the base is e, which represents the value 2.718281828….

The graph of the function $f(x) = a^x$ has the x-axis as an **asymptote.** The graph always contains the point (0, 1). (See Figure A.8.)

a.

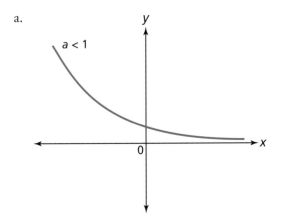

b.

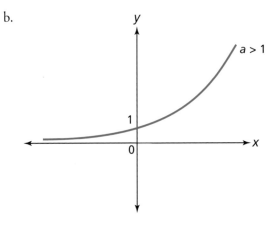

FIGURE A.8 Exponential Function

Logarithmic

Another way of writing $x = a^y$ is $y = \log_a x$, or $f(x) = \log_a x$. The function $f(x) = \log_a x$ is called a **logarithmic function.**

For $f(x) = \log_a x$, x can be any real numbers greater than 0, while the function values can be any real number. (See Figure A.9.)

a. $y = \log$ base 3 of x

b. $y = \log$ base 0.5 of x

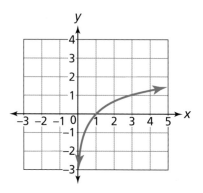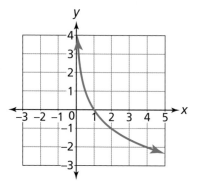

FIGURE A.9 Logarithmic Functions

APPENDIX B

SOLUTIONS TO END OF CHAPTER REVIEW QUESTIONS

CHAPTER 1 REVIEW OF MATHEMATICS FUNDAMENTALS

Addition and Subtraction of Integers

1.1 Add: $(-92) + 92 + (-10)$

Solution:

$(-92) + 92 + (-10) = (-92 + 92) + (-10) = 0 + (-10) = -10$

1.2 Add: $-2 + (-7) + 4 + (-6)$

Solution:

$$\begin{aligned} -2 + (-7) + 4 + (-6) &= -9 + 4 + (-6) \\ &= -5 + (-6) \\ &= -11 \end{aligned}$$

1.3 Add: $-126 + (-247) + (-358) + 338$

Solution:

$$\begin{aligned} -373 + (-358) + 338 &= -731 + 338 \\ &= -393 \end{aligned}$$

1.4 Subtract: $-28 - (-28)$

Solution:

$$\begin{aligned} -28 - (-28) &= -28 + 28 \\ &= 0 \end{aligned}$$

1.5 Subtract: $-8 - 30 - 11 - 7$

Solution:

$$\begin{aligned} -8 + (-30) + 11 + (-7) &= -38 + 11 + (-7) \\ &= -27 + (-7) \\ &= -34 \end{aligned}$$

1.6 Subtract: $42 - 30 - 65 - (-11)$

Solution:

$$\begin{aligned} 42 - 30 + (-65) + 11 &= 12 + (-65) + 11 \\ &= -53 + 11 \\ &= -42 \end{aligned}$$

1.7 The record high in a certain city in the month of June is 109°F, and the record low in the month of January is −21°F. What is the difference between the two temperatures?

Solution:

Set up the subtraction problem $109 - (-21)$ and solve as follows:
$109 + 21 = 130°F$

Multiplication and Division of Integers

1.8 Multiply: $4\,(-5)\,(-2)\,(-6)$

Solution:
$$-20\,(-2)\,(-6) = 40\,(-6)$$
$$= -240$$

1.9 Multiply: $3\,(-5)\,(-4)\,(9)$

Solution:
$$-15\,(-4)\,(9) = 60\,(9)$$
$$= 540$$

1.10 Find $(-7)^2$.

Solution:
$$(-7)^2 = (-7)\,(-7) = 49$$

1.11 Find $(-5)^3$.

Solution:
$$(-5)^3 = (-5)\,(-5)\,(-5) = 25\,(-5) = -125$$

1.12 Find $(-1)^9$.

Solution: -1

Since there are an odd number of negative factors, the answer will be negative.

1.13 Find -8^2.

Solution:
$$-8^2 = -(8)(8) = -64$$

1.14 Divide: $-156 \div (-13)$

Solution: 12

1.15 Find the quotient of 144 and −24.

Solution: $144 \div (-24) = -6$

1.16 The combined scores of the top 11 golfers in a tournament equaled −44. What was the average score of each of the 11 players?

Solution:

$-44 \div 11 = -4$
Hence the average score is 4 under par.

Operations with Rational Numbers

1.17 Solve: $\dfrac{1}{8} + \dfrac{3}{16} - \left(-\dfrac{1}{2}\right)$

Solution:

Note the LCD $(8, 16, 2) = 16$; then the above becomes:

$$\dfrac{2}{16} + \dfrac{3}{16} - \left(-\dfrac{8}{16}\right) = \dfrac{5}{16} + \dfrac{8}{16} = \dfrac{13}{16}$$

1.18 Multiply: $\left(\dfrac{1}{2}\right)\left(-\dfrac{3}{8}\right)\left(\dfrac{2}{5}\right)$

Solution:

$$\left(-\dfrac{3}{16}\right)\left(\dfrac{2}{5}\right) = -\dfrac{6}{80}$$
$$= -\dfrac{3}{40}$$

1.19 Multiply: $25.355 \times (-0.5)$

Solution:

-12.6775

1.20 Divide: $-26.22 \div (-6.9)$

Solution: 3.8

1.21 Eleanor had a balance in her bank account of \$1,369.23. She paid her bills with checks written for \$679.65, \$567.35, and \$240.34. What is her current account balance?

Solution:

Her balance is giving by the expression:
$$1369.23 - 679.65 - 567.35 - 240.34 = 689.58 - 567.35 - 240.34$$
$$= 122.23 - 240.34$$
$$= -118.11$$

Using Order of Operations

1.22 Solve: $-5 \cdot (3 - 9)$

Solution:

$$-5 \cdot (3 - 9) = -5 \cdot (-6) = 30$$

1.23 Solve: $-12 - 3 + 7$

Solution:

$$-12 - 3 + 7 = -12 + (-3) + 7$$
$$= -15 + 7$$
$$= -8$$

1.24 Solve: $18 \div 2 \cdot (-3)$

Solution:

$$18 \div 2 \cdot (-3) = 9 \cdot (-3) = -27$$

1.25 Solve: $10 + 2 \cdot (15 + (-5))$

Solution:

$$\begin{aligned} 10 + 2 \cdot (15 + (-5)) &= 10 + 2 \cdot (10) \\ &= 10 + 20 \\ &= 30 \end{aligned}$$

1.26 Solve: $(-2)^3 - 20$

Solution:

$$\begin{aligned} (-2)^3 - 20 &= (-2)(-2)(-2) - 20 \\ &= -8 - 20 \\ &= -8 + (-20) \\ &= -28 \end{aligned}$$

1.27 Solve: $-23 - (6 + (-9))$

Solution:

$$\begin{aligned} -23 - (6 + (-9)) &= -23 - (-3) \\ &= -23 + 3 \\ &= -20 \end{aligned}$$

1.28 Solve: $12 - 2 \cdot (9 - 8)$

Solution:

$$\begin{aligned} 12 - 2 \cdot (9 - 8) &= 12 - 2 \cdot (1) \\ &= 12 - 2 \\ &= 10 \end{aligned}$$

1.29 Solve: $-1.5 \cdot (7 - 8)^2$

Solution:

$$\begin{aligned} -1.5 \cdot (7 - 8)^2 &= -1.5 \cdot (-1)^2 \\ &= -1.5 \cdot (-1)^2 - 1.5 \cdot (1) \\ &= -1.5 \end{aligned}$$

1.30 Solve: $-4^2 - 5 \cdot (-2)^2$

Solution:

$$\begin{aligned} -4^2 - 5 \cdot (-2)^2 &= -16 - 5 \cdot (4) \\ &= -16 - 20 \\ &= -16 + -20 \\ &= -36 \end{aligned}$$

1.31 Solve: $\dfrac{(6-8)}{(12-9)}$

Solution:

$$\frac{(6-8)}{(12-9)} = \frac{(6+(-8))}{(12+(-9))} = -\frac{2}{3}$$

1.32 Solve: $\dfrac{(15-9)}{(9-1)}$

Solution:

$$\frac{(15-9)}{(9-1)}=\frac{6}{8}=\frac{3}{4}$$

1.33 Solve: $\dfrac{[(2^2)+(-1)]}{(6-3)}$

Solution:

$$\frac{[(2^2)+(-1)]}{(6-3)}=\frac{[(4)+(-1)]}{(6-3)}=\frac{3}{3}=1$$

1.34 Solve: $\dfrac{1}{5}\cdot(16-21)$

Solution:

$$\frac{1}{5}\cdot(16-21)=\frac{1}{5}\cdot(-5)=-\frac{5}{5}=-1$$

1.35 Solve: $\dfrac{2}{3}\cdot(7-10)$

Solution:

$$\frac{2}{3}\cdot(7-10)=\frac{2}{3}\cdot(-3)=-2$$

Chapter 2 Introduction to Algebra

2.1 Use the Distributive Law to rewrite the following expression: $8(z+3)$

Solution:
$$8(z+3)=8\cdot z+8\cdot 3$$
$$=8z+24$$

2.2 Use the Distributive Law to rewrite the following expression: $-9(c-2)$

Solution:
$$-9(c-2)=(-9)\cdot c+(-9)\cdot(-2)$$
$$=-9c+18$$

2.3 Write the following expression without parentheses: $-(4u-7v+w)$

Solution:
$$-(4u-7v+w)=(-1)(4u-7v+w)$$
$$=-(-1)(4u)+(-1)(-7v)+(-1)(w)$$
$$=-4u+7v-w$$

2.4 Combine the like terms in the following expression: $20s + 14t - 10s + t$

Solution:

$$
\begin{aligned}
20s + 14t - 10s + t &= 20s - 10s + 14t + t \\
&= (20 - 10)s + (14 + 1)t \\
&= 10s + 15t
\end{aligned}
$$

2.5 Combine the like terms in the following expression: $3x^2 + 5xy - 6xy - 2x^2$

Solution:

$$
\begin{aligned}
3x^2 + 5xy - 6yx - 2x^2 &= 3x^2 - 2x^2 + 5xy - 6yx \\
&= 3x^2 - 2x^2 + 5xy - 6xy \\
&= (3 - 2)x^2 + (5 - 6)xy \\
&= 1x^2 + (-1)xy \\
&= x^2 - xy
\end{aligned}
$$

2.6 Simplify the following expression using the Distributive Law and combining like terms:

$6x - 7[4(x + 3) - (x - 8)] - 2$

Solution:

$$
\begin{aligned}
6x - 7\big[4(x + 3) - (x - 8)\big] - 2 &= 6x - 7\big[4x + 12 - (x - 8)\big] - 2 \\
&= 6x - 7\big[4x + 12 - x + 8\big] - 2 \\
&= 6x - 7\big[4x - x + 12 + 8\big] - 2 \\
&= 6x - 7\big[3x + 20\big] - 2 \\
&= 6x - 21x - 140 - 2 \\
&= -15x - 142
\end{aligned}
$$

2.7 Solve: $3(1 - x) + 10 = 14 - 2(x + 3)$

Solution: $x = 5$

2.8 Solve: $\dfrac{2}{3}(x - 2) + \dfrac{3}{4} = \dfrac{5}{4}(2x + 3)$

Solution: $x = -\dfrac{26}{11}$

2.9 Solve using the Addition Property of Equations: $x - 8 = 14$

Solution:

$$
\begin{aligned}
x - 8 &= 14 \\
x - 8 + 8 &= 14 + 8 \\
x &= 22
\end{aligned}
$$

Check solution:

$$
\begin{aligned}
x - 8 &= 14 \\
(22) - 8 &= 14? \\
14 &= 14? \\
&\quad Yes!
\end{aligned}
$$

2.10 Solve using the Addition Property of Equations: $z + \dfrac{5}{8} = \dfrac{15}{16}$

Solution:

$$z + \frac{5}{8} = \frac{15}{16}$$

$$z + \frac{5}{8} - \frac{5}{8} = \frac{15}{16} - \frac{5}{8}$$

$$z = \frac{15}{16} - \frac{10}{16}$$

$$z = \frac{5}{16}$$

Check solution:

$$z + \frac{5}{8} = \frac{15}{16}$$

$$\left(\frac{5}{16}\right) + \frac{5}{8} = \frac{15}{16}?$$

$$\frac{5}{16} + \frac{10}{16} = \frac{15}{16}?$$

$$\frac{15}{16} = \frac{15}{16}?$$

$$Yes!$$

2.11 Solve using the Multiplication Property of Equations: $16c = -48$

Solution:

$$16c = -48$$

$$\left(\frac{1}{16}\right)(16c) = \left(\frac{1}{16}\right)(-48)$$

$$\left(\frac{16}{16}\right)c = \frac{-48}{16}$$

$$c = -3$$

Check solution:

$$16c = -48$$

$$16(-3) = -48?$$

$$-48 = -48?$$

$$Yes!$$

2.12 Solve using the Multiplication Property of Equations: $-\dfrac{2}{3}y = 24$

Solution:

$$-\frac{2}{3}y = 24$$

$$\left(-\frac{3}{2}\right)\left(-\frac{2}{3}y\right) = \left(-\frac{3}{2}\right)(24)$$

$$\left(\frac{3}{2} \cdot \frac{2}{3}\right)y = -\frac{3 \cdot 24}{2}$$

$$y = -36$$

Check solution:

$$-\frac{2}{3}y = 24$$

$$-\frac{2}{3}(-36) = 24?$$

$$24 = 24?$$

$$Yes!$$

Solve for the variable

2.13 Solve: $5p - 4 = 16$

Solution:

$$5p - 4 = 16$$

$$5p - 4 + 4 = 16 + 4$$

$$5p = 20$$

$$\left(\frac{1}{5}\right)(5p) = \left(\frac{1}{5}\right)(20)$$

$$\frac{5p}{5} = \frac{20}{5}$$

$$p = 4$$

Check solution:

$$5p - 4 = 16$$

$$p = 4$$

$$5(4) - 4 = 16?$$

$$20 - 4 = 16?$$

$$16 = 16?$$

$$Yes!$$

2.14 Solve: $-6x + 7 = -41$

Solution:

$$-6x + 7 = -47$$

$$-6x + 7 - 7 = -41 - 7$$

$$-6x = -48$$

$$\frac{-6x}{-6} = \frac{-48}{-6}$$

$$x = 8$$

2.15 Solve: $-\dfrac{1}{4}y - 1 = 15$

Solution:

$$-\frac{1}{4}y - 1 = 15$$

$$-\frac{1}{4}y - 1 + 1 = 15 + 1$$

$$-\frac{1}{4}y = 16$$

$$(-4)\left(-\frac{1}{4}\right)y = (-4)(16)$$

$$y = -64$$

2.16 Solve: $2(x - 3) = 9$

Solution:

$$2(x - 3) = 9$$

$$2x - 6 = 9$$

$$2x - 6 + 6 = 9 + 6$$

$$2x = 15$$

$$\frac{2x}{2} = \frac{15}{2}$$

$$x = \frac{15}{2}$$

2.17 Solve: $3(2y + 1) = 27$

Solution:

$$3(2y + 1) = 27$$

$$6y + 3 = 27$$

$$6y + 3 - 3 = 27 - 3$$

$$6y = 24$$

$$\frac{6y}{6} = \frac{24}{6}$$

$$y = 4$$

2.18 Solve: $-2(z + 4) = -12$

Solution:

$$-2z - 8 = -12$$

$$-2z - 8 + 8 = -12 + 8$$

$$-2z = -4$$

$$\frac{-2z}{-2} = \frac{-4}{-2}$$

$$z = 2$$

2.19 Solve: $-5(-3x + 1) = -45$

Solution:

$$-5(-3x + 1) = -45$$
$$15x - 5 = -45$$
$$15x - 5 + 5 = -45 + 5$$
$$15x = -40$$
$$\frac{15x}{15} = -\frac{40}{15}$$
$$x = -\frac{8}{3}$$

2.20 Solve: $\left(-\dfrac{1}{2}\right)(4x + 6) = 10$

Solution:

$$\left(-\frac{1}{2}\right)(4x + 6) = 10$$
$$\left(-\frac{1}{2}\right)(4x) + \left(-\frac{1}{2}\right)(6) = 10$$
$$-2x - 3 = 10$$
$$-2x - 3 + 3 = 10 + 3$$
$$-2x = 13$$
$$\frac{-2x}{-2} = \frac{13}{-2}$$
$$x = -\frac{13}{2}$$

2.21 Solve: $-2(x + 1) + x = 12$

Solution:

$$-2(x + 1) + x = 12$$
$$-2x - 2 + x = 12$$
$$-x - 2 = 12$$
$$-x - 2 + 2 = 12 + 2$$
$$-x = 14$$
$$(-1)(-x) = (-1)(14)$$
$$x = -14$$

2.22 Solve: $4x + 11 = 6x - 3$

Solution:

$$4x + 11 = 6x - 3$$
$$4x + 11 - 11 = 6x - 3 - 11$$
$$4x = 6x - 14$$
$$4x - 6x = 6x - 6x - 14$$
$$-2x = -14$$
$$\frac{-2x}{-2} = \frac{-14}{-2}$$
$$x = 7$$

Check solution:

$$4x + 11 = 6x - 3$$
$$x = 7?$$
$$4(7) + 11 = 6(7) - 3?$$
$$28 + 11 = 42 - 3?$$
$$39 = 39?$$
$$Yes!$$

2.23 Solve: $-\frac{1}{2}z + \frac{2}{5} = \frac{7}{5}$

Solution:

$$-\frac{1}{2}z + \frac{2}{5} = \frac{7}{5}$$
$$-\frac{1}{2}z + \frac{2}{5} - \frac{2}{5} = \frac{7}{5} - \frac{2}{5}$$
$$-\frac{1}{2}z = \frac{5}{5}$$
$$-\frac{1}{2}z = 1$$
$$(-2)\left(-\frac{1}{2}z\right) = (-2)(1)$$
$$z = -2$$

Check solution:

$$-\frac{1}{2}z + \frac{2}{5} = \frac{7}{5}$$
$$z = -2?$$
$$-\frac{1}{2}(-2) + \frac{2}{5} = \frac{7}{5}?$$
$$1 + \frac{2}{5} = \frac{7}{5}?$$
$$\frac{5}{5} + \frac{2}{5} = \frac{7}{5}?$$
$$\frac{7}{5} = \frac{7}{5}?$$
$$Yes!$$

2.24 Solve: $-3x + 4 = 2x - 14$

Solution:

$$-3x + 4 = 2x - 14$$
$$-3x + 4 + 3x = 2x - 14 + 3x$$
$$4 = 5x - 14$$
$$4 + 14 = 5x - 14 + 14$$
$$18 = 5x$$
$$\frac{18}{5} = \frac{5x}{5}$$
$$\frac{18}{5} = x$$
$$x = \frac{18}{5}$$

2.25 Solve: $9x - 1 = -x + 49$

Solution:

$$9x - 1 + x = -x + 49 + x$$
$$10x - 1 = 49$$
$$10x - 1 + 1 = 49 + 1$$
$$10x = 50$$
$$\frac{10x}{10} = \frac{50}{10}$$
$$x = 5$$

2.26 Solve: $11x + 3 = 3x + 35$

Solution:

$$11x + 3 = 3x + 35$$
$$11x + 3 - 3x = 3x + 35 - 3x$$
$$8x + 3 = 35$$
$$8x + 3 - 3 = 35 - 3$$
$$8x = 32$$
$$\frac{8x}{8} = \frac{32}{8}$$
$$x = 4$$

2.27 Solve: $4p - 9 = -2p + 21$

Solution:

$$4p - 9 = -2p + 21$$
$$4p - 9 + 2p = -2p + 21 + 2p$$
$$6p - 9 = 21$$
$$6p - 9 + 9 = 21 + 9$$
$$6p = 60$$
$$\frac{6p}{6} = \frac{60}{6}$$
$$p = 10$$

2.28 Solve: $5m + 1 = -10m - 19$

Solution:

$$5m + 1 = -10m - 19$$
$$5m + 1 + 10m = -10m - 19 + 10m$$
$$15m + 1 = -19$$
$$15m + 1 - 1 = -19 - 1$$
$$15m = -20$$
$$\frac{15m}{15} = -\frac{20}{15}$$
$$m = -\frac{4}{3}$$

2.29 Solve: $-3(x - 4) = 9x$

Solution:

$$-3(x - 4) = 9x$$
$$-3x + 12 = 9x$$
$$-3x + 12 + 3x = 9x + 3x$$
$$12 = 12x$$
$$\frac{12}{12} = \frac{12x}{12}$$
$$1 = x$$
$$x = 1$$

2.30 Solve: $7(x - 3) = 5(x + 3)$

Solution:

$$7(x - 3) = 5(x + 3)$$
$$7x - 21 = 5x + 15$$
$$7x - 21 - 5x = 5x + 15 - 5x$$
$$2x - 21 = 15$$
$$2x - 21 + 21 = 15 + 21$$
$$2x = 36$$
$$\frac{2x}{2} = \frac{36}{2}$$
$$x = 18$$

2.31 Solve: $-2(2x - 3) = 3(x + 1) + 10$

Solution:

$$-2(2x - 3) = 3(x + 1) + 10$$
$$-4x + 6 = 3x + 3 + 10$$
$$-4x + 6 = 3x + 13$$
$$-4x + 6 + 4x = 3x + 13 + 4x$$
$$6 = 7x + 13$$
$$6 - 13 = 7x + 13 - 13$$
$$-7 = 7x$$
$$-\frac{7}{7} = \frac{7x}{7}$$
$$-1 = x$$
$$x = -1$$

2.32 Solve: $2m - 3(m + 1) = 4(m + 3)$

Solution:

$$2m - 3(m + 1) = 4(m + 3)$$
$$2m - 3m - 3 = 4m + 12$$
$$-m - 3 = 4m + 12$$
$$-m - 3 + m = 4m + 12 + m$$
$$-3 = 5m + 12$$
$$-3 - 12 = 5m + 12 - 12$$
$$-15 = 5m$$
$$-\frac{15}{5} = \frac{5m}{5}$$
$$-3 = m$$
$$m = -3$$

2.33 Solve: $-4(b + 1) + 2b = 3(2b - 1)$

Solution:

$$-4b - 4 + 2b = 6b - 3$$
$$-2b - 4 = 6b - 3$$
$$-2b - 4 + 2b = 6b - 3 + 2b$$
$$-4 = 8b - 3$$
$$-4 + 3 = 8b - 3 + 3$$
$$-1 = 8b$$
$$-\frac{1}{8} = \frac{8b}{8}$$
$$-\frac{1}{8} = b$$
$$b = -\frac{1}{8}$$

Solve

2.34 Five times a number is equal to 3 less than twice the number. Find the number.

Solution:

Let $x =$ the number.

$$5x = 2x - 3$$
$$5x - 2x = 2x - 3 - 2x$$
$$3x = -3$$
$$\frac{3x}{3} = -\frac{3}{3}$$
$$x = -1$$

2.35 Frog Pond Golf Course charges non-members $60.00 for each round of golf. The membership fee is $100.00, and members pay $40.00 for each round of golf. For how many rounds will the total of charges be the same for members and non-members?

Solution:

Let x represent the number of rounds of golf.
The cost for non-members is $60x$, and the cost for members is $100 + 40x$

$$60x = 100 + 40x$$
$$60x - 40x = 100 + 40x - 40x$$
$$20x = 100$$
$$\frac{20x}{20} = \frac{100}{20}$$
$$x = 5$$

CHAPTER 3 LINEAR EQUATIONS AND INEQUALITIES

Introduction to Linear Equations

3.1 Solve: $2x - 3 = 15$

Solution: $x = 9$

3.2 Solve: $0.3x + 20 = 1.2x - 25$

Solution: $x = 50$

Application: Solving Problems Using Formulas

3.3 Set up an equation and solve. The length of a rectangle is twice its width. If the perimeter is 36 meters, what are its dimensions?

Solution:

6 m $\times$ 12 m

3.4 Set up an equation and solve. The width of a rectangle is 3 more than twice its length. The perimeter is 60 feet. Find the width and length of the rectangle.

Solution:

If x is the length, and $2x + 3$ is the width, then

$$2(x) + 2(2x + 3) = 60$$
$$2x + 4x + 6 = 60$$
$$6x + 6 = 60$$
$$6x + 6 - 6 = 60 - 6$$
$$6x = 54$$
$$\frac{6x}{6} = \frac{54}{6}$$
$$x = 9$$

Length = 9 feet, width = 2(9) + 3 = 21 feet

3.5 Set up an equation and solve. Three consecutive odd integers have a sum of 51; find the integers.

Solution:

15, 17, and 19 are the integers.

3.6 Set up an equation and solve. Find three consecutive even integers such that twice the largest is equal to two more than three times the smallest.

Solution:

Represent the three integers as x, $x + 2$, and $x + 4$.
x is the smallest, and $x + 4$ is the largest, so $2(x + 4) = x$

$$2x + 8 = 3x + 2$$
$$2x + 8 - 2x = 3x + 2 - 2x$$
$$8 = x + 2$$
$$8 - 2 = x + 2 - 2$$
$$6 = x$$
$$x = 6$$

The three integers are 6, 8, and 10

Translating Sentences into Equations

3.7 Translate the following English phrase into an algebraic expression: three more than twice some number.

Solution: $2x + 3$

3.8 Translate the following English phrase into an algebraic expression: four less than five times some number.

Solution: $5x - 4$

3.9 Translate and solve. Nine more than three times a number is -3. Find the number.

Solution:

$$3x + 9 = -3$$
$$3x + 9 - 9 = -3 - 9$$
$$3x = -12$$
$$\frac{3x}{3} = -\frac{12}{3}$$
$$x = -4$$

3.10 Translate and solve. Four less than twice the sum of a number and 2 is 10. Find the number.

Solution:

$$2(x + 2) - 4 = 10$$
$$2x + 4 - 4 = 10$$
$$2x = 10$$
$$\frac{2x}{2} = \frac{10}{2}$$
$$x = 5$$

3.11 Translate and solve. Twice a number is fifteen less than three times the number. Find the number.

Solution:

$$2x = 3x - 15$$
$$2x - 3x = 3x - 15 - 3x$$
$$-x = -15$$
$$(-1)(-x) = (-1)(-15)$$
$$x = 15$$

3.12 If a person invested a third of her money at 6% and two thirds at 9% and received \$450 in interest, find the total money invested.

Solution:

Step 1: Identify the variable.
Let x be the total money invested.
Step 2: Translate.

Then , $\frac{1}{3}x$ is the money invested at 6% and, $\frac{2}{3}x$ is the money invested at 9%. Hence,

$0.06\left(\frac{1}{3}x\right)$ is the interest at 6% and $0.09\left(\frac{2}{3}x\right)$ is the interest at 9%.

Step 3: Write the linear equation.

$$0.06\left(\frac{1}{3}x\right) + 0.09\left(\frac{2}{3}x\right) = 450.$$

Step 4: Solve.

$$0.06\left(\frac{1}{3}x\right) + 0.09\left(\frac{2}{3}x\right) = 450$$

$$0.02x + 0.06x = 450 \qquad \text{Remove parentheses.}$$

$$0.08x = 450 \qquad \text{Combine like terms.}$$

$$\frac{0.08x}{0.08} = \frac{450}{0.08} \qquad \text{Divide both sides by 0.08.}$$

$$x = \$5625$$

3.13 A coffee shop has two types of coffee: Coffee A sells for \$4 per pound and Coffee B sells for \$13 per pound. Mix 90 pounds of Coffee B with Coffee A to get a mixture that will sell for \$10 per pound. How many pounds of Coffee A should be used?

Solution:

Step 1: Identify the variable.
Let x be the number of pounds of Coffee A to be used.

Step 2: Translate.
We want to add x pounds of the \$4 coffee A to 90 pounds of the \$13 coffee B to obtain a total of $x + 90$ pounds of the \$10 per pound mix.

Step 3: Write the linear equation.
$4x + 13(90) = 10(x + 90)$

Step 4: Solve.

$$4x + 13(90) = 10(x + 90)$$

$$4x + 1170 = 10x + 900 \qquad \text{Remove parentheses.}$$

$$1170 - 900 = 10x - 4x \qquad \text{Move variables to one side, values to other}$$

$$270 = 6x$$

$$\frac{270}{6} = \frac{6x}{6} \qquad \text{Divide both side by 6.}$$

$$45 = x$$

Therefore, 45 pounds of the \$4 Coffee A should be used for the mixture.

Mixture and Uniform Motion Problems

3.14 Set up an equation and solve. How much 20% acid must be mixed with 5% acid to make 30 mL of 12% acid?

Solution:

14 mL of 20% acid and 16 mL of 5% acid

3.15 Set up an equation and solve. A plane leaves Chicago flying due east at 200 mph while a train that left two hours earlier is going due west at 70 mph. How much time will it take for them to be 545 miles apart?

Solution:

1.5 hours from the plane's departure or 3.5 hours from the train's

3.16 On a 425 mile trip, John drove for 4 hours and Barry drove for 3 hours. John's rate of speed was 10 mph faster than Barry's rate. Find the rates in miles per hour. How many miles did each drive?

Solution:

Let x represent Barry's rate, and $x + 10$ represent John's rate. Using the distance formula,

Rate	$\times$	Time	$=$	Distance
x		3		$3x$
$x + 10$		4		$4(x + 10)$

Since the total distance is 425 miles,

$$3x + 4(x + 10) = 425$$
$$3x + 4x + 40 = 425$$
$$7x + 40 = 425$$
$$7x + 40 - 40 = 452 - 40$$
$$7x = 385$$
$$\frac{7x}{7} = \frac{385}{7}$$
$$x = 55$$

Barry's rate is 55 mph and John's rate is $55 + 10 = 65$ mph.
Barry drove $55 \times 3 = 165$ miles, and John drove $65 \times 4 = 260$ miles.

3.17 Set up an equation and solve. There are 125 cast members for the play Oliver! 30 members came down with the flu. What percent of cast members had the flu?

Solution:

Let x represent the percent of cast members that had the flu.

$$125x = 30$$
$$x = \frac{30}{125}$$
$$x = .24$$

Since the equation gives the percent as a decimal, multiply by 100 to convert to percent.
24% of the cast had the flu.

3.18 A team lost 8 of the 40 games the played. What percent of games did they win?

Solution:

Since 8 games were lost, $40 - 8 = 32$ games were won.
Let x represent the percent of games won.

$$40x = 32$$
$$x = \frac{32}{40}$$
$$x = 0.8$$

Multiply by 100 to convert to percent.
80% of the games were won.

3.19 How much needs to be invested into a simple interest account paying 4% for 3 years that would result in $540 in interest?

Solution:

$$I = PRT$$
$$540 = P(.04)(3)$$
$$540 = P(.12)$$
$$\frac{540}{(.12)} = P\left(\frac{.12}{.12}\right)$$
$$4500 = P$$

$4500 would need to be invested.

3.20 Brand A of herbal tea costs $2.00 per ounce, and Brand B costs $4.00 per ounce. A merchant would like to create a mixture of the teas to yield 100 ounces that would sell for $2.70 per ounce. How much of each brand would be needed?

Solution:

Let x represent the number of ounces of Brand A, and $100 - x$ represent the number of ounces of Brand B. The total cost of the teas can be represented as $2.00x + 4.00 (100 - x) = 2.70 (100)$

$$2x + 400 - 4x = 270$$
$$-2x + 400 = 270$$
$$-2x + 400 - 400 = 270 - 400$$
$$-2x = -130$$
$$\frac{-2x}{-2} = \frac{-130}{-2}$$
$$x = 65$$

65 ounces of Brand A, and $100 - 65 = 35$ ounces of Brand B would be needed.

First Degree Inequalities

3.21 Solve and graph the solutions: $3x + 1 < 10$

Solution: $x < 3$

3.22 Solve and graph the solutions: $10x + 9 > -15x + 34$

Solution:

$$10x + 9 > -15x + 34$$
$$10x + 9 - 9 > -15x + 34 - 9$$
$$10x > -15x + 25$$
$$10x + 15x > -15x + 25 + 15x$$
$$25x > 25$$
$$\frac{25x}{25} > \frac{25}{25}$$
$$x > 1$$

x > 1

3.23 Solve and graph the solutions: $3(6 - x) \leq -12$

Solution:

$$3(6 - x) \leq -12$$
$$18 - 3x \leq -12$$
$$18 - 3x - 18 \leq -12 - 18$$
$$-3x \leq -30$$
$$\frac{-3x}{(-3)} \leq \frac{-30}{(-3)}$$
$$x \leq 10$$

$x \leq 10$

3.24 Solve and graph the solutions: $9x - 7 > 5(x + 5)$

Solution:

$$9x - 7 > 5(x + 5)$$
$$9x - 7 > 5x + 25$$
$$9x - 7 - 5x > 5x + 25 - 5x$$
$$4x - 7 > 25$$
$$4x - 7 + 7 > 25 + 7$$
$$4x > 32$$
$$\frac{4x}{4} > \frac{32}{4}$$
$$x > 8$$

$x > 8$

3.25 Solve and graph the solutions: $-2(2x - 9) + 3 < 6x + 5$

Solution:

$$-2(2x - 9) + 3 < 6x + 5$$
$$-4x + 18 + 3 < 6x + 5$$
$$-4x + 21 < 6x + 5$$
$$-4x + 21 + 4x < 6x + 5 + 4x$$
$$21 < 2x + 5$$
$$21 - 5 < 2x + 5 - 5$$
$$16 < 2x$$
$$\frac{16}{2} < \frac{2x}{2}$$
$$8 < x$$
$$x > 8$$

$x > 8$

3.26 Solve and graph the solutions: $2 - 3(x - 4) \leq 11$

Solution: $x \geq 1$

3.27 Solve and graph the solutions: $5(4 - x) - 2x \geq 3 - (x - 1)$

Solution:

$$-5(4 - x) - 2x \geq 3 - (x - 1)$$
$$-20 + 5x - 2x \geq 3 - x + 1$$
$$-20 + 3x \geq 4 - x$$
$$-20 + 3x + x \geq 4 - x + x$$
$$-20 + 4x \geq 4$$
$$-20 + 4x + 20 \geq 4 + 20$$
$$4x \geq 24$$
$$\frac{4x}{4} \geq \frac{24}{4}$$
$$x \geq 6$$

x ≥ 6

3.28 Solve and graph the solutions: $12x - 7(x - 3) + 3 > 4 - (2x + 1)$

Solution:

$$12x - 7(x - 3) + 3 > 4 - (2x + 1)$$
$$12x - 7x + 21 + 3 > 4 - 2x - 1$$
$$5x + 24 > 3 - 2x$$
$$5x + 24 + 2x > 3 - 2x + 2x$$
$$7x + 24 > 3$$
$$7x + 24 - 24 > 3 - 24$$
$$7x < -21$$
$$\frac{7x}{7} < \frac{-21}{7}$$
$$x < -3$$

x < -3

Absolute Value Equations and Inequalities

3.29 Solve and graph the solutions: $|x+5|=8$

Solution:

$$x+5=8 \qquad \text{or} \qquad -(x+5)=8$$
$$-x-5=8$$
$$x+5-5=8-5 \qquad \text{or} \qquad -x-5+5=8+5$$
$$x=3 \qquad \text{or} \qquad -x=13$$
$$(-1)(-x)=(-1)(13)$$
$$x=3 \qquad \text{or} \qquad x=-13$$

x = 3 or x = -13

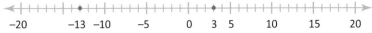

3.30 Solve and graph the solutions: $|2x-3|=5$

Solution: $x=4, -1$

3.31 Solve and graph the solutions: $|x+3|<2$

Solution: $-5<x<-1$

3.32 Solve and graph the solutions: $|x-3|+7=15$

Solution:

$$|x-3|+7-7=15-7$$
$$|x-3|=12$$

$$x-3=12 \qquad \text{or} \qquad -(x-3)=12$$
$$-x+3=12$$
$$x-3+3=12+3 \qquad \text{or} \qquad -x+3-3=12-3$$
$$x=15 \qquad \text{or} \qquad -x=9$$
$$(-1)(-x)=(-1)(9)$$
$$x=15 \qquad \text{or} \qquad x=-9$$

x = 15 or x = -9

3.33 Solve and graph the solutions: $x \leq -1$ or $\geq \dfrac{11}{3}$

Solution: $|3x-4| \geq 7$

3.34 Solve and graph the solutions: $-|x-6| > -13$

Solution:

$$(-1)\left(-|x-6|\right) > (-1)(-13)$$
$$|x-6| < 13$$

$x - 6 < 13$	and	$-(x - 6) < 13$
		$-x + 6 < 13$
$x - 6 + 6 < 13 + 6$	and	$-x + 6 - 6 < 13 - 6$
$x < 19$	and	$-x < 7$
$x < 19$	and	$x > 7$

x < 19 and x > 7

3.35 Solve and graph the solutions: $|x-1| + 9 \geq 20$

Solution:

$$|x-1| + 9 - 9 \geq 20 - 9$$
$$|x-1| \geq 11$$

$x - 1 \geq 11$	or	$-(x - 1) \geq 11$
		$-x + 1 \geq 11$
$x - 1 + 1 \geq 11 + 1$	or	$-x + 1 - 1 \geq 11 - 1$
$x \geq 12$	or	$-x \geq 10$
		$(-1)(-x) \geq (-1)(10)$
$x \geq 12$	or	$x \leq -10$

x ≥ 12 or x ≤ -10

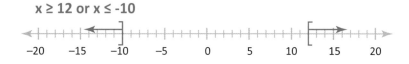

Chapter 4 Graphing Linear Equations and Inequalities

Introduction to the Cartesian Plane

Graph the following ordered pairs on a coordinate axes and indicate in which quadrant they are located.

4.1 $(4, 7)$

4.2 $(0, -8)$

4.3 $(-2, 5)$

Solutions:

See the graph for the graphed points. Coordinate (4, 7) lies in Quadrant I; coordinate (0, −8) no quadrant; coordinate (−2, 5) lies in Quadrant II.

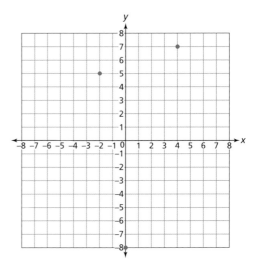

Give the coordinates of the following points in the plane.

4.4 Point A

4.5 Point B

4.6 Point C

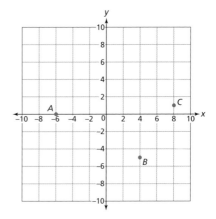

Solutions:

4.4 (−6, 0)

4.5 (4, −5)

4.6 (8, 1)

Introduction to Functions

Evaluate the following functions for the given values of the variables.

4.7 $f(x) = 11 - 2x$, for $x = 5$ and $x = -3$

4.8 $g(x) = x^2 - 4x - 15$, for $x = 0$ and $x = 2$

Solutions:

4.7 1 and 17

4.8 −15 and −19

4.9 Determine whether or not each of the following is a function and explain why or why not.

a.

x	y
2	4
3	8
2	−3

b.

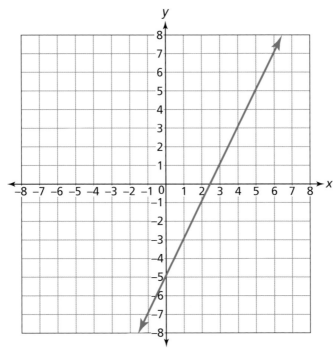

Solutions:

4.9a is not a function because each x is not paired with one and only one y.

4.9b is a function since its graph passes the vertical line test.

Linear Functions

4.10 Find three points that satisfy the equation, plot them, and graph the line: $y = -2x + 5$.

Solutions:

The points will vary; following is the graph.

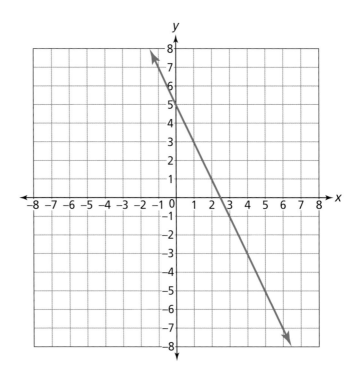

4.11 Use the *x*-intercept and *y*-intercept to graph the linear equation $2x - y = 4$.

Solution:

Find the *x*-intercept using $y = 0$.

$$2x - 0 = 4$$
$$2x = 4$$
$$\frac{2x}{2} = \frac{4}{2}$$
$$x = 2$$

The *x*-intercept is at the point $(2, 0)$

Find the *y*-intercept using $x = 0$.

$$2(0) - y = 4$$
$$0 - y = 4$$
$$-y = 4$$
$$-y(-1) = 4(-1)$$
$$y = -4$$

The *y*-intercept is at the point $(0, -4)$

Plot the coordinates $(2, 0)$ and $(0, -4)$ and draw the line of the equation through the coordinates.

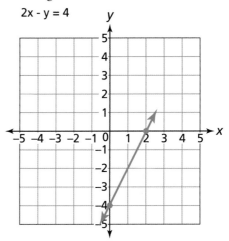

2x - y = 4

4.12 Use the *x*-intercept and *y*-intercept to graph the linear equation $-3x + y = -6$.

Solution:

Find the *x*-intercept using $y = 0$.

$$-3x + 0 = -6$$
$$-3x = -6$$
$$\frac{-3x}{-3} = \frac{-6}{-3}$$
$$x = 2$$

The *x*-intercept is at the point $(2, 0)$

Find the *y*-intercept using $x = 0$

$$-3(0) + y = -6$$
$$0 + y = -6$$
$$y = -6$$

The *y*-intercept is at the point $(0, -6)$

Plot the coordinates (2, 0) and (0, −6) and draw the line of the equation through the coordinates.

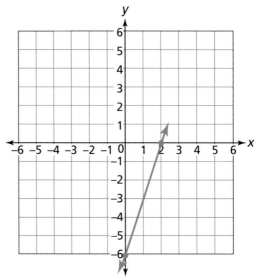

4.13 Use the *x*-intercept and *y*-intercept to graph the linear equation $5x - 2y = -10$.

Solution:

Find the *x*-intercept using $y = 0$.

$$5x - 2(0) = -10$$
$$5x = -10$$
$$\frac{5x}{5} = -\frac{10}{5}$$
$$x = -2$$

The *x*-intercept is at the point $(-2, 0)$

Find the *y*-intercept using $x = 0$

$$5(0) - 2y = -10$$
$$0 - 2y = -10$$
$$-2y = -10$$
$$\frac{-2y}{-2} = \frac{-10}{-2}$$
$$y = 5$$

The *y*-intercept is at the point $(0, 5)$

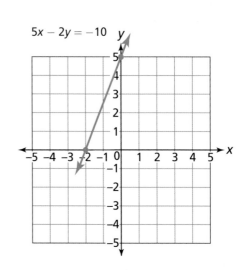

4.14 Graph the linear equation $y = -3x + 1$ using the slope and y-intercept.

Solution:

Plot the y-intercept at the point $(0, 1)$. The slope is -3, indicating a move of 3 units down and 1 unit to the right, to arrive at the point $(1, -2)$. Plot this point and draw a line through the points.

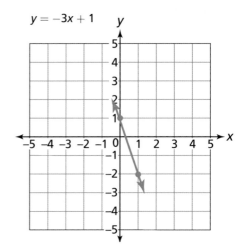

4.15 Graph the linear equation $y = \left(\dfrac{2}{3}\right)x - 4$ using the slope and y-intercept.

Solution:

Plot the y-intercept at the point $(0, -4)$. The slope is $\dfrac{2}{3}$, indicating a move of 2 units up and 3 unit to the right, to arrive at the point $(3, -2)$. Plot this point and draw a line through the points.

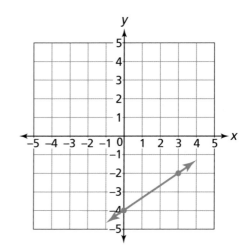

4.16 Graph the linear equation $2y = -x + 6$ using the slope and y-intercept.

Solution:

Solve for y:

$$\frac{2y}{2} = -\frac{x}{2} + \frac{6}{2}$$

$$y = -\frac{1}{2}x + 3$$

Plot the y-intercept at the point $(0, 3)$. The slope is $-\dfrac{1}{2}$, indicating a move of 1 unit down and 2 unit to the right, to arrive at the point $(2, 2)$. Plot this point and draw a line through the points.

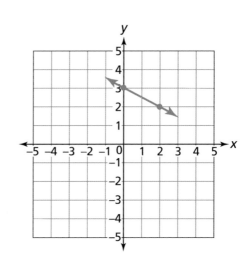

4.17 Graph the linear equation $4x - 3y = 9$ using the slope and y-intercept.

Solution:

Solve for y:

$$-3y = -4x + 9$$

$$\frac{-3y}{-3} = \frac{-4x}{-3} + \frac{9}{-3}$$

$$y = \frac{4}{3}x - 3$$

Plot the y-intercept at the point $(0, -3)$. The slope is $-\dfrac{4}{3}$, indicating a move of 4 units down and 3 unit to the right, to arrive at the point $(3, 1)$. Plot this point and draw a line through the points.

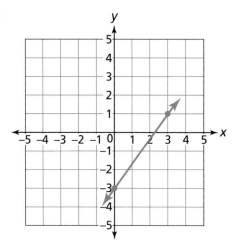

4.18 Graph the linear equation $y = -3$ using the slope and y-intercept.

Solution:

The equation can be rewritten as $y = 0x - 3$. Plot the y-intercept at the point $(0, -3)$. The slope is zero, indicating a horizontal line. Draw a horizontal line through the point $(0, -3)$

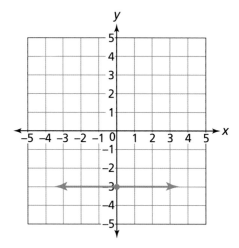

4.19 Write the equation of the line that has a slope of $\dfrac{1}{2}$ and y-intercept of $(0, -3)$.

Solution:

Substitute the values $x = 0$, $y = -3$, and slope $= \dfrac{1}{2}$. Then solve for b.

$$-3 = \frac{1}{2}(0) + b$$

$$-3 = b$$

Rewrite the equation in slope-intercept form: $y = \dfrac{1}{2}x - 3$

4.20 Write the equation of the line that has a slope of -2 and passes through the point (2, 1).

Solution:

Substitute the values $x = 2$, $y = 1$, and slope $= -2$. Then solve for b.

$$1 = -2(2) + b$$
$$1 = -4 + b$$
$$1 + 4 = -4 + b + 4$$
$$5 = b$$

Rewrite the equation in slope-intercept form: $y = -2x + 5$

4.21 Write the equation of the line that has a slope of $\frac{2}{3}$ and passes through the point (−3, 1).

Solution:

Substitute the values $x = -3$, $y = 1$, and slope $= \frac{2}{3}$. Then solve for b.

$$1 = (-3)(1) + b$$
$$1 = -3 + b$$
$$1 + 3 = -3 + b + 3$$
$$4 = b$$

Rewrite the equation in slope-intercept form: $y = \frac{2}{3}x + 4$

4.22 The corporate jet cost $400,000 new in 2005. By 2009, it had depreciated to a value of $260,000. Write a linear equation for the value of the plane in terms of the number of years after its purchase ($V = mt + b$). Use this equation to estimate the value of the plane in 2012.

Solutions:

$V = -35,000 \times t + 400,000$; the plane has depreciated to a value of $155,000 in 2012.

Slope of a Straight Line

4.23 Determine the slopes of the lines joining the following pairs of points:
   a. (2, 5) and (−3, 10)
   b. (2, 5) and (2, 10)

Solutions:

4.23a $m = -1$
4.23b m is undefined.

4.24 Write the equation of the line that passes through the points (0, 2) and (−1, −1).

Solution:

Step 1: Find the slope

$$m = \frac{(-1-2)}{(-1-0)} = \frac{-3}{-1} = 3$$

Step 2: Choose one set of coordinates and substitute for x and y.
Using $x = 0$ and $y = 2$, rewrite the equation as $2 = 3(0) + b$, giving $b = 2$

Rewrite the equation in slope-intercept form: $y = 3x + 2$

4.25 Write the equation of the line that passes through the points (1, 1) and (−2, 10).

Solution:

Step 1: Find the slope

$$m = \frac{(10-1)}{(-2-1)} = \frac{9}{-3} = -3$$

Step 2: Choose one set of coordinates and substitute for x and y.
Using $x = 1$ and $y = 1$, rewrite the equation as $1 = -3(1) + b$

$$1 = -3 + b$$
$$1 + 3 = -3 + b + 3$$
$$4 = b$$

Rewrite the equation in slope-intercept form: $y = -3x + 4$

4.26 Write the equation of the line that passes through the points (3, 2) and (2, 3).

Solution:

Step 1: Find the slope

$$m = \frac{(3-2)}{(2-3)} = \frac{1}{-1} = -1$$

Step 2: Choose one set of coordinates and substitute for x and y.
Using $x = 3$ and $y = 2$, rewrite the equation as $3 = 2(-1) + b$

$$3 = -2 + b$$
$$3 + 2 = -2 + b + 2$$
$$5 = b$$

Rewrite the equation in slope-intercept form: $y = -x + 5$

4.27 Write the equation of the line that passes through the points (2, −4) and (−2, −2)

Solution:

Step 1: Find the slope

$$m = \frac{(-2-(-4))}{(-2-2)} = \frac{2}{(-4)} = -\frac{1}{2}$$

Step 2: Choose one set of coordinates and substitute for x and y.

Using $x = -2$ and $y = -2$, rewrite the equation as $-2 = -\frac{1}{2}(-2) + b$

$$-2 = 1 + b$$
$$-2 - 1 = 1 + b - 1$$
$$-3 = b$$

Rewrite the equation in slope-intercept form: $y = -\frac{1}{2}x - 3$

4.28 Find the slope of a line that is parallel to the line $2x - y = 3$.

Solution:

Rewrite the equation in slope-intercept form:

$$-y = -2x + 3$$
$$(-1)(-y) = (-2x)(-1) + 3(-1)$$
$$y = 2x - 3$$

The slope of a line that is parallel to $2x - y = 3$ is 2.

4.29 Write the equation of the line that passes through the point $(-2, 1)$ and is parallel to the line $y = 3x - 2$.

Solution:

Substitute using slope $= 3$, $x = -2$, and $y = 1$ to find b.

$$1 = 3(-2) + b$$
$$1 = -6 + b$$
$$1 + 6 = -6 + b + 6$$
$$7 = b$$

Write the equation in slope-intercept form: $y = 3x + 7$

4.30 Give the slopes of the lines that are perpendicular to the following lines:
  a. $3x + 5y = 15$
  b. $x = 7$

Solutions:

4. 30a $m = \dfrac{5}{3}$

4.30b $m = 0$

4.31 Write the equation of the line that passes through the point $(1, 3)$ and is perpendicular to the line $y = \dfrac{1}{2}x - 1$.

Solution:

The slope of the perpendicular line is the negative reciprocal of $\dfrac{1}{2}$, which is -2.
Substitute using slope $= -2$, $x = 1$, and $y = 3$ to find b.

$$3 = -2(1) + b$$
$$3 = -2 + b$$
$$3 + 2 = -2 + b + 2$$
$$5 = b$$

Write the equation in slope-intercept form: $y = -2x + 5$

Graphing Inequalities

4.32 Graph the inequality $y \leq \frac{1}{2} x + 3$.

Solution:

The shaded and labeled region in the graph at right is the solution.

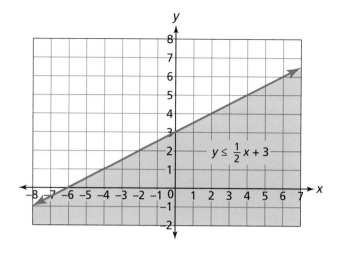

4.33 Graph the inequality $2x + y > 1$.

Solution:

Solve for y:

$$2x + y - 2x > 1 - 2x$$
$$y > -2x + 1$$

Plot the y-intercept at the point $(0, 1)$. The slope is -2, indicating a move of 2 units down and 1 unit to the right, to arrive at the point $(1, -1)$. Plot this point and draw a dotted line through the points.

Since the Inequality symbol is a $>$, shade the region above the line.

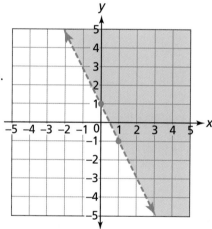

4.34 Graph the inequality $3x - y > 2$.

Solution:

Solve for y:

$$3x - y - 3x > 2 - 3x$$
$$-y > -3x + 2$$
$$(-1)(-y) < -3x(-1) + 2(-1)$$
$$y < 3x - 2$$

Plot the y-intercept at the point $(0, -2)$. The slope is 3, indicating a move of 3 units up and 1 unit to the right, to arrive at the point $(1, 1)$. Plot this point and draw a solid line through the points.

Since the inequality symbol is a $<$, shade the region below the line.

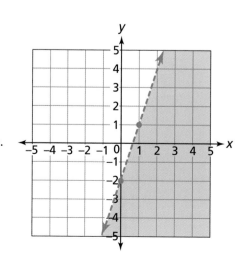

4.35 An insurance company has policies that cost $40 and $60 per month. Graph the inequality that shows the region where the number of polices sold will generate a monthly revenue in excess of $5,000.

Solution:

Graph the inequality $40x + 60y > 5000$. (See following graph.)

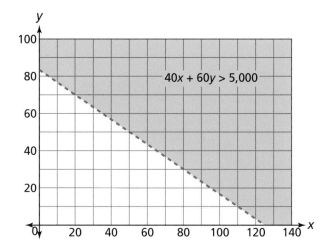

Chapter 5 Systems of Linear Equations and Inequalities

5.1 Determine if the point $(5, 1)$ is a solution to the systems of equations.

$x + y = 6$
$x - y = 4$

Solution:

Plug in both equations $x = 5$ and $y = 1$ and verify if the equation is true.
$x + y = 6 \rightarrow 5 + 1 = 6 \rightarrow 6 = 6$ *True*
$x - y = 4 \rightarrow 5 - 1 = 4 \rightarrow 4 = 4$ *True*

5.2 Determine if the point $(3, -1)$ is a solution to the system of equations.

$x - 2y = 1$
$2x - y = 5$

Solution:

Substitute the values $x = 3$ and $y = -1$ to the first equation:

$3 - 2(-1) = 1$
$3 - (-2) = 1$
$3 + 2 = 1$
$5 = 1$

Since the result is a false statement, the point $(3, -1)$ is not a solution to the system.

5.3 Graph the following systems of equations to determine the solution.

$2x - y = 2$

$-x + y = -1$

Solution:

From the graph we find the solution at (1, 0).

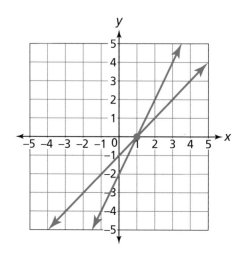

5.4 Graph the following systems of equations to determine the solution.

$2x - y = 2$

$6x - 3y = -18$

Solution:

From the graph we find the lines are parallel and thus no solution. Note that parallel lines have the same slope and solving both equations for y gives a slope = 2.

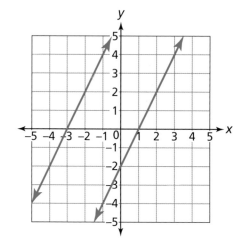

5.5 Graph the following systems of equations to determine the solution.

$2x - y = 2$

$4x - 2y = 4$

Solution:

From the graph we find these are the same lines and only differ by a constant of 2 times each value. Therefore, there are infinite solutions.

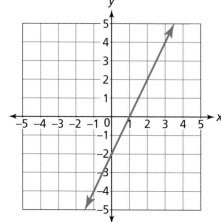

5.6 Use the substitution method to solve the following system of equations.

$y = 2x + 6$

$-3x - y = 4$

Solution:

Substitute $2x + 6$ for y in the equation $-3x - y = 4$ and solve for x:

$$-3x - (2x + 6) = 4$$

$$-3x - 2x - 6 = 4$$

$$-5x - 6 = 4$$

$$-5x - 6 + 6 = 4 + 6$$

$$-5x = 10$$

$$\frac{-5x}{(-5)} = \frac{10}{(-5)}$$

$$x = -2$$

5.7 Substitute $x = 2$ in the equation $y = 2x + 6$:

$y = 2(-2) + 6$

$y = -4 + 6$

$y = 2$

The solution to the system is $(-2, 2)$

5.8 Use the substitution method to solve the following system of equations.

$x = y - 3$

$-4x - y = -8$

Solution:

Substitute $y - 3$ for x in the equation $-4x - y = -8$ and solve for y:

$$-4(y - 3) - y = -8$$

$$-4y + 12 - y = -8$$

$$-5y + 12 = -8$$

$$-5y + 12 - 12 = -8 - 12$$

$$-5y = -20$$

$$\frac{-5y}{(-5)} = \frac{-20}{(-5)}$$

$$y = 4$$

Substitute $y = 4$ in the equation $x = y - 3$:

$x = 4 - 3$

$x = 1$

The solution for the system is $(1, 4)$

5.9 Use the substitution method to solve the following system of equations.

$4x + 2y = 6$

$y = -2x + 3$

Solution:

Substitute $-2x + 3$ for y in the equation $4x + 2y = 6$:

$4x + 2(-2x + 3) = 6$

$\quad 4x - 4x + 6 = 0$

$\quad\quad\quad\quad\quad 6 = 0$

Since this is a false statement, there is no solution to the system.

5.10 Use the substitution method to solve the following systems of equations.

$3x + y = 4$

$x - 2y = 4$

Solution:

Step 1: Solve the second equation for x.

$x - 2y = 4 \rightarrow x = 4 + 2y$

Step 2: Plug in $4 + 2y$ for x into the first equation and solve for y.

$3x + y = 4 \rightarrow 3(4 + 2y) + y = 4 \rightarrow 12 + 6y + y = 4 \rightarrow 12 + 7y = 4 \rightarrow 7y = 4 - 12 \rightarrow 7y = -8 \rightarrow y = -\dfrac{8}{7}$

Step 3: Now plug in $y = -\dfrac{8}{7}$ into the second equation and solve for x.

$x - 2y = 4 \rightarrow x - 2\left(-\dfrac{8}{7}\right) = 4 \rightarrow x + \dfrac{16}{7} = 4 \rightarrow x = 4 - \dfrac{16}{7} \rightarrow x = \dfrac{28}{7} - \dfrac{16}{7} = \dfrac{12}{7}$

Therefore the solution is $\left(\dfrac{12}{7}, -\dfrac{8}{7}\right)$.

5.11 Use the elimination method to solve the following systems of equations.

$5x + y = 5$

$5x + 3y = 15$

Solution:

Step 1: Multiply the second equation by -1.

$(-1)5x + (-1)3y = (-1)15$

$\quad\quad -5x - 3y = -15$

Step 2: Add the first equation and the newly formed second equation together to eliminate the x's.

$\quad\ 5x + y = 5$

$\underline{-5x - 3y = -15}$

$\quad\quad -2y = -10 \quad\quad\quad$ Divide both sides by -2.

$\quad\quad \dfrac{-2y}{(-2)} = \dfrac{-10}{(-2)}$

$\quad\quad\quad\quad y = 5$

Step 3: Plug $y = 5$ into the first equation and solve for x.

$$5x + y = 5$$
$$5x + 5 = 5$$
$$5x + 5 - 5 = 5 - 5$$
$$5x = 0$$
$$\frac{5x}{5} = \frac{0}{5}$$
$$x = 0$$

Therefore the solution is (0, 5).

5.12 Use the elimination method to solve the following system of equations.

$$6x - 2y = 2$$
$$-3x + 3y = 9$$

Solution:

To eliminate x, multiply both sides of the equation $-3x + 3y = 9$ by 2:

$$(2)(-3x + 3y) = 9(2)$$
$$-6x + 6y = 18$$

Add the equations $6x - 2y = 2$ and $-6x + 6y = 18$ and solve for y;

$$6x - 2y = 2$$
$$+ \quad -6x + 6y = 18$$
$$\overline{\qquad\qquad}$$
$$4y = 20$$
$$\frac{4y}{4} = \frac{20}{4}$$
$$y = 5$$

Substitute $y = 5$ in the equation $6x - 2y = 2$ and solve for x:

$$6x - 2(5) = 2$$
$$6x - 10 = 2$$
$$6x - 10 + 10 = 2 + 10$$
$$6x = 12$$
$$\frac{6x}{6} = \frac{12}{6}$$
$$x = 2$$

The solution to the system is (2, 5)

5.13 Use the elimination method to solve the following system of equations.

$$5x - 2y = -1$$
$$-2x + 3y = -4$$

Solution:

To eliminate y, multiply both sides of the first equation by 3, and both sides of the second equation by 2:

$$(3)(5x - 2y) = -1(3) \quad \text{and} \quad (2)(-2x + 3y) = -4(2)$$
$$15x - 6y = -3 \qquad\qquad\qquad -4x + 6y = -8$$

Add the resulting equations:

$$\begin{array}{r} 15x - 6y = -3 \\ + \quad -4x + 6y = -8 \\ \hline 11x = -11 \end{array}$$

$$\frac{11x}{11} = -\frac{11}{11}$$

$$x = -1$$

Substitute $x = -1$ in the equation $-2x + 3y = -4$:

$$-2(-1) + 3y = -4$$
$$2 + 3y = -4$$
$$2 + 3y - 2 = -4 - 2$$
$$3y = -6$$
$$\frac{3y}{3} = -\frac{6}{3}$$
$$y = -2$$

The solution to the system is $(-1, -2)$

5.14 Use the elimination method to solve the following system of equations.

$$5x - 5y = 40$$
$$x + 3y = 0$$

Solution:

To eliminate x, multiply both sides of the equation $x + 3y = 0$ by -5:

$$(5)(x + 3y) = 0(-5)$$
$$-5x - 15y = 0$$

Add the equations $5x - 5y = 40$ and $-5x - 15y = 0$ and solve for y:

$$\begin{array}{r} 5x - 5y = 40 \\ + \quad -5x - 15y = 0 \\ \hline -20y = 40 \end{array}$$

$$\frac{-20y}{(-20)} = \frac{40}{(-20)}$$

$$y = -2$$

Substitute $y = -2$ in the equation $x + 3y = 0$ and solve for x:

$$x + 3(-2) = 0$$
$$x - 6 = 0$$
$$x - 6 + 6 = 0 + 6$$
$$x = 6$$

The solution to the system is $(6, -2)$

5.15 Use the elimination method to solve the following system of equations.

$-4x + 2y = 20$

$3x + 5y = -15$

Solution:

To eliminate *x*, multiply both sides of the first equation by 3, and both sides of the second equation by 4:

$(3)(-4x + 2y) = 20(3)$ and $(4)(3x + 5y) = -15(4)$

$\quad -12x + 6y = 60 \qquad\qquad\qquad 12x + 20y = -60$

Add the equations $-12x + 6y = 60$ and $12x + 20y = -60$:

$$
\begin{array}{r}
-12x + 6y = 60 \\
+\quad 12x + 20y = -60 \\
\hline
26y = 0 \\
\dfrac{26y}{26} = \dfrac{0}{26} \\
y = 0
\end{array}
$$

Substitute $y = 0$ in the equation $-4x + 2y = 20$ and solve for *x*:

$-4x + 2(0) = 20$

$\quad -4x = 20$

$\quad \dfrac{-4x}{(-4)} = \dfrac{20}{(-4)}$

$\quad\quad x = -5$

The solution to the system is $(-5, 0)$

5.16 Use the elimination method to solve the following system of equations.

$3x - y = 12$

$-6x + 2y = 6$

Solution:

To eliminate y, multiply both sides of the equation $3x - y = 12$ by 2:

$(2)(3x - y) = 12(2)$

$\quad 6x - 2y = 24$

Add the equations $-6x + 2y = 6$ and $6x - 2y = 24$:

$$
\begin{array}{r}
-6x + 2y = 6 \\
+\quad 6x - 2y = 24 \\
\hline
0 = 30
\end{array}
$$

The result is a false statement, so there is no solution to the system.

5.17 Solve the systems of equations with method of choice.

$\dfrac{1}{5}x + \dfrac{2}{5}y = 1$

$\dfrac{1}{4}x - \dfrac{1}{3}y = -\dfrac{5}{12}$

Solution:

Step 1: One method would be to get rid of the fractions by multiplying each equation by its LCD. Multiply equation 1 by 5.

$$5\left(\frac{1}{5}\right)x + 5\left(\frac{2}{5}\right)y = 5(1)$$
$$x + 2y = 5$$

Multiply equation 2 by 12.

$$12\left(\frac{1}{4}\right)x - 12\left(\frac{1}{3}\right)y = -12\left(\frac{5}{12}\right)$$
$$3x - 4y = -5$$

Step 2: Use the substitution method by solving $x + 2y = 5$ for x.
$x + 2y = 5 \rightarrow x = 5 - 2y$

Step 3: Plug in $5 - 2y$ for x into the second equation and solve for y.
$3x - 4y = -5 \rightarrow 3(5 - 2y) - 4y = -5 \rightarrow 15 - 6y - 4y = -5 \rightarrow 15 - 10y = -5 \rightarrow -10y = -20 \rightarrow y = 2$

Plug in $y = 2$ into the first equation and solve for x.
$x + 2y = 5 \rightarrow x + 2(2) = 5 \rightarrow x + 4 = 5 \rightarrow x = 1$

Therefore the solution is $(1, 2)$.

5.18 Solve the systems of equations with method of choice.

$0.2x + 0.3y = 1$
$x - 0.5y = 3$

Solution:

Step 1: One method would be to remove the decimals by multiplying both equations by 10 since the least decimal values are 10ths:

$$10(0.2x) + 10(0.3y) = 10(1)$$
$$10(x) - 10(0.5y) = 10(3)$$

which gives

$$2x + 3y = 10$$
$$10x - 5y = 30$$

Step 2: Using elimination multiply the first equation by -5.

$$(-5)(2x) + (-5)(3y) = (-5)(10)$$
$$-10x - 15y = -50$$

Step 3: Add the newly formed first equation and second equation together.

$$-10x - 15y = -50$$
$$\underline{10x - 5y = 30}$$
$$-20y = -20$$
$$y = 1$$

Step 4: Now plug in $y = 1$ into the first equation and solve for x.

$$2x + 3y = 10 \rightarrow 2x + 3(1) = 10 \rightarrow 2x = 7 \rightarrow x = \frac{7}{2} \text{ or } 3.5$$

Therefore, the solution is (3.5, 1).

5.19 The demand and supply for a certain product is given by the following systems of equations:

$D(p) = 1500 - 5p$

$S(p) = 300 + p$

Find the price at the equilibrium point for each function and then find the value of the demand at this price.

Solution:

The equilibrium point is where the two functions are equal, that is, $D(p) = S(p)$. Setting the two functions equal and solving for p gives:

$$1500 - 5p = 300 + p$$
$$1500 - 5p + 5p = 300 + p + 5p$$
$$1500 = 300 + 6p$$
$$1500 - 300 = 6p$$
$$1200 = 6p$$
$$\frac{1200}{6} = \frac{6p}{6}$$
$$200 = p$$
$$D(200) = 1500 - 5(200) = 1500 - 1000 = 500$$

5.20 Graph the systems of inequalities and shade the feasible solution.

$y > -3$

$x < 2$

Solution:

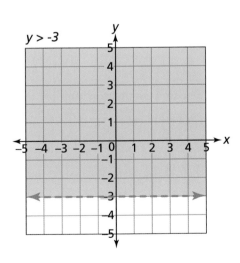

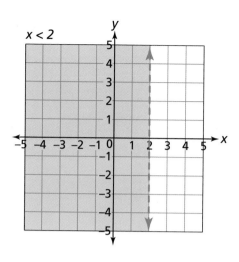

x < 2

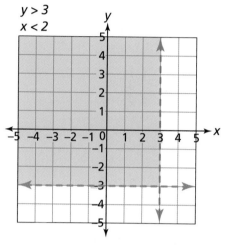

y > 3
x < 2

5.21 Graph the systems of inequalities and shade the feasible solution.

$y \geq 3x - 2$

$y < -2x + 3$

Solution:

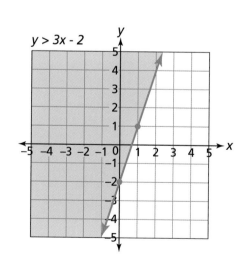

y > 3x - 2

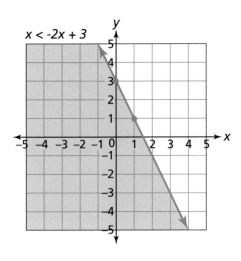

$x < -2x + 3$

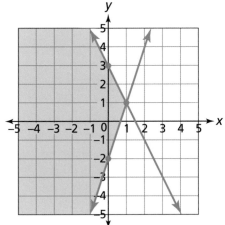

5.22 Graph the systems of inequalities and shade the feasible solutions:

$x - y \geq 2$

$x + y \leq 6$

Solution:

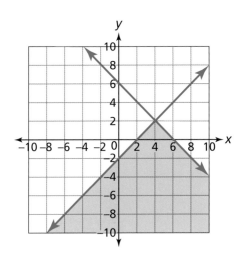

5.23 Graph the systems of inequalities and shade the feasible solution.

$2x - y < -1$

$x - y > -2$

Solution:

Convert both inequalities to slope-intercept form:

$$2x - y < -1 \qquad\qquad \text{and} \qquad\qquad x - y > -2$$

$$2x - y - 2x < -1 - 2x \qquad\qquad x - y - x > -2 - x$$

$$-y < -2x - 1 \qquad\qquad\qquad -y > -x - 2$$

$$(-1)(-y) > (-2x - 1)(-1) \qquad\qquad (-1)(-y) < (-x - 2)(-1)$$

$$y > 2x + 1 \qquad\qquad\qquad\qquad y < x + 2$$

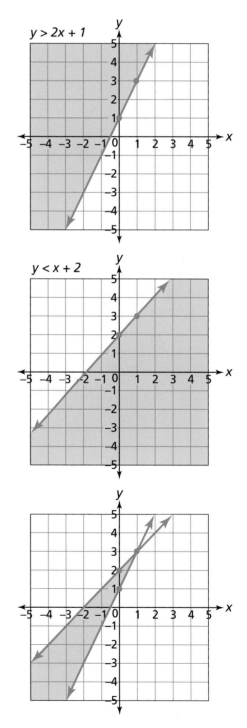

5.24 Graph the systems of inequalities and shade the feasible solution.

$y \geq -4$

$x - y < 5$

Solution:

Convert $x - y < 5$ to slope-intercept form:

$x - y - x < 5 - x$

$\qquad -y < -x + 5$

$(-1)(-y) > (-x + 5)(-1)$

$\qquad\quad y > x - 5$

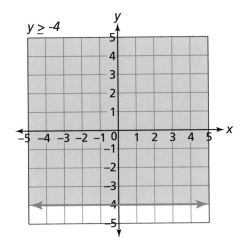

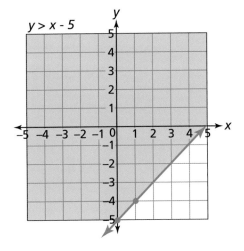

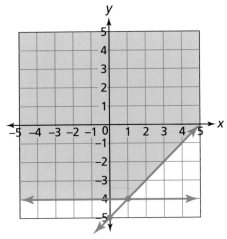

5.25 Graph the systems of inequalities and shade the feasible solution.

$x \leq -2$

$x - y \geq 2$

Solution:

Convert $x - y \geq 2$ to slope-intercept form:

$x - y - x \geq 2 - x$

$\qquad -y \geq -x + 2$

$(-1)(-y) \leq (-x + 2)(-1)$

$\qquad\qquad y \leq x - 2$

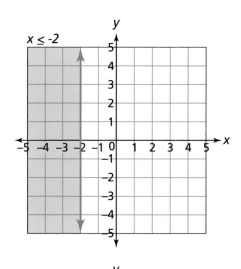

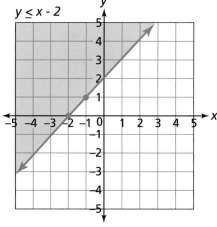

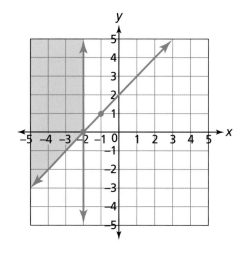

5.26 Graph the systems of inequalities and shade the feasible solution.

$2x - 3y < -6$

$x + 2y \leq 1$

Solution:

Convert both inequalities to slope-intercept form:

$$2x - 3y < -6 \qquad \text{and} \qquad x + 2y \leq 1$$

$$2x - 3y - 2x < -6 - 2x \qquad\qquad x + 2y - x \leq 1 - x$$

$$-3y < -2x - 6 \qquad\qquad\qquad 2y \leq -x + 1$$

$$\frac{-3y}{(-3)} > \frac{-2}{(-3)}x\frac{-6}{(-3)} \qquad\qquad \frac{2y}{2} \leq \frac{-x}{2} + \frac{1}{2}$$

$$y > \frac{2}{3}x + 2 \qquad\qquad\qquad y \leq \frac{-1}{2}x + \frac{1}{2}$$

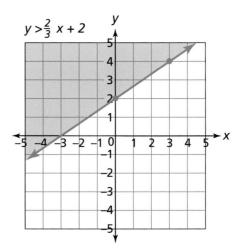

$y > \frac{2}{3}x + 2$

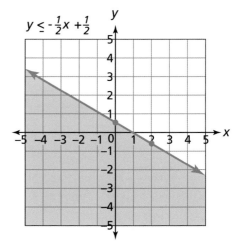

$y \leq -\frac{1}{2}x + \frac{1}{2}$

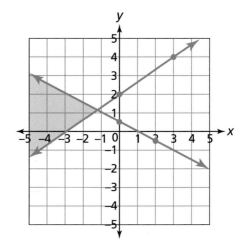

5.27 Graph the systems of inequalities and shade the feasible solutions:

$x \geq 1$

$y \geq 2$

$4 \leq 2x + y$

$2x + y \leq 6$

Solution:

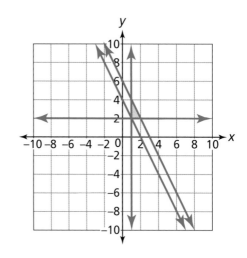

5.28 Solve the systems of equations using matrix row operations.

$2x + y = 2$

$x - y = 7$

Solution:

$$\begin{bmatrix} 2 & 1 & | & 2 \\ 1 & -1 & | & 7 \end{bmatrix} \Longrightarrow \begin{bmatrix} 2 & 1 & | & 2 \\ 1 & -1 & | & 7 \end{bmatrix}$$

$$\begin{bmatrix} 1 & -1 & | & 7 \\ 2 & 1 & | & 2 \end{bmatrix} \longleftarrow \boxed{-2\text{Row1} + \text{Row2}}$$

$$\begin{bmatrix} 1 & -1 & | & 7 \\ 0 & 3 & | & -12 \end{bmatrix} \longleftarrow \boxed{(1/3) * \text{Row 2}}$$

$$\begin{bmatrix} 1 & -1 & | & 7 \\ 0 & 1 & | & -4 \end{bmatrix} \longleftarrow \boxed{1\text{Row2} + \text{Row1}} \qquad \begin{bmatrix} 1 & 0 & | & 3 \\ 0 & 1 & | & -4 \end{bmatrix}$$

Thus, the solution is $(x, y) = (3, -4)$

5.29 Members of book clubs purchased a total of about 110 million books in 2010. Paperback sales exceeded sales of hardbacks by about 40 million books. How many copies of each type of book were published?

Solution:

Let $x =$ hardback books and $y =$ paperback books.

Total: $x + y = 110$

Exceeded: $y = x + 40$

$$\begin{bmatrix} 1 & 1 & | & 110 \\ -1 & 1 & | & 40 \end{bmatrix}$$

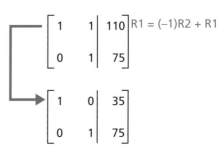

Therefore, 35 million hardback and 75 paperback books were published.

5.30 Solve the following systems of equations:

$3x + y - 2z = 13$
$x - 2y + 3z = -9$
$2x + 2y + z = 3$

Solution:

To eliminate z:

Multiply the both sides of the third equation by 2 and add to the first equation:

$$\begin{array}{ll} 3x + 2y - 2z = 13 & \quad 3x + y - 2z = 13 \\ (2)(2x + 2y + z) = 3(2) & \quad + \quad 4x + 4y + 2z = 6 \\ \hline & \quad\quad\quad 7x + 5y = 19 \end{array}$$

Multiply both sides of the third equation by -3 and add it to the second equation:

$$\begin{array}{ll} x - 2y + 3z = -9 & \quad\quad x - 2y + 3z = -9 \\ (-3)(2x + 2y + z) = 3(-3) & \quad + \quad -6x - 6y - 3z = -9 \\ \hline & \quad\quad -5x - 8y = -18 \end{array}$$

To eliminate y, multiply both sides of $7x + 5y = 19$ by 8, and multiply both sides of $-5x - 8y = -18$ by 5:

$$(8)(7x + 5y) = 19(8)$$
$$(5)(-5x - 8y) = (-18)(5) \quad \rightarrow$$

$$\begin{array}{r} 56x + 40y = 152 \\ + \quad -25x - 40y = -90 \\ \hline 31x \quad\quad = 62 \end{array}$$

Solve for x:

$$\frac{31x}{31} = \frac{62}{31}$$
$$x = 2$$

Choose an equation to solve for y.

Substitute $x = 2$ in the equation $7x + 5y = 19$ and solve for y:

$$7(2) + 5y = 19$$
$$14 + 5y = 19$$
$$14 + 5y - 14 = 19 - 14$$
$$5y = 5$$
$$y = 1$$

Substitute $x = 2$ and $y = 1$ into an original equation and solve for z:

$$2x + 2y + z = 3$$
$$2(2) + 2(1) + z = 3$$
$$4 + 2 + z = 3$$
$$6 + z = 3$$
$$6 + z - 6 = 3 - 6$$
$$z = -3$$

The solution to the system of equations is $(2, 1, -3)$

5.31 Solve the following systems of equations:

$$-2x + 3y + z = -10$$
$$5x + y - z = 19$$
$$2x - y + 2z = -2$$

Solution:

To eliminate z, add the first and second equations together:

$$\begin{array}{r} -2x + 3y + z = -10 \\ + \quad 5x + \; y - z = 19 \\ \hline 3x + 4y \quad\quad = 9 \end{array}$$

Then multiply both sides of the equation $-2x + 3y + z = -10$ by -2 and add to the equation $2x - y + 2z = -2$:

$$(-2)(-2x + 3y + z) = -10(-2) \quad \rightarrow$$

$$\begin{array}{r} 4x - 6y - 2z = 20 \\ + \; 2x - \; y + 2z = -2 \\ \hline 6x - 7y \quad\quad = 18 \end{array}$$

To eliminate x, multiply both sides of the equation $3x + 4y = 9$ by (-2) and add to the equation $6x - 7y = 18$:

$$(-2)(3x + 4y) = 9(-2) \qquad \rightarrow$$

$$-6x - 8y = -18$$
$$+ \quad 6x - 7y = 18$$
$$\overline{\overline{\qquad -15y = 0 \qquad}}$$
$$y = 0$$

Substitute $y = 0$ in the equation $3x + 4y = 9$ and solve for x:

$$3x + 4(0) = 9$$
$$3x = 9$$
$$\frac{3x}{3} = \frac{9}{3}$$
$$x = 3$$

Substitute $x = 3$ and $y = 0$ into one of the original equations and solve for z:

$$-2x + 3y + z = -10$$
$$-2(3) + 3(0) + z = -10$$
$$-6 + 0 + z = -10$$
$$-6 + z = -10$$
$$-6 + z + 6 = -10 + 6$$
$$z = -4$$

The solution to the system of equations is (3, 0, -4)

5.32 Solve the following systems of equations:

$$2x - y + 4z = -3$$
$$x - 2y - 10z = -6$$
$$3x + 4z = 7$$

Solution:

First write the system of equations in a matrix.

$$\begin{bmatrix} 2 & -1 & 4 & | & -3 \\ 1 & -2 & -10 & | & -6 \\ 3 & 0 & 4 & | & 7 \end{bmatrix}$$

Step 1: Interchange rows 1 and 2.

$$\begin{bmatrix} 1 & -2 & -10 & | & -6 \\ 2 & -1 & 4 & | & -3 \\ 3 & 0 & 4 & | & 7 \end{bmatrix}$$

Step 2: Multiply row 1 by -2 and add to the second row.

$$\begin{bmatrix} -2 & 4 & 20 & | & 12 \\ (-2)+2 & 4+(-1) & 20+4 & | & 12+(-3) \\ 3 & 0 & 4 & | & 7 \end{bmatrix}$$

$$\begin{bmatrix} 1 & -2 & -10 & | & -6 \\ 0 & 3 & 24 & | & 9 \\ 3 & 0 & 4 & | & 7 \end{bmatrix}$$

Step 3: Multiply the first row by -3 and add to third row.

$$\begin{bmatrix} 1 & -2 & -10 & | & -6 \\ 0 & 3 & 24 & | & 9 \\ 0 & 6 & 34 & | & 25 \end{bmatrix}$$

Step 4: Multiply row 2 by $\dfrac{1}{3}$.

$$\begin{bmatrix} 1 & -2 & -10 & | & -6 \\ 0 & 1 & 8 & | & 3 \\ 0 & 6 & 34 & | & 25 \end{bmatrix}$$

Step 5: Multiply row 2 by -6 and add to row 3.

$$\begin{bmatrix} 1 & -2 & -10 & | & -6 \\ 0 & 1 & 8 & | & 3 \\ 0 & 0 & -14 & | & 7 \end{bmatrix}$$

Step 6: Multiply row 3 by $\dfrac{-1}{14}$.

$$\begin{bmatrix} 1 & -2 & -10 & | & -6 \\ 0 & 1 & 8 & | & 3 \\ 0 & 0 & 1 & | & -\dfrac{1}{2} \end{bmatrix}$$

Step 7: Multiply row 3 by 10 and add to row 1.

$$\begin{bmatrix} 1 & -2 & 0 & | & -11 \\ 0 & 1 & 8 & | & 3 \\ 0 & 0 & 1 & | & -\dfrac{1}{2} \end{bmatrix}$$

Step 8: Multiply row 3 by -8 and add to row 2.

$$\begin{bmatrix} 1 & -2 & 0 & | & -11 \\ 0 & 1 & 0 & | & 7 \\ 0 & 0 & 1 & | & -\dfrac{1}{2} \end{bmatrix}$$

Step 9: Multiply row 2 by 2 and add to row 1.

$$\begin{bmatrix} 1 & 0 & 0 & | & 3 \\ 0 & 1 & 0 & | & 7 \\ 0 & 0 & 1 & | & -\dfrac{1}{2} \end{bmatrix}$$

Therefore, the solution is $(x, y, z) = (3, 7, -\dfrac{1}{2})$

5.33 Solve the following system of equations:

$x + y + z = 2$

$6x - 4y + 5z = 31$

$5x + 2y + 2z = 13$

Solution: First write system of equations in matrix.

$$\begin{bmatrix} 1 & 1 & 1 & | & 2 \\ 6 & -4 & 5 & | & 31 \\ 5 & 2 & 2 & | & 13 \end{bmatrix}$$

Step 1: R2 = −6R1 + R2

$$\begin{bmatrix} 1 & 1 & 1 & | & 2 \\ 0 & -10 & -1 & | & 19 \\ 5 & 2 & 2 & | & 13 \end{bmatrix}$$

Step 2: R3 = −5R1 + R3

$$\begin{bmatrix} 1 & 1 & 1 & | & 2 \\ 0 & -10 & -1 & | & 19 \\ 0 & -3 & -3 & | & 3 \end{bmatrix}$$

Step 3: $R2 = \left(-\dfrac{1}{10}\right) R2$

$$\begin{bmatrix} 1 & 1 & 1 & | & 2 \\ 0 & 1 & \dfrac{1}{10} & | & -\dfrac{19}{10} \\ 0 & -3 & -3 & | & 3 \end{bmatrix}$$

Step 4: R3 = 3R2 + R3

$$\begin{bmatrix} 1 & 1 & 1 & | & 2 \\ 0 & 1 & \dfrac{1}{10} & | & -\dfrac{19}{10} \\ 0 & 0 & -\dfrac{27}{10} & | & -\dfrac{27}{10} \end{bmatrix}$$

Step 5: $R3 = \left(-\dfrac{10}{27}\right) R3$

$$\begin{bmatrix} 1 & 1 & 1 & | & 2 \\ 0 & 1 & \dfrac{1}{10} & | & -\dfrac{19}{10} \\ 0 & 0 & 1 & | & 1 \end{bmatrix}$$

Step 6: R1 = −1R3 + R1

$$\left[\begin{array}{ccc|c} 1 & 1 & 1 & 1 \\ 0 & 1 & \dfrac{1}{10} & -\dfrac{19}{10} \\ 0 & 0 & 1 & 1 \end{array}\right]$$

Step 7: $R2 = \left(-\dfrac{1}{10}\right)R3 + R2$

$$\left[\begin{array}{ccc|c} 1 & 1 & 0 & 1 \\ 0 & 1 & 0 & -2 \\ 0 & 0 & 1 & 1 \end{array}\right]$$

Step 8: R1 = −1R2 + R1

$$\left[\begin{array}{ccc|c} 1 & 0 & 0 & 3 \\ 0 & 1 & 0 & -2 \\ 0 & 0 & 1 & 1 \end{array}\right]$$

Therefore the solution is $(x, y, z) = (3, -2, 1)$.

5.34 Find the determinants of the following system of equations:

$2x - 3y = -9$

$-3x + 4y = 10$

Solution:

$(2)(4) - (-3)(-3) = 8 - 9 = -1$

5.35 Find the determinants of the following system of equations:

$5x - 2y = 10$

$3x + 2y = 6$

Solution:

$(5)(2) - (3)(-2) = 10 - (-6) = 10 + 6 = 16$

5.36 Use the Gaussian method to solve the system of equations:

$2x + y = 2$

$-x + y = 5$

Solution:

Write the system as a matrix:

$$\begin{bmatrix} 2 & 1 & 2 \\ -1 & 1 & 5 \end{bmatrix}$$

Multiply the bottom row by 2 and add it to the top row to get 0 In the second row, first column:

$$\begin{bmatrix} 2 & 1 & 2 \\ 2(-1)+2 & 2(1)+1 & 2(5)+2 \end{bmatrix} \rightarrow \begin{bmatrix} 2 & 1 & 2 \\ 0 & 3 & 12 \end{bmatrix}$$

This gives $3y = 12$. Solve for y:

$$\frac{3y}{3} = \frac{12}{3}$$
$$y = 4$$

Substitute $y = 4$ into one of the original equations:

$$2x + y = 2$$
$$2x + 4 = 2$$
$$2x + 4 - 4 = 2 - 4$$
$$2x = -2$$
$$x = -1$$

The solution to the system is $(-1, 4)$

Chapter 6 Polynomials

6.1 Simplify: 5^{-3}

Solution:

$$5^{-3} = \frac{1}{5^3} = \frac{1}{125}$$

6.2 Simplify: $\dfrac{2}{x^{-4}}$

Solution:

$$\frac{2}{x^{-4}} = 2x^4$$

6.3 Simplify: $\dfrac{1}{2x^0}$

Solution:

$$\frac{1}{2x^0} = \frac{1}{2(1)} = \frac{1}{2}$$

6.4 Simplify: $(3m^2n^4)(-2mn^6)$.

Solution:
$$(3m^2n^4)(-2mn^6) = -6m^3n^{10}$$

6.5 Simplify: $(4x^6y^4)(-3x^{-1}y^2)$

Solution:
$$(4x^6y^4)(-3x^{-1}y^2) = -12x^5y^6$$

6.6 Simplify: $(x^2y^{-4})^2$

Solution:

$$(x^2y^{-4})^2 = x^4y^{-8} = \frac{x^4}{y^8}$$

6.7 Simplify: $\left(\dfrac{2}{3}\right)^3$

Solution:

$$\left(\dfrac{2}{3}\right)^3 = \dfrac{2^3}{3^3} = \dfrac{8}{27}$$

6.8 Simplify: $\dfrac{x^3 y}{xy^4}$

Solution:

$$\dfrac{x^3 y}{xy^4} = \dfrac{x^2}{y^3}$$

6.9 Simplify: $\dfrac{2x^{-3}}{6x^{-2}}$

Solution:

$$\dfrac{2x^{-3}}{6x^{-2}} = \dfrac{1}{3x}$$

6.10 Write .000057 in scientific notation.

Solution:

$$.000057 = 5.7 \times 10^{-5}$$

6.11 Write 2.72×10^{-3} in decimal notation.

Solution:

$$2.72 \times 10^{-3} = .00272$$

6.12 Evaluate the polynomial: $2x^3 - 5x + 11$ for $x = -2$

Solution:

$$2(-2)^3 - 5(-2) + 11 = 2(-8) + 10 + 11 = -16 + 21 = 5$$

6.13 Evaluate the polynomial: $15 + 2x - x^2$ for $x = 5$

Solution:

$$15 + 2(5) - 5^2 = 15 + 10 - 25 = 25 - 25 = 0$$

6.14 Perform the indicated operation and simplify: $(2x^2 - 5x + 7) + (3x^2 - 11x - 17)$

Solution:

$2x^2 + 3x^2 - 5x - 11x + 7 - 17$	Group like terms.
$5x^2 - 16x - 10$	Collect like terms.

6.15 Perform the indicated operation and simplify: $(3x^3 - x + 8) - (x^3 - 2x^2 - 5x - 11)$

Solution:

$3x^3 - x + 8 - x^3 + 2x^2 + 5x + 11$	Distribute negative.
$3x^3 - x^3 + 2x^2 + 5x - x + 8 + 11$	Group like terms.
$2x^3 + 2x^2 + 4x + 19$	

6.16 Perform the indicated operation and simplify: $2x(x - 3)$

Solution:

$2x(x - 3) = 2x^2 - 6x$

6.17 Perform the indicated operation and simplify: $4x(x^2 - 3x + 5)$

Solution:

$4x^3 - 12x^2 + 20x$ Distribute $4x$.

6.18 Perform the indicated operation and simplify: $-4ab(5a - 3b)$

Solution:

$-4ab(5a - 3b) = -20a^2b + 12ab^2$

6.19 Perform the indicated operation and simplify: $4a^3 + 2a(a^2 - 5a - 3)$

Solution:

$4a^3 + 2a(a^2 - 5a - 3) = 4a^3 + 2a^3 - 10a^2 - 6a = 6a^3 - 10a^2 - 6a$

6.20 Perform the indicated operation and simplify: $(2x - 5)(x + 3)$

Solution:

$2x \cdot x + 2x \cdot 3 + (-5) \cdot x + (-5) \cdot 3$ FOIL
$2x^2 + 6x - 5x - 15$ Multiply terms.
$2x^2 + x - 15$ Collect like terms.

6.21 Simplify $(x - 2y)(x + 5y)$

Solution:

$(x - 2y)(x + 5y) = x^2 + 5xy - 2xy - 10y^2$
$= x^2 + 3xy - 10y^2$

6.22 Perform the indicated operation and simplify: $(x^2 + 2)(x^2 - x - 3)$

Solution:

$x^2 \cdot x^2 + x^2 \cdot (-x) + x^2 \cdot (-3) + 2 \cdot x^2 + 2 \cdot (-x) + 2 \cdot (-3)$ Distribute.
$x^4 - x^3 - 3x^2 + 2x^2 - 2x - 6$ Multiply.
$x^4 - x^3 - x^2 - 2x - 6$ Collect like terms.

6.23 Perform the indicated operation and simplify: $(3x - 5)(3x + 5)$

Solution:

$(3x - 5)(3x + 5)$
$3x \cdot 3x + 3x \cdot 5 + (-5) \cdot 3x + (-5) \cdot 5$ FOIL
$9x^2 + 15x - 15x - 25$ Multiply.
$9x^2 - 25$ Collect like terms.

6.24 Perform the indicated operation and simplify: $(x^2 - 3)(x^2 - 3)$

Solution:

$(x^2 - 3)(x^2 - 3)$
$x^2 \cdot x^2 + x^2 \cdot (-3) + (-3) \cdot x^2 + (-3)(-3)$ FOIL
$x^4 - 3x^2 - 3x^2 + 9$ Multiply.
$x^4 - 6x^2 + 9$ Collect like terms.

6.25 Perform the indicated operation and simplify: $y^2 - (x - y)^2$

Solution:

$y^2 - (x - y)^2 = y^2 - (x - y)(x - y) = y^2 - [x^2 - 2xy + y^2] = -x^2 + 2xy$

6.26 Divide: $\dfrac{5m^4 n^2}{25mn^2}$

Solution:

$\dfrac{5m^4 n^2}{25mn^2} = \dfrac{m^3}{5}$

6.27 Divide: $\dfrac{4m^3 n^5 - 20m^2 n^2}{4m^2 n^2}$

Solution:

$\dfrac{4m^3 n^5 - 20m^2 n^2}{4m^2 n^2} = \dfrac{4m^3 n^5}{4m^2 n^2} - \dfrac{20m^2 n^2}{4m^2 n^2} = mn^3 - 5$

6.28 Divide: $\dfrac{3pq^3 + 18p^2 q^2 - pq}{3pq}$

Solution:

$\dfrac{3pq^3 + 18p^2 q^2 - pq}{3pq} = \dfrac{3pq^3}{3pq} + \dfrac{18p^2 q^2}{3pq} - \dfrac{pq}{3pq} = q^2 + 6pq - \dfrac{1}{3}$

6.29 Divide: $(x^2 + 3x - 40) \div (x - 5)$

Solution:

$$\begin{array}{r} x + 8 \\ x - 5 \overline{)\, x^2 + 3x - 40} \end{array}$$

$(x^2 + 3x - 40) \div (x - 5) = x + 8$

6.30 Divide: $(x^2 + 5x - 7) \div (x + 3)$

Solution:

$(x^2 + 5x - 7) \div (x + 3) = x + 2 - \dfrac{13}{x + 3}$

6.31 The following polynomial describes the height of an object t seconds after being thrown straight up with an initial velocity of 96 feet per second:

$H(t) = -16t^2 + 96t$

Find the height of the object after 5 seconds.

Solution:

$\begin{aligned} H(5) &= -16(5)^2 + 96(5) \\ &= -16(25) + 480 \\ &= -400 + 480 \\ &= 80 \text{ feet} \end{aligned}$

6.32 The demand for a particular item is given by $x = 100 - p$, where p is the price of the product. Revenue can be found by taking the number of items sold times the price of each item. Find the revenue. Then find the revenue if the particular item sold for $28.

Solution:

Revenue = Number of items sold · Price of each item = $(100 - p) \cdot p = 100p - p^2$
Revenue = $100(28) - 28^2 = \$2016$

Chapter 7 Factoring Polynomials

7.1 Factor completely: $8x - 24$

Solution:

$8x - 24 = 8(x - 3)$

7.2 Factor a monomial from a polynomial: $16 - 8x^2$

Solution:

$16 - 8x^2 = 8(2 - x^2)$

7.3 Factor a monomial from a polynomial: $2x^4 - 4x$

Solution:

$2x^4 - 4x = 2x(x^3 - 2)$

7.4 Factor the monomial from a polynomial: $9x^2 + 81$

Solution:

$9x^2 + 81 = 9(x^2 + 9)$

7.5 Factor completely: $\dfrac{x}{2} + \dfrac{3x^2}{4}$

Solution:

$\dfrac{x}{2}\left(1 + \dfrac{3x}{2}\right)$

7.6 Factor completely: $10x^2 - 25x^3$

Solution:

$5x^2(2 - 5x)$

7.7 Factor completely: $x(y + 2) + 4(y + 2)$

Solution:

$(y + 2)(x + 4)$

7.8 Factor completely: $3x^2 (c - d) + 5(c - d)$

Solution:

$(c - d)(3x^2 + 5)$

7.9 Factor completely: $x(x - 1) + y(1 - x)$

Solution:

$(x - 1)(x - y)$

7.10 Factor completely: $2x^4 - 4x^3 - x^2 + 2x$

Solution:

$2x^3(x - 2) - x(x - 2) = (x - 2)(2x^3 - x) = x(x - 2)(2x^2 - 1)$

7.11 Factor completely: $x^2 + 7x + 12$

Solution:

$(x + 4)(x + 3)$

7.12 Factor completely: $x^2 + 8x + 16$

Solution:

$(x + 4)(x + 4)$

7.13 Factor completely: $t^2 - 8t + 15$

Solution:

$(t - 5)(t - 3)$

7.14 Factor completely: $b^2 + 12b + 27$

Solution:

$(b + 9)(b + 3)$

7.15 Factor completely: $y^2 - y - 2$

Solution:

$(y - 2)(y + 1)$

7.16 Factor completely: $x^2 + 27x + 72$

Solution:

$(x + 24)(x + 3)$

7.17 Factor completely: $2x^2 + 10x + 8$

Solution:

$2x^2 + 10x + 8 = 2(x^2 + 5x + 4) = 2(x + 4)(x + 1)$

7.18 Factor completely: $xy^2 + 5xy + 6x$

Solution:

$xy^2 + 5xy + 6x = x(y^2 + 5y + 6) = x(y + 3)(y + 2)$

7.19 Factor completely: $5x^2 + 7x + 2$

Solution:

$(x + 1)(5x + 2)$

7.20 Factor completely: $2x^2 - 5x + 3$

Solution:

$(2x - 3)(x - 1)$

7.21 Factor completely: $6x^2 + 5x - 1$

Solution:

$(6x - 1)(x + 1)$

7.22 Factor completely: $7x^2 + 50x + 7$

Solution:

$(7x + 1)(x + 7)$

7.23 Factor completely: $6y^2 - 7y - 3$

Solution:

$(3y + 1)(2y - 3)$

7.24 Factor completely: $-2x^2 - 7x - 5$

Solution:

$-1(2x^2 + 7x + 5) = -(2x + 5)(x + 1)$

7.25 Factor the following expression: The equivalent resistance R of two electric circuits is given by $2R^2 - 3R + 1$.

Solution:

$(2R - 1)(R - 1)$

7.26 Factor completely: $4x^2 - 25$

Solution:

Difference of two squares is $(2x - 5)(2x + 5)$.

7.27 Factor completely: $125x^3 + 64y^3$

Solution:

Sum of two cubes is $(5x + 4y)(25x^2 - 20xy + 16y^2)$.

7.28 Factor completely: $8x^3 - 27$

Solution:

Difference of two cubes is $(2x - 3)(4x^2 + 6x + 9)$.

7.29 Solve: $(x + 3)(x + 2) = 0$

Solution:

Two possible solutions: $x = -3$ and $x = -2$

7.30 Solve: $x^2 - 81 = 0$

Solution:

Two possible solutions: $x = -9$ and $x = 9$

7.31 Solve the following by factoring: $x^2 + 6x + 8 = 0$

Solution:

Two possible solutions: $x = -4$ and $x = -2$

7.32 Solve the following by factoring: $2x^2 + x - 36 = 0$

Solution:

$$2x^2 + x - 36 = 0$$
$$(2x + 9)(x - 4) = 0 \qquad\qquad \text{Factor.}$$

$2x + 9 = 0$	or	$x - 4 = 0$	Set both $= 0$.
$2x + 9 - 9 = 0 - 9$		$x - 4 + 4 = 0 + 4$	Solve.
$2x = -9$		$x = 4$	
$\dfrac{2x}{2} = -\dfrac{9}{2}$			
$x = -\dfrac{9}{2}$			

Two possible solutions: $x = -\dfrac{9}{2}$ or $x = 4$

7.33 Solve the following by factoring: $12x^2 + 5x - 3 = 0$

Solution:

$$12x^2 + 5x - 3 = 0$$
$$(4x + 3)(3x - 1) = 0 \qquad\qquad \text{Factor.}$$

$4x + 3 = 0$	or	$3x - 1 = 0$	Set both $= 0$.
$4x + 3 - 3 = 0 - 3$		$3x - 1 + 1 = 0 + 1$	Solve.
$4x = -3$		$3x = 1$	
$\dfrac{4x}{4} = -\dfrac{3}{4}$		$\dfrac{3x}{3} = \dfrac{1}{3}$	
$x = -\dfrac{3}{4}$		$x = \dfrac{1}{3}$	

Two possible solutions: $x = -\dfrac{3}{4}$ or $x = \dfrac{1}{3}$

7.34 The square of a positive number is four more than three times the positive number. Find the number.

Solution:

The number is 4.

7.35 Find the dimensions of a rectangle with width $= 2x + 1$ and length $= x + 3$ and an area of 7 square feet.

Solution:

$$\text{Area} = \text{Length} \times \text{Width} \qquad\qquad \text{Formula}$$

$$7 = (x + 3)(2x + 1)$$

$$7 = 2x^2 + 7x + 3 \qquad\qquad \text{FOIL}$$

$$0 = 2x^2 + 7x - 4 \qquad\qquad \text{Set equation} = 0.$$

$$0 = (2x - 1)(x + 4) \qquad\qquad \text{Factor.}$$

$$2x - 1 = 0 \qquad \text{or} \qquad x + 4 = 0 \qquad\qquad \text{Set factors} = 0.$$

$$2x - 1 + 1 = 0 + 1 \qquad\qquad x + 4 - 4 = 0 - 4$$

$$2x = 1 \qquad\qquad\qquad x = -4$$

$$\frac{2x}{2} = \frac{1}{2}$$

$$x = \frac{1}{2}$$

Because the negative would not make sense, we discard $x = -4$ and use $x = \dfrac{1}{2}$.

Therefore, the dimensions are $L = x + 3 = \dfrac{1}{2} + 3 = 3\dfrac{1}{2}$ feet and $W = 2x + 1 = 2\left(\dfrac{1}{2}\right) + 1 = 2$ feet.

Chapter 8 Quadratic Functions

8.1 Write the quadratic function with coefficients $a = 8$, $b = 3$, and $c = 4$ in general form.

Solution:

Inset the constants in to the general form of the quadratic equation.
$y = 8x^2 + 3x + 4$

8.2 What are the coefficients of the quadratic function $y = 2x^2 + 3x + 10$

Solution:

By analogy to the general form $a = 2$, $b = 3$, and $c = 10$.

8.3 The parabola $y = x^2$ is shifted 2 units to the left and 5 unit up from the origin. Write its equation in vertex form.

Solution:

The vertex of $y = x^2$ is $(0, 0)$. If the parabola is shifted 2 units to the left, then $h = -2$. A shift of 2 units up means $k = 5$. Therefore, $y = (x + 2)^2 + 5$

8.4 The parabola $y = x^2$ shifts 1 unit down and 3 units to the right from the origin. It is stretched to be three times as steep as the original parabola. Write its equation in vertex form.

Solution:

A shift of 1 unit down means that $k = -1$, and a shift of 3 units to the right mean $h = 3$. If the parabola is three times as steep, this indicates that $a = 3$.
In vertex form, the equation is $y = 3(x - 3) - 1$

8.5 If $f(x) = x^2$ is shown in the graph below, graph $f(x) + 5$.

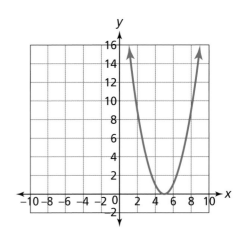

Solution:

$f(x) = x^2$. $f(x) + 5 = x^2 + 5$. This transforms the original function by moving the vertex up 5 units on the y-axis.

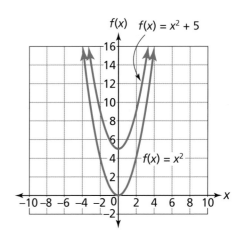

8.6 If the graph of $f(x) = 2x^2$ is shown below, graph $f(x - 1)$.

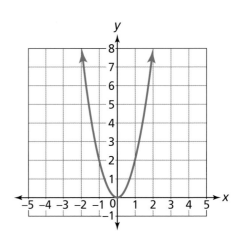

Solution:

$f(x - 1) = 2(x - 1)^2$. This will transform the graph by shifting it to the right.

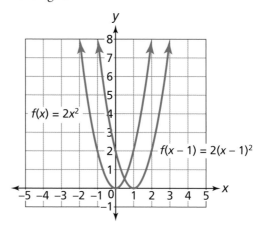

8.7 Below is the graph of $f(x) = x^2 + 2$. Graph $-f(x)$.

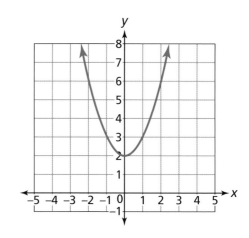

Solution:

$-f(x) = -(x^2 + 2) = -x^2 - 2$. This reflects the curve about the x-axis, so the new curve is as shown below.

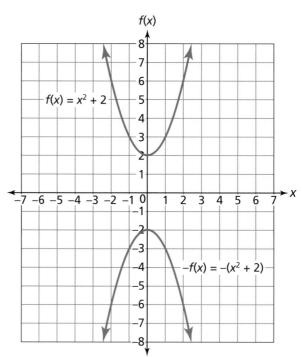

8.8 What is the axis of symmetry of the quadratic function $f(x) = -\dfrac{1}{2}x^2$?

Solution:

Because there are no terms of lower order than 2, the parabola will have the y-axis ($x = 0$) as its axis of symmetry.

8.9 What is the axis of symmetry of the function $f(x) = (x-3)^2 - 4$

Solution:

Since $h = 3$ in this equation the axis of symmetry is the line $x = 3$.

8.10 What is the axis of symmetry of the function $f(x) = x^2 + 4x + 4$?

Solution:

Factoring $f(x) = x^2 + 4x + 4 = (x+2)^2$. Therefore the axis of symmetry will be the line $x = -2$.

8.11 What is the axis of symmetry of the function $f(x) = 2x^2 + 3x + 1$

Solution:

For a quadratic function in standard form, the axis of symmetry is $x = -\dfrac{b}{2a}$.

In this case, we have $-\dfrac{3}{2 \cdot 2} = -\dfrac{3}{4}$

8.12 Does the parabola given by $x^2 - 3x + 2$ open up or down?

Solution:

In this case $a = 1$, so the parabola opens up.

8.13 Does the quadratic function $f(x) = -3x^2 + 2x + 5$ open up or open down?

Solution:

Because the sign of the coefficient of the x^2 term is negative, the parabola will open down.

8.14 Will the graph of the function $f(x) = \dfrac{3}{4}(x-7)^2$ open upward or downward?

Solution:

$$f(x) = \frac{3}{4}(x-7)^2 = \frac{3}{4}x^2 - \frac{21}{2} + \frac{147}{4}$$

Since the coefficient of the x^2 term is positive, the parabola will open upward.

8.15 Find the vertex of the quadratic function $y = (x+2)^2 - 4$

Solution:

$y = (x+2)^2 - 4$
$y = (x - (-2)^2 + (-4)$
By analogy of the definition, see that $h = -2$ and $k = -4$
Vertex of the quadratic function is $(-2, -4)$

8.16 Find the vertex of the equation $y = 3(x-2)^2 + 3$

Solution:

In vertex form, $(h, k) = (2, 3)$

8.17 How many *x*-intercepts can the graph of $f(x) = ax^2 + bx + c$ have?

Solution:

Zero, one or two

8.18 How many *y*-intercepts does the graph of $f(x) = ax^2 + bx + c$ have?

Solution:

One

8.19 Use the discriminant to determine the number of solutions of $3x^2 + 2x - 2 = 0$.

Solution:

In $3x^2 + 2x - 2 = 0$, $a = 3$, $b = 2$, and $c = -2$. Then $b^2 - 4ac = (2)^2 - 4(3)(-2) = 4 + 24 = 28$. Since the discriminant is 28, a positive number, this equation has two distinct real solutions.

8.20 Use the discriminant to determine the number of solutions of $x^2 - 6x + 9 = 0$.

Solution:

In $x^2 - 6x + 9 = 0$, $a = 1$, $b = -6$, and $c = 9$
$b^2 - 4ac = (-6)^2 - 4(1)(9) = 36 - 36 = 0$
The discriminant is 0, so the equation has one root.

8.21 Use the discriminant to determine the number of solutions of $5x^2 + 1 = 0$.

Solution:

In $5x^2 + 1 = 0$, $a = 5$, $b = 0$, and $c = 1$
$b^2 - 4ac = 0^2 - 4(5)(1) = 0 - 20 = -20$
Since the discriminant is -20, a negative number, this equation has no real solution.

8.22 Determine the coordinate of the vertex for the quadratic function $f(x) = \dfrac{3}{4}(x - 7)^2$.

Solution:

The vertex form of a quadratic is $f(x) = a(x - h)^2 + k$, where (h, k) is the vertex. The function is already in this form: $f(x) = \dfrac{3}{4}(x - 7)^2 + 0$.

So, $h = 7$, $k = 0$. The vertex is at $(7, 0)$.

8.23 Determine the coordinates of the vertex for the quadratic function $f(x) = x^2 + 4x + 6$.

Solution:

To get the function into the form $f(x) = a(x - h)^2 + k$, we need to notice that $x^2 + 4x + 4 = (x + 2)^2$.
We can rewrite the function as follows (called completing the square):

$f(x) = x^2 + 4x + 4 + 2$

$f(x) = (x + 2)^2 + 2$

$f(x) = (x - (-2))^2 + 2$

This is now in the vertex form with $h = -2$ and $k = 2$. The vertex of the parabola is $(-2, 2)$.

8.24 What number completes the square in the expression $x^2 + 18x$?

Solution:

We are trying to find "b" in the special form $(a + b)^2 = a^2 + 2ab + b^2$:

$x^2 + 18x + b$

$a = x$

$18x = 2xb$

Solve for b:

$$\frac{18x}{2x} = \frac{2xb}{2x}$$

$$9 = b$$

Finally we square b:
$b^2 = 9^2 = 81$

So the completed square is:
$x^2 + 18x + 81$

8.25 Find the number that will make the following a perfect square: $y^2 - \frac{1}{5}y + ?$

Solution:

To complete the square, we need the b in $(a - b)^2 = a^2 - 2ab + b^2$:

$$\frac{1}{5} = 2b$$

$$\left(\frac{1}{2}\right)\left(\frac{1}{5}\right) = \left(\frac{1}{2}\right)(2b)$$

$$\frac{1}{10} = b$$

Square b:

$$b^2 = \left(\frac{1}{10}\right)^2 = \frac{1}{100}$$

The completed square is:

$$y^2 - \frac{1}{5}y + \frac{1}{100}$$

8.26 Complete the square for $x^2 + 10x$ then factor to the resulting perfect square trinomial.

Solution:

The coefficient of the x-term is 10. Half of 10 is 5 and $5^2 = 25$. Thus, add 25.
$x^2 + 10x + 25 = (x + 5)^2$

8.27 Solve the following quadratic equation by completing the square: $x^2 - 8x = -12$.

Solution:

To complete the square, we need to find b such that

$2bx = 8x$

$b = 4$

We square b to get the constant term:
$b^2 = 4^2 = 16$

We must add 16 to each side of the equation to complete the square:

$x^2 - 8x + 16 = -12 + 16$

$x^2 - 8x + 16 = 4$

Factor the polynomial:

$(x - 4)^2 = 4$

Take the square root of each side:

$\sqrt{(x-4)^2} = \sqrt{4}$

$x - 4 = \pm 2$

First solution:

$x - 4 = 2$

$x - 4 + 4 = 2 + 4$

$x = 6$

Second solution:

$x - 4 = -2$

$x - 4 + 4 = -2 + 4$

$x = 2$

$x = 2, 6$

Check $x = 2$

$x^2 - 8x = -12$

$(2)^2 - 8(2) = -12?$

$4 - 16 = -12?$

$-12 = -12?$

 *Yes!*

Check $x = 6$

$x^2 - 8x = -12$

$(6)^2 - 8(6) = -12?$

$36 - 48 = -12?$

$-12 = -12?$

 *Yes!*

Solution $x = 2, 6$ is correct.

8.28 Solve by completing the square: $x^2 - 14x - 4 = 0$.

Solution:

$x^2 - 14x - 4 + 4 = 0 + 4$

$x^2 - 14x = 4$

$x^2 - 14x + \left(\dfrac{14}{2}\right)^2 = 4 + \left(\dfrac{14}{2}\right)^2$

$x^2 - 14x + 7^2 = 4 + 49$

$(x - 7)^2 = 53$

$\sqrt{(x-7)^2} = \sqrt{53}$

$x - 7 = \pm\sqrt{53}$

First solution:

$$x - 7 = \sqrt{53}$$
$$x - 7 + 7 = 7\sqrt{53}$$

Second solution:

$$x - 7 = -\sqrt{53}$$
$$x - 7 + 7 = 7 - \sqrt{53}$$

8.29 Solve by completing the square: $2x^2 - 13x - 5 = 0$.

Solution:

$$2x^2 - 13x - 5 + 5 = 0 + 5$$
$$2x^2 - 13x = 5$$
$$\frac{2x^2 - 13x}{2} = \frac{5}{2}$$
$$x^2 - \frac{13}{2}x = \frac{5}{2}$$
$$x^2 - \frac{13}{2}x + \left(\frac{1}{2}, \frac{13}{2}\right)^2 = \frac{5}{2} + \left(\frac{1}{2}, \frac{13}{2}\right)^2$$
$$x^2 - \frac{13}{2}x + \left(\frac{13}{4}\right)^2 = \frac{5}{2} + \frac{169}{16}$$
$$\left(x - \frac{13}{4}\right)^2 = \frac{5}{2} + \frac{169}{16}$$
$$\left(x - \frac{13}{4}\right)^2 = \frac{40 + 169}{16}$$
$$\left(x - \frac{13}{4}\right)^2 = \frac{209}{16}$$
$$\sqrt{\left(x - \frac{13}{4}\right)^2} = \sqrt{\frac{209}{16}}$$
$$x - \frac{13}{4} = \pm\frac{\sqrt{209}}{4}$$

First solution:

$$x - \frac{13}{4} = \frac{\sqrt{209}}{4}$$
$$x - \frac{13}{4} + \frac{13}{4} = \frac{13}{4} + \frac{\sqrt{209}}{4}$$
$$x = \frac{13 + \sqrt{209}}{4}$$

Second solution:

$$x - \frac{13}{4} = -\frac{\sqrt{209}}{4}$$

$$x - \frac{13}{4} + \frac{13}{4} = \frac{13}{4} - \frac{\sqrt{209}}{4}$$

$$x = \frac{13 - \sqrt{209}}{4}$$

8.30 Identify the value of a, b, and c in the quadratic equation $x^2 - 7 = 0$.

Solution:

$a = 1$, $b = 0$, $c = -7$

8.31 Use the quadratic formula to solve $9x^2 - 7x - 3 = 0$.

Solution:

$a = 9$

$b = -7$

$c = -3$

Substituting into the quadratic formula:

$$x = \frac{-b \pm \sqrt{b^2 - 4ac}}{2a}$$

$$x = \frac{-(-7) \pm \sqrt{(-7)^2 - 4(9)(-3)}}{2(9)}$$

$$x = \frac{7 \pm \sqrt{49 + 108}}{18}$$

$$x = \frac{7 \pm \sqrt{157}}{18}$$

The solutions are:

$$x = \frac{7 + \sqrt{157}}{18}$$

$$x = \frac{7 - \sqrt{157}}{18}$$

8.32 Use the quadratic formula to solve $0.6x^2 = 1.2x + 0.06$.

Solution:

$$0.6x^2 - 1.2x - 0.6 = 1.2x + 0.06 - 1.2x - 0.6$$

$$0.6x^2 - 1.2x - 0.6 = 0$$

$$10(0.6x^2 - 1.2x - 0.6) = 10(0)$$

$$6x^2 - 12x - 6 = 0$$

$$a = 6$$

$$b = -12$$

$$c = -6$$

$$x = \frac{-b \pm \sqrt{b^2 - 4ac}}{2a}$$

$$x = \frac{-(-12) \pm \sqrt{(-12)^2 - 4(6)(-6)}}{2(6)}$$

$$x = \frac{12 \pm \sqrt{144 - (-144)}}{12}$$

$$x = \frac{12 \pm \sqrt{288}}{12}$$

$$x = 1 \pm \frac{\sqrt{288}}{\sqrt{(12)^2}}$$

$$x = 1 \pm \frac{\sqrt{288}}{\sqrt{144}}$$

$$x = 1 \pm \sqrt{\frac{288}{144}}$$

$$x = 1 \pm \sqrt{2}$$

First solution:

$$x = 1 + \sqrt{2}$$

Second solution:

$$x = 1 - \sqrt{2}$$

8.33 Use the square root property to solve $x^2 = -4$.

Solution:

No real solution

8.34 Use the square root property to solve $x^2 - 16 = 0$.

Solution:

$$x^2 - 16 = 0$$
$$x^2 = 16$$
$$x = \pm 4$$

8.35 Use the square root property to solve $3x^2 = 9$.

Solution:

$$3x^2 = 9$$
$$x^2 = 3$$
$$x = \pm\sqrt{3}$$

8.36 Use the square root property to solve $(x - 4)^2 = 25$.

Solution:

Instead of x^2, we have $(x - 4)^2$. But the square root property can still be used.

$$(x - 4)^2 = 25$$

$$x - 4 = \sqrt{25} \quad \text{or} \quad x - 4 = -\sqrt{25}$$
$$x - 4 = 5 \qquad\qquad x - 4 = -5$$
$$x = 9 \qquad\qquad\quad x = -1$$

Chapter 9 Graphing Higher-Order Polynomials

For the following polynomials:

    a. Classify the polynomial functions as constant, linear, quadratic, cubic, or quartic.

    b. Find the leading term.

    c. Find the leading coefficient.

    d. Give the degree of the polynomial.

9.1 $f(x) = -x^2 - 3x + 5$.

Solution:

    a. Quadratic

    b. $-x^2$

    c. -1

    d. 2

9.2 $f(x) = 5 - x$.

    a. Linear

    b. $-x$

    c. 1

    d. 1

9.3 $f(x) = -0.7x^4 - 3x^2 + 5x - 7$.

    a. Quartic

    b. $-0.7x^4$

    c. -0.7

    d. 4

9.4 $f(x) = -\dfrac{2}{3}$.

    a. Constant

    b. $-\dfrac{2}{3}$

    c. $-\dfrac{2}{3}$

    d. 0

9.5 $f(x) = x^3 + 5x^2 - x + 9$.

    a. Cubic

    b. x^3

    c. 1

    d. 3

9.6 Given $f(x) = 5x - 3$, evaluate $f(3)$.

Solution:

$f(3) = 5(3) - 3 = 12$

9.7 Given $F(x) = x^2 + 3x - 4$, evaluate $F(-3) =$

Solution:

$(-3)^2 + 3(-3) - 4 = 9 - 9 - 4 = -4$

9.8 Given $H(x) = \dfrac{3x}{x+2}$, evaluate $H(-3)$.

Solution:

$\dfrac{3(-3)}{-3+2} = 9$

9.9 Determine which of the following are polynomials. For those that are polynomials, give the degree, and for those that are not polynomials, explain why not.

    a. $f(x) = 2 - 3x^2$
    b. $f(x) = 5$
    c. $f(x) = \dfrac{x-2}{x^2+5}$

Solution:

    a. Yes, degree $= 2$
    b. Yes, degree $= 0$ because $5 = 5x^0 = 5(1) = 5$
    c. No, because it is the ratio of two polynomials and cannot be written in standard form

9.10 Graph the following power functions and determine if they are even or odd functions.

    a. $f(x) = x^2$
    b. $f(x) = x^4$
    c. $f(x) = x^3$

Solution:

    a. $f(x) = x^2$ is an even function. See the graph.

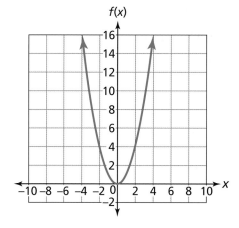

    b. $f(x) = x^4$ is an even function. See the graph.

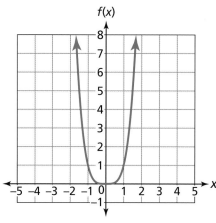

c. $f(x) = x^3$ is an odd function. See the graph.

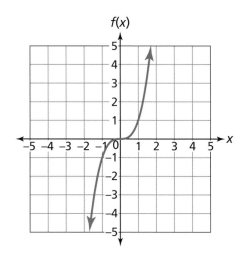

9.11 Determine algebraically whether the function $f(x) = -2x^2$ is even, odd or neither.

Solution:

$f(x) = -2x^2$
$f(-x) = -2(-x)^2 = -2(x^2) = -2x^2$
The function is even.

9.12 Determine algebraically whether the function $f(x) = 2x^3 - 2x$ is even, odd or neither.

Solution:

$f(x) = 2x^3 - 2x$
$f(-x) = 2(-x)^3 - 2(-x) = 2(-x^3) + 2x = -2x^3 + 2x$
The function is odd.

9.13 Determine algebraically whether the function $f(x) = -3x^2 + 2$ is even, odd or neither.

Solution:

$f(x) = -3x^2 + 2$
$f(-x) = -3(-x)^2 + 2 = -3x^2 + 2$
The function is even.

9.14 Graph $f(x) = \dfrac{3}{4}x + 1$

Solution:

Step 1: Make a table of several values of x and $f(x)$.

x	f(x)
−4	−2
−1	.25
0	1
1	1.75
4	4

Step 2: Plot these points on a coordinate plane.

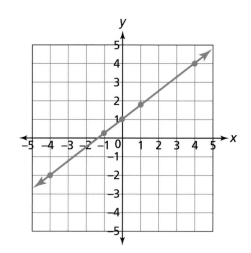

9.15 Graph $f(x) = -\dfrac{1}{2}x + 3$.

Solution:

Step 1: Make a table of several values of x and $f(x)$.

x	f(x)
−4	5
0	3
2	2

Step 2: Plot these points on a coordinate plane.

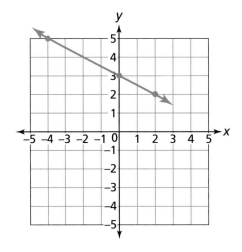

9.16 Graph the polynomial $f(x) = \dfrac{1}{2}(x-1)^4$ using transformations. Show each stage of the function being transformed and explain the transformation.

Solution:

Step 1: Graph $f(x) = x^4$.

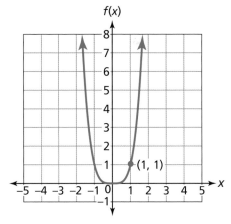

Step 2: Shift 1 unit to the right to graph $f(x) = (x-1)^4$.

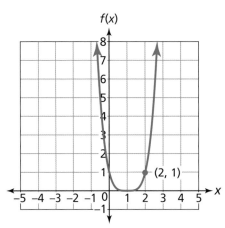

Step 3: Compress by a factor of ½.

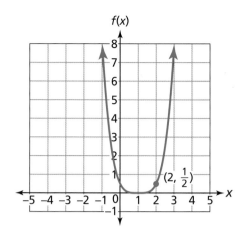

9.17 Graph the polynomial $f(x) = 1 - x^3$ using transformations. Show each stage of the function being transformed and explain the transformation.

Solution:

Step 1: Graph $f(x) = x^3$.

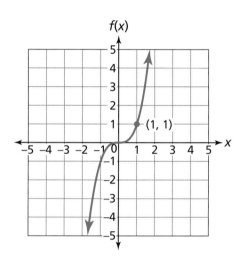

Step 2: Reflect about the *x*-axis by multiplying by -1 to graph $f(x) = -x^3$.

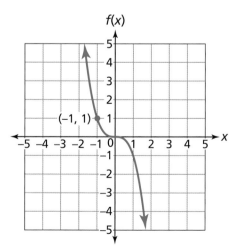

Step 3: Shift function up 1 unit to graph $f(x) = 1 - x^3$.

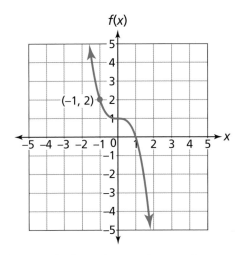

9.18 Find a polynomial of degree 3 whose zeros are -2, 3, and 4. Then graph the polynomial to verify your result.

Solution:

$(x - (-2))(x - 3)(x - 4) = (x + 2)(x - 3)(x - 4) = x^3 - 5x^2 - 2x + 24$

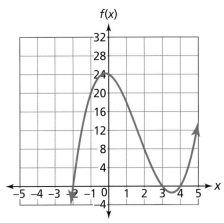

9.19 Find a polynomial of degree 4 whose zeros are -4, -1, 2, 3. Then graph the polynomial to verify your result.

Solution:

$(x - (-4))(x - (-1))(x - 2)(x - 3) = (x + 4)(x + 1)(x - 2)(x - 3) = x^4 - 15x^2 + 10x + 24$

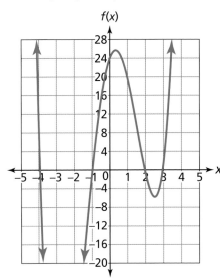

9.20 Find the zeros and state the multiplicity of the polynomial $f(x) = -2(x-4)^3(x+5)$.

Solution:

$x - 4 = 0$
$x = 4$ with a multiplicity of 3.

$x + 5 = 0$
$x = -5$ with a multiplicity of 1.

9.21 Find the zeros and state the multiplicity of the polynomial $f(x) = x^2(x+2)(x+2)(x+2)$.

Solution:

$x^2 = 0$
$x = 0$ with a multiplicity of 2.

$x + 2 = 0$
$x = -2$ with a multiplicity of 3.

9.22 Find a polynomial of degree 3 whose zeros are -2, multiplicity 2; 4, multiplicity 1. Then graph the polynomial to verify your result.

Solution:

$f(x) = (x+2)^2(x-4) = x^3 - 12x - 16$

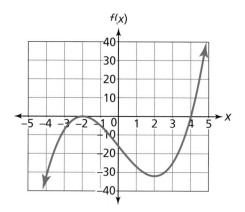

9.23 Find and identify the number of turning points for the function $f(x) = x^2(x-2)$. Verify with the graph of the function.

Solution:

The function is degree 3 since $f(x) = x^2(x-2) = x^3 - 2x^2$ and thus has $3 - 1 = 2$ turning points. One at $(0, 0)$ and the other between $x = 0$ and $x = 2$.

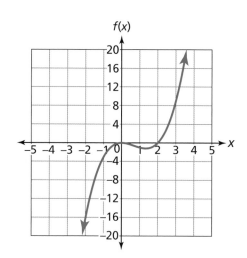

9.24 For the polynomial, $f(x) = x^3 - x^2 - 12x$ find the intercepts and determine the maximum number of turning points.

Solution:

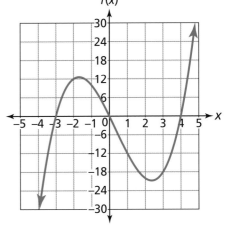

To find the x-intercepts, first factor the polynomial.
$f(x) = x^3 - x^2 - 12x = x(x-4)(x+3)$

Thus $x = 0$, $x = 4$ and $x = -3$ or the points $(0, 0)$, $(4, 0)$ and $(-3, 0)$ are all x-intercepts.
To find the y-intercepts, set $x = 0$, that is
$f(0) = 0^3 - 0^2 - 12(0) = 0$

Thus the origin $(0, 0)$ is the only y-intercept.

The function is of degree 3 so it will contain at most $3 - 1 = 2$ turning points.

9.25 For the function $f(x) = 3(x - 7)(x + 3)^2$:
  a. List each real zero and its multiplicity
  b. Find the x and y intercepts
  c. Determine the maximum number of turning points

Solution:
  a. 7, with multiplicity of 1 and -3 with multiplicity of 2
  b. Crosses the x-axis at 7 and -3
  c. $n - 1 = 3 - 1 = 2$

9.26 Find the turning point of $f(x) = x^2 - 2x$ and graph its function.

Solution:

Step 1: Make a table of the points along the graph.

x	f(x)
−1	3
0	0
1	−1
2	0
3	3

Step 2: Plot the points and use them to form the graph.

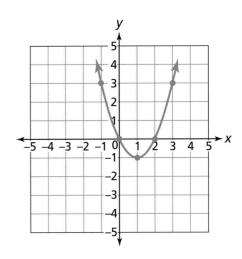

Step 3: The turning point of this function is located at $x = 1$

Chapter 10 Rational Expressions and Equations

10.1 Write $\dfrac{3}{8a^2}$ with a denominator of $16a^4$.

Solution:

$$\frac{3}{8a^2} = \frac{3}{8a^2} \cdot 1 = \frac{3}{8a^2} \cdot \frac{2a^2}{2a^2} = \frac{6a^2}{16a^4}$$

10.2 Simplify the following: $\dfrac{12x^2}{15x^4}$

Solution:

$$\frac{12x^2}{15x^4} = \frac{(2)(2)(3)(x)(x)}{(3)(5)(x)(x)(x)(x)} = \frac{4}{5x^2}$$

10.3 Simplify the following: $\dfrac{3x-2}{2-3x}$

Solution:

$$\frac{3x-2}{2-3x} = -1$$

10.4 Simplify the following: $\dfrac{(x+2)^2}{(x+2)^3}$

Solution:

$$\frac{(x+2)^2}{(x+2)^3} = \frac{(x+2)(x+2)}{(x+2)(x+2)(x+2)} = \frac{1}{x+2}$$

10.5 Simplify the following: $\dfrac{6x-8}{9x^2-16}$

Solution:

$$\frac{6x-8}{9x^2-16} = \frac{2(3x-4)}{(3x+4)(3x-4)} = \frac{2}{3x+4}$$

10.6 Simplify the following: $\dfrac{2a^2-ab-b^2}{a^2-b^2}$

Solution:

$$\frac{2a^2-ab-b^2}{a^2-b^2} = \frac{(2a+b)(a-b)}{(a+b)(a-b)} = \frac{2a+b}{a+b}$$

10.7 Simplify the following: $1 + \dfrac{x}{1 + \dfrac{1}{1+x}}$

Solution:

$$1 + \frac{x}{1 + \dfrac{1}{1+x}} = 1 + \frac{x}{\dfrac{1+x}{1+x} + \dfrac{1}{1+x}} = 1 + \frac{x}{\dfrac{2+x}{1+x}} = 1 + \frac{x(1+x)}{2+x}$$

$$\frac{2+x}{2+x} + \frac{x+x^2}{2+x} = \frac{x^2+2x+2}{2+x}$$

10.8 Find the LCM of $2x^3y^2$ and $3x^2y^4$.

Solution:

$2x^3y^2 = (2)(x)(x)(x)(y)(y)$

$3x^2y^4 = (3)(x)(x)(y)(y)(y)(y)$

$\text{LCM} = 6x^3y^4$

10.9 Find the LCM of $x^2 + 3x$ and $x^2 + 8x + 15$.

Solution:

$x^2 + 3x = x(x+3)$

$x^2 + 8x + 15 = (x+5)(x+3)$

Thus the LCM $= x(x+3)(x+5)$

10.10 Perform the Indicated operation and simplify $\dfrac{3}{5} + \dfrac{1}{10}$

Solution:

A common denominator of 5 and 10 is 10, as a result we obtain

$$\frac{3}{5} + \frac{1}{10} = \frac{6}{10} + \frac{1}{10} = \frac{7}{10}$$

10.11 Simplify the following: $\dfrac{5}{3x} + \dfrac{2}{3x}$

Solution:

$$\frac{5}{3x} + \frac{2}{3x} = \frac{7}{3x}$$

10.12 Simplify the following: $\dfrac{x}{x+2} - \dfrac{3x+1}{x+2}$

Solution:

$$\frac{x}{x+2} - \frac{3x+1}{x+2} = \frac{x-(3x+1)}{x+2} = \frac{x-3x-1}{x+2} = \frac{-2x-1}{x+2}$$

10.13 Add: $\dfrac{3}{2x+4} + \dfrac{2}{x+2}$

Solution:

$$\frac{3}{2x+4} + \frac{2}{x+2} = \frac{3}{2(x+2)} + \frac{2}{x+2} \cdot \frac{2}{2} = \frac{3+4}{2(x+2)} = \frac{7}{2(x+2)}$$

10.14 Subtract: $\dfrac{4x}{x+1} - \dfrac{3}{x-1}$

Solution:

$$\frac{4x}{x+1} - \frac{3}{x-1} = \frac{4x}{x+1} \cdot \frac{x-1}{x-1} - \frac{3}{x-1} \cdot \frac{x+1}{x+1} = \frac{4x(x-1) - [3(x+1)]}{(x+1)(x-1)}$$

$$\frac{4x^2 - 4x - [3x+3]}{(x+1)(x-1)} = \frac{4x^2 - 4x - 3x - 3}{(x+1)(x-1)} = \frac{4x^2 - 7x - 3}{(x+1)(x-1)}$$

10.15 Multiply: $\dfrac{3}{x} \cdot \dfrac{5}{y}$

Solution:

$$\dfrac{3}{x} \cdot \dfrac{5}{y} = \dfrac{15}{xy}$$

10.16 Multiply: $\dfrac{4x}{3y} \cdot \dfrac{5}{8x^2}$

Solution:

$$\dfrac{4x}{3y} \cdot \dfrac{5}{8x^2} = \dfrac{20x}{24x^2 y} = \dfrac{5}{6xy}$$

10.17 Multiply: $\dfrac{2x^2 - 4x}{x^2 - 5x + 6} \cdot \dfrac{x^2 - 9}{2x^2}$

Solution:

$$\dfrac{2x^2 - 4x}{x^2 - 5x + 6} \cdot \dfrac{x^2 - 9}{2x^2}$$

$$\dfrac{2x(x-2)}{(x-2)(x-3)} \cdot \dfrac{(x+3)(x-3)}{2x^2} \qquad \text{Factor.}$$

$$\dfrac{2x(x-2)}{2x^2(x-2)} \cdot \dfrac{(x+3)(x-3)}{(x-3)} \qquad \text{Group common terms.}$$

$$\dfrac{1}{x} \cdot \dfrac{(x+3)}{1} \qquad \text{Cancel common terms}$$

$$\dfrac{x+3}{x} \qquad \text{Complete.}$$

10.18 Divide: $\dfrac{4}{y} \div \dfrac{x}{2}$

Solution:

$$\dfrac{4}{y} \div \dfrac{x}{2} = \dfrac{4}{y} \cdot \dfrac{2}{x} = \dfrac{8}{xy}$$

10.19 Divide: $\dfrac{x^2}{y^2 - 1} \div \dfrac{x^2}{y+1}$

Solution:

$$\dfrac{x^2}{y^2 - 1} \div \dfrac{x^2}{y+1} = \dfrac{x^2}{(y+1)(y-1)} \cdot \dfrac{y+1}{x^2} = \dfrac{1}{y-1}$$

10.20 Divide: $\dfrac{8x^3 + 27y^3}{64x^3 - y^3} \div \dfrac{4x^2 - 9y^2}{16x^2 + 4xy + y^2}$

Solution:

$$\dfrac{8x^3 + 27y^3}{64x^3 - y^3} \div \dfrac{4x^2 - 9y^2}{16x^2 + 4xy + y^2}$$

$$\dfrac{8x^3 + 27y^3}{64x^3 - y^3} \cdot \dfrac{16x^2 + 4xy + y^2}{4x^2 - 9y^2}$$ Flip second fraction and multiply.

$$\dfrac{(2x + 3y)(4x^2 - 6xy + 9y^2)}{(4x - y)(16x^2 + 4xy + y^2)} \cdot \dfrac{16x^2 + 4xy + y^2}{(2x - 3y)(2x + 3y)}$$ Factor.

$$\dfrac{(4x^2 - 6xy + 9y^2)}{(4x - y)(2x - 3y)}$$ Cancel common terms.

10.21 Solve: $\dfrac{x}{4} + 5 = \dfrac{2x}{3}$

Solution:

$$12\left(\dfrac{x}{4} + 5\right) = 12\left(\dfrac{2x}{3}\right)$$

$$3x + 60 = 8x$$

$$x = 12$$

10.22 Solve the following: $\dfrac{1}{x} = \dfrac{1}{3x} + \dfrac{1}{2}$

Solution:

$$\dfrac{1}{x} = \dfrac{1}{3x} + \dfrac{1}{2} \rightarrow 6x\left(\dfrac{1}{x}\right) = 6x\left(\dfrac{1}{3x}\right) + 6x\left(\dfrac{1}{2}\right) \rightarrow 6 = 2 + 3x$$

$$6 - 2 = 2 + 3x - 2$$

$$4 = 3x$$

$$\dfrac{4}{3} = \dfrac{3x}{3}$$

$$\dfrac{4}{3} = x$$

10.23 Solve the following: $\dfrac{4}{9} = \dfrac{x}{27}$

Solution:

$$(4)(27) = (9)(x)$$

$$108 = 9x$$

$$x = 12$$

10.24 Solve the following: $\dfrac{4}{x} = \dfrac{8}{x + 1}$

Solution:

$$4(x + 1) = 8x$$

$$4x + 4 = 8x$$

$$4 = 4x$$

$$x = 1$$

10.25 Solve the following: $\dfrac{3}{2} = \dfrac{6}{x+5}$

Solution:

$$\dfrac{3}{2} = \dfrac{6}{x+5}$$

$\quad 3(x+5) = 6(2)$ Cross product.

$\quad 3x + 15 = 12$ Multiply.

$3x + 15 - 15 = 12 - 15$

$\quad\quad\quad 3x = -3$

$\quad\quad\quad\quad x = -1$

10.26 Solve the following: $\dfrac{4}{x-1} = \dfrac{14}{2x+1}$

Solution:

$4(2x+1) = 14(x-1)$

$\quad 8x + 4 = 14x - 14$

$\quad\quad\quad 18 = 6x$

$\quad\quad\quad\; x = 3$

10.27 The total amount of time t that is required for two workers to complete a job working together, if one worker can complete it alone in c hours and the other in d hours, can be expressed with the following equation: $\dfrac{1}{t} = \dfrac{1}{c} + \dfrac{1}{d}$. Solve the equation for t. Then use the solved equation to answer the following. If Mark can mow his lawn in 2 hours and his brother can mow it in 3 hours, if they work together how long will it take them to mow the lawn?

Solution:

$$\dfrac{1}{t} = \dfrac{1}{c} + \dfrac{1}{d}$$

$(tcd)\dfrac{1}{t} = (tcd)\dfrac{1}{c} + (tcd)\dfrac{1}{d}$ Multiply by LCD.

$\quad cd = td + tc$

$\quad cd = t(d + c)$ Factor out t.

$\dfrac{cd}{d+c} = t$ Divide both side by $d + c$.

Part 2: $\dfrac{cd}{d+c} = t$

$\quad\quad\quad\quad \dfrac{(3 \cdot 2)}{3+2} = t$

$\quad\quad\quad 1.2 \text{ hours} = t$

10.28 A blueprint uses a scale of $\frac{3}{4}$ inch = 2 feet. Find the scaled-down dimensions of a room that is 10 feet by 12 feet.

Solution:

$$\frac{\frac{3}{4}\,\text{in}}{2\,\text{ft}} = \frac{\text{width}}{10} \qquad \text{Width proportion}$$

$$\frac{3}{8} = \frac{w}{10}$$

$$3(10) = 8w \qquad \text{Cross product}$$

$$30 = 8w$$

$$\frac{30}{8} \text{ or } 3.75 \text{ feet} = w$$

$$\frac{\frac{3}{4}\,\text{in}}{2\,\text{ft}} = \frac{\text{length}}{12} \qquad \text{Length proportion}$$

$$\frac{3}{8} = \frac{l}{12}$$

$$3(12) = 8l \qquad \text{Cross product}$$

$$36 = 8l$$

$$\frac{36}{8} \text{ or } 4.5 \text{ feet} = l$$

10.29 A boat travels 30 miles downstream in the same time it takes to go 20 miles upstream. If the river current flows at 5 miles per hour, what is the boat's speed in still water?

Solution:

$$\frac{30}{R+5} = \frac{20}{R-5}$$

$$30(R-5) = 20(R+5)$$

$$30R - 150 = 20R + 100$$

$$30R - 150 + 150 = 20R + 100 + 150$$

$$30R - 20R = 20R + 250 - 20R$$

$$10R = 250$$

$$\frac{10R}{10} = \frac{250}{10}$$

$R = 25$ miles per hour

10.30 Graph the following rational equations:

a. $y = \dfrac{1}{x}$

Solution:

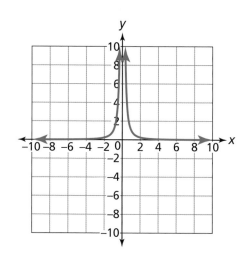

b. $y = \dfrac{1}{x^2}$

Solution:

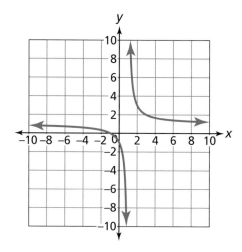

10.31 Graph the rational equation: $y = \dfrac{x+1}{x-1}$

Solution:

Chapter 11 Rational Exponents and Radical Functions and Equations

Rational Exponents/Connection between Powers and Roots

11.1 Evaluate: $625^{\frac{1}{4}}$

Solution:

$$625^{\frac{1}{4}} = \sqrt[4]{625}$$
$$= 5$$

11.2 Evaluate: $1024^{\frac{1}{5}}$

Solution:

$$1024^{\frac{1}{5}} = \sqrt[5]{1024} = 4$$

11.3 Evaluate: $25^{\frac{3}{2}}$

Solution:

$$25^{\frac{3}{2}} = \left(\sqrt[2]{25}\right)^3$$
$$= 5^3$$
$$= 125$$

11.4 Evaluate: $27^{\frac{5}{3}}$

Solution:

$$27^{\frac{5}{3}} = \left(\sqrt[3]{27}\right)^5 = 3^5 = 243$$

11.5 Evaluate: $32^{\frac{3}{4}}$

Solution:

$$32^{\frac{3}{4}} = \left(2^5\right)^{\frac{3}{4}}$$
$$= (2^4 \cdot 2)^{\frac{3}{4}}$$
$$= (2^4)^{\frac{3}{4}}(2)^{\frac{3}{4}}$$
$$= (2^{4 \cdot \frac{3}{4}})(2^3)^{\frac{1}{4}}$$
$$= (2^3)(2^3)^{\frac{1}{4}}$$
$$= 8 \cdot 8^{\frac{1}{4}}$$
$$= 8 \cdot \sqrt[4]{8}$$

11.6 Evaluate: $243^{\frac{3}{4}}$

Solution:

$$243^{\frac{3}{4}} = (3^5)^{\frac{3}{4}}$$

$$= (3^4 \cdot 3)^{\frac{3}{4}}$$

$$= (3^4)^{\frac{3}{4}} (3)^{\frac{3}{4}}$$

$$= \left(3^{4 \cdot \frac{3}{4}}\right) (3^3)^{\frac{1}{4}}$$

$$= (3^3)\left(27^{\frac{1}{4}}\right)$$

$$= 27\sqrt[4]{27}$$

11.7 Evaluate: $\left(\sqrt{10x}\right)^2$

Solution:

$$\left(\sqrt{10x}\right)^2 = \left((10x)^{\frac{1}{2}}\right)^2$$

$$= (10x)^{\frac{1}{2} \cdot 2}$$

$$= (10x)^1$$

$$= 10x$$

11.8 Evaluate: $\sqrt{500}$

Solution:

$$\sqrt{500} = \sqrt{125 \cdot 4}$$

$$= \sqrt{5^3 \cdot 2^2}$$

$$= \sqrt{5 \cdot 5^2 \cdot 2^2}$$

$$= 5 \cdot 2\sqrt{5}$$

$$= 10\sqrt{5}$$

11.9 Evaluate: $\left(\sqrt{(x+6)}\right)^2$

Solution:

$$\left(\sqrt{(x+6)}\right)^2 = (x+6)$$

11.10 Evaluate: $\left(\sqrt[3]{x^2 + 5x - 9}\right)^3$

Solution:

$$\left(\sqrt[3]{x^2 + 5x - 9}\right)^3 = x^2 + 5x - 9$$

11.11 Evaluate: $\sqrt[3]{64x^5yz^7}$

Solution:

$$\sqrt[3]{64x^5yz^7} = \sqrt[3]{4^3\,x^2x^3\,yzz^3z^3}$$
$$= 4xz^2\sqrt[3]{x^2yz}$$

11.12 Simplify: $9\sqrt{8z} - 4\sqrt{50z}$

Solution:

$$9\sqrt{8z} - 4\sqrt{50z} = 9\sqrt{(4)(2z)} - 4\sqrt{(25)(2z)}$$
$$= 9\left(\sqrt{4}\right)\left(\sqrt{2z}\right) - 4\left(\sqrt{25}\right)\left(\sqrt{2z}\right)$$
$$= 9(2)\left(\sqrt{2z}\right) - 4(5)\left(\sqrt{2z}\right)$$
$$= 18\left(\sqrt{2z}\right) - 20\left(\sqrt{2z}\right)$$
$$= -2\sqrt{2z}$$

11.13 Simplify: $\sqrt{18} - \sqrt{50}$

Solution:

$$\sqrt{18} - \sqrt{50} = \sqrt{9\cdot 2} - \sqrt{25\cdot 2}$$
$$= \sqrt{3^2\cdot 2} - \sqrt{5^2\cdot 2}$$
$$= 3\sqrt{2} - 5\sqrt{2}$$
$$= -2\sqrt{2}$$

11.14 Simplify: $3\sqrt{32x} + 5\sqrt{50x}$

Solution:

$$3\sqrt{32x} + 5\sqrt{50x} = 3\sqrt{16\cdot 2x} + 5\sqrt{25\cdot 2x}$$
$$= 3\sqrt{4^2\cdot 2x} + 5\sqrt{5^2\cdot 2x}$$
$$= 3\cdot 4\sqrt{2x} + 5\cdot 5\sqrt{2x}$$
$$= 12\sqrt{2x} + 25\sqrt{2x}$$
$$= 37\sqrt{2x}$$

11.15 Simplify: $\sqrt[3]{216x^4y^7} - \sqrt[3]{125x^4y^{10}}$

Solution:

$$\sqrt[3]{216x^4y^7} - \sqrt[3]{125x^4y^{10}} = \sqrt[3]{6^3\,xx^3\,yy^6} - \sqrt[3]{5^3\,xx^3\,yy^9}$$
$$= 6xy^2\sqrt[3]{xy} - 5xy^3\sqrt[3]{xy}$$
$$= (6xy^2 - 5xy^3)\sqrt[3]{xy}$$

11.16 Simplify: $\dfrac{\sqrt{8y^{21}}}{\sqrt{2y}}$

Solution:

$$\dfrac{\sqrt{8y^{21}}}{\sqrt{2y}} = \sqrt{\dfrac{8y^{21}}{2y}}$$

$$= \sqrt{4y^{20}}$$

$$= 2y^{10}$$

11.17 Simplify: $\left(\dfrac{125}{729}\right)^{\frac{2}{3}}$

Solution:

$$\left(\dfrac{125}{729}\right)^{\frac{2}{3}} = \left(\sqrt[3]{\dfrac{125}{729}}\right)^2$$

$$= \left(\dfrac{\sqrt[3]{125}}{\sqrt[3]{729}}\right)^2$$

$$= \left(\dfrac{5}{9}\right)^2$$

$$= \left(\dfrac{5^2}{9^2}\right)$$

$$= \left(\dfrac{25}{81}\right)$$

11.18 Simplify: $\dfrac{\sqrt{12x^{18}}}{\sqrt{3x^2}}$

Solution:

$$\dfrac{\sqrt{12x^{18}}}{\sqrt{3x^2}} = \sqrt{\dfrac{12x^{18}}{3x^2}}$$

$$= \sqrt{4x^{16}}$$

$$= 2x^8$$

11.19 Simplify: $\dfrac{\sqrt{20}}{\sqrt{3}}$

Solution:

$$\dfrac{\sqrt{20}}{\sqrt{3}} \cdot \dfrac{\sqrt{3}}{\sqrt{3}} = \dfrac{\sqrt{60}}{\sqrt{9}}$$

$$= \dfrac{\sqrt{4*15}}{3}$$

$$= \dfrac{2\sqrt{15}}{3}$$

Solving Equations with Radicals

11.20 Solve: $\sqrt{x} = 11$

Solution:

$$\sqrt{x} = 11$$
$$\left(\sqrt{x}\right)^2 = 11^2$$
$$x = 121$$

11.21 Solve: $\sqrt{x} = 18$

Solution:

$$\sqrt{x} = 18$$
$$\left(\sqrt{x}\right)^2 = 18^2$$
$$x = 324$$

11.22 Solve: $\sqrt{x} - 3 = 22$

Solution:

$$\sqrt{x} - 3 = 22$$
$$\sqrt{x} - 3 + 3 = 22 + 3$$
$$\sqrt{x} = 25$$
$$\left(\sqrt{x}\right)^2 = 25^2$$
$$x = 625$$

11.23 Solve: $\sqrt{x} - 6 = 30$

Solution:

$$\sqrt{x} - 6 = 30$$
$$\sqrt{x} = 36$$
$$\sqrt{x}^2 = 36^2$$
$$x = 1296$$

11.24 Solve: $\sqrt{z + 12} = 3$

Solution:

$$\sqrt{z + 12} = 3$$
$$\left(\sqrt{z + 12}\right)^2 = 3^2$$
$$z + 12 = 9$$
$$z + 12 - 12 = 9 - 12$$
$$z = -3$$

11.25 Solve: $\sqrt{z-10} = 4$

Solution:

$$\sqrt{z-10} = 4$$
$$\left(\sqrt{z-10}\right)^2 = 4^2$$
$$z - 10 = 16$$
$$z = 26$$

11.26 Solve: $\sqrt{5y+6} = 6$

Solution:

$$\sqrt{5y+6} = 6$$
$$\left(\sqrt{5y+6}\right)^2 = 6^2$$
$$5y + 6 = 36$$
$$5y + 6 - 6 = 36 - 6$$
$$5y = 30$$
$$\frac{5y}{5} = \frac{30}{5}$$
$$y = 6$$

11.27 Solve: $\sqrt{3y+1} = 5$

Solution:

$$\sqrt{3y+1} = 5$$
$$\left(\sqrt{3y+1}\right)^2 = 5^2$$
$$3y + 1 = 25$$
$$3y = 24$$
$$y = 8$$

11.28 Solve: $\sqrt[3]{3x-7} = 2$

Solution:

$$\sqrt[3]{3x-7} = 2$$
$$\left(\sqrt[3]{3x-7}\right)^3 = 2^3$$
$$3x - 7 = 8$$
$$3x = 15$$
$$x = 5$$

11.29 Solve: $\sqrt{x} = \sqrt{4x-6}$

Solution:

$$\sqrt{x} = \sqrt{4x-6}$$
$$\left(\sqrt{x}\right)^2 = \left(\sqrt{4x-6}\right)^2$$
$$x = 4x-6$$
$$x - 4x = 4x - 4x - 6$$
$$-3x = -6$$
$$\frac{-3x}{-3} = \frac{-6}{-3}$$
$$x = 2$$

11.30 Solve: $\sqrt{5x-3} = \sqrt{2x}$

Solution:

$$\sqrt{5x-3} = \sqrt{2x}$$
$$\left(\sqrt{5x-3}\right)^2 = \sqrt{2x}^2$$
$$5x - 3 = 2x$$
$$-3 = -3x$$
$$x = 1$$

11.31 Solve: $\sqrt{z+10} - z = 8$

Solution:

$$\sqrt{z+10} - z = 8$$
$$\sqrt{z+10} - z + z = 8 + z$$
$$\sqrt{z+10} = z + 8$$
$$\left(\sqrt{z+10}\right)^2 = (z+8)^2$$
$$z + 10 = z^2 + 16z + 64$$
$$z + 10 - 10 = z^2 + 16z + 64 - 10$$
$$z = z^2 + 16z + 54$$
$$z - z = z^2 + 16z - z + 54$$
$$0 = z^2 + 15z + 54$$
$$0 = (z+6)(z+9)$$
$$z + 6 = 0$$
$$z + 6 - 6 = 0 - 6$$
$$z = -6$$
$$or$$
$$z + 9 = 0$$
$$z + 9 - 9 = 0 - 9$$
$$z = -9$$
$$z = -6, -9$$

Since a binomial was squared, check the possible solutions. $z = -9$ is not a solution.

11.32 Solve: $\sqrt{x-1}+3=x$

Solution:

$$\sqrt{x-1}+3=x$$

$$\sqrt{x-1}=x-3$$

$$\left(\sqrt{x-1}\right)^2=(x-3)^2$$

$$x-1=x^2-6x+9$$

$$0=x^2-7x+10$$

$$0=(x-2)(x-5)$$

$$x=2,5$$

Check: $\sqrt{2-1}+3=2$

$$\sqrt{1}+3=2$$

$$1+3=2$$

$$4\neq2$$

$$\sqrt{5-1}+3=5$$

$$\sqrt{4}+3=5$$

$$2+3=5$$

$$5=5$$

Therefore, there is one solution, $x=5$.

11.33 Solve: $2\sqrt{y-4}-y=-4$

Solution:

$$2\sqrt{y-4}-y=-4$$

$$2\sqrt{y-4}-y+y=-4+y$$

$$2\sqrt{y-4}=y-4$$

$$\frac{2\sqrt{y-4}}{2}=\frac{y-4}{2}$$

$$\sqrt{y-4}=\frac{y-4}{2}$$

$$\left(\sqrt{y-4}\right)^2=\left(\frac{y-4}{2}\right)^2$$

$$y-4=\frac{(y-4)^2}{4}$$

$$4(y-4)=4\left(\frac{y^2-8y+16}{4}\right)$$

$$4y-16=y^2-8y+16$$

$$4y - 4y - 16 = y^2 - 8y - 4y + 16$$
$$-16 = y^2 - 12y + 16$$
$$-16 + 16 = y^2 - 12y + 16 + 16$$
$$0 = y^2 - 12y + 32$$
$$0 = (y - 4)(y - 8)$$
$$y - 4 = 0$$
$$y - 4 + 4 = 0 + 4$$
$$y = 4$$
$$or$$
$$y - 8 = 0$$
$$y - 8 + 8 = 0 + 8$$
$$y = 8$$
$$y = 4, 8$$

Both solutions check.

Radical Functions

11.34 Given the formula for the base of a square pyramid $b = \sqrt{\dfrac{3V}{h}}$, where b is the length of the side of the base, h is the height of the pyramid, and V is the volume of the pyramid. What is the volume of the pyramid if the base is 8 feet and the height is 6 feet?

Solution:
Solve for V:

$$b = \sqrt{\frac{3V}{h}}$$
$$b^2 = \left(\sqrt{\frac{3V}{h}}\right)^2$$
$$b^2 = \frac{3V}{h}$$
$$b^2 h = \left(\frac{3V}{h}\right) h$$
$$b^2 h = 3V$$
$$\frac{b^2 h}{3} = \frac{3V}{3}$$
$$V = \frac{b^2 h}{3}$$

Substitute the values for and b and h.

$$V = \frac{(8\,ft)^2 (6\,ft)}{3}$$
$$V = 128\,ft^2$$

11.35 Given the following formula: $y = \sqrt{x - h} + k$. Solve for x if $h = 2$ and $k = 0$, and $y = 5$.

Solution:

$$y = \sqrt{x - h} + k$$
$$y - k = \sqrt{x - h} + k - k$$
$$y - k = \sqrt{x - h}$$
$$(y - k)^2 = \left(\sqrt{x - h}\right)^2$$
$$y^2 - 2ky + k^2 = x - h$$
$$y^2 - 2ky + k^2 + h = x - h + h$$
$$x = y^2 - 2ky + k^2 + h$$

Substitute the values of y, h, and k into the equation:

$$x = y^2 - 2ky + k^2 + h$$
$$x = (5)^2 - 2(0)(5) + 0^2 + 2$$
$$x = 25 + 2$$
$$x = 27$$

Graphing Radical Functions

11.36 Describe what happens to the graph of $y = -(x + 6)^{\frac{1}{2}} - 4$ as compared to the parent function $y = x^{\frac{1}{2}}$.

Solution:

As compared to the parent function, the graph is reflected over the x-axis, shifted to the left 6 units, and shifted down 4 units.

Chapter 12 Exponential and Logarithmic Functions

12.1 Find the inverse for the equation $y = 5x + 3$.

Solution:

Simply interchange x and y and solve for y:

$$y = 5x + 3$$
$$x = 5y + 3$$
$$x - 3 = 5y$$
$$\frac{(x - 3)}{5} = y$$

12.2 Graph the following functions and determine if they are increasing or decreasing:

    a. $f(x) = 2^x$

    b. $f(x) = \left(\dfrac{1}{2}\right)^x$

Solution:

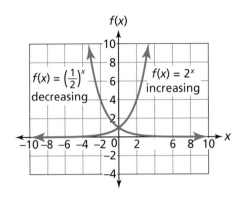

12.3 Graph the following functions and determine if they are increasing or decreasing:

    a. $f(x) = e^x$

    b. $f(x) = e^{-x}$

Solution:

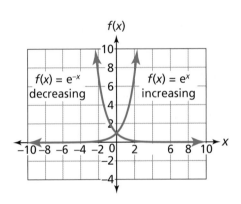

12.4 Explain why the two functions are similar in problems 12.2 and 12.3.

Solution:

Because e represents the number $2.71828...$, these are both exponential functions. Also $\left(\dfrac{1}{2}\right)^x$ is the same as 2^{-x}.

12.5 The formula $A = Pe^{rt}$ is used in business for calculating interest on an invested (or owed) amount that is compounded continuously, where P is the amount invested (or owed), r is the interest rate, and t is the time in years the amount has been invested. If an individual invests $1,000 compounded continuously for three years at 6%, what is the amount of the investment at the end of the three years? Round to the nearest cent.

Solution:

$A = Pe^{rt} = 1000e^{(0.06*3)} = \$1197.22$

12.6 The formula $A = Pe^{rt}$ is used in business for calculating interest on an invested (or owed) amount that is compounded continuously, where P is the amount invested (or owed), r is the interest rate, and t is the time in years the amount has been invested. If an individual invests $3,300 compounded continuously for four years at 2%, what is the amount of the investment at the end of the four years? Round to the nearest cent.

Solution:

$A = Pe^{rt}$

$A = 3300e^{(0.02 \cdot 4)}$

$A = 3300e^{0.08}$

$A = 3300(1.083287)$

$A = 3574.85$

At the end of four years the investment is worth $3,574.85.

12.7 The formula $A = Pe^{rt}$ is used in business for calculating interest on an invested (or owed) amount that is compounded continuously, where P is the amount invested (or owed), r is the interest rate, and t is the time in years the amount has been invested. If an individual invests $6,000 at a rate of 3.5% compounded continuously, how long will it take to double their money?

Solution:

Doubling $6,000 will be $12,000, therefore we let $A = 12000$.

$$A = Pe^{rt}$$

$$12000 = 6000e^{0.035t}$$

$$2 = e^{0.035t}$$

$$\ln 2 = \ln e^{0.035t}$$

$$\ln 2 = 0.035t$$

$$\frac{\ln 2}{0.035} = t$$

$$\frac{0.693147}{0.035} = t$$

$$19.8 = t$$

It will take 19.8 years to double the investment.

12.8 The formula $A = P\left(1 + \dfrac{r}{n}\right)^{nt}$ is used in business for calculating interest on an invested (or owed) amount that is compounded a certain number, n, times per year, where P is the amount invested (or owed), r is the interest rate, and t is the time in years the amount has been invested. If an individual invests $1,000 compounded quarterly for three years at 6%, what is the amount of the investment at the end of three years? Round to the nearest cent.

Solution:

$n = 4$ since compounded quarterly or four times per year

$$A = P\left(1 + \frac{r}{n}\right)^{nt} = 1000\left(1 + \frac{0.006}{4}\right)^{4 \cdot 3} = \$1195.62$$

12.9 The formula $A = P\left(1 + \dfrac{r}{n}\right)^{nt}$ is used in business for calculating interest on an invested (or owed) amount that is compounded a certain number, n, times per year, where P is the amount invested (or owed), r is the interest rate, and t is the time in years the amount has been invested. If an individual invests \$4,200 compounded semiannually for three years at 4.1%, what is the amount of the investment at the end of three years? Round to the nearest cent.

Solution:

$$A = P\left(1 + \frac{r}{n}\right)^{nt}$$

$$A = 4200\left(1 + \frac{0.041}{2}\right)^{2 \cdot 3}$$

$$A = 4200(1 + 0.0205)^6$$

$$A = 4200(1.0205)^6$$

$$A = 4200(1.12948)$$

$$A = 4743.81$$

At the end of three years, the investment will be worth \$4,743.81.

12.10 If the population for a certain town is given by the equation $P = 1500(2^{0.3t})$, where t is the time in years from 1980, find the population in 1985.

Solution:

$t = 5; P = 1500(2^{0.3*5}) \approx 4242$

12.11 Simplify the following:

    a. $\log_2(16)$
    b. $\log_5(25)$
    c. $\log_{10}(0.001)$
    d. $\log_4\left(\dfrac{1}{4}\right)$

Solutions:

    a. 4 because $2^4 = 16$
    b. 2 because $5^2 = 25$
    c. -3 because $10^{-3} = 0.001$
    d. -1 because $4^{-1} = \dfrac{1}{4}$

12.12 Simplify $\log_3 243$

Solution:

$\log_3 243$

$3^x = 243$

$x = 5$

12.13 Simplify $\log_9 81$

Solution:

$\log_9 81$

$9^x = 81$

$x = 2$

12.14 Simplify $\log_3 \dfrac{1}{27}$

Solution:

$\log_3 \dfrac{1}{27}$

$3^x = \dfrac{1}{27}$

$\ln 3^x = \ln \dfrac{1}{27}$

$x\ln 3 = \ln \dfrac{1}{27}$

$x = \dfrac{\ln \dfrac{1}{27}}{\ln 3}$

$x = -3$

12.15 Solve the following equations for x.

   a. $\log_3(x) = 2$
   b. $\log_2(x) = -3$
   c. $\log_{32}(x) = \dfrac{1}{5}$

   d. $\log_4(x) = \dfrac{1}{2}$

Solutions:

   a. 9

   b. $\dfrac{1}{8}$

   c. 2
   d. 2

12.16 Solve $\log_{27} x = \dfrac{1}{3}$

Solution:

Write in exponential form. $27^{\frac{1}{3}} = x$

$\sqrt[3]{27} = x$

$3 = x$

12.17 Solve $\log_4 x = 5$

Solution:

Write in exponential form. $4^5 = x$

$1024 = x$

12.18 Solve $\log_4 2x = 3$

Solution:

Write in exponential form. $4^3 = 2x$

$64 = 2x$

$32 = x$

12.19 Solve $\log_5 (3x + 7) = 2$

Solution:

Write in exponential form. $5^2 = 3x + 7$

$25 = 3x + 7$

$18 = 3x$

$6 = x$

12.20 Solve the following for x:

$\log_3(4x - 7) = 2$

Solution:

$$4x - 7 = 3^2$$
$$4x - 7 = 9$$
$$4x - 7 + 7 = 9 + 7$$
$$4x = 16$$
$$\frac{4x}{4} = \frac{16}{4}$$
$$x = 4$$

12.21 Solve the following for x:

$\log_x(64) = 2$

Solution:

$$x^2 = 64$$
$$x = \pm\sqrt{64}.$$

$x = \pm 8$ Logarithm bases are always positive, therefore $x = 8$.

12.22 Solve $\log_x 81 = 4$

Solution:

Write in exponential form. $x^4 = 81$

$x = 3$

12.23 Solve the following for x:

$2^x = 5$

Solution:

$2^x = 5$

$x = \log_2(5)$

$x = \dfrac{\ln(5)}{\ln(2)}$ Change of base formula

$x \approx 2.322$

12.24 Solve $4^x = 10$

Solution:

Take the natural log of both sides. $\ln 4^x = \ln 10$

$x \ln 4 = \ln 10$

$x = \dfrac{\ln 10}{\ln 4}$

$x = \dfrac{2.302585}{1.386294}$

$x = 1.661$

12.25 Solve $e^x = 9$

Solution:

Take the natural log of both sides. $\ln e^x = \ln 9$

$x = \ln 9$

$x = 2.197$

12.26 Solve $8^{2x+5} = 30$. Round to three decimal places.

Solution:

Take the natural log of both sides

$\ln 8^{2x+5} = \ln 30$

$(2x+5)\ln 8 = \ln 30$

$2x + 5 = \dfrac{\ln 30}{\ln 8}$

$2x + 5 = 1.635630$

$2x = -3.36437$

$x = -1.682$

12.27 Solve $9e^{(x+1)} = 108$

Solution:

$9e^{x+1} = 108$

$e^{x+1} = 12$

$x + 1 = \ln 12$

$x = \ln 12 - 1$

$x = 1.485$

12.28 The following formula represents the number N of cells in a culture after a time t has passed, where N_0 is the initial number of cells and k represents the positive growth rate of the cells.
$N(t) = N_0 e^{kt}$ where $k > 0$
If a colony of bacteria is modeled by the function $N(t) = 130 e^{0.045t}$, determine the initial amount of bacteria.

Solution:
$N(0) = 130 e^{0.045(0)} = 130$

12.29 The following formula represents the number N of cells in a culture after a time t has passed, where N_0 is the initial number of cells and k represents the positive growth rate of the cells.
$N(t) = N_0 e^{kt}$ where $k > 0$
If a colony of bacteria is modeled by the function $N(t) = 130 e^{0.045t}$, what is the growth rate of the bacteria?

Solution:
$.045 = 4.5\%$

12.30 The following formula represents the number N of cells in a culture after a time t has passed, where N_0 is the initial number of cells and k represents the positive growth rate of the cells.
$N(t) = N_0 e^{kt}$ where $k > 0$
If a colony of bacteria is modeled by the function $N(t) = 130 e^{0.045t}$, how long will it take the population to reach 160 grams?

Solution:
$$130 e^{0.045t} = 160$$
$$e^{0.045t} = \frac{160}{130}$$
$$0.045t = \ln\left(\frac{160}{130}\right) \approx 0.2076$$
$$t = \frac{0.2076}{0.045}$$
$$t \approx 4.6 \text{ days.}$$

12.31 The formula $A = Pe^{rt}$ is used in business for calculating interest on an invested (or owed) amount that is compounded continuously, where P is the amount invested (or owed), r is the interest rate, and t is the time in years the amount has been invested.
If an individual invests \$4,000 compounded continuously at 3%, how many years was the money invested if the return was \$5,399.44

Solution:

Plug the values into the formula $A = Pe^{rt}$

$$5399.44 = 4000 e^{0.03t}$$
$$1.349859 = e^{0.03t}$$
$$\ln 1.349859 = 0.03t$$
$$\frac{\ln 1.349859}{0.03} = t$$
$$\frac{0.3}{0.03} = t$$
$$10 = t$$

It will take 10 years to reach a return of \$5,399.44.

12.32 The following formula represents exponential growth, where $k > 0$. A is the amount after time t has passed, A_0 is the initial amount and k is the growth constant. $A = A_0 e^{kt}$ where $k > 0$
There were 10 rabbits living on an island. After 7 months there were 50 rabbits. Determine how many rabbits there will be in 15 months.

Solution:

Plug the given values into the formula $A = A_0 e^{kt}$ to find the growth constant.

$$50 = 10 e^{k7}$$
$$5 = e^{7k}$$
$$\ln 5 = 7k$$
$$\frac{\ln 5}{7} = k$$
$$0.22992 = k$$

Next use the value $k = 0.22992$ and $t = 15$.

$$A = A_0 e^{kt}$$
$$A = 10 e^{(0.22992)(15)}$$
$$A = 10 e^{3.4488}$$
$$A = 10(31.4625)$$
$$A = 314.62$$

In 15 months there will be 315 rabbits on the island.

12.33 The following formula represents exponential depreciation of worth, where $k < 0$. A is the amount of worth after time t has passed, A_0 is the initial amount and k is depreciation constant. $A = A_0 e^{kt}$ where $k < 0$
If Christina purchases a car for \$45,000 and two years later it has depreciated exponentially to \$30,000, find the depreciation constant. Round to three decimal places.

Solution:

Plug in the values into the formula $A = A_0 e^{kt}$

$$30000 = 45000 e^{k2}$$
$$0.666667 = e^{2k}$$
$$\ln 0.666667 = \ln e^{2k}$$
$$\ln 0.666667 = 2k$$
$$\frac{\ln 0.666667}{2} = k$$
$$\frac{-0.405465}{2} = k$$
$$-0.203 = k$$

12.34 The following formula represents exponential depreciation of worth, where $k < 0$. A is the amount of worth after time t has passed, A_0 is the initial amount and k is depreciation constant. $A = A_0 e^{kt}$ where $k < 0$
If James purchases a car for \$36,000 and two years later it has depreciated exponentially to \$26,000, how much will the car be worth five years from the date of purchase? Round to three decimal places.

Solution:

Find the depreciation constant by plugging the values into the formula $A = A_0 e^{kt}$.

$$26000 = 36000 e^{k2}$$

$$0.722222 = e^{2k}$$

$$\ln 0.722222 = 2k$$

$$\frac{\ln 0.722222}{2} = k$$

$$-0.162711 = k$$

Now use the value $k = -0.162711$ and $t = 5$ to find the value of the car five years from date of purchase.

$$A = 36000 e^{-0.162711(5)}$$

$$A = 36000 e^{-0.813556}$$

$$A = 36000(0.4432789)$$

$$A = 15958.04$$

In five years James' car will be worth \$15,958.04.

12.35 The population of a country is increasing at a rate of 2.5% per year. If the population is currently 5,000,000, how many years will it take for the population to reach 6,500,000?

Solution:

Plug the numbers into the formula $N = N_0 (1 + r)^t$.

$$6500000 = 5000000(1 + 0.025)^t$$

$$1.3 = (1.025)^t$$

$$\ln 1.3 = \ln(1.025)^t$$

$$\ln 1.3 = t \ln(1.025)$$

$$\frac{\ln 1.3}{\ln 1.025} = t$$

$$10.63 = t$$

The population will reach 6,500,000 in 10.63 years.

GLOSSARY

A

absolute value (of a number): Distance of the number from zero.

A-C method: A method that uses the product of the a and c constants in the general quadratic equation to aid in factoring.

addition property of equations: Adding (or subtracting) the same quantity to (or from) the expressions on both sides of an equation keeps the expressions equivalent (keeps the equation *balanced*).

annuity: An investment that involves someone making and/or receiving monthly payments over a specified period.

asymptote: A line to which the graph of a function becomes arbitrarily close for appropriate values of the variable.

average cost: The quotient of the total of fixed and variable costs and the number of items made.

axis of symmetry: A vertical line through the vertex of a parabola.

B

ballistics equation: The equation of motion $x(t) = \frac{1}{2}at^2 + v_0 t + x_0$, where t is time in seconds and $x(t)$ is the height of the object at time t.

base: The number on which an exponent acts.

box method: A method similar to the A-C method.

C

cartesian plane: A two-dimensional coordinate system consisting of a horizontal number line called the x-axis and a vertical number line called the y-axis. Their intersection at their 0 points is the origin of the coordinate system.

common factor: A factor common to all terms of an expression.

common logarithm: Logarithm with base equal to 10.

completing the square: A method of transforming a quadratic function from standard form into vertex form.

compound inequality: Inequalities joined by either "and" or "or."

compound interest: Interest earned when interest is reinvested at the beginning of each investment period.

compound interest (general formula): $A = P\left(1 + \frac{r}{n}\right)^{nt}$

continuous function: Graph has no breaks, jumps, or holes. All polynomial functions are continuous.

continuously compounded interest formula: $A = Pe^{rt}$

coordinates: The x-coordinate and y-coordinate of a pair of numbers, one from each axis, corresponding to a point in the plane.

Cramer's Rule: A method of using determinants to solve a system.

D

degree (of a single-variable polynomial): Value of the greatest exponent of the polynomial; also called order.

determinant: A number representing a square matrix.

direct variation: Quantities y and x vary directly, or are directly proportional, when $y = kx$ or or $\frac{y}{x} = k$, where $k \neq 0$.

discriminant: The quantity $b^2 - 4ac$, which indicates the number of roots of the quadratic equation related to a quadratic function in standard form.

E

e: A constant with an approximate value of 2.71828; base of natural logarithms.

elimination method (for solving a system): A procedure that requires adding a multiple of one equation to the other in order to eliminate one variable.

equation: Two expressions set equal to each other.

equivalent exponential and radical expressions: $\left(\sqrt[n]{a}\right)^m = a^{\frac{m}{n}} = \sqrt[n]{a^m}$

equivalent expressions: Have the same value for every value of their variables.

even function f: Satisfies $f(-x) = f(x)$.

exponent: Superscript to upper right of base.

exponential function: A function in the form $f(x) = a^x$, where the base a is a positive number.

exponential growth formula: $N = N_0(1 + r)^t$; another formula for continuous exponential growth is $N = N_0 e^{kt}$.

extraneous solution: A solution of an equation that does not make sense.

F

factoring: Rewriting an expression in an equivalent form to show a common factor as a factor of the entire expression.

FOIL: Shortcut for finding the product of two binomials.

formula: An equation that describes the relationship between several variables.

function f: A collection of ordered pairs $(x, f(x))$ for which every first coordinate is paired with a unique second coordinate.

function notation $f(x)$: Read "f of x" or "f is a function of (the variable) x"; x is the input, $f(x)$ is the output.

future value: The amount a person will receive in the future if he or she makes a certain monthly payment now.

G

gaussian elimination: A procedure for finding the solution to a system of equations.

greatest common factor (of an expression): The product of all the common factors of the terms in the expression.

I

index: The integer, n, greater than 1 in the expression $\sqrt[n]{x}$; it identifies the type of root.

inequality: A sentence using one of the four symbols: $<$ (is less than), $>$ (is greater than), $\leq$ (is less than or equal to), or $\geq$ (is greater than or equal to).

integers: The set consisting of whole numbers and their opposites.

inverse variation: Quantities y and x vary inversely when $y = \dfrac{k}{x}$ or $xy = k$, where $k \neq 0$.

irrational numbers: The set of decimal numbers that do not terminate or repeat.

J

joint variation: Quantity y varies jointly with x and z when $y = kxz$, where $k \neq 0$.

L

light intensity equation: $I = \dfrac{k}{4\pi r^2}$ describes light intensity where I is the intensity, k is the power of the light source, and r is the distance to the light source.

like terms: Terms that have the same variables raised to the same powers.

linear equation: An equation that can be written in the form $y = mx + b$.

linear function: A function $f(x)$ for which 1 is the greatest power of x in the equation.

linear inequality: A linear equation in two variables with the $=$ symbol replaced by one of the four inequality symbols.

logarithmic function: Function of the form $y = f(x) = \log_a x$.

M

marginal cost: The difference between successive costs as production increases by one unit.

marginal quantities: Functions derived from the cost, revenue, and profit functions.

markdown: Decrease in price.

markup: Increase in price.

matrix: A rectangular array of numbers.

maximum (local): The pointing the greatest function value (in its immediate neighborhood).

minimum (local): The point having the least function value (in its immediate neighborhood).

monomial: Any one term expression of the form $ax_1 r^1 x_2 r^2 x_3 r^3 \cdots x_n r^n$.

multiplication property of equations: Expressions on either side of an equation remain equivalent when each is multiplied or divided by the same quantity.

multiplicity (of a factor): The power to which that factor is raised in a completely factored polynomial function.

N

natural logarithm: Has base equal to e.

negative number: Any number less than zero; the opposite of a positive number.

nth root of x: $\sqrt[n]{x}$; the quantity r such that $r^n = (\sqrt[n]{x})^n = x$.

number line: Represents real numbers in order, with every point representing a real number and every real number corresponding to a point on the line.

O

odd function: A function g that satisfies $g(-x) = -g(x)$ for all x.

opposite: *See* negative number.

order (of a single-variable polynomial): *See* degree.

origin: The intersection of the x- and y-axes at their 0 points; the point with the coordinates (0, 0).

P

parabola: The name of the graph of a quadratic function.

parent function: A function in its most basic standard form.

polynomial: Sum of monomials.

polynomial function (in one variable): A function of the form $f(x) = a_n x^n + a_{n-1} x^{n-1} + a_{n-2} x^{n-2} + \ldots + a_1 x + a_0$, where n is a nonnegative integer and a_n through a_0 are constant coefficients. The constant coefficients of a polynomial function can be any real numbers.

positive number: Any number greater than zero.

power function: A polynomial function with only one term. A power function has the form $f(x) = ax^n$.

present value: The amount that a person has to invest now in order to receive a certain monthly payment in the future.

principal: An initial amount of investment money.

product property of radicals: $\sqrt[n]{a^m} \cdot \sqrt[n]{b^m} = \sqrt[n]{(ab)^m}$

proportion: An equation setting two ratios equal to each other.

Q

quadratic equation: A quadratic function set equal to zero.

quadratic formula: For a quadratic equation $ax^2 + bx + c = 0$, the quadratic formula is.

$$x = -\frac{b}{2a} \pm \frac{\sqrt{b^2 - 4ac}}{2a}$$

$$= \frac{-b \pm \sqrt{b^2 - 4ac}}{2a}.$$

quadratic function: A polynomial function of degree 2.

quotient property of radicals:

$$\sqrt[n]{\frac{a}{b}} = \frac{\sqrt[n]{a}}{\sqrt[n]{b}}$$

R

radical: The symbol $\sqrt{}$ used to indicate finding a root of a number; also expressions such as $\sqrt[4]{16}$ or $\sqrt{3t}$.

radical expression: Any expression that contains a radical.

radicand: The value under the radical symbol.

rate, r: The percent used to compute the interest earned by the principal for a given period of time.

ratio: A fraction comparing two quantities.

rational expression: A function of the form $f(x) = \frac{a(x)}{b(x)}$, where $a(x)$ and $b(x)$ are polynomials and $b(x)$ can never equal zero.

rational numbers: Set of all fractions and all decimals that can be written in fractional form.

real numbers: The set of all rational numbers and irrational numbers.

root: A number that makes an equation true or satisfies a radical expression.

S

scientific notation: Shorthand representation of a decimal.

simple interest: Amount of interest earned on the principal only.

simplified radical form: The radicand has no factors with power greater than or equal to the index, there is no radical in the denominator, and the radicand is not a fraction.

simplify (an expression): Rewrite the expression as an equivalent expression using algebraic rules.

slope: The measure of a line's steepness; for (x_1, y_1) and (x_2, y_2) on the line, the slope is $\frac{y_2 - y_1}{x_2 - x_1}$.

slope-intercept form: $y = mx + b$, where m is the slope of the line and b is the y-intercept.

solution of a system: The collection of points or their coordinates that satisfy all the equations of the system.

square matrix: An $n \times n$ matrix.

square root (of x): The number r such that $r^2 = (\sqrt{x})^2 = x$.

square root method: A method of solving quadratic equations by taking the square root of both sides of the equation.

standard form (of a quadratic function): $f(x) = ax^2 + bx + c$

subscript: A number written below and to the right of a variable to distinguish it from another variable.

substitution method (for solving a system): A procedure that requires solving for a variable in one equation and substituting that value in another equation of the system.

synthetic division: Shortcut for dividing a polynomial by $x - d$.

system of linear equations: A group of linear equations (in the same plane) that uses the same variables.

system of linear inequalities: A group of linear inequalities that uses the same variables.

T

term: Any addend in an expression.

time, t: The number of periods for which the principal will earn interest.

transformation of a parabola: A change in the basic graph $y = x^2$ of a quadratic function related to one of the constants a, h, or k.

translation: A vertical or horizontal shift of a graph reflecting a change in its basic equation.

trial method: A method of factoring polynomials using equal parts practice and educated guesses.

turning points: The local maximums/minimums of a graph.

V

variable: A letter or symbol used to represent an unknown number.

variable expression: An expression that contains a variable.

vertex: The maximum point of a parabola that opens downward or the minimum point of a parabola that opens upward.

vertex form (of a quadratic function): $y = a(x - h)^2 + k$; the point (h, k) is the vertex.

X

x-axis: The horizontal number line of a Cartesian coordinate system.

x-coordinate: A point's distance in the x direction from the y-axis.

x-intercept: The point (or the coordinate value) where a line intersects the x-axis.

Y

y-axis: The vertical number line of a Cartesian coordinate system.

y-coordinate: A point's distance in the y direction from the x-axis.

y-intercept: The point (or the coordinate value) where a line intersects the y-axis.

Z

zero (of a function): A value of the variable that makes the value of the function zero.

zero product property: If $xy = 0$, then either x or y (or both) are equal to 0.

PHOTO CREDITS

Chapter 1 Opener, p. 2: © forestpath (Fotolia); p. 10: © scotttnz (Fotolia); p. 21: © McCarony (Fotolia).

Chapter 2 Opener, p. 32: © mangostock (Fotolia); p. 49: © VILevi (Fotolia); p. 53: © WavebreakMediaMicro (Fotolia).

Chapter 3 Opener, p. 68: © Jashin (Fotolia); p. 75: © Pavel Losevsky (Fotolia); p. 76: © isyste (Fotolia); p. 79: © Avantgarde (Fotolia).

Chapter 4 Opener, p. 100: © PhotoAlto Photography (Veer).

Chapter 5 Opener, p. 148: © Robert Kneschke (Fotolia).

Chapter 6 Opener, p. 206: © olly (Fotolia); p. 220: © florin1961 (Fotolia).

Chapter 7 Opener, p. 240: © dzain (Fotolia); p. 257: © Blend Images Photography (Veer); p. 258: © ristoviitanen (Fotolia).

Chapter 8 Opener, p. 274: © Corbis Photography (Veer); p. 295: © TEMISTOCLE LUCARELLI (Fotolia).

Chapter 9 Opener, p. 312: © diego cervo (Fotolia).

Chapter 10 Opener, p. 350: © vision images (Fotolia); p. 371: © .shock (Fotolia).

Chapter 11 Opener, p. 386: © Lisa F. Young (Fotolia).

Chapter 12 Opener, p. 412: © bociek666 (Fotolia); p. 429: © LittleMan (Fotolia).

REFERENCES

Arny, T., & Schneider, S. (2010). Explorations: *An introduction to astronomy* (6th ed.). New York, NY: McGraw-Hill.

Burzynski, D., & Ellis, W. (2009). Factoring polynomials: Factoring two special products. Retrieved from http://cnx.org/content/m21903/latest/

Cajori, F., & Odell, L. R. (1917). *Elementary algebra*. New York, NY: Macmillan.

Definitions. (n.d.). In *Encarta online dictionary*. Retrieved from http://encarta.msn.com

Dodge, W. (1998). Worksheets of algebra 1. New Trier High School, Winnetka, IL.

Harris, T. (n.d.). How cameras work. Retrieved from http://electronics.howstuffworks.com/camera2.htm

Larson, R., Boswell, L., Kanold, T., & Stiff, L. (2007). *Algebra 2*. Evanston, IL: McDougal Littell.

Major, N. (2004). Algebra I, 2nd semester [Lecture notes]. Cherry Creek High School, Greenwood Village, CO.

Math Forum @ Drexel. (n.d.). Distance, rate, and time. Retrieved from http://mathforum.org/dr.math/faq/faq.distance.html

Rietz, H. L., & Crathorne, A. R. (1909). *College algebra*. New York, NY: Henry Holt and Company.

Stapel, E. (n.d). Factoring quadratics: The hard case (examples). Retrieved from Purplemath website: http:// www.purplemath.com/modules/factquad3.htm

INDEX

M

Notes